ISBN 978-0-265-97608-1
PIBN 10918222

✓ United States

REPORTS.

OF

CASES ARGUED AND ADJUDGED

IN

THE SUPREME COURT.

OF

THE UNITED STATES.

DECEMBER TERM, 1855.

By BENJAMIN C. HOWARD,

COUNSELLOR AT LAW AND REPORTER OF THE DECISIONS OF THE SUPREME
COURT OF THE UNITED STATES.

VOL. XVIII.

BOSTON:
LITTLE, BROWN, AND COMPANY,
Law Publishers and Booksellers.
1866.

This volume is printed on acid free paper by
WILLIAM S. HEIN & CO., INC.

SUPREME COURT OF THE UNITED STATES.

LIST OF ATTORNEYS AND COUNSELLORS,

ADMITTED DECEMBER TERM, 1855.

THOMAS C. JOHNSON,	Missouri.
O. H. BROWNING,	Illinois.
GEORGE M. WESTON,	Maine.
J. MURRAY RUSH,	Pennsylvania.
EDWARD WALN,	Pennsylvania.
DAVID K. BOYLAN,	New Jersey.
THOMAS T. EVERETT,	District of Columbia.
THOMPSON CAMPBELL,	California.
JAMES THORINGTON,	Iowa.
GEORGE ROBERTSON,	Kentucky.
JAMES MORRIS,	New York.
PAUL WILLARD, JR.,	Massachusetts.
CHARLES BELLINGHURST,	Wisconsin.
ALEX. W. BUEL,	Michigan.
THOMAS H. BAIRD,	Pennsylvania.
LINTON STEPHENS,	Georgia.
ALBERT B. CAPWELL,	New York.
ZEBULON BAIRD,	Indiana.
GEORGE G. DUNN,	Indiana.
W. L. UNDERWOOD,	Kentucky.
JAMES R. DOOLITTLE,	Wisconsin.
JOHN R. SHARPSTEIN,	Wisconsin.
SYDNEY L. JOHNSON,	Louisiana.
FRANKLIN A. DICK,	Missouri.
J. YOUNG SCAMMON,	Illinois.
WM. H. ROGERS,	Delaware.
ALEXANDER CLARKE,	New York.
CONRAD BAKER,	Indiana.
EVANS CASSELBERRY,	Missouri.
JOHN PYNE,	New York.
SAMUEL CRAWFORD,	Wisconsin.
SAMUEL W. HOLLADAY,	California.
JOHN M. PARKER,	New York.
JOHN IVAN ALLEN,	New York.
A. T. RAINEY,	Texas.

MARCUS J. PARROTT,	*Kansas Territory.*
JOHN UPFOLD PETITT,	*Indiana.*
ELZA JEFFORD,	*Ohio.*
ROBERT LOWRY,	*Indiana.*
JAMES A. ABBOTT,	*Massachusetts.*
GEORGE F. BETTS,	*New York.*
STEPHEN I NOBLE,	*Ohio.*
W. P. REID,	*Ohio.*
R. A. LOCKWOOD,	*California.*
JAMES S. BROWN,	*Wisconsin.*
WILLIAM H. KELSEY,	*New York.*
JACKSON W. GREEN,	*Tennessee.*
THOMAS H. LEWIS,	*Louisiana.*
THOMAS WILLIAMS,	*Pennsylvania.*
SAMUEL H. HEMPSTEAD,	*Arkansas.*
PHILIP VAN TRUMP,	*Ohio.*
ABSALOM FOWLER,	*Arkansas.*
JOHN T. BRADY,	*Kansas Territory.*
SAMUEL CARUTHERS,	*Missouri.*
W. B. WEBB,	*District of Columbia.*
MILTON ANDROS,	*Massachusetts.*
HORACE E. SMITH,	*New York.*
LUCIAN BARBOUR,	*Indiana.*
JOHN G. VOSE,	*New York.*
J. C. HALL,	*Iowa.*
W. T. REID,	*Iowa.*
IVERS J. AUSTIN,	*Massachusetts.*
DENNIS McMAHON,	*New York.*

a *

LIST OF ATTORNEYS AND COUNSELLORS,

ADMITTED AT ADJOURNED DECEMBER TERM, 1855.

GEORGE S. YERGER,	*Mississippi.*
S. TEACKLE WALLIS,	*Maryland.*
JOHN H. THOMAS,	*Maryland.*
CLINTON RICE,	*New York.*
JAMES C. CARTER,	*New York.*
MOSES A. DROPSIE,	*Pennsylvania.*
A. BROWNING,	*New Jersey.*
J. M. SMILEY,	*Louisiana.*
C. J. WALKER,	*Michigan.*
GEORGE HOWE,	*Vermont.*
JAMES M. JOHNS,	*Delaware.*
LUCIUS N. BANGS,	*New York.*
ABRAM WAKEMAN,	*New York.*
GEORGE GALE,	*Wisconsin.*
WILLIAM L. BURT,	*Massachusetts.*
ASA OWEN ALDIS,	*Vermont.*
WILLIAM G. HAMMOND, JR.,	*New York.*
JOHN A. GODFREY,	*California.*
PETER H. WATSON,	*District of Columbia.*
P. B. WILCOX,	*Ohio.*
CHARLES H. RHETT,	*South Carolina.*

LIST OF CASES REPORTED.

LIST OF CASES REPORTED.

ERRATUM.

In 16 Howard, page 371, on the top line of the page, for *Veriton* read *Vinton*, so that the passage will read thus:

"The case was argued by Mr. Stanberry and Mr. Vinton," &c.

THE DECISIONS

OF THE

SUPREME COURT OF THE UNITED STATES,

AT

DECEMBER TERM, 1855.

THE UNITED STATES, APPELLANTS, *v.* PEARSON B. READING.

Where there was a grant of land in California, subject to the condition that the
grantee should build a house upon it, and have it inhabited within a year from the
date of the grant, and also that he should obtain a judicial possession and measurement or survey of it, the evidence shows sufficient reasons for a non-compliance on
the part of the grantee.

This court again decides, as in Frémont *v.* United States, 17 How. 560, that a mere
omission to comply with these conditions would not necessarily amount to a forfeiture, unless there were circumstances which showed an intention to abandon the property.

Although the title did not become definitive until the grant was approved by the departmental assembly, yet an immediate interest passed by the grant from the governor,
whose duty it was (and not that of the grantee) to submit the case to the departmental assembly, and if they should reject it, then to lay the case before the supreme
government of the Republic.

If the governor failed to execute this duty, the title remained as it was after the grant
was issued, and is sufficient for confirmation under the act of congress, passed on
March 3, 1851, (9 Stats. at Large, 631.)

The evidence in the present case shows that the grantee was a naturalized citizen of
the Mexican Republic, and the fact that he joined the troops of the United States
when war broke out with Mexico, furnishes no evidence of his intention to abandon
the property, nor any reason why the grant should be forfeited.

THIS was an appeal from the district court of the United States
for the northern district of California.

The claim was originally presented to the board of commissioners, who confirmed it in December, 1852, to the extent and
quantity of six square leagues and no more, as described in the
Mexican grant, if that quantity be contained within the boundaries called for in the grant; and if less, then they confirmed it
for that smaller quantity.

The United States appealed to the district court, which affirmed the decision of the commissioners. An appeal brought
the case up to this court.

The title of Reading is set forth in the opinion of the court, except the conditions of the grant, which were as follows, namely.

"In the name of the Mexican nation I have granted to him said land, subject to the approval of the most excellent departmental assembly, and to the following conditions: —

1. He shall not sell, alienate, or hypothecate it, nor impose on it any tax, entail any other incumbrance, nor shall he donate it.

2. He shall not hinder the cultivation or other profits which the natives of that region may derive from said land.

3. He may inclose it without prejudice to the crossing roads and public uses; he may enjoy it freely, appropriating it to the cultivation which best suits him, but within a year he shall build a house and it shall be inhabited.

4. The land which has been granted is of the extent of which mention has already been made. The judge who shall give the possession shall cause it to be measured according to ordinance, and the overplus which may result shall remain to the nation for convenient uses.

5. If he contravene these conditions, he shall lose his right to the land, and it shall be denounced by any other person."

The case was argued by *Mr. Cushing,* (attorney-general,) for the United States, and by *Mr. Lawrence* and *Mr. Bibb,* for the appellee. There was also a brief filed upon the side of the appellee, by *Mr. Volney E. Howard.*

Mr. Cushing made the following points: —

1. Reading not being a Mexican citizen, could not take and hold a grant of land in a Mexican territory.

For the rule of naturalization prior to 10th September, 1846, see Scmidt's Laws of Spain and Mexico, 353. For additional provisions made then, see Leyes y Decretos, 1844–1846, p. 423.

2. Reading was not entitled to take and hold lands in California, which was frontier territory.

3. The grant was not approved by the departmental assembly.

4. Without the approbation of the departmental assembly, there was no grant passing any title. Fifth regulation of November 21, 1828.

5. Reading would have no claim, in law or equity, upon Mexico to complete and confirm his incipient title, if she had not transferred California to the United States by treaty.

6. Reading abandoned whatever claim he had, before the final conquest by the United States.

Mr. Bibb contended that, with respect to the condition of obtaining the approval of the departmental assembly, it was the duty of the governor, and not the grantee, to lay the case before that body. Fifth and sixth regulations of 1828. The omission or neglect of the governor to do this, could not deprive the grantee of his vested interest. 5 Cranch, 242; 9 How. 833.

So also are the legal maxims, *Nemo punitur sine injuria, facto, seu defalta. Nul prenada advantage de son tort demesne.* Coke's 2 Inst. 287, 718, and maxims at the end of that volume. Domat's Civil Law, Book I. title 1, § 5, par. 17, p. 29; Pothier on Obligations, part 2, chap. 8, par. 212; Co. Litt. 205 *b*; 2 Comyn's Dig. Condition, (D. 7,) p. 827; 5 Viner, Condition, (N. *c*,) pleas 23, 25, p. 246.

With respect to the other condition subsequent, namely, the judicial mensuration and marking out of the boundaries, the evidence shows that the grantee was not to blame.

The United States have not claimed nor attempted to exert the power to annul Mexican grants for non-performance of conditions. 9 Stats. at Large, 633, § 11, *et seq.*

Mr. Justice WAYNE delivered the opinion of the court.

We find in the record of this appeal, that Reading, the appellee, was an immigrant from the United States, in the then Mexican territory of California, in the year 1842, and that he afterwards became a citizen of the Mexican republic. After residing there for two years, he petitioned the governor, Michel Torena, for a grant of land called Buena Ventura, situated on the bank of the River Sacramento, bounded on the north by vacant lands; on the east by the River Sacramento, and on the south and west by vacant lands, according to a plat annexed to his petition. The governor referred the petition to the secretary of state for information concerning it. The secretary, in reply, says, the petitioner was a proper person for the governor's favor, and, upon the official certificate of Jno. A. Sutter, (who was military commandant of the northern frontier of California, and charged with civil jurisdiction also,) he declares that the land asked for was vacant, and could be granted. The governor directed the title to be issued, and it was prepared for his signature.

It is as follows: —

" Citizen Michel Torena, General of Brigade of the Mexican Army, Adjutant-General of the Staff of the same, Governor, Commandant-General, and Inspector of the Department of the Californias.

" Whereas, Don Pearson B. Reading — a Mexican by naturalization — has made application, for his personal benefit, for the land known by the name of Buena Ventura, on the margin of the River Sacramento, from the creek called Lodo, (Lodoso, *Muddy*,) which is on the north as far as the Island de Sangre, with six square leagues in extent; and the proper proceedings and investigations having been previously complied with, according to the provisions of the laws and regulations concerning the matter, by virtue of the authority vested in me, in the name of the Mexican nation, I have granted to him said land, subject to the approval of the most excellent departmental assembly."

There are also conditions annexed to the grant, which may be seen in the reporter's statement of the case. The grant was signed by the governor, and countersigned by the secretary of state, on the 4th of December, 1844, and entered into the archives of the Territory on the same day, with an order from the governor that the title, "being held as valid," should be delivered to the interested party for his security and other purposes.

The power of the governor to make such a grant of land is admitted. The regularity and genuineness of the entire proceeding, and its entry into the archives of the Territory, are not disputed; but Reading's right to a confirmation of it is denied, upon several grounds. Each objection shall have due consideration, not because all of them require it, but to prevent the same points from being urged again in cases of a like kind.

It is said, the grant was provisional only, having been made subject to the approval of the departmental assembly; and, as that had not been given, that it passed no such interest in the land to Reading as entitled him to a confirmation of the grant. Other objections were urged against the confirmation of it, arising out of the national status of Reading when he received the grant, and also out of the fact, that, in the war between Mexico and the United States, he left the standard of the former, and joined the American forces which invaded California. And it was said, as it had been in Frémont's case, that he lost whatever right he had to the land, and subjected it to be denounced by any other person, because he had not complied with the condition to build a house upon it, and to have it inhabited within a year from the date of the grant, and because he had omitted to obtain a judicial possession and measurement, or survey of it. The last two objections are charges of negligence, which must be determined by the proofs in the cause. In our opinion, they do not show either negligence or omission in the particulars mentioned. The witness, Hensley, says, it was upon his suggestion that Reading applied for the land. He knew the locality of it, from having been there. After stating that he had seen a paper purporting to be a grant of the land, dated in December, 1844, he says that Reading visited it in August, 1845, and that they were ten days together upon the land, looking for suitable locations for fields and building sites. That Reading then put upon it a Frenchman named Julian, to build a house for him and to keep possession of it; that, at that time, Reading placed upon the land horses and cattle. That the house was built. It was afterwards burnt by the Indians, and Julian was killed by them. Ford, another witness, who went to that part of the country in March, 1846, as one of a military company to quell an outbreak of the Indians, confirms Hensley's statement in respect to Julian's possession of the land for Reading, but says that he had been forced by the Indians to abandon the house he had built; and that the horses which had been put upon the land, or others belonging to Reading, had been driven from it by Julian, as it was impossible to keep them there on account of the hostilities of the Indians. And Sutter accounts very satisfactorily for Reading's absence from the land during the years of 1845 and 1846, in his reply to the question, if it would have been safe for Reading to have resided personally on his ranche during the revolution and hostilities of those years, when he says, Major Reading had hardly time to do so, as he was nearly all the time required by me to do service. Sutter had said before, in his answer to another question, that he had been, in the years 1844–1846, military commandant of the northern frontier of California, and was also charged with the civil jurisdiction in all that region of country; and, as such, that he had official power to order Reading upon military duty, and that he had done so. It appears also from his testimony, that he kept Reading so employed in the service of Mexico, with the exception of short intervals, from the early part of the spring of 1845 into a part of the year 1846, until Col. Frémont invaded Upper California, when, shortly afterwards, Reading joined him. The facts of the case, in respect to the occupation and cultivation of the land by Reading's agent, disprove the objection. Such an agency for building a house, and having it inhabited by the agent, was as good a compliance with the condition requiring that to be done, as if it had been done personally by Reading. The objection, that he had disregarded the condition of the grant, in not having obtained judicial possession and a survey of the land, is answered by the declaration of Sutter, the only person officially authorized to give it, and without whose permission no survey could have been made. He says, that Reading applied to him in the spring of the year 1845, to be put in judicial possession of the land, but that he had not complied, because his military engagements in the field against the Indians, just before and following the application, had disabled him from doing so; and that the revolution which followed Col. Frémont's coming was his reason for not having given to Read-

1 *

ing judicial possession, according to the prayer of his petition for that purpose.

We have noticed these minor objections against the confirmation of this grant, that the real merits of the transaction might be known, and not because it was essential to the decision of the case. For, even if the proofs in the case, in respect to the grantee's occupancy of the land, had been otherwise than they have been shown to have been, his title to it would not have been lost, because the conditions annexed to the grant had not been fulfilled ; unless it could be shown that there had been on his part such unreasonable delay or want of effort to fulfil those conditions as would amount to an intention "to abandon his claim" before the Mexican power had ceased to exist, and that he was now endeavoring to resume it, from its enhanced value under the government of the United States. This court, considering, in Frémont's case, 17 How. 560, the same objections which are now under our consideration in this, uses the following language : "Regarding the grant to Alvarado, therefore, as having given him a vested interest in the quantity of land therein specified, we proceed to inquire whether there was any breach of the conditions annexed to it, during the continuance of the Mexican authorities, which forfeited his right, and revested the title in the government. The main objection on this ground is the omission to take possession, to have the land surveyed, and to build a house on it within the time limited in the conditions. It is a sufficient answer to this objection to say, that negligence in respect to these conditions and others annexed to the grant, does not, of itself, always forfeit the right of the grantee."

"It subjects the land to be denounced by another, but the conditions do not declare the land forfeited to the State upon the failure of the grantee to perform them. The chief objects of these grants was to colonize and settle the vacant lands. The grants were usually made for that purpose, without any other consideration and without any claim of the grantee on the bounty or justice of the government. But the public had no interest in forfeiting them, even in these cases, unless some other person desired and was ready to occupy them, and thus carry out the policy of extending its settlements. They seem to have been intended to stimulate the grantee to prompt action in settling and colonizing the land, by making it open to appropriation by others in case of his failure to perform them. But, as between him and the government, there is nothing in the language of the conditions, taking them altogether, nor in their evident object and policy, which would justify the court in declaring the land forfeited to the government, where no other person sought to appropriate them, and their performance had not been unreasonably delayed. Nor do we find anything in the practice and usages of the Mexican tribunals, as far as we can ascertain, that would lead to a contrary conclusion."

It was also urged, that no title passed by the grant, as it had not received the approval of the departmental assembly. Our examination of the decrees of the 18th of August, 1824, and of the 21st of November, 1828, leads us to a different result. A right and title passed by the governor's grant, but its definitive validity was suspended for the approval of the assembly; and so it continued to be suspended, until its approbation had been given, when the title became definitive. But if that was refused, it did not take away, nor in any way qualify, the grantee's title, but only kept its final validity in suspense until the grant had been rejected by the supreme government of the republic; it being the duty of the governor, after its rejection by the assembly, to forward the documents of title to the supreme government for its decision.

Further, we must infer from the same decrees, and particularly from the 5th article of that of the 21st of November, 1828, that it was the duty of the governor, and not that of the grantee, to forward grants of land given by him to the departmental assembly. The latter might very well, after that had been done by the governor, solicit the approval of the assembly, personally or by an agent, by all those considerations which had gained him the governor's favor. But if the governor failed to transmit the documents, from any cause whatever, the grantee's title continued to be just what it was when the grant was given. Nor could any neglect or refusal of the governor to transmit his grantee's documents of title to the assembly take from him his right in the land, if the grant had been made with a due regard to what the decree of the 18th of August, 1824, required, and in conformity with the cautionary regulations of that of the 21st of November, 1828. In other words, from our reading of those decrees, the governor could not either directly recall a grant made by him, or indirectly nullify it when it had been conferred conformably with them. Those decrees prescribe a course of action for such grants, and impose upon the governor the execution of it. When, then, the archives of the Territory of the Californias do not show that the governor's grants of land had been sent to the departmental assembly; or that, having been sent, they had been rejected, and that after such rejection they had not been sent, by the governor making the grants, to the supreme executive government for its final decision — the titles of the grantees are just what they were in their beginnings, and are sufficient, now that the territory has been transferred to the United States, for confirmation under its statute of the 3d of March, 1851. Such grants, so circumstanced, are equitable titles, protected by the treaty of Guadalupe Hidalgo, and by the laws and usages of nations concerning the rights of property, real and personal, of the inhabitants of a ceded or conquered country. And, we may add, they are protected by the usages of Mexico in respect to such grants, the archives of California showing that a very large portion of the land in the occupation of its inhabitants was held by titles wanting the approval of the departmental assembly. And we entirely concur with Mr. Commissioner Hall, in the opinion given by him in the case, that the want of such approval in so many instances, as are shown by the archives of the territory, was owing to the fact that the political affairs of the territory had been in confusion for several years preceding its cession to the United States. That the assembly had seldom been called together, and when assembled its sessions had been brief, and occupied with the consideration of pressing matters of a public character; and that the governors making grants had very much neglected to present them to the assembly for approval. We are of the opinion that Reading's right to a confirmation of his grant cannot be refused on account of its not having had the approval of the departmental assembly.

We will now dispose of the objections to a confirmation of this grant, connected with Reading's national status, when he received his documentary title, and with his having subsequently joined the forces of the United States in the war with Mexico. It is said he was not a naturalized citizen of the Mexican republic when the grant was conferred, and that, if he was, his title was forfeited to Mexico, for having fought against her; and, if not forfeited, that his course in that particular should be taken as full proof of his intention to abandon all right and title to the land.

The case, as it is made in the record, does not require from us a particular consideration of the circumstances under which foreigners might receive and retain grants of land, by the decrees of 1824 and 1828. It is enough to say, that the Mexican republic, from the time of its emancipation from Spain, always dealt most liberally with foreigners in its anxiety to colonize its vacant lands. It invited them to settle upon her territory, by promises of protection of them and their property. And, by the first article of the decree of 1828, for colonizing her vacant lands, foreigners were included with those to whom the governors of the territories might make grants of land for the purpose of cultivating and inhabiting them.

But the fact of Reading's Mexican naturalization is not an

open question in this case. The record admits the regularity and genuineness of his documentary title for the land. The admission is as good for all of the necessary recitals in them, as it is for the main purpose for which they were inserted in those documents. That was a grant of the land. The recitals are those "requisite conditions," stated in the second and third paragraphs of the decree of November 21, 1828, concerning which, the governor is enjoined to seek for information, which, when affirmatively ascertained, make the foundation for the governor's exercise of his power to grant vacant lands.

In his petition for a grant, Reading says he is a native of the United States, and had resided in the country since the year 1842. The governor states him to be a Mexican by naturalization, in the grant, and "that as the proper proceedings and investigations had been previously complied with, according to the provisions and laws and regulations concerning the matter," he, in virtue of the authority vested in him, grants to the petitioner the land known as Buena Ventura, on the margin of the River Sacramento, from the creek called Lodo, (Lodoso, Muddy,) which is on the north as far as the Island de Sangre, with six square leagues in extent, subject to the approval of the departmental assembly, and on the conditions annexed to the grant. Now this is not merely the language of clerical formality, though it might be the same from usage in like cases, but it is a declaration of the governor's official and judicial conscience; that his power to make the grant has been used in a fit case, for the approval of it by the departmental assembly, or for the decision of the supreme executive government, in case the action of the assembly should make it necessary for him to carry it there for its decision.

We consider it conclusive of the fact of the petitioner's Mexican naturalization, precluding all other inquiries about it, in our consideration of this case, by the record.

The last objection was that Major Reading having joined the forces of the United States in the war with Mexico, had forfeited his right to the approval of his grant by the authorities of Mexico, which the United States might take advantage of to defeat his claim; and, if not so, that the fact itself raised a strong presumption that he meant to abandon it. As to the last, there is nothing in the record from which such an intention can be inferred, and the fact itself is insufficient for such a purpose. There is much to show the reverse, if the circumstances and condition of the country are considered, when Reading joined Colonel Frémont. There had been in the year 1845 a successful revolution in California, by which Torena, the governor, had been deposed; his powers had been assumed by Colonel Don

José Castro, without any authority from the supreme executive
government of Mexico. It was followed by Indian outbreaks,
with marked hostility to the foreigners who had settled in California, and more so against those from the United States than
to any other class. If they were not instigated, they certainly
were not discouraged by the existing government. Its conduct
indicated its wishes, if not a fixed design, to drive the naturalized immigrants from the United States from their homes and
from the territory. In such a state of things Col. Frémont carried the war into California. Neither the supreme government,
nor the territorial, gave protection to its inhabitants, and it had
become part of the war policy of Mexico to suspect the fidelity
of settlers from the United States to their Mexican allegiance,
and plans were formed to get rid of them. We take the fact
from other authentic sources, and Sutter speaks of it in the
record, with positiveness as to himself. Reading had good
cause for like apprehensions, and having joined Colonel Frémont
under such circumstances, his conduct may be said to have been
blameless of all treachery to Mexico.*

But if they were otherwise, and Reading had voluntarily, and
without circumstances to excuse it, abandoned his Mexican
allegiance for that of his nativity, the United States could not
urge it as a cause for the forfeiture of his title to land acquired
from Mexican laws, and in the mode in which those laws had
been executed by the governors of the states and territories of
that republic.

War has its incidents and rights for persons and for nations,
unlike any that can occur in a time of peace, and they make the
law applicable to them. One of them is, that by the law of
war either party to it may receive and list among his troops such
as quit the other, unless there has been a previous stipulation
that they shall not be received. But when they have been
received, a high moral faith and irrevocable honor, sanctioned
by the usages of all nations, gives to them protection personally,
and security for all that they have or may possess. They are
exempt also from all reproach from the sovereignty to which
their services have been rendered. Nothing that they claim as
their own can be taken from them, upon the imputation that
they had forfeited or meant to relinquish it by the abandonment
of their allegiance to the sovereignty which they had left.

The reverse would partake of Sir Guy Carleton's "impossible
infamy," † though when used by him in reply to a letter from

---

* See Senate Document, report by General Cass, of 23d of February, 1848, on Cal-
ifornia claims. Statement of Samuel I. Hensley, Richard Owens, and deposition of
Wm. N. Lokes.
† Col. Benton's Thirty Years' View, vol. i. p. 90.

General Washington, not so well applied, as it might be, if the United States was allowed to interpret the treaty of Guadalupe Hidalgo, so as to take for itself Reading's land, because he had joined its forces in the war with Mexico.

Having considered every objection made to the confirmation of this grant, and believing no one available for such a purpose, it only remains for us to declare our affirmance of the award of the commissioners, and the decree of the district court.

Mr. Justice DANIEL dissented.

Mr. Justice CATRON.

I agree that the grant to Major Reading describes the land he applied for so that it can be ascertained and surveyed; and secondly, that he took possession and built a house on it within a year after the execution of the grant, in compliance with its material condition, and that the judgments of the board of commissioners, and of the district court of California, were proper. But there are no facts in the case on which any question can be raised, whether the grantee, Reading, was subject to be denounced for failing to take possession and building a house; and therefore I cannot agree that the doctrine should be introduced into the opinion here, as it may embarrass the court in other cases in which the question will properly arise.

Nor can I be committed to the assumption extracted from the Frémont case, and sought to be sanctioned in the principal opinion, that a Spanish concession, authorizing the grantee to occupy and cultivate, is indefeasible in its operation, although the land was never possessed nor occupied, unless some person shall denounce the land as forfeited, and obtain a second concession for it from the governor. The assumption signifies that every incipient concession made by Mexican authority secured the land to the claimant without the performance of any one condition; that the claimant is only bound to prove that the concession was signed by a person holding the office of governor at the time; or, in other words, that the grant was not forged. How ruinous such an assertion may eventually prove in the cases of old and abandoned claims is quite manifest, as it must apply in all cases where the same land is covered by different grants; the oldest will of course be the better title, unless the younger grantee can show that the land had been denounced, and the first grant revoked by the authority that made it. When such a case is presented, and we are called on to consider this doctrine of a "denouncement," I wish to be free to do so, unaffected by previous assertions and *dicta* in cases that did not involve the question, and in which it was never considered by me.

That the Frémont case did not involve the doctrine is manifest; it was a floating claim for 50,000 arpens of land, subject to be located by selection and survey in any part of a large section of country bounded by rivers and mountains; and the opinion of this court was, that Alvarado took, and Colonel Frémont held, as assignee of Alvarado, a pervading interest in the entire section of country, and that the land might be taken anywhere within it, so that the rights of others were not disturbed. The rule is, so far as I know, throughout the former dominions of Spain on this continent, where donations of land have been made for the purposes of cultivation or pasturage, and where the donations imposed the condition that the grantee should occupy and cultivate the land, and he failed to do so or abandoned it, that the claim under it was defeated.

It is assumed that the Frémont claim stood on the footing of that of General Greene, for 25,000 acres derived from North Carolina, to be located and surveyed within the military district by commissioners designated for that purpose.

General Greene's grant, in effect, was a floating claim, just such an interest in the lands as was reserved for the officers and soldiers of the North Carolina line, by virtue of warrants issued to them, and which might be located in a land-office in any part of the military district. This is the doctrine held by the courts of Tennessee, where the land lies, in reference to General Greene's grant, and the interest that warrant holders had in common with General Greene, as will be seen by the case of Neal v. E. T. College, 6 Yerger, 190.

General Greene acquired no specific land; he acquired by the act of the legislature a promise of the specified quantity, to be ascertained by a subsequent survey and allotment. And this was the condition of the Frémont title, as this court decided.

Now, how was it possible for any one to apply to a Mexican governor, and ask for Alvarado's land, because he did not inhabit or cultivate it, or because he had abandoned it? He never had any land; he only had a promise of land, or a common interest in a large tract of country; and the idea of any one denouncing a holder of this floating claim, and asking for the particular land it covered, would have been unmeaning and idle.

The Frémont case, therefore, furnished no grounds for raising or deciding the question of denouncement, and the repeal of the first grant and of re-grant to another. What is now claimed for the opinion in that case, as part of the court's legitimate decision, can only be treated as an assertion, and as part of the reasoning of the court in coming to a conclusion on other questions involved in the controversy.

Cases of denouncement in advance of a second grant for the

same land are unknown in California, so far as we are advised; and the result of holding this proceeding necessary before a second grant could be made, (although no survey of the first had been secured, nor any possession taken,) must result in the conclusion that, among several concessions for the same land, the oldest will hold it; and those in possession under younger grants must yield the possession. This is the common-law doctrine on which the Frémont case is supposed to have been decided. But is this the true rule as regards double grants, according to the Spanish law, as administered in countries formerly owned and governed by Spain?

The law has been established in Louisiana for nearly forty years, that where the Spanish authorities have granted the same land twice, and the younger grantee has taken possession and performed the conditions of inhabitation and cultivation, he is entitled to hold the land; and this was held in contests between the first and second grantees, and in cases where no denouncement had been made in favor of the younger grantee. Boissier et al. *v.* Metayer, 5 Mar. R. 678, (1818;) Gonsanlier's Heirs *v.* Brashear, 5 Martin's N. S. 83; Baker *v.* Thomas, 2 Louisiana R. 634; Brossard *v.* Gonsanlier, 12 Robinson's R. 1.

The correctness of these decisions I have never doubted; and they have been substantially followed by this court, when it held, as it has often done, that a concession or first decree for land, over which no ownership was exercised or possession taken during the existence of the Spanish government, was inoperative, and imposed no obligation on the United States to confirm the title. It was so held in the case of The United States *v.* Boisdoré, 11 How. 96, which has been followed in various other cases since.

With this explanation, I concur in the affirmance of the judgment.

Mr. Justice CAMPBELL. I concur.

Mr. Justice DANIEL, dissenting.

I am unable to concur in the decision of the court in this case.

Waiving in its consideration every exception to the proofs of the naturalization of the appellee, and those also taken to the locality of the subject claimed by him as being forbidden territory, there are other grounds of objection which appear to be conclusive against the pretensions of the appellee.

This was an application to the board of commissioners, for the confirmation of a grant or title alleged to have been made to the appellee by the Mexican government, anterior to the cession of

California to the United States. To entitle the applicant to such confirmation, it was indispensable for him to show that he occupied such a position with respect to the Mexican government as would have enabled him to perfect his title, had there been no relinquishment of the sovereignty of the country by the granting power. It cannot be denied, that a necessary ingredient in a complete title under the Mexican government, was the approbation of the departmental assembly; and the very act itself of the application to the commissioners for a confirmation of title concedes the position, that without such an approval the title must be defective. I cannot concur with the court in thinking that the excuse offered for not obtaining the approbation of the departmental assembly, was a sufficient one; and much less can I suppose that, by such an excuse, an indispensable requisite to the completion of titles could be wholly dispensed with. To tolerate such a position, would render the validity of titles to any and every extent dependent upon the ignorance, the diligence, or the corruption of persons interested in reducing them to such an attitude of uncertainty. Even should it be admitted that there was no particular limit prescribed as to the time of obtaining the sanction of the departmental assembly, and that the appellee might have been excusable for omitting or failing in this requisite, for the time being, still, the conclusion remains unshaken, that, without such approbation, there could by the law of Mexico be no title. If this be true, the objection operates *à multo fortiori* if it be shown that not only was that requisite of approbation wanted, but that its obtention was, by the conduct of the appellee himself, rendered impossible; and under this aspect of the case is presented the stronger ground upon which the claim of the appellee should have been condemned and rejected. This is an application for the confirmation of a grant or title alleged to have been made by the Mexican government to the appellee, as one of the citizens of the Mexican republic.

In order to have invested the appellee with any right as derived from that republic, had its sovereignty over the country remained unchanged, he surely would have been bound to show the continuation of his allegiance to that republic, and the maintenance of those relations, and the fulfilment of those duties, in the existence of which the bounty of the State to him had its origin and motive; at all events, he would be compelled to show himself exempt from the violation of the most sacred obligations which any citizen or subject can sustain to that country and government to which his allegiance is owing. Should he violate such obligation, and become a rebel or traitor to that government, he not only can have no merits in the view of that government, but he becomes obnoxious to the forfeiture of both property and life.

In this case, the appellee seeks the confirmation of a claim derived confessedly from the republic of Mexico; at the same time, by his own showing, and by the testimony of others, it is established undeniably, that before his title was perfected, he became a rebel against that republic, and made every exertion for its destruction. Nay, this case exhibits the inconsistency of urging a right founded on duties sustained to the Mexican republic, with the assumption at the same time of merit deduced from the admitted facts of hostility and faithlessness to that government. The appellee can have no rights to be claimed from or through the Mexican government, to which he became an open enemy. By his conduct he completely abrogated every such right, and became, as respects that government, punishable as a state criminal; and thus not only failed to obtain that sanction without which his title was defective, namely, the approbation of the departmental assembly of Mexico, but, by his own voluntary conduct, rendered its procurement, upon every principle of public law, public or political policy or necessity, or of private morality, altogether impossible.

Were the appellee urging a claim as one deduced from the government of the United States, and originating in services rendered to them, he might then plead his merits with reference to this government in support of his title; but he is claiming a title from Mexico under the stress of Mexican laws; and he proves that by those laws, as they would be under like circumstances by the laws of every country — by the first of all laws, that of self-preservation — his pretensions must be repudiated and condemned. Strange as it may be, we have heard it earnestly pressed as commending this claim to the favorable consideration of this court, that the appellee, after obtaining his incipient grant as a Mexican citizen, and upon the foundation and principles of duty to Mexico, deserted that country when in flagrant war with an enemy, and contributed his utmost exertions for her conquest by that enemy. Were the pretensions of the appellee based upon services rendered to the United States, and were the origin and character of these pretensions to be sought for in the bounty and power of the United States, there might be consistency and integrity in this argument; but so far is this from being true as to the origin and nature of these pretensions, it is shown that these had their origin in that bounty which he has forfeited, and under those obligations which were binding upon the appellee, and which he has deserted and betrayed. The only obligations sustained by the United States to the citizens of Mexico are those which, by their substitution for the government of Mexico, the former have by express stipulation or by necessary implication assumed.

The appellee, then, having unquestionably forfeited every pretension of right as against Mexico, deserted and assailed by him, the United States, as the successors to the sovereignty of Mexico, can sustain no obligation with respect to him in connection with this claim. I think, therefore, that the decision of the court below should be reversed, and petition of the appellee dismissed.

WILLIAM J. McLEAN AND JOHN M. BASS, EXECUTORS OF HENRY R. W. HILL, DECEASED, THE SAID HENRY R. W. HILL AND WILLIAM J. McLEAN BEING THE SURVIVING PARTNERS OF THE FIRM OF N. AND J. DICK AND CO., APPELLANTS, *v.* JAMES L. MEEK, ADMINISTRATOR OF JOSEPH MEEK, AND JAMES L. MEEK AND JOSEPH MEEK.

The record of a debt against an administrator in one State is not sufficient evidence of the debt against an administrator of the same estate in another State.

The case of Stacy *v.* Thrasher, 6 How. 44, examined and affirmed.

In this case, even if there were other evidence of a demand, it would be for a debt upon open account, which would be barred by the statute of limitations in Mississippi, and therefore the decree of the circuit court, dismissing the bill, is affirmed.

THIS was an appeal from the circuit court of the United States for the southern district of Mississippi.

The case was this.

Joseph Meek, a citizen and resident of Davidson county, State of Tennessee, died on the 12th of February, 1838, leaving property in the States of Tennessee and Mississippi. He left three children, namely: James L. Meek, Joseph Meek, and a daughter, who was married to John Munn.

Jesse Meek, the brother of the deceased, was appointed his administrator in both States, namely, in Mississippi on the 30th February, 1838, and in Tennessee in September, 1838.

The estate in Tennessee was insolvent, and in November, 1840, a bill was filed in the chancery court at Franklin, in the State of Tennessee, by Jesse the administrator, and by John Munn and wife, alleging the insolvency of the estate and praying for its administration according to the laws of that State in case of insolvent estates. To this bill the creditors were made parties defendants. The minor sons were also made defendants by their guardian.

Jesse Meek's letters of administration in Mississippi were revoked on 28th December, 1841, and John Munn appointed on the same day administator *de bonis non.* He continued to administer until 12th February, 1849, and on the next day James L. Meek was appointed in his place.

In the progress of the administration in insolvency in Tennessee, the claim of N. and J. Dick and Co., (the surviving partners of which firm were the appellants,) for $21,460.80 was presented to the clerk and master, who had been directed by the court to report on the debts filed against the estate. The claim was allowed for $20,445.67, which report was confirmed by the court. Upon this claim, Dick and Co. received two sums, namely, one of $300 and the other of $1,987.13.

On the 29th of August, 1850, Hill and McLean, as surviving partners of the firm of Dick and Co., filed their bill in the circuit court of the United States for the southern district of Mississippi against James L. Meek, as administrator, which was afterwards so amended as to be against said Meek in his individual capacity, and also against Joseph Meek, one of the heirs.

The only evidence relied upon by the complainants was a transcript of the record from the chancery court of Tennessee.

The circuit court dismissed the bill, and the complainants appealed to this court.

It was submitted on printed arguments by *Mr. Benjamin,* for the appellant, and *Mr. Harris,* for the appellee.

Mr. Benjamin referred to the cases of Aspden *v.* Nixon, 4 How. 467, and Stacy *v.* Thrasher, 6 How. 44, and said: —

These authorities, rightly construed, are conclusive against the appellees. In the present case, the administrator in Tennessee and in Mississippi is the same person; and in the proceedings in chancery in Tennessee, which resulted in a decree establishing the claim of the appellants, the present defendants were parties, as shown by the foregoing statement of facts.

In addition to this consideration, the present defendant, James L., as administrator *de bonis non* of Joseph Meek, is privy with his predecessor, Jesse, in the trust resulting from the administration. The principle is ruled expressly in Stacy *v.* Thrasher, as being the law of Mississippi. See the language of Judge Grier, at page 60.

Mr. Harris referred to the case of Stacy *v.* Thrasher, and contended that, as a simple contract debt, it was barred by the statute of limitations. Hutch. Miss. Code, 830-3.

Mr. Justice CATRON delivered the opinion of the court.

Hill and McLean sued James L. Meek, administrator of

2 *

Joseph Meek, by bill in equity, in the circuit court of the United States for the southern district of Mississippi, for upwards of $20,000, alleged to be due the complainants by Joseph Meek at the time of his death.

He died in February, 1838, and was then domiciled in Davidson county, Tennessee. In September, 1838, Jesse Meek was appointed administrator of Joseph Meek's estate in said county. In November, 1840, the estate was alleged to be insolvent, and a bill was filed in the chancery court exercising jurisdiction in Davidson county, by Jesse Meek, the then administrator, and John Munn and his wife, who was a daughter of Joseph Meek, setting forth the insolvency, and praying for judicial administration of the assets among the creditors of the deceased, according to the statute of that State. To this bill the creditors were the proper defendants, and entitled to share the assets ratably. The other children of the deceased were also made defendants, and acted by their guardian.

Nathaniel and James Dick and Co. presented a claim for allowance of $21,445, and which was allowed by the chancery court in May, 1846, and about $2,000 of it was afterwards paid out of the assets distributed; and for the balance remaining unpaid the present bill was filed, seeking a discovery of assets from the administrator in Mississippi, and payment therefrom.

The evidence relied on to sustain the suit and establish the demand, was a copy of the record from the chancery court of Tennessee; and the principal question is, whether this proceeding bound the administrator or affected the assets in Mississippi.

There is one circumstance worthy of explanation. Jesse Meek administered in Mississippi, 30th February, 1838, on Joseph Meek's estate, but his letters were revoked in 1841, and John Munn was appointed administrator *de bonis non*, and afterwards James L. Meek was appointed, and superseded Munn; and James L. is here sued.

During the contest in the Tennessee court, when Dick and Co. established their demand, Jesse Meek was the Tennessee administrator, and Munn and Joseph L. Meek were successively administrators in Mississippi.

These administrations were independent of each other; the respective administrators represented Meek, the deceased intestate, by an authority coextensive only with the State where the letters of administration were granted, and had jurisdiction of the assets there, and were accountable to creditors and distributees according to the laws of the State granting the authority. No connection existed, or could exist, between them, and therefore a recovery against the one in Tennessee was no evidence against the other in Mississippi. Stacy *v.* Thrasher, 6 How. 44, lays down this distinct rule.

But if there was evidence of the demand, as alleged, and which we do not doubt exists, yet it is only evidence of an open account existing at the time of Joseph Meek's death, in 1838, and therefore subject to be barred by the act of limitations in Mississippi barring such claims, if suit is not brought to enforce them within three years next after the cause of action accrued. The answers of the administrator and heirs of Joseph Meek rely on the act of limitations as a bar to relief, and which bar would necessarily be allowed, if the cause was remanded, so that further evidence might be introduced. As it now stands, however, there is no evidence of the demand, and therefore we order that the decree of the circuit court shall be affirmed.

JACOB KISSELL, PLAINTIFF IN ERROR, *v.* THE BOARD OF THE PRESIDENT AND DIRECTORS OF THE ST. LOUIS PUBLIC SCHOOLS.

The act of congress passed on the 13th of June, 1812, (2 Stats. at Large, 748,) reserved for the support of schools in the respective towns or villages in Missouri "all town or village lots, out-lots or common-field lots, included in such surveys," (which the principal deputy-surveyor was directed in a preceding section to make,) "which are not rightfully owned or claimed by any private individuals, or held as commons belonging to such towns or villages, or that the President of the United States may not think proper to reserve for military purposes, provided that the whole quantity of land contained in the lots reserved shall not exceed one twentieth part of the whole lands included in the general survey of such town or village."

The act of 26th of May, 1824, (4 Stats. at Large, 65,) directed the individual claimants to present their claims within a specified time, after which the surveyor-general was to designate and set apart the lots for the support of schools.

The act of 27th of January, 1831, (4 Stats. at Large, 435,) relinquished the title of the United States in the above lots to the inhabitants of the towns, and also in the lots reserved for the support of schools, to be disposed of or regulated as the legislature of the State might direct.

In 1833, the legislature incorporated a board of commissioners of the St. Louis public schools, and, in 1843, the surveyor returned a plat in conformity with the above laws.

The title to the lots thus indicated by the surveyor as school lots enured to the benefit of the school commissioners. Until the survey, the title was like other imperfect titles in Louisiana, waiting for the public authority to designate the particular land to which the title should attach.

The certificate of the surveyor is record evidence of title, and the question is not open whether or not these lots were out-lots or common-field lots, or other lots described in the statute. The title is good until some person can show a better.

Such a better title was not found in an entry under the pre-emption laws of April 12, 1814, and 29th of April, 1816. The land in question was within the limits of the town of St. Louis, and was also reserved from sale. For both reasons it was not subject to pre-emption.

The ignorance of the pre-emptioner that the land was reserved, does not prevent the entry from being void.

THIS case was brought up from the supreme court of Missouri by a writ of error issued under the 25th section of the judiciary act.

It was an ejectment, brought by the board of school commissioners, to recover from Kissell the following lot in St. Louis county, namely: Beginning on the west side of a street running parallel with and next east of Carondelet Avenue, called Lawrence street or Short street, at a point 120 feet south of the intersection of said street with Wood street; thence westwardly in a line parallel with Wood street 120 feet to an alley; thence southwardly along the said alley 90 feet; thence easterly in a line parallel with Wood street 120 feet, and thence to the place of beginning.

The suit was brought in the St. Louis circuit court, (state court,) where there was a judgment for the plaintiffs. Kissell carried it to the supreme court, where the judgment was affirmed, and a writ of error brought the case up to this court.

The school commissioners claimed title under the three acts of congress mentioned in the head note of the case, and the survey made in 1843, a copy of which was produced in court. Kissell claimed under an entry of fractional section 26, made by Robert Duncan, on the 2d of May, 1836, by virtue of a preemption right.

Without a copy of the map, it is difficult to convey to those members of the profession who are not familiar with Missouri land cases, a clear idea of the nature of this case. It may be proper, however, to mention that it contained numerous long and narrow parallelograms, which, it was contended, were the only lots referred to by the statutes as out-lots, &c., whilst the pieces of land designated by the surveyor as school lands were in detached pieces, scattered about in various places.

It was argued by *Mr. Lawrence* and *Mr. Johnson*, for the plaintiff in error, for whom there was also a printed argument filed by Mr. Thomas C. Johnson, of St. Louis. For the defendants in error, it was argued by *Mr. Geyer*.

The points made on behalf the plaintiff in error, were: 1. That, by the terms of the act of 1812, lots reserved for school purposes were such only as had a previous existence under the Spanish government. 2. That it was to the limits of the Spanish, and not to the limits of the American town, that reference is made in the proviso to the second section, limiting the lots reserved for the support of schools to one twentieth of the land within such town or village; and, 3. That by the term "out boundary," used in the first section, reference is not made to a continuous out boundary or "ring survey," but to the out boundary res ect ve of the town, common-fields, and commons, separately. p   i ly

The points made by *Mr. Geyer* were the following, namely:

1. The act of congress of the 13th of June, 1812, making further provision for settling the claims to land in the Territory of Missouri, and the acts supplementary thereto, of the 26th of May, 1824, and 27th of January, 1831, together with the certificate of the surveyor-general of the survey, designation, and setting apart of the land in controversy, for the support of schools, constitute a complete legal title, equivalent to a patent, conclusive upon the United States, to which the mere entry of the same land with the register and receiver must yield.

2. The survey of the out-boundaries of the town of St. Louis, given in evidence, having been made and certified by the surveyor-general, in pursuance of authority vested in him by law, neither its accuracy nor its validity was open to question in the case at bar.

3. The certificate of the surveyor-general, of the survey, designating and setting apart the land in question, is evidence not only that it is within the out-boundaries, but that it was, at the time of designation, a vacant lot, reserved by the act of 1812, had not been selected for military purposes by the President, and does not, together with the lands before assigned, exceed the maximum limit; and, unless it appeared that the United States had no title, or the surveyor-general no authority to make the survey and designation, it is conclusive, upon a principle applicable alike to all official acts of public officers in the disposition of public lands.

4. The "Plat and description of the survey of the out-boundaries of the town (now city) of St. Louis," made and certified by the surveyor-general, if not absolutely conclusive, is at least *primâ facie* evidence that it is in conformity with the requirements of the act of 1812, and, for the purpose of this case, *that* is all-sufficient. No evidence is necessary to support the survey, and there is none on the record competent to overthrow it.

5. If the survey and designation of the lot in question to the use of schools shall be held to be subject to review in a collateral action at law, still, it requires the production of no evidence in aid of it. It stands for proof until it is rebutted; and, in this case, there is no testimony produced by the defendant below, competent to repel or impair its force.

Mr. Justice CATRON delivered the opinion of the court.

In this case, the school commissioners were plaintiffs in their corporate capacity, and, in order to eject the defendant below, were bound to produce a legal title to the land claimed. Their title depends on three acts of congress, passed in 1812, 1824, and 1831.   The act of 1812 confirmed, to private owners at St. Louis and other villages in Missouri, town lots, out-lots, and common-field lots, in, adjoining, and belonging to the towns, and it also confirmed to the towns their commons.

This act made it the duty of the principal surveyor to survey, or cause to be surveyed and marked, (where the same had not already been done according to law,) the out-boundary lines of the said several towns and villages, so as to include the *out-lots*, common-field lots, and commons thereto respectively belonging.

The second section provides, " that all town or village lots, out-lots, or common-field lots, included in such surveys, which are not rightfully owned or claimed by any private individuals, or held as commons belonging to such towns or villages, or that the President of the United States may not think proper to reserve for military purposes, shall be, and the same are thereby, reserved for the support of schools in the respective towns and villages : *Provided*, the whole quantity of land contained in the lots reserved for the support of schools shall not exceed one twentieth of the whole lands included in the general survey of any town or village."

The first section of the act of the 26th of May, 1824, requires the owners of lots which are confirmed by the act of the 13th of June, 1812, within eighteen months after the passage of the act, " to designate their said lots by proving, before the recorder of land titles, the fact of inhabitation, cultivation, or possession of their said lots, and the boundaries and extent of each claim, so as to enable the surveyor-general to distinguish the private from the vacant lots appertaining to said towns and villages."

The second section of this act makes it the duty of the surveyor-general, immediately after the expiration of the time allowed for private owners to prove the inhabitation, cultivation, and possession of their lots, " to proceed, under the instruction of the commissioner of the general land-office, to survey, designate, and set apart to the said towns and villages, respectively, so many of the said vacant town or village lots, out-lots, and common-field lots, for the support of schools in said towns and villages, respectively, as the President shall not, before that time, have reserved for military purposes, and not exceeding one twentieth part of the whole lands included in the general survey of such town or village, according to the provision of the second section of the act of the 13th of June, 1812; and also to survey and designate, as soon after the passage of this act as may be, the commons belonging to the said towns and villages, according to their respective claims and confirmations under said act of congress, where the same has not already been done."

By the third section of the act, the recorder of land titles is required to issue a certificate of confirmation for each (private) claim confirmed, " and, as soon as the said term (eighteen months) shall have expired, furnish the surveyor-general with the list of lots proved to have been inhabited, cultivated, or possessed, to serve as his guide in distinguishing them from the vacant lots to be set apart as above described, (for the use of schools,) and shall transmit a copy of such list to the commissioner of the general land-office."

On the 27th of January, 1831, an act of congress was passed, for the purpose of transferring the title of the United States (if any) remaining in the property belonging to the several towns and villages embraced by the act of the 13th of June, 1812.

. The first section relinquishes to the inhabitants of the several towns and villages all the right, title, and interest of the United States in and to the town and village lots, out-lots, and common-field lots confirmed to them by the first section of the act of the 13th of June, 1812. The second section relinquishes all right, title, and interest of the United States in and to the town and village lots, out-lots, and common-field lots reserved for the support of schools, by the act of 1812, in the respective towns and villages, and provides that " the same shall be sold or disposed of, or regulated, for the said purpose, in such manner as may be directed by the legislature of the State of Missouri."

The defendants in error were incorporated by a public act of the legislature of Missouri, approved the 13th of February, 1833, entitled " An act to establish a corporation in the city of St. Louis, for the purpose of public education." By the ninth section of this act, the title, possession, charge, and control of all lands and lots in or near St. Louis, granted to the inhabitants for school purposes by any act of congress, is vested in the board of school commissioners, with power to dispose of and apply the same to the purpose of education.

At the trial, the (then) plaintiff gave in evidence the following documents, among others : —

1. A plat called and known as map X, being certified by the surveyor-general to be " a plat and description of the survey of the out-boundary lines of the town (now city) of St. Louis, in the Territory (now State) of Missouri, as it stood incorporated on the 13th of June, 1812, including the out-lots, common-field lots, and commons thereto belonging, made in pursuance of the first section of the act of congress approved the 13th of June, 1812, entitled ' An act making further provision for settling the claims to land in the Territory of Missouri,' which was approved and certified by the surveyor-general, December 8, 1840."

2. A certificate of the surveyor-general, in pursuance of instructions of the commissioner of the general land-office, as follows : —

"*Assignment and Survey, No.* 367.

"Office of the surveyor of public lands in the States of Illinois and Missouri, St. Louis, June 15, 1843.

"Under the instructions of the commissioner of the general land-office, the piece of land, the survey of which is herein platted and described, has been legally surveyed, and under the instructions aforesaid it is hereby designated and set apart to the town (now city) of St. Louis, for the support of schools therein, in conformity with the second section of the act of congress, approved the 26th of May, 1824, entitled an act supplementary to an act passed on the 13th day of June, one thousand eight hundred and twelve, entitled 'An act making further provisions for settling the claims to land in the Territory of Missouri'; the said piece of land hereby designated and set apart as aforesaid is situated within the bounds of the survey directed to be made by the first section of the act of the 13th of June, 1812, aforesaid, so as to include the town-lots, out-lots, common-field lots and commons of the town of St. Louis; and is also within the limits of the said town of St. Louis, as it stood incorporated on the 13th day of June, 1812; and does not, together with all other land designated and set apart to the town of St. Louis for the support of schools, under the aforesaid second section of the act of congress of the 26th of May, 1824, amount to one twentieth of the whole lands included in the general survey directed to be made of said town of St. Louis, by the aforesaid first section of the act of congress of the 13th day of June, 1812; the said piece of land was not, so far as the records of the office show, rightfully owned or claimed by any private individual on the said 13th day of June, 1812; nor was it held as common belonging to the said town of Saint Louis; neither has it been reserved by the President of the United States for military purposes."

Similar certificates are found in the record for other parcels of lands assigned to the use of schools, but not involved in controversy.

When Louisiana was acquired, the lands included in the outboundary survey, comprising St. Louis, its fields and commons, were held by imperfect rights, the legal title being vested in the United States, as they had previously been in the government of Spain. As this government could not be sued in its own courts, nor coerced to perfect equitable claims and rights, claimants had to rely on its justice; and as congress had the full and sole power by the constitution to dispose of the public lands, and to make needful rules and regulations for that purpose, it followed that those who sought titles must obtain them on the terms that congress might prescribe; and more especially were the donations made by the act of 1812, to promote education, regulated by this rule.

By the act of 1812, the towns acquired the promise of, and an imperfect title to, certain vacant lands that might be found to exist within an out-boundary survey, but the government reserved to itself the power to make this survey, and the board of school directors was therefore compelled to remain passive until it was completed, and the private claims within it ascertained, and until the United States designated the school lands comprehended within it.

This survey was completed in 1840 by the surveyor-general, and in 1843 he fulfilled the duty of designating the school lands, whereby they became vested in the authorities of Missouri. These proceedings exhausted the powers of the surveyor-general under the acts we have quoted; and whatever controversies may now arise, in reference to these lands, must be subject to judicial cognizance. See Elliott v. Piersol, 1 Pet. 341.

Our opinion is, that the school lands were in the condition of Spanish claims after confirmation by the United States, without having established and conclusive boundaries made by public authority, and which claims depended for their specific identity on surveys to be executed by the government. The case of West v. Cochran, 17 How. 413, lays down the dividing line between the executive and judicial powers in such cases, to wit: That until a designation, accompanied by a survey or description, was made by the surveyor-general, the title attached to no land, nor had a court of justice jurisdiction to ascertain its boundaries.

We are furthermore of opinion that the certificate of the surveyor-general, above set forth, and which was accepted by the grantees, is record evidence of title, by the recitals in which the government and the board of school directors are mutually bound and concluded. And this instrument, declaring that the land prescribed was reserved for the support of schools, and the courts of justice having no power to revise the acts of the surveyor-general under these statutes, as respects the school lands, it is not open to them to inquire whether the lands set apart were or were not lots of the description referred to in the statutes. The parties interested have agreed that this land was a school lot, and here the matter must rest, unless some third person can show a better title. And the plaintiff in error insists that he has shown a better one by the production of Duncan's entry covering the land. It was allowed by the register and receiver at St. Louis, May 2, 1836, for the fractional section No. 26, by virtue of a pre-emption claim set up by Duncan.

Of this land, the designated school lot claimed by the plaintiff below includes five acres and $\frac{66}{100}$ths of an acre.

The entry was contested, and was brought to the consideration of the commissioner of the general land-office, and upon August 1, 1845, he instructed the register and receiver that only $8\frac{20}{100}$ acres was vacant at that spot; the residue of the $85\frac{49}{100}$ acres surveyed as fractional section 26, had been located on private claims; nor was there evidence that any part of the $8\frac{66}{100}$ acres had been inhabited as required by the pre-emption laws. This inquiry, he remarks, was however unnecessary, because the $8\frac{66}{100}$ acres had been reserved for the support of schools in the town of St. Louis by the act of 1812, and a selection of said land, for that purpose, having been made under the act, "it cannot, therefore, be subject to the operation of the subsequent pre-emption laws of 1814 and 1816."

He further declared: "In addition to the above objection, the said land is within the corporate limits of the city of St. Louis, as established in 1809, and, if not so reserved, would not have been subject to pre-emption subsequent to that time, — the principle having been early settled in a pre-emption case for land within the limits of the town of Mobile, that the right of preemption, designated for the benefit of agriculturists, could not be regarded as applicable to residents within the bounds of an incorporated city or town." For the foregoing reasons, the entry of fractional section 26, for $35\frac{49}{100}$ acres, was cancelled, and the register and receiver were ordered to refund the purchasemoney.

On these facts, the circuit court gave to the jury the following charge: —

"The court is asked to instruct you, that the claims of the respective parties to the land in controversy must depend mainly upon the question, whether the land was reserved for the use of schools by the act of the 13th of June, 1812. In this view the court concurs; but without advising you more at large upon that subject, as requested, gives the case the direction indicated by two of the propositions submitted, one on either side, designed to effect a comparison between the titles of the parties. These are as follows: —

"On the part of the defendant, ' that the pre-emption to Robert Duncan conferred a valid claim under the pre-emption laws, and that he, having settled upon the land before any survey thereof was actually made, is entitled to hold it, and that the persons deriving title from said Duncan have a title superior to the plaintiffs.'

"On the other hand, it is insisted 'that the title of the plaintiffs, under the act of the surveyor-general, designating and setting apart the ground in controversy to the plaintiffs, is superior to the title of the defendant, under an entry with the register and receiver of the land-office'; and of this opinion is the court. The jury is therefore instructed, that, upon the titles exhibited in testimony by the parties, the plaintiff is entitled to recover.

"The court adds, that the defendant has the right to impeach the title of the plaintiff, the same and to the same extent as if the entry of Duncan, under which he claims, had not been vacated by the commissioner of the general land-office. And the court further instructs the jury, that no evidence has been adduced on the part of the defendant competent to invalidate or overthrow the plaintiff's title, and therefore the jury should find for the plaintiff."

The conflicting titles both depend on acts of congress, and are submitted to this court on the whole record; and which we are called on to compare, as was done in the cases of Matthews v. Zane, 4 Cranch, 382; Ross v. Barland, 1 Pet. 664; and Jackson v. Wilcox, 13 Pet. 509. This follows from the instruction given, which maintains that the title of the board of public schools, under the certificate of the surveyor-general, setting apart the land in dispute to the plaintiffs below, was superior to the defendants' title under Duncan's entry with the register and receiver; and that, therefore, the jury was directed to find for the plaintiff. This general instruction raises the question, whether the land was subject to sale, to one claiming a preference of entry under the pre-emption laws.

To which it may be answered, that when the act of 1812 dedicated certain lands for the purposes of education to the use of the village of St. Louis, and the act of 1831 vested the title to these lands in the city, such lands were appropriated, and not subject to sale; they were beyond the reach of the officers of the government, nor could their action lawfully extend to them, with the exception that they could be ascertained and designated within the power reserved. Nor could Duncan be heard to say that he did not know that this parcel of land was reserved. The same excuse might be made, and with a much greater claim to justice and propriety, by one who obtained an entry on land reserved from sale for military purposes, or for some other public use, by the President; the fact of which reservation was hardly known beyond the general and local land-offices; yet such entries have constantly been set aside as absolutely void, or as voidable, by the department of public lands. The case of Wilcox *v.* Jackson, 13 Pet., was an instance of the first kind, where the entry was pronounced as absolutely void, it being in the notorious limits of a reservation for military purposes; and so here the entry of Duncan was within the notorious limits of the city of St. Louis, according to the record of incorporation made by the court of common pleas for St. Louis county, in 1809, and which city limits are recognized by the department of public lands and by the out-boundary survey, as the existing limits when the act of 1812 was passed. This appears from the documents offered in evidence, on which the instruction to the jury was founded. We, therefore, concur with the views expressed by the state courts and those of the commissioner of the general land-office, that Duncan's entry was invalid.

As this concurrence with the state courts is conclusive of the controversy, we do not deem it necessary to examine further into the titles and instructions given to the jury.

It is proper to remark, that we are here dealing with the survey, (marked X,) and ascertaining its effect as regards the lands granted and allotted for school purposes, and are not to be understood as having expressed any opinion on the effect of this out-boundary survey on titles situated beyond it, and claimed to have been confirmed by the act of 1812, or which were subject to be identified by the recorder of land titles, under the act of 1824.

For the reasons above stated, it is ordered that the judgment of the supreme court of Missouri be affirmed.

———

ISAAC HARTSHORN, PLAINTIFF IN ERROR, *v.* HORACE H. DAY.

If the defendant in error files a copy of the record before the expiration of the time which is allowed to the plaintiff in error to file it, and afterwards the plaintiff in error files the record in proper time, the case made by the defendant in error will be dismissed.

THIS case was brought up, by writ of error, from the circuit court of the United States for the District of Rhode Island.

The defendant in error filed the record, and docketed the case on the 24th of November, 1855, and on the ensuing 1st of December the plaintiff in error filed his copy of the record, within the period allowed him by the 63d rule of court.

Mr. Gillett, for the defendant in error, moved the court for leave to withdraw the record filed by him in order to have the same forthwith printed at his own expense.

Upon which motion, Mr. Justice McLEAN delivered the opinion of the court.

In the above case, a motion was made by the defendant that he be permitted to withdraw the record filed and docketed by him, and have it printed at his own expense, without losing its place on the docket.

Rule 63, published in 16 How. requires that, when an appeal on writ of error shall be taken to this court thirty days before the commencement of the ensuing term, the record shall be filed within the first six days of the term ; and if the plaintiff in error or appellant shall fail to comply with this rule the defendant in error or appellee may have the cause docketed and dismissed, upon producing a certificate of the clerk of the court wherein the judgment or decree was rendered, stating the cause, and certifying that such writ of error or appeal has been duly sued out and allowed.

But the rule states, the defendant in error or appellee may, at his option, docket the case and file a copy of the record with the clerk of the court; and if the case is docketed and a copy of the record filed with the clerk of this court, by either party, within the periods of time above limited and prescribed by this rule, the case shall stand for argument at the term.

The above case was docketed in this court, by the defendant in error, before the expiration of the time allowed the plaintiff to file the record.

The plaintiff in error filed the record and had the cause docketed, before the expiration of the six days after the commencement of the term ; he was therefore within the rule, and was guilty of no laches. Had he failed to do this, the defendant, on the certificate of the clerk, might have docketed and dismissed the cause, or he might have procured the record and docketed the case which, under the rule, would stand for argument at the present term. But the case cannot be dismissed or docketed by the defendant, unless the plaintiff in error or appellant shall be in default.

The above cause is, therefore, dismissed.

Order.

Mr. *Gillet*, of counsel for the defendant in error having moved the court on a prior day of the present term, for leave to withdraw this record in order to have the same printed forthwith, and it appearing to the court that this record was filed and docketed at the instance of the defendant in error, on the 24th

3 *

day of November last, and it also appearing that the plaintiff in error had filed the record and docketed the case, on the 1st of December last, within the period allowed him by the 68d rule of court, it is considered by the court that this cause was filed and docketed prematurely by the defendant in error, and should be dismissed — whereupon it is now here ordered by this court that this cause be stricken from the docket and that the record thereof be delivered to the defendant in error.

The United States, Appellants, *v.* John C. Fremont.

Where the record is not filed by the appellant, within the time prescribed by the rules of this court, and the appellee files a copy of it, the appeal will be dismissed upon his motion.

Also, where a mandate went down from this court to the district court of the United States for the northern district of California, and that court entered a decree according to the mandate, this furnishes no ground for an appeal, and the case will be dismissed upon that ground.

This was an appeal from the district court of the United States, for the northern district of California, and was a sequel to the same case reported in 17 How. 553.

As the case involved a principle somewhat novel, and especially an important point of practice, the reporter thinks it proper to insert the papers upon which the motion to dismiss the appeal was founded.

The appellee, J. C. Fremont, (by his counsel,) moves to dismiss this appeal, and brings here into court the certificate of the clerk of the district court of the United States for the northern district of California, stating the case, and certifying the appeal as prayed, allowed, and sued, (at the instance and prayer of the attorney for the United States for the district aforesaid,) for and on behalf of the United States, in the month of July of the present year 1855 —

And for causes of dismissal, the following are assigned and shown.

1. That the said appeal is, in fact and truth, nothing but an appeal from the opinion and decree and mandate of this supreme court of the United States, pronounced between the same parties, at December term, 1854, (reported in 17 How. 553, 576,) entered of record in the said district court of the United States for the northern district of California, in strict conformity with the opinion and mandate of this supreme court, and made the decree of said district court. Wherefore the

appeal, so as aforesaid prayed and allowed, is subversive of order and due subordination, in derogation of the supreme judicial power and authority of the supreme court of the United States as established by the constitution, unlawful in the inception, tending in its consequences, (if indulged,) to vexatious delay and endless litigation.

2. Because the party appellant has failed to docket the case and file the record thereof with the clerk of this court within the first six days of this term, as required by the rules of this court.

The appellee further moves for permission to take out a copy of the dismission, when granted, forthwith, in order to prevent further delay.

JONES, CRITTENDEN, and BIBB,
Dec. 14, 1855.   for Appellee.

MANDATE SUPREME COURT UNITED STATES.

United States of America, ss.

The President of the United States of America, to the Honorable the judge of the district court of the United States for the northern district of California : Greeting : —

Whereas lately, in the district court of the United States for the northern district of California, before you, in a cause between the United States, appellants, and John C. Fremont, claimant and appellee; the decree of the said district court was in the following words, namely : —

This cause coming on to be heard at the above stated term, on appeal from the final decision of the commissioners to ascertain and settle private land claims in the State of California, under the act of congress approved March 8, 1851, upon the transcript of the proceedings and decision, and the papers and evidence on which said decision was founded, and also upon the testimony and depositions taken before this court, and the arguments of counsel for the United States and for the claimant being heard, it is ordered, adjudged, and decreed, that the decision of the said commissioners be in all things reversed and annulled, and that the said claim be held invalid and rejected, " as by the inspection of the transcript of the record of the said district court which was brought into the supreme court of the United States, by virtue of an appeal agreeably to the act of congress in such cases made and provided, fully and at large appears.

And whereas in the present term of December, in the year of our Lord one thousand eight hundred and fifty-four, the said cause came on to be heard before the said supreme court on the said transcript of the record, and was argued by counsel, on

United States v. Fremont.

consideration whereof it is the opinion of this court that the claim of the petitioner to the land as described and set forth in the record is a good and valid claim. Whereupon it is now here, ordered, adjudged, and decreed, by this court, that the decree of the said district court in this case be and the same is hereby reversed, and that this cause be and the same is hereby remanded to the said district court for further proceedings to be had therein, in conformity to the opinion of this court.

You, therefore, are hereby commanded that such further proceedings be had in said cause, in conformity to the opinion and decree of this court as according to right and justice, and the laws of the United States, ought to be had, the said appeal notwithstanding.

Witness the Honorable Roger B. Taney, chief justice of said supreme court, the first Monday of December, in the year of our Lord one thousand eight hundred and fifty-four.

Wm. Thomas Carroll,
Clerk Supreme Court of the United States.

Indorsed: Filed June 4, 1855.
    John A. Monroe, *Clerk.*
    By W. H. Chevers, *Deputy.*

Decree of United States District Court.

The United States, appellants,
    v.   } Stated term, June 27, 1855.
John C. Fremont, appellee. }

Comes now the said John C. Fremont, by his attorney, and the United States by theirs, also come, and the mandate of the supreme court of the United States having been filed in this court, duly authenticated under the seal of the said supreme court, and certified by the clerk thereof—whereby it appears that at the December term of said supreme court, 1854, that is to say, on the 10th day of March, 1855, upon the appeal by the said John C. Fremont, from the decree of this court, reversing the decision of the said commissioners, and holding invalid and rejecting the claim of the said John C. Fremont, (the said appeal having come on to be heard before the said supreme court, upon the transcript of the record of this court,) the said supreme court rendered, and pronounced a judgment and decree in the following words to wit: " It is the opinion of this court that the claim of the petitioner to the land as described and set forth in the record, is a good and valid claim. Whereupon, it is now here adjudged and decreed by this court that the decree of the said district court in this cause be and the same is hereby reversed, and that this cause be and the same is hereby remanded to the

United States v. Fremont.

said district court for further proceedings to be had therein in conformity to the opinion of this court.

It is therefore ordered, adjudged, and decreed, by this court, that the claim of the said John C. Fremont, to the land as described and set forth in the record, is a good and valid claim, and that the said claim be and the same is hereby confirmed to the extent of ten square leagues, the quantity specified in the original grant, set forth in the record, and within the limits therein mentioned, the said land to be surveyed in the form and divisions prescribed by law for surveys in California and in one entire tract.

M. HALL McALLISTER,
Circuit Judge United States District of California.
OGDEN HOFFMAN, Jr.
United States District Judge.

Indorsed : Filed June 27, 1855.
  JOHN A. MONROE, *Clerk.*
  By W. H. CHEVERS, *Deputy.*

<hr>

Notice of Appeal.

District court of the United States in and for the northern district of California.

The United States, appellants, }
  v.
John C. Fremont, appellee. }

Sir: The United States intend to appeal from the final decree of the court in this cause.

S. W. INGE,
United States District Attorney.

To JOHN A. MONROE, Esq., *Clerk.*

Indorsed : Filed, June 27, 1855.
  JOHN A. MONROE, *Clerk.*
  By W. H. CHEVERS, *Deputy.*

<hr>

District court of the United States in and for the northern district of California.

The United States, appellants, }
  v.
John C. Fremont, appellee. } .

Sir: The United States intend to appeal from the final decree of the court in this cause.

S. W. INGE,
United States District Attorney.

To VOLNEY E. HOWARD, Esq.

Marshal's Return.

I served this notice in person, by copy, on V. E. Howard, this 27th day of June, 1855.

W. H. RICHARDSON, *United States Marshal.*
By Q. E. SEWELL, *Deputy.*

Indorsed: Filed, June 28, 1855.
JOHN A. MONROE, *Clerk.*
By W. H. CHEVERS, *Deputy.*

In the district court of the United States for the northern district of California.

The United States *v.* John C. Fremont.	Appeal from the board of commissioners to ascertain and settle private land-claims in California.

Be it remembered that on the return of the mandate from the supreme court of the United States, (in the appeal from the decision of this court heretofore rendered in this cause,) the said John C. Fremont moved the court to pronounce a decree in pursuance of said mandate, in the form of the decree in that behalf in the record of this cause appearing, (except-*Bill of ex-* ing the following words, to wit: "The said land to *ceptions.* be surveyed in the form and divisions prescribed by law for surveys in California, and in one entire tract,") to which motion the attorney for the United States objected, and after arguments, the court, on June 27, 1855, refused to render the decree as prayed by the said John C. Fremont, but added thereto the words above quoted, as to the mode of survey, and rendered the decree in this behalf accordingly, to which decision of the court (adding the above quoted words) and to the said portion of said decree directing the mode of survey, the said John C. Fremont by his counsel, at the proper time, duly excepted, and prayed that this his exception be signed and sealed by the court, and made a part of the record of this cause, which is accordingly done.

M. HALL MCALLISTER,
Circuit Judge United States for the District of California, and Presiding Officer United States District Court.
OGDEN HOFFMAN, Jr.
United States District Judge, Northern District of California.

Indorsed: Filed, June 28, 1855.
JOHN A. MONROE, *Clerk.*
By W. H. CHEVERS, *Deputy.*

Order granting Appeal.

At a stated term of the district court of the United States of America, for the northern district of California, held at the court-house in the city of San Francisco on Monday, the 23d day of July, in the year of our Lord one thousand eight hundred and fifty-five.

Present: —

HON. M. H. MCALLISTER, *Circuit Judge.*
HON. OGDEN HOFFMAN, JR., *District Judge.*

The United States, appellants, }
             v.   }
John C. Fremont, appellee. }

In this case, on application of the United States attorney, made in open court, it is ordered by the court, that an appeal on behalf of the United States from the final decision of this court rendered in said cause at the present term be and the same is hereby granted.

And that a certified transcript of the pleadings, evidence, depositions, and proceedings in the said cause be sent to the supreme court of the United States, without delay.

Indorsed: Filed July 23, 1855.

JOHN A. MONROE, *Clerk.*
By W. H. CHEVERS, *Deputy.*

UNITED STATES OF AMERICA.

Northern District of California.

I, John A. Monroe, clerk of the district court of the United States of America for the northern district of California, do hereby certify that the annexed pages from one to one hundred and twenty inclusive, contain a full, true, and correct transcript of the record on file from the Board of Land Commissioners, together with the pleadings, depositions, orders, opinion, decrees, bond, mandate of the supreme court of the United States, and the proceedings thereon in this court, filed in this office in the case entitled: The United States, appellants, *v.* John C. Fremont, appellee.

In testimony whereof I have hereunto set my hand and affixed the seal of the said court, this 18th day of October, in the year of our Lord one thousand eight hundred and fifty-five, and of our Independence the eightieth.

JOHN A. MONROE, *Clerk.*
By W. H. CHEVERS, *Deputy.*

Mr. Justice McLEAN delivered the opinion of the court.

This is an appeal from the northern district of California.

A final decree was entered in this case at the last term, and a mandate was issued to the district court, directing such further proceedings in conformity to the opinion and decree of this court, as according to right and justice, and the laws of the United States, ought to be had.

This court reversed the decision of the district court, and ordered, adjudged, and decreed, that the claim of the said John C. Fremont, to the land as described, and set forth in the record, is a good and valid claim; and that the said claim be, and the same is hereby confirmed to the extent of ten square leagues, the quantity specified in the original grant, set forth in the record and within the limits therein mentioned, the said land to be surveyed in the form and divisions prescribed by law for surveys in California, and in one entire tract."

The mandate was filed in the district court, and the counsel of Fremont moved the court for an order in pursuance of said mandate, in the form of the decree in that behalf elsewhere in the record of the case appearing, excepting the following words, " the said land to be surveyed in the form and divisions prescribed by law, for surveys in California, and in one entire tract," which motion was opposed by the district attorney of the United States. The district court entered the decree upon its record, refusing to omit the words, moved by the appellee, and to this refusal his counsel excepted.

No further proceedings were had, as appears from the record; and at a subsequent day of the district court, the attorney of the United States applied for an appeal in open court, in behalf of the United States, from the final decision of that court, at the above term, which was granted.

The appeal was allowed the 23d of July, 1855, more than three months before the commencement of the present term of this court; and no record of the case having been filed within six days, after the commencement of the term, as the rule requires, a record of the case being filed by the appellee, a motion is made to dismiss the appeal on the ground that there was no action of the district court on which an appeal could be taken. And also, on the ground that the appellants have failed to file the record within the rule.

It was the duty of the appellants to file the record and docket the cause, within the first six days of the present term; the decree appealed from having been entered sixty days before the commencement of the present term. With the exception of California, Oregon, Washington, New Mexico, and Utah, appeals or writs of error allowed are required to be docketed within the first six days of the term, if entered or allowed, thirty days before its commencement.

The appellants having failed to file the record, it was filed by the appellee, which entitles him, under the rule, to have the cause dismissed.

But the counsel for the appellee insist that the appeal should be dismissed, on the ground that it was taken with the intent to bring before this court a review of its decree entered at the last term. As there was no action by the district court, except the entry of the mandate upon its records, the appeal brings before us only, that which was transmitted to the district court by the mandate. This is an irregular procedure; and it must have been entered without a particular examination by the court.

The appeal is dismissed, and the clerk is directed, forthwith, to certify this decision to the district court.

Mr. Justice CATRON.

I agree that, by the 19th, 30th, 43d, and 63d rules governing the practice of this court, the record presented was not filed in time, and that therefore the appeal must be dismissed for want of prosecution. But I do not concur that, on the present motion to dismiss, we ought to decide the question, whether the district court could or could not allow the appeal on the decree made there, on the ground that the decree did not conform to the mandate of this court.

The motion to dismiss for want of prosecution, and the motion to dismiss for want of jurisdiction, to entertain the appeal, are different and distinct in their character; the one only dismisses the appeal and allows a second; and the other bars it.

The practice has been, when the record was not filed in time, for the defendant in error, or appellee, to produce a certificate from the clerk, or a copy of the record duly certified, showing that the writ of error or appeal had been ytaken, and that it operated as a *supersedeas*, when the cause was docketed' and dismissed. But when a motion was made to dismiss the cause for want of jurisdiction in this court to entertain the writ of error or appeal; or in other words, want of authority in the court below to allow it, (which is the question here,) then the record was ordered to be printed, briefs filed, and the question discussed in the usual way. Nor has it ever occurred in my experience in this court, to set down a cause to be heard at the same time, on both motions. The consequence must be in such a proceeding, that if the plaintiff in error is turned out of court for his neglect, in not filing the record in time, he has no power to move for a *certiorari* to amend the record, filed by the other

side, and then this court bars a second appeal by further adjudg-
ing that no jurisdiction existed in the inferior court to allow it.
And such is the judgment in this case.

Some of the most stringent controversies that have come
before us, have arisen on motions to dismiss for want of jurisdiction, and especially in causes brought here from state courts
under the 25th section of the judiciary act.

The idea in such cases, that a state court decision should in
effect be affirmed, and the plaintiff in error barred, by dismissing case for want of jurisdiction, on the presentment of a manuscript record, without furnishing the court with even a brief (as
was done here) is not only contrary to our established practice,
but is calculated to do great mischief to suitors.

In the instance before us, I never saw the papers until after I
heard the opinion of the majority of the court read. I deemed
it unimportant, on the first question, to read the record, as it had
not been filed in time, nor was a valid excuse offered for the
delay. On the second question, I had then formed no opinion.
In his remarks, the attorney-general referred us to a letter of the
district attorney of the United States for the northern district
of California, which was officially written to the secretary of the
interior, and presented to us, as part of the attorney-general's
argument, setting forth the reasons why the appeal was prosecuted. These reasons, in substance, are, that this court, in its
opinion delivered by the chief justice at the last term (17 How.
565), remanded the cause, and directed the court below to enter
a decree conformably to that opinion; which opinion (ibid. 558)
declared: "That if any other person within the limits where the
quantity granted to Alvarado should be located had afterwards
obtained a grant by specific boundaries before Alvarado had
made his survey, the title of the latter grantee could not be
impaired by any subsequent survey for Alvarado; and that as
between individual claimants from the government, the title of
the party who had obtained a grant for the specific land would
be the superior and better one."

And it is insisted, in this argument, that the district court
should have inserted in its decree the foregoing conclusions,
and have protected individual titles and rights in the region of
country where Colonel Fremont's claim might be located, ordering that such lands should be excluded from the survey as
Fremont's land, although they were embraced within its out-
boundaries. And, secondly, that, in the opinion of this court,
the district court was directed to cause the grant to Alvarado to
be surveyed, " in the form and divisions prescribed by law for
surveys in California." But that it had made no decree as to
the form of the survey, and disregarded the instruction, leaving

it to the surveyor to ascertain the law, and to locate the land, according to the law of California, whether it was Mexican or United States law; whereas, it is insisted that the true construction of the grant to Alvarado, (as to the manner in which it shall be surveyed,) was a judicial question; and that, as the concession was for the purposes of cultivation and pasturage, a survey should be made of lands suited to these purposes, and that the district court ought so to have adjudged and decreed and to have excluded a survey of barren mountains, including improved gold-mines, contrary to the plain intention of the parties to the grant as originally made.

The questions presented were supposed to be of grave importance and much difficulty, and, therefore, no imputation of unfair and oppressive conduct should be cast on the officer of the government who prayed this appeal, under the express sanction of the district court.

It is manifest that Fremont, the appellee, believed he might appeal, if he saw proper to do so. He took a bill of exceptions, and had it signed by the court, to its ruling, that his claim should be surveyed in one tract. As no bill of exceptions lies, in cases of this description, an appeal could have been prosecuted, on the affirmative fact, that too much had been inserted in the decree, contrary to the mandate of this court; so, on the other hand, if not enough was put into the decree, to execute the mandate, an appeal would equally lie. As a general rule, this is undoubted. It is plainly apparent that both parties, and the court, believed that an appeal would lie.

I hold it to be true, however, that the appeal should not have been allowed. By the treaty of peace with Mexico, the legal title to the public lands in California was vested in the United States, onerated with private claims to parts thereof. Alvarado's claim was presented as one of this character, and being brought before this court, was pronounced to be a good and subsisting claim; and furthermore, that all the conditions it contained were subsequent conditions, which, by the treaty, ceased to have any binding force; and, therefore, they were struck from the grant as being no necessary part thereof. It was also held that the claim, in this condition, was assignable, and properly assigned to Colonel Fremont; and, as there was no grant to any specific tract of land, that Colonel Fremont held a common interest in the public lands generally, lying within a large section of country described in the grant.

This decision reduced the claim to the condition of a mere floating land-warrant, that could not be located by judicial authority, more than an ordinary floating warrant can be located by the decree of a court; and, therefore, when seeking location it must, of necessity, address itself to the executive or legislative power.

The district court, having entered the decree as directed, had no jurisdiction to take any further step in the cause. It follows that the executive department must determine for itself whether any law exists authorizing that branch of the government to ascertain and survey the land, and issue a patent for it, by which the title of the United States will be devested, and transferred to the grantee.

Order.

This cause came on to be heard on the transcript of the record from the district court of the United States for the northern district of California, filed by the appellee, John C. Fremont, and, on the motion of Messrs. Crittenden and Bibb, of counsel for the appellee, to docket and dismiss this appeal, pursuant to the 63d rule of this court, and was argued by counsel, as well against as in support of the said motion. On consideration whereof, it appearing to this court that the appellants have altogether failed to prosecute their appeal pursuant to the rules of this court. And, also, as the mandate only was entered on the records of the district court, no action being had thereon, that there was no ground for an appeal in this cause from the said district court, it is thereupon now here ordered, adjudged, and decreed by this court, that this appeal be and the same is hereby docketed and dismissed, and that this cause be and the same is hereby remanded to the said district court, with directions to proceed therein according to law and in conformity to this decision. And it is further ordered by this court here, that the clerk do forthwith issue a writ of *procedendo* in this cause to the said district court.

EX PARTE IN THE MATTER OF LATHROP L. STURGESS *v.* CHRISTIAN HARROLD. ALSO, GEORGE BUCKLEY *v.* CHRISTIAN HARROLD.

A certificate from the clerk of the circuit court, that he cannot make out the record in time to comply with the 63d rule of this court, does not furnish a sufficient reason for an extension of the time prescribed by that rule.

Mr. Lawrence, of counsel for the plaintiffs in error in these cases, filed certificates of the clerk of the circuit court of the United States for the eastern district of Louisiana, stating that judgments were entered against the plaintiffs in error in that court, on the 16th day of November, 1855, and that writs of error were duly applied for, and allowed on the 21st of November, 1855, returnable to the December term, 1855, of the supreme court of the United States. The certificates further stated that the clerk could not, consistently with the other duties of his office, make out and have ready the transcripts of the records and proceedings at the opening of the term of the supreme court, nor within less than ninety days thereafter.

Whereupon, *Mr. Lawrence* applied for an extension of time under the 63d rule of this court.

Mr. Justice McLEAN delivered the opinion of the court.

In the above cases writs of error were allowed on the 21st day of November last, the judgments having been entered on the 16th of that month. The clerk of the circuit court certifies that he cannot, consistently with the other duties of his office, make out and have ready the transcript of the record and proceedings in the said causes, in time for the same to reach Washington City at the opening of the term of the supreme court, nor within less than ninety days thereafter.

On this statement of the clerk, a motion is made for longer time to certify the record.

At the December term, 1853, this court adopted a rule requiring, where a judgment or decree was entered thirty days before the succeeding term of this court, that the writ of error or appeal should be entered on the record of this court, and the record filed within the first six days of the term. But if less than thirty days intervene between the entry of the judgment or decree and the sitting of this court, the case should be entered on the docket of this court, and the record filed, within thirty days from the commencement of the term.

The above rule was adopted to prevent unnecessary and improper delays, in prosecuting writs of error or appeals in this court from the inferior courts. Thirty days from the commencement of this term affords ample time to the clerk, to make out and forward the records in the above cases. The rules of this court can, in no respect, depend upon the convenience of the clerks of the inferior courts.

Extension denied, and motion overruled.

4*

JAMES B. PECK ET AL., APPELLANTS, *v.* JOHN SANDERSON, LIBELLANT.

This court cannot grant a motion for the rehearing of a cause which has been transmitted to the court below.

THIS case was argued and decided at the last term, and is reported in 17 Howard.

Mr. Rush, of counsel for the appellee, now stated to the court that a petition from the appellee was on file, verified by affidavit, and moved for a rehearing, which was opposed by *Mr. Wahr*, counsel for the appellant.

Mr. Justice McLEAN delivered the opinion of the court.

This case was decided at the last term, on an appeal from the circuit court of the United States for the eastern district of Pennsylvania, and a motion is now made by *Mr. Rush*, counsel for the appellee, for a reargument, on the ground that he was prevented by sickness from attending the court at the time of the hearing.

It is a subject of regret that any cause should be heard in the absence of counsel, and especially where the cause of absence, by a failure in the mail, was unknown to the court.

In the above case, the brief of the counsel was before the court, and it is not probable that an oral argument would have changed the result.

But in the case of Browder *v.* McArthur, 7 Wheat. 58, it was held that this court cannot grant a rehearing in a case which has been remitted to the court below; and in the case of the Washington Bridge Company *v.* Stewart et al. 3 How. 413, the same principle was recognized. The motion is overruled.

Barnard's Heirs v. Ashley's Heirs et al.

ELIZABETH J. BARNARD, MARY A. BARNARD, CORRINE BARNARD, WILLIAM S. BARNARD, AND THOMAS BARNARD, INFANT CHILDREN AND SOLE HEIRS OF THOMAS BARNARD, DECEASED, BY WILLIAM CANNON, THEIR GUARDIAN AND NEXT FRIEND, COMPLAINANTS AND APPELLANTS, v. MARY W. W. ASHLEY, EXECUTRIX, AND WILLIAM E. ASHLEY, AND FRANCES A. ASHLEY, AND HENRY C. ASHLEY, AN INFANT, BY MARY W. W. ASHLEY, HIS GUARDIAN, HEIRS, &c. OF CHESTER ASHLEY, DECEASED, AND SILAS CRAIG'S REPRESENTATIVES.

The act of congress passed on the 4th of July, 1836, (5 Stats. at Large, 107,) provided for a direct supervision by the commissioner of the general land-office over registers and receivers of the land-offices, and therefore their judgment is not conclusive in a case where additional proceedings were had before them in 1837.

The cases of Wilcox v. Jackson, 13 Pet. 511, and Lytle v. Arkansas, 9 How. 333, commented on and explained.

Where a survey was approved on June 4, 1834, a selection made, under the authority of congress, by Governor Pope, on June 6, 1834, the lands thus selected were not open to pre-emptions under the act of June 19, 1834.

Where there was an erroneous survey, a selection of a section did not attach until a correct survey was returned, which was not until the 19th of July, 1834. As the pre-emption law was passed on the 19th of June, 1834, an occupant of the selection would have had the better title, if he could have brought himself within the conditions of the law. But the evidence shows that he could not do so.

By the act of congress passed on January 6, 1829, (4 Stats. at Large, 329,) a donation claim could not be located upon land occupied by an actual settler. But in this case, the evidence shows that the land in question was not so occupied.

THIS was an appeal from the circuit court of the United States for the southern district of New York.

The case is stated in the opinion of the court.

It was argued by *Mr. Pike*, for the appellants, and by *Mr. Lawrence* and *Mr. Crittenden*, for the appellees.

The points of law made by the respective counsel were so interwoven with the facts, that they cannot be explained without an elaborate statement of the case.

Mr. Justice CATRON delivered the opinion of the court.

The proceedings in the court below consisted of a bill filed by Barnard against Ashley and Craig, praying that certain patents for lands issued to the defendants might be decreed to be cancelled, upon the ground of a violation of pre-emption rights on part of the complainant, to the following tracts, namely: N. E. ¼ and S. W. fr. ¼ of sec. 27; S. E. fr. ¼ of sec. 28, T. 18 S., R. 1 W.; S. W. fr. ¼ of sec. 15, T. 19 S., R. 1 W.; S. E. ¼ of sec. 22, T. 18 S., R. 1 W.; and a cross-bill on part of Ashley to be quieted in his title to the S. E. qr. of sec. 22, against the right set up by Barnard to that tract, under a junior patent therefor, upon the ground that Barnard had no right to this tract, and that the patent was issued to him improperly.

The title of Ashley and Craig (the appellees) to the first four tracts is derived from a sale to them of the land in controversy by the governor of Arkansas, in consequence of a selection made by him of the land under certain provisions of the acts of congress of the 2d of March, 1831, and the 4th of July, 1832, (4 Stats. at Large, 478, 563,) upon which selection and sale patents were issued by the United States. The title to the S. E. ¼ of sec. 22, T. 18 S., R. 1 W., is derived from the location of what is called a "Lovely donation claim" on this quarter section, by virtue of the provisions of the 8th section of the acts of the 24th of May, 1828, (4 Stats. at Large, 306,) and 6th of January, 1829, (Ibid. 829.)

According to the conceded facts, it is insisted, on the part of Ashley and Craig, that the register and receiver having, on due proof and examination, rejected Barnard's claims to a preference of entry of the four quarter sections, he is thereby concluded from setting them up in a court of equity, because the register and receiver acted in a judicial capacity, and their judgment, being subject to no appeal is conclusive of the claim. And the cases of Jackson v. Wilcox, and Lytle v. The State of Arkansas are relied on to maintain this position.

In cases arising under the pre-emption laws of the 29th of May, 1830, and of the 19th of June, 1834, the power of ascertaining and deciding on the facts which entitled a party to the right of pre-emption was vested in the register and receiver of the land district in which the land was situated, from whose decision there was no direct appeal to higher authority. But, even under these laws, the proof on which the claim was to rest was to be made "agreeably to the rules to be prescribed by the commissioner of the general land-office"; and, if not so made, the entry would be suspended, when the proceeding was brought before the commissioner by an opposing claimant. In cases, however, like the one before us, where an entry had been allowed on *ex parte* affidavits, which were impeached, and the land claimed by another, founded on an opposing entry, the course pursued at the general land-office was to return the proofs and allegations, in opposition to the entry, to the district office, with instructions to call all the parties before the register and receiver, with a view of instituting an inquiry into the matters charged; allowing each party, on due notice, an opportunity of cross-examining the witnesses of the other, each being allowed to introduce proofs; and, on the close of the investigation, the register and receiver were instructed to report the proceeding to the general land-office, with their opinion as to the effect of the proof, and the case made by the additional testimony. And, on this return, the commissioner does in fact exercise a supervision over the acts of the register and receiver. This power of revision is exercised by virtue of the act of July 4, 1836, § 1, which provides " that, from and after the passage of this act, the executive duties now prescribed, or which may hereafter be prescribed by law, appertaining to the surveying and sale of the public lands of the United States, or in anywise respecting such public lands; and also such as relate to private claims of land, and the issuing of patents for all grants of land under the authority of the government of the United States, shall be subject to the supervision and control of the commissioner of the general land-office, under the direction of the President of the United States." The necessity of " supervision and control," vested in the commissioner, acting under the direction of the President, is too manifest to require comment, further than to say that the facts found in this record show that nothing is more easily done than apparently to establish, by *ex parte* affidavits, cultivation and possession of particular quarter sections of land, when the fact is untrue. That the act of 1836 modifies the powers of registers and receivers to the extent of the commissioner's action in the instances before us, we hold to be true. But if the construction of the act of 1836, to this effect, were doubtful, the practice under it for nearly twenty years could not be disturbed without manifest impropriety.

The case relied on, of Wilcox v. Jackson, 13 Pet. 511, was an ejectment suit, commenced in February, 1836; and as to the acts of the register and receiver, in allowing the entry in that case, the commissioner had no power of supervision, such as was given to him by the act of July 4, 1836, after the cause was in court.

In the next case, 9 How. 333, all the controverted facts on which both sides relied had transpired, and were concluded before the act of July 4, 1836, was passed; and therefore its construction, as regards the commissioner's powers, under the act of 1836, was not involved. Whereas, in the case under consideration, the additional proceedings were had before the register and receiver in 1837, and were subject to the new powers conferred on the commissioner.

In Lytle's case, we declared that the occupant was wrongfully deprived of his lawful right of entry, under the pre-emption laws, and the title set up under the selection of the governor of Arkansas was decreed to Cloyes, the claimant, this court holding his claim to the land to have been a legal right, by virtue of the occupancy and cultivation, subject to be defeated only by a failure to perform the conditions of making proof and tendering the purchase-money. There the facts were examined to ascertain which party had the better right; and, following out that precedent, we must do so here.

Governor Pope was authorized to select lands equal to ten sections in the Territory of Arkansas, in tracts not less than a quarter section each, and to sell the same for the purpose of raising a fund to erect public buildings in the territory. The three first-named quarter sections lie in township 18, the survey of which was made and returned to the local land-office, and approved June 4, 1834, when the lands therein were subject to entry by the governor.

He made his final amended selections of the three tracts in township 18, June 6, 1834. The bill claims title to these tracts under the occupant law of June 19, 1834. As Governor Pope's assignees, Craig and Ashley had a vested right when the act of June 19 was passed; it did not operate on these lands, which were appropriated to the use of the United States; and patents for them were properly awarded to the purchasers from the governor.

The condition of the S. W. quarter of sec. 15, T. 19, differs from the preceding lands in this: the township survey of No. 19 was found to be inaccurate when first returned to the land-office at Little Rock, and a resurvey was ordered as to some of the section lines, which were not finally adjusted till the 19th of July, 1834.

Governor Pope had selected the S. W. quarter of sec. 15 on the 29th of May preceding, relying on the inaccurate survey; and it is insisted for Barnard's heirs, that the selection was invalid, as it could not be made of unsurveyed lands; and that township No. 19 could not be legally recognized as surveyed, until the survey was settled and adopted by the surveyor-general of the district.

Our opinion is, that the selection could only take effect from the 19th of July, 1834, when the township survey was sanctioned, and became a record in the district land-office. As the occupant law passed June 19, 1834, Barnard's assignor, Richmond, could lawfully enter the quarter section, if he had occupied the same as required by law; that is to say, if he was in possession when the act was passed, and cultivated any part of the land in the year 1833.

The bill alleges that Richmond occupied the quarter section June 19, 1834; that he had cultivated the same in 1833, and made due proof of his right of pre-emption.

It is further alleged, that on the 20th day of January, 1834, some five months before the occupant law was passed, Barnard purchased from Richmond the quarter section in dispute, and took his title bond for a conveyance when Richmond should obtain a patent for the land; and by force of this bond the bill prays to have the patent to Craig and Ashley adjudged to have been for Barnard's benefit, and that the land be decreed to Barnard's heirs.

The act of 1834 revived the act of 29th of May, 1830, "to grant pre-emption rights to settlers." That act provides, (§ 8,) "that all assignments and transfers of rights of pre-emption given by this act, prior to the issuing of patents, shall be null and void."

The act of January 28, 1832, allowed a transfer of the certificate of purchase. Here, however, the assignment was made in January, 1834, when no law allowing of a preference of entry existed; but, as no reliance seems to have been placed in the pleadings on this ground of defence, we will not rest our decree on it.

As respects Richmond's occupation according to the act of 1834, John Monholland, Edward Doughty, and Daniel Kuger each swear, in similar language, "that Richmond, in the year 1833, cultivated part of the S. W. fractional quarter, sec. 15, in T. 19 S., R. 1 W. of the principal meridian, and raised a corn crop on the same in that year, (1833,) and was in possession of the same on the 19th day of June, 1834." Kuger says Richmond had his dwelling-house on the quarter section, and resided there on the 19th of June, 1834.

Jacob Silor, examined on part of the respondents, Ashley and Craig, states that he resided on Grand Lake, quite near the quarter section in dispute, since 1830. He says: "In February, 1833, when I arrived on the aforesaid lake, there was a turnip-patch on the southwest fractional quarter of fractional section 15, in township 19 south, of range 1 west, claimed by one Edward Doughty, which I believe he abandoned in consequence of the location of the ten-section claim on the land. After Doughty left the aforesaid fractional quarter, William Richmond, in December, 1833, built a cabin where the turnip-patch claimed by the said Edward Doughty was made, and planted some eschallots. The aforesaid William Richmond lived in the same township, on the Mississippi River, on the lands owned by Mr. Cummins or Mr. Shaw, on the 19th of June, 1834; and never did live on section 15, from the time I went on the lake to the present day."

Benjamin Taylor deposes, that he settled with his negroes on township 18, in February, 1834; that in the spring of that year he examined with care the several tracts of land of Ashley and Craig, with a view to purchase them; and, being asked what the situation of the southwest quarter of section 15 was, when he examined it, answers, that " there was a small burn of cane, perhaps twenty yards square, uninclosed, without the appearance of ever having been cultivated, and no house was thereon." We suppose that it had been burnt up by fire in the woods, or removed during the winter of 1833, 1834.

We hold the truth to be, that Richmond built a cabin in 1833, and in January, 1834, sold out his improvements to Barnard and removed away, and resided elsewhere in June, 1834, and consequently was not entitled to a preference of entry.

The next subject of controversy is the S. E. qr. of sec. 22, T. 18. Ashley, by cross-bill, prayed to have his title quieted to this quarter section against Barnard's heirs, and the circuit court granted him the relief he asked.

The half of section 22 was entered by Ashley on a floating warrant, known as a Lovely claim. By the act of January 6, 1829, no one was permitted to enter the improvement of an actual settler in the territory, by virtue of such floating warrant; and it is alleged that Barnard was such an actual settler, and had an improvement on the S. E. qr. sec. 22, T. 18, before Ashley entered it.

The cross-bill alleges that Barnard had improvements on sec. 23, but that they did not extend to the S. E. qr. of sec. 22 previous to the 4th of June, 1834, when Ashley entered the land. It was shortly before that time that Martin had corrected the eastern boundary of sec. 22, locating it about one hundred yards further west, and which was adopted as the true line at the land-office. In support of the bill, Benjamin Taylor deposes, as already stated, that he removed to the immediate neighborhood of the lands in dispute in February, 1834, when he examined the half sec. 22, with a view to purchase it from Ashley. He states that Thomas Barnard cultivated the S. W. qr. of fractional sec. 23, in 1834; but that his cultivation and improvement did not extend to the south half of sec. 22, nor had any other person residence or cultivation thereon.

Philip Booth states that Barnard showed him (Booth) an improvement on the S. E. qr. of sec. 22 early in 1834; thinks it was an extension of his farm of two or three acres. It had been cleared the year before, but there was no cultivation. The witness does not recollect whether the clearing extended beyond the old line or the new one.

Silas Craig, who was a competent witness for Ashley in this separate proceeding, deposes that he was with Martin, the surveyor, when the lines were run and adjusted, late in February, 1834; that the new and proper line bounding the section east is about one hundred yards west of the first line, which was rejected by the surveyor-general; that when he was at the southeast corner of the section he examined Barnard's improvement, and ascertained that it did not extend west to the new line at any place. He seems to have made it his business to see if the improvement of Barnard extended to the S. E. qr. in dispute.

Romulus Payne was called on to prove the value of mesne profits and improvements; he says that Barnard commenced the cultivation on the S. E. qr. of sec. 22, in 1837.

John Monholland, Edward Doughty, and several other witnesses, swear on behalf of the defendants to the cross-bill, in general terms, that Barnard had possession of the S. E. qr. sec. 22, on the 19th of June, 1834, and that he had an improvement on part of it in 1833.

Barnard, in proving up his pre-emption right, swore that he was cultivating the quarter section in 1833, and in possession on the 19th June, 1834. And this affidavit is indorsed by two witnesses, Harrison and Butler, who merely say that they have heard Barnard's affidavit read, and that it is true.

So, likewise, Jacob Silor indorsed William Richmond's affidavit, made before a justice of the peace, and intended to secure a preference of entry for Barnard in Richmond's name, and which was declared sufficient by the register and receiver; and yet, when Silor was re-examined as a witness in this cause, he conclusively proved that Richmond left the land, and resided elsewhere when the occupant law of June 19, 1834, was passed.

The *ex parte* affidavits of Butler and Harrison, and those of Monholland and Doughty, were obviously written out for them to swear to as matter of form, but made with so little knowledge, on part of the witnesses, of the section lines, and the number of quarter sections on which they deposed improvements existed in 1833 and 1834, as to be of little value. And the same may be safely said of other witnesses whose affidavits were taken without cross-examination.

It is most obvious that these loose affidavits obtained by the interested party have been made, as to the improvement being on the quarter section claimed, on the information of him who sought the preference of entry; the witnesses not knowing, of their own knowledge, where the true section line was, over which they swear Barnard's improvement extended in the year 1833.

When the last examination was had before the register and receiver in 1837, Barnard's own witnesses, Philip Booth and John F. Harrison, swore the facts to be, that Barnard had "deadened the timber and cleared away the cane," on a part of S. E. qr. sec. 22; that he fenced it early in 1834, and made a crop of corn on it that year, and was in possession June 19, 1834. Booth, in a subsequent affidavit, contradicts his first statement. That there was no cultivation on the quarter section in 1833, we think is satisfactorily established; nor had Barnard any right to enter it. And such was the final opinion of the register and receiver, which the commissioner of the general land-office reversed, and ordered a patent to issue to Barnard.

The circuit court were obviously of opinion, as appears from the decree it made, that Craig and Taylor's evidence established the fact that Barnard had no part of the quarter section in possession in 1833 or 1834, and hence decreed for the complainants in the cross-bill. And, in the doubtful state of the evidence, we are not prepared to say that this court can hold otherwise, and, therefore, affirm the decree, and order the cause to be remanded for further proceedings, as respects the profits and improvements.

JOEL WRIGHT, PLAINTIFF IN ERROR, v. SCHUYLER H. MATTISON.

A statute of the State of Illinois, passed in 1839, declared: "That hereafter every person in the actual possession of land or tenements under claim and color of title made in good faith, and who shall, for seven successive years after the passage of this act, continue in such possession, and shall, also, during said time, pay all taxes legally assessed on such land or tenements, shall be held and adjudged to be the legal owner of said land or tenements, to the extent and according to the purport of his or her paper title."

What constitutes color of title, explained.

What is color of title is matter of law, and when the facts exhibiting the title are shown, the court will determine whether they amount to color of title.

But good faith in the party, in claiming under such color, is a question of fact for the jury.

Hence, where the court decided that the color of title was not made in good faith, such decision was erroneous. It should have been left to the jury.

An act of 1835, upon the same subject, passed by the State of Illinois, also examined and explained.

꜀ THIS case was brought up by writ of error from the circuit court of the United States for the district of Illinois.

The case is stated in the opinion of the court.

It was argued by *Mr. Browning*, for the plaintiff in error, and *Mr. Williams*, for the defendant in error.

Mr. Browning said that he felt some embarrassment in consequence of the decision of this court in Moore v. Brown, 11 How. 434; but he thought that a different construction had since been given to the statute by the supreme court of Illinois, in Irving v. Brownell, 11 Illinois, 402, 414. These cases were then discussed.

Wright also claimed under an auditor's deed in 1838, which was within the protection of the act of 1835, and which would have furnished a sufficient defence, if he had been in possession for seven years. Whether he was so or not, was a question of fact for the jury. But the court withdrew it from them. Wright had clearly had possession of one and a half acres, and yet the court decided that he was entitled to the protection of the statute of 1835, or that of 1839.

Mr. Browning then contended that Wright was within the act of 1839, holding under claim and color of title made in good faith, and cited Cro. Jac. 122; 9 Watts, 78; 5 Barr, 300; 8 Serg. & Rawle, 298; 6 Barr, 325; 8 ibid. 506; 7 S. & R. 173; 2 Caines, 188; 4 Johns. 202; 9 Cow. 557; 4 Paige, 199; 6 Johns. 47; 16 ibid. 299; 18 ibid. 44, 360; 13 ibid. 119; 8 Conn. 246, 402; 4 Georgia, 115; 4 Hayw. 185; 5 ibid. 288; 5 Pet. 402; 11 ibid. 41; 10 ibid. 442; 8 ibid. 244, 253.

Mr. Browning then commented on Irving v. Brownell, admitting that the court said in that case that the words, "claim and color of title made in good faith," in the statute of 1839, meant title of higher character and superior dignity to that intended by the words, "connected title in law or equity, deducible of record," in the statute of 1835. But he contended that this *dictum* was virtually overruled by Davis v. Easley et al. 13 Illinois, 192, 199; and then cited cases to show that the title of Wright was acquired in good faith. 16 Johns. 299; 8 Pet. 253; 9 Cow. 558.

Mr. Williams contended that the acts of 1835 and 1839 require occupancy under a title *primâ facie* good; the first-named act requiring residence on the land, and the other the payment of taxes, and that the claim of title be made in good faith. It is not denied that this construction is according to the fair import of the terms of these acts, nor that it is the settled construction of the Kentucky limitation law, from which the terms, "a connected title in law or equity, deducible of record," &c., are copied, as well as of similar acts in Kentucky, Louisiana, and Tennessee. Moore v. Brown et al. 11 How. 424; Skyle's Heirs v. King's Heirs, 2 A. K. Marsh. 387; Frique v. Hopkins et al. 4 Martin, N. S. 224; Barlow v. Bill, 4 Bibb, 106; Clay v. Miller, ibid. 461; Young v. Murray, 3 A. K. Marsh. 58; Powell v. Harrison, 2 Pet. 241; Walker v. Turner, 5 ibid. 668; Poage's Heirs v. Chinn's Heirs, 4 Dana, 50.

He then argued to show that the following consequences did not result from his construction of the laws, as was contended for by the opposite counsel: —

1. That it renders the acts altogether inoperative.

2. That it was obviously the intention of the legislature to protect the possession of a person purchasing upon the faith of conveyances made by the officers of the State who were authorized to sell and convey lands.

8. That these acts were intended to protect actual settlers and cultivators, whose titles were liable to exception, against speculators having better titles.

Mr. Justice DANIEL delivered the opinion of the court.

The questions determined by the circuit court, whose decision we are called on to review, arose upon the construction of two statutes of the State of Illinois, which limit the right of action against the possessors of lands, held by purchasers in virtue of sales and conveyances under the authority of the State, for the non-payment of taxes.

The provisions of the statutes in question are as follow: —

January 17, 1835. Sect. 1. " That, hereafter, no person who now has, or hereafter may have, any right of entry into any lands of which any person may be possessed by actual residence thereon, having a connected title in law or equity, deducible of record from this State or the United States, or from any public officer authorized by the laws of the State to sell such lands for the non-payment of taxes, or from any sheriff, marshal, or other person authorized to sell such lands on execution, or under any order, judgment, or decree of any court of record, shall make any entry therein except within seven years from the time of such possession being taken; but when the possessor shall acquire such title after taking such possession, the limitation shall begin to run from the time of acquiring title."

By the statute of 1839 it is enacted, " That, hereafter, every person in the actual possession of lands or tenements, under claim and color of title made in good faith, and who shall, for seven successive years after the passage of this act, continue in such possession, and shall also during the said time pay all the taxes legally assessed on such lands or tenements, shall be held and adjudged to be the legal owner of said lands or tenements, to the extent and according to the purport of his or her paper title. All persons holding under such possession, by purchase, devise, or descent, before said seven years shall have expired, and shall continue such possession, and continue to pay the taxes as aforesaid, so as to complete the possession and payment of the taxes for the term aforesaid, shall be entitled to the benefit of this section."

In this case in the circuit court, which was an action of ejectment, the plaintiff's lessee, the defendant in error here, exhibited in proof a release from the widow of the patentee from the United States, of the premises in question; also deeds of conveyance from the heirs of the patentee, with the exception of one of those heirs, who was a minor, and whose estate or interest in the premises there seems to have been no attempt to transfer.

The lessee of the plaintiff further proved the possession of the premises by the defendant at the commencement of the action on the 15th of July, 1851.

The defendant, to maintain the issue on his part, offered to read in evidence to the jury a deed of the 20th of December, 1828, from the auditor of public accounts of the State of Illinois, to Nathaniel Wright and Joel Wright, for the land in controversy, reciting the public sale of those lands by the auditor, in pursuance of the several acts of the general assembly of the State, and of the act entitled, "An act for levying and collecting a tax on land and other property, approved February 18, 1823," and the bidding off the said lands to Nathaniel Wright and Joel Wright, as the best bidders, for the sum of eleven dollars and six cents, being the tax and costs due thereon for the years 1821 and 1822.

In connection with the aforegoing deed from the auditor, the defendant offered to read in evidence to the jury a deed, properly executed and recorded, from the said Nathaniel Wright to the defendant, Joel Wright, for the northeast quarter of section thirty-four, (the premises claimed;) and offered further to prove to the jury, that the said defendant had been in the actual possession of the premises for more than seven years next preceding the commencement of this suit, and had paid all the taxes assessed thereupon; and the defendant stated by his counsel, that the purpose of offering the evidence was to secure to the defendant the benefit and protection of the seven years' limitation laws of 1835 and 1839.

To the introduction of this evidence by the defendant, the plaintiff objected, assigning for his objection the following causes: —

1. That the defendant had neither proved, nor offered to prove, that the requisitions of the revenue law of 1823 had been complied with, prior to the sale of said land for taxes as stated in the auditor's deed, and that the deed was not *primâ facie* evidence of these facts.

2. That said deed was void upon its face.

The court excluded the evidence thus tendered by the defendant, who excepted to the opinion of the court.

The defendant next offered in evidence a deed from the auditor of public accounts to the defendant, dated on the 10th day of January, 1833, in which it is stated, that, in conformity with all the requisitions of the several laws in such cases made and provided, the auditor had, on the 11th day of January, 1831, exposed to sale a certain tract of land, being the northeast quarter of section thirty-four, in township seven north, in range four east of the fourth principal meridian, for the sum of

5 *

one dollar and eighty-two cents, being the amount of the tax for
the year 1830, with the interest and costs chargeable on the said
lands; and that the said Joel Wright had offered to pay the
aforesaid sum for the whole of the said land; and the said
Wright having paid the said sum into the treasury of the State,
the auditor thereby granted and conveyed to the said Wright
the whole of the northeast quarter of section thirty-four as above
described, (being the land in controversy,) subject to the right
of redemption, as provided by law.

This last-mentioned deed from the auditor was admitted in
evidence without objection, and as well as the former deed from
the auditor to Nathaniel and Joel Wright, bearing date on the
20th of December, 1823, was shown to have been regularly recorded in the proper recording office.

By a statement of facts agreed between the counsel, it was in
proof on the trial, that Joel Wright, claiming that he and his
brother, Nathaniel, were owners and tenants in common in fee-
simple of the land in controversy, took possession of it in 1829,
by inclosing and putting under actual cultivation a portion thereof, and that, from time to time, he had extended his inclosures,
until, in 1841, he had all the said quarter section under actual
cultivation, with the exception of about twenty acres; and that,
from the date last mentioned forward, he had continued in actual
possession and cultivation of the said land; and had paid all the
taxes assessed upon the said land from the year 1840 to 1851,
inclusive of both years, and that the land was of the value of more
than three thousand dollars.

The evidence having been closed on the part of the plaintiff,
and on that of the defendant, the plaintiff moved the court for
the following instructions to the jury, namely: —

"That the deed offered in evidence by the defendant, of the
10th of January, 1838, from the auditor to the defendant, is
of itself such a title as will protect a party in the possession
of land under the act of 1839, provided it is made in good faith,
and connected with the payment of taxes for seven successive
years, and a continued possession for that time; but if the jury
believe from the evidence that the defendant was in possession
of the land in controversy, claiming to be the owner in fee, in
the year 1829, and so continued to remain in possession until the
year 1838, then he could acquire no title by permitting the land
to be sold for taxes, and becoming the purchaser thereof in
1831; and the auditor's deed to the defendant on the sale of
1831 for the taxes of 1830, given in evidence by the defendant,
conveys no title, and is not a title obtained in good faith; and
such a deed, if obtained in the manner aforesaid, is not such a
title as brings his possession within the protection of the limitation acts of 1835 and 1839.

This last instruction having been given as prayed by the plaintiff, was excepted to by the defendant.

After the closing of the testimony, there were on the part of the defendant, five several instructions prayed of the court. Of these, the first two having been granted, and no exception to them having been reserved, they are therefore not properly subjects for comment here.

The third one of these instructions being deemed unimportant, under the view which we take of this cause, will be dismissed without particular remark.

The 5th instruction prayed for by the defendant below, the materiality of which will hereafter be shown, was in the following words, namely: "That the questions whether the deed given in evidence was made in good faith, and whether the defendant has occupied the said land under said deed in good faith, are questions of fact which must be decided by the jury upon consideration of all the facts and circumstances given in evidence upon the trial in this cause." This fifth instruction the court refused to grant, except with the following qualification, namely: "That this, as a general proposition, is true, but as a matter of law, the court charges the jury, that any man who is in possession of land, claiming to be the owner thereof, and who permits the land to be sold for the non-payment of taxes, and who himself becomes the purchaser, and acquires a deed under such purchase, such title cannot be said within the meaning of the law, to be made in good faith."

To the above refusal and qualification by the court the defendant in the ejectment excepted.

From the sketch which has been given of the proceedings in this cause in the circuit court, it is shown that the defendant did not found his title either exclusively or principally upon the provisions of the statute of 1835, but relied in defence of that title, and of his possession, equally, if not chiefly, upon the statute of 1839, and the acts of the auditor performed in the execution and under the authority of the latter law. And it is in viewing this cause as controlled by the provisions of the statute of 1839, that we regard it as entirely disembarrassed of any doubt or perplexity, which might surround an attempt to rest its decision upon a construction of the law of 1835. Hence we have dismissed from our consideration the several questions discussed and ruled in the circuit court, with reference to the law of 1835, as being irrelevant to the points regularly involved in this cause, which depend essentially upon the statute of Illinois of 1839.

By the 1st section of this statute, as we have already seen, it is declared: "That hereafter every person in the actual possession of land or tenements under claim and color of title made in good faith, and who shall for seven successive years after the passage of this act continue in such possession, and shall also during said time pay all taxes legally assessed on such land or tenements, shall be held and adjudged to be the legal owner of said land or tenements, to the extent and according to the purport of his or her paper title."

There exists no controversy in this case as to the facts, that the defendant in the ejectment proved the actual possession by him of the land, and the payment of all the taxes assessed thereon, for seven successive years previously to the institution of this suit. The proof of these facts by the defendant, therefore, left open under the 1st section of the statute of 1839 the single inquiry, whether it was shown or attempted to be shown by him that he held under claim and color of title made in good faith.

We deem it unnecessary to examine in detail the numerous decisions adduced in the argument for the plaintiff in error, to define and establish the meaning of the phrase, " color of title." The courts have concurred, it is believed, without an exception, in defining " color of title " to be that which in appearance is title, but which in reality is no title. They have equally concurred in attaching no exclusive or peculiar character or importance to the ground of the invalidity of an apparent or colorable title ; the inquiry with them has been, whether there was an apparent or colorable title, under which an entry or a claim has been made in good faith.

We refer to a few decisions by this court which are deemed conclusive to the point, that a claim to property, under a conveyance, however inadequate to carry the true title to such property, and however incompetent might have been the power of the grantor in such conveyance to pass a title to the subject thereof, yet a claim asserted under the provisions of such a deed is strictly a claim under color of title, and one which will draw to the possession of the grantee the protection of the statutes of limitation, other requisites of those statutes being complied with. We will lastly, upon this point, refer to a recent decision of the supreme court of the State of Illinois, which not less for its intrinsic strength than on account of the circumstance that it is an interpretation by the highest judicial authority of the State, of the peculiar local legislation of that State, is entitled to special attention and respect.

In the case of Gregg v. The Lessee of Sayre and wife, 8 Pet. 253, 254, in which the question was raised as to the effect of a deed impeached either for fraud in the grantor, or want of estate in him coextensive with the terms of the instrument, this court say: " It is not necessary to decide whether these conveyances were fraudulently made by Ormsby, (the grantor,) or not. The important point is to know whether Gregg and wife (the grantees) had knowledge of the fraud if committed, or participated in it. This knowledge the circuit court charged the jury was immaterial, as the fraud of Ormsby rendered the deeds void, and consequently they could give no color of title to an adverse possession. This construction is clearly erroneous. If Ormsby be justly chargeable with fraud, yet if Gregg and wife did not participate in it; if, when they received their deeds, they had no knowledge of it, there can be no doubt that the deeds do give color of title under the statute of limitations. Upon their face the deeds purport to convey a title in fee; and having been accepted in good faith by Gregg and wife, they show the nature and extent of their claim to the premises."

The case of Ewing *v.* Burnett, 11 Pet. 41, was one in which plaintiff and defendant claimed under conveyances from the same grantor. The grantee in the junior deed relied upon his title as being protected by proof of adverse possession for the time of limitation. The introduction of this deed was objected to, because, as it was alleged, the defendant had notice of the claim of the grantee in the elder conveyance. To an objection thus urged to the introduction of the junior deed, this court said, that there were two answers: first, that the jury might have negatived the proof of such notice; secondly, though there was such notice of a prior deed as would make a subsequent one inoperative to pass a title, yet an adverse possession for twenty-one years, under claim and color of title merely void, is a bar."

So late as the year 1851, in the case of Pillow *v.* Roberts, in the 18th of Howard, 472, speaking of the protection extended by statutes of limitation to a possession held under claim of color of title, this court say, " statutes of limitation would be but of little use if they protected those only who could otherwise show an indefeasible title to the land. Hence color of title, even under a void and worthless deed, has always been received as evidence that the person in possession claims adversely to all the world." And again, in the same case, it is said, in order to entitle the defendant to set up the bar of the statute after five years' adverse possession, he had only to show that he and those under whom he claimed held under a deed from a collector of the revenue of lands sold for the non-payment of taxes; he was not bound to show that all the prerequisites of the law had been complied with in order to make the deed a valid and indefeasible conveyance of the title. If the court should require such proof before the defendant could have the benefit of this law, it would require him to show that he had no need of the protection of the statute before he could be entitled to it. Such a construction would annul the statute altogether, which was evidently intended to save the defendant from the difficulty, after such a length of time, of showing the validity of his tax title.

The case of Woodward *v.* Blanchard, decided by the supreme court of Illinois within a few months past, was like the case at present under review,—an action of ejectment against a purchaser of land sold for the non-payment of taxes.

The defendant in the ejectment relied, for the maintenance and protection of his title and possession, upon the statute of Illinois of 1839, already quoted; professing to hold under claim and color of title as expressed in that statute, all the other requirements of the law being fulfilled. The defence thus alleged superinduced necessarily a construction of the statute as to the signification of the phrase, "claim or color of title made in good faith," and in their interpretation the court institute a comparison between its provisions and those of the statute of 1835, and point out the distinctive features of each. With respect to the law of 1839, they say: "There is in this act not only a change in the facts, but an evident intention to dispense with part of the requirements of the former act, and to relax the strictness required in others. Possession is retained in one case, but residence is dispensed with; connection in the chain to be deduced of record, and its deduction from specified sources, are dispensed with; in place of these, claim and color of title made in good faith, with the payment of taxes, are substituted as to lands in possession. But, as to another class of lands, (vacant and unoccupied,) possession and claim are both dispensed with, and the party is only required to show color of title in good faith." Further on, the court say: "We are therefore, under this defence, not driven to the springs or sources of the title, to inquire if they be pure, nor to the successive channels through which it may pass, for the purpose of removing obstructions to or difficulties in its course and transmission. But we come at once to the party defendant, to inquire if he had a claim and color of title with his possession, at the beginning of this period; if they were made in good faith, and his possession continued and was accompanied by the payment of taxes for seven successive years." What say the court is claim? The act of taking possession, if otherwise unexplained, will be referable to the paper title, and understood as making claim under it. Color of title may be made through conveyances, or bonds, or contracts, or bare possession under parol agreements.

Nor is it at all important, whether the title be weak or strong; for color of title is acquired to establish an adverse possession for the operation of the statute, which commences by disseisin of the rightful owner with a claim of a land. But our statute requires this color of title to be accompanied by a written evidence, "a paper title," and an act or motion of the mind. It must be in good faith. Defects in the title may not be urged against it as destroying color, but, at the same time, might have an important and legitimate influence in showing a want of confidence and good faith in the mind of the vendee, if they were known to him, and he believed the title therefore to be fraudulent and void. What is color of title is matter of law, and when the facts exhibiting the title are shown, the court will determine whether they amount to color of title. But good faith in the party in claiming under such color is purely a question of fact, to be found and settled as other facts in the cause. We can entertain no doubt in this case that the auditor's deed to the purchaser at the tax sale is color of title in Woodward, in the true intent and meaning of the statute, and without regard to its intrinsic worth as a title. "Good faith," (say the court,) "is doubtless used here in its popular sense, as the actual existing state of the mind, whether so from ignorance, scepticism, sophistry, delusion, or imbecility, and without regard to what it should be from given legal standards of law or reason."

We have quoted at some length from the opinion of the supreme court of Illinois, both on account of the clearness and accuracy of its reasoning, and on account of the respect which is due to it, as an interpretation of a statute of the State by her supreme judicial authority. We entirely approve of the exposition of the supreme court of Illinois, in its opinion of what constitutes color of title, upon well-established general principles, and within the scope and meaning of the statute of 1839, and in relation to the nature of the question of what constituted good faith in the possessor of such colorable title, and also as to the manner in which that question should be determined, namely: as a question of fact determinable by the jury, and not by the court.

But the court in the case before us withdrew from the jury, and assumed upon itself the right of deciding upon the motives and intention of the defendant in the ejectment; and it was with the view, doubtless, of exercising this function, that the qualification to the fifth prayer of the defendant was added by the court, and that the court had previously at the instance of the plaintiff, instructed the jury, that although the deed of the 10th of January, 1833, from the auditor to the defendant, was of itself such a title as would protect the party in possession under the act of 1839, connected with payment of taxes, and continued possession for the period of limitation, yet, if the

Graham v. Bayne.

defendant, being in possession of the land in controversy, had permitted it to be sold for taxes, and had himself become the purchaser thereof, the deed of the auditor in pursuance of such sale could convey no title to the defendant, and was not a title obtained in good faith. The accuracy or inaccuracy of the legal positions taken by the court in this instruction we deem it not necessary at present to determine.

We hold, that, in assuming to decide upon the question of good faith on the part of the defendant, the court exerted an authority not legitimately belonging to it; a power exclusively appertaining to the jury. We further hold, that it was error in the court to decide as it did upon the prayer of the plaintiff in the ejectment, and by its qualification annexed to the fifth prayer of the defendant, that the deed from the auditor of the 10th of January, 1833, was not such an instrument as could be adduced in evidence under the statute of 1839, in order to show color of title. We are therefore of the opinion that the decision of the circuit court be reversed, and that this cause be remanded to that court, with directions to order a *venire facias de novo* for the trial thereof, in conformity with the law as herein expounded.

JOHN G. GRAHAM, PLAINTIFF IN ERROR, *v.* ALEXANDER BAYNE.

A statute passed by the State of Illinois, on 3d March, 1845, permits matters both of fact and law to be tried by the court, if both parties agree.

Where a case was tried in the circuit court of the United States, in which both parties agreed that matters of law and fact should be submitted to the court, and it was brought to this court upon a bill of exceptions which contained all the evidence, this court will remand the case to the circuit court with directions to award a *venire de novo.*

A bill of exceptions must present questions of law. Where there is no dispute about the facts, counsel may agree on a case stated in the nature of a special verdict. But to send the whole evidence up is not the same thing as agreeing upon the facts.

Even if a special verdict be ambiguous or imperfect, if it find but the evidence of facts and not the facts themselves, or finds but parts of the facts in issue, and is silent as to others, it is a mis-trial, and the court of error must order a *venire de novo.* They can render no judgment on an imperfect verdict or case stated.

THIS case was brought up by writ of error, from the circuit court of the United States for the district of Illinois.

It was an action of ejectment brought by Bayne against Graham, to recover the southeast quarter of section 15, in townships seven, range four east.

The circumstances under which the case came up are stated in the opinion of the court. It was argued by *Mr. Browning* for the plaintiff in error, and *Mr. Williams,* for the defendant; but as their arguments were directed to the merits of the case, which were not decided by this court, they are omitted.

Mr. Justice GRIER delivered the opinion of the court.

This case was tried in the circuit court for the district of Illinois, without the intervention of a jury, and under the following agreement of counsel:—

" Be it remembered, that upon the calling of this cause for trial, by the mutual agreement of the parties, and in accordance with the laws and practice of this State, a jury was waived, and both matters of law and fact were submitted to the court, upon the distinct understanding that the right of either party should be full and perfect to object to the admission of improper evidence, and to insist upon the admission of competent evidence, with the same privilege of excepting to the rulings of the court in either case, as though the cause were tried by a jury; and with the right to either party to avail himself in the supreme court of any erroneous ruling in this court, precisely as though the cause had been submitted to a jury, and with liberty to either party, if it should be necessary to a hearing of this cause in the supreme court, to treat the evidence in this cause in the nature of a special verdict."

The common law has been adopted by Illinois, and all the States except Louisiana. In that State, the courts of the United States have been compelled to adopt the forms of pleading and practice peculiar to the civil law and the code. That system knows no distinction between law and equity. All cases are tried alike, on petition and answer, with or without the intervention of a jury, as the parties may elect.

This court having separate jurisdiction, both in equity and law, is compelled to distinguish. They can review cases in common law by writ of error only, and on bills of exception presenting questions of law. The circuit courts may adopt the forms of pleading and practice of the state courts, but no state legislation can be applied to the practice of this court, and the mode in which causes shall be brought into it for review.

The very numerous cases on this subject, (from Field v. United States, 9 Pet. 182, to Arthurs and Hart, 17 How. 6,) show the difficulties we have had to encounter in reconciling our modes of review to the civil code of practice as used in the courts of Louisiana.

But in the States governed by the common law, and where the circuit courts are not compelled to adopt every new code of practice invented for the benefit of state courts, there is no reason why the strict rules of the common law should be in anywise relaxed or changed in this court, to suit the anomalies in practice thus introduced in the circuit courts. That the courts of the United States should not be hasty in adopting new codes of practice, which attempt to ingraft the civil law system of pleading and practice on the stalk of the common law, the cases of Butterworth v. Burnet, and Toby v. Randon, 11 How., most amply demonstrate.

The 11th section of the practice act of Illinois, (March 8, 1845,) permits matters both of fact and law to be tried by the court, if both parties agree.

Counsel may agree, as in this case, to submit both fact and law to the decision of the court; but they cannot, by agreement, introduce a new practice into this court, or compel us to adopt the provisions of the 22d section of the same act, as to the mode in which such cases shall be reviewed in error. The practice of this court is regulated by the common law and acts of congress only. See Bayard v. Lombard, 9 How. 530.

If the parties agree to submit the trial both of fact and law to the judge, they constitute him an arbitrator, or referee, whose award must be final and conclusive between them; but no consent can constitute this court appellate arbitrators. When the error alleged does not appear on the face of the record, or on a demurrer, a bill of exceptions to the ruling of the court on questions of law, either in admitting or rejecting testimony, or in their instructions to the jury, constitutes the only mode of bringing a case before this court for review.

It is true, that when there is no dispute as to the facts, counsel may agree on a case stated in the nature of a special verdict; and the judgment of the court below on such case stated, or verdict, may be reviewed here on a writ of error. See Stimpson v. The Railroad, 10 How. 329.

The counsel in this case have agreed, that "if it should be necessary to a hearing of this cause in the supreme court, to treat the evidence in the nature of a special verdict," this agreement may be good as between themselves, and point out the source from which the facts for a case stated, or special verdict, may be drawn, but it cannot compel this court to search through the evidence to find out the facts. The record exhibits the testimony and evidence laid before the judge. It is evidence of facts, but not the facts themselves as agreed or found. The court below decided that a certain deed given in evidence did not show sufficient "color of title" under the limitation law of Illinois. The act referred to requires not only "color of title," but a possession taken and held "in good faith," with payment of taxes. The question of "good faith" is one of fact, or of mixed fact and law, to be decided by the jury under proper instructions from the court. It is one necessary to be ascertained before the court can give a judgment.

Even if we should consent to review this loose statement of evidence as a case stated, it contains no finding or agreement whatever as to this material fact. Where there is a case stated, or special verdict, the court of error must not only reverse the judgment below, if found erroneous, but enter a correct and final judgment.

If a special verdict be ambiguous, or imperfect,—if it find but the evidence of facts, and not the facts themselves, or finds but part of the facts in issue, and is silent as to others,—it is a mistrial, and the court of error must order a *venire de novo.* They can render no judgment on an imperfect verdict, or case stated. See Prentice *v.* Zane, 8 How. 484.

No mere agreement of counsel can substitute evidence of facts in place of facts, or require the opinion of this court on an imperfect statement of them. A writ of error cannot by these methods be converted into a chancery appeal, nor a court of error into appellate arbitrators.

The judgment of the circuit court is therefore reversed, and a *venire de novo* awarded.

NEHEMIAH CARRINGTON, LIBELLANT AND APPELLANT, *v.* THE BRIG ANN C. PRATT, LEONARD B. PRATT, CLAIMANT.

Where a bottomry bond was taken for a larger amount than was actually advanced, with a fraudulent purpose to enable the owner of the vessel to recover the amount of the bond from the underwriters, the bond was void.
Not only so, but the lender of the money loses his maritime lien upon the vessel for the sum actually advanced.

THIS was an appeal in admiralty from the circuit court of the United States for the district of Maine.

The case is stated in the opinion of the court.

It was argued by *Mr. Rowe,* for the appellant, and *Mr. Fessenden,* for the appellee.

Mr. Rowe made the following points, namely:—

1. Airey was rightfully in possession and command of the brig at St. Thomas, and had power to hypothecate her.

2. Airey's conduct, if wrong in this respect, cannot affect the libellant's claim. 3 Sumn. 228.

3. The attempt at deception was not for the purpose of wronging or injuring any party.

4. It does not appear that Carrington was *particeps criminis.*

5. The bond is not void *in toto,* but valid to the extent of the actual advances and interest. 1 Dodson, 389; 8 Pet. 228; 1 Wheat. 107.

6. The fraud, even if Carrington be *particeps criminis*, was not such as to render the bond void *in toto.* 8 C. Robinson, 240, 276.

7. If the bond is invalid *in toto* now, it was void *ab initio*, not voidable merely; and the rights of the parties are the same as if the instrument had not been drafted. 8 Camp. 119; Abbott on Shipping, Pt. II. 142, 151; 11 Mass. 359; 1 Pick. 415.

8. The libellant had a lien upon the brig for his advances, at the date of the bond. 8 Pet. 538, 550; The Hunter, Ware's Rep. 249.

9. The lien has never been extinguished or waived. 7 Pet. 324, 345; 4 Wheat. 255, 290, 291.

10. The lien was not lost by the subsequent fraud.

Mr. Fessenden made the following points:—

1. This was peculiarly a contract of bottomry, having all its characteristics and incidents. Kent's Comm. (7th ed.) 3, 429, 430; 3 Sumn. 228; 4 Law & Eq. Rep. 589.

The draft and agreement do not affect its character. Kent, 3, 423, 424; The Hunter, Ware's R. 249; The Nelson, 1 Hag. 169.

2. Being perfected, and in due form, it forms an express lien upon the vessel. Bottomry is a lien of the strictest kind, only seamen's wages having precedence of it. The Dowthorpe, 2 W. Rob. 73; 9 Eng. Ad. Rep. 79.

Having stipulated for and obtained an express lien of the highest character, as by bottomry, the material man, or lender, necessarily loses, or waives, the implied or tacit hypothecation, which he might otherwise have had.

Because the two liens are inconsistent, being of a different nature. One may coexist with a claim upon the owner; the other cannot. A bottomry bond binding the owner is held void as to that part, in order to sustain the express lien. The common law maxim applies, *Expressum facit cessare tacitum.* The Nestor, 1 Sumn. 1, 78, 83, 86; Abbott on Ship. from Molloy, 198; The Nelson, before cited; The Tartar, 1 Hag.

Maritime, like common-law liens, are lost by acts inconsistent with the lien,—taking other securities and the like. Ramsay *v.* Allegre, 12 Wheat. 611; The William Money, 2 Hag. 136; The Betsey and Rhoda, Davies, 112; Paul *v.* Hayford, 22 Maine, 234; Story on Bailments, § 360; Swett *v.* Brown, 5 Mass. 180; Buck *v.* Ingersoll, 11 Met. 226; Libby *v.* Cushman, 29 Maine, 432.

3. The libellant having selected his security, must rely upon that alone, so far as the lien is concerned. And this security is lost by its fraudulent character. The Tartar, 1 Hag. 14; The

Nelson, 1 Hag. 176; The Sydney Cove, 2 Dods. 1; Bouvier, Law. Dic. Tit. Fraud; Willis v. Baldwin, Doug. 450; Smith v. Bromley, Doug. 696; Alsager v. Spalding, 4 Bing. N. C. 407; Smith v. Hubbs, 10 Maine, 70; The Ann C. Pratt, Curtis, 845; Lowry v. Pierson, 2 Bailey, 824.

A court of equity will not aid a party to enforce such a contract, or to escape from the consequences. Story's Eq. 1, § 59; Cases cited in note to same, 2, § 697.

This is equally true in the admiralty. Courts of admiralty act as courts of equity. Brown v. Lull, 2 Sumn. 449; The Betsey and Rhoda, Daveis, 119.

The fraud attempted in this case, if intended for the underwriters only, was upon a party directly interested, and for whom the master was agent, in the state of facts then existing. Bryant v. Com. Ins. Co. 6 Pick. 181; Douglass v. Moody, 9 Mass. 548.

4. The contract, being void for fraud, cannot be sustained for any part. The cases where a bottomry bond has been sustained for a part, go no further than to reject such portion as is inconsistent with the contract of bottomry, in order to give effect to the express contract. They do not reject the contract, and give another remedy. The Hunter, Ware, 249, stands alone, opposed to legal principles, and that was not a case of fraud. The libellant cannot, therefore, resort to the lien he might have had but for the bond. The Ann C. Pratt, and cases cited, Curtis, 852.

The libellant could only claim under a tacit hypothecation by alleging his own turpitude in the matter of the bond. This the law never permits.

Mr. Justice NELSON delivered the opinion of the court.

This is an appeal in admiralty from a decree of the circuit court of the United States for the district of Maine.

The original libel, filed by Carrington in the district court against the brig, was founded upon a bottomry bond executed by Airey, the mate and acting master, at the island of St. Thomas, by which the vessel was hypothecated to the libellant for the payment of the sum of $4,591.42, advanced by him for her necessary repairs and supplies, she having arrived at that port in a disabled condition, together with ten per cent maritime interest, the whole sum amounting to $5,050.56.

The defence set up to the libel, so far as it is material to be noticed, was that the bond had been executed for a much larger sum than was loaned, and was received by the lender knowing the same, and in fraud of the rights of the parties interested.

Upon the coming of the proofs, it appeared that the sum really advanced to the acting master was but $3,877.25, it

6*

Carrington *v.* Pratt.

being $714.17 less than the amount for which the bond was given.

The proofs further showed that two sets of accounts and vouchers were made out by the clerk of the libellant; the one corresponding with the truth of the case, the other with the fictitious amount of the bottomry bond; both of which sets were forwarded to the father of the captain of the brig, with letters of advice, both from the lender and Airey, the mate, informing him that the bond was given for the larger sum, and the false accounts and vouchers sent, to enable the owner to make a claim for the same against the underwriters upon the vessel. Captain Pratt, the master of the brig, was on shore with the ship's papers, at St. Michael, when the storm occurred that disabled the vessel, and became separated from her, when Airey, the mate, took the command and proceeded to St. Thomas. By an arrangement between Airey and the libellant, it was agreed that the former should draw a bill in favor of the latter, upon the father of Captain Pratt, for the actual sum advanced, and, if paid at maturity, (thirty days' sight,) the maritime interest of ten per cent would be relinquished. This accounts for the communication of the parties with the father on the subject, instead of with Captain Pratt himself.

The district court, after allowing an amendment of the libel at the sitting, setting up a claim upon the vessel for the true sum advanced, with the maritime interest, held that a lien existed upon the brig, in favor of the libellant, for this amount, by operation of the general admiralty law, and decreed accordingly.

The claimant appealed to the circuit court; that court reversed the decree below, and dismissed the libel, concurring with the district judge that the bottomry bond was fraudulent and void, and could not be admitted as the foundation of a decree in favor of the libellant, for any amount; but differed with him upon the other question in the case, and held that the contract between Airey and the lender, for security by bottomry, and fulfilment of that agreement by the execution of the bond, were acts wholly inconsistent with the idea of a general or implied maritime lien on the vessel, and that none therefore existed.

Upon full consideration, we all agree that the decree of the circuit court is right, and should be affirmed.

As it respects the right to a recovery upon a bottomry bond, the libellant is met by the defence resting upon the familiar principle, that a court administering justice upon principles of equity will not lend its aid to enforce the fulfilment of a contract in favor of a party to it, which is founded in fraud. 2 Story's Eq. § 298, and cases. In such cases, the court leaves both parties where the law finds them, giving no relief or countenance to claims of this description. Here, the underwriters, who were sought to be defrauded by the use of the fictitious accounts and vouchers, were directly interested in the transaction, as the fair expenses of the repairs of the brig fell within one of the perils insured against. Any contrivance, therefore, to exaggerate them, or by which evidence could be furnished to enable the owner to recover on his policy a greater amount than actually advanced, was dishonest and fraudulent, and can receive no countenance in a court of justice.

It is insisted, however, that the security should be held valid for the amount actually advanced, conceding it to be void for the excess. It is true, that a bottomry bond may be good in part and bad in part, and may be upheld even in cases when taken for a sum in the aggregate larger than that which properly constitutes a lien upon the vessel within this species of security. There are many cases to this effect. Abbot, 126, n.; 1 Wheat. 107; 8 Pet. 228. These are cases, however, in which the items rejected were not properly chargeable on the ship, or were embraced within the bond from inadvertence or mistake, and entirely consistent with the good faith of the parties in the transaction. They stand upon widely different principles from those where the objectionable items are fictitious, and inserted in the bond with the intent to defraud third persons. The entire security in such cases becomes tainted with the fraud, and a *particeps criminis* is not allowed to come into court to enforce it, even for the money advanced or expended; for to permit it would afford countenance to the fraud by giving partial effect to it.

By holding the security valid to the extent of the loan, rejecting the excess, the guilty party would risk nothing; for, when detected in the fraud, he would still be enabled to reimburse himself for the amount really due. We have seen that the rule of equity — and which is the rule of admiralty in such cases — refuses to interfere for relief, and leaves the parties where the law finds them.

Assuming, then, the bond to be void, as an hypothecation for the money advanced, and, therefore, not available to charge the vessel, can the lender resort to the general or implied maritime lien that it is claimed attaches in cases of repairs or advances in the foreign port, in the absence of any special agreement to the contrary?

We think not. The contract of hypothecation, by bottomry, under which the money was loaned, is different from that implied by the general admiralty law. In the one case, the money advanced is payable only in the event of the safe arrival of the vessel at the port of destination, the lender taking the responsibility of the sea-risk, and entitled to charge extraordinary inter-

Carrington *v.* Pratt.

est. According to the terms of the bond in this case, Carrington and Company, the lenders, "agreed to stand to and bear the
hazard and adventure thereof, on the hull or body of the said
brig, during her voyage"; and the condition is, "to pay or
cause to be paid at the expiration of five days after first arrival
of said brig," &c.; but, "if, during the said voyage, an utter
loss of said brig, by fire, enemies, or other casualty, shall unavoidably happen, &c., then this obligation to be void"; and in
the case of hypothecation the owner is not personally liable for
the advance or repairs. In the other — the case of an implied
lien — the obligation to pay the money is absolute; and to secure the payment, the vessel, the credit of the owner and of the
master himself, are pledged.

Now, it is well settled that the lien implied by the general
admiralty law, may be waived by the express contract of the
parties, or by necessary implication; and the implication arises
in all cases where the express contract is inconsistent with an
intention to rely upon the lien. A familiar instance is where the
money is advanced or repairs made, looking solely to the personal responsibility of the owner or master. Abbot, 125, n.;
ibid. 116, n., Story's Ed. 1829. In that case, no credit being
given to the vessel as a security, the implied lien is necessarily
displaced.

It is true, in this case credit was given to the vessel by the
lenders, and a lien thus provided for; but it was one altogether
different from that implied by the admiralty law, and inconsistent
with an intention to look to that as a security for the loan, as
much so as if he had agreed to look solely to the personal responsibility of the owners.

It is insisted, however, assuming the bond to be void and
inoperative, that the lender is then remitted to his implied lien,
the same as if no bond had been given. How this might be in
a case where the instrument was defective and void, for want
of authority to execute it, or for any other cause consistent with
the good faith of the parties, it is not now necessary to inquire,
or express any opinion. But we think it clear that no such principle can be admitted in a case where the bond has been avoided
on the ground that it was entered into in bad faith, and with
intent to defraud, on the part of the lenders. Any other conclusion would be giving to a party the benefit of his own turpitude, which the law forbids.

The admiralty law treats this species of security with a good
deal of indulgence, and properly so, as the advances to the master at the foreign port by the merchant is oftentimes essential, to
enable the vessel to earn her freight, and is for the general interest of commerce. The advance is made also frequently at great

risk, on the part of the lender, he being a stranger to the owner
and master, and must look, from necessity, mainly to the pledge
of the vessel for his security.   The court, therefore, leans in
favor of upholding these hypothecations, disregarding technical
objections and nice distinctions, which sometimes invalidate instruments at common law; but, they are the creatures of necessity
and distress, and are entered into in the absence of the owner,
who has no opportunity to guard his interests; and the transactions, therefore, out of which they arise should be strictly
watched, and the observance of the utmost good faith exacted
from all the parties concerned.

It has been recently held, in the court of exchequer in England, that the master can pledge the ship for repairs, or loan of
money for that purpose, in the foreign port, only by bottomry
security; and that, in the absence of this, the merchant must
look to the personal responsibility of the owner or master.   78
Eng. Com. Law R. 417; Stainbank and Ambler v. Shepherd.

As this question does not necessarily arise in this case, it is
not important to inquire as to the rule of the admiralty in this
country in this respect.

Judgment of the court below affirmed.

JOHN HOLROYD, PLAINTIFF IN ERROR, v. LEVI PUMPHREY.

Where property stood assessed upon the books of the corporation of Washington in
     the name of James Thomas, and was sold for taxes, the sale was good, although
     James Thomas was dead when the taxes were levied.
Nor was such sale invalid upon the ground that the corporation had, in a prior year,
     sold the property as belonging to the heirs of James Thomas, which sale was not
     carried out to completion.
The act of congress, passed on 26th May, 1824, (4 Stats. at Large, 76,) provides for
     the case.

THIS case was brought up by writ of error from the circuit
court of the United States for the District of Columbia, holden
in and for the county of Washington.

The case is stated in the opinion of the court.

It was argued by *Mr. Davis* and *Mr. Lawrence*, for the plaintiff in error, and *Mr. Carlisle* and *Mr. Bradley*, for the defendant
in error.

The points did not involve any general principles of law, and
are, therefore, omitted.

Mr. Justice CAMPBELL delivered the opinion of the court.

This action was commenced by the plaintiff, to recover a lot of land situate within the city of Washington, in possession of the defendant.

His title is derived from a sale by the city collector of taxes, in the year 1846, at which he was the purchaser; and to sustain it he produced, on the trial of the cause, evidence from the corporation records that the lot had been assessed for taxes as the property of James Thomas, for the years 1844 and 1845; that the taxes for those years were not paid; that the lot had been advertised for sale twelve weeks in one of the city papers, and that he purchased and obtained a deed for the lot from the mayor.

It appeared in the evidence, that James Thomas, to whom the lot had been assessed, had died in 1842; and that the lot had been advertised for sale in 1844, by the collector of taxes, to raise the taxes of that year, as the property of " the heirs of James Thomas," and bid off, but it did not appear that the taxes had been paid on this bid, or that there was any deed to the purchaser, nor was there an assessment of the lots as the property of the heirs.

The circuit court gave the following instruction to the jury:—

" If, from the whole evidence aforesaid, the jury shall find that the said lots in the said declaration mentioned were, up to the year 1844, assessed on the tax-books, at the city of Washington, in the name of James Thomas; that the said James Thomas, to whom they were so assessed, in his lifetime held and claimed the same as his own; that he resided in the said city of Washington, and there died in November, 1842, and letters of administration on his personal estate were granted to his son by the orphans' court of Washington county, in December, 1842; that the said lots were, in December, 1844, advertised and sold by said corporation for taxes due thereon, in the name of the ' heirs of James Thomas,' and afterwards were advertised and sold as stated in said plaintiff's evidence, then the plaintiff is not entitled to recover in this action."

Our opinion is, that the sale in 1844, as the property of the " heirs of James Thomas," was inoperative upon the title of the plaintiff. The advertisement did not express the name of the person to whom the lot was assessed on the books of the corporation at the time of such assessment, as was required by the act of congress of the 26th May, 1824, amending the city charter; (4 Stats. at Large, 75, § 2;) nor were the taxes due for that year collected by means of its sale; at most, it was an abortive effort to do so, which, failing, left the lien of the corporation on the lot for the assessed taxes, and its legal remedies to enforce it, unimpaired; nor will the fact of the assessment to James Thomas after his death, nor the advertisement of the property as assessed to him, defeat the conveyance under the sale.

The act of congress, above referred to, provides for the case. It declares, " that no sale of real property, for taxes hereafter made, shall be impaired or [made] void, by reason of such property not being assessed or advertised in the name or names of the lawful owner or owners thereof, provided the same shall be advertised as above directed." We have seen that the corporation was directed to advertise the name of the person to whom the lot appeared to be assessed on the books of the corporation.

The judgment of the circuit court is reversed, and the cause remanded for a *venire*, &c.

ISAAC R. SMITH, OWNER OF THE SLOOP VOLANT, PLAINTIFF IN ERROR, *v.* THE STATE OF MARYLAND.

The soil below low-water mark in the Chesapeake Bay, within the boundaries of Maryland, belongs to the State, subject to any lawful grants of that soil by the State or the sovereign power which governed its territory before the Declaration of Independence.

But this soil is held by the State not only subject to, but in some sense in trust for, the enjoyment of certain public rights, among which is the common liberty of taking fish, as well shell-fish as floating fish.

The State has a right to protect this fishery by making it unlawful to take or catch oysters with a scoop or drag, and to inflict the penalty of forfeiture upon the vessel employed in this pursuit.

Such a law is not repugnant to the constitution of the United States, although the vessel which is forfeited is enrolled and licensed for the coasting trade under an act of congress.

Neither is it repugnant to the constitution as interfering with the admiralty and maritime jurisdiction of the judicial power of the United States.

Nor is the law liable to an objection that no oath is required before issuing a warrant to arrest the vessel. That clause of the constitution refers only to process issued under the authority of the United States.

THIS case was brought up by writ of error from the circuit court of the second judicial circuit of the State of Maryland, in and for Anne Arundel county.

The case is stated in the opinion of the court.

It was argued by *Mr. Latrobe*, for the plaintiff in error, and *Mr. Campbell*, for the State of Maryland.

Mr. Latrobe contended that all the laws of Maryland, namely : 1833, ch. 254 ; 1837, ch. 310 ; 1846, ch. 38 ; 1849, ch. 217, and a law passed in 1854, should be taken in connection as forming a body of legislation in *pari materia*.   12 How. 299.

These laws were said to be unconstitutional on these grounds, namely : —

1. Because they are repugnant to the 8th section of the first

article of the constitution of the United States, which grants to
congress the power to regulate commerce with foreign nations,
and among the several States, and with the Indian tribes.

2. Because they are repugnant to the 2d section of the third
article, which declares that the judicial powers of the United
States shall extend to cases of admiralty and maritime jurisdiction.

8. Because the said laws contain (with the exception of the
law of 1854) no provision for an oath or affirmation as to probable cause before issuing a warrant, nor was such oath or
affirmation, in fact, made, or any warrant issued prior to the
seizure.

4. Because the said laws are repugnant to the second section
of article fourth, which declares that the citizens of each State
shall be entitled to all privileges and immunities of citizens in the
several States.

Mr. Campbell made the following points:—

1. That the soil of the Chesapeake Bay is vested in the State
of Maryland as the successor of the lord proprietary, and that
the object and effect of the laws assailed is to protect the oysters
while fixed in such soil, and for which it alone has title to them
before they become articles of commerce; and that the protection thus extended does not obstruct the free use of the waters
of Maryland for commerce or navigation. Browne and Kennedy,
5 Harris & Johnson, 195; Casey and Inloes, 1 Gill, 512; Corfield and Coryell, 4 Wash. C. C. R. 371; Bennett and Boggs,
Baldwin, 72; Martin and Waddell, 16 Pet. 367; 8 Kent's Commentaries, 439.

2. That the offences punished by the laws in question are not
within the admiralty or maritime jurisdiction of the United
States. Corfield and Coryell, (above cited;) United States v.
Bevans, 8 Wheat. 886; 2 Brown's Civ. and Adm. Law, Appen-
dix, 420.

Mr. Justice CURTIS delivered the opinion of the court.

This is a writ of error to the circuit court for Anne Arundel
county, in the State of Maryland, under the 25th section of the
judiciary act of 1789. It appears by the record that the plaintiff in error, being a citizen of the State of Pennsylvania, was
the owner of a sloop called The Volant, which was regularly
enrolled at the port of Philadelphia, and licensed to be employed
in the coasting trade and fisheries; that, in March, 1853, the
schooner was seized by the sheriff of Anne Arundel county,
while engaged in dredging for oysters in the Chesapeake Bay,
and was condemned to be forfeited to the State of Maryland,

by a justice of the peace of that State, before whom the proceeding was had; that on appeal to the circuit court for the county, being the highest court in which a decision could be had, this decree of forfeiture was affirmed; and that the plaintiff in error insisted, in the circuit court, that such seizure and condemnation were repugnant to the constitution of the United States.

This vessel being enrolled and licensed, under the constitution and laws of the United States, to be employed in the coasting trade and fisheries, and while so employed having been seized and condemned under a law of a State, the owner has a right to the decision of this court upon the question, whether the law of the State, by virtue of which condemnation passed, was repugnant to the constitution or laws of the United States.

That part of the law in question containing the prohibition and inflicting the penalty, which appears to have been applied by the state court to this case, is as follows: (1833, ch. 254:) —

"*An Act to prevent the Destruction of Oysters in the Waters of this State.*

"Whereas, the destruction of oysters in the waters of this State is seriously apprehended, from the destructive instrument used in taking them, therefore —

SEC. 1. *Be it enacted by the general assembly of Maryland,* That it shall be unlawful to take or catch oysters in any of the waters of this State with a scoop or drag, or any other instrument than such tongs and rakes as are now in use, and authorized by law; and all persons whatever are hereby forbid the use of such instruments in taking or catching oysters in the waters of this State, on pain of forfeiting to the State the boat or vessel employed for the purpose, together with her papers, furniture, tackle, and apparel, and all things on board the same."

The question is, whether this law of the State afforded valid cause for seizing a licensed and enrolled vessel of the United States, and interrupting its voyage, and pronouncing for its forfeiture. To have this effect, we must find that the State of Maryland had power to enact this law.

The purpose of the law is, to protect the growth of oysters in the waters of the State, by prohibiting the use of particular instruments in dredging for them. No question was made in the court below whether the place in question be within the territory of the State. The law is, in terms, limited to the waters of the State. If the county court extended the operation of the law beyond those waters, that was a distinct and substantive ground of exception, to be specifically taken and presented on the record, accompanied by all the necessary facts to enable this court to determine whether a voyage of a vessel, licensed and enrolled for the coasting trade, had been interrupted by force of a law of a State while on the high seas, and out of the territorial jurisdiction of such State.

To present to this court such a question upon a writ of error to a state court, it is not enough that it might have been made in the court below; it must appear by the record that it was made, and decided against the plaintiff in error.

As we do not find from the record that any question of this kind was raised, we must consider that the acts in question were done, and the seizure made, within the waters of the State; and that the law, if valid, was not misapplied by the county court by extending its operation, contrary to its terms, to waters without the limits of the State. What we have to consider under this writ of error is, whether the law itself, as above recited, be repugnant to the constitution or laws of the United States.

It was argued that it is repugnant to that clause of the constitution which confers on congress power to regulate commerce, because it authorizes the seizure, detention, and forfeiture of a vessel enrolled and licensed for the coasting trade, under the laws of the United States, while engaged in that trade.

But such enrolment and license confer no immunity from the operation of valid laws of a State. If a vessel of the United States, engaged in commerce between two States, be interrupted therein by a law of a State, the question arises whether the State had power to make the law by force of which the voyage was interrupted. This question must be decided, in each case, upon its own facts. If it be found, as in Gibbon v. Ogden, 9 Wheat. 1, that the State had not power to make the law, under which a vessel of the United States was prevented from prosecuting its voyage, then the prevention is unlawful, and the proceedings under the law invalid. But a State may make valid laws for the seizure of vessels of the United States. Such, among others, are quarantine and health laws.

In considering whether this law of Maryland belongs to one or the other of these classes of laws, there are certain established principles to be kept in view, which we deem decisive.

Whatever soil below low-water mark is the subject of exclusive propriety and ownership, belongs to the State on whose maritime border, and within whose territory it lies, subject to any lawful grants of that soil by the State, or the sovereign power which governed its territory before the declaration of independence. Pollard's Lessee v. Hagan, 3 How. 212; Martin v. Waddell, 16 Pet. 367; Den v. The Jersey Co. 15 How. 426.

But this soil is held by the State, not only subject to, but in some sense in trust for, the enjoyment of certain public rights,

among which is the common liberty of taking fish, as well shell-
fish as floating fish. Martin v. Waddell; Den v. Jersey Co.;
Corfield v. Coryell, 4 Wash. R. 376; Fleet v. Hagemen, 14
Wend. 42; Arnold v. Munday, 1 Halst. 1; Parker v. Cutler
Milldam Corporation, 2 Appleton (Me.) R. 353; Peck v. Lock-
wood, 5 Day, 22; Weston et al. v. Sampson et al. 8 Cush. 347.
The State holds the propriety of this soil for the conservation
of the public rights of fishery thereon, and may regulate the
modes of that enjoyment so as to prevent the destruction of the
fishery. In other words, it may forbid all such acts as would
render the public right less valuable, or destroy it altogether.
This power results from the ownership of the soil, from the
legislative jurisdiction of the State over it, and from its duty to
preserve unimpaired those public uses for which the soil is held.
Vattel, b. 1, c. 20, s. 246; Corfield v. Coryell, 4 Wash. R. 376.
It has been exercised by many of the States. See Angell on
Tide Waters, 145, 156, 170, 192–3.

The law now in question is of this character. Its avowed,
and unquestionably its real, object is to prevent the destruction
of oysters within the waters of the State, by the use of particular
instruments in taking them. It does not touch the subject of
the common liberty of taking oysters, save for the purpose of
guarding it from injury, to whomsoever it may belong, and by
whomsoever it may be enjoyed. Whether this liberty belongs
exclusively to the citizens of the State of Maryland, or may lawfully be enjoyed in common by all citizens of the United States;
whether this public use may be restricted by the State to its own
citizens, or a part of them, or by force of the Constitution of the
United States must remain common to all citizens of the United
States; whether the national government, by a treaty or act of
congress, can grant to foreigners the right to participate therein;
or what, in general, are the limits of the trust upon which the
State holds this soil, or its power to define and control that trust,
are matters wholly without the scope of this case, and upon
which we give no opinion.

So much of this law as is above cited may be correctly said
to be not in conflict with, but in furtherance of, any and all
public rights of taking oysters, whatever they may be; and it is
the judgment of the court, that it is within the legislative power
of the State to interrupt the voyage and inflict the forfeiture of
a vessel enrolled and licensed under the laws of the United
States, for a disobedience, by those on board, of the commands
of such a law. To inflict a forfeiture of a vessel on account of
the misconduct of those on board, — treating the thing as liable
to forfeiture, because the instrument of the offence is within
established principles of legislation, which have been applied

by most civilized governments. The Malek Adhel, 2 How. 233–4, and cases there cited. Our opinion is, that so much of this law as appears by the record to have been applied to this case by the court below, is not repugnant to the clause in the constitution of the United States which confers on congress power to regulate commerce.

It was also suggested, that it is repugnant to the second section of the third article, which declares that the judicial power of the United States shall extend to all cases of admiralty and maritime jurisdiction. But we consider it to have been settled by this court, in United States v. Bevans, 3 Wheat. 386, that this clause in the constitution did not affect the jurisdiction, nor the legislative power of the States, over so much of their territory as lies below high-water mark, save that they parted with the power so to legislate as to conflict with the admiralty jurisdiction or laws of the United States. As this law conflicts neither with the admiralty jurisdiction of any court of the United States conferred by congress, nor with any law of congress whatever, we are of opinion it is not repugnant to this clause of the constitution. The objection that the law in question contains no provision for an oath on which to found the warrant of arrest of the vessel, cannot be here maintained. So far as it rests on the constitution of the State, the objection is not examinable here, under the twenty-fifth section of the judiciary act. If rested on that clause in the constitution of the United States which prohibits the issuing of a warrant but on probable cause supported by oath, the answer is, that this restrains the issue of warrants only under the laws of the United States, and has no application to state process. Barron v. Mayor, &c. of Baltimore, 7 Pet. 243; Lessee of Livingston v. Moore et al. 7 Pet. 469; Fox v. Ohio, 5 How. 410.

The judgment of the circuit court of Maryland in and for Anne Arundel county is affirmed, with costs.

WILLIAM H. JONES, JAMES B. WELLS, JOHN CHAIN, JONAS A. CASTALINE, PHILIP C. PAUL, WILLIAM R. ROBERTS, AND JAMES W. BYRNE, PLAINTIFFS IN ERROR, v. THOMAS M. LEAGUE.

Formerly, it was held, in some of the circuit courts, that the averment of citizenship in a different State from the one in which the suit was brought, and which it is necessary to make in order to give jurisdiction to the federal courts, must be proved on the general issue. But the rule now is, that if the defendant disputes the allegation of citizenship which is made in the declaration, he must so plead in abatement.

Jones et al. v. League.

The change of citizenship from one State to another must be made with a *bond fide* intention of becoming a citizen of the State to which the party removes.

It was not such a *bond fide* change where the plaintiff only made a short absence, and it appeared from the deed under which he claimed that he was in fact prosecuting the suit for the benefit of his grantor, (who could not sue,) receiving a portion of the land recovered as an equivalent for paying one third of the costs and superintending the prosecution of the suit.

In such a case, the federal court has no jurisdiction.

THIS case was brought up, by writ of error, from the district court of the United States for the district of Texas.

It was an action of trespass to try title brought by League against Jones and the other plaintiffs in error. League averred himself to be a citizen of Maryland, in his original petition, or declaration, and claimed title to a tract of land in the county of Refugio, on St. Joseph's Island, in the State of Texas.

League claimed under a deed made to him on the 11th of May, 1850, by one John Power, a citizen of Texas, acting for himself and Hewetson and the representatives of Walker. This deed contained the following trust, namely:—

That League would commence the necessary suits to try title; that if decided adversely, he would carry the cases to the supreme court of the United States; that when the litigation should be finally determined, he would convey two thirds of the lands recovered to the grantors; that League should pay one third of the expenses of litigation heretofore incurred, and all costs and expenses for the future; that League might make sales and divide the proceeds in the proportion of one third to himself and two thirds to the grantors, &c., &c.

The defendants pleaded four pleas in abatement to the jurisdiction of the court. The first plea set forth the substance of the above deed, and then alleged that Power was, at the time of the commencement of the suit, a citizen of Texas; that League was also a citizen of Texas, but went to Maryland for the purpose of setting up a pretence of being a citizen of that State, and after remaining less than four months in Maryland, he returned to Texas: that it was a fraudulent device to enable him to bring the suits which Power could not have brought, &c.

The second and third pleas need not be noticed, as no question arose upon them in this court. The fourth alleged that, at the time of the commencement of the suit, League was a citizen of the State of Texas.

With respect to the first plea, the plaintiff demurred to it, and the demurrer was sustained by the court. On the fourth plea, the plaintiff took issue upon it, and a trial was had, which resulted, under the instructions of the court, which will presently be mentioned, in a verdict of the jury for the plaintiff. In order to understand the instructions, it is necessary to say that it was

7 *

admitted of record by the plaintiff, for the purposes of the trial, that he was a citizen of the Republic of Texas from 1838 up to the time of annexation of the United States; that he remained domiciled in the State of Texas; and that he was a citizen of the State of Texas, on the first day of July, A. D. 1850; and he waived the necessity of proving the above facts.

And thereupon the court instructed the jury, that it is incumbent on the defendants on the issue made to show that the said plaintiff was a citizen of the State of Texas at the time of filing the petition in this cause; that the admission made by the plaintiff as above stated was, in law, presumptive proof that, at the time of filing the petition, the said plaintiff was a citizen of the State of Texas; but that on the other hand the allegation in the petition, that the plaintiff was, at the time of filing the same, a citizen of the State of Maryland was *primâ facie*, or presumptive proof that he was, as alleged, a citizen of the said State of Maryland at that time: That these two contradictory presumptions, one arising from the plaintiff's admission, the other from the allegation in his petition, were equivalent in weight, and counterbalanced or destroyed each other: And that if there was no other testimony beside the admissions of the plaintiff adduced on the part of the defendants to show that the said plaintiff was, at the time of filing the petition, a citizen of the State of Texas, the jury would on this point find for the plaintiff; to each and every part of which charge (except the first and second clauses thereof, to wit: That the burden of proof was upon the defendants, and that the plaintiff's admissions was presumptive proof of his being a citizen of Texas at the date of filing the petition) the said defendants by their counsel excepted, and tender this their first bill of exceptions, which they pray may be signed, sealed, and made a part of the record in this cause, and the same is now done accordingly.

    [SEAL.]   JOHN C. WATROUS.
January 28, 1854.

Other exceptions were taken in the progress of the trial, but it is not necessary to notice them.

The case was argued by *Mr. Hale*, for the plaintiffs in error, and *Mr. Hughes*, for the defendant. All other points are omitted except the one relating to jurisdiction. This point was stated by *Mr. Hale* as follows: —

The judicial power vested by the constitution extends to controversies — not merely suits — between citizens of different States; and in determining the limits of this power, we are to look to things, not names. McNutt *v.* Bland, 2 How. 9. The true rule as to the matters presented by the plea, is well settled to be that, when a conveyance is made for a valuable consideration, by a citizen of one State to a citizen of another State, it is effective to give the right to sue, although the principal motive, which influenced both parties, may have been a desire to give jurisdiction to courts of the United States; Smith *v.* Kernochen, 7 How. 215–217; McDonald *v.* Smalley, 1 Pet. 623. But the converse is equally true, that when no valuable consideration passes, and the grantee receives the legal title for the avowed purpose of giving jurisdiction to courts of the United States, while the real party in interest remains a citizen of the same State as the defendants, then, the court will not permit such a fraud upon the laws and the policy of the government, but will look into the transaction, on a plea in abatement, and ascertain the real party to the suit, without regard to the form of the conveyance, or of the action. Maxfield's Lessee *v.* Levy, 2 Dall. 381; S. C. 4 Dall. 330; Hurst's Lessee *v.* Neil, 1 Wash. C. C. R. 70–81; Smith *v.* Kernochen, 7 How. 215–217.

Mr. Hughes contended that the court had jurisdiction by the averments of the petition; and the plea made the deed part of the plea, by which deed it was shown that League took the estate for a valuable consideration; that the instruction of the court was correct, because as this court had established the rule in 14 How. 510, that the averment of citizenship in the petition is *primâ facie* evidence of the fact averred, which defendant must remove by proof, it necessarily followed that the two presumptions counteracted each other, and the jury were constrained to find that the plaintiff was a citizen of Maryland at the commencement of the action, 9 Wheat. 537.

Mr. Justice McLEAN delivered the opinion of the court.

This is a writ of error to the district court of the United States of the district of Texas.

The plaintiff filed his petition in the district court, alleging that he was seized in fee of a certain tract of land in the county of Refugio, on St. Joseph's island, in the State of Texas; beginning, on said island, at the point nearest the Aransas bar; thence in a northeasterly direction with the sea-shore to the inlet from the sea into the bay; thence north forty-five degrees west to the shore of the bay or lagoon; thence, with the meanders of the bay, to the place of beginning, containing three and one-half leagues, be the same more or less. That the defendants entered the same by force, and ejected the plaintiff.

And the petition further represents, that the plaintiff having possession of several other tracts of lands of which he was seized, the defendants forcibly entered and dispossessed him, &c.; and the petitioner prayed that after due trial, according to the forms of law, he may have judgment for his damages aforesaid, for the recovery of the lands aforesaid.

The defendants plead that the court ought not to take further cognizance of the action of the plaintiff, because they say that the plaintiff claims title under and through a pretended indenture, purporting to be made and entered into on the 11th of May, 1850, by a certain John Power, of the county of Refugio, and State of Texas, a certain James Hewetson, of the State of Coahuila, and Republic of Mexico, by his attorney in fact, James Power; and the said James Power, acting for and in behalf of the representatives of Duncan S. Walker, deceased, of the one part, and Thomas M. League, of the city of Galveston, and State of Texas, aforesaid, of the other part, but really, and in law and fact, only by the said James Power, of the one part, and the plaintiff, of the other part; which said indenture purported to convey from James Power unto the plaintiff, his heirs and assigns forever, the said tracts and parcels of land described in the petition, and which the plaintiff seeks to recover in this action.

The said conveyance being made to the plaintiff in trust, for the following purposes: that the said League should commence all such suit, or suits, as might be necessary to settle the title to said lands, in the district court, and, should a decision be made adversely in said court, that he would prosecute a writ of error or appeal to the supreme court of the United States; and when the litigation was finally determined, the said League would convey two-thirds of the land recovered, in which the title should be settled, to said Power and Hewetson, and the representatives of the said Walker, and their heirs and assigns; and, until such conveyances were made, should hold said lands for the benefit of said parties; and the plaintiff agreed to pay one-third of the expense of litigation, and the expense before that time incurred, which it was agreed amounted to one thousand dollars.

And the defendants allege, that the said Power, at the time of the conveyance, and for years before and ever since, has been a citizen of Texas; and that the said plaintiff has resided in the State of Texas for twelve years, and is a citizen of that State. That before commencing suit he went to Maryland and other States, and remained absent about four months, and on his return brought this suit as a citizen of Maryland; and that the said conveyance was colorable, and was made to give jurisdiction to the courts of the United States.

Three other pleas were filed representing that the conveyance was made by Power, a citizen of Texas, and who is the real plaintiff in the case, to give jurisdiction to the federal courts, and that League is a nominal plaintiff.

The plaintiff admits, for the purposes of this cause, that the only legal title which he claims to have to the several tracts of land in his petition described, is that conveyed to him by James Power, of the State of Texas.

A demurrer was filed to the first plea, and issues joined as to the others.

At an early period of this court, it was held in some of the circuit courts, that the averment of citizenship, to give jurisdiction, must be proved on the general issue. And as a consequence of this view, if at any stage of the cause it appeared that the plaintiff's averment of citizenship was not true, he failed in his suit. But it is now held, and has been so held for many years, that if the defendant disputes the allegation of citizenship in the declaration, he must plead the fact in abatement of the suit; and that this must be done in the order of pleading, as at common law.

In this case, jurisdiction is claimed by the citizenship of the parties. The plaintiff avers that he is a citizen of Maryland, and that the defendants are citizens of Texas.

In one of the pleas, it is averred that the plaintiff lived in Texas twelve years and upwards, and that, for the purpose of bringing this suit, he went to the State of Maryland, and was absent from Texas about four months.

The change of citizenship, even for the purpose of bringing a suit in the federal court, must be with the *bonâ fide* intention of becoming a citizen of the State to which the party removes. Nothing short of this can give him a right to sue in the federal courts, held in the State from whence he removed. If League was not a citizen of Maryland, his short absence in that State without a *bonâ fide* intention of changing his citizenship, could give him no right to prosecute this suit.

But it very clearly appears from the deed of conveyance to the plaintiff, by Power, that it was only colorable, as the suit was to be prosecuted for the benefit of the grantor, and the one-third of the lands to be received by the plaintiff was in consideration that he should pay one-third of the costs, and superintend the prosecution of the suit. The owner of a tract of land may convey it in order that the title may be tried in the federal courts, but the conveyance must be made *bonâ fide*, so that the prosecution of the suit shall not be for his benefit.

The judgment of the district court is reversed, for want of jurisdiction in that court.

DAVID BUSH, PLAINTIFF IN ERROR, *v.* JAMES I. PERSON, AD-
MINISTRATOR DE BONIS NON OF MABORN COOPER, DECEASED.
+2

Where a person mortgaged land, which was at the time subject to a judgment lien,
the deed containing what was equivalent to a covenant of warranty; then took the
benefit of the bankrupt act of 1841; and then purchased the property which was
sold under the judgment lien, he is estopped by his covenant from setting up his
after-acquired title to defeat the mortgage.
The bankrupt act does not annul a covenant in such a case.

THIS case was brought up from the high court of errors and
appeals of the State of Mississippi, by a writ of error issued
under the 25th section of the judiciary act.
The case is stated in the opinion of the court.

It was argued by *Mr. Bayard,* for the plaintiff in error, and
Mr. Crittenden, for the defendant.

Mr. Bayard explained the doctrine of estoppel at common
law, and referred to Williams *v.* Saunders, 80, note. But where
there is no covenant of warranty there is no estoppel, 11 How.
298; and in this case there was none. The law of the State
implies such a covenant from a deed of bargain and sale, but
not as between mortgagor and mortgagee.

Mr. Crittenden contended that the second section of the bankrupt act excepted mortgages and other securities for debt. It
says that mortgages must remain unimpaired, but if Bush is
allowed to hold, the mortgage certainly is impaired.

Mr. Justice CURTIS delivered the opinion of the court.
A bill to foreclose a mortgage on a lot of land in Mississippi
was filed by the administrator of the assignee of the mortgage,
in the superior court of chancery in that State. The complainant obtained a decree of foreclosure, and the respondent appealed
to the high court of errors and appeals, where the decree of the
superior court of chancery was affirmed. The appellant then
prosecuted the writ of error, which brings the case before this
court.
The case was, shortly, this: The appellant was one of two
mortgagors. When the mortgage was executed, the land was
encumbered by a lien from a judgment previously recovered
against the mortgagors.
After executing the mortgage the appellant became a bankrupt, under the act of congress of August 19, 1841, 5 Stats. at
Large, 440, and received his discharge. The land was exposed
to sale to satisfy the judgment lien, and the appellant, after his

discharge, purchased it. The court of appeals of Mississippi decided: —

1. That though the deed of mortgage contained no express covenant of warranty, the words "grant, bargain and sell," which were in the deed, under the law of that State, imported covenants of warranty of title, and against encumbrances, and for quiet enjoyment, as effectually as though such covenants had been expressly set out in the deed.

2. That, under the law of Mississippi, if there had been no discharge in bankruptcy, the appellant would be estopped by his covenants from setting up his after-acquired title to defeat the mortgage.

3. That the discharge in bankruptcy did not enable him to do so.

This last position is the only one re-examinable here; the decision by the state court, of all matters depending exclusively upon the law of the State, being conclusive, on a writ of error, under the 25th section of the judiciary act of 1789.

The question for our consideration is, what effect the discharge of a bankrupt has upon estoppels, arising by law from covenants of warranty contained in his deeds of conveyance of land.

To determine this, it is necessary to have in view the different modes of operation of such covenants. They are contracts, and an action lies for recovery of the damages sustained by their breach. At law, they run with the land; and if the covenantor subsequently acquire an outstanding paramount title, it enures by force of the covenant to him who claims under the deed of the covenantor. This rule is now established in the law of this country, and has been affirmed in numerous decisions in this and other courts. Many of them may be found collected in a note to 2 Smith's Leading Cases, 545, &c.

In equity, the covenantor is treated as estopped by his covenant to assert that any outstanding title existed inconsistent with what he undertook to sell and convey.

The argument on the part of the appellant is, that, under the 4th section of the bankrupt act, he was discharged from all debts, contracts, and other engagements provable under the act; that not only the debt secured by this mortgage, but the covenant of warranty itself, was provable under the act. And, consequently, the covenantor, being released from the covenant, it could no longer have the operation allowed to it by the courts of Mississippi.

It must be admitted, that if the covenantee or his assignee had released the covenant, it would be difficult to maintain that it could continue in existence for any purpose. But it must be considered, that whatever discharge has taken place in this case, is by force of a statute, which may have so qualified and limited its effect as still to leave the covenant in existence for one purpose, though not for others; and that the question, whether it has done so, can be determined only by examining the act, and ascertaining the will of the legislature in this particular.

The second section of the act contains this proviso: "That nothing in this act contained shall be construed to annul, destroy, or impair any lawful rights of married women, or minors, or any liens, mortgages, or other securities on property, real or personal, which may be valid by the laws of the States respectively, and which are not inconsistent with the provisions of the second and fifth sections of this act." There does not appear to have been anything in this mortgage inconsistent with those sections; and it is not denied that the mortgage itself, considered simply as a conveyance of the land, remained unaffected by the act.

It is therefore obvious, that though the bankrupt, personally, was released by the act, the debt due from the land continued undischarged. In this particular, beyond all doubt, the discharge by the act differs from a release by the creditor; since, if the latter had released the debtor, the mortgage would thereby have been satisfied, and the charge on the land destroyed.

The intention of the legislature to carry out this distinction between the personal liability of the debtor and the liability of the land, and to preserve the latter in full force, unaffected by the discharge of the debtor, is clearly declared by the act. The act says, in so many words, that a mortgage, valid by the law of the State, shall not be impaired by anything in the act.

We think there is sufficient reason why this proviso should be so construed as completely to save the effect and operation of all estoppels running with the land and operating at law to pass the legal title, or in equity to conclude the grantor from asserting the existence of a title inconsistent with what he undertook to sell and convey. The purpose of the legislature to afford complete and effectual protection to mortgage titles, against anything which was to be done under the act, and the broad and strong terms in which this purpose is expressed, require us to say, that the debtor cannot derive from the act an enabling power to do or assert anything which will impair a mortgage otherwise valid. Nor is there any incongruity with established principles, in holding that the personal discharge of the debtor does not free him from the estoppel.

If this obligation could rest solely upon a covenant, effectual in law to charge the grantor in a personal action, it would follow, that when such personal liability was released by the bankrupt act, the estoppel would naturally fall with it; and that an intention to preserve the estoppel ought to be clearly indicated, to induce the court to say it was not destroyed ; but such estoppels do not depend on personal liability for damages. This is apparent, when we remember that estoppels bind, not only parties, but privies in blood and estate, though not personally liable on the covenants creating the estoppel. See Carver v. Jackson, 4 Pet. 85, 87 ; White v. Patten, 24 Pick. 324 ; Mark v. Willard, 18 New Hamp. R. 889 ; Baxter v. Bradbury, 20 Maine R. 260.

Indeed, it is the settled doctrine of this court, not only that no existing personal liability is necessary to work an estoppel, but that none need have existed at any time. In Van Rensselaer v. Kearney et al. 11 How. 322, it was held, after great consideration and a full examination of the authorities, that " if a deed bear on its face evidence that the grantors intended to convey, and the grantee expected to become invested with, an estate of a particular description or quality, and that the bargain had proceeded upon that footing between the parties ; then, although it may not contain any covenants of title, in the technical sense of the term, still, the legal operation and effect of the instrument will be as binding on the grantor and those claiming under him, in respect to the estate thus described, as if a formal covenant to that effect had been inserted ; at least, so far as to estop them from ever afterwards denying that he was seized of the particular estate at the time of the conveyance."

It is familiar law, also, which was applied in Carver v. Jackson, 4 Pet. 86, 88, that a mere recital of a fact in a deed is as effectual an estoppel as a covenant. There is no necessary connection, therefore, between the personal liability of the debtor on his covenant, and the estoppel which arises therefrom ; and it is not an incongruity for the legislature to preserve the latter while they discharge the former.

Estoppels which run with the land and work thereon are not mere conclusions ; they pass estates, and constitute titles ; they are muniments of title, assuring it to the purchaser. Their operation is highly beneficial, tending to produce security of titles ; and if a discharge under the bankrupt law were allowed to destroy this mode of assurance, it would in an important particular impair the operation of deeds containing it. This, by the express words of the bankrupt law, is prohibited.

In Stewart v. Anderson, 10 Alabama R. 504, the supreme court of Alabama had this precise question before them, and held the bankrupt estopped. A similar decision was made by the court of appeals of Maryland in reference to the effect of a discharge under the insolvent law of that State. Dorsey v. Gasaway, 2 H. and J. 411.

Our opinion is, that the decree of the high court of errors and appeals of Mississippi should be affirmed, with costs.

SAMUEL VERDEN, PLAINTIFF IN ERROR, v. ISAAC COLEMAN.

This court again decides that a decree upon a motion to dissolve an injunction in the course of a chancery cause, and where the bill is not finally disposed of, is not such a final decree as can be re-examined in this court, under the 25th section of the judiciary act.

THIS case was brought up from the supreme court of Indiana, by a writ of error issued under the 25th section of the judiciary act.

The case is explained in the opinion of the court.

It was argued by *Mr. Gillett*, for the plaintiff in error, no counsel appearing for Coleman.

Mr. Justice CAMPBELL delivered the opinion of the court.

The plaintiff filed his bill in the circuit court of Benton county, Indiana, sitting in chancery, to obtain a decree to cancel a mortgage and the mortgage note, and also to restrain, by injunction, the mortgagee from proceeding upon the power of sale contained in the mortgage until the final hearing, and from thence perpetually.

A temporary injunction was granted in vacation upon the usual conditions, which was dissolved, on the coming in of the answers upon the motion of the defendants, by the circuit court.

From the order dissolving the injunction there was an appeal to the supreme court of Indiana, where, after argument, the decree of the circuit court was affirmed. Upon this decree this writ of error is prosecuted.

This court has repeatedly decided that a decree upon a motion to dissolve an injunction in the course of a chancery cause, and where the bill is not finally disposed of, is not such a final decree as can be re-examined in this court, under the terms of the 25th section of the judiciary act of the 24th September, 1789. McCollum v. Eager, 2 How. 61; Gibbons v. Ogden, 6 Wheat. 448.

The writ of error is dismissed.

Minter et al. v. Crommelin.

WILLIAM J. MINTER, HIRAM F. SALTMARSH, AND ASHLEY PARKER, PLAINTIFFS IN ERROR, v. CHARLES CROMMELIN.*

Where a patent for land is issued by the officers of the United States, the presumption is that it is valid and passes the legal title. But this may be rebutted by proof that the officers had no authority to issue it on account of the land's not being subject to entry and grant.

The act of March 3, 1817, which was passed to carry into effect the treaty of August 9, 1814, with the Creek Indians, provided in the 6th section that no land reserved to a Creek warrior should be offered for sale by the register of the land-office, unless specially directed by the secretary of the treasury.

The secretary was authorized to decide whether or not the Indian had abandoned the land. If abandoned, it became forfeited to the United States.

Hence, where such a reservation was offered for sale, and a patent issued for it, the presumption is that the secretary had decided the fact of abandonment, and issued the order for the sale.

THIS case was brought up from the supreme court of Alabama, by a writ of error issued under the 25th section of the judiciary act.

The case is stated in the opinion of the court.

It was argued by *Mr. Phillips,* for the plaintiffs in error, and *Mr. Bradley,* for the defendant.

Mr. Justice CATRON delivered the opinion of the court.

The material facts of this case are as follows: —

On the 12th April, 1820, a certificate, No. 28, issued from the land-office of the United States to Tallasse Fixico, a friendly chief of the Creeks, appropriating to his use and occupancy fraction 24, T. 18, R. 18, east of Coosa River, in pursuance of the act of congress of 3d March, 1817, passed to carry into effect the treaty of Fort Jackson, of August 9, 1814, with the Creek Indians.

The reservee, Tallasse Fixico, was in possession of the land, and while in possession, in 1828, he sold it, for a valuable con- sideration, to George Taylor, to whom he gave a deed and the possession of the land at the time of sale.

The said Taylor, while in possession, in July, 1834, sold to C. Crommelin, the defendant in error, a portion of the land, about forty acres. The purchaser received deeds for the same at the time of sale, dated 12th and 14th July, 1834, and immediately, or a short time thereafter, entered into possession, and has con- tinued in possession until the present time.

On the 4th June, 1839, Isham Bilberry and Samuel Lee obtained from the land-office at Cahawba, a pre-emption certifi- cate, No. 35,014, in their favor, under the pre-emption act of

---

* Mr. Justice CAMPBELL did not sit in this cause.

1834, for southeast fractional quarter of sec. 24, T. 18, R. 18, being a part of Tallasse Fixico's reservation, and embracing the land in possession of the defendant in error, and which is the land sued for, namely: the forty acres purchased by him from Tay or.

On the same day, namely: 4th June, 1839, Bilberry and Lee assigned the pre-emption certificate to the plaintiffs in error, Hiram F. Saltmarsh, William T. Minter, and Ashley Parker, in whose favor a patent was subsequently issued.

The state court charged the jury " that if they found the defendant held for a series of years, and continued to hold possession under deeds from Taylor, and that Taylor held possession under Tallasse Fixico, and that the plaintiffs were never in possession; that then, the defendant held under color of title, and was in a condition to contest the validity of the patent.

" 2. That the certificate of possession which issued to Tallasse Fixico, was an· appropriation of the land by the government of the United States to a particular purpose; and that if Tallasse Fixico, in 1828 or 1829, did abandon said land, it was not subject to entry under the pre-emption laws. That the patent, under which the plaintiffs claimed title, was issued under the pre-emption laws of the United States; that the land conveyed by said patent was not subject to entry under pre-emption, and that, therefore, said patent had issued contrary to law, and was void."

To this charge the plaintiffs excepted.

A verdict and judgment were rendered for the defendant, and the plaintiffs took up the cause to the supreme court of Alabama, where the judgment was affirmed, to bring up which judgment a writ of errror was prosecuted out of this court.

The state court in effect pronounced the patent, under which the plaintiffs claimed title, to be void for want of authority in the officers of the United States to issue it, on the supposition that the land was reserved from sale when it was entered and granted. The presumption is, that the patent is valid, and passed the legal title; and, furthermore, it is *primá facie* evidence of itself that all the incipient steps had been regularly taken before the title was perfected by the patent. It has been so held by this court in many instances, commencing with the case of Polk *v.* Wendell, 9 Cranch, 98, 99.

But if the executive officers had no authority to issue the patent because the land was not subject to entry and grant, then it is void, and the want of power may be proved by a defendant at law, 9 Cranch, 99. And the question here is, whether the defendant has proved the want of authority?

The 6th section of the act of 1817 provides that no land

reserved to a Creek warrior should be offered for sale by the register of the land-office, unless specially directed by the secretary of the treasury. Both by the treaty and the act of congress it was declared that if the Indian abandoned the reserved land, it became forfeited to the United States. The fact of abandonment, the secretary was authorized to decide, and if he did so find, he might then order the land to be sold as other public lands. The rule being that the patent is evidence that all previous steps had been regularly taken to justify making of the patent; and one of the necessary previous steps here being an order from the secretary to the register to offer the land for sale, because the warrior had abandoned it, we are bound to presume that the order was given. That such is the effect, as evidence, of the patent produced by the plaintiffs, was adjudged in the case of Bagnell v. Broderick, 13 Pet. 450, and is not open to controversy anywhere, and the state court was mistaken in holding otherwise.

The defendant being in possession, without any title from the United States, we deem it unnecessary to discuss the effect of the parol proof introduced in the state circuit court to defeat the patent.

It is therefore ordered that the judgment of the supreme court of Alabama, be reversed.

ROBERT H. McCREADY AND OTHERS, CLAIMANTS OF THE STEAMBOAT BAY STATE, HER TACKLE, MACHINERY, &C., APPELLANTS, v. GOLDSMITH, WELLS, AND OTHERS.

Where a large steamer was coming down Long Island Sound, on a foggy morning, with a speed of sixteen or seventeen miles per hour, in the direct track of the coasting trade, and run down a vessel which was lying at anchor, (the weather being perfectly calm,) the steamer was grossly in fault.

The vessel at anchor cannot be considered in fault for omitting to have horns blown or empty barrels beaten. The usage that this is done in such a case is not established; and, moreover, it is doubtful whether such a precaution would have been of any service.

THIS was an appeal from the circuit court of the United States for the southern district of New York.

The case is stated in the opinion of the court.

The district court decreed that the collision was caused by the fault, want of precaution, and blamable conduct of the persons on board of and managing each of the vessels, and ordered the damages to be borne in equal moieties by them. Both par-

McCready et al. v. Goldsmith et al.

ties appealed to the circuit court. Mr. Justice Nelson reversed the decree of the district court, and ordered that the libellants should recover against The Bay State the sum of $6,411, with interest from the 8th of October, 1849, and costs in both courts.

An appeal from this decree brought the case up to this court.

It was submitted on printed arguments, by *Mr. Lord*, for the appellants, and *Mr. Cutting*, for the appellees.

The arguments of the counsel upon both sides consisted of comments upon the facts and evidence in the cause, which it would not be possible to explain without an abstract of the testimony.

Mr. Justice NELSON delivered the opinion of the court.

This is an appeal in admiralty, in a case of collision, from a decree of the circuit court of the United States for the southern district of New York.

The collision occurred on Long Island Sound, off Watch Hill light, on the Connecticut shore, between the schooner Oriana and the steamer Bay State, on the 18th of August, 1847, when the former was run down and sunk. The schooner was laden with coal, and on her way to New Bedford. The steamer was engaged in one of her usual trips from Fall River, through the Sound to the city of New York. On the morning of the accident the weather was thick and foggy, and so dark that a vessel could not be seen over two or three hundred feet off, and the wind at a dead calm. The schooner lay helpless on the water.

The steamer is a large vessel, some sixteen hundred tons burden, with powerful engines, and of great speed, and was coming down the Sound at the time at the rate of sixteen or seventeen miles the hour. The hands on board the schooner heard the noise of her paddle-wheels before she appeared in sight; she was within less than her length when they could first discern her; and she had approached within that distance of the schooner before that vessel was discerned by the hands on board the steamer.

The place where this collision occurred is in the direct track of the coasting trade between the Eastern States, New York, and Pennsylvania, and where the waters are greatly frequented by vessels engaged in it.

We agree, that it is not for this court to lay down any fixed and inflexible rule as it respects the rate of speed of steam vessels navigating these waters. This must depend upon the circumstances attending each particular case. These may justify a rate deemed prudent navigation at one time, that would be wholly unjustifiable at another. But we feel no difficulty in

McCready et al. v. Goldsmith et al.

saying, that, in a case circumstanced as the present one, a fog so dense that the most vigilant look-out would be unable to discern a vessel at a distance of more than sixty or one hundred yards — navigating, at the time, waters frequented with sailing vessels — a rate of sixteen or seventeen miles the hour is altogether inadmissible as prudent or reasonably safe navigation. According to the testimony of the pilot, it would take four or five minutes to stop The Bay State at this rate of speed; at a reduced rate, it would of course take a proportionably less time. This, in addition to the better opportunity for each vessel approaching to adopt the proper manœuvre to avoid the collision, should admonish those engaged in navigating vessels of this description, of the propriety, if not necessity, of slacking their speed in thick weather, and especially in a track where other water-craft are usually to be met.

Some of the officers on board this steamer, as is apparent from the evidence, were laboring under a very imperfect appreciation of their whole duty as regarded her proper navigation.

A passenger on board, who witnessed the collision, was struck with the impropriety of the rate of speed, and asked why they ran so fast in a fog, and was answered that it was necessary, in order to enable them to keep their reckoning in going from place to place. And we learn also from the testimony of the pilot and some others, that they make no difference in the rate of speed in consequence of a fog; that they go slow when making land, or a light, or in narrow passages, and when sounding the lead, as if the only precautions they were bound to observe in the navigation were as it respected the safety of their own vessel.

We will only repeat what we said in the case of Newton v. Stebbins, 10 How. 606: "That it may be matter of convenience that steam vessels should proceed with great rapidity; but the law will not justify them in proceeding with such rapidity, if the property and lives of other persons are thereby endangered."

We are all satisfied that this vessel was grossly in fault, on account of the rate of speed with which she was moving, under the circumstances, at the time of the collision.

The remaining question is, whether or not the schooner was also in fault. And this, in the present case, depends upon another, namely, whether she omitted any precautionary measures which she was bound to observe under the circumstances, such as beating empty casks or blowing a fog-horn, with a view to give notice to vessels approaching, of her position.

A good many witnesses have been examined as to the usage of vessels navigating the Sound, in respect to the blowing of horns, beating of empty barrels, and the like, in thick and foggy weather; but, on looking carefully into the testimony, it will be found that no such general or established usage has been proved.

The evidence of most of the experienced masters who have been examined goes to disprove the prevalence of any such usage. The practice is occasionally resorted to in the navigation of the Sound, but with what advantage or security against accidents, does not distinctly appear. Without much more evidence of the usage, and of its utility in preventing collisions, than is shown in this case, we cannot say that the omission to comply with it is of itself chargeable as a fault against the schooner. It may well be, that the use of these means should be entitled to consideration upon a nice question of proper vigilance and caution, in a case of collision between two vessels, like any other precautionary measure that might tend to prevent its occurrence. Beyond this, we do not think the evidence as disclosed in the case would justify us in carrying the effect of the omission.

Besides, we are not satisfied, upon the evidence, that the precautionary measure of blowing horns, or ringing a fog-bell, would have been of any avail under the circumstances of this case. The witnesses on the part of the steamer agree that the noise of the motion of the vessel in the water is so great that it could be heard at a much further distance than their own fog-bell; and several of them consider the bell useless for this reason; and one of them states expressly that he did not recollect ever hearing a horn while on a steamboat when she was under way, but had after she stopped. A horn, it is said by some of the witnesses, cannot be heard, at the furthest, over a mile and a half; and if so, it certainly could not be heard anything like that distance, if at all, on board a steamboat in motion. The steamer, as we have seen, was moving at a rate of more than a mile in four minutes; and taking into view the size of The Bay State, with her powerful engines, together with this rate of speed, it is quite apparent that if a horn could have been heard at all, it could not, upon any reasonable conclusion, in time to have materially influenced the result.

We are satisfied the decree of the court below is right, and should be affirmed.

THE UNITED STATES, PLAINTIFFS IN ERROR, *v.* CATESBY AP. ROGER JONES.

Where an officer of the navy was detached on special duty in France, and a sum of money was transmitted to him by the secretary of the navy, to be disbursed for medical attendance, the propriety of this act was peculiarly within the jurisdiction and discretion of the head of the department; and the officer cannot be charged with the amount so transmitted, by the accounting officers of the treasury department.

THIS case was brought up, by writ of error, from the circuit court of the United States, for the District of Columbia, holden in and for the county of Washington.

The facts are stated in the opinion of the court.

It was argued by *Mr. Cushing,* (attorney-general,) for the United States, and by *Mr. Carlisle,* and *Mr. Jones,* for the defendant.

Mr. Cushing's points were:—

1. The expenses incurred by Lieutenant Jones while in France, on leave of absence, were not chargeable to the United States. The act of 3d March, 1835, (4 Stats. at Large, 755, 757,) fixed the annual compensation of officers, and prohibited all other allowances.   When absent on leave, the government is not bound to provide medical attendance.

2. The secretary of the treasury was not authorized to advance the money in question to Lieutenant Jones.

The act of January 31, 1823, (3 Stats. at Large, 723,) only allows advances to officers employed on distant stations.   This was when they received emoluments, which were cut off by the act of 1835.

3. The accounting officers are not bound to allow, in a settlement of an account with an officer, a credit for money unlawfully received or expended, without authority of law.

The act of 3d March, 1849, (9 Stats. at Large, 419,) applies to pursers and storekeepers only, and the disbursement must be made in pursuance of an order from an officer in command. The opinions of the following attorneys-general, do not a [ ]ly to the case.   Mr. Berrien, Parker's case, 1 Opinions Attorney-General, 679; Mr. Taney, Thorp's case, 1 Opinions Attorney-General, 785; Mr. Butler, Parker's case, 1 Opinions Attorney-General, 913; Mr. Johnson, (Miami claim,) Lassell's case, 2 Opinions Attorney-General, 1998; Mr. Crittenden, commissioner of customs, November 13, 1852, MS.

4. Money belonging to the government, which has been wrongfully received, can be recovered back in an action at law.

5. The President is not authorized to expend marine hospital money in a foreign country.

The counsel for defendant in error, contended that the above opinions of attorneys-general were applicable, and

1. That the payment of the medical attendance of an officer,

is not such an allowance to the officer, as was contemplated in the prohibition of the act of 1835.

2. That the act of 1828, provides " that the President of the United States may direct such advances as he may deem necessary and proper, to such persons in the military and naval service as may be employed on distant stations, where the discharge of the pay and emoluments to which they may be entitled, cannot be regularly effected." Medical attendance is one of these emoluments.

3. Under the acts (1 Stats. at Large, 606, c. 77, § 3; Ib. 729, c. 36, §§ 2 and 3) providing for hospital money, the President is authorized to provide for sick and disabled officers in such manner as he shall direct, in ports where no United States hospitals exist. The order of the navy department was conclusive on the fourth auditor.

4. The act of 1849 (9 Stats. at Large, 419, Res. 17, § 2) requires the disbursement to be allowed and the commanding officer to be held responsible. In this case, it would be the President.

5. Money paid under such circumstances with a full knowledge of the facts, cannot be recovered back. 2 East, 469; 4 Dallas, 109; Starkie's Ev. pt. 4, p. 112.

Mr. Justice GRIER delivered the opinion of the court.

The action in this case is for money had and received by the defendant, Jones. It was entered amicably, and submitted on a case stated.

The defendant is a lieutenant in the navy of the United States. In December, 1851, he was in Paris, on leave of absence, and was severely and dangerously wounded by accident, during the emeute or revolutionary outbreak in that month. In July, 1852, he was placed by the secretary of the navy on special duty, for the collection of information relative to the steam navy of France. Afterwards, in August, 1852, the sum of one thousand dollars was transmitted to him by the secretary of the navy, with orders to apply it " to discharge the expenses attending the injuries received by him in Paris." It is admitted that this money was disbursed according to the orders of the secretary. The accounting officers of the treasury have charged the amount so disbursed by the defendant against him on his pay account, " and have refused to recognize the authority of the secretary of the navy in the premises."

The reason alleged for this refusal by the accounting officer is, that by his construction of the second section of the act of 3d of March, 1835, c. 27, the secretary of the navy had no authority to make such appropriation of the funds of the government in his hands. The act, so far as it is material, is in these words: "That the yearly allowance provided in this act is all the pay, compensation, and allowance which shall be received under any circumstances whatever by any such officer, &c.".

Notwithstanding an opinion of a late attorney-general to the contrary, the accounting officer "entertains no doubt" that the expenses attending the medical treatment of a sick and disabled officer or seaman are among the "allowances" prohibited by this act, and has consequently felt bound to repudiate the secretary's construction of the law, and his opinion as to the powers and duties of his department.

For the purposes of this case, however, it will not be necessary for the court to decide between these discordant opinions as to what things come within the category of "allowances," according to the true intent and meaning of the act of congress.

It is the peculiar province and duty of the navy department to provide medical stores and attendance for the officers and seamen attached to that service. It may truly be said, also, to enter into the contract of the government with persons so employed by them. For this purpose, a bureau of medicine is attached to this department, and numerous medical officers appointed. The law, moreover, exacts from every officer and seaman a monthly contribution from their wages to make provision for the sick and disabled. These contributions are applied, under the supervision of the President, to the erection and maintenance of marine hospitals, and similar institutions for the benefit of seamen.

The exigencies of the service often require the employment of soldiers and sailors at a distance from public hospitals, and when the attendance of the medical officers cannot be obtained; or, consequently, in fulfilment of the humane policy of the government, it frequently becomes necessary to employ temporarily physicians not regularly commissioned. For in this way alone can the department perform the duty assumed by the government of providing the necessary medical attendance for those who become sick or disabled in its service. The executive department of the government, to which is intrusted the control of the subject-matter, must necessarily determine all questions appertaining to the employment and payment of such temporary agents, and the exigency which demands their employment. The secretary of the navy represents the President, and exercises his power on the subjects confided to his department. He is responsible to the people and the law for any abuse of the powers intrusted to him. His acts and decisions, on subjects submitted to his jurisdiction and control by the constitution and laws, do not require the approval of any officer of another department to make them valid and conclusive. The accounting officers of the treasury have not the burden of responsibility cast upon them of revising the judgments, correcting the supposed mistakes, or annulling the orders of the heads of departments.

In the case before us, the defendant has not come before the accounting officers of the treasury, claiming from the government an "allowance" for medical attendance while on leave of absence, and submitting to these officers the propriety and legality of such "allowance." On the contrary, the agreed case shows, that a sum of money had been transmitted to the defendant by the secretary of the navy to be disbursed, and that he had disbursed it according to his orders; and whether it was for paying for services acknowledged by the secretary to have been rendered to the government for medical attendance on the defendant himself, or on another, could make no difference. The liability of the defendant to refund this money to the government is founded on the act of the accounting officer charging him with it, because, in his opinion, the secretary of the navy had mistaken the law or abused his discretion.

We are of opinion that he was not bound to assume this responsibility.

The propriety of detaching the defendant on special duty in France, of furnishing him with medical attendance while so employed, and of adopting and ratifying his act in the employment of such physician, under all the circumstances, are all subjects peculiarly within the jurisdiction and discretion of the head of the navy department, and not subject to revision or correction by the officers of any other department.

The judgment of the circuit court is therefore affirmed.

Mr. Justice CATRON, and Mr. Justice DANIEL, dissented.

Mr. Justice DANIEL dissenting.

I am unable to concur in the opinion of the court just pronounced in this cause, for the reason that this opinion upon mere assumed and hypothetical considerations of hardship or motives by which the legislature may have been influenced, undertakes directly to contravene, and in reality to annual a law, than which there is not one more clear or more positive in its provisions to be found upon the statute book.

With respect to considerations of hardship in the operation of a positive law, or of the motives of those by whom it has been enacted, I can, in expounding its provisions, assume no power which is legitimate; those are subjects exclusively within the province of the lawmakers, and to them it belongs to control them.

The statute here referred to as being affected by the opinion in this case, is that bearing date on the 3d of March, 1835, (4 Stats. at Large, 755, 757,) regulating the pay of the navy of the United States.

If it were by me deemed regular to seek for the objects of congress in the changes by this law of the provisions of previous statutes, those objects might perhaps be correctly inferred from the fact that, by the law of 1835 now under consideration, the compensation previously made to officers of the navy was in many, if not in every instance, at least doubted. But I deem it proper to confine myself to the language of the statute of 1835; and to expound its clear and unambiguous terms without reference to any thing *dehors* those terms, and especially freed from any rule of interpretation so uncertain as mere conjecture.

By this law, after regulating the pay of naval officers of every grade, it is declared, section 2: " That no allowance shall hereafter be made to any officer in the naval service of the United States for drawing bills, for receiving or disbursing money, or transacting any business for the government of the United States, nor shall he be allowed servants, or pay for servants, or clothing, or rations for them, or pay for the same, nor shall any allowance be made to him for rent of quarters, or to pay rent for furniture, or for lights or fuel, or transporting baggage." After the above enumeration, comprehensive as it is, we find in the law the following exclusion of any and every allowance which might be claimed, upon the ground of its having been omitted in the enumeration preceding it : " It is hereby expressly declared, that the yearly allowances provided by this act, is all the pay, compensation, and allowance that shall be received, under any circumstances whatsoever, by any such officer or person, except for travelling expenses when under orders, for which ten cents per mile shall be allowed."

That the officers of the navy were cognizant of the mandate of this law must be presumed ; but, in addition to this legitimate conclusion, it is known as an historical fact in the public administration of the government, that, by a circular addressed to them, they were severally informed of the provisions of the law ; besides which, they must unavoidably have learned them by every settlement for their pay at the treasury.

How, then, it can be possible to escape from the comprehensive language of the statute, which may well be styled " the exclusion of every conclusion " in favor of the claim by Lieutenant Jones, it passes my power to perceive. It will not be pretended by any one, that the advance made to him was a portion of his yearly pay, yet the statute declares that the yearly pay shall be " all the pay, compensation, and allowance that shall be received by any such officer or other person, under any circumstances whatsoever, except for travelling expenses, for which ten cents per mile may be allowed."

Surely the phrase, " under any circumstances whatsoever," is broad enough to comprehend any casualty to which any person may be exposed.

But it has been alleged, in excuse for the retention of this money by Lieutenant Jones, that there was no naval surgeon in Paris, and that the money was advanced by the secretary of the navy. To the first part of this apology it is a sufficient reply to state: first, that the statute has declared the pay of the officer to be a sufficient allowance under all circumstances whatsoever, and, therefore, under the circumstances of this case, no allowance beyond that graduated by the law itself could properly be claimed; second, that the government could be under no conceivable obligation, even independently of the express exclusion of the law, to provide medical or surgical attendance to wait upon an officer off duty, and not necessarily exposed to any of the perils of duty; that had Lieutenant Jones been on duty, he would have been attended by a portion of the medical staff, and been, if in reach of them, entitled to the benefit of the naval hospitals; and thus, under the regular usages of the service, been supplied with those aids for which the law and the usages of the service has made provision. Every one can perceive the danger of abuse attendant on a practice, by an officer, of employing a surgeon or physician, *ad libitum*, to attend him when off duty, and to charge the expense of such employment to the government as a legitimate allowance to the officer when off duty.

It is no excuse for an irregularity like this to say, that where troops or vessels are employed on distant service there may be resort to medical or surgical aid; in such an instance, the persons called in would be engaged for the army, the fleet, or the corps generally, at regulated rates, and the account for such services would be settled and certified in conformity with such rules or rates; but an instance of this kind, justified by necessity alone, and conducted by rule, can bear no similitude to the advance, without authority of law or usage, of a round sum of money to one whose compensation had already been provided, and to be expended by him according to his own tastes or ideas, without known regard to any other criterion, and to be accounted for to nobody.

The secretary of the navy had no authority of law for making the advance in question. It was not within the provisions of the law for the creation and application of the hospital fund. That fund, by the law which created it, is to be applied to objects and in modes designated, and the present instance falls not within either of the directions of the law.

But it has been insisted that the secretary of the navy, having ordered the payment of this money, the subordinate or beneficiary cannot be called on for reimbursement; first, because the payment having been voluntarily made by the government, the money could not be recovered back upon ·the rules governing actions for money had and received; and, secondly, that the secretary himself, if any one, and not his subordinates, should be made accountable. These two excuses do not appear to be altogether. consistent; for if the money was paid under a competent authority, and with full knowledge and in good faith, there could be no recovery on any account. But it is denied that the secretary had the power to make the payment or advance, or that he can be looked upon as being the government, or in any respect as being identified with the government, except so far as he is acting within his regular constitutional and legal sphere. To hold the converse of this, would be to justify the most irregular and flagrant abuses, and to cover them with the excuse that they were the acts of the government itself which had been wronged.

Well, then, with respect to any protection which can be extended to the recipient of this money, upon the mere ground that it was paid to him under an order from the secretary of the navy. The officers of the navy must, like all others, be presumed to be cognizant of the law. If, then, with this necessary imputation of knowledge, an officer, either through the ignorance, or carelessness, or mistake, or connivance of the agent of the government, get possession of and apply to his own advantage the funds of that government, and seek to protect himself by alleging a voluntary payment to him, such a defence would seem 'to be warranted neither by law, nor equity, nor good faith.

Again, it has been insisted that the sum of money having been advanced by direction of the secretary of the navy, the auditor, by whom, according to law, the accounts of Lieutenant Jones were to be settled, could have no right to question the legality or regularity of such advance, or to charge it to the officer who had used it; and this position seems to be rested upon the naked position that the auditor, being subordinate to the secretary of the navy, has no right or power to examine into his acts, although such are necessarily complicated or connected with the actings and doings of those transactions the law requires him to examine and adjust. To such a rule of proceeding as this I can by no means subscribe; I know of no rule of subordination which can justify, much less demand, a departure from the law, or from integrity, in obedience merely to the fact of inferiority in the gradation of place. Each and every officer has his duties to perform, and is bound to their performance with independence and good faith; and no matter whose acts may be brought before him, whether those of his immediate superior or one much higher in power, he is bound to bring them all to the test of the law, and to pronounce upon all, from the greatest to the least, by one inflexible rule,—the rule of duty; and surely, when an appeal is made to tribunals of justice, they should recognize no standard but that of the law itself.

My opinion is, that the decision of the circuit court should be reversed, and judgment entered for the plaintiffs.

THE UNITED STATES, USE OF JAMES MACKEY ET AL. PLAINTIFFS IN ERROR, v. RICHARD S. COXE.

Administrators upon an estate who were appointed in the Cherokee nation had a right to maintain a suit or prosecute a claim for money in the District of Columbia, and a payment to a person acting under a power of attorney from them would have been valid.

But where this person, instead of receiving the money under his power of attorney, took out letters of administration in the District of Columbia, and then signed a receipt as attorney for money paid by himself as administrator to himself as attorney for the Cherokee administrators, this receipt is good, and the surety upon his administration bond is not responsible to the Cherokee heirs.

The Cherokee nation are so far under the protection of the laws of the United States, that they may be considered, for the purposes above named, as a State or territory of the United States.

THIS case was brought up by writ of error, from the circuit court of the United States for the District of Columbia, holden in and for the county of Washington.

The case is stated in the opinion of the court.

It was argued by *Mr. Chilton*, for the plaintiffs in error, and by *Mr. Carlisle* and *Mr. Bradley*, for the defendant.

Mr. Justice McLEAN delivered the opinion of the court.

This is a writ of error to the circuit court for the District of Columbia.

The action was brought against the defendant as surety in the administration bond of Austin J. Raines, administrator of Samuel Mackey, late of the Cherokee nation.

Raines received from James Mackey, Joseph Talley, and Preston T. Mackey, as administrators of Samuel Mackey, deceased, a power of attorney for them and in their names to petition the congress of the United States to settle and release the claim of the United States against the said Samuel Mackey, deceased, as principal, and John Drenner, Lewis Evans, and Hiro T. Wilson, as securities; and after the passage of any law in relation to said claim by congress, to receive all moneys that may be due the estate of the said Mackey, deceased, from the treasurer of the United States, and full receipts, acquittances, and relinquishments thereof to make in their name ; and further, to adjust and settle with the treasurer of the United States, or other officers of the government, all other claims of said Mackey against the United States, and to receive all moneys due from the United States to said Mackey on any account whatever.

Raines came to Washington and procured a settlement of the accounts between the government and Samuel Mackey, deceased ; but the treasury department refused to pay him the balance due Mackey upon the power of attorney, and required him to take out letters of administration. He thereupon applied to the orphans' court of the county of Washington, in the District of Columbia, for letters of administration, which were granted upon his executing bond, with the defendant and James Reeside as sureties. He then received from the treasury the sum of $10,518.05, out of which he paid the expense of administration, and for the balance he executed the following receipt : —

" 7th July, 1841. Received of Austin J. Raines, administrator of Samuel Mackey, deceased, the sum of ten thousand five hundred and thirteen dollars and five cents, being the amount due to the representatives next of kin and distributees of said Samuel Mackey, from said administrator.

Signed,   JAMES MACKEY,
JOSEPH TALLEY,
PRESTON T. MACKEY.

By their attorney in fact, A. J. RAINES."

Reeside, the co-obligor in the administration bond, having died several years ago, the process was served only on the defendant.

The declaration contained several counts, stating that the said Samuel Mackey died intestate, leaving Sarah Mackey, his widow, and James Mackey, Preston T. Mackey, William Mackey, George Mackey, Nancy Talley, wife of Joseph Talley, and Corine Mackey, all being citizens of the Cherokee nation, and that, by the laws of said Cherokee nation, the widow and children were distributees of the deceased.

The defendant filed a general plea of performance, on which issue was joined.

On the trial before the jury, among other prayers for instruction was the following : " If the jury find from the evidence that Austin J. Raines, as administrator of Samuel Mackey, deceased, received from the treasury of the United States the sum of $10,518.05, and after deducting the expenses of administration there remained in his hands the clear sum of $10,505.20$\frac{1}{4}$,

9 *

and no debts of said deceased are shown payable by said administrator; and James Mackey, Joseph Talley, and Preston T. Mackey were the original administrators of said Samuel Mackey, under the laws of the Cherokee nation, the burden of proof is on the defendant to show that said Raines paid said sum of $10,505.20¼ to said James Mackey, Joseph Talley, and Preston T. Mackey, or the survivors of them; and although the jury may find that the paper offered in evidence, purporting to be a power of attorney from said James Mackey, Joseph Talley, and Preston T. Mackey to said Raines is genuine, yet the said Raines had no authority to receipt for said parties by himself, as their attorney in fact, to himself as administrator, and that such receipt is not a payment by him as administrator of said parties; and unless such payment be proved otherwise than by such receipt, the said Raines has not performed the condition of this bond as administrator of Samuel Mackey, and the said defendant is liable in this action to the said James Mackey, Joseph Talley, and Preston T. Mackey, or the survivors of them, for the said sum of $10,505.20¼, with interest thereon from the date when the same was received"; which instruction was refused, and to which an exception was taken.

There were other exceptions, but this one presents the material points in the case.

By the treaty made between the United States and the Cherokee nation, dated March 14, 1835, in article 5, the United States covenanted and agreed that "the lands ceded to the Cherokee nation in the foregoing article shall, in no future time, without their consent, be included within the territorial limits or jurisdiction of any State or territory. But they shall secure to the Cherokee nation the right of their national councils to make and carry into effect all such laws as they may deem necessary for the government and protection of the persons and property within their own country belonging to their people, or such persons as have connected themselves with them : provided always, that they shall not be inconsistent with the constitution of the United States, and such acts of congress as have been or may be passed regulating trade and intercourse with the Indians," &c.

The Cherokees are governed by their own laws. As a people, they are more advanced in civilization than the other Indian tribes, with the exception, perhaps, of the Choctaws. By the national council their laws are enacted, approved by their executive, and carried into effect through an organized judiciary. Under a law "relative to estates and administrators," letters of administration were granted to the persons above named on the estate of Samuel Mackey, deceased, by the probate court, with as much regularity and responsibilities as letters of administration are granted by the state courts of the Union.

This organization is not only under the sanction of the general government, but it guarantees their independence, subject to the restriction that their laws shall be consistent with the constitution of the United States, and acts of congress which regulate trade and intercourse with the Indians. And whenever congress shall make provision on the subject, the Cherokee nation shall be entitled to a delegate in the national legislature.

It is refreshing to see the surviving remnants of the races which once inhabited and roamed over this vast country as their hunting-grounds, and as the undisputed proprietors of the soil, exchanging their erratic habits for the blessings of civilization.

A question has been suggested whether the Cherokee people should be considered or treated as a foreign State or territory. The fact that they are under the constitution of the Union, and subject to acts of congress regulating trade, is a sufficient answer to the suggestion. They are not only within our jurisdiction, but the faith of the nation is pledged for their protection. In some respects they bear the same relation to the federal government as a territory did in its second grade of government, under the ordinance of 1787. Such territory passed its own laws, subject to the approval of congress, and its inhabitants were subject to the constitution and acts of congress. The principal difference consists in the fact that the Cherokees enact their own laws, under the restriction stated, appoint their own officers, and pay their own expenses. This, however, is no reason why the laws and proceedings of the Cherokee territory, so far as relates to rights claimed under them, should not be placed upon the same footing as other territories in the Union. It is not a foreign, but a domestic territory,—a territory which originated under our constitution and laws.

By the 11th section of the act of 24th of June, 1812, it is provided "that it shall be lawful for any person or persons to whom letters testamentary or of administration hath been or may hereafter be granted, by the proper authority in any of the United States or the territories thereof, to maintain any suit or action, and to prosecute and recover any claim in the District of Columbia, in the same manner as if the letters testamentary or administration had been granted in the District. Under this law the money due to Mackey might have been paid, and, indeed, should have been paid, to Raines, the attorney in fact of the administrators of Mackey. But, through abundant caution, letters of administration were required to be taken out in this District, as a prerequisite to the payment of the money by the treasury department.

Mackey et al. v. Coxe.

No question could arise as to the validity of the Cherokee law under which letters of administration were granted on the estate of Mackey, and as the power of attorney given by the administrators to Raines seems to have been duly authenticated and proved, a payment to the administrator, by the government, would have been a legal payment. The Cherokee country, we think, may be considered a territory of the United States, within the act of 1812. In no respect can it be considered a foreign State or territory, as it is within our jurisdiction and subject to our laws.

Although an executor or administrator cannot sue in a foreign court, in virtue of his original letters of administration, yet he may lawfully, under that administration, receive a debt voluntarily paid in any other State. Stevens v. Gaylord, 11 Mass. R. 256. In Doolittle v. Lewis, 7 John. Ch. 49, Chancellor Kent held, that a voluntary payment to a foreign executor or administrator was a good discharge of the debt. Shultz v. Pulver, 3 Paige, 182; Hooker v. Olmstead, 6 Pick. 481.

This suit is brought in the name of the surviving administrators of Mackey and of the distributees. Regularly, an action by the distributees could not be sustained, unless an application had been made to the orphans' court in this District to order a distribution, and authorize or direct the administrator, Raines, to pay the same. This administration being ancillary to that of the domicile of the deceased, the distribution would be governed by the law of the domicile.

There appears to have been no creditors, of the estate of Mackey, in the District of Columbia, and letters of administration were obtained here, as necessary under the decision of the treasury department. This object being accomplished, and the costs of the administration paid, Raines, as agent of the administrators of the domicile, receipted for the money in their behalf, under the power of attorney from the administrators. And the question arises, whether this discharges the defendant as surety on the administration bond of Raines.

Under the power of attorney he was authorized to receive all moneys that may be due the estate of Mackey from the treasurer of the United States, and receipt for the same. He received and receipted for the money as administrator in this District, and then executed a receipt to himself as agent, under the power of attorney as agent for the administrators.

Under the circumstances, it would be a hardship fraught with injustice, to hold the defendant liable as surety on the administration bond. Raines was the confidential agent of the administrators of Mackey — the money was placed in his hands, under full authority to receive it. It has never been paid over,

Mackey et al. *v.* Coxe.

it is said, by reason of the bursting of a boiler, by which Raines lost his life and the money which he had received. But whether this be true or not, the money went into the hands of Raines, who was the agent of the administrators, duly authorized to receive it; and we think, under the peculiar circumstances of the case, the defendant was thereby discharged. Whether for the payment of creditors or distribution among the heirs, the domicile of the deceased was the place to which the money should be transmitted. It would add to the conditions of the administration bond, to hold the defendant responsible for the safe transmission of the money, after it was placed in the hands of the agent of the administrators.

Had the receipt of Raines been duly filed and acted upon, in the court of probate, his surety on his administration bond would have been discharged. The action of the probate court only is wanting, but we think such action was not essential, and that the equity of the case is equally clear without it. The parties are estopped from denying the agency of Raines.

In Vaughan *v.* Northup et al., 15 Pet. 6, this court say: "The debts due from the government of the United States have no locality at the seat of government. The United States, in their sovereign capacity, have no particular place of domicile, but possess in contemplation of law an ubiquity throughout the Union; and the debts due by them are not to be treated like the debts of a private debtor, which constitute local assets in his own domicile. On the contrary, the administrator of a creditor of the government, duly appointed in the State where he was domiciled at the time of his death, has full authority to receive payment, and give a full discharge of the debt due to his intestate, in any place where the government may choose to pay it."

We think there is no error in the ruling of the court, and the judgment of the circuit court is therefore affirmed.

Justices NELSON and CURTIS stated that they concurred in the decision of the court to affirm the judgment of the circuit court, upon the ground that, as no final account had been settled by the administrator in the orphans' court, and no order had been made by that court, either directing the administrator to pay the balance in his hands to the principal administrators, for distribution by them, or directing a distribution to be made here, there was no breach of the bond. That this being an ancillary administration, it depended upon the discretion of the orphans' court, which granted it, whether the money, remaining in the hands of the ancillary administrator, after the satisfaction of all claims in this jurisdiction, should be distributed here, by the ancillary administrator, or remitted to the principal administrators for distribution; and until that discretion shall be exercised, and the ancillary administrator directed which of these courses to pursue, he is in no default, and his surety is not liable.

RICHARD H. SESSIONS, DANIEL H. SESSIONS, AND SANDFORD C. FAULKNER, APPELLANTS, *v.* JOHN M. PINTARD.

Where there was a decree in the court below for the payment of a certain sum of money, (land being held as security,) from which decree an appeal was taken, the sureties upon the appeal bond are not entitled to a *pro rata* credit upon their responsibility, the land having proved insufficient to pay the amount of the decree.

The entire proceeds of the sale of the land must be deducted from the amount of the decree, and the sureties upon the appeal bond must be responsible for the balance.

THIS was an appeal from the circuit court of the United States for the eastern district of Arkansas.

It was a sequel to the case of Goodloe's Administrator *v.* Pintard, decided in this court and reported in 12 How. 24. The subsequent proceedings are stated in the opinion of the court.

It was submitted on printed argument by *Mr. Pike,* for the plaintiffs in error, and argued by *Mr. Carlisle* and *Mr. Crittenden,* for the defendants.

Mr. Pike stated the question which arose in the case in this way:—

The question in the case may be very briefly stated thus: Where, in a suit to enforce a lien on land for the purchase-money due the vendor, there is a decree ascertaining the amount due by the vendee, and recognizing the lien, and ordering payment or sale of the land, and, on appeal from this decree, sureties enter into a bond conditioned to prosecute the appeal with effect and make good all damages and costs, how far does the land stand as *their* security? If, when it is sold, the amount decreed, with interest, is more than the penalty of their bond, and the land sells for less than the penalty, in what way are the proceeds to be applied? Shall they be credited upon the aggregate of the decree, perhaps leaving the sureties to pay the whole penalty, or against the penalty, or proportionally against the penalty and the excess over it?

The condition of the bond was to prosecute the appeal with effect, and pay all damages and costs in case of failure to make the appeal good. The damages were the interest which accrued between the dates of the decree against Goodloe and the judgment against the bail, amounting to less than $7,000. This should have been the extent of the recovery, and not the whole penalty of $12,000.

The surety who pays money for the principal is entitled to all the securities which the plaintiff has for the debt. Union Bank of Maryland v. Edwards, 2 Gill & Johnson, 358; 7 Serg. & R. 9; 8 Serg. & R. 309; 10 J. R. 524; 2 J. Cas. 227; 2 J. C. R. 554.

The counsel for Pintard contended that the credits had been properly applied and given.

Mr. Justice McLEAN delivered the opinion of the court.·

This is an appeal from the circuit court of the eastern district of Arkansas.

Pintard, on the 10th of April, 1847, obtained a decree against Archibald Goodloe for $10,552, with ten per cent interest per annum on the amount decreed. There was also an order that a certain tract of land should be sold, and the proceeds applied to the payment of the decree.

An appeal was taken from this decree to this court, by which the decree was affirmed. On the 20th of February, 1852, Pintard commenced an action against Sessions and others on the appeal bond, and at April term, 1853, obtained a judgment on the bond for the penalty thereof; amounting to the sum of $12,000.

At the same time, Pintard procured an order for the sale of the land specified in the decree, which was sold on the 15th of November, 1852, for the sum of $8,025, which, after paying the expense of the sale, left a balance of $7,525 as a credit on said decree, as of the 15th of November, 1852. The interest, with the sum decreed, up to that period, amounted to $16,877. The proceeds of the sale of the land being deducted from this sum, leaves a balance on the decree of $8,912, with interest from the 17th day of April, 1853. The interest on this sum, up to the time judgment was rendered on the appeal bond, makes the sum of $9,283, as the amount to be collected on the judgment.

An execution was issued on the judgment the 14th of May, 1853, for $12,000 with an indorsement of a credit of $2,717. This execution was levied on a number of slaves, of the value of $12,000, as the property of Sessions, the defendant. A delivery bond was taken for the slaves, with Daniel H. Sessions as security; but the slaves not being delivered on the day of the sale, an execution was issued against principal and surety on the delivery bond.

At this stage of the proceedings, a bill was filed by the appellants, complaining that the distribution which had been made of the proceeds of the sale of the land was inequitable, and that such proceeds should be credited on the judgment entered upon the appeal bond, *pro rata*, and not exclusively on the decree; and the complainants pray that Pintard may be decreed to enter a credit upon the judgment as aforesaid, as of its date, for the sum of $5,323.35; and that a perpetual injunction might be granted to prevent him from collecting any more than the residue of the judgment, after deducting the above sum.

A temporary injunction was granted, Pintard filed his answer, and, upon the final hearing, the injunction was dissolved and the bill dismissed, at the costs of the complainants. From this decree an appeal was taken, and that brings the case before us.

The complainants in their bill allege no fraud nor mistake, as a ground of relief. They claim that the money received under the decree for the sale of the land shall be applied, *pro rata*, in the discharge of the judgment against them, and the balance of the decree which remains after deducting the judgment. This would give to them a credit on the judgment of $5,724; and that Pintard, in claiming the whole amount of the judgment, seeks to recover from them $8,568.99 more than in equity he is entitled to.

This claim of the appellants rests upon the ground that there was a lien on the land sold by the original decree, which operated as an inducement to them to become sureties on the appeal bond. The land, by the original decree, was directed to be sold; consequently, the proceeds of the sale could be applied only in discharge of the decree. On what ground could the appellants claim a *pro rata* distribution of this fund? They were bound to the extent of the penalty of their bond, on which a judgment was entered. They had a direct interest in the application of the proceeds of the land to the payment of the original decree, including the interest and costs; and so much as such payment reduced the original decree below the amount of the judgment against them, they were entitled to a credit on the judgment. The judgment has been so made, and the credit entered, and beyond this they have no claim, either equitable or legal.

In the argument, a subrogation of the land or its proceeds, for the benefit of complainants, is urged; but on what known principle of equity does not satisfactorily appear. Had the appellants paid the decree in full, they might have claimed a control over the land decreed to be sold, or its proceeds. They made no payment, but assert a general equity to have the fund applied, *pro rata*, on their judgment. This would leave a large amount of the original decree unsatisfied. On what ground could Pintard be subjected to such a loss? He looked to the land and

Curtis et al. v. Petitpain et al.

the surety on the appeal bond, which more than covered his decree, including interest and cost.

The condition of the appeal bond was "for the prosecution of said appeal to effect, and to answer all damages and costs, if" there should be a failure to make the plea good in the supreme court. There was a failure to do this, and the penalty of the bond was incurred. Whatever hardship may be in this case is common to all sureties who incur responsibility and have money to pay. Beyond that of a faithful application of the proceeds of the land in payment of the decree, the appellants have no equity. They cannot place themselves in the relation of two creditors having claims on a common fund, which may be distributed *pro rata* between them. Pintard has a claim on both funds; first, on the proceeds of the land, and second, on the judgment entered on the appeal bond for the satisfaction of the original decree.

The decree of the circuit court is affirmed, with costs.

LOUIS CURTIS, BENJAMIN CURTIS, JOHN L. HUBBARD, JAMES D. B. CURTIS, AND HENRY A. BOORAINE, PLAINTIFFS IN ERROR, *v.* MADAME THERESE PETITPAIN, WIFE OF VICTOR FESTE, AND MANDERVILLE MARIGNY, LATE UNITED STATES MARSHAL FOR THE EASTERN DISTRICT OF LOUISIANA.

Where the record contains only an agreed statement of facts, it is not in conformity with the eleventh and thirty-first rules of this court, and the case will be dismissed.

Where different parties claimed a fund in the hands of the marshal, which had arisen from sales under an execution, a judgment of the circuit court on rules as to whom the money should be paid, is not such a judgment as can be re-examined in this court.

THIS case was brought up by writ of error from the circuit court of the United States for the eastern district of Louisiana. It is stated in the opinion of the court.

It was argued by *Mr. Taylor*, for the plaintiffs in error, and *Mr. Benjamin* for the defendants.

The point of practice, upon which the case went off, was raised by *Mr. Benjamin*, who contended that the transcript was not such a complete record as was required by the 11th and 81st rules of court.

The points made relating to the merits of the cause are omitted.

Mr. Justice CAMPBELL delivered the opinion of the court.

The record certified in this cause consists of "an agreed statement of facts," which the parties submitted to the court on the rules taken by the plaintiffs against the defendants, and the judgment rendered thereon, and a judgment rendered on a motion for a new trial, being the proceedings after the submission of the case.

The case stated is, that the plaintiffs recovered a judgment against Victor Feste in the circuit court of the United States. That an execution issued thereon, and a seizure was made of immovable as well as movable property; which was sold, and the proceeds held by the marshal.

While these proceedings were pending, Madame Feste recovered, in one of the state courts, a decree against her husband, Victor Feste, for the separation of property and the amount of dowry brought in marriage; and thereupon served a notice upon the marshal, claiming to have satisfaction of her legal mortgage, in preference to the execution creditor, from the moneys in his hands, and obtained a rule from the court requiring him to answer her claim. The plaintiffs, upon their part, (as the case states,) also obtained a rule, to enforce the payment of the money to them on their execution. To settle these conflicting claims was the object of the agreed case thus submitted to the court.

Two questions arise *in limine*, either of which is, in our opinion, decisive of this cause: 1st. That this is not such a transcript as will satisfy the 11th and 31st rules of this court, under the decision of Keene v. Whittaker, 13 Pet. 459; and, 2d, that this is not such a judgment as this court can re-examine, according to the principle of Bayard v. Lombard, 9 How. 530. And we agree with the defendants upon both these questions.

The cause is dismissed with costs.

JECKER, TORRE, AND CO., ET AL., CLAIMANTS OF THE CARGO OF THE SHIP ADMITTANCE, AND FESSENDEN AND FAY, CLAIMANTS OF THE SHIP ADMITTANCE, v. JOHN B. MONTGOMERY, LIBELLANT.

In a state of war, the nations who are engaged in it, and all their citizens or subjects, are enemies to each other. Hence, all intercourse or communication between them is unlawful.

Cases mentioned, by way of illustration, in which property of a subject or citizen, found trading with an enemy, has been adjudged to be forfeited as prize.

The interposition of a neutral port through which the property is to pass, does not prevent it from being confiscated.

In the present case, the evidence shows that the owners of the ship and cargo knew that the destination of the voyage was to an enemy's port. Even if the owner of the

Jecker et al. v. Montgomery.

vessel was ignorant of it, the fate of the vessel must be decided by the acts of those persons who had her in charge.

It is generally the duty of the captor to send his prize home for adjudication ; but circumstances may render such a step improper, and of these he must be the judge. In making up his decision, good faith and reasonable discretion are required. In the present case he was excusable for not sending home the vessel.

Generally, the proceedings for the condemnation of property as prize ought to be instituted in the name of the United States. The circumstances, which led to the use of the name of the captor, and the fact that no objection was made to it in the court below, prevent this court from pronouncing the objection to be fatal.

The proceeds of sale were properly deposited in the treasury of the United States.

THIS was an appeal from the circuit court of the United States for the District of Columbia, holden in and for the county of Washington.

The case is stated in the opinion of the court.

It was argued by *Mr. Coxe* and *Mr. Nelson*, for the appellants, and *Mr. Key* and *Mr. Johnson*, for the appellees. The arguments consisted chiefly in comments upon the evidence upon both sides, and, for the appellants, in the legal objection that the libel should have been filed in the name of the United States, instead of an individual.

Mr. Justice DANIEL delivered the opinion of the court.

This is an appeal from a decree in admiralty by the circuit court of the United States for the District of Columbia, by which decree the ship Admittance, claimed by the appellants, Charles B. Fessenden and Richard S. Fay, as owners, and the cargo of the same ship claimed by the appellants, Jecker, Torre, and Co. and Manuel Quintana, were upon a libel filed by the appellee, John B. Montgomery, condemned as prize of war.

It will serve to explain the nature of the present controversy, and the character of the decree of the circuit court above mentioned, to refer to the proceedings heretofore had therein upon a libel filed by the claimants of the cargo for restitution, and to the decision of this court upon cross-appeals from those proceedings, both by the claimants and the captor, out of which last-mentioned decision the case before us has arisen.

By the decision of this court just referred to, (see 13 Howard, p. 498,) we hold the following propositions to have been expressly ruled : —

1. That the admiralty court of the District of Columbia had jurisdiction of the libel for the condemnation of the property in contest, although such property was not brought within its jurisdiction ; and if they found the subject liable to condemnation, might proceed to condemn, although not in fact within the custody or control of the court.

2. That the admiralty court in the District of Columbia, having jurisdiction of the case, it was its duty to order the captors

to institute proceedings in that court to condemn the property as prize, by a day to be named in the order; and in default thereof to be proceeded against upon a libel for an unlawful seizure; because the property of the claimant is not devested by the capture, but by condemnation in a prize court — is not devested until condemnation, though such condemnation will relate back to the capture.

3. That the grounds alleged for the seizure of the vessel and cargo, namely, that the vessel sailed from New Orleans with the design of trading with the enemy, and did in fact hold illegal intercourse with them, are sufficient, if supported by testimony, to subject both vessel and cargo to condemnation.

4. And if they were liable to condemnation, the reasons assigned in the answer for not bringing the vessel and cargo into a port of the United States for trial — namely: that it was impossible so to do consistently with the public interest — is sufficient, if supported by proofs, to justify the captors in selling vessel and cargo in California, and to exempt the captors from damages on that account.

5. That to a libel for restitution, probable cause for seizure is no defence; but is so only against a claim for damages, in cases in which the property has been restored or lost after seizure.

Under the authority of the rulings just enumerated, and in obedience to the mandate founded thereupon, the libel in the cause now before us was filed; and the case made by the parties presents, as the material questions for consideration, the inquiries: 1. Whether the vessel sailed with the design of trading with the enemy, and did in fact hold illegal intercourse with them. 2. Admitting that the vessel and cargo were in the first instance liable to condemnation, whether the reasons assigned for not bringing them within the United States were so supported by proof, as to justify the captor in not bringing them within the United States, and in selling them in California, without a forfeiture of their rights as captors.

As a principle applicable to the first of these inquiries, it may be averred as a part of the law of nations — forming a part, too, of the municipal jurisprudence of every country — " that in a state of war between two nations, declared by the authority in whom the municipal constitution vests the power of making war, the two nations and all their citizens or subjects are enemies to each other." The consequence of this state of hostility is, that all intercourse and communication between them is unlawful. *Vide* Wheaton on Maritime Captures, cap. 7, p. 209, quoting from Bynkershoeck this passage : " *Ex natura belli commercia inter hostes cessare, non est dubitandum. Quamvis nulla specialis sit commerciorum prohibitio, ipso tamen jure belli, commercia inter hostes esse vetita, ipsæ indictiones bellorum satis declarant.*

Upon this principle of public law, it has been the established rule of the high court of admiralty in England, that a trading with the enemy, except by a royal license, subjects the property to confiscation. The decisions of that court show that the rule has been rigidly enforced, as, for instance, where the government had authorized a homeward trade from the enemy's possessions, but had not specifically protected an outward trade to the same; and again, in instances where cargoes have been laden before the war, but where the parties had not used all possible diligence to countermand the voyage after the first notice of hostilities; and this rule has been enforced, not only against subjects of the Crown, but likewise against those of its allies in the war, upon the assumption that the rule was founded on the universal principle which states allied in war had a right to apply to each other's subjects. *Vide* Wheaton on Captures, p. 212; and 1 C. Robinson's Adm. R. 196, The Hoop.

The same rule has been adopted with equal strictness by this court. In the case of The Rapid, reported in 8 Cranch, 155, the claimant, a citizen of the United States, had purchased goods in the enemy's country a long time before the declaration of war, and had deposited them on an island near the boundary line between the two countries. Upon the breaking out of hostilities, his agents had hired the vessel to proceed to the place of deposit and bring away these goods. Upon her return the vessel was captured, and, with the cargo, was condemned as prize of war for trading with the enemy. In applying the law to this state of facts, this court said, and said unanimously: "That the universal sense of nations has acknowledged the demoralizing effects that would result from the admission of individual intercourse. The whole nation are embarked in one common bottom, and must be reconciled to submit to one common fate. Every individual of the one nation must acknowledge every individual of the other nation as his own enemy, because the enemy of his country. But, after deciding what is the duty of the citizen, the question occurs, what is the consequence of a breach of that duty? The law of prize is a part of the law of nations. In it, a hostile character is attached to trade, independently of the character of the trader who pursues or directs it. Condemnation to the use of the captor is equally the fate of the property of the belligerent and of the property engaged in anti-neutral trade. But a citizen or an ally may be engaged in a hostile trade, and thereby involve his property in the fate of those in whose cause he embarks." Again, the court say: "If by trading, in prize law was meant that signification of

10*

the term which consists in negotiation or contract, this case
would not come under the penalties of the rule. But the object and spirit of the rule is to cut off all communication or
actual locomotive intercourse between individuals of the belligerent nations. Negotiation or contract has, therefore, no
necessary connection with the offence. Intercourse inconsistent
with actual hostility is the offence against which the operation of
the rule is directed."

The case of The Joseph, reported in 8 Cranch, p. 451, was
that of a vessel owned by citizens of the United States, that
sailed from thence before the war, with a cargo on freight on a
voyage to Liverpool and the north of Europe, and thence back
to the United States. After arriving and discharging her cargo
at Liverpool, she took in another at Hull, and sailed for St.
Petersburg. At St. Petersburg, she received news of the war
with England, and sailed to London with a Russian cargo consigned to British merchants; delivered her cargo and sailed for
the United States in ballast, under a British license, and was
captured. In the opinion of this court in this case, delivered by
Washington, Justice, it is said : "That after the decision in the
cases of The Rapid and of The Alexander, it is not to be contended, that the sailing with a cargo on freight from St. Petersburg to London, after a full knowledge of the war, did not
amount to such a trading with the enemy as to have subjected
both the vessel and cargo to condemnation as prize of war, had
she been captured on that voyage. The alleged necessity of
undertaking that voyage to enable the master out of the freight
to discharge his expenses at St. Petersburg — countenanced, as
the master declares, by the opinion of our minister at St. Petersburg, that by undertaking such a voyage he would violate no
law of the United States — although these considerations, if
founded in truth, present a case of peculiar hardship, yet they
afford no legal excuse which it is competent to this court to admit as the basis of its decision."

The same course of decision which has established that property of a subject or citizen taken trading with the enemy is forfeited, has decided also that it is forfeited as prize. The ground
of the forfeiture is, that it is taken adhering to the enemy, and
therefore the proprietor is *pro hac vice* to be considered as an
enemy. *Vide* also Wheaton on Captures, p. 219, and 1 C. Robinson, 219, the case of The Nelly.

Attempts have been made to evade the rule of public law, by
the interposition of a neutral port between the shipment from
the belligerent port and their ultimate destination in the enemy's
country; but in all such cases the goods have been condemned,
as having been taken in a course of commerce rendering them

liable to confiscation; and it has been ruled that, without license from g vernment, no communication, direct or indirect, can be carried on with the enemy; that the interposition of a prior port makes no difference; that all trade with the enemy is illegal, and the circumstance that the goods are to go first to a neutral port will not make it lawful. 8 C. Robinson, 22, The Indian Chief; and 4 C. Robinson, 79, The Jonge Pieter.

Having thus stated the law with regard to maritime captures, it remains to be ascertained how far the case before us upon the pleadings and proofs, falls within the scope or the terms of that law.

The libel propounds, that the libellant, as the commander of the United States ship Portsmouth, did, on the 7th of April, 1847, at the port of San José in lower California, in the Republic of Mexico, seize and take possession of as lawful prize, a certain ship or vessel called The Admittance — one Peter Peterson being the master — with her cargo, provisions, tackle, and all other appurtenances to the said ship belonging. That the said ship is a merchant vessel belonging to citizens of the United States, and that the cargo of said ship is believed by the libellant to have belonged to certain merchants resident in Mexico. That about the month of October, 1846, the said ship with her cargo, left the port of New Orleans for a port in the Republic of Mexico, into which port the captain intended to discharge the cargo. That for some time prior to the sailing of this ship, and upon the day of her seizure, open and public war existed between the United States and the Republic of Mexico and its dependencies. That in consequence of said state of war, and in discharge of his duty, the ship Admittance, with her cargo, was seized by the libellant as prize of war.

The libellant further propounds, that Peterson, as master of the said ship, did sail from the United States with the intention of trading, and in fact did trade and otherwise hold illegal intercourse with the enemies of the United States, whereby the said ship, her cargo, tackle, and appurtenances, became subjects of lawful prize. All which illegal intention and acts of the master more fully appear by the papers of the said ship, and by other papers received from the master by the libellant, numbered from one to fifteen inclusive; from the deposition of William Bell, the first mate of The Admittance, and from the log-book — all of which it is prayed may be made parts of the libel; which concludes with a prayer for condemnation of ship and cargo, and for the dismission of the libel previously filed by Torre, Jecker, and Co., praying restitution of a portion of the cargo.

To the libel of Captain Montgomery were filed an answer on

behalf of Fessenden and Fay, who intervened as owners of the ship, and separate answers on behalf of Jecker, Torre, and Co., and of Manuel Quintana, as owners of the cargo.

These answers, so far as they are made up merely of general denials of the charges propounded in the libel, require no special animadversion. So far, however, as the specific facts alleged in them by way of exculpation, the compatibility of those facts with the established law of prize, or with the proofs adduced in the case, become a question, the statements in these answers are matters of essential importance, requiring particular examination.

The respondents Fessenden and Fay have in their answers observed an entire silence with respect to a knowledge on their part as to the destination of the ship or cargo; whilst they are very explicit in the assertion of their belief, that the cargo was put on board by the charterer, and that the ship sailed under a full persuasion that a treaty of peace would speedily terminate the then existing war between the United States and Mexico, and that they never were informed, nor do they believe, that the cargo was to be landed or disposed of in Mexico until after the termination of the war. Personally they say, that they know nothing of what occurred in relation to the ship and cargo in the Pacific; but from what they have learned they believe, and therefore aver, that there was no trading with the enemy at any time during the voyage. This statement, which implies knowledge in the respondents of the existence of war between the United States and Mexico at the time of chartering of their ship, and knowledge likewise that the cargo put on board was destined for the port of a nation, at the time of the shipment at any rate, in open hostility with the United States, will, as to its verity, be further tested by a comparison with the testimony furnished by the papers found in the captured vessel and by the examination of witnesses. And in this connection it may be observed, that the bare permission by the owners of the use of their vessel in hostile or piratical enterprises renders such vessel liable to capture and condemnation equally with her employment in similar offences under the immediate command of such owners themselves. *Vide* the case of The United States v. The Brig Maleck Adel, 2 How. 234; The United States v. The Schooner Little Charles, 1 Brok. Rep. 347; The Palmyra, 12 Wheat. 14; 1 C. Rob. R. 127; The Vrow Judith.

Comparing this answer with the papers found on board the captured vessel, we see it expressly stipulated in the charter-party, the very contract by which the ship was hired, and which was signed by these respondents, that the ship shall proceed to New Orleans, and there take from the charterers Wylie and

Ygana, 1,100 bales of cotton, to be delivered at the port of San Blas to the order of the shipper, the consignee paying freight for the room occupied in the ship by the cotton, eleven hundred dollars, payable on delivery of the cargo; the cargo to be received at New Orleans and discharged at San Blas with despatch. The charter-party further provides, that if on the arrival of the ship off San Blas, the port is blockaded, or other obstructions prevent the discharge of the ship, she shall proceed to the Sandwich Islands, and there remain until the port is open, the said Wylie and Ygana paying in addition to the charter the further sum of one thousand dollars per month during such detention. We will hereafter state what is c nce ve by this court to be the proper construction of this phrase, i " If the port is blockaded, or other obstructions prevent the discharge of the ship." Independently of this phrase, however, we have, on the face of this contract, the declaration that the shipment was made to an enemy's port; that the delivery was to take place at that port; that the interposition of the neutral island of Honolulu was not for the purpose of trade with, or transshipment at that island, but solely for the purpose of affording an opportunity to enter into and discharge at a port known to be an enemy's port, in which the consignees of the cargo resided, and the delivery at which port was made a precedent and necessary condition to the payment of freight.

Upon a comparison of the bill of lading with the charter-party, the *terminus* of the voyage and the destination of the cargo are more clearly shown. The language of the bill of lading runs thus: "Shipped in good order and well conditioned, by Wylie and Ygana, on board the good ship Admittance, whereof is master for the present voyage Peterson, and now lying at New Orleans, and bound for Honolulu, two thousand seven hundred and seven small bales of cotton, being marked and numbered as in the margin, and are to be delivered." Where? Not at Honolulu, where there was no consignee, apparent or mentioned — not at San Blas, as an incidental point in the track of the voyage to Honolulu, but at " the aforesaid port of San Blas," the predetermined limit of the voyage, and to Don Lewis Rivas Gongora, resident at San Blas, the correspondent and consignee of the shipper.

Taking, in connection with the charter-party and the bill of lading, the instructions from the respondent, Fessenden, to the master of the ship before sailing from New Orleans, it seems almost incredible that the owners should have been ignorant of the character of the voyage, and of the hazards incurred by their vessel resulting from that character. How, upon any other view, can be accounted for the extreme caution enjoined upon the

master with respect to the danger of entering a Mexican port —
danger expressly distinguished from that arising from the probability of capture by vessels of the United States; such as it is
said might arise from the disposition of the Mexican government, under the plea of the right of war to confiscate the vessel,
notwithstanding the consignees might have obtained permission
to land the cargo? It is absurd to suppose that this caution
could have had any possible reference to a state of re-established
amity between Mexico and the United States, as the vessel of a
friendly nation could incur no risk of confiscation by entering
the port of a friend. We think that it was to dangers and
hazards which might proceed from the Mexican authorities —
hazards and dangers incident to an existing and known state of
war, which were in the contemplation of the owners when, in the
charter-party, they speak of " other obstructions," (beyond that
of blockades,) " which might prevent the discharge of the ship at
San Blas," an enemy's port. This interpretation of the conduct
and purposes of the owners and charterers is strongly corroborated by, and explains that portion of the instructions to the master
which tells him, " you will perceive from this that you must be
very cautious about going into a Mexican port, for, although the
consignees may have authority to land the cotton, yet they might
seize the vessel after being discharged, unless the vessel as well
as the cargo had permission from the Mexican government."
This language would be unintelligible, unless it had reference to
a known belligerent attitude of the two nations, forbidding intercourse or traffic between their respective citizens, and to a contemplated dispensation from the existing prohibitions by one of
the belligerents. We are, therefore, upon a just construction
of the answer of the claimants of the vessel, of the charter-party
signed by them, of the bill of lading, and of the instructions to
the master, impelled to the conclusion, that these claimants of
the vessel were aware of the character of the voyage for which
they had hired her, and were willing, nevertheless, to incur the
hazards of the enterprise in consideration of the profits it promised them.

Looking next beyond the evidence of intention and knowledge as deducible from the ship's papers proper, to the acts of
the master in execution of the objects and purposes of the voyage, the following facts are shown by the testimony of the witnesses, Bell, Martin, and Graves, all of them belonging to the crew
of The Admittance, and the first-named being the mate of the
ship: That she sailed directly to San Blas; that upon her arrival
off this port, then being an enemy's port, and in the possession
of the enemy, she remained before it three days and nights, during which time the master opened an intercourse with the port,

Jecker et al. v. Montgomery.

receiving at different times communications therefrom, to which he replied; that whilst off San Blas the captain showed no American ensign, but after receiving the communications from the shore he ordered the chief mate not to head the log-book, and also directed the concealment of the ship's name by covering her stern with painted canvas, and proceeded along the coast as far as 188 north, looking for some bay or inlet on the coast of Mexico where the cargo might be delivered; but finding no suitable place, the ship was headed for San José, California. It is further proved by the witnesses, Mesroon and Bell, that The Admittance entered the port of San José before it was captured by the forces of the United States, and when it was still a Mexican port, in the possession of the enemies of the United States; and the witnesses, Bell and Graves, both of the crew of The Admittance, swear that the captain, before the seizure, landed goods at this hostile port. Upon every correct view, then, of the facts of this case, and of the law of prize as applicable to these facts, it is clear that the ship Admittance was properly subject to seizure and condemnation as prize of war.

We have seen, by the authorities cited, that intercourse with the enemy is sufficient cause for personal punishment, and for the confiscation of property; that it is a cause originating in, and inflexibly enforced by necessity for guarding the public safety. In this cause are established against the claimants of this vessel, not only intercourse, but trading, in its common acceptation. Moreover, it is a settled principle, that if the owners had not anticipated a violation of the public law, the fate of their vessel, with respect to an infraction of that law, must depend upon the conduct of the agent with whom they have intrusted its management.

With respect to the respondents, Jecker, Torre, and Co., and Quintana, claimants of the cargo, the written documents found on board the captured vessel, and surrendered to the libellant by the master, fasten upon these claimants not only a knowledge of the design, under the pretext of a voyage to the Sandwich Islands, of trading with citizens of the United States, a belligerent nation, but they fix upon those parties strenuous and active efforts to possess themselves of the fruits of that traffic — the cargo of the ship; and to obtain them not even by the circuitous voyage to Honolulu, but by direct transit to and within the territory of the enemy's nation. It is a circumstance of much significance disclosed by these papers, that there appears to have existed a perfect understanding and preconcert between these claimants, the charterers of the vessel, and the master. The arrival of the master is anticipated and waited for, and no sooner does his vessel appear on the Mexican coast, (the war still continuing,) than she is boarded from the shore by the agents of the claimants, bringing assurances of arrangements made for the violation of the law of war, and of the safety with which that violation might be accomplished.

Thus, on the 12th of February, 1847, a letter, from which the following extracts are taken, was addressed by the agent of the claimants, Jecker, Torre, and Co., Louis Rivas Gongora, to the master of The Admittance: —

"Capt. P. Peterson, Ship Admittance, off San Blas.

"Sir: I have been informed of your sailing from New Orleans with a cargo of cotton to my consignment, and have also received a copy of Messrs. Wylie and Ygana's instructions for your guidance; also a copy of your charter-party. But as it will be more for the convenience of all parties concerned, that in case of your not being allowed by the blockading vessels to enter San Blas or Manzanilla, you should not proceed to the Sandwich Islands, which are very distant, but in the first place to San José near Cape San Lucas, which is in possession of the Americans, I have to request that if you find the port of San Blas blockaded, and should be warned off, you will, as is directed in your instructions, proceed to Manzanilla, where, if you are allowed to enter, you will find an agent meeting you there, who will receive your cargo. If San Blas is open when you arrive, you will come into the bay immediately and anchor, putting yourself under the orders of Don Eustaquio Pasiere, who will proceed to discharge your cargo; and as it is of much importance that the cotton should be on shore as soon as possible, I hope you will do everything on your part to commence and to finish discharging with the least possible delay. If you are permitted to enter San Blas or Manzanilla, you must come in under British colors, the name of the vessel and your own remaining without alteration, still reporting yourself from New Orleans; but you will be careful not to deliver any of the papers of the ship or cargo to any one except to Don Eustaquio Pasiere."

Again, on the 27th of the same month, this person thus addresses the master from Tepic: —

"Capt. P. Peterson, Ship Admittance, off San Blas.

"Sir: I had the pleasure to write to you on the 12th of this month, which will be delivered to you along with this. But as at present certain circumstances have taken place which, I think, make it too dangerous for you to come into San Blas, I have to request that you will proceed immediately to Manzanilla, and put yourself under the orders of Don Manuel de la Quintana, who has gone to meet you there, and who will deliver to you a letter, authorizing him to act as your consignee. He will discharge your vessel, pay your freight, and transact all the business of your vessel the same as if I was present. You will please enter Manzanilla under English colors, and, as the war continues, you will take care that it shall not be known that your vessel is American."

In proof of the agency of Rivas, as the representative of Jecker, Torre, and Co., and as affecting them by his acts, reference may be made to a communication from that firm, dated Mazatlan, April 1, 1847, addressed to the master of The Admittance, which communication was doubtless prepared on entire ignorance of the seizure of that vessel, which had occurred only three days previously at San José. In this communication it is said : "Should this find you at San José, we have to request you to proceed at once to San Blas, referring you at the same time to the accompanying letter for you from Don Luis Rivas de Gongora, of Tepic. Mr. Rivas has furnished us with copies of your letters to him, of the dates of the 3d and 4th of March, by which it appears you entertain fears of being seized by an English or American cruiser should you follow his recommendation to discharge under English colors." They then refer the master to Mr. Mott and Mr. Bolton, for assurances that his apprehensions are groundless, and state, " that in less than a month previously an American vessel discharged at San Blas without let or hindrance ; that the difficulty with regard to the vessel in a Mexican port had been overcome by an order of the supreme government, by which vessels of any nation were permitted to enter, provided that the captain would make a declaration to the effect that he belonged to a friendly or neutral nation, no papers confirming that assertion being required of him."

We think, then, that by the evidence found in the possession of the master of The Admittance, there is shown a complicity in all the respondents in premeditating, and as far as they had power in executing, a scheme for effecting intercourse and trade with the open enemies of the United States — an offence such as rendered all the means and instruments for the accomplishment of such a scheme lawful prize of war.

But it has been insisted, that should it be conceded that there existed originally sufficient grounds for capture and condemnation, still, the captor had forfeited all right of prize by omitting to send the vessel and cargo to the United States for adjudication, and by selling them without the justification of necessity in a foreign country. The libellant has alleged, in justification of the disposition of the vessel and cargo, " that he was at the time of the capture of The Admittance at a great distance from the United States, and, without weakening inconveniently the force under his command in his own ship, he could not have spared a sufficient prize crew and officers to command the captured ship, and to bring her into the United States."

The exception here taken brings up the inquiry, as to the duty and power of a captor to send in his prize for adjudication, and as to the discretion vested in him in deciding upon the extent of that duty, and the feasibility of that power under existing circumstances. This inquiry has been treated with so much force and perspicuity by Mr. Justice Curtis, in a case adjudged by him between a portion of these respondents as claimants of the ship, and the libellants, that it cannot be more clearly and at the same time more succinctly elucidated than it will be by reference to the opinion of that judge in the case alluded to, (*vide* Fay et al. v. Montgomery, 1 Curtis's R. 266.) In that case, the judge remarks : " The grounds on which restitution is claimed are thus stated in the libel, ' that the seizure and detention were without any legal, justifiable, reasonable, or probable cause ; and even if there had been probable cause for the seizure of the said vessel, the said Montgomery was legally bound to send the same to the United States for trial, which might easily have been done, but which the said Montgomery illegally and unjustifiably omitted to do, and thereby illegally converted the same to his own use.' Here (says the judge) are two distinct grounds : the first being that the seizure was an act of illegal violence ; and the second, that, by not sending the vessel to the United States for trial, the respondent had illegally converted it to his own use." After commenting upon the evidence which led his mind to the conclusion that there was properly a question of prize to be tried, the judge remarks : " And this brings me to consider the other ground stated in the libel, that by his omission to send the vessel to the United States for trial, the respondent illegally converted the vessel to his own use. That captors may so act towards prize property as to forfeit their rights as captors, and render themselves liable to make restitution, with or without damages, is clear. But before the court can so declare, a case of forfeiture of rights, free from all reasonable doubt, must be made out. In considering this part of the case, the question is, whether the allegation that the respondent omitted to send the vessel to the United States for trial, when he could safely and properly have done so, and thereby illegally converted the property to his own use, is made out in proof." The answer of the respondent to this part of the libel states : " That it was impossible for him, consistently with the public interests committed to his direction, to have sent the ship Admittance to any port of the United States." The judge proceeds to say: "Before considering the facts upon which the forfeiture is asserted, one principle should be stated, which is entitled to an important effect on this part of the case. It is, that an honest exercise of discretion, necessarily arising out of his command, cannot be treated as such misconduct in the commander of a public ship of war, as will forfeit his fair title, and render him liable to be treated as a trespasser. This principle is too obviously just to require the support of authority; but it will be found to have been laid down and applied in the case of Dinsman v. Wilkes, in 12 How. 890.

"Now it must be admitted, that the question whether the necessities of the public service will allow the commander of a ship of war, in time of war, upon a remote station on the other side of the globe, to spare one of his officers to go home in command of a prize, is one depending on his discretion, necessarily arising out of his command. In the first instance, he alone has the power to decide the question—he alone has the needful knowledge of facts, and he is bound to exercise his judgment upon them. Certainly his judgment is not conclusive — good faith and reasonable discretion are requisite; but it would not only be a hardship, but injustice, to impose on the commander the duty of determining such a question, and, when he has determined it, to attribute to him as an act of misconduct that he did not come to a different conclusion. It is true, that it is a clear duty of a commander to send in his prize for adjudication, but this is not an absolute obligation. It depends on his ability to perform it; and of this, as already said, he must judge in the first instance; and if he decides with reasonable discretion and an honest purpose to do his duty, I cannot consider him as guilty of misconduct which works a forfeiture."

The judge then, after an examination of the proofs in the case, and of the law as above expounded by him, comes to the following conclusion: "Keeping these principles in view, I am not satisfied that, in omitting to send the vessel to the United States, Captain Montgomery violated any known duty, or acted with so little discretion as to render him liable as a trespasser." And he closes his review of the evidence with this very forcible view of its just import and character: "One of the lieutenants of The Portsmouth was serving on shore — two only remained; and it does not appear that a single passed-midshipman was on board. Lieutenant Revere [one of the remaining lieutenants on board] has given an opinion—no doubt an honest one—that he might have been spared; but it is an opinion formed under no responsibility of command; and I am not prepared to say that a sloop of war on that coast, at that time, officered by only two lieutenants, ought to have been left with only one, in order to send home a prize—and still less, that the commander erred so grossly, in not detaching this officer on such service as to forfeit his legal rights thereby."

The facts which are applicable to this part of the case now before us are essentially, if not literally, those adduced in the trial before the judge whose opinion has been just quoted; and the very clear exposition of those facts, with the legal deductions from them, as set forth in that opinion, command our entire approbation, and are regarded as conclusive against the appellants upon the question of forfeiture by the appellee of his right of prize.

Another exception urged in the argument as fatal to the decree of the circuit court demands our notice, and it is this: That the proceedings instituted in the district court for the condemnation of the vessel and cargo as prize of war were in the name of the libellant, the captor, whereas they should have been commenced and prosecuted in the name of the United States. This irregularity, for such it must be admitted to be, may have proceeded from a misapprehension of the opinion of this court in the case of Jecker, Torre, and Co. *v.* Montgomery; (see 18 How. 498;) in which opinion it is stated to be the duty of the district court to order the captor to institute proceedings in that court for the condemnation of the property as prize of war, by a certain day to be named by the court. The exception thus urged is not raised in the answers or in any other form of pleading in the court below. The parties have gone to trial upon allegations connected with the merits, and upon such testimony as they have chosen to introduce. It would seem to be a sufficient answer to this exception to say, that after its waiver or after an omission to urge it in the court below, and after going into an extended range of testimony as applicable to the merits of the case, to permit an exception entirely distinct from the merits, in the appellate court, would be extending an improper license to the party starting such exception, and might be productive of injustice to his opponent. The exception is unquestionably technical or formal. It embraces neither the question of power of the captor to seize, nor that of the character of the subjects of capture as lawful prize of war. Moreover, this exception, if allowable, would seem to have no other object or purpose, but that of securing the ends which the proceedings and decree of the court have in fact accomplished; for it is seen that the libel, though filed in the name of the captor, was founded upon the public authority of the United States, and the decree pronounced in the case is in favor and in the name of the government, by whom it is shown the proceeds of the condemned

Jecker et al. v. Montgomery.

subject have been actually received. It is plain, therefore, that every purpose which the most formal proceeding could have effected, and nothing beyond this, has been accomplished by the decree in this case; and the proposal now pressed upon the court is, that in virtue of a formal exception, which either has been waived or omitted in the proper time and place, the merits of this controversy voluntarily submitted, and fully examined, should be entirely lost sight of, and that the party who alone, within the purview of the exception itself, could regularly claim the subject of the controversy, should for the mere form be required to surrender that subject. Such a proposal should be regarded as neither equitable nor reasonable, and should be especially discountenanced by a tribunal which acts upon principles of an enlarged public policy — less fettered perhaps that any other by narrow technical rules.

This case bears a strong resemblance to that of Benton v. Woolsey and the Bank of Utica, reported in 12 Pet. 27, in which the district attorney of the United States filed an information in his own name, in behalf of the United States, in the district court for the northern district of New York, to enforce a mortgage given to the United States by Woolsey, one of the defendants. This court in that case hold this doctrine: "Some doubts were at first entertained by the court whether this proceeding could be sustained in the form adopted by the district court. It is a bill of information and complaint in the name of the district attorney, in behalf of the United States. But on carefully examining the bill, it appears to be in substance a proceeding by the United States, although in form it is in the name of the officer; and we find that this form of proceeding in such cases has been for a long time used without objection in the courts of the United States held in New York, and was doubtless borrowed from analogous cases in the courts of the State where the State was plaintiff in the suit. No objection has been made to it either in the court below or in this court, and we think that the United States may be considered as the real party, although in its form it is the complaint of the district attorney."

The objection which has been made to the deposit in the treasury of the money arising from the sale of the captured property in this case appears to be without weight. Since the act of congress of the 3d of March, 1849, it appears to be the intention and the positive mandate of congress, that all prize money arising from captures by vessels of the navy of the United States, whether received by marshals for the sale of prizes, or in the hands of prize agents, should be deposited in the treasury of the United States. *Vide* § 8th of the act, Stats. at

11 *

Large, vol. ix. p. 878. It does not clearly appear in whose hands the proceeds of the sale of The Admittance and her cargo were at the date of the above statute. But if they were in the possession of Captain Montgomery at or after that time, either as captor or prize-master, or whether they were in the hands of any other person, it was within the scope and objects of the law to place the proceeds of the prize sale in the treasury of the United States; and accordingly it is shown by the certificate of the treasurer of the United States, that the sum of sixty-seven thousand dollars, as the proceeds of the sale of The Admittance, were on the 26th of December, 1849, by William Speiden, purser of the navy of the United States, deposited in the treasury of the United States.

Upon a consideration of the facts and the law of this case, we are of the opinion that the decree of the circuit court be affirmed.

ADAM HAM, PLAINTIFF IN ERROR, v. THE STATE OF MISSOURI.

The act of congress passed on the 6th of March, 1820, (3 Stats. at Large, 547,) accepted by an ordinance declaring the assent of the people of Missouri thereto, adopted on the 19th of July, 1820, granted to the State for the use of schools the sixteenth section of every township in the State, which had not been sold or otherwise disposed of.

This expression, "otherwise disposed of," does not include the case of an imperfect title, claimed to be derived from the Spanish governor, which had been rejected by the board of commissioners in 1811.

The claim was confirmed in 1828 so far as to relinquish all the title which the United States then had; but at that time the United States had no title, having granted the land to Missouri in 1820, which they had a right to do.

The proviso in the act of March 3, 1811, which forbade lands claimed before the board of commissioners from being offered for sale until after the decision of congress thereon, did not prevent a donation for schools, and, moreover, contemplated only a temporary suspension for the purposes of investigation.

THIS case was brought up from the supreme court of the State of Missouri, by a writ of error issued under the 25th section of the judiciary act.

It is fully stated in the opinion of the court.

It was argued by *Mr. Geyer*, for the plaintiff in error, no counsel appearing for the defendant.

Mr. Geyer made the following points: —

1. The reservation by the act of March 3, 1811, is something more than "a direction" to the officers to refrain from selling the land claimed. It severed the land embraced by the claim from the public domain, and appropriated it to the satisfaction

of the claim in the event of confirmation; being so set apart and appropriated, it was "disposed of," and therefore not granted nor promised to be granted by the act of March 6, 1820.

2. The State did not acquire a complete title to the 16th section by force of the compact, even where the land had not been sold, reserved, appropriated, or otherwise disposed of; in such case it was reserved and appropriated to the use of schools; "but the title to the land being still in the United States, could be passed by the government to any person for any consideration," and in this case was passed by the confirmatory act of May 24, 1828, and the patent deed of the United States of March 25, 1839.

The propositions offered to the convention having been accepted, became obligatory upon the United States; "the compact was complete between the sovereignties," and the United States became bound to grant and convey the lands embraced by the first proposition, but there is no present conveyance, no word of present grant, and, therefore, no complete title vested by the terms of the compact.

The engagement on the part of the United States is executory, precisely as is the obligation to perfect inchoate titles, or to make a final decision thereon, and hold the lands reserved by law to abide the decision. No time is appointed for the fulfilment of the engagement in either case, and in both the title remains in the United States, subject to the legislative power of congress.

3. The second proviso in the confirmatory act, (repeated in the patent,) to which some importance was attached by the supreme court of Missouri in this case, has no effect whatever upon the title of either party. The act and patent, if they have any effect whatever, pass all the title which the United States had or could convey at the date, and no form of conveyance could accomplish more. Neither the confirmatory act nor the patent would prejudice the rights of third persons, nor any title theretofore derived from the United States, by purchase or donation, if the proviso had been omitted; but while the rights and titles of others are not prejudiced or impaired, they are not enlarged or improved. The executory engagement of the 6th of March, 1820, is not executed or converted into a complete title of that date by the saving, in the confirmatory act and patent. If the legal title was not vested in the State by the compact, it remained in the United States until it was vested in the claimants by the confirmatory act and patent, and the grantees are not liable to be indicted and punished for entering upon the land granted, by reason of the proviso.

Mr. Justice DANIEL delivered the opinion of the court.

Upon a writ of error to the supreme court of the State, under the authority of the 25th section of the judiciary act.

The proceedings now under review were founded upon an indictment in the circuit court of the county of St. Francis, against the plaintiff in error, for having committed waste and trespass on the sixteenth section of lands situated in congressional township number thirty-four, range seven east, as being school lands belonging to the inhabitants of the township aforesaid.

Upon this indictment the plaintiff was convicted, and condemned to pay a fine assessed by the jury, of four hundred dollars, together with the costs of the prosecution. From the judgment of the circuit court, the plaintiff in error having taken an appeal to the supreme court of Missouri, by the latter tribunal that judgment was in all things affirmed ; the same plaintiff now seeks its reversal here, in virtue of several acts of congress alleged to be applicable to this case.

Upon the trial in the circuit court, the following facts were either established in proof or admitted by the parties : —

1. A joint petition on the part of Jean Batiste Vallé, and the heirs of François Vallé, Jean Batiste Pratte, and St. Geunne Beauvais, presented on the 15th of October, 1800, to Delassus, the lieutenant-governor of upper Louisiana, praying for a grant of two leagues square of land on the River St. François, including the mine, known by the name of Mine à la Motte, and the lands adjacent.

2. An acknowledgment by the lieutenant-governor, dated January 22, 1801, of his want of power to grant a concession of the extent prayed for, and the fact of his having transmitted the petition to the intendant-general, with the expression of an opinion favorable to the grant, and to the character of the applicants.

3. An order by the intendant-general, that the documents presented in behalf of the petitioners should be translated into the Castilian language, and then be laid before the fiscal agent.

4. A plat and survey for 28,224 arpens, or 24,142 acres of land, situated on the river St. Francis, certified by Nathaniel Cook, as deputy surveyor of the district of St. Genevieve, said by him to have been made by virtue of a concession by Delassus to J. B. and François Vallé, Beauvais, and Pratte, on the 22d of January, 1801.

5. The proceedings of the board of commissioners for the examination of land titles, on the 27th of December, 1811, setting forth the claim of Jean Batiste and François Vallé, Jean Batiste Pratte, and St. Geunne Beauvais, for two leagues of land, including the La Motte Mine, founded on the recommendation from Lieutenant-Governor Delassus for a concession, bearing

date on the 22d of January, 1801, and the order of the intendant-general already mentioned, and the rejection of the claim by the commissioners.

6. The first section of an act of congress, approved May 24, 1828, confirming to François Vallé, Jean Batiste Vallé, Jean Batiste Pratt, and St. Geunne Beauvais, their heirs or legal representatives, a tract of land not exceeding two leagues square, situated in the county of Madison in the State of Missouri, commonly known by the name of the Mine la Motte, according to a field-plat and survey made by Nathaniel Cook, deputy surveyor of St. Genevieve, on the 22d day of February, 1806, with a proviso in the said first section, that the confirmation thus granted shall extend only to a relinquishment of title on the part of the United States, nor prejudice the rights of third persons, nor any title heretofore derived from the United States, either by purchase or donation.

7. A plat and survey made by Jenifer Sprigg, deputy-surveyor, in the months of March, 1829, and August, 1830, of the La Motte Mine tract of land, stated to contain 23,728.02 acres of land, confirmed to François Vallé, Jean Batiste Vallé, Jean Batiste Pratte, by an act of congress approved on the 24th of December, 1828.

8. A patent from the President of the United States, bearing date on the 25th of March, 1839, granted under the authority of the act of congress last mentioned, (and in virtue of a title derived from the confirmees,) to Lewis F. Linn and Evariste Pratte, for the La Motte Mine, and the land surrounding the same, containing 23,728.02 acres of land, in conformity with the survey of Sprigg, as certified from the general land-office; this patent, containing literally the proviso in the act of congress limiting the grant to the patentees, to a relinquishment of the title of the United States at the date of the act of congress of 1828.

9. An admission on the part of the State, that all the right, title, and claim of the original proprietors of the Mine la Motte tract of land had regularly passed to and was vested in Thomas Fleming, as fully as those proprietors had or could have had the same.

10. A lease from Thomas Fleming, of the 9th of April, 1849, to Ham, the plaintiff in error, for a portion of the Mine la Motte land.

11. An admission further on the part of the State, that the sixteenth section claimed as school lands, was within the lines of the original survey of the tract made by Nathaniel Cook, and of the other surveys given in evidence.

Upon the trial of the indictment, the circuit court, at the instance of the counsel for the State, instructed the jury, "that the act of the 6th of March, 1820, entitled 'An act to authorize the people of Missouri Territory to form a constitution and state government, &c.,' taken in connection with an ordinance declaring the assent thereto by the people of Missouri, by their representatives assembled in convention on the 19th of July, 1820, operated as a grant by congress to the State of Missouri for the use of schools, of the 16th section in controversy, unless such 16th section had been previously disposed of by government.

"That, although the land claimed by the proprietors of Mine la Motte was, by the several acts of congress, reserved from sale, and that the survey of said claim includes the 16th section in controversy, yet such reservation is not such disposition of said section by the government, as is within the saving clause of the 6th section of the act of 1820, and cannot operate to prevent the title from vesting in the State, by virtue of said grant."

The defendant in the prosecution prayed of the court the following instructions, which were refused:—

"That if the jury believe the land in question is included within the original grant by the Spanish government, and within the lines of the survey made by N. Cook, in 1806, and within the lines of the lands confirmed by the act of congress to the original grantees and those claiming under them, then this land never was public land, subject or liable to be donated by congress to the State for the use of schools.

"That the several acts of congress reserving section 16 for the support of schools, could only refer to the public lands proper, and could not attach to private claims, which had previous to such donation been claimed by individuals, and reserved by congress to satisfy those claims.

"That the confirmation of the claim by the act of congress of 1828 conferred and gave a superior title to the lands in question, over the title of the State for the use of schools."

Upon the accuracy or inaccuracy of the instructions given by the court at the instance of the State, and of those denied by it upon the prayer of the defendant in the prosecution, the decision of this cause must depend.

It would seem not to admit of rational doubt, that the act of congress, of March 6, 1820, authorizing the people of the Territory of Missouri to form a constitution and state government, taken in connection with the ordinance of the state convention of the 19th of July, 1820, amounted not merely to a grant for the use of schools, of the 16th section of every township of public lands in the Territory, but, further, to a positive condition or mandate, so far as congress possessed the power to impose it, for the dedication of those sections to that object. The assertion of the court, then, of the existence and character of such grant, whilst it recognized any proper limitation or qualification imposed thereon, either by previous acts of congress or by the investiture of any rights arising therefrom, can be obnoxious to no just criticism, but was in all respects proper.

Whether or not the lands claimed by the proprietors of the Mine la Motte, so far as they cover a portion of the sixteenth section of township 34, range 7 east, are exempted from the operation of the act of March 6, 1820, and of the ordinance of July 19, 1820, must depend upon the correct interpretation of the previous legislation of congress, and upon the acts and position of the claimants with reference to that legislation.

By the 10th section of the act of congress, approved March 3, 1811, authorizing the President of the United States to offer for sale such portions of the public lands lying in the State of Louisiana as shall have been surveyed under the direction of the 8th section of the same statute, it is provided, that " all such lands, with the exception of section number sixteen, which shall be reserved in each township for the use of schools," (and with the exception, further, of a township of land granted by the 7th section of the same statute for the use of a seminary of learning, and of certain salt-springs and lead-mines,) " shall be offered for sale to the highest bidder, under the direction of the register of the land-office, the receiver of public moneys, and principal deputy-surveyor." In this 10th section is contained a proviso, " that till after the decision of congress thereon, no tract of land shall be offered for sale, the claim to which has been in due time and according to law presented to the recorder of land titles in the district of Louisiana, and filed in his office for the purpose of being investigated by the commissioners appointed to ascertain the rights of persons claiming lands in the Territory of Louisiana."

Upon this 10th section of the act of 1811, and the proviso thereto annexed, is founded the position taken by the plaintiff in error, that the sixteenth section of township 34 did not, and could not, vest in the State of Missouri, in virtue of the act of March 3, 1820, and of the ordinance of July 19 of the same year, so far as that section fell within the proviso. In comparing the enacting part of § 10 of the statute of 1811 with the proviso annexed thereto, it will strike the attention, that the limitation or restriction contained in the proviso has no connection, by its terms, with lands granted or donated for schools, but relates altogether to such lands as it was designed and declared should be sold at public auction to the highest bidder.

Such, certainly, were not the lands appropriated to a specific, ultimate, and permanent purpose, namely, the support of schools.

As to these lands, sales, and every other disposition inconsistent with such dedication, were expressly inhibited. But, putting aside the literal meaning of the 10th section and its proviso, it may well be asked whether the language and objects of the latter can be made to import anything beyond a temporary suspension of the sales of the lands intended for sale, for the simple purposes of investigation ; and much more, whether the 10th section of the act of 1811, and the proviso thereto, can be interpreted to mean a denial to itself by congress of the right and power to sell or to give, either upon satisfactory evidence of the invalidity of any opposing claim, or upon considerations of public policy, the land embraced within the suspension.

Such an interpretation, as it is not warranted by the language of the acts of congress, seems not to accord either with considerations of justice or policy. Suppose that congress, after the passage of the law of 1811, should become satisfied of the groundless nature of a claim presented to the commissioners, and should be convinced further, not only of the benefits to result from appropriating the subject of that claim to purposes of education, but also of their having pledged that subject to such purposes ; it cannot be questioned that the power to reject or disregard an unfounded claim, and to comply with a previous and just obligation, remained in a plenary and unimpaired extent in congress ; and that this right and obligation could in no degree be affected by a mere agreement to investigate.

Let it be remembered, too, that the application of those under whom the plaintiff in error deduces his alleged title was for a simple gratuity, founded on no consideration whatever but the bounty of the donor. The opinion and the action by congress with respect to the rights of the parties to that controversy seem to have been entirely coincident with the views herein suggested. Under the provision of the act of 1811, the proprietors of the Mine la Motte presented their claim, together with such evidence as they deemed essential to its support, to the tribunal created by law for the investigation of land titles. By this tribunal, the claim of these proprietors was rejected on the 27th of December, 1811. From the period last mentioned until the 24th of May, 1828, an interval of seventeen years, this claim remains dormant or quiescent, when it is confirmed at the date last mentioned.

The nature and effect of this confirmation will presently be considered ; but in the interval above mentioned, the government, (the undoubted possessor of the title,) after the lapse of nine years from the rejection by its agent of this slumbering title, by express compact with the State of Missouri, grants to that State, for the use of schools, the sixteenth section of every township in the State which had not been sold " or otherwise disposed of."

Upon recurring to the law of May 24, 1828, it will be borne in mind that the confirmation to the proprietors of the Mine la Motte is extended merely to a relinquishment of the title of the United States at the date of that law, and is declared to have no influence to prejudice the rights of third persons, nor any title heretofore derived from the United States, either by purchase or donation.

It is proper to keep in view this proviso in this confirmation, in order to ascertain its effect, if any, upon the proper meaning of the qualification in the grant to the State of Missouri comprised in the phrase "or otherwise disposed of."

In our construction of the act of congress of March 3, 1811, we have interpreted the proviso to the 10th section of that act as neither declaring nor importing a final and permanent devestiture, or any devestiture whatsoever, of the title of the United States, but as a provision prescribing a temporary arrangement merely for the purposes of investigation, leaving the title still in the government, to be retained or parted with according to the dictates of justice or policy, as these might be developed by such investigation. Nothing is here ordained which is definite in its character. Inquiry is all that is directed. The language and plain import of the 6th section of the act of the 3d of March, 1820, confer a clear and positive and unconditional donation of the sixteenth section in every township; and, when these have been sold or otherwise disposed of, other and equivalent lands are granted. Sale, necessarily signifying a legal sale by a competent authority, is a disposition, final and irrevocable, of the land. The phrase "or otherwise disposed of" must signify some disposition of the property equally efficient, and equally incompatible with any right in the State, present or potential, as deducible from the act of 1820, and the ordinance of the same year. Upon any other hypothesis, the right to the sixteenth section would attach under the provision of the act of 1820; the State would still have the title, and could recover the section specifically, and there would be no necessity for providing an equivalent for that section.

Under our interpretation of the acts of March 3, 1811, and of May 24, 1828, no title can have passed to the proprietors of the La Motte Mine lands. The reply of the lieutenant-governor, Delassus, to the petition of the applicants for the mine, acknowledges explicitly the absence of all power in that officer to make the grant asked for, and refers those petitioners to the intendant-general, as the only functionary possessing authority to make it. This officer took no further action upon the petition than to order its translation into the Castilian language.

On the 27th of December, 1811, this claim was before the commissioners for the examination of land titles in the State of

Louisiana, and was rejected by them. From this period of time down to the 24th of May, 1828, no grant from the United States, nor evidences of title from any source, except those already referred to, have been shown by the plaintiff or those under whom he claims. In the mean time, the United States, the undoubted legal owners of the land in controversy, by the act of March 3, 1820, bestow it on the State, as they had full authority so to do, —bestow the specific section, it never having been disposed of within the intent and meaning of the 6th section of the act last mentioned.

The confirmation in 1828, and the patent of the 25th of March, 1839, professing to confer no title but such as remained in the United States at those periods respectively, and the grant of the sixteenth section in township 34, range east, comprised within the survey of the Mine la Motte, having been made seven years anterior to the confirmation, which constitutes the only ground of title in the claimants of the mine, the pretensions of the confirmees to the section in controversy must be regarded as without foundation and utterly null.

The view which this court has taken of the evidence in this cause, and of the law as applicable to that evidence, dispenses with any necessity for an examination *seriatim* of the instructions asked by the plaintiff in error upon the trial of the indictment, and refused by the court. It is sufficient to remark, that the positions assumed in the instructions so prayed for, being incompatible with the law of this case as expounded by this court, we deem those instructions to have been properly refused. It is the opinion of this court, that the decision of the supreme court of the State of Missouri, pronounced in this cause, sustaining that of the circuit court, is correct, and ought to be, as it is hereby, affirmed.

Mr. Justice NELSON. I concur in the judgment of the court upon the ground that, though the 10th section of the act of March 3, 1811, had the effect to prevent the title of Missouri to this land from vesting, until the final decision by congress upon the claim of Vallé and others, yet the act of May 24, 1828, confirming lands to Vallé and others, operated as such final decision, and, by its true construction, excepted out of the confirmation so much of the land as was included in section sixteen, the public surveys of the township having been made before the passage of the last-mentioned act. I do not know that the opinion of the court is intended to go further than this. If it does, I do not assent thereto.

Mr. Justice CURTIS concurred with Mr. Justice Nelson.

Mr. Justice GRIER also concurred with Mr. Justice Nelson.

ALBERT H. GUILD AND JOHN F. LIGHTNER, PARTNERS IN TRADE, UNDER THE FIRM OF GUILD AND LIGHTNER, AND HENRY HUGG AND ROBERT G. HANNA, PARTNERS IN TRADE, UNDER THE STYLE AND FIRM OF HENRY HUGG AND CO., PLAINTIFFS IN ERROR, *v.* JOSEPH FRONTIN.

Where a trial by jury is waived in the court below, and there is no special verdict or agreed statement of facts or bill of exception upon a point of law, this court cannot review the judgment of the court below.

But having jurisdiction of the cause, and no error appearing upon the face of the record, the judgment will be affirmed.

THIS case was brought up by writ of error from the district court of the United States for the northern district of California.

The point of practice involved in it is stated in the opinion of the court.

It was argued by *Mr. Blair*, for the plaintiffs in error, and submitted on a printed brief by *Mr. Cutting*, for the defendant.

Mr. Justice GRIER delivered the opinion of the court.

The record and proceedings in this case are in conformity with the practice of the state courts of California. It was tried without the intervention of a jury, and the testimony, together with the opinion of the court, filed of record. But there is no special verdict, or agreed statement of facts, on which the judgment was rendered; nor is there any bill of exceptions, sealed by the court, to their decision on any question of law. We are, in fact, called upon to review the case on the pleadings, exhibits, and testimony, as if it were a bill in chancery. Our very frequent decisions on this subject seem not to have come to the knowledge of the bar in the court below. Parties may, by consent, waive the trial of issues of fact by a jury, and submit the trial of both facts and law to the court. It will not be a mistrial. But if they wish the judgment of the court to be reviewed on a writ of error, a special verdict or agreed statement of facts must be put on record. The issues of fact must be ascertained, and made certain, before a court of error can review the decision of an inferior court. If the verdict do not find all the issues, or the agreed statement in the nature of a special verdict be imperfect or incomplete, this court may order a *venire de novo*, because of the mistrial, as in the case of Graham *v.* Bayne, *ante*, p. 60, at this term. But having jurisdiction of the cause, and no error appearing on the face of the record, the judgment of the court below must be affirmed.

The case of Prentice *v.* Zane, 8 How. 470, is directly in point on this subject.

ALFRED SAVIGNAC, PLAINTIFF IN ERROR, v. ABRAHAM GARRISON.

The act of congress passed on the 13th of June, 1812, confirmed the titles to out-lots
in the town of St. Louis, in Missouri, upon certain conditions, and the act of 26th
of May, 1824, required the performance of these conditions, and the boundaries of
the lot to be proved before the recorder of land titles.
Whether the lot and conditions came within the purview of the act of 1812 were questions of fact for the jury. The neglect to procure the survey and location under the
act of 1824 did not forfeit the title acquired under the act of 1812.
The case of Guitard et al. v. Stoddard, 16 How. 494, controls this case.

THIS case was brought up by writ of error from the circuit
court of the United States for the district of Missouri.
The case is stated in the opinion of the court.

It was argued by *Mr. Baxter*, for the plaintiff in error, and
Mr. Ewing, for defendant.

The decision of the court being that the case of Guitard et
al. *v.* Stoddard controls this one with respect to the instructions
given by the court below, it is not thought advisable to report
the arguments of counsel, which covered the whole case.

Mr. Justice NELSON delivered the opinion of the court.
This is a writ of error to the circuit court of the United States
for the district of Missouri.
The plaintiff below, Garrison, brought an action of ejectment
against Savignac, to recover the possession of a lot of land in
the city of St. Louis, claiming title derived from the confirmation of Mordecai Bell's Spanish claim by the act of congress
of 1835.
The defendant claimed title to the lot under the 1st section
of the act of 13th of June, 1812, which provided "that the
rights, titles, and claims to town or village lots, out-lots, common field lots, and commons, in, adjoining, and belonging to the
several towns or villages, (enumerating several, of which St.
Louis was one,) which lots have been inhabited, cultivated, or
possessed prior to the 20th December, 1803, shall be, and the
same is hereby confirmed to the inhabitants of the respective
towns or villages, according to their several right or rights in
common thereto."
Evidence was given on the trial, by the defendant, deducing
a title or claim to the lot in question, derived from Charles
Simoneau, and also evidence tending to prove that the lot was
an out-lot within the purview of the act of 1812, and that
Simoneau was in possession and cultivation of it prior to the
20th December, 1803.

After the testimony closed, the court instructed the jury that " there was no evidence that Simoneau cultivated any out-lot or common-field lot; nor that any one existed at the place where the cultivation was; nor had the act of 1812 application to this land, so far as Simoneau, or those claiming under him, are concerned. And further, that if there had existed an out-lot or common-field lot, undefined by boundaries, which was claimed on the ground of inhabitation, cultivation, or possession, then the act of the 26th May, 1824, required that the fact of inhabitation, cultivation, or possession, and the boundaries and extent of such claim, should be proved before the recorder of land titles, to enable the surveyor-general to distinguish the private from the vacant lots. And no steps having been taken under the act of 1824, nor any authoritative location or survey of the land, at any time, either under the Spanish government or the government of the United States, the evidence given in this case will not enable the defendant to resist a recovery by the plaintiff."

The case of Guitard et al. *v.* Stoddard, 16 How. 494, decided since this case was tried at the circuit, disposes of both branches of the instructions to which we have referred, holding that whether or not the lot, and the inhabitation, cultivation, or possession thereof came within the purview of the act of 1812, were questions of fact for the jury; and that the neglect to procure the survey and location, under the act of 1824, did not operate to impair or forfeit the title acquired under that of 1812.

As the judgment of the court below must be reversed for errors in the instructions referred to, it is unimportant to take notice of any other questions raised on the trial or in the argument.

Judgment reversed, and *venire de novo* to issue.

ROBERT A. PARKER AND MILES WHITE, APPELLANTS, *v.* WILLIAM OVERMAN.

A statute of Arkansas directs, that, where lands are sold by a sheriff, or other public officer, the purchaser is authorized to institute proceedings in a court, calling upon all persons to come in and show cause why the sale should not be confirmed.

Such a proceeding, when instituted in a state court and removed into the circuit court, conformably to the act of congress, constitutes a case over which this court will take jurisdiction.

In such petition for removal, it is not enough to allege that the petitioners were residents in another state. They must allege that they were citizens.

The statute makes the deed sufficient evidence of the authority, the description, and the price. The term " sufficient," is equivalent to *primâ facie.*

Before the sheriff can assess land, he is required to file an affidavit before a certain

Parker et al. *v.* Overman.

day, and to file his assessment before another given day. A non-compliance with these requisitions makes the assessment, and of course the sale for taxes, invalid; and the deed must be set aside.

THIS was an appeal from the circuit court of the United States for the District of Arkansas.

The case is stated in the opinion of the court.

It was argued by *Mr. William Shepard Bryan*, for the plaintiffs in error, and *Mr. Lawrence*, for defendant.

The points made by *Mr. Bryan*, which are decided by the court, were the following: —

1. That by the true construction of the act, such a deed is made evidence only of those facts which are recited in it.

2. That in order to establish the regularity and validity of a sale of land for taxes, the deed should show, upon its face, that every essential preliminary required by the statute has been performed.

8. That the deeds set out in the record, fail to recite several of these essential preliminaries; and that, therefore, they do not furnish evidence of the validity of the sale in question.

There are no recitals in the deeds, that the sheriff filed his assessment list, on or before March 25; that he gave ten days' notice in each township, that the list would be laid before the next county court; that he laid the list before the county court, at the term next succeeding March 25; that the court, at that term, adjusted this tax to be paid; that on or before the first Monday in August, he filed a list of the lands of non-residents with the auditor; that the list was corrected by the auditor, and advertised when corrected. 18 How. 472; 8 Eng. (Ark. Rep.) 242; 14 Pet. 322; 4 Wheat. 77; Arkansas Revenue Act, (Dig. c. 189, § 112.)

6. That all the testimony taken together (even if the incompetent testimony on the part of the petitioner be considered) shows that the sheriff and collector did not strictly pursue the authority to sell the land for taxes, given him by the revenue act, but that he omitted several important particulars.

He filed his assessment list too late; he neglected to give the ten days' notice required by law; he laid the list before the county court one term too late; and he was too late in filing with the auditor a list of the lands of non-residents.

Mr. Lawrence: —

The deed which was given in evidence was *primâ facie*, and, in the absence of positive proof of irregularity, conclusive evidence of the regularity and legality of the tax sale. Rev. Stats. c. 128, § 96, p. 687. Roberts *v.* Pillow, 18 How. 472.

By the 97th section of the Revenue act, p. 687, Rev. Stats., it is enacted, that "no exception shall be taken to any deed made by a collector," &c., "but such as shall apply to the real merits of the case, and are consistent with a liberal and fair interpretation of the intention of the general assembly."

It is insisted that no objection which is taken to the proceedings in this case has any merit, considered with regard to the intention of the general assembly.

So far as the proceedings connected with the sale are concerned, a strict compliance with the statute is shown.

The only want of compliance with the literal requirements of the act, is in the fact that the affidavit of the assessor, required by section 7, was not filed till the 15th March, 1845, and the assessment list was not filed in the office of the county clerk, on or before the 25th March, as required by section 26.

Dallas County was created by act approved January 1, 1845, which act passed the lower house, 24th December, 1844, and the senate, on the 28th of the same month.

By the 9th section of that act, an election was to be held on the fourth Monday of January, of all the officers necessary for the organization of the county, except justices and constables.

The first officers of Dallas county were sworn in about the 1st March, 1845.

The sheriff filed his affidavit as assessor, 15th March, 1845, and on the 28th April, 1845, filed his assessment list in the county court. The county court at its first term, adjudged the list as required by law, and all the proceedings thereafter were in strict accordance with the revised statutes.

It is submitted, first, that the objection, that the assessor's oath was not filed on the 10th day of January, and the assessment list on the 25th of March, has no substantial merit, because the list was to be made out and filed, in order to be adjusted by the court, upon the appeal of any one aggrieved by the amount assessed on his property.

So far as regards the land in question, they were assessed at the lowest amount permitted by the law. Of course no advantage would have happened from an earlier notice of that which he could not object to.

And, secondly, it is submitted that the act erecting Dallas county was a legislative suspension of such portions of the revised statutes as the act, by its requirements, rendered impossible.

Mr. Justice GRIER delivered the opinion of the court.

As some doubts were entertained, and have been expressed by some members of the court, as to its jurisdiction in this case, it will be necessary to notice that subject, before proceeding to examine the merits of the controversy. It had its origin in the state court of Dallas county, Arkansas, sitting in chancery. It is a proceeding under a statute of Arkansas, prescribing a special remedy for the confirmation of sales of land by a sheriff or other public officer. Its object is to quiet the title. The purchaser at such sales is authorized to institute proceedings by a public notice in some newspaper, describing the land, stating the authority under which it was sold, and "calling on all persons who can set up any right to the lands so purchased, in consequence of any informality, or any irregularity or illegality connected with the sale, to show cause why the sale so made should not be confirmed."

In case no one appears to contest the regularity of the sale, the court is required to confirm it, on finding certain facts to exist. But if opposition be made, and it should appear that the sale was made "contrary to law," it became the duty of the court to annul it. The judgment or decree, in favor of the grantee in the deed, operates "as a complete bar against any and all persons who may thereafter claim such land, in consequence of any informality or illegality in the proceedings."

It is a very great evil in any community, to have titles to land insecure and uncertain; and especially in new States, where its result is to retard the settlement and improvement of their vacant lands. Where such lands have been sold for taxes, there is a cloud on the title of both claimants, which deters the settler from purchasing from either. A prudent man will not purchase a lawsuit, or risk the loss of his money and labor upon a litigious title. The act now under consideration was intended to remedy this evil. It is in substance a bill of peace. The jurisdiction of the court over the controversy is founded on the presence of the property; and, like a proceeding *in rem*, it becomes conclusive against the absent claimant, as well as the present contestant. As was said by the court in Clark *v.* Smith, (18 Pet. 203,) with regard to a similar law of Kentucky: "A State has an undoubted power to regulate and protect individual rights to her soil, and declare what shall form a cloud over titles; and having so declared, the courts of the United States, by removing such clouds, are only applying an old practice to a new equity created by the legislature, having its origin in the peculiar condition of the country. The state legislatures have no authority to prescribe forms and modes of proceeding to the courts of the United States; yet having created a right, and at the same time prescribed the remedy to enforce it, if the remedy prescribed be substantially consistent with the ordinary modes of proceeding on the chancery side of the federal courts, no reason exists why it should not be pursued in the same form as in the state court."

In the case before us, the proceeding, though special in its form, is in its nature but the application of a well-known chancery remedy; it acts upon the land, and may be conclusive as to the title of a citizen of another State. He is therefore entitled to have his suit tried in this court, under the same condition as in other suits or controversies.

In the petition to remove this case from the state court, there was not a proper averment as to the citizenship of the plaintiff in error. It alleged that Parker "resided" in Tennessee, and White in Maryland. "Citizenship" and "residence" are not synonymous terms; but as the record was afterwards so amended as to show conclusively the citizenship of the parties, the court below had, and this court have, undoubted jurisdiction of the case.

What we have already stated sufficiently shows the nature of the present controversy. The decree appealed from "adjudges the absolute title to the land to pass and be confirmed to, and vest in, said William Overman, his heirs, &c., free, clear, and discharged from the claim of said defendants, and all persons whatsoever; and that the said sale thereof for taxes, so made by the sheriff of Dallas county to said Overman, is hereby confirmed in all things, and said defendants perpetually enjoined from setting up or asserting any claim thereto, &c."

The plaintiffs in error allege that this decree is erroneous, and should have been for defendants below.

Much of the argument of the learned counsel in this case was wasted on the effect to be attributed to the recitals in the deed, and the decision of this court in the case of Pillow *v.* Roberts, 18 How. 472.

That was an action of ejectment, in which this court decided that, under the 96th section of the revenue law, the sheriff's or collector's deed was made *primâ facie* evidence of the regularity of the previous proceedings. The effect of that section of the act, and of the decision in that case, was to cast the burden of proof of irregularity in the proceedings on the party contesting the validity of the deed; but as the present controversy is for the purpose of giving an opportunity "to all persons who can set up any right or title to the land so purchased, in consequence of any informality or illegality connected with such sale," to contest its validity, it would be absurd to make the deed, whose validity is in question, conclusive evidence of that fact. Consequently, the statute enacts that in this proceeding "the deed shall be taken and considered by the court as·sufficient evidence of the authority under which said sale was made, the description of the land, and the price at which it was purchased. The deed is to be received as *primâ facie* evidence of these three facts, and casts the burden of proof as to them on the defendant. The term "sufficient" is evidently used in the statute as a synonyme for "*primâ facie*," and not for "conclusive."

In judicial sales under the process of a court of general jurisdiction, where the owner of the property is a party to the proceedings, and has an opportunity of contesting their regularity at every step, such objections cannot be heard to invalidate or annul the deed in a collateral suit. But one who claims title to the property of another under summary proceedings where a special power has been executed, as in case of lands sold for taxes, is bound to show every fact necessary to give jurisdiction and authority to the officer, and a strict compliance with all things required by the statute.

The principal objection to the regularity of the sale in this case, and the only one necessary to be noticed, is, that the land was not legally assessed. A legal assessment is the foundation of the authority to sell; and if this objection be sustained, it is fatal to the deed.

In order to qualify the sheriff to fulfil the duties of assessor, the statute requires that, "on or before the tenth day of January, in each year, the sheriff of each county shall make and file in the office of the clerk of the county an affidavit in the following form," &c.: "And if any sheriff shall neglect to file such affidavit within the time prescribed in the prece ng section, his office shall be deemed vacant, and it shall be the duty of the clerk of the county court, without delay, to notify the governor of such vacancy," &c.

The statute requires, also, "that on or before the 25th day of March, in each year, the assessor shall file in the office of the clerk of the county the original assessment, and immediately thereafter give notice that he has filed it," &c. This notice is required, that the owner may appeal to the county court "at the next term after the 25th day of March, and have his assessment corrected, if it be incorrect." If the assessor shall fail to file his assessment within the time specified by this act, he is deemed guilty of a misdemeanor and subjected to a fine of five hundred dollars.

These severe inflictions upon the officer, for his neglect to comply with the exigencies of the act, indicate clearly the importance attached to his compliance in the view of the legislature, and that a neglect of them would vitiate any subsequent proceedings, and put it out of the power of the sheriff to enforce the collection of taxes by a sale of the property.

The record shows that Peyton S. Bethel, the then sheriff of

the county of Dallas, did not file his oath as assessor on or before the 10th of January, as required by law. He did file an oath on the 15th of March, but this was not a compliance with the law, and conferred no power on him to act as assessor. On the contrary, by his neglect to comply with the law, his office of sheriff became *ipso facto* vacated, and any assessment made by him in that year was void, and could not be the foundation for a legal sale. The neglect, also, to file his assessment and give immediate notice on the 25th of March, so that the purchaser might have his appeal at the next county court, was an irregularity which would have avoided the sale even if the assessment had been legally made.

The statute makes the time within which these acts were to be performed material; and a strict and exact compliance with its requirements is a condition precedent to the vesting of any authority in the officer to sell.

We are of opinion, therefore, that the sale of the land of the appellants was " contrary to law," and that the deed from Edward M. Harris, sheriff and collector of Dallas county, to William Overman, set forth and described in the pleadings and exhibits of this case, is void, and should be annulled.

EDWARD C. RICHARDS, ISAAC BASSETT, AND ROBERT W. ABORN, COMPLAINANTS AND APPELLANTS, *v.* SYLVANUS HOLMES, A. H. HARPER, GEORGE A. DWIGHT ET AL.

Where there was a deed of trust to secure the payment of a note which had two years to run, and the trustee was empowered to sell in case any default should be made in payment of any part of the debt and interest, the trustee could sell the property if the interest for the first year was not paid when due.

It was not necessary that the trust deed should describe the interest as being annual.

The trustee had power to adjourn the sale from time to time, if duly advertised, and it should seem to him necessary in order to secure a fair price.

The creditor for whose benefit the sale was made had a right to request the auctioneer to make a bid for him, if fairly used.

Assignors who did not indorse the note, but assigned it by deed, and covenanted that it should be first paid out of the proceeds of sale of the property conveyed in the deed of trust, cannot be held personally responsible. The covenant in the assignment was only that the note assigned should have a preference.

THIS was an appeal from the circuit court of the United States for the District of Columbia, holden in and for the county of Washington.

The case is stated in the opinion of the court.

It was argued by *Mr. Bibb*, for the appellants, and by *Mr.*

Fendall and *Mr. Tracy*, for the appellees. There was also a brief filed by *Mr. Bradley*, as counsel for Southworth, Litchfield, and Beach.

Mr. Bibb made the following points: —

1. That the note was dated on the 1st of May, 1846, and payable in two years. The trustee had no right to sell until the 1st of May, 1848, whereas he sold on the 21st of October, 1847.

2. The allegation set up that Holmes had verbally agreed with Harper to pay the interest semi-annually, &c., cannot be permitted to vary the deed or enlarge the powers of the trustee. Nor could the consent of Holmes impair the rights of Richards, Bassett, and Aborn. They had a right to redeem the property when the note became due, the property being worth more than the lien upon it.

8. The notice of sale was not properly given.

4. The auctioneer was seller and bidder for Harper.

The trustee could not purchase the estate himself; he could not buy as the agent of another; he could not employ the auctioneer to bid for the estate on behalf of Harper. *Ex parte* Bennett, 10 Ves. 393; Coles *v.* Trecothick, 9 Ves. 248; *Ex parte* James, 8 Ves. 345, 348, 350; *Ex parte* Lacey, 6 Ves. 625; Lister *v.* Lister, 6 Ves. 631, 632; Twining *v.* Morris, 2 Brown Ch. Ca. 326; The York Buildings Co. *v.* McKenzie, 8 Brow. Par. Ca., Appen.; Davoue *v.* Fanning, 2 Johns. Ch. Rep. 254, 257, 268, 269, 270.

According to established principles, such a sale as this cannot stand in a court of equity.

The counsel for the appellees, after justifying the sale in other respects, thus noticed one of the points of alleged defectiveness: —

The trustee did not bid at all; Harper's bid was regular. His rights as a creditor, whose only security for his whole fortune was the property advertised for sale, stood on ground as strong, at least, as that of the owner of it. And, though it is not lawful for an owner to employ an agent " to take advantage of the eagerness of bidders, to screw up the price," yet, as a " defensive precaution," " a bidder may be privately appointed by the owner, to prevent the estate from being sold at an under-value." 1 Sugden on Vendors, (9th ed.) 26, 27; Fonbl. Eq. Bk. 1, ch. 4, § 4, n. X; 1 Mad. Ch. Pr. (4th Am. ed.) 324, 825; Smith *v.* Clarke, 12 Ves. 477; Steele *v.* Ellmaker, 11 Serg. & R. 86; Jenkins *v.* Hogg, 2 Const. Rep. (S. C.) 821; Wolfe *v.* Luyster, 1 Hall, N. Y. R. 146; Phippen *v.* Stickney, 3 Metc. 384. Harper made only one bid, and that for " defensive precaution." The bid was made through the auctioneer, who was the agent of both parties.

Smith's Mercantile Law, 801, and the cases there cited; Conelly *v.* Parsons, 3 Ves. 625, n.

It is denied that the property was sold at "a very inadequate price," or that the amount at which it is said to have been assessed on the books of the corporation of Washington (of which there is no evidence) is a true test of its value. But even if the price were "very inadequate," the inadequacy would be no ground for annulling this sale. 1 Fonbl. Eq. 128; 1 U. S. Digest, 344, pl. 88, and the cases there cited. It will be contended that the sale was in all respects regular; and that, if it were not so, yet the complainants cannot avail themselves of the imputed irregularities.

Mr. Justice CURTIS delivered the opinion of the court.

This is an appeal from a decree of the circuit court for the District of Columbia. The appellants filed their bill in that court to set aside a sale, made to satisfy a prior incumbrance on land, upon which they claimed to have a second incumbrance. In the court below, some question appears to have been made concerning the priority of the incumbrances; but none is made here, it being conceded, that though that claimed by the complainants was the earliest in date, the other was first recorded, and takes precedence.

The sale in question was made under a deed of trust, whereby Holmes, the debtor, conveyed to the defendant, Philip R. Fendall, in trust to secure the payment of a promissory note, bearing date May 1, 1846, payable in two years from date, for $2,800 and interest, payable annually.

It is objected that the sale, which was made on the 21st of October, 1847, after one year's interest had become due, but before the principal sum was payable, was premature. This depends upon the meaning and effect of the power of sale contained in the deed. It was competent for the parties to agree to a foreclosure by sale for non-payment of interest, and the question is, whether they did so agree. The event in which the trustee is empowered to sell is thus described in the deed: —

"But if the hereinbefore described promissory note, with the interest legally due thereon, shall not be fully paid off and discharged when said note shall be due and payable, and payment of the same shall be demanded, or if any note or notes given in substitution for or renewal of the hereinbefore described promissory note shall not be fully paid off and discharged according to the tenor and effect of the said substitute or new note or notes, together with the interest legally due on such substitute or note or notes, so that any default be made in payment of any part of the aforesaid debt of two thousand eight hundred dollars and interest, then so soon after such default, &c."

The omission to pay the first year's interest was a default within the express words of this power. That interest was part of the interest secured by the note, and a failure to pay it was a "default in payment of part of the aforesaid interest." The deed authorizes the trustee to sell for any such default, and, consequently, the sale was not premature.

It was argued that the trust deed does not describe the note as bearing annual interest, and, consequently, that the subsequent incumbrancer has a right to insist that, as against him, there was no power to sell for non-payment of such interest.

It is true the deed does not purport to describe the interest which is to become due on the note; but it clearly shows that it bore interest at some rate, and payable at some time or times, and this was sufficient to put a subsequent incumbrancer on inquiry as to what the rate of interest and the time or times of its payment were. The deed, in effect, declares, and its record gives notice to subsequent purchasers, that its purpose is to secure the payment of such interest as has been reserved by the note; the amount, and date, and time of payment of which are mentioned. We do not think the mere omission to describe in the deed what that interest was to be, is a defect of which advantage can be taken by the complainants.

The complainants further insist that the property was not duly advertised. The provision in the deed of trust upon this subject is as follows: "It shall be the duty of the said Philip R. Fendall or his heirs to enter upon the hereinbefore conveyed piece or parcel of ground and appurtenances, and sell the same at public auction to the highest bidder, or at private sale, for cash or credit, according to his or their discretion, after having given public notice of such sale, by advertisement, at least thirty days previously thereto, in the National Intelligencer, or in some other newspaper printed or published in the city of Washington aforesaid."

Inasmuch as the trustee was empowered to sell at private sale as well as at public auction, his power extended to a private sale made at any time after thirty days' notice. Having given notice for the space of thirty days that he was about to sell the property, he might, at any time after the expiration of that thirty days, have proceeded to sell it at private sale. But this notice should be such as to call for purchasers at private sale. The notice given was of a sale at public auction. This did not call for purchasers, except at the time and place mentioned in the notice. No sale was made at the time and place designated in the thirty days' notice, published in the National Intelligencer.

At that time and place the attendance of bidders was so small, that the trustee believed an attempt to sell for a fair price would be fruitless; and he adjourned the sale for the space of fourteen days, giving notice of such adjournment in the same newspaper of the next day. At the time and place thus fixed for the adjourned sale another postponement took place, for the same reasons, for one week; and the place of sale was changed from the premises to the rooms of the auctioneer. Of this postponement, also, public notice was given on the next day, in the same newspaper.

There is no reason to suspect the least unfairness on the part of the trustee, or any one concerned. His conduct seems to have been dictated solely by an honest desire to obtain the best price for the property. Nor is there any ground for believing that either of these postponements prejudiced the interest of the complainants. They stand upon the objection, that though the trustee might have sold on the first day, of which thirty days' notice was given, he could not on that day adjourn the sale.

But we consider that a power to a trustee to sell at public auction, after a certain public notice of the time and place of sale, includes the power regularly to adjourn the sale to a different time and place, when, in his discretion fairly exercised, it shall seem to him necessary to do so in order to obtain the fair auction price for the property.

If he has not this power, the elements or many unexpected occurrences may prevent an attendance of bidders, and cause an inevitable sacrifice of the property. It is a power which every prudent owner would exercise in his own behalf under the circumstances supposed, and which he may well be presumed to intend to confer on another. This power of sale does not undertake to prescribe the particular manner of making the sale. It is to be at public auction, and "after having given public notice of such sale by advertisement at least thirty days"; but it assumes that the sale will be conducted as such sales are usually conducted. A sale regularly adjourned, so as to give notice to all persons present of the time and place to which it is adjourned, is, when made, in effect the sale of which previous public notice was given.

The courts of several States have gone further in this direction than we find necessary, though we do not intend to intimate any doubt of the correctness of their decisions. They have held that a public officer, upon whom a power of sale is conferred by law, may adjourn an advertised public sale to a different time and place, for the purpose of obtaining a better price for the property. Tinkom v. Purdy, 5 Johns. 345; Russell v. Richards, 11 Maine, 371; Lantz v. Worthington, 4 Barr, 153; Warren v. Leland, 9 Mass. 265. If such a power is implied where the law, acting *in invitum*, selects the officer, *à fortiori* it may be presumed to be granted to a trustee selected by the parties.

The remaining objection is, that the defendant Harper, the creditor for whose benefit the sale was made, through the trustee, requested the auctioneer to bid for him the sum of twenty-five hundred dollars; that the auctioneer did so, and there being no higher bid, the property was struck off to Harper. It is insisted that this renders the sale void.

We do not deem it necessary to examine the numerous and somewhat conflicting decisions upon the subject of by-bidding, or bidding by persons standing in fiduciary capacities. This case stands clear of those decisions and of the principles upon which they rest. No decision lays down a positive rule that such sales, though affected by such bidding, are, *per se*, and as between all persons, void. They may be avoided by parties whose just interests have been injuriously affected by such misconduct, provided the rights of innocent third persons are not thereby disturbed.

It was for the advantage of these complainants, as subsequent incumbrancers, that this property should sell for the best price which could be obtained. Even improper practices to enhance the price, if any such had been resorted to, could not be complained of by them. It is only some practice to prevent bidding, or procure a sale for less than the property would have otherwise brought, which can be relied on by them to avoid the sale. We have no doubt the creditor, for the satisfaction of whose debt the sale was made, had a right to compete fairly at the sale; but whether he had or not, his doing so could not be injurious to the complainants.

It is true he employed the auctioneer to bid for him; but this fact alone could not depreciate the price. Such an authority may be used for fraudulent purposes; but, if fairly used, its tendency is to enhance the price; and in this case there is no evidence that it was intended to be, or in fact was, unfairly used. On the contrary, there seems to be no room for doubt that the price bid by the auctioneer for Harper was more than any other person was willing to give. It must be remembered, that the auctioneer was not employed as the agent of the creditor to purchase the property for him at the least price at which it could be obtained. Such an agency an auctioneer should not undertake. It is inconsistent with his relation to the seller, and with the faithful discharge of his duty to the seller.

But an agency simply to bid a particular sum for a purchaser, amounting to no more than receiving from the purchaser, before the auction, a bid which is to be treated as if made there by the purchaser himself, is not necessarily inconsistent with any duty

Richards et al. *v.* Holmes et al.

of the auctioneer, and does not enable any one to avoid the sale.

And the same remark applies to the trustee. It was his duty to obtain for the property the best price he could by the use of due diligence in a fair sale. It would have been improper for him, in behalf of the creditor, to employ the auctioneer to buy at anything short of that best price. But there was no impropriety in his employing him to bid a particular sum for the creditor, to prevent a sacrifice of the property.

We have considered all the objections to this sale made by the complainants, and finding neither of them valid, the decree of the court below is, in that respect, affirmed.

As to so much of the complainants' bill as seeks relief against their assignors, in the event of not obtaining satisfaction from the land, we are of opinion that these assignors are under no such liability as is asserted by the complainants. The complainants purchased a negotiable note which was overdue. The assignors did not indorse it, but simply assigned it by deed. They entered into certain specific covenants concerning the subject-matter assigned; and their liability depends exclusively on these covenants. Neither of these covenants appears to have been broken. The only one concerning which any doubt has been raised is the following:—

"And we do in like manner covenant, promise, and agree, that the said note of three thousand dollars, hereinbefore assigned, shall be and is entitled to payment out of any sale of the premises conveyed in and by the deed of trust aforesaid, before the other note therein specified, and shall have a prior lien on the said premises, or the proceeds thereof."

We think the purpose and effect of this covenant was, not to secure payment out of any sale which might be made by any party under any title to the premises, but only to assure the priority of payment of the note assigned, in preference to the other note, out of any sale made under the particular title to the premises described in the deed of assignment.

The covenant that the note assigned is due, is shown to have been kept by the note itself, in the absence of other evidence. The answer admits the receipt of moneys from the maker on account of other debts, but denies any payment on account of this note; and there is no evidence to the contrary.

The decree of the circuit court is affirmed, with costs.

WILLIAM JONES AND SYLVESTER MARSH, PLAINTIFFS IN ERROR,
v. WILLIAM S. JOHNSTON.

Where reference was made in deeds to 'a recorded plat, and in an ejectment suit, evidence was offered to show that this plat differed from the original plat, the evidence
ought not to have been admitted. If an error existed, the proper remedy was in
chancery to reform the deeds.

And where the deeds under which both parties claimed, referred to this plat, it was of
no consequence, whether or not the plat was recorded precisely according to the
requisitions of a statute of the state.

The true rule for the jury would have been to ascertain whether the lot claimed by
the plaintiff had any water front at the time the deed, under which he claimed was
executed, and not whether it had a water front at the time when the lot was originally laid out.

In case it should be found that the lot in question was entitled to a water front at the
time of the execution of the deed to the plaintiff, then the rule adopted by the court
below for dividing the made ground, was not a correct rule.

The true rule pointed out.

THIS case was brought up by writ of error, from the circuit
court of the United States, for the District of Illinois.

The case is stated in the opinion of the court, but it is difficult for the reader to understand the points, unless with the
assistance of an explanatory map. Many of these were used
during the argument, but the sketch here presented may convey
some idea of the locality.

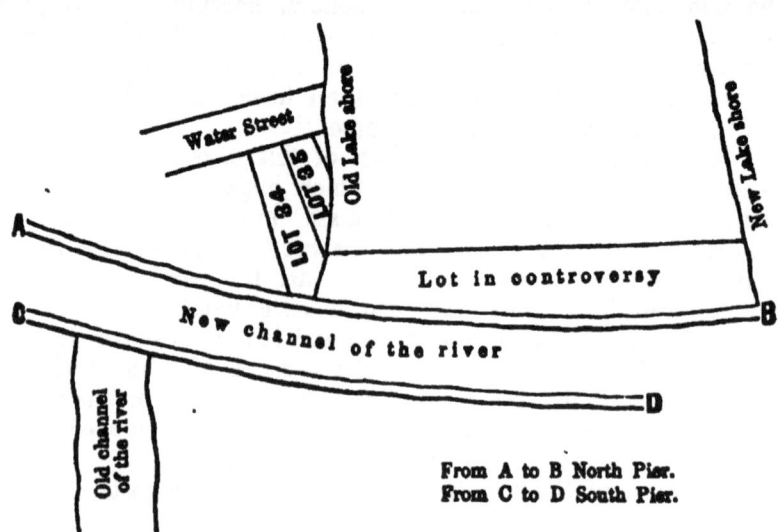

From A to B North Pier.
From C to D South Pier.

Johnston, who brought the ejectment in the court below, was
the owner of lot No. 84. Jones and Marsh claimed that lot
No. 85 was entitled to the whole benefit of the alluvion. There

were three trials in the court below, the last of which resulted in a verdict and judgment for the plaintiff as follows : —

Beginning at a point on the line between lots thirty-four and thirty-five, in Kinzie's addition to Chicago, Cook county, Illinois, three hundred feet southerly of the south line of North Water street, measuring on that line for distance ; thence south, eleven degrees and thirty minutes, east, one hundred and thirty-five feet, to the north pier; thence easterly along the north pier to the shore of Lake Michigan; thence northwardly along the Lake shore two hundred and twenty-two feet; thence westerly in a straight line to the place of beginning.

The instructions given to the jury by the circuit court are stated in the opinion of the court.

It was argued by *Mr. Scammon* and *Mr. Johnston*, for the plaintiffs in error, and by *Mr. Lawrence* and *Mr. Chase*, for the defendant.

On the trial in the circuit court, the counsel for the defendant made twelve prayers to the court; some of which were granted, others with reservations and qualifications. The counsel for the plaintiff made seven prayers, which were qualified in the same way ; and then the court gave other instructions to the jury of its own accord. The arguments of counsel in this court discussed all these points; and it would not be possible to explain them, without giving too extended a statement of all the points.

Mr. Justice NELSON delivered the opinion of the court.

This is a writ of error to the circuit court of the United States for the district of Illinois.

The suit below, was an action of ejectment, brought by *Johnston*, against Jones and Marsh, to recover a tract of alluvial land in the city of Chicago, formed in Lake Michigan, adjoining the north pier of Chicago harbor, and which is claimed as an accretion to water-lot No. 34, in Kinzie's addition. The defendant, Jones, is owner of lot. No. 35, in said addition, lying east, and adjoining 34, and between that and the lake.

Both parties claim under Robert A. Kinzie, the patentee of the north fractional section 10, in township 39, which was situate in the bend of the Chicago River, at its mouth, and bounded southerly by that river, and easterly by the Michigan Lake. Kinzie, the patentee, in February, 1833, laid out an addition to the town of Chicago upon this fractional section, and made a plat of the same, which was recorded in the recorder's office of the county, on the 18th of January, 1834, according to the requirements of the laws of the State of Illinois. On this plat, lot No. 34 is one of a series of water-lots, bounded on the south side of North

Water street, sixty feet, as its northerly boundary, and is included within lines dropped from the fixed corners on that street
at right angles with the same, and extended until they intersect
the lake shore. Lot No. 35 is the next lot east, of the same
width, on Water street, and extended in like manner to the lake,
its west line being the east line of 34.

On the 25th of February, 1833, R. A. Kinzie conveyed to
John H. Kinzie several lots in this addition, and among others
lot No. 35. And on the 1st September, 1834, John H. conveyed
the same to Jones, the defendant, describing it in the deed as in
Kinzie's addition, and as " being water-lot No. 35," &c., " agreeably to the town plat, recorded in the office of the recorder of
the said county of Cook, to which reference may be had if
necessary."

On the 22d of October, 1835, R. A. Kinzie conveyed to Johnston, the plaintiff, lot No. 34, describing it as lying in Kinzie's
addition, and known as water-lot No. 34, " as will more fully
appear, reference being had to said plat as recorded in the recorder's office of the town of Chicago, in the county of Cook,"
&c.

In the summer of 1833, the general government commenced
the construction of the harbor of the city of Chicago, which is
formed by an erection of two piers across this fractional section
10, from the curve of the Chicago River, as it takes a direction
southerly to the lake, and for a considerable distance into the
lake, the effect of which was to turn the river from its sweep
southerly across the sand-bar to the waters of the lake between
the two piers, and thus opening a passage for vessels into the
town.

The south pier was built in 1833, and the north in 1834. The
harbor thus constructed, divided several of the lots in Kinzie's
addition that bounded on Water street, east and west, and, among
others, as is claimed by the defendant, No. 34, leaving a part of
it as originally laid out, south of the harbor.

Since the construction of the harbor and extension of the
piers into the waters of the lake, the shore above, or north of
the piers, has greatly changed, the firm land having increased
by the washing up of sand and earth, and the recession of the
waters to the extent of some twelve hundred feet in width, and
for a considerable distance in length northward along the shore.
The present suit is brought to recover a portion of this alluvion
or new-formed land, as an increment or accession to lot No. 34.
The plaintiff claims that a part of its southern termination on
the lake was north of the piers, and contiguous to the new-
formed land, and therefore entitled to its share of the increment.
The defendant contends that no part of its boundary was on

the lake north of the harbor, and therefore no part connected with or adjoining this land newly formed. On the contrary, that part of his own lot, No. 85, which lies between 84 and the lake, was bounded on the lake south of the north pier, and hence cut off No. 84 from any portion of the alluvial accession.

The plaintiff insisted, on the trial, that the plat of Kinzie's addition, as recorded in the recorder's office in January, 1834, was incorrect, and produced what was claimed to be the original, but which was not recorded when the conveyances of the lots in question were executed. According to this original plat, as the side lines were laid down, lot No. 84 appeared to be partially bounded on the lake north of the harbor. In this respect, it differed from the plat recorded; as, according to the side lines as there extended, its entire boundary on the lake was south of the harbor.

. In laying out the addition by the surveyor in 1883, the only lines of the lots run out or measured on the ground were those butting on Water street, the north lines of the lots. The side lines depend upon their protraction on the plat of the addition; and which, as we have already said, were formed by dropping them at right angles from the corners on Water street, and extending them till they intersected the lake. And even the lake shore, as laid down on the plat — as appears from the testimony of the surveyor — was ascertained without survey or measurement, and with little more accuracy than could be obtained from the eye.

The case was a good deal embarrassed on the trial, arising out of the evidence in respect to this original plat, and some consideration and effect were given to it by the court in submitting it to the jury. We think the court erred in admitting it as evidence to control, or in any way to affect, the recorded plat. Both lots in controversy were conveyed with express reference to that, and without such reference there is not a sufficient description given in the deeds of the boundaries to admit of a location of either.

If there was in fact any error or mistake in this reference, by way of description of the premises conveyed, the remedy was in chancery to reform the deed. So long as that remained unreformed, the description of the lot by the reference to the recorded plat was conclusive upon the parties.

The acts of the State of Illinois regulating the laying out of town-lots, and the recording of the plats of the same, were supposed by the court below to have a bearing upon the questions involved, and influenced the instructions given and refused to the jury. It seemed to be admitted that the plat recorded did not conform in all respects to the requirement of the statutes.

But it is not pretended that the omission in any way operated to invalidate the deeds, or affect prejudicially the rights of the parties under them.   Both parties stand upon the same footing in this respect, as each claims under the same survey of the town, and by reference to the same plat.   We do not perceive that these acts of the State have any material bearing upon the case, and should not have been allowed to influence the trial.   If the description in the deeds was sufficiently certain, by a reference to the plat on record, to identify and locate the lots, the title passed to the grantees, whether the plat conformed to the acts of the legislature or not.   This is all that was material so far as the plat is concerned.

The court, in instructing the jury, observed that the controversy turned upon the length of the line dividing lot 34 from 35, before the north pier was constructed — that whether in point of fact it touched the shore of the lake before it reached the pier, or the place where the pier was; in other words, whether there was any water-line of lot 34 north of the north pier, and if so, what was the extent of the water-line.

Again, the court charged, after adverting to the recorded plat, and to the question whether or not it was made in conformity to the statutes of Illinois, that, if the jury should find the plat was not so made and recorded, then they should determine, under all the evidence in the case, whether or not, prior to the construction of the north pier, the dividing line between lots 34 and 35 touched the water at a point north of where the north pier was subsequently placed; if it did, then the court was of opinion that the owner of 34 had a right to follow the water as the accretions were formed on his water-line.

In these instructions we think the court erred.

As we have seen, this lot No. 34 was conveyed to the plaintiff the 22d October, 1835, and described as included within side lines dropped at right angles from the northwest and northeast corners on Water street, which were sixty feet apart, and fixed, and extended in right lines till they intersected the shore of the lake below.   The boundaries, therefore, including and locating the lot were specific and complete.   The north boundary was marked on the south side of Water street; the side lines extended according to the plat at right angles from Water street to the lake; the lake was the southern boundary which closed the lines of the lot.

Now, in order to determine what land was conveyed to the plaintiff by his deed of 22d October, 1835, all that was necessary was to locate the lot upon the ground in conformity to the description at that date.   The calls in the deed having reference to the plat, furnished the necessary data for the location.   There was the fixed line north on the ground, the lake, a natural object south, and the lot enclosed between two lines extending at right angles from the corners on Water street to the lake.

If the call for the southern boundary, instead of being a lake, which is a shifting line, had been a permanent object, such as a street or wall, there could not be two opinions as to the location. And yet the water-line, though it may gradually and imperceptibly change, is just as fixed a boundary in the eye of the law as the former. I speak not now of sudden and considerable changes, which are governed by different principles.

The court below, as appears from the instructions referred to, assumed that lot No. 34 should be located on the ground as of the time of the survey and plat of February, 1838, some two years and nine months previous to the conveyance to the plaintiff, and not at the date of that conveyance; and if at that time the dividing line between 34 and 35 would strike the lake north of where the north pier of the harbor was subsequently built, so as to give a like boundary at that time above the pier, the plaintiff would be enabled to take under his deed not only lot 34, as laid down on the plat, but all subsequent accretions by alluvion or dereliction, whatever might be the extent of the new-formed land. By the like assumption and process of reasoning, if the present plaintiff should convey the lot with the same specific boundaries, the north line sixty feet on Water street, and side lines extending at right angles to the lake, the deed would carry with it the whole of the new-made land outside the lines of the deed which is now in dispute — it being a tract from one hundred and thirty to two hundred and twenty-two feet one way, and some twelve hundred the other.

Now, one answer to this assumption is, that a grantee can acquire by his deed only the lands described in it by metes and bounds, and with sufficient certainty to enable a person of reasonable skill to locate it, and cannot acquire lands outside of the description by way of appurtenance or accession.

Lord Coke says: "A thing corporeal cannot properly be appurtenant to a thing corporeal, nor a thing incorporeal to a thing incorporeal." Coke Litt. 121, B.

And this court in Harris et al. v. Elliot, 10 Pet. 54, after approving of the maxim of Coke, observed, that, according to this rule, land cannot be appurtenant to land. In the case of Jackson v. Hathaway, 15 Johns. R. 454, the court say, a mere easement may, without express words pass, as an incident to the principal object of the grant; but it would be absurd to allow the fee of one piece of land not mentioned in the deed to pass as appurtenant to another distinct parcel which is expressly granted by precise and definite boundaries. See also 7 Mass. 6.

Land gained from the sea either by alluvion or dereliction, if the same be by little and little, by small and imperceptible degrees, belongs to the owner of the land adjoining. 2 Bl. Com. 261-2. If, therefore, the rule be as supposed by the court below, that the boundaries of lot 84 must be taken as it would have been located at the time of the plat, and the southern limit to stop at the water-line as it then existed, and the subsequent gain by alluvion or dereliction to pass as appurtenant to the land conveyed, the grantee would find it difficult upon this construction to reach the lake at all. Certainly he could not, if the water-line as it then existed is to be deemed the southern limit as described in his deed, provided alluvial accretions had taken place between the survey and plat and the date of the deed. The land thus formed belonged to the adjoining owner for the time being, and we have seen that the deed would not pass it as appurtenant or incidental to the land granted.

But the true answer to the position assumed, and which governed the trial below, is, that the water boundary on the lake is to be deemed the true southern boundary of the lot at the date of the conveyance, as much so as North Water street was its northern boundary. And the plaintiff is carried by his deed to it, not because of the alluvial deposit, if any, between the water-line at the time of the survey and plat and the line at the date of the deed, having passed as appurtenant to the lot, but because one of the calls given in the deed requires that the side lines should be thus extended. Any alluvial accretions since the deed belong to the plaintiff as owner of the adjoining land. Any past accretions belonged to the then owner, and whoever sets up a title to them must show a deed of the same as in the case of any other description of land.

The case of Robert M. Lamb v. Thomas C. Rickets, 11 Ohio, 311, exemplifies the principle for which we are contending. The defendant had agreed to convey a piece of land called the Hamlin lot, containing forty-two acres more or less, and also two other small lots of ten acres, with a proviso if the Hamlin lot and the two others contained more than fifty-two acres the excess was reserved. The defendant conveyed the Hamlin lot, and refused to convey the other two. A bill was filed to compel a conveyance. The Hamlin lot was bounded by one of its lines on the bank of the Tuscarawas River, and had been originally conveyed to the defendant, and by him to the plaintiff, as containing forty-two acres more or less.

The defence set up to the bill was, that before the defendant conveyed the lot to the plaintiff large accessions had been made from the river to the lot, and that these alluvial formations made up the quantity of fifty-two acres.

The plaintiff claimed that the quantity should be determined according to the old boundary of the lot upon the bank of the river, which would be but some forty-two acres. But the court held that the question was, not as the bank of the river was twenty-five or thirty years ago, but as it was' when the Hamlin tract was conveyed to the plaintiff, and estimated the quantity of land conveyed accordingly.

The case of Giraud's Lessee v. Hughes et al. 1 Gill & Johnson, 249, asserts a similar principle. There Gist's inspection, a grant as early as 1782, was bounded by one of its lines in the waters of the Patapsco River, afterwards a basin of Baltimore; the lines, however, were given in the grant by courses and distances, and did not call for the river. Hughes held under this grant by deed in 1782.

Before 1812, the waters of the Patapsco had gradually receded, and formed a body of firm land, which had been surveyed and patented by the State to the plaintiff. The question was, whether or not Hughes was entitled to this alluvial deposit as the adjoining owner to the river. It was not doubted by the counsel or court but that, if the grant of Gist's inspection had been bounded on the river, this boundary of the tract would have included the land made by the recession of the water; and the court even held, that as the original location of the tract extended into the river, it entitled those holding under it to the land, on the ground that the principle governing these alluvial accretions gave them to the adjoining owner. In other words, the description in the original grant gave, in legal effect, to the grantee, a water boundary; and if so, the boundary included the accretions.

The jury, therefore, in this case, should have been directed to inquire whether or not, at the time of the deed to the plaintiff, lot No. 84 had a water-line upon the lake north of the north pier of the Chicago harbor; — in other words, whether the line between that lot and No. 85 struck the shore of the lake before it reached this pier. If it did, then the question would properly arise in respect to its right to a share of the alluvial accretions formed since that period. If it did not, then no question of the kind could arise in the case.

We think the court also erred in the rule laid down to govern the jury in the division of the new-made land. That was, the jury should ascertain the extent of the water-line of 84 between the piers and the point where the line dividing 84 and 85 touched the water. They should also ascertain the extent of the water-line of the fraction of land south of North Water street and east of 85, and also of 85 to the point dividing 84 and 85; they would then have the plaintiffs' and the defendant's front on the lake. They must then ascertain the front on the lake shore, as it at present exists, and divide that into as many equal parts as there are feet on the old shore from North Water street to the piers, and give to each of the parties as many of these parts as he had feet on the old shore, and then draw a straight line from the point of division on the old lake shore to the point thus determined as the point of division on the present one.

We do not perceive why North Water street should have been adopted as the northern limit upon the old shore, as the basis in making the division, as it appears from the evidence and maps that the alluvial accretions extended much farther north. The northern limit on the old shore should have been carried as far as the new-made land extended, as each riparian proprietor was entitled to his proper share, and it was essential that the entire line be regarded, in order that each might obtain his proportional part. Neither do we perceive any reason for excluding the pier shore of the lake — that is, the shore along the line of the piers — from measurement, in ascertaining the extent of the newly made shore. If we disregard the artificial construction which occasioned the accretions, the lake there is as much new shore as any other portion of it, and should have been taken into the estimate.

As no question was made below whether or not the alluvial accretions in question were formed under such circumstances as gave to adjoining owners a title to them, we do not intend to express any opinion upon that question.

The judgment of the court below is reversed, with directions that a *venire de novo* issue.

JOSIAH SIDDONS GRIFFITH, JAMES S. CHEW, AND MARY E. CHEW, HIS WIFE, PLAINTIFFS IN ERROR, v. JOHN B. BOGERT, ABRAHAM MYER, AND THADDEUS SMITH.

The law of Missouri allows the lands of a deceased debtor to be sold under execution, but prohibits it from being done until after the expiration of eighteen months from the date of the letters of administration upon his estate.

Where the letters of administration were dated on the 1st of November, 1819, and the sale took place on the 1st of May, 1821, the sale was valid. In this case the *terminus a quo* should be included.

Moreover, the sale was ordered to take place on that day by a court of competent jurisdiction, and this makes the matter *rem judicatam*, and is evidence of the construction which the courts of Missouri place upon their laws.

And, besides, the question of the regularity of a judicial sale cannot be raised collaterally, except in case of fraud, in which the purchaser was a participant.

Griffith et al. v. Bogert et al.

This case came up by writ of error, from the circuit court of the United States for the district of Missouri.

The case is stated in the opinion of the court.

It was argued by *Mr. Crittenden*, for the plaintiffs in error, and *Mr. Geyer*, for the defendants.

Those of *Mr. Crittenden's* points, which were included in the decision of the court, were the two following: —

1. Because the judgments themselves were void, so far as they related to, or affected the lands, tenements, or hereditaments of the intestate; or, if not, that the executions issued thereon, dated respectively, the 28th of February, and 9th of April, 1821, under or in virtue of which the sheriff sold the land in question, were illegal, null and void, because issued before the expiration of eighteen months from the date (1st of November, 1819) of the letters of administration of the estate of said intestate, and were therefore issued in direct violation of the express provisions of the before-recited act of the 25th of January, 1817; 8 Metcalf, 502.

2. Because the sale, in virtue of which said deed purports to have been executed, was made on the 1st day of May, 1821, and before the expiration of eighteen months from the date, (1st of November, 1819,) of the said letters of administration, contrary to the express terms of the said act of 1817, and was, therefore, illegal and void.

The only questionable part of this proposition is, whether the 1st of May, 1821, is a day after the expiration of eighteen months from the 1st of November, 1819, or included in, and part of the period. The reasonable and legal rule of computation of time in such cases, is to exclude the first day, that is, the day of the event or act from which the computation is to be made. It is but the fraction of a day, and the law takes no notice or account of it. This is believed to be the rule as now settled by judicial discussions in Missouri. Gantly *v.* Ewing, 3 How. 707; Kennon *v.* Osgood, 19 Mo. R. 60; Blaine *v.* Beehler, 12 Mo. R. 477.

Upon the principal point in the case, *Mr. Geyer* said: —

The sale was made on the 1st of May, 1821, which was after the expiration of eighteen months, from the death of the intestate, or the date of the letters of administration, (1st of November, 1819,) construing the act of 1817 according to the rules and principles which have been recognized and applied in analogous cases.

It has been laid down in many cases as a general rule, that where time is to be computed from an event or an act, the day of the event or the performance of the act is to be included.

Norris *v.* The Hundred of the Gawthry, Hobart, 139; King *v.* Adderly, Douglass, 463; Castle *v.* Burdett, 8 Term R. 623; Glassington *v.* Rawlings, 8 East, 407; Priest *v.* Tarlton, 3 N. H. Rep. 93; Thomas *v.* Afflick, 16 Pa. R. 14; Robinet *v.* Compton, 2 La. An. R. 856; Pierpoint *v.* Graham, 4 Wash. C. C. Rep. 232; Arnold *v.* United States, 9 Cranch, 104.

In some cases, the rule has been held to be, to exclude the day of the act or event from the computation; in others, the day has been excluded without laying down any general rule. King *v.* Cumberland, 4 Nov. and M. 375; Judd *v.* Fulton, 10 Barl. 117; Wing *v.* Davis, 7 Maine, 31; *Ex parte v.* Deane, 2 Cowen, 605; Cornell *v.* Moulton, 8 Denio, 12; Snydor *v.* Warren, 2 Cowen, 518; S. B. Mary Blane *v.* Beehler, 12 Mo. R. 477; Kimm *v.* Osgood's Administrators, 19 Mo. R. 60.

But it has been denied that there is any general rule, that the day of the act or event from which time is to be computed is to be included or excluded, and held that whether it is to be taken inclusive or exclusive, depends upon the reason of the thing, the context, and subject-matter. Lester *v.* Garland, 15 Vesey, Jr., 248; Dowling *v.* Foxall, 1 Ball & Bealty, 196; Windsor *v.* China, 4 Maine, 298; Bigelow *v.* Wilson, 1 Peck, 485; Presbury *v.* Williams, 15 Mass. 193; Jones *v.* Planters' Bank, 5 Humphries, 619; O'Conner *v.* Towns, 1 Texas, 107.

In the earlier cases, "from the date" was generally held to be inclusive, and "from the day of the date," exclusive, but the doctrine now most generally received is, that there is no difference in the two forms of expression, both meaning the same thing; and in the computation of time on promissory notes and bills of exchange, the day of the date has generally been excluded; in other instances, it is held to be inclusive or exclusive, according to the context and subject-matter. Pugh *v.* Duke of Leeds, Cowper, 714, and cases there cited and reviewed; Rand *v.* Rand, 4 N. H. 267; Moore *v.* Bond, 18 Maine, 142; Wilcox *v.* Wood, 9 Wend. 346.

It appears to have been very generally agreed that either the first or the last day shall be included in the computation, and in no case are both to be excluded or included, unless the contract or statute upon which the question arises will admit of no other construction. *Ex parte v.* Deane, 2 Cow. 605; Thomas *v.* Afflick, 16 Pa. R. 14; Sander's Heirs *v.* Norton, 4 Monroe, 474.

Upon a review of the cases, it appears that there is no general rule in computing time from an act done or an event, or from a date or the day of the date, that the day is to be inclusive or exclusive; but, according to the adjudged cases, whether the day in either case is to be included or excluded, depends upon the reason of the thing, the subject-matter, and the context.

Griffith et al. *v.* Bogert et al.
___

But the title of a *bonâ fide* purchaser, at judicial sales, is not affected by any irregularities in the proceedings of the officer, or in the process under which he sold; therefore, if the eighteen months limited by the statute had not expired at the time of the sale, under which the defendants hold, the sheriff's deed would not, on that account, be void; at most, it would be voidable, and could be impeached only in a direct proceeding, and not in a collateral action. All that is necessary to support the title of a purchaser in an action of ejectment, is the judgment, execution, levy, and sheriff's deed. Jackson *v.* Steinburg, 1 J. C. 158; Jackson *v.* Bartlett, 8 J. R. 361; Jackson *v.* Rosevelt, 13 J. R. 97; Same *v.* Delaney, 13 J. R. 585; Same *v.* Robbins, 16 J. R. 587; Brown *v.* Miller, 3 J. J. Marsh, 439; Lawrence *v.* Sheed, 2 Bibb, 401; Webber *v.* Stith & Cox, 6 Monroe, 101; Day *v.* Graham, 1 Gel. (6 Ill.) R. 435; Swigart *v.* Harber, 4 Scam, 364; Ware *v.* Bradford, 2 Al. R. 676; 19 do. 132; State Bank *v.* Noland, 13 Ark. R. 299; Newton *v.* State Bank, 14 Ark. R. 9; Byers *v.* Fowler, 12 Ark. 218; Wheaton *v.* Sexton, 4 Wheat. 506; Hart *v.* Rector, 7. Mo. R. 531; Reed *v.* Heirs of Austin, 9 Mo. R. 722; Landes *v.* Perkins, 12 Mo. R. 254; Draper *v.* Bryson, 17 Mo. R. 71; Carson *v.* Walker, 16 Mo. R. 68; Robinett *v.* Compton, 2 La. An. R. 856.

All the questions now raised were before the court, which was a court of competent jurisdiction, and its acts cannot now be impeached. 1 Baldwin, 246; 1 Serg. & Rawle, 101; 8 Serg. & Rawle, 397; 2 Pet. 257; 10 Pet. 473; 2 How. 343.

Mr. Justice GRIER delivered the opinion of the court.

The plaintiffs claim the land which is the subject of controversy in this suit, as heirs of Isaac W. Griffith, who died seised of the same in 1819. His estate was insolvent. Judgments were obtained against his administrators in 1820, executions were issued thereon, and the property sold by the sheriff. The defendants claim under the purchaser at this sale.

On the trial, the court below instructed the jury "that the sheriff's deed, read in evidence under the judgments and executions also in evidence, was effectual to devest the title of the heirs of Isaac H. Griffith to the land mentioned in said deed."

It is admitted, that in the State of Missouri the lands of a deceased debtor may be taken in execution, and sold by the sheriff, in satisfaction of a judgment against the administrator. And also that such deed vests in the purchaser all the estate and interest which the deceased had in the property at the time of his death. But it is alleged that this sale is "without authority of law and void," because the execution was issued and sale made before the time limited for stay of execution against the

14 *

Griffith et al. v. Bogert et al.

real estate of a decedent. The law and the facts, on which this objection to the validity of the sale is founded, are as follows: —

By an act of 1817, it is provided that "all lands, tenements, and hereditaments shall be liable to be seized or sold upon judgment and execution obtained against the defendant or defendants, in full life, or against his or her heirs, executors, or administrators, after the decease of the testate, or intestate; provided no such land, tenements, or hereditaments shall be seized and sold until after the expiration of eighteen months from the death of such ancestor, or the date of the letters testamentary or letters of administration, and execution may issue against such lands, tenements, and hereditaments, after the death, testate or intestate, and after the time aforesaid, in the same manner as if such person were living."

The letters of administration on the estate of Griffith are dated on the 1st of November, 1819. The sale was made by the sheriff on the 1st of May, 1821, on executions previously issued.

It is contended that the term of eighteen months from the 1st of November, 1819, had not expired on the 1st of May, 1821, and consequently the sale was without authority of law, and void.

But we are of opinion that the assumption on which this inference is based is not correct; nor the inference correct, if the assumption were granted.

If the day on which the letters of administration be counted in the calculation, the term of eighteen months had "expired" on the 1st of May, 1821.

Whether the *terminus a quo* should be so included, it must be admitted, has been a vexed question for many centuries, both among learned doctors of the civil law and the courts of England and this country. It has been termed by a writer on civil law (Tiraqueau) the *controversia controversissima*.

In common and popular usage, the day *a quo* has always been included, and such has been the general rule both of the Roman and common law. The latter admits no fractions of a day; the former, in some instances, as in cases of minority, calculated *de momento en momentum*. The result of this subdivision was to comprehend a part of the *terminus a quo*. But in cases where fractions of a day were not admitted, as in those of usucaption or prescription, a possession commencing on the 1st of January, and ending on the 31st of December, was counted a full year. It was in consequence of the uncertainty introduced on this subject by the disquisitions and disputes of learned professors, that Gregory IX., in his decretals, introduced the phrase of " a year and a day," in order to remove the doubts thus created, as to whether the *dies a quo* should be included in the term. It thus maintained the correctness of the common usage, while it satisfied the doubts of the doctors.

The earlier cases at common law show the adoption of the popular usage as the general rule, but many exceptions were introduced in its application to leases, limitations, &c., where a forfeiture would ensue. But the cases are conflicting, and have established no fixed rule as to such exceptions. Lord Mansfield reviews the cases before his time, in Pugh v. Leeds, Cowp. 714, and comes to the conclusion "that the cases for two hundred years had only served to embarrass a point which a plain man of common sense and understanding would have no difficulty in construing."

The rule he lays down in that case is, "that courts of justice ought to construe the words of parties so as to effectuate their deeds and not destroy them; and that, 'from' the date, may in vulgar use, and even in strict propriety of language, mean either inclusive or exclusive."

It would be tedious and unprofitable to attempt a review of the very numerous modern decisions, or to lay down any rules applicable to all cases. Every case must depend on its own circumstances. Where the construction of the language of a statute is doubtful, courts will always prefer that which will confirm rather than destroy any *bonâ fide* transaction or title. The intention and policy of the enactment should be sought for and carried out. Courts should never indulge in nice grammatical criticism of prepositions or conjunctions, in order to destroy rights honestly acquired.

In the present case there is no reason for departing from the general rule and popular usage of treating the day from which the term is to be calculated, or *"terminus a quo,"* as inclusive. The object of the legislature was to give a stay of execution for eighteen months, in order that the administrator might have an opportunity of collecting the assets of the deceased and applying them to the discharge of his debts. The day on which the letters issue may be used for this purpose as effectually as any other in the year. The rights of the creditor to execution are restrained by the act, for the benefit of the debtor's estate. The administrator has had the number of days allowed to him by the statute to collect his assets and pay the debts. The construction which would exclude the day of the date is invoked, not to avoid a forfeiture or confirm a title, but to destroy one, obtained by a purchaser in good faith under the sanction of a public judicial sale.

If the statute in question were one of limitation, whereby the remedy of the creditor would have been lost, unless execution had issued and sale been made within the eighteen months, probably a different construction might have prevailed. Yet, even in such a case, the precedents conflict. (See Cornell v. Moulton, 3 Denio, 12; and Presbury v. Williams, 15 Mass. 193.)

But, if the correct application of the rule to the present case were doubtful, the fact that this question was raised and decided by the court between the parties to the judgment, and that the court after considering the question, ordered the sale to be made on the 1st of May, would be conclusive, not only as *res judicata inter partes*, but as evidence of the received construction by the courts of Missouri, which it would be an abuse of judicial discretion now to overturn.

Finally, there is another view of this case which is conclusive, as regards this and all other objections taken by the counsel to the validity of the sheriff's deed. It is the well-known and established rule of law in Missouri and elsewhere, that a judicial sale and title acquired under the proceedings of a court of competent jurisdiction cannot be questioned collaterally, except in case of fraud, in which the purchaser was a participant. (See Grignon v. Astor, 2 How. 319.) The cases of Reed v. Austin, 9 Mo. R. 722; of Landes v. Perkins, 12 Mo. 239; Carson v. Walker, 16 Mo. 68, and Draper v. Bryson, 17 Mo. 71, show that this principle of the common law is the received and established doctrine of the courts of Missouri.

The sheriff's deed in the present case is founded on a regular judgment in a court of competent jurisdiction, and an execution on said judgment issued by authority of the court, and levied on property subject by law to be taken and sold to satisfy the judgment. The writ authorized the sheriff to sell; a sale was made in pursuance thereof by the sheriff, and a deed executed to the purchaser, which was afterwards acknowledged in open court according to law. At this time, all parties interested could and would have been heard to allege any irregularity in the proceedings that would justify the court in setting it aside. The objections to this sale do not reach the power of the court, or the authority of the sheriff to sell. The issuing of an execution on a judgment before the stay of execution has elapsed, or after a year and day without reviving the judgment, the want of proper advertisements by the sheriff, and other like irregularities, may be sufficient ground for setting aside the execution or sale, on motion of a party to the suit, or any one interested in the proceedings; but when the objections are waived by them, and the judicial sale founded on these proceedings is confirmed by the court, it would be injurious to the peace of the community and the security of titles to permit such objections to the title to be heard in a collateral action.

On every view of the case, we are of opinion that the title of the purchaser is protected by the established rules of law, and that there was no error in the instructions given to the jury by the court below.

The judgment of the circuit court is therefore affirmed.

EDWIN C. LITTLE AND OLIVER SCOVILL, APPELLANTS, *v.* LEVI W. HALL, ANTHONY GOULD, DAVID BANKS, WILLIAM GOULD, AND DAVID BANKS, JR.

On the 27th of December, 1847, George F. Comstock was appointed state reporter, under a statute of the State of New York, which office he held until the 27th of December, 1851.

During his term of office, viz. in 1850, he, in conjunction with the comptroller and secretary of the State, acting under the authority of a statute, made an agreement with certain persons, that for five years to come they should have the publication of the decisions of the court of appeals and the exclusive benefit of the copyright.

At the expiration of Mr. Comstock's term, viz. on the 27th of December, 1851, he had in his possession sundry manuscript notes, and the decisions made at the ensuing January term were also placed in his hands to be reported. Out of these materials he made a volume, and sold it upon his own private account.

Whatever remedy the first assignees may have had against Mr. Comstock individually, they are not to be considered as the legal owners of the manuscript, under the copyright act of congress, and are not entitled to an injunction to prevent the publication and sale of the volume.

THIS was an appeal from the circuit court of the United States for the northern district of New York.

The case is stated in the opinion of the court.

It was argued by *Mr. Seward,* for the plaintiffs in error, and *Mr. Haven,* for the defendants.

Mr. Seward made the following points: —

1. Comstock, by accepting the office of state reporter, and acting under it, and by uniting with the secretary of state and comptroller in the contract with the appellants of April 20, 1850, must be deemed to have accepted the terms and conditions of the act of April 11, 1848, and of April 9, 1850. And those statutes operated, by reason of such acquiescence on his part, to vest in the State of New York all the interest and right which he might have, as author, in any reports of decisions of the court of appeals which should be prepared by him as reporter; and the State became the absolute owner thereof.

2. By the contract made by the state reporter, the secretary of state, and the comptroller, on behalf of the State, with the appellants, the interest of the State in all matter constituting the reports to be made by Comstock, as reporter, was equitably

Little et al. *v.* Hall et al.

and legally vested in the appellants, for the purpose of being published exclusively by them during the term specified in the contract.

3. The appellants, by the operation of the contract, and of the laws of the State in pursuance of which it was made, became the legal assignees and proprietors of the manuscript matter prepared by Comstock as state reporter, under the ninth section of the law of congress of 1831, which right was exclusive of all others during the continuance of the contract. The exclusive copyright was the exclusive right to publish the manuscripts.

This proposition is a legal deduction from the two former propositions already established.

4. Volume 4 of Comstock's Reports was covered by the contract, as to all the matter that it contained, and so was subject to the exclusive right of the appellants to the manuscript matter prepared by the reporter, and incorporated into the work.

. The expiration of Comstock's term of office did not alter his liability in this respect. True, he could not be required to prepare the decisions for publication, and to furnish notes and references ; but,

1. If he did not do this, he must hold the materials subject to the order of his successor, who must do the labor ; or, if he did use them, and prepare them for publication with notes and references, then the materials and additional matter, being incorporated together, and so prepared according to the contract, must pass, under the contract, to the appellants.

Had Comstock died during his term of office, the trust and bailment would have remained attached to the materials in the hands of his executors. A trust would have resulted to the State a right of action, legal or equitable, to the appellants, when the purpose for which he received the materials failed to take effect. (2 Fonblanque, 118.)

It is wholly unimportant that Comstock might, either while in office, or after going out of office, have acquired similar materials by other means.

1st. As he would in that case have used similar materials, as the basis for labor to be performed for the appellants under the contract, and as he had received an equivalent in advance for that labor, either the labor must be done for their benefit or not at all.

2d. But in point of fact, he received these specified materials as a trustee and bailee, and he must be held to the obligations they created.

These are principles so familiar, and they so fully pervade every branch of jurisprudence, equally the law and equity, that references to authorities would seem superfluous. But for con-

venience, refer to Hill on Trustees, 172, 282, 509, 2 Vesey, 498;
Taylor *v.* Plumer, 3 Maule & Selwyn, 562, 567, 574; Adair *v.*
Shew, 1 Schoale & Lefroy, 262 ; Story on Equity Jurisprudence, § 588, &c., 1,257, 1,258, 1,261; Kane *v.* Bloodgood, 7
Johnson's Ch. Reports, 110, where it is held that every deposit
is a trust, and that every person who receives money to be paid
to another, or to be applied to a particular purpose to which he
does not apply it, is a trustee. So the principle adopted in the
case of a tenant, that he cannot deny the title of his landlord so
long as he retains possession, but must surrender the premises,
and place himself in hostility to his landlord, before he can set
up a title in himself, is founded on the very contract of tenancy
itself. (Nelson, Ch. J. ; Phelan and wife *v.* Kelly, 25 Wend.
392. See also Massey *v.* Davis, 2 Vesey, Jr., 818, 820 ; East
India Co. *v.* Hinchman, 1 Vesey, Jr., 289.)

5. It is in evidence, that Mr. Comstock has commenced, and
still has pending, an action to establish his right to the office of
state reporter, at this time. This claim of continuance in office
is utterly inconsistent with the position of individual and
private right, action, and interest, in regard to volume 4, set up
by the respondents, and is conclusive against him and them,
that volume 4 was prepared by him as state reporter, and subject to the operation of the contract, Exhibit A.— (Lord Chancellor, in 2 Vesey, Jr., 696 ; 1 Swanston, Note (a) to p. 381;
Comyn's Digest, Election, C. I.)

Comstock has made his election to claim and hold the office
of state reporter, with full knowledge of his rights, and he is
bound by it.

6. There is no proof of any acquiescence by the appellants in
the claim of Mr. Comstock, by which he was misled or induced
to incur expense.

Mr. Haven, for defendants in error, made the following
points : —

1. There is no question of copyright or of property in manuscripts involved in the case, and the plaintiffs' claim does not
fall within the provisions of any of the acts of congress, and
this is fatal to the plaintiffs' case.

I. The laws of the United States afford remedies, and the
federal courts have jurisdiction only in favor of the "author" of
a book or "his legal assigns," or the "author or legal proprietor"
of a manuscript. Of course, a book or manuscript belongs pri-
marily under the copyright laws to the author. The plaintiffs
not being the "author," must therefore deduce from him a
"legal" right and title to the book or manuscript, or else they
cannot sustain their bill in the federal courts. If they can allege

Little et al. *v.* Hall et al.

any other rights which have been violated, these must be asserted in the state courts, and on some general principle of
equity or of law. See the opinion of the circuit court, which
proceeds very much on this ground. See also laws of the United
States, 2 sess. 21 Cong. 1831, p. 11, §§ 1, 9; 2 Kent, Comm. (6th
ed.) 379. Clark *v.* Price, 2 Wilson, Ch. R. 157. Jollie *v.* Jaques,
1 Blatch. 618, 627.

II. But the strongest manner in which the plaintiffs can state
their case is to allege that the notes, references, and manuscript
matter composed by Mr. Comstock, and contained in the book
in question, fall within the purview of their contract for the
publication of the State Reports to be composed by the state
reporter. We say the strongest, because this assumes the precise fact controverted, to wit, that Mr. Comstock's labors upon
this book were official and not private. It is not pretended of
course that the plaintiffs, under their contract with the state
officers, could have any interest in the labors of Mr. C., or any
one else as a private reporter.

III. Assuming then this, the best statement of the plaintiffs'
case, to be true, it only follows that the contract with the plaintiffs has been violated, affording perhaps a just ground of action
or claim against the State of New York, or its agents who made
the contract. But it by no means follows that the plaintiffs
have the "legal" title to, or are "the legal proprietors" of the
book or of the manuscript in question. At the time of the contract, no part of the work was composed. The agreement,
therefore, was simply executory, and could vest no title or actual
property in that which had no existence.

2. But the case is not such as has been thus far assumed. In
fact, Mr. Comstock was not in the service of the State. He
was a private citizen, and another person held the office of state
reporter, and received the salary annexed thereto. In fact, also,
Mr. Comstock, at no period of his labors on this book, pretended
to be acting for the State, or the plaintiffs. Being a private citizen, in fact, before he began, he distinctly announced that he
should not prepare the work for the State or the plaintiffs, but
should do it in his private character, and would sell it as his own
property. After he began, he employed the stereotype printer
on his private account. Still later, he invited proposals to buy
the work as his own, and, among others, invited the plaintiffs;
and finally he sold it as his own, thus maintaining from the beginning to the end an open consistency of conduct, a course of
conduct at the time called in question by no one, not even the
plaintiffs, who now seek to appropriate the result of his labors
as their property.

3. What has been thus far said, it is believed, shows that the

plaintiffs, in the most favorable views which can be taken of their case, have no such title as will sustain their bill, nor indeed any title at all, whatever may be said of the defendants, their position, and that of their vendor, Mr. Comstock. We shall now speak of them and of him, especially of his position and relations to the subject, placing the facts and circumstances of the case in the light in which we regard them, and demonstrating, if we can, that, upon every principle of law and justice, the copyright of the book in question is with the defendants.

4. The complainants are equitably estopped from claiming the relief asked for in their bill.

Mr. Justice McLEAN delivered the opinion of the court.

This is an appeal from the decree of the circuit court of the United States for the northern district of New York.

A want of jurisdiction to sustain this appeal was alleged by counsel, as it does not appear from the record that the amount in controversy exceeds the sum of two thousand dollars; but this objection was obviated by an affidavit, which stated that the amount claimed by the plaintiffs exceeds that sum.

This bill was filed under the copyright act, to enjoin the defendants from publishing and selling the fourth volume of Comstock's Reports.

The plaintiffs, who are publishers and booksellers at Albany, New York, represent that, on the 20th of April, 1850, they entered into an agreement with Washington Hunt, comptroller, Christopher Morgan, secretary, and George F. Comstock, reporter, of the State of New York, as required by statute, that they should have the publication, for the term of five years, of the decisions of the court of appeals, and the exclusive benefit of the copyright, to be taken out in behalf of the State, of the notes and references, and other matter furnished by the reporter, connected with said decisions; and that instrument was declared to be an assignment and transfer of the copyright of the matter so published, which should consist of volumes of not less than five hundred pages each.

On the 27th of December, 1847, George F. Comstock was appointed state reporter for three years, and until his successor was appointed and qualified, at a salary of $2,000 per annum. He was to have, under the law, no interest in the reports, but the copyright of his notes, references, and abstracts of arguments, was to be taken in the name of the secretary of state, for the benefit of the people of New York. The law forbade the reporter and all other persons from acquiring a copyright in the reports, but declared they might be republished by any person.

Mr. Comstock's term of office expired on the 27th of December, 1850, and his successor, Henry R. Selden, Esq., was appointed to succeed him on the 17th of January, 1851. Mr. Comstock questioned the validity of his appointment, and the matter was referred to the judges of the court of appeals, then in session at Albany, who decided that Mr. Selden was duly appointed. He took the oath on the 21st of January, 1851, and immediately entered upon the duties of his office.

Mr. Comstock published three volumes of his reports; and having in his hands, at the expiration of his office, opinions of the court to make half or more of another volume, on the suggestion of the judges, and with the consent of Mr. Selden, the opinions of the January term were delivered to him, that he might complete his fourth volume. At the time of this arrangement, he had made no preparation, by notes, &c., for this volume, and did not commence the work until some months afterwards.

After he had made considerable advance in the preparation of this volume, he invited proposals for the purchase of the copyright; and although the plaintiffs, in conversation with him, said they would give as much as any other persons; yet they made no proposal, as they were apprehensive it might affect the contract for the publication of the reports, as above stated. The defendants purchased the copyright, for which they paid $ 2,500. At a large expense, they prepared stereotypes for the work, and printed it.

The plaintiffs, so soon as the volume was published, commenced a republication of it, and filed this bill to enjoin the defendants from selling their edition. Previous to the publication of the third volume of Comstock's Reports, the secretary of state had the copyright of the head-notes, references, &c., entered by the clerk of the district court of the United States, for the benefit of the State; and the complainants had a similar entry made, to secure the copyright to the State, of the fourth volume. This was not done by the secretary of state, as the law directed, and it seems it was not sanctioned by him, as he was doubtful whether he had the power to do so.

The 9th section of the copyright act of the 3d of February, 1831, provides " that any one who shall print or publish any manuscript whatever without the consent of the author or legal proprietor first obtained as aforesaid," " shall be liable to suffer and pay to the author or proprietor all damages occasioned by such injury," &c.

At common law, an author has a right to his unpublished manuscripts the same as to any other property he may possess, and this statute gives him a remedy by injunction to protect this right.

Little et al. v. Hall et al.

A formal transfer of a copyright by the supplementary act of the 30th of June, 1834, is required to be proved and recorded as deeds for the conveyance of land, and such record operates as notice.

After the expiration of his official term, Comstock did not and could not act as reporter. His successor, having been appointed and qualified, discharged the duties of the office and received the salary. As many of the opinions of the court were in the hands of Comstock when his office expired, it might have been made a question whether he could not publish the fourth volume as reporter. This would have given to the State a continuous report of the decisions of the court of appeals, as the law contemplated, with the copyright of the notes, &c., secured for the benefit of the people of the State. If the opinions of the court came into his hands during his continuance in office, there would seem to be no impropriety in his publishing them, as filling up the measure of his term.

But it seems a different view was taken by the late reporter. As his term of office had expired, he was unwilling to publish the fourth volume without compensation for his labor. This changed his relations with the plaintiffs, as that contract was made as reporter, and on the supposition that he would be continued in that office. Under that contract, the complainants had the advantage of publishing the reports for the price stipulated, but any one was at liberty to republish them.

The fourth volume was published by Mr. Comstock as an individual, he having secured to himself the copyright. This probably insured to the purchaser of the right the republication of the work for the term of twenty-eight years. Under the agreements made with the plaintiffs, they had only the profit of their contract.

Whether the plaintiffs may not have a remedy on their contract with Mr. Comstock in the local tribunals of the State, is not a question before us. Our only inquiry is, whether any relief can be given by this court under the copyright act. Where a case arises under that act, we have jurisdiction, though both the parties, as in this case, are citizens of the same State. But if the act do not give the remedy sought, we can only take jurisdiction on the ground that the controversy is between citizens of different States.

Were the plaintiffs the legal proprietors of the manuscript from which the fourth volume of Comstock's Reports was published? The plaintiffs rely upon their contract with the comptroller, the secretary of state, and Mr. Comstock, the reporter. In that contract it is said, " this instrument is declared to be an assignment and transfer of the copyright of the matter so published to the parties of the second part."

This contract was made with Mr. Comstock as reporter, and the plaintiffs agreed to publish the work in volumes containing five hundred pages each, to have them well bound in calf, the types, paper, and the entire execution, to be equal to Denio's Reports; the work to be done under the superintendence of the reporter; copies to be furnished to certain officers of the State, and the publishers were to keep the volumes for sale at two dollars and fifty cents per copy; and in all things they were bound to comply with the statutes of the State.

Comstock could not have published the work as reporter without the consent of the court of appeals, and also the secretary of state, who was required to secure the copyright to the State; and for his labor in preparing the notes, references, &c., and superintending the printing, he could have received no compensation.

Without saying what effect might have been given to the contract had the relation of the parties remained unchanged, we are unable to say, as the case now stands before us, that the plaintiffs were the legal owners of the manuscript within the copyright law. The contract was made by Comstock as reporter, whose duties were regulated by law; and the obligations of the complainants as publishers were embodied in the contract, and were incompatible with any publication on private account.

The entire labor of the work was performed by Comstock, not as reporter, but on his own account. It is, we think, not a case for a specific execution of the contract; and, in effect, that is the object of the bill. This result has not been brought about by the acts of Comstock. He may have been imprudent in extending his contract unconditionally beyond the term of his office. But in doing so he has an apology, if not an excuse, by being associated in making the contract with two high functionaries of the State. Under the changed relation of the parties, the plaintiffs cannot be considered as the legal owners of the manuscript for the purposes of the contract under the copyright law.

Whatever obligation may arise from the contract under the circumstances as against Comstock must be founded on his failure to furnish the manuscripts to the plaintiffs, and of such a case we can take no jurisdiction as between the parties on the record.

The decree of the circuit court is affirmed.

JAMES M. COOPER, PLAINTIFF IN ERROR, v. ENOCH C. ROBERTS.

It has always been a cherished policy with the government of the United States to appropriate the section numbered sixteen in every township of land for the use of schools.

Reservations were made in the sale of other lands which contained salt springs or lead mines, but not in the appropriation of section sixteen for schools.

When the State of Michigan was admitted into the Union, it was upon the condition that every section numbered sixteen in every township of the public lands, and where such section has been sold or otherwise disposed of, other lands equivalent thereto, and as contiguous as may be, shall be granted to the State for the use of schools.

When the lands are surveyed and marked out, the title of the State attaches to No. 16, and if there be no legal impediment, becomes a legal title.

The act of March 1, 1847, (9 Stats. at Large, 146,) providing for the sale of mineral lands, does not include section sixteen, which remains subject to the compact with Michigan.

Under the operation of that act, and also the act of September, 1850, (9 Stats. at Large, 472,) a lease made in 1845, by the secretary of war, of some mineral land (including section sixteen,) did not confer a right upon the mining company, who were the assignees of the lease, to enter their lands and obtain a patent for section sixteen.

It was not necessary for the State of Michigan to obtain the consent of congress before making a sale of the section.

Whether or not the officers of the State of Michigan pursued the laws of the State in effecting the sale, is a question which the occupant of the land cannot raise in this suit.

THIS case was brought up, by writ of error, from the circuit court of the United States for the district of Michigan.

It is stated in the opinion of the court.

It was argued by *Mr. Buel* and *Mr. Vinton*; for the plaintiff in error, and *Mr. Truman Smith*, for the defendant.

Such of the points only as were included within the decision of the court will be noticed.

The counsel for the plaintiff in error first considered the questions which arose relative to the act of 23d June, 1836, granting school lands to Michigan.

1. Is it simply a law in the ordinary meaning of the term, and, as such, repealable at the will of the law-making power, or does it belong to that class of laws which are legislative compacts?

The counsel contended that it was a compact.   5 Stats. at Large, 59, 60.

2. If it be of the latter class, when did it take effect as a compact, and become obligatory on the parties to it?

It became obligatory on 25th July, 1836, that being the day on which the legislature of Michigan passed the act of acceptance.   Revised Code of Michigan for 1846, 748; 2 Wheat. 196; 4 Harrington, 479; 9 Wheat. 469.

15 *

8. Does either possess the power to annul or change any of the essential terms of it, without the assent of the other?

Whether the grant of section 16 operated as a present grant, or was only a promise that it should be granted *in futuro*, makes no difference in the obligation of the United States.

4. Viewed as a compact, what are the rules and principles that govern it? And what are the obligations which the article respecting section 16 imposes on the United States?

The rules and principles which govérn it are those which regulate contracts generally. 1 Pet. Cond. R. 453; 1 Tenn. 819; 8 Ohio, 572.

That the government cannot resume its grant, and that a grant is a contract executed, see New Orleans *v.* De Armas, 9 Pet. 286. There the court say: "It is a principle applicable to every grant, that it cannot affect pre-existing titles." In Terrett *v.* Taylor, 9 Cranch, 43, (same case, 2 Pet. Cond. R. 321,) held, that where the legislature had the authority to make a grant of lands, such grant, when made, vests an indefeasible and irrevocable title. And in Fletcher *v.* Peck, 6 Cranch, 87, Chief Justice Marshall said: "A grant in its own nature amounts to an extinguishment of the right of the grantor, and implies a contract not to reassert that right; a party, therefore, is always estopped by his own grant." Pollard's Lessee *v.* Hogan, 3 How. 212.

Whether a contract be executed or executory, it is equally binding on the parties to it. Fletcher *v.* Peck, 2 Pet. Cond. R. 321.

5. What is the meaning and effect of that clause in the article which provides, that where section sixteen has been sold or otherwise disposed of, other lands equivalent thereto and as contiguous as may be, shall be granted to the State?

This was to provide for prior and not subsequent sales. Assuming that the act of 1836 was only a promise, and that the act of March 1, 1847, embraced section sixteen, still, Michigan has the better right to it. But that act did not dispose of the mineral lands without reference to the school reservation.

1. Instead of the mineral lands being reserved by the act in pursuance to an established policy, it was a primary object of that act to put an end to the policy that had theretofore prevailed of reserving mineral lands from sale, and to dispose of them by sale as soon as practicable, and for the best price that could be obtained.

2. By the true interpretation of the second section of the act, section sixteen in every township of the district is expressly reserved from sale; and also such reservations as the President shall deem necessary for public uses, whether the same are mineral lands or not.

8. As the interpretation of the court conflicts with prior and existing legislative grants and obligations, those grants and obligations are entitled to the benefit of every legal presumption and inference in their favor; and such effect ought not to be given to the law, unless the intent to produce this conflict be expressed in manifest and undoubted language.

4. If the act had, in general terms, directed the sale of all the lands in the district, but was silent as to the lands previously dedicated and granted to schools, it would not have the effect to divert them from this special use.

Mr. Smith, for the defendants in error, contended:—

1. That the article in the act of 1886 was conceived in words of the future tense; and that the plaintiff below could not make out a title without a patent. 13 Pet. 516; 15 How. 438; 1 Qp. Att. Gen. 273; 12 How. 76; 14 ibid. 274.

But if we assume that the first article of this compact operated to vest in the State of Michigan the fee, or a good and perfect title to these lands, then the next question is, whether that title has, through Williams, been transferred to the plaintiff? To answer which we must, as already mentioned, turn our attention both to the laws of the United States and of the State of Michigan.

Michigan had no power to sell this section without the assent of congress. The income of each section is to be applied to the support of schools in the township where it is situated and the State has no power, without the consent of congress, to sell it for the purpose of creating a general fund. 14 How. 274.

This is shown by the numerous acts of congress granting permission to sell. 4 Stats. at Large, 237, 298; 5 ibid. 600; 10 ibid. 6.

The United States, in granting these lands, are the founders of a charity; 9 Cranch. 292; and their assent is necessary for a sale. 4 Wheat. 518.

But, assuming that the State of Michigan has the entire control of the lands, and can sell them without consulting either the United States or the inhabitants of the townships where situated; then the question arises, whether these lands were sold in conformity with the laws of the State?

The argument upon this point is omitted.

Mr. Justice CAMPBELL delivered the opinion of the court.

The plaintiff sued in ejectment to recover a portion of section No. 16, in township No. 50 north, of range 39 west, lying within the mineral district south of Lake Superior, in Michigan.

His case affirms that this section had been appropriated by the

United States to the State of Michigan for the use of schools, in
their compact, by which that State became a member of the
Union; that the governor of Michigan issued, in November,
1851, to Alfred Williams, a patent, evincing a sale of that section under the laws of Michigan, in February, 1851; that he has
a conveyance from the patentee, and that the defendant is a
tenant in possession, withholding the *locus in quo* from him.
The defendant, to support his issue, relies upon a license given
in 1844, by the mineral agent of the United States for that district, empowering the donee to examine and dig for lead, and
other ores, for the term of one year, and within that term to
mark out and define a specific tract of land, not to exceed three
miles square, for mining purposes; and, if he should fulfil this
and other conditions, he was to become entitled to a lease for
three years, with a privilege of one or two renewals, under restrictions. The secretary of war, in September, 1845, executed
a lease for a tract three miles square, which the donee of the
license had selected, and which included the *locus in quo*, and
stipulated to renew it, if congress shall not have passed a law
"directing the sale, or other disposition, of these lands," and if
the lessee shall have complied with all the conditions of the
present lease, and tendered a bond for the fulfilment of the conditions of the new lease, as described in the act. This lease
came to the Minnesota Mining Company by assignment, and
that company in 1847, and from thence till 1851, held possession
of the land described in the declaration, erected valuable improvements, and made successful explorations for copper upon
it. In November, 1850, the company applied to the proper officers of the land-office to enter the land comprised in the lease,
and from thence, till the date of their patent in 1852, the right
of the company to secure the *locus in quo* by entry was in dispute in the land-office of the United States. In September, 1851,
the secretary of the interior determined adversely to the claim
of the company, and in favor of the claim of Michigan; and in
1852, upon proofs that the company had complied with the lease,
while he reaffirmed his conclusions in favor of Michigan, allowed
the entry of the company, but with a reservation of the rights of
Michigan. The section No. 16, aforesaid, was surveyed in the
summer of 1847, and the portion in controversy, in the report of
the geological survey of the district, was returned to the land-
office as containing mines of copper. There was no application
to the department of public lands to renew the lease held by the
company, for the reason (it is said) that the system of letting
mineral lands of this kind had been abandoned, upon the doubts
expressed by the attorney-general, in 1846, of the legality of such
leases. Upon the trial of the cause in the circuit court, the

plaintiff moved the court for instructions to the jury, that, upon the facts, he was entitled to a verdict, and that the defendant's patent was invalid. The court refused the prayer, and told the jury, " that by the act of congress of 1st March, 1847, all the mining lands within the district, reported, were taken out of the operation of the general law for the disposal of the public lands, in pursuance of an established policy to reserve from the ordinary mode of disposing of public lands those that contained valuable salt springs, lead mines, &c., that they might be leased or disposed of to purchasers having full knowledge of their value, by reason of the salt springs or mineral ores they contained, at their full value, for the public benefit. That, by the above act, all the mineral lands reported by the geologist within the district, in pursuance of this settled policy of the government, were appropriated and disposed of without reference to the school reservation, the appropriation of the land being made before the surveys were executed, and before the locality of section 16 could be known. And as it appears from the report of the geologist that the land in controversy contains valuable minerals, and was within the boundaries of the lease under which the Minnesota Company claim, and that they had made large expenditures thereon for mining, were entitled to the right of purchase, as provided in the third section of the above law ; and having paid for the same, it was a disposition of the land which congress had a right to make, and was an exercise of power within the grant. That the setting apart of another section adjacent will satisfy the grant to the State."

Our first inquiry will be into the nature of the right of the State of Michigan to section No. 16 in the townships of that State, and the effect of the discovery of minerals in such a section upon that right. The practice of setting apart section No. 16 of every township of public lands, for the maintenance of public schools, is traceable to the ordinance of 1785, being the first enactment for the disposal by sale of the public lands in the western territory. The appropriation of public lands for that object became a fundamental principle, by the ordinance of 1787, which settled terms of compact between the people and States of the northwestern territory, and the original States, unalterable except by consent. One of the articles affirmed that "religion, morality, and knowledge, being necessary for good government and the happiness of mankind "; and ordained that " schools, and the means of education, should be forever encouraged." This principle was extended, first, by congressional enactment, (1 Stats. at Large, 550, § 6,) and afterwards, in 1802, by compact between the United States and Georgia to the southwestern territory. The earliest development of this article, in practical legislation, is to be found in the organization of the State of Ohio, and the adjustment of its civil polity, according to the ordinance, preparatory to its admission to the Union. Proposals were made to the inhabitants of the incipient State to become a sovereign community, and to accept certain articles as the conditions of union, which, being accepted, were to become obligatory upon the United States. The first of these articles is, " that the section No. 16 in every township, and where such section has been sold, granted, or disposed of, other lands equivalent thereto and most contiguous to the same, shall be granted to the inhabitants of such township, for the use of schools."

A portion of this territory had been encumbered in the articles of cession by the States, and another portion by congress for the fulfilment of public obligations, prior to the ordinance of 1785, and without reference to the school reservations; therefore, uniformity in the appropriation of the section No. 16 was partially defeated. The southwestern territory was similarly burdened in the compact of cession by Georgia, with the fulfilment of antecedent obligations, and similar paramount obligations have arisen in treaties with the Indian tribes who inhabited it. The rights of private property vested in the inhabitants, ceded with Louisiana and Florida, and guaranteed to them in the treaties of cession, created an obstruction to the same policy within them. But the constancy with which the United States have adhered to the policy in the various compacts with the people of the newly-formed States, and the care which congress has manifested to prevent the accumulation of prior obligations which might interrupt it, fully display their estimate of its value and importance. There is, obviously, a definite purpose declared to consecrate the same central section of every township of every State which might be added to the federal system, to the promotion " of good government and the happiness of mankind," by the spread of " religion, morality, and knowledge," and thus, by a uniformity of local association, to plant in the heart of every community the same sentiments of grateful reverence for the wisdom, forecast, and magnanimous statesmanship of those who framed the institutions for these new States, before the constitution for the old had yet been modelled. Has the discovery of minerals of value upon this section been deemed a sufficient cause for its withdrawal from the operation of this policy, and the compacts which develop it?

The ordinance of 1785 dedicated the section No. 16 for the maintenance of public schools, and in each sale of the public lands there was by the same ordinance a reservation of one third part of all gold, silver, lead, and copper mines within the township or lot sold. No reservations were afterwards made of gold, silver, or copper mines until the acts of March, 1847. By the act of March 26, 1804, and the act of March, 1807, every "grant of a salt-spring or a lead-mine thereafter to be made, which had been discovered previously to the purchase from the United States, was to be considered as null and void." (2 Stats. at Large, 279, § 6; 449, § 6.) These statutes indicate a policy to withdraw from sale lands containing these minerals. But the compacts have been made without such a reservation, nor has the usage of the land-office interpolated such an exception to the general grant of the section No. 16 for the use of schools.

The grant of the section No. 16 for the use of schools can be executed without violating the spirit of the legislation upon salt-springs or lead-mines, and, as we have seen, no statute prior to the admission of Michigan to the Union contains an appropriation or reservation of other mineral lands. The State of Michigan was admitted to the Union, with the unalterable condition " that every section 'No. 16,' in every township of the public lands, and where such section has been sold or otherwise disposed of, other lands equivalent thereto, and as contiguous as may be, shall be granted to the State for the use of schools." We agree, that until the survey of the township and the designation of the specific section, the right of the State rests in compact — binding, it is true, the public faith, and dependent for execution upon the political authorities. Courts of justice have no authority to mark out and define the land which shall be subject to the grant. But when the political authorities have performed this duty, the compact has an object, upon which it can attach, and if there is no legal impediment the title of the State becomes a legal title. The *jus ad rem* by the performance of that executive act becomes a *jus in re*, judicial in its nature, and under the cognizance and protection of the judicial authorities, as well as the others. Gaines v. Nicholson, 9 How. 356.

The question now arises whether the act of March 1, 1847, created a legal impediment to the operation of this principle, either by the reservation of the land for public uses, or by its appropriation to superior claims. In March, 1847, congress established a land district in this region for the disposal of the public lands. It directed a geological survey for the ascertainment of those containing valuable ores, whether of lead or copper, and a report to the land-office. It provided for the advertisement and sale of such lands, departing in a measure from that usual mode, as to the length of the notice and the amount of price; and in reference to the remainder of the lands, it applied the usual regulations. To the section containing these directions, (9 Stats. at Large, 146, § 2,) there is added an

tainly of universal interest, but of municipal concern, over which the power of the State is plenary and exclusive. In the present instance, the grant is to the State directly, without limitation of its power, though there is a sacred obligation imposed on its public faith. We think it was competent to Michigan to sell the school reservations without the consent of congress.

The defendant further objects, that the officers of the State violated the statutes of Michigan in selling these lands, after they were known, or might have been known, to contain minerals. Without a nice inquiry into these statutes, to ascertain whether they reserve such lands from sale, or into the disputed fact whether they were known, or might have been known, to contain minerals, we are of the opinion that the defendant is not in a condition to raise the question on this issue. The officers of the State of Michigan, embracing the chief magistrate of the State, and who have the charge and superintendence of this property, certify this sale to have been made pursuant to law, and have clothed the purchaser with the most solemn evidence of title. The defendant does not claim in privity with Michigan, but holds an adverse right, and is a trespasser upon the land, to which her title is attached.

Michigan has not complained of the sale, and retains, so far as the case shows, the price paid for it. Under these circumstances, we must regard the patent as conclusive of the fact of a valid and regular sale on this issue.

Upon the whole record, we think the jury should have been instructed, that if they found the facts thus given in evidence to be true, the plaintiff was entitled to recover the premises in question.

Judgment reversed; cause remanded — a *venire* to issue.

THE SCHOONER FREEMAN, HER TACKLE, &C., CHARLES HICKOX, CLAIMANT AND APPELLANT, v. ALVAH BUCKINGHAM, PHILO BUCKINGHAM, BENJAMIN H. BUCKINGHAM, AND JAMES W. McCULLOK, LIBELLANTS.

Under the admiralty law of the United States, contracts of affreightment, entered into with the master in good faith, and within the scope of his apparent authority as master, bind the vessel to the merchandise for the performance of such contracts, wholly irrespective of the ownership of the vessel, and whether the master be the agent of the general or the special owner.

If the general owner has allowed a third person to have the entire control, management, and employment of the vessel, and thus become owner *pro hac vice*, the general owner must be deemed to consent that the special owner or his master may create liens binding on the interest of the general owner in the vessel, as security for the performance of such contracts of affreightment.

Schooner Freeman, &c. v. Buckingham et al.

But no such implication arises in reference to bills of lading for property not shipped, designed to be instruments of fraud; and they create no lien on the interest of the general owner, although the special owner was the perpetrator of the fraud.

Though in such a case the special owner would be estopped, in favor of a *bonâ fide* holder of the bill of lading, from proving that no property was shipped, yet the general owner is not estopped.

THIS was an appeal from the circuit court of the United States for the northern district of New York.

The case is stated in the opinion of the court.

It was argued by *Mr. Haven*, for the appellant, and *Mr. Ganson*, for the appellee.

Mr. Haven made the following points: —

1. Hickox, the claimant, was the owner of the schooner Freeman. He agreed to sell her to John Holmes for $4,500, payable in five instalments, at various times from June, 1851, to December, 1853. And on such payments being made, and other conditions complied with, he agreed to give John Holmes a good and sufficient bill of sale of her, &c. By this agreement, the property of the claimant in the schooner was not devested. Hilliard on Sales, title "Conditional Sales," pp. 18–23; Barrett *v.* Pritchard, 2 Pick. 512; Ayer *v.* Bartlett, 9 Pick. 156; West *v.* Bolton, 4 Verm. Rep. 558; Herring *v.* Willard, 2 Sandf. Sup. Ct. Rep. 418.

Mem. — Kent, in his Commentaries, (vol. ii. p. 497,) says: "When there is a condition precedent attached to a contract of sale and delivery, the property does not vest in the vendee on delivery, until the performance of the condition, or the seller waives it; and the right continues in the vendor, even against the creditors of the vendee."

He cites Strong *v.* Taylor, 2 Hill, 326, which is in point, and was decided by Justice Nelson.

2. (Second point omitted.)

3. If Hickox, the owner, had directed the master to sign the bills of lading, or given him authority to do so, without having the flour on board, the schooner would have been bound, or the owner would have been estopped from denying the shipment had been made; but in a case where there is no fraud, and the master has only general authority as such, he cannot sign a bill of lading for goods not delivered so as to charge the owner or vessel, even when the bill of lading has been assigned or indorsed, for value. Grant and others *v.* Norway and others, 70 Eng. Com. Law Rep. 664, fully in point.

4. The signatures of Ramsdell, the master, to the bills of lading, were procured by S. Holmes by fraud, by false representations, and by substitution of false papers, amounting to a fel-

ony, or were forged. And as between Holmes and Hickox, the bills were void and of no validity. This being so, the libellants, if they had been indorsees of the bills for value, would take nothing under them, as they make title to the pretended flour only by showing Holmes shipped it; and bills of lading procured by a felony, by fraud, or forgery, are no evidence of that fact, nor do they estop any one. And this case must stand as though S. Holmes forged the bills. King v. Richards, 6 Whart. Penn. Rep. 418; Berkley v. Wattling, &c., 7 Ad. & El. 29, and 34 Eng. Com. Law Rep. 22; Bates v. Todd, 1 Moody & Robinson, 106; Angell on Carriers, §§ 231–337; Abbott on Shipping, 324, 325, original paging; Bates v. Stanton, 1 Duer Sup. Ct. Rep. 79, and cases cited.

5. But the pretended flour was consigned to the libellants as factors of S. Holmes & Co., and not as owners. By the bills, they were not interested in it; the consignment was "for account of S. Holmes & Co." This would have given the libellants no right or title to the flour had it been on board the schooner, and Holmes could have sold it or given a good title to a stranger at any time before it actually reached the libellants. Patten v. Thompson, 5 Maule & Selw. 350; Russell on Factors and Brokers, 202, 203, republished in Law Library, vol. 48; Grove v. Brien, 8 How. 429, 438; Conrad v. Atlantic Ins. Co. 1 Pet. 345, 386; Kinloch v. Craig, 3 Term Rep. 119.

Mr. Ganson made the following points: —

1. The appellees were the consignees of the property, acknowledged in the contracts of affreightment to have been shipped on the schooner, and, as such, had advanced money upon the faith of the shipment therein declared, and the contract therein contained.

2. By such consignment and advance, the appellees acquired a property in the flour mentioned and referred to in those contracts. The delivery of the bills of lading to the appellees, by which the flour was to be delivered to them, and the advancement of money upon the faith thereof, was equivalent to an actual delivery of the property to them, as a security for the advance. Gibson v. Stevens, 8 How. 384; Conard v. Atlantic Insurance Co. 1 Pet. 445; Bank of Rochester v. Jones, 4 Comstock, 497.

3. It is a well-established rule of the maritime law of this country, that the ship is bound to the merchandise, and the well-established practice of our admiralty courts to entertain proceedings *in rem* for the non-performance of contracts of affreightment. The Rebecca, Ware's Rep. 188; New Jersey Steam Navigation Co. v. Merchants' Bank, 6 How. 344; The Volunteer, 1 Sumn. R. 551.

4. If the two contracts in question were made under such circumstances as to bind the vessel, it must answer for their non-performance. The question then arises, were they so made ?

5. Had the master of The Freeman any authority to sign these bills of lading? He was acting under the employment of Sylvanus Holmes. The vessel was in the possession of Holmes. He was running her at his own expense and risk, and for his own benefit. The appellant had not any interest in her earnings, and was not liable for her debts. Sylvanus Holmes, therefore, and not the appellant, was the owner of the vessel, within the signification of that term as used by the maritime law, with reference to determining who is responsible personally for the master's contracts. Reynolds v. Toppan, 15 Mass. 370; Hallet v. Columbian Insurance Co. 8 John. 272; The Phebe, Ware's R. 263; Cutler v. Windsor, 6 Pick. 385.

A person in possession of a vessel, under a conditional contract of purchase, is the owner within the rule referred to. Leonard v. Huntington, 15 John. 298; Hinton v. Hogeboon, 7 John. 308; Thorn v. Hicks, 7 Cowen, 797.

It is upon this rule that the courts hold that a mortgagee out of possession is not liable for supplies; but, if in possession, is liable. McIntyre v. Scott, 8 John. 159; Phillips v. Ledley, 1 W. C. C. R. 226; Miln. v. Spinola, 4 Hill, 177; Champlin v. Butler, 18 John. 169.

Hence, also, a person running a vessel under a charter-party, is liable for its debts, and the general owner is not; and the vessel is liable for the contracts of the charterer's master. Drinkwater v. The Brig Spartan, Ware's R. 149; The Phebe, Ib. 263.

If, under the contract for a conditional sale, there be a forfeiture, and the property reverts, and in case of a charter-party, at its expiration, the vessel goes back to the general owner, subject to the admiralty liens created in the hands of the conditional vendee or charterer.

6. The appellant was a mere mortgagee out of possession, holding, as a mortgagee does, the legal title as a security for the payment of the purchase-money; he, therefore, is not personally responsible for the master's contracts, nor is the vessel liable for the appellant's contracts.

7. The master, therefore, was not the agent of the appellant, but derived all his authority over the vessel, and to make contracts binding upon her, from his employer, Sylvanus Holmes. The master derived his authority from Sylvanus Holmes, in his character as owner, within the signification of that term as used by the maritime law.

8. The contracts of affreightment are such as bind the vessel to answer *in specie* for their non-performance. If they were

16 *

made by the master under such circumstances as to render the
person who was *pro tempore* the owner personally responsible
for their performance, then it follows the vessel is liable also; for
the liability of each proceeds upon the basis that the contracts
are made by one having authority to make them as the agent of
the owner of the vessel. The Druid, 1 W. Rob. 899.

9. Sylvanus Holmes would be liable personally upon the contracts, and the master had authority to make them; for they
were executed by the procurement of, and used by the owner of
the vessel, Sylvanus Holmes, himself.

10. The owner, Sylvanus Holmes, is, therefore, estopped from
denying the master's authority to execute the contracts of
affreightment; and if the master did execute them with the
sanction of the owner of the vessel, his authority to do so cannot be questioned.

11. The master and the owner, Sylvanus Holmes, as against
these appellees, cannot deny even the receipt of the property on
board, for it would be bad faith in them to do so; much less can
they deny the contract to carry the flour, upon the faith of which
contract, as well as upon the shipment and receipts declared in
the bills of lading, the appellees parted with their money. Niles
v. Culver, 8 Barb. S. C. R. 205; Abbot on Shipping, 328, (margin;) Foster *v.* Newland, 21 Wend. 94.

12. The appellant cannot impeach these contracts as between
him and the appellees, —

I. Because he was not the owner of the schooner, at the time
the contracts were made and broken, in the eye of the maritime
law.   That law only recognizes the person who employed the
vessel, and was *pro hac vice* the owner, to determine the liability of the vessel; and if the contracts presented hold good as
against such owner, then the vessel is held to be bound to answer, *in specie*, for the non-performance of the contracts, and the
rights of the general owner are subject to the lien and operation
of the contracts so made.

II. Because he, by the contract with Holmes for the sale of
the vessel, and the delivery of the vessel to him under and in
pursuance of the provisions of that contract, is, in law, deemed
to have taken the risks of its becoming hypothecated, to answer
for the breach of any and all maritime contracts, as well as damages sustained by collision and all other marine torts. If it became so hypothecated, it would, in case of a forfeiture of the
conditional contract, revert to him *cum onere*.

III. Because he allowed Holmes to hold himself out to the
world as the owner of the vessel. He will not, therefore, be permitted to gainsay his acts, especially as against these appellees
who are innocent parties, and have no power to prevent his

wrongful doings. If any one is to suffer, it should be the appellant. The liens of the maritime law should not be in this way avoided when contracted by third parties, in the ordinary course of business, with the master of the vessel, relative to her ordinary employment, under the sanction of the ostensible owner. The rights of parties would be far better guarded, and the interests of commerce be far better subserved, by protecting persons who deal with the ostensible owner of a vessel, than by favoring those who seek to reap the rewards of the business, but avoid its risks and responsibilities under the cover of a contract like that set up in this case.

13. The provisions of the decree, relative to the securities given to Mr. Morrison, are right. This court cannot marshal these assets, and the decree gives the appellant all the rights to the securities that the appellees have, and this is all he can claim in equity.

14. The appellant should be required to pay the costs personally, because the fund realized from the sale of the vessel is insufficient to pay the appellee's claim; and if their costs were decreed to be paid from that fund, it would be in effect to decree that they pay their own costs, which would be manifestly inequitable.

15. The decree should be affirmed, with costs to be paid by the appellant personally.

Mr. Justice CURTIS delivered the opinion of the court.

This is an appeal from a decree of the circuit court of the United States for the northern district of New York.

The appellees filed their libel in the district court, alleging that they are the consignees named in two bills of lading, signed by the master of the Schooner Freeman, which certify that certain quantities of flour had been shipped on board the schooner by S. Holmes and Company, at Cleveland, in the State of Ohio, to be carried to Buffalo, in the State of New York, and there safely delivered — dangers of navigation excepted — to an agent named in the bills of lading, to be by him forwarded to the libellants, in the city of New York. That though this merchandise was thus consigned to the libellants for account of the shipper, yet, on receipt of the bills of lading, and on the faith thereof, the libellants made advances to the shippers. That thirteen hundred and sixty barrels of the flour mentioned in the bills of lading were not delivered at Buffalo, though the delivery was not prevented by any danger of navigation.

In accordance with the prayer of the libel, the schooner was arrested, and the appellant intervened as claimant.

It appeared that, a short time before these bills of lading were signed, the claimant, being the sole owner of the schooner, contracted with John Holmes to sell it to him for the sum of $ 4,000, payable by instalments of $ 500, at different dates; that, by the contract, John Holmes was to take possession of the vessel, and if he should make all the agreed payments, the claimant was to convey to him; that only one instalment had become payable, and had been paid, when the vessel was arrested; that the vessel was delivered to John Holmes, under this contract, and he allowed his son, Sylvanus Holmes, to have the entire control and management of the schooner, which was in his employment, and victualled and manned by him, and commanded by a master whom he appointed, at the time the bills of lading in question were signed.

It further appeared that Sylvanus Holmes transacted business under the style of S. Holmes and Company; that the flour mentioned in these bills of lading as having been shipped by him, and which the master failed to deliver, never was in fact shipped — nor, so far as appeared, had Sylvanus Holmes any such flour; and that he induced the master to sign the bills of lading by fraud and imposition, intending to use them — as he did use them — as instruments to impose on the libellants, and obtain advances on the faith thereof.

To state succinctly the legal relations of these parties, it may be said, that the claimant was the general owner of the vessel; that Sylvanus Holmes was owner *pro hac vice;* that the libellants are holders of the bills of lading, for a valuable consideration parted with, in good faith, on the credit of the bills of lading; but that the bills of lading themselves are not real contracts of affreightment, but only false pretences of such contracts; and the question is, whether they can operate, under the maritime law, to create a lien, binding the interest of the claimant in the vessel.

Under the maritime law of the United States the vessel is bound to the cargo, and the cargo to the vessel, for the performance of a contract of affreightment, but the law creates no lien on a vessel as a security for the performance of a contract to transport cargo, until some lawful contract of affreightment is made, and a cargo shipped under it.

In this case there was no cargo to which the ship could be bound, and there was no contract made, for the performance of which the ship could stand as security.

But the real question is, whether, in favor of a *bona fide* holder of such bills of lading procured from the master by the fraud of an owner *pro hac vice*, the general owner is estopped to show the truth, as undoubtedly the special owner would be. This question does not appear to have been made in the court below, the distinction between the special and general owner not having been insisted on. So large a part of the carrying trade of this country is carried on in vessels of which the masters, or other persons, are owners *pro hac vice*, and the practice of taking security by way of mortgage of vessels has become so common, while, at the same time, the confidence placed in bills of lading as the representatives of property is so great and so important to commerce, that the relative rights of the holders of such documents, and of the general owners and mortgagees of vessels, which are involved in this case, are subjects of magnitude; and the case has received the attentive consideration of the court.

The first and most obvious view which presents itself is, that the claimant in this case is not personally liable on these bills of lading. The master who signed them was not his agent, and they created no contract between him and the consignor or consignee, or any third person who might become their holder. Abbot on Shipping, 42 and note, 57 and note. And it has been laid down by the high court of admiralty in England, (The Druid, 1 Wm. Rob. 399,) that "in all causes of action which may arise during the ownership of the persons whose ship is proceeded against, I apprehend that no suit could ever be maintained against a ship, where the owners were not themselves personally liable, or where their personal liability had not been given up, as in bottomry bonds by taking a lien on the vessel. The liability of the ship, and the responsibility of the owners in such cases, are convertible terms; the ship is not liable if the owners are not responsible; and, *vice versâ*, no responsibility can attach on the owners if the ship is exempt and not liable to be proceeded against." See also The Bold Buccleugh, 2 Eng. Law and Eq. 537.

Though this language is broad enough to cover all cases, whether of contract or tort, it should be observed that the case before the court was one of wilful tort by the master, and that there was no occasion to advert to any distinction between a general and special owner, or to consider whether the interest of the former in the vessel could be bound by the act of the latter, or of the master appointed by him.

We are of opinion that, under our admiralty law, contracts of affreightment, entered into with the master, in good faith, and within the scope of his apparent authority as master, bind the vessel to the merchandise for the performance of such contracts, wholly irrespective of the ownership of the vessel, and whether the master be the agent of the general or the special owner.

In the case of The Phebe, Ware's R. 263, Judge Ware has traced the power of the master to bind the vessel by contracts of affreightment to the maritime usages of the middle ages. So far as respects such contracts made by the master in the usual course of the employment of the vessel, and entered into with a party who has no notice of any restriction upon that apparent authority, those maritime usages may safely be considered to make part of our law; though we should hesitate to declare that their effect has not been modified by our own commercial law, which has recognized interests and rights unknown to the commercial world when those usages obtained. And we desire to be understood as not intending to say that all contracts made by a master within the usual scope of his employment, which, by the ancient maritime law, would have created liens on the vessel, will now do so, in such manner as to bind the interests in the vessel of parties whom he does not represent as agent. For the ground on which we rest the authority of a master, who is either special owner or agent of the special owner, is, that when the general owner intrusts the special owner with the entire control and employment of the ship, it is a just and reasonable implication of law that the general owner assents to the creation of liens binding upon his interest in the vessel, as security for the performance of contracts of affreightment made in the course of the lawful employment of the vessel. The general owner must be taken to know that the purpose for which the vessel is hired, when not employed to carry cargo belonging to the hirer, is to carry cargo of third persons; and that bills of lading, or charter-parties, must, in the invariable regular course of that business, be made, for the performance of which the law confers a lien on the vessel.

He should be considered as contemplating and consenting that what is uniformly done may be done effectually; and he should not be allowed to say that he did not expect, or agree, that third persons, who have shipped merchandise and taken bills of lading therefor, would thereby acquire a lien on the vessel which he has placed under the control of another, for the very purpose of enabling him to make such contracts to which the law attaches the lien. See The Cassius, 2 Story, 93; Webb v. Pierce, 1 Curtis, 107.

But if this be the ground upon which the interest of the general owner is subjected to liens, by the act of those who are not so his agents as to bind him personally, this ground wholly fails in the case at bar.

There can be no implication that the general owner consented that false pretences of contracts, having the semblance of bills of lading, should be created as instruments of fraud; or that, if so created, they should in any manner affect him or his property. They do not grow out of any employment of the vessel; and there is as little privity or connection between him, or his vessel, and such simulated bills of lading, as there would be between him and any other fraud or forgery which the master or special owner might commit.

Nor can the general owner be estopped from showing the real character of the transaction, by the fact that the libellants advanced money on the faith of the bills of lading; because this change in the libellant's condition was not induced by the act of the claimant, or of any one acting within the scope of an authority which the claimant had conferred. Even if the master had been appointed by the claimant, a wilful fraud committed by him on a third person, by signing false bills of lading, would not be within his agency. If the signer of a bill of lading was not the master of the vessel, no one would suppose the vessel bound; and the reason is, because the bill is signed by one not in privity with the owner. But the same reason applies to a signature made by a master out of the course of his employment. The taker assumes the risk, not only of the genuineness of the signature, and of the fact that the signer was master of the vessel, but also of the apparent authority of the master to issue the bill of lading. We.say the apparent authority, because any secret instructions by the owner, inconsistent with the authority with which the master appears to be clothed, would not affect third persons. But the master of a vessel has no more an apparent unlimited authority to sign bills of lading, than he has to sign bills of sale of the ship. He has an apparent authority, if the ship be a general one, to sign bills of lading for cargo actually shipped; and he has also authority to sign a bill of sale of the ship, when, in case of disaster, his power of sale arises. But the authority in each case, arises out of, and depends upon, a particular state of facts. It is not an unlimited authority in the one case more than in the other; and his act, in either case, does not bind the owner, even in favor of an innocent purchaser, if the facts upon which his power depended did not exist; and it is incumbent upon those who are about to change their condition, upon the faith of his authority, to ascertain the existence of all the facts upon which his authority depends.

Though the law on this point seems to have been considered in Westminster Hall not to have been settled, when the eighth edition of Abbot on Shipping was published, in 1849, (Ab. on Sh. 325,) we take it to be now settled, by the cases of Grant v. Norway, 2 Eng. Law and Eq. 337; Hubbersty v. Ward, 18 ibid. 551; and Coleman v. Riches, 29 ibid. 823.

The same law was much earlier laid down in Walter v. Brewer, 11 Mass. 99.

But the case at bar is much stronger in favor of the claimant, because the master was not appointed by him, and the signature of the bills of lading was obtained by the fraud of the special owner.

In Gracie *v.* Palmer, 8 Wheat. 605, the question came before this court, whether the charterer and the master could, by a contract made with a shipper who acted in good faith, destroy the lien of the owner on the goods shipped, for the freight due under the charter-party. It was held they could not; and the decision is placed upon the ground of want of authority to do the act. It was admitted by the court that the charterer and master might impose on a shipper in a foreign port, by making him believe the charterer was owner, and the master his agent. But it was considered that so far as respected the owner, the risk of loss from such imposition lay on the shipper. So, in this case, even if the special owner and the master had combined to issue these simulated bills of lading, they could not create a lien on the interest of the general owner of the vessel. Upon the actual posture of the facts, the master having been defrauded by the special owner into signing the bills of lading, it would be difficult to distinguish them, so far as respects the rights of the claimant, from bills forged by the special owner. On these grounds, we are of opinion that, upon the facts as they appear from the evidence in the record, the maritime law gives no lien on the schooner; that the claimant is not estopped from alleging and proving those facts; and, consequently, that the decree of the court below must be reversed, and the cause remanded, with directions to dismiss the libel, with costs.

THE WIDOW AND HEIRS OF BENJAMIN POYDRAS DE LA LANDE, PLAINTIFFS IN ERROR, *v.* THE TREASURER OF THE STATE OF LOUISIANA.

The laws of Louisiana impose a tax of ten per cent upon what an heir, legatee, or donee may receive upon the succession to an estate of a person deceased, where such heir, legatee, or donee is not domiciliated in Louisiana, and is not a citizen of any State or Territory of the Union. They also provide that the executor, &c., shall pay the tax.

Where the state court decided that this tax was properly imposed upon the succession accruing to persons who were born in France, had always lived in France, without ever having been in Louisiana, this is not such a decision as can be reviewed by this court under the 25th section of the judiciary act.

No question was made in the court below that these laws conflicted with any provision of the constitution of the United States. In a petition for rehearing, several grounds were alleged as reasons for granting it; but the record does not show why the court refused it.

THIS case was brought up from the supreme court of Louisiana, by a writ of error issued under the 25th section of the judiciary act.

The case is stated in the opinion of the court.

It was argued by *Mr. Janin*, for the plaintiffs in error, and *Mr. Benjamin*, for defendant.

Mr. Janin made the following points : —

It is important to ascertain what points the supreme court of Louisiana really decided, for upon this depends the jurisdiction of this court. The decision turned principally upon the construction of the statutes of 1842 and 1850, and sums up a review of these statutes in the following words: " From this view of the statute, we conclude that the tax attaches not only to property falling to alien heirs, who are non-residents, but also to the property falling to citizens of our own State who reside abroad."

(*Mr. Janin* contended that under the 911, 912, 918, and 914th articles of the Code of Practice, a decision upon a petition for rehearing could be reviewed by this court.)

The Louisiana statutes, as expounded by the supreme court of the State, are contrary to two provisions of the constitution of the United States, namely: —

" Art. IV. sect. 2. The citizens of each State shall be entitled to all privileges and immunities of citizens in the several States."

" Art. I. sect. 8. The congress shall have power to regulate commerce with foreign nations, and among the several States, and with the Indian tribes." 4 Wash. C. C. R. 380 ; Story on the Constitution, § 1806 ; 9 Wheat. 190.

Mr. Benjamin contended that the record did not show that the questions stated in the 25th section arose in the case, much less that they were decided as that section requires. A petition for rehearing can bring up no new question. 6 La. R. 198 ; 19 La. R. 48 ; 1 Rob. R. 830 ; 1 Annual, 406.

The defence in the state court assumed the position, that the state law, properly construed, applies only to heirs alien and non-resident, and alleged that the defendants were citizens of Louisiana and residents. The court, without determining whether defendants were citizens of Louisiana or not, held, that the proper construction of the law embraced them as non-residents, whether they were citizens of Louisiana or of France.

The alleged error is that, if the defendants are citizens of Louisiana, and if the court construed the statute aright, then the statute is unconstitutional. But the court below did not decide the defendants to be citizens of Louisiana, and this court therefore cannot examine the first question suggested, and it is equally without power to examine the second question, being without jurisdiction to revise a decision of a state court for error in the construction of a state statute.

The question of the jurisdiction of this court, in cases similar to the present, was again very recently passed on by the court, and its former decisions reviewed and affirmed, in a case from Louisiana, which cannot be distinguished in principle from the one now under consideration.

Grand Gulf Co. *v.* Marshall, 12 How. 166, and other cases still later, affirm the previous jurisprudence. Lawler et al. *v.* Walker et al. 14 How. 158; Robertson *v.* Coulter, 16 How. 106.

Mr. Justice McLEAN delivered the opinion of the court.

This is a writ of error to the supreme court of Louisiana.

The treasurer of the State of Louisiana instituted a suit in the second district of New Orleans, claiming, in behalf of the State, a tax of ten per cent on the amount of the succession of Benjamin Poydras de la Lande, inherited by persons alleged to be citizens and residents of France.

This tax was claimed by virtue of two acts of the legislature. of Louisiana, one passed on the 26th of March, 1842, which provided " that each and every person, not being domiciliated in this State, and not being a citizen of any State or Territory of the Union, who shall be entitled — whether as heir, legatee, or donee — to the whole or any part of the succession deceased, whether such person shall have died in this State or elsewhere, shall pay a tax of ten per cent on all sums, or on the value of all property which he may actually receive, or so much thereof as is situated in this State."

The 76th section of the act of March 21, 1850, provides, that "every executor, curator, tutor, or administrator, having the charge or administration of succession property belonging in whole or in part to a person residing out of this State, and not being a citizen of any other State or Territory of the United States, shall be bound to retain in his hands the amount of the tax imposed by law, and to pay over the same to the state treasurer."

Benjamin Poydras, an old and wealthy naturalized citizen of Louisiana, having died in 1851, in France, leaving a widow and three minor children in that country, the treasurer of the State of Louisiana filed, on the 27th of February, 1852, a petition in the second district court of New Orleans against the widow, as tutrix of her minor children, claiming ten per cent on the amount of the property left by the deceased in Louisiana. The grounds for this claim, as alleged in the petition, are, "that the said tutrix, as well as her said minor children, are all citizens of France, and reside in that country."

The answer of the defendants denied their liability for the payment of the tax, alleging that they were citizens of the State of Louisiana, legally domiciliated therein. The lower court gave judgment for the State, which judgment, on appeal, was affirmed by the supreme court of the State.

This being a writ of error, under the 25th section of the judiciary act of 1789, the defendant in error insists that there is no jurisdiction. That section provides, that on " a final judgment or decree in any suit in the highest court of law or equity in which a decision in the suit could be had, where is drawn in question the validity of a treaty or statute of, or an authority exercised under, any State, on the ground of their being repugnant to the constitution or laws of the United States, and the decision is in favor of such their validity, may be re-examined, and reversed or affirmed in the supreme court of the United States, upon a writ of error.

In the petition, the respondents are alleged to be citizens and residents of France. In their answer, they allege, that the deceased, in the year 1804, settled in Louisiana, and became a citizen of the United States, and maintained his residence and citizenship in Louisiana; that his last visit to France was intended to be temporary, but he was involved in lawsuits in that country for years, though he intended to return to Louisiana, and would have done so, had he not died. During his absence he acquired a large amount of property in Louisiana, and he continued to express his determination to return to that country during his life. And they alleged that they were citizens of the State of Louisiana.

In the final judgment in the lower court, the judge says: —

" The deceased was a French subject, who was born and died in France; and his heirs, now residents and natives of France, who have never been in this State, claim his estate. It appears to me that they came within the purview of the act of 1842." A judgment for $45,208.80 and costs of suit was entered against the defendants. An appeal was taken to the supreme court of the State, where the judgment of the inferior court was affirmed.

It does not appear from the pleadings, and procedure in the inferior or in the supreme court, that the question was made whether the acts of 1842 and 1850 were in conflict with any provision of the constitution of the United States.

The supreme court held, that the tax in question "attaches not only to property falling to alien heirs, who are non-residents, but also to the property falling to citizens of our own State residing abroad." And they say the object of the law is to discourage absenteeism. The court held that neither the act of

1842 nor that of 1850 is repugnant to the 187th article of the constitution of the State, of 1845.

Up to the final judgment in this case, in the supreme court of Louisiana, no question was raised by the counsel nor decided by the court, involving the constitutionality of either of the acts before us, under the constitution of the United States. Indeed, this is not asserted by the counsel; but it is contended that such a question was raised and decided on the petition for a rehearing. If this were admitted, does it bring the case within the 25th section? It must appear from the record, that one or both the acts referred to are not only repugnant to some provision of the constitution of the United States, but that the point was presented to the court, and it decided in favor of the unconstitutional act or acts.

The points, which the defendants requested the court to review, were:—

1. That a citizen of Louisiana, whether native or naturalized, who absents himself, even for temporary purposes, from the State for more than two years, thereby loses his domicile and residence, and is bound to pay to the State ten per cent on any inheritance, legacy, or donation to which he may be entitled as intestate or under a will, if the estate of which he is heir and legatee is opened in the State after his aforesaid absence of more than two years; but that he would not be liable to this tax, if during his absence he had become a citizen of another State or Territory of the Union.

2. That the act of March 26, 1842, which establishes the tax of ten per cent upon foreign non-resident heirs, is not contrary to the 12th article of the constitution of 1845.

8. That Benjamin Poydras, by his prolonged residence in France, during the latter part of his life, had lost his domicile in Louisiana.

In neither of the above grounds is there an intimation of any conflict with the federal constitution in the decision. Whether there was a repugnancy between the tax-acts and the state constitution, is a matter which belongs, exclusively, to the state court.

The court refused the rehearing, on what ground does not appear.

This court can exercise no appellate power over the supreme court of a State, except in a few specified cases; and the ground of jurisdiction must be stated with precision, and the ruling of the court to bring the case under the 25th section must appear, on the record, to have been against the right claimed. Any reason assigned for a rehearing or a new trial is not sufficient.

The case is dismissed for want of jurisdiction.

THE HEIRS OF GENERAL LAFAYETTE, PLAINTIFFS IN ERROR, v. JOSEPH KENTON ET AL. THE HEIRS OF GENERAL LA-FAYETTE, PLAINTIFFS IN ERROR, v. EDWARD C. CARTER ET AL.

By acts of congress passed in 1803 and 1805, General Lafayette was authorised to locate land warrants upon any lands which were the property of the United States; to
have surveys executed, and to obtain a certificate from the register of the land office,
that the land surveyed was not rightfully claimed by any other person.
The location was made upon land in the vicinity of New Orleans, and included land
which was vacant, and also land which was claimed by individuals. But the entry
contained no exterior boundaries.
It was not until 1825 that the location was surveyed; and then there were marked
upon the plat such lands as were vacant, and such as were claimed by individuals.
The register certified that the lands contained in the survey were vacant, with the
exception of the parts designated as private claims; and a patent was issued for
such vacancies, having the survey attached to it.
These claims of individuals having been confirmed by operation of acts of congress,
are excepted from the grant of the patent. Apart from the documents which establish the titles of these individual claimants, the patent shows that nothing was
granted except the lands which were marked as vacant.

THESE cases were brought up by writ of error from the circuit court of the United States, for the eastern district of Louisiana.

They were argued by *Mr. Taylor*, for the plaintiffs in error, and *Mr. Benjamin* and *Mr. Janin*, for defendants.

The arguments of counsel were so connected with the maps which were produced in court, that it would be difficult to present to the reader a clear explanation of them without the map.

Mr. Justice CATRON delivered the opinion of the court.

By an act of 1803, congress authorized the secretary of war, to issue to Major-General Lafayette land warrants, amounting in all, to 11,520 acres. By the act of March 2, 1805, he was author-ized to locate his warrants on any lands, "the property of the United States," within the Orleans territory; the locations to be made with the register of a land-office established there, and the surveys were to be executed under the authority of the sur-veyor of the public lands south of Tennessee. Patents were directed to be issued, when surveys of the respective tracts were presented to the secretary of the treasury, "together with a cer-tificate of the proper register, (in each case,) stating that the land surveyed was not rightfully claimed by any other person." And the act further provided, that no location should include any improved lands or lots.

By an act passed in 1806, entries were authorized for any quantity of land not less than five hundred acres.

17 *

On the 26th day of November, 1807, General Lafayette (by his agent) located 503 acres, calling for "vacant land situated beyond the line of six hundred yards lately abandoned by congress to the corporation of the said city, round the fortifications of the same."

Owing to the unsettled state of private land claims near the city of New Orleans, the location was not surveyed until March, 1825, when the principal surveyor certified to the register that he had surveyed for General Lafayette, "a tract of land situate in the parish of Orleans, beyond the line of six hundred yards abandoned by congress to the corporation of the city of New Orleans, having such courses, distances, boundaries, and contents as are represented in the annexed plat of survey."

Pursuant to the act of March 2, 1805, the register certified that "the lands contained in the survey returned to his office were vacant, with the exception of the parts designated as private claims."

On the 4th day of July, 1825, a patent issued, which, by its recitals, describes the out-boundaries of the 503 acres, and then the granting clause declares that there is "granted to said General Lafayette, and to his heirs, all such PARTS OR PARCELS of the tract of land above described as are 'not legally claimed' by any other person or persons whomsoever."

From the recitals in the patent, it might be inferred that General Lafayette's entry had the same boundaries as described in the patent; the fact, however, is, that the description contained in the patent is the first description, in words, of the land claimed under the entry; the patent being, in fact, founded on the figurative plan, which is attached to and forms an essential part of the patent, and to this plan we are forced to look for a certificate of the register, "stating that the land is not rightfully claimed by any other person."

Until the certificate was made, the secretary was not authorized to issue the patent, and, to enable the register to make the proper certificate, he was compelled to delay till congress, either directly or indirectly, through commissioners, ascertained the rightful claims of others lying within the limits supposed to be covered by General Lafayette's location; and as the location, in the form it was surveyed, (and no doubt as claimed to exist when it was made,) notoriously interfered with claims of different private individuals, and covered possessions protected by the act of March 3, 1807, no reason could be urged, on behalf of the locator, why a survey and certificate should be made and returned to the secretary of the treasury before the private claims were duly ascertained; it being the obvious object of the locator to obtain "the parts or parcels of land," within his out-bound-

Craighead et al. *v.* J. E. and A. Wilson.

aries, that should chance to be found vacant, after the private claims had been acted on and confirmed, or rejected.

As respected these private rights and pretensions, congress reserved to itself the power to deal with them by such means as were deemed appropriate; and by the course of action it prescribed, General Lafayette was compelled to abide. The case of West *v.* Cochran (17 How. 408) lays down the governing rule on the subject.

The courts of justice have no power to revise what congress, or commissioners acting by its authority, have done in their confirmations of the titles here assailed. Against the United States these confirmations are conclusive, and they are equally so against General Lafayette; this being a condition imposed on his location by the act of 1805, above quoted, and which is affirmed in his patent. Titles, covering the lands sought to be recovered by the petitioners below, were confirmed to others before the patent to General Lafayette was issued, which appears by documents found in the record. But, if these documents were wanting, we are of opinion that the patent, and the figurative plan, with the designations on it, where the private confirmed titles and the vacant lands are laid down on the plot, and noted as private property or as vacant, furnish evidence that nothing passed by the grant but the lands noted as being vacant. It is, therefore, ordered that the judgment in the circuit court be affirmed in the respective cases cited in the caption.

JOHN B. CRAIGHEAD ET AL., APPELLANTS, *v.* JOSEPH E. AND ALEXANDER WILSON.

Where a case in chancery was referred to a master to state accounts between the plaintiffs and defendants, to ascertain how much property remained in the hands of the latter, and how much had been sold, with the prices; to make allowances to the defendants for payments made or incumbrances discharged, and to ascertain what might be due from either defendant to the plaintiffs, this was not such a final decree as could be appealed from to this court.

Although the decree settles the equities of the bill, yet the amount to be distributed amongst the parties depends upon the facts to be reported by the master; and until the allotment to each one of the share to which he might be entitled, the decree cannot be considered as final.

THIS was an appeal from the circuit court of the United States, for the eastern district of Louisiana.

There were briefs filed in this case by *Mr. Robertson* and *Mr. Taylor*, for the appellants, and by *Mr. Benjamin* and *Mr. Janin*, for the appellees; but the question of jurisdiction was not raised.

Craighead et al. *v.* J. E. and A. Wilson.

Mr. Justice McLEAN delivered the opinion of the court.

This is an appeal from the circuit court of the United States for the eastern district of Louisiana.

During the opening argument of this case, doubts were suggested whether the decree of the circuit court was final within the act of congress, and the attention of the court was directed to that question.

The complainants filed their bill in the circuit court, claiming as heirs a part of the property of Joseph and Lavinia Erwin, deceased. Erwin died in 1829, in the parish of Iberville, having made his will in 1828. His property, real and personal, was much embarrassed; the persons claiming an interest in the succession were numerous; and, from the loose manner in which the property was managed by the testator in his lifetime, and by those who succeeded him, great difficulty was found in the distribution of the estate.

The circuit court, having ascertained the heirship of the claimants and their relative rights in the succession, referred the matter to a special master, "to take an account of the successions of the said Joseph Erwin, sen., Joseph Erwin, jr., and Lavinia Erwin, in so far as it may be necessary to state the accounts between the plaintiffs and the heirs at law, defendants in this suit, to ascertain the property in kind that remains in the possession and control of either of the defendants, except Adams and Whiteall, as aforesaid — what has been sold, and the prices of the same and the profits thereof; and he will report all the encumbrances that have been discharged by either of the defendants on the same, and make to them all just allowances for payments, and permanent and useful improvements, and just expenses, and to ascertain what may be due to the said plaintiffs from either defendant; and the said master may make a special report of any matters that may be requisite to a full adjustment of the questions in the cause."

By the 22d section of the judiciary act of 1789, it is provided, that final decrees of the circuit court, where the amount in controversy exceeds two thousand dollars, may be brought before this court by an appeal. The law intended that one appeal should settle the matter in controversy between the parties; and this would be the result in all cases where the appeal is taken on a final decree, unless it should be reversed or modified by this court.

The cases are numerous which have been dismissed on the ground that the appeals were taken from interlocutory decrees. In Perkins *v.* Fourniquet, 6 How. 206, it was held, " where the circuit court decreed that the complainants were entitled to two sevenths of certain property, and referred the matter to a master in chancery, to take and report an account of it, and then reserved all other matters in controversy between the parties until the coming in of the master's report," was not a final decree on which an appeal could be taken. And, in the same volume, 209, Pulliam et al. v. Christian, where "a decree of the circuit court, setting aside a deed made by a bankrupt before his bankruptcy; directing the trustees under the deed to deliver over to the assignee in bankruptcy all the property remaining undisposed of in their hands, but without deciding how far the trustees might be liable to the assignee for the proceeds of sales previously made and paid away to the creditors; directing an account to be taken of these last-mentioned sums in order to a final decree," was held not to be a final decree, and the appeal was dismissed.

The above cases are sufficient to show the grounds on which appeals in chancery are dismissed. To authorize an appeal, the decree must be final in all matters within the pleadings, so that an affirmance of the decree will end the suit. To apply this test, in all cases, cannot be difficult.

In no legal sense of the term, is the decree now before us a final one. The basis of the decree, embracing the equities in the bill, is found, but the distribution among the parties in interest depends upon the facts to be reported by the master. It is his duty, under the interlocutory decree, to balance the equities by ascertaining what has been expended on the property, and what has been received by each of the claimants; and also every other matter which should have a bearing and influence in the distribution of the pr ert . Until the court shall have acted upon this report and sanctiyned it, giving to each of the devisees his share of the estate under the will, the decree is not final.

There may be cases in which the attention of the court has not been drawn to the character of the decree appealed from; but such an inadvertence cannot constitute an exception to the rule. The decision of the court, under the law, establishes the rule which must govern in appeals from the circuit courts.

The case of Whiting v. Bank of the United States, 13 Peters, 6, is supposed to conflict with the above rule; but that was a decree of foreclosure and sale of the mortgaged premises. This was held to be a final decree, the order for sale having an effect similar to that of an execution on a judgment.

The case of Michaud et al. v. Girod et al. 4 How. 503, was an interlocutory decree in the circuit court, and which case, being appealed, was heard and decided by this court. But, from the report, there appears to have been no exception taken to the appeal, and it may be presumed to have escaped the notice of the court.

Abbott et ux. *v.* Essex Company.

The case of Forgay et al. *v.* Conrad, 6 How. 201, was an appeal from an interlocutory decree, which was sustained, though objected to. But this decision was made under the peculiar circumstances of that case. The decree was, that certain deeds should be set aside as fraudulent and void; that certain lands and slaves should be delivered up to the complainant; that one of the defendants should pay a certain sum of money to the complainant; that the complainant should have execution for these several matters; that the master should take an account of the profits of the lands and slaves, and also an account of certain money and notes, and then said decree concluded as follows, viz.: "And so much of said bill as contains or relates to matters hereby referred to the master for a report, is retained for further decree in the premises," &c.

It will be observed, that two deeds for lots in New Orleans were declared to be null and void, and certain slaves owned by Forgay, one of the appellants, were directed to be sold on execution, as also the real estate and the proceeds distributed among the bankrupt's creditors; and if the defendants principally interested could not take an appeal until the return of the master, their property, under the decree, would have been disposed of beyond the reach of the appellate court, so that an appeal would be useless. This was the principal ground on which the appeal was sustained, although it was stated that this part of the decree was final.

The court say: "The decree upon these matters might and ought to have awaited the master's report; and when the accounts were before the court, then every matter in dispute might have been adjudicated in one final decree; and if either party thought himself aggrieved, the whole matter would be brought here and decided in one appeal, and the object and policy of the acts of congress upon this subject carried into effect."

The decree before us is not final, consequently it must be dismissed.

----- · ------- · -----

JAMES A. ABBOTT AND HANNAH K., HIS WIFE, DEMANDANTS AND PLAINTIFFS IN ERROR, *v.* THE ESSEX COMPANY, TENANTS.

The following clause in a will, namely: "I give to my two sons, viz. John and Jacob, all my lands, &c., live stock, &c., tools, &c., bonds, &c., to be equally divided between them, and the executor is ordered to pay debts out of that part of the estate. *Item.* — It is my will that if either of my said sons, John and Jacob, should happen to die without any lawful heirs of their own, then the share of him who may first decease shall accrue to the other survivor and his heirs," gave an estate in fee simple to John and Jacob, and the share of the one who first died without issue passed over to the other son by way of executory devise.

THIS case was brought up by writ of error from the circuit court of the United States for the district of Massachusetts.

The part of the will which gave rise to the question is stated in the opinion of the court.

It was admitted by the parties that said testator died in the year 1775; that his will was duly proved August 5, 1776; that his two sons, John Kittredge and Jacob Kittredge, survived him; that said John Kittredge died in the year 1826, never having been married; that said Jacob Kittredge died in the lifetime of his brother John, on July 15, 1807, leaving the following children, namely: John Kittredge, his oldest child, who died, without ever having had issue, on the 10th of January, 1823; Jacob Kittredge, his next oldest child, who died December 18, 1831, having had issue one child, who is the demandant, Hannah Kittredge Abbott; Thomas W. Kittredge, his next child, who is now alive; Hannah Kittredge, his next child, who died intestate on the 28th of October, 1815, never having had issue; George W. Kittredge, his next child, who died July 4, 1836, intestate, having had issue one child, Jacob Kittredge, who is now alive; and William H. Kittredge, his last child, who died intestate on the 1st of October, 1849, never having had issue. The marriage of the demandants was also admitted, and that the surviving son of Jacob Kittredge, the devisee named in said will, and also his surviving grandchild, had, before the commencement of the suit, released and conveyed to demandants all their interest and title in the demanded premises.

The demandants thereupon submitted, and requested the judge to instruct the jury, that, by the said will of John Kittredge, his two sons John and Jacob, therein named, took and became seised as to the real estate therein devised to them in equal moieties of an estate tail general, with cross remainder in fee-simple, it being material and necessary, to enable the demandants to maintain the issue on their part, to prove that estates tail as aforesaid were so devised by the said will. But the judge refused so to instruct the jury, but did instruct them that, under said will, the testator's said sons, John Kittredge and Jacob Kittredge, took and became seised of an estate in fee simple, and that the share of the one of the said sons who should first die without issue in the lifetime of the other of said sons, would in that event go over to said other son by way of executory devise.

A writ of error brought up this ruling for review.

The case was argued by *Mr. Abbott* and *Mr. Fessenden*, for the plaintiffs in error, and *Mr. Merwin* and *Mr. Loring*, for the defendants.

The points made by the counsel for the plaintiffs in error were the following, namely: —

The plaintiffs in error claim that the estate which the two sons, John and Jacob, took under this will were estates in fee tail general, with cross remainders in fee-simple.

Rule of Interpretation.

The rule by which this court is to be governed, in the interpretation of this will, is the rule of law which has been established by the highest judicial tribunal of the State or district in which the land lies, or the suit originated. Hinde *v.* Vattier, 5 Pet. U. S. Rep. 397; Jackson *v.* Chew, 12 Wheat. 153; Bank of the United States *v.* Daniels, 12 Pet. 83; Webster *v.* Cooper, 14 How. 488.

Propositions.

1. The testator, by the first clause in the will, gave to John and Jacob an estate for life only; and, although he directed the executor, John, to see that the debts and legacies were paid out of that part of the estate given to John and Jacob, this was a charge upon the estate or fund given to John and Jacob, and not upon the sole executor personally; and therefore the charge does not enlarge the estate for life to an estate in fee-simple. 2 Jarman on Wills, 126, and note; Denn *v.* Slater, 5 D. & E. 335; Doe *v.* Owens, 1 Barn. & Adolph. 318; Denn *v.* Mellor, 5 D. & E. 558; Clark *v.* Clark, 1 Crompt. & Mees. 89; Lithgow *v.* Kavanagh, 9 Mass. 161; Cook *v.* Holmes, 11 Mass. 528; Wait *v.* Belding, 24 Pick. 129; Parker *v.* Parker, 5 Met. 134; Gardner *v.* Gardner, 3 Mason, 209; Legh *v.* Warrington, 1 Br. Parl. C. 511; Williams *v.* Chitty, 3 Ves. jr. 552; Miles *v.* Leigh, 1 Atk. 573.

2. Having given each of his two sons an estate for life, the next item in the will (namely, the proviso " that if either of said sons, John or Jacob, should happen to die without any lawful heirs of their own ") enlarges the estate for life to an estate tail in each of the two sons; and, by the use of such language, the testator intended an indefinite failure of issue. Purefoy *v.* Rogers, 2 Saunders, 380; Sonday's Case, 9 Coke, 127; King *v.* Rumball, Cro. Jac. 448; Chaddock *v.* Crowley, Cro. Jac. 695; Holmes *v.* Meynel, T. Ray. 452; Forth *v.* Chapman, 1 P. Will. 663; Brice *v.* Smith, Willes's Rep. 1; Hope *v.* Taylor, 1 Burr. 268; Doe *v.* Fonnereau, Doug. 504; Denn *v.* Slater, 5 Term Rep. 335; Doe *v.* Rivers, 7 Ibid. 276; Doe *v.* Ellis, 9 East, 382; Goodridge *v.* Goodridge, 7 Mod. 453; Tenney *v.* Agar, 12 East, 253; Kirkpatrick *v.* Kirkpatrick, 13 Ves. jr. 476; Barlow *v.* Slater, 17 Ves. 479; Romily *v.* James, 6 Taunt. 263; Atkinson *v.* Hutchinson, 3 .P. Will. 258; Sheffield *v.* Orrery, 3 Atk. 282;

Lampley v. Blower, Ibid. 896; Shepperd v. Lessingham, Amb. 122; Gordon v. Adolphus, 3 Bro. P. C. 806; Geering v. Shenton, Cowper, 410; Peake v. Pegden, 2 T. R. 720; Cadogan v. Ewart, 7 Ad. & E. 636; Walter v. Drew, Com. Rep. 292; Dansey v. Griffiths, 4 M. & S. 61; Wallers v. Andrews, 2 Bing. 196; Crooke v. De Vandes, 9 Ves. 197; Elton v. Eason, 19 Ves. 77; Todd v. Duesbury, 8 M. & W. 514; Sampson v. Sampson, 4 N. C. 833; 2 Fearne, Ex. Dev. 5 Ed. 200; Bamford v. Lord, 14 Com. Bench, 707; Newton v. Griffiths, 1 Har. & Gill. 111; Bells v. Gillespie, 5 Rand, 273; Broaddus v. Turner, Ibid. 308; Sydnor v. Sydnor, 2 Munf. 263; Cruger v. Hayward, 2 Dessaus, 94; Erwin v. Dunwood, 17 Serg. & Rawle, 61; Caskey v. Brewer, Ibid. 441; Heffner v. Knepper, 6 Watts, 18; Patterson v. Ellis, 11 Wend. 259; Hunter v. Haynes, 1 Wash. 71; Lillebridge v. Adie, 1 Mason, 285; Dallam v. Dallam, 7 Harr. & John. 220; Eichelberger v. Barnitz, 9 Watts, 447; Waples v. Harmon, 1 Harring. 223; Jiggetts v. Davis, 1 Leigh. 368; Ide v. Ide, 5 Mass. 500; Hawley v. Northampton, 8 Mass. 3; Nightingale v. Burrill, 15 Pick. 104; Adams v. Cruft, 14 Pick. 25; Parker v. Parker, 5 Met. 134; Wight v. Thayer, 1 Gray, 286.

3. Where, by one clause in a will, an estate for life, or an estate in fee-simple, is given by plain words, if it appear in other parts of the will, by explanatory words or by implication, that it was the intent of the testator in such devise that the issue should take the estate in succession after him, then the life estate is enlarged in the one case, and the estate in fee reduced in the other, to an estate tail. Nightingale v. Burrill, 15 Pick. 104; Parker v. Parker, 5 Met. 134.

4. The words " lawful heirs of their own," mean " heirs of the body lawfully begotten "; and in this will they are technical, and used as words of limitation, restraining the devise to a certain class of heirs, namely, the heirs of the body of either John or Jacob. See authorities under second proposition.

5. That the meaning and intention of the testator, by the use of the words " first decease," was, the one that should so first decease; namely, should first decease without heirs of the body lawfully begotten.

6. The testator, by the use of the words " other survivor," meant and intended " other " simply, and thereby showed his especial reference to the children or heirs of the body of either of the devisees; meaning and intending, if either left heirs of the body at any time, they were to take their father's estate according to the will of the testator. •2 Jarman on Wills, 609, 785; Doe v. Wainewright, 5 Durn. & E. 427; Anderson v. Jackson, 16 Johns. 415; Cole v. Sewall, 2 Conn. & Law. 844; Aiton v. Brooks, 7 Sim. 204; Harmon v. Dickinson, 1 Brown C. C. 82.

7. In a devise of real and personal property, the law makes a distinction as to the two estates, in the construction of devisees; and, when technical language is used, the devisee takes an absolute estate in the personal, and a limited estate, or an estate tail, in the real property. Forth *v.* Chapman, 1 P. Will. 663; Bamford *v.* Lord, 14 Com. Bench, 707, in which all the English cases are collated; Hawley *v.* Northampton, 8 Mass. 3; Nightingale *v.* Burrill, 15 Pick. 104; Adams *v.* Cruft, 14 Pick. 25; Parker *v.* Parker, 5 Met. 134.

8. The use of the word "estate" in the first clause, or in other parts of the will, is not for any technical or specific purpose, but simply directory and descriptive. It was used to designate the fund only out of which the debts and legacies were to be paid. Gardner *v.* Gardner, 3 Mason, 209, and other authorities cited under first proposition.

9. If the testator had not referred to John and Jacob any further than to have given them all his land, &c., to be equally divided between them, and directed John to see that the debts and legacies were paid, they might each have taken a fee-simple by implication; but, having controlled this intent by the proviso in the will, that if either should happen to die without heirs of the body, this creates an estate tail in each son, with cross-remainders in fee-simple absolute. Parker *v.* Parker, 5 Met. 134; Bells *v.* Gillespie, 5 Rand. 273; Caskey *v.* Brewer, 17 Serg. & Rawle, 441.

10. If the testator's sons, John and Jacob, took and became seised of an estate in fee-simple, the share of him who should first die without issue would, in that event, go to the other, if living, by way of executory devise; and if the other son was not living, it would go to his heirs.

Points of Defendants in Error.

The defendants submit, as the proper construction of this will, that it gave to the two sons a fee-simple conditional, with executory devises over, and not an estate tail general, with cross remainders in fee.

That each son took a fee-simple, upon this single contingency: that if the son who died first left no issue, then that his share was to pass to the surviving brother, by way of executory devise.

I. By the first clause, independent of that which devised the estate over, a fee-simple absolute was given to the two sons.

1. Although the devising clause contains no words of inheritance, yet it charges personally one of the devisees with the payment of debts and legacies, by reason of the estate devised, and

therefore carries a fee by implication. Lithgow *v.* Kavenagh, 9 Mass. 165, 166; Wait *v.* Belding, 24 Pick. 189.

And as the intent of the testator is clear, that both sons should take the same estate, if John, the executor, took a fee, then Jacob did also. Roe *v.* Dow, 3 M. & S. 518.

(*a.*) The direction to pay the debts and legacies out of the estate devised, creates a charge upon the devisee personally, as well as upon the estate. Doe *v.* Richardson, 3 Term R. 356; Doe *v.* Snelling, 5 Ibid. 87; Spraker *v.* Van Alystyne, 18 Wend. 205; Gardner *v.* Gardner, 3 Mason, 178; 2 Jarman on Wills, 172.

(*b.*) Moreover, the charge is here imposed "in consideration of what is given the said sons," clearly importing that a personal liability was intended.

(*c.*) The rule is the same, although the devisee charged is named as executor. Goodtitle *v.* Maddern, 4 East, 496; Doe *v.* Holmes, 8 Term R. 1; Doe *v.* Phillips, 3 B. & Adolph. 753; Dolton *v.* Hewer, 6 Madd. Ch. R. 9; 2 Jarman on Wills, 172.

2. One of the legacies given is the maintenance of Sarah Dwinnel, a granddaughter, "out of that part of my estate I give to my sons, John and Jacob Kittredge, until she arrives to the age of eighteen years." (Record, p. 6.)

If life estates only were given to the two sons, then the manifest intention of the testator might be defeated, by their dying before she reached that age.

3. The testator directs the legacies to be paid "out of that part of my estate I have given to my two sons."

It is well settled, that a devise of one's "estate" includes all the testator's interest in the subject devised; and this is true, although it is accompanied with words descriptive only of the *corpus* of the property. Godfrey *v.* Humphrey, 18 Pick. 537; Paris *v.* Miller, 5 M. & S. 408; Gardner *v.* Harding, 3 J. B. Moore, 565; 2 Jarman on Wills, 181, 182.

If then, this expression, "this part of my estate," &c., had been used in the clause making the gift, it would clearly have carried a fee.

But the testator's intention to give a fee is as fairly inferable from his subsequently describing what he has given, as "that part of my estate," &c., as if he had used those words in making the gift.

If the intention to give a fee appears from any part of the will, a fee will pass.

II. The next inquiry is, whether the fee-simple thus given is reduced by the succeeding clause of the will, to an estate tail by implication: Item, "It is my will that if either of my said sons should happen to die without any lawful heirs of his own, then the share of him who may first decease shall accrue to the other survivor and his heirs."

This depends upon whether the testator has provided for a definite or indefinite failure of issue.

If he intended a failure of issue at the death of the first taker, then the will gives a fee-simple conditional, and not an estate tail; and the limitation over, not being too remote, is good as an executory devise. Pells v. Brown, Cro. Jac. 590, and cases cited *post*.

The defendants contend that this is the proper construction of the will.

The demandants rely upon this rule of construction, namely, that, in a devise, words referring to the death of a person without issue are construed to import an idefinite failure of issue, instead of a failure at the death of such person. 2 Jarman on Wills, 418.

But this rule, taken with its proper qualifications, will not justify the construction which the demandants seek to give this will. This involves, —

1. A brief examination of the rule itself, and of some of its established qualifications.

2. The inquiry, what, if any, is the rule of construction as settled in Massachusetts; and how far it conforms to the rule as established elsewhere.

3. A consideration of the provisions of this will, and the in quiry whether, under the application of the rule thus ascertained, they do not plainly refer to a definite failure of issue.

I. The rule itself is entirely artificial, giving an arbitrary meaning to certain forms of expression, as "dying without issue," and the like. Its application, therefore, should be limited to these settled forms of expression. 2 Jarman on Wills, 418.

1. It is generally conceded that the rule violates the natural meaning of language, and in most cases tends to defeat rather than to give effect to the intentions of testators. 2 Jarman on Wills, 418; Keily v. Fowler, Ch. J. Wilmot Notes, &c., 298; Hall v. Chaffee, 14 N. H. 216, and cases *post*.

Insomuch, that in England and several of the States, the rule has been abolished by express legislation. 1 Vict. c. 26, § 29; New York R. St.; Virginia, 1819; Miss. 1824; N. C. 1827.

2. Its qualifications.

A limitation "if T. died without issue, living his brother W., then to W." refers to a failure of issue at the death of T. Pells v. Brown, Cro. Jac. 590.

So also the words, if one die, "leaving no issue behind him," Porter v. Bradley, 3 Term R. 143; and, if one leave no issue, then life estates, " to the survivor or survivors." Roe v. Jeffrey, 7 Term R. 585.

The limitation, in bequests, "to the survivor," has been uniformly held in England to denote a definite failure of issue. Hughes v. Sayer, 1 P. Wm. 584; Ranelagh v. Ranelagh, 2 M. & K. 441; Radford v. Radford, 1 Keen, 486; Lewis on Perpetuities, 218.

Although it may not have been so held in reference to devisees of real estate. See Lewis on Perp. 221.

In the United States, it is settled by numerous authorities that a limitation, "to the survivor," imports a definite failure of issue, in gifts both of real and personal estate. Fosdick v. Cornell, 1 Johns. R. 440; Anderson v. Jackson, 16 Johns. 382; Jackson v. Chew, 12 Wheat. 153; Wilkes v. Lyon, 2 Cowen, 333; Cutter v. Doughty, 23 Wend. 513; Dawson v. De Forest, 3 Sandf. Ch. R. 456; Heard v. Horton, 1 Denio, 165; Dew v. Schenk, 3 Hals. 29; Cordle v. Cordle, 6 Munf. 455; Rapp v. Kapp, 6 Barr. 45; Johnson v. Currier, 10 Barr. 498; Morgan v. Morgan, 5 Day, 517; Couch v. Gorham, 1 Conn. 36.

II. The rule in Massachusetts is, that although a devise to one and his heirs, and if he die without issue, then to another, will create an estate tail, with remainder over, yet that this construction will be controlled by other words, showing that the testator referred to a failure at the death of the first taker. Hawley v. Northampton, 8 Mass. 41.

And in conformity with the American doctrine, it has been held, that a limitation to the survivor denotes a definite failure of issue. Richardson v. Noyes, 2 Mass. 56. See Ide v. Ide et al. 5 Mass. 500.

The case of Parker v. Parker, 5 Met. 134, cannot be considered as having established a rule of construction which controls this case, for these reasons. 12 Wheat. 153.

1. The construction of a will by a state court does not constitute a rule of decision for this court, unless it has been long acquiesced in as a rule of real property. Lane et al. v. Vick et al. 3 How. 476; Comer v. Brown, 16 How. 354.

2. That decision was made on the ground that the testator did not intend to give more than an estate tail to the sons; whereas, in this case, as already shown, the sons were intended to have a fee.

8. That decision was based upon erroneous principles, and is obviously the result of inadvertence.

(a.) The rule of Purefroy r. Rogers, 2 Saund. 388, on which the opinion was founded, is not a rule of construction, favoring the presumption that the particular estate is an estate tail, rather than a fee-simple. See also Doe v. Morgan, 3 Term R. 763; Nightingale v. Burrill, 15 Pick. 111.

(b.) The opinion proceeded on the mistaken idea, that a limitation over on the failure of issue, necessarily implied that the first taker was to have an estate tail, without referring to the decisive distinction, whether the limitation was upon a definite or indefinite failure of issue. (p. 139.) But see Nightingale v. Burrill, 15 Pick. 118.

(c.) The conclusion, that the will created an estate tail, was entirely inconsistent with what the court had previously declared, p. 137, to be "the manifest object of the testator"; and that was, to give a fee-simple conditional.

4. That decision cannot control the construction of this will, because the single question upon which this depends was neither passed upon nor adverted to; namely, whether a definite or indefinite failure of issue was intended.

If it had been, it is utterly improbable that the court would have come to the result they did; for it is undoubted law everywhere, that a limitation over upon the first taker's dying without issue, and under twenty-one years of age, is clearly upon a definite failure of issue. Pells v. Brown, Cro. Jac. 590; Glover v. Monckton, 3 Bingh. 13; Doe v. Johnson, 16 L. & E. 550; Lippett v. Hopkins, 1 Gall. 454; Barnitz v. Casey, 7 Cranch, 456; Ray v. Enslin, 2 Mass. 554.

5. The provisions of the will in that case, and of the will in this are materially different.

III. This will provides for a definite failure of issue.

1. The language, "if either son should happen to die without heirs," denotes that the testator was contemplating a contingency which would occur, if at all, at the death of such son.

2. The limitation is "to the other survivor."

According to the decision supra, a limitation to the "survivor" denotes a definite failure of issue.

But here the limitation is "to the other survivor."

The term survivor, as here employed, cannot be construed to mean "other"; for, as the term "other" is also used, such a construction would deprive "survivor" of all force.

This language shows that the testator referred to the other, personally, as the survivor.

3. It is clear, that a fee-simple, and not an estate tail, is devised over, "to the survivor and his heirs."

It is highly improbable that the testator intended, in the event of the limitation over taking effect, that the son should hold one half the estate in fee-simple, and the other in fee-tail.

4. It is "the share" of him who may die first, that is devised over.

(a.) The term "share," in a devise, denotes all one's interest, and will pass a fee. Paris v. Miller, 5 M. & S. 408; Doe v. Bacon, 4 M. & S. 366.

(*b.*) Here, a fee-simple is clearly devised over, and it is called " the share " of the first taker. This certainly implies that that " share " was a fee-simple.

(*c.*) The true import of this language is, and the understanding of the testator undoubtedly was, that what is given over, (*i. e.* a fee-simple,) is just exactly what the first taker would have held, had he not died without issue.

5. The devise includes both real and personal estate.

(*a.*) It is very certain that the testator did not intend to limit over the personal property, on an indefinite failure of issue, and from uniting the two in the same clause and in the same contingency, the inference is equally as strong as to the real estate. Porter *v.* Bradley, 3 Term R. 146, and Richardson *v.* Noyes, 2 Mass. 68, are direct authorities.

(*b.*) A distinction has indeed been sometimes made between real and personal estate, but the soundness of this distinction is denied by the weight of authority. *Vide* cases *supra.*

6. Lastly, it is the share of him " who may first decease " that is devised over.

(*a.*) This language cannot be taken literally, for then the share of the one dying first would go over, although he left issue.

(*b.*) Nor does it mean merely the share of him who may die without issue ; for this would disregard the plain provision of the will, that it must be the share of him who dies first.

(*c.*) The testator's meaning is clear ; the share of him " who may first decease " is devised over, " if he happens to die without lawful heirs," (*i. e.* issue ;) but in no event is any other share devised over but his who may first decease.

These words, in connection with the fact that the limitation is to the survivor, demonstrate that the testator referred to the period of the death of the first taker.

Mr. Justice GRIER delivered the opinion of the court.

The questions submitted to our consideration in this case arise on the construction of the will of John Kittredge, deceased, and on the following devise to his sons : —

" *Item.* I give to my two sons, namely, John and Jacob Kittredge, all my lands and buildings in Andover aforesaid, excepting the land I gave to my son Thomas aforesaid, which buildings consist of dwelling-houses, barns, corn-house, gristmill, and cider-mill, all of every denomination ; also, all my live stock of cattle, horses, sheep and swine, and all my husbandry utensils of every denomination, and all my tools that may be useful for tending the mills aforesaid ; and also all my bonds and notes of hand and book accounts, together with what money I may leave at my decease ; and my wearing apparel, I

give the same to my said sons, John and Jacob Kittredge, to
be equally divided between them; and in consideration of what
I have given my said sons, John and Jacob Kittredge, the executor of this testament, hereinafter named, is hereby ordered
to see that all my just debts and funeral charges, together with
all the legacies in this will mentioned, be paid out of that part
of my estate I have given to my two sons, John and Jacob Kittredge, to whom I give each one bed and bedding.

"*Item.* It is my will, that if either of my said sons, namely,
John and Jacob Kittredge, should happen to die without any
lawful heirs of their own, then the share of him who may first
decease shall accrue to the other survivor and his heirs."

On the trial, the demandants requested the court to instruct
the jury, " that John and Jacob took the real estate therein devised in equal moieties of an estate tail general, with cross-
remainders in fee-simple." But the court instructed the jury,
" that the testator's said sons, John and Jacob, took an estate in
fee-simple, and that the share of the one of the sons, who
should first die without issue, in the lifetime of the other, should,
in that event, go over to the other son, by way of executory de
vise." To this instruction the plaintiffs excepted, and now contend: —

1. That the testator, by the first clause of his will, gave to
John and Jacob an estate for life only.

2. That the next clause of the will enlarges the estate for life
to an estate-tail in each of the two sons, and, by the use of such
language, the testator intended an indefinite failure of issue.

The defendants, on the contrary, maintain that, independent
of the last clause, by which the estate is given over, the sons
took a fee-simple. And, secondly, that the clear intention of the
testator is, that both real and personal estate should pass on a
definite contingency, namely, the decease of one brother without
issue in the lifetime of the other.

There is, perhaps, no point of testamentary construction which
has undergone such frequent discussion, and is so fruitful in cases
not easily reconciled, as that now brought under our consideration. This has arisen, in a great measure, from the discrepancy between the popular acceptation of the phrases, " if he die
without issue," " in default of issue," and similar expressions,
from the established legal acceptation of them in courts of justice. It is often necessary to construe these expressions as con-
veying an estate tail by implication, in order to carry out the
evident general intent of the testator. Such is, or ought to be,
the object of all rules of interpretation; but court rules, however
convenient in the disposition of cases where the intention is
doubtful, cannot claim to be absolute or of universal application.

Abbott et ux. v. Essex Company.

Hence it has been said, "that courts have been astute to defeat the application of this rule of construction, harsh in itself, and often producing results contrary to the testator's intention." If wills were always drawn by counsel learned in the law, it would be highly proper that courts should rigidly adhere to precedents, because every such instrument might justly be presumed to have been drawn with reference to them. But, in a country where, from necessity or choice, every man acts as his own scrivener, his will is subject to be perverted by the application of rules of construction of which he was wholly ignorant.

The rule laid down in Purefoy v. Rogers, 2 Saund. 388, "that where a contingency is limited to depend on an estate of freehold which is capable of supporting a remainder, it shall never be construed to be an executory devise," has been received and adopted in Massachusetts.

In England, and in some of the States here, it has been abolished by legislative interposition, as harsh and injurious. This rule, however, has never been construed, either in England or this country, to include cases where the title of the first taker is a fee-simple, and the contingency is definite.

In the case of Pells v. Brown, Cro. Jac. 590, where there was a devise "to A in fee, and, if he die without issue living, then C shall have the land," it was held to be an executory devise to C, on the contingency of A dying in the lifetime of C without issue. There is no necessary conflict between this case and that of Purefoy v. Rogers. It is true, also, that this rule has been applied where the first taker had an estate in fee; and it is conceded, "that, unless there are expressions or circumstances from which it can be collected that these words, 'without issue,' are used in a more confined sense, they are to have their legal sense of an indefinite failure of issue"; but whenever such "expressions or circumstances" show the intention of the testator that the estate is to go over only on a definite contingency, courts will give effect to such intention. Notwithstanding the expressions in Plunket v. Holmes, Sid. 47, derogatory of the case of Pells v. Brown, it has always been considered "a leading case, and the foundation of this branch of the law." See Williams's Saunders, 388, b, in note.

In Porter v. Bradley, 8 T. R. 143, where lands were devised to A and his heirs, and if he die leaving no issue behind him, then over, it was decided that the limitation over was good by way of executory devise; and Lord Kenyon acknowledges the case of Pells v. Brown to be "the foundation and *magna charta* of this branch of the law," deciding that the words, "leaving no issue behind him," showed clearly that the testator did not contemplate an indefinite failure of issue.

In the case of Roe v. Jeffery, 7 T. R. 589, where the devise was to "A and his heirs, and in case he should depart this life and leave no issue, then to B, C, and D, and the survivor or survivors of them, share and share alike," it was held that the devise to B, C, and D was a good executory devise. In delivering the opinion of the court in that case, Lord Kenyon observes: "This is a question of construction, depending on the intention of the party; and nothing can be clearer than if an estate be given to A in fee, and by way of an executory devise, an estate be given over, which may take place within a life or lives in being, &c., the latter is good by way of executory devise. The question, therefore, in this and similar cases is, whether, from the whole context of the will, we can collect when an estate is given to A and his heirs forever, but if he die without issue, then over, the testator meant without issue living at the death of the first taker. The rule was settled as long ago as in the reign of James I., in the case of Pells v. Brown. That case has never been questioned or shaken, and is considered as a cardinal point on this head of the law."

Without referring to any more of the numerous English and American cases brought to our notice by the learned counsel, of like tenor, it will be sufficient to notice the case of Richardson v. Noyes, 2 Mass. 56. There the devise was "to my three sons, A, B, and C, all my other lands, &c.; also my will is, that if either of them should die without children, the survivor or survivors of them to hold the interest or share of each or any of them so dying without children as aforesaid"; and it was held to pass an estate in fee-simple, determinable on the contingency of either of them dying without issue, and vesting by way of executory devise. See also the case of Ray v. Enslen, 2 Mass. 554. Those cases fully adopt the principles of the English cases we have just referred to. The case of Parker v. Parker, 5 Metc. 134, has been quoted as containing a contrary doctrine; but it does not appear that the question of definite or indefinite failure of issue was made by the counsel or adverted to by the court in the decision.

Our inquiry must be, therefore, from an examination of the whole context of this will: —

1. Whether, independent of the second clause, by which the estate is limited over, the sons took an estate in fee-simple or only a life estate; and,

2. Whether he intended to give over the share of each son to the other, on the contingency of his death, without issue living at the time of his decease, or upon an indefinite failure of issue.

1. There are no words of inheritance, in this first clause of the devise, to John and Jacob, but such words are not absolutely

necessary in a will to the gift of a fee. The subject of this devise is described as "that part of my estate." The word "estate," or "that part of my estate," has always been construed to describe not only the land devised, but the whole interest of the testator in the subject of the devise; thus, a devise of "my estate, consisting of thirty acres of land, situate, &c.," will carry a fee. Moreover, the legacy given for the maintenance of Sarah Devinny, "to be paid out of that part of my estate given to John and Jacob," would be defeated by their death before she arrived at the age of eighteen, if the devise to them was a life estate only. The intention of a testator must be drawn from the whole context of his will. And it is not necessary to look alone at the words of the gift itself to ascertain the intention of the testator as to the *quantum* of the estate devised, if it can be gathered, from expressions used in any part of it, what he supposed or intended to be the nature and extent of it. It will not admit of a doubt, also, that the testator intended that both of his sons should have the same estate in the devised premises, which were "to be equally divided between them." John is charged personally, in respect of the estate given him, with the payment of all the debts and legacies. The testator calls it the "consideration" to be paid for that part of his estate given to his two sons; and though John was appointed executor, whose duty it became, as such, to see to the payment of the debts and legacies, the charges are to be paid by him at all events out of the estate devised to him and Jacob, and not out of the rents and profits only. By their acceptance of the devise, they became personally liable. In such cases, it is well settled that the devisee takes a fee, without words of inheritance.

On this point, therefore, we are of opinion that John and Jacob each took a fee in their respective "share" or moiety of the estate devised to them.

2. It remains to consider the effect of the second clause of the will, which is in these words: "It is my will, that, if either of my said sons, namely, John or Jacob, should happen to die without any lawful heirs of their own, then the share of him who may first decease shall accrue to the other survivor and his heirs."

Viewing this clause free from the confusion of mind produced by the numerous conflicting decisions of courts, and untrammelled by artificial rules of construction, we think that no two minds could differ as to the clear intention of the testator. By "lawful heirs of their own," he evidently meant lineal descendants or "issue."

The contingency contemplated is as definite as language can make it — "if either son should happen to die without heirs of their own during the life of the other."

The person to take, on the happening of this contingency, is precisely described — "the other survivor." It is true, that cases may be found which decide that the term "survivor" does not of itself necessarily import a definite failure of issue, and no doubt there are many cases where it would be necessary to disregard the obvious import of this term, in order to carry out the general intent of a testator, otherwise apparent; but a large number of English, and nearly all the American, cases acknowledge the force of this term as evidence of the testator's intending a definite contingency. The other words of this clause, connected with it, clearly describe a definite contingency, and the individual who is to take on its happening: "the share of him who shall first decease without heirs shall accrue to the other survivor"; — on the death of one, the other is to take — a definite contingency and a definite individual.

Again, it is the "share," or the estate previously given, not of him who dies without issue, generally, but of him who may first decease, that is given over to the other survivor. This "share" also consisted of personal and real property. As to the former, the testator could certainly not mean an indefinite failure of issue, yet both, personalty and realty, are within the same category, and, as one "share," they are subject to the same contingency. It is said to be a rule of construction, that the words "dying without issue," will be construed to mean "an indefinite failure of issue" as to real estate; but with regard to personalty, it shall be taken to mean "a failure at the death." There are several cases to this effect. Lord Kenyon, in speaking of them in Roe v. Jeffrey, very justly remarks that "the distinction taken in Forth v. Chapman, 1 P. Wms. 663, that the very same words in a will should receive one construction when applied to one portion of the devise, and another construction as applied to another, is not reconcilable with reason." Without making an array of cases, we may state that many of the English, and nearly all the American cases, seem to concur in the truth and force of this observation; and consider a "share" of an estate, consisting of both realty and personalty, given over on a contingency to the "survivor," as clear evidence that the testator did not intend an indefinite failure of issue. A rule of construction which would give different meanings to the same words, in the same sentence, could only be tolerated where, from the whole context of the will, it is evident that without such construction the general intent of the testator as to the disposition of his realty would be frustrated.

Lastly, construing this clause as providing for an indefinite failure of issue, and as vesting each of the sons with an estate tail by implication, the survivor would take an estate in fee-simple in his brother's share, while he had an estate in tail in his own ; a result most improbable, which could hardly have been contemplated by the testator, and which ought not to be imputed to him without clear expressions indicating such an intention.

On the whole, we are of opinion that the instructions given to the jury by the court below are correct, and that the judgment should be affirmed.

PATRICK MCLAUGHLIN, PLAINTIFF IN ERROR, *v.* JAMES SWANN AND JOHN S. GITTINGS, GARNISHEES OF THE CHESAPEAKE AND OHIO CANAL COMPANY.[*]

The attachment law of Maryland allows an attachment by way of execution to be issued upon a judgment and levied upon the credits (*inter alia*) of the defendant.

Where an attachment of this nature was laid in the hands of garnishees who were trustees, and it appeared that, after performing the trust, there was a balance in their hands due to the defendant, the attachment will bind this balance.

The defendant might have brought an action to recover it, and wherever he can do this, the fund is liable to be attached.

A bill filed in the court of chancery by another creditor against the garnishees and the defendant, filed after the laying of the attachment, and the opinion and decree of the chancellor thereon, do not change the rights of the plaintiff in the attachment. The decree was passed without prejudice to his rights. If these things were made evidence by consent in the court below, it does not so appear in the bill of exceptions.

Whatever legal or equitable defences the garnishees might have set up in an action brought against them by the defendant to recover the balance in their hands, can be set up, by bill of interpleader or otherwise, against the plaintiff in the attachment.

The different modes of presenting these legal and equitable defences in different states referred to.

THIS case was brought up by writ of error from the circuit court of the United States, for the District of Maryland.

The case is stated in the opinion of the court.

The instructions given by the circuit court to the jury, and which were excepted to by the plaintiff, were as follows : —

And the court directed the jury that the plaintiff was not entitled to recover, and their verdict must be for the defendants :

1. Because the rights of the parties claiming as *cestui que trusts*, under the deed of April 15, 1840, and the rights of those claiming an interest in the surplus after the *cestui que trusts* are satisfied, cannot be adjusted and determined in the proceeding

---

[*] Mr. Chief Justice TANEY was prevented by sickness from taking his seat on the bench, at the present term, until the 4th of February, and was not present when this case was argued and decided in this court.

McLaughlin *v.* Swann et al.

by attachment against the trustees in a court of law, and there
is no evidence that any specified sum ascertained by the accounts
of the trustees, or by judicial decision, was due to the Chesapeake and Ohio Canal Company at the time this attachment was
laid, or at any time since, after satisfying all legal or equitable
claims on the fund placed in the hands of the trustees.

2. Because there is no evidence that anything remained in
the hands of the trustees, after satisfying the trust mentioned in
the deed, more than sufficient to satisfy the claim of the Alexandria Canal Company and others, having prior and superior
claims on the fund to the plaintiff in this attachment.

8. The plaintiff having become a party to the proceedings in
the chancery court of Maryland, in the suit in which this fund
was in litigation, and the trustees in the fund being all before
the court, he is concluded by its decision while the decree remains in force.

It was argued in this court by *Mr. Davis*, for the plaintiff in
error, and by *Mr. Campbell*, for the defendants.

Mr. Davis made the following points: —

1. That under the circumstance of this case, the process of
attachment was a proper process to reach, and affect any surplus
in the hands of the trustees remaining after gratifying the trusts
of the deed, and not needed to satisfy the demands of others
having prior and superior claims on the fund.

2. That there was evidence of a large surplus existing in the
hands of the trustees, after satisfying the trusts of the deed, the
claim of the Bank of Potomac, and all others superior and prior
to the claim of the present plaintiff.

8. That the decree of the court of chancery of Maryland alluded to, cannot prejudice the plaintiff's right to recover, if it
can be shown that at the time of passing the decree, the trustees
had in hand a surplus, which was liable to be affected by process
of attachment.

Under the first head he cited 5 Har. & John. 812–815; 8 Har.
& McH. 535, and maintained that every equitable interest in
Maryland, except a trust in process of execution, is liable to be
attached under the act of 1715.   See act of 1881, c. 821, which
is a declaratory act.

The trust had expired in this case, and an action for money
had and received could have been maintained against the trustees.

Mr. Campbell contended, that when the attachment was issued,
the whole surplus was in controversy between the Chesapeake
Bank and the Bank of Potomac.

McLaughlin v. Swann et al.

How could the court below settle the conflict between these rival claimants, neither of them before it, or weigh in legal scales their respective equities?

Case v. Roberts, 8 Eng. Comm. Law, 172. The action for money had and received must not be turned into a bill of equity for the purpose of discovery. While the matter remains in account and is charged with the specific trust, the action for money had and received will not lie. Roper v. Holland, 30 Eng. Comm. Law, 37; Edwards v. Bates, 49 Ib. 598; Pardoe v. Price, 18 Mees. & Welsby, 282, 283; Bartlett v. Dimmond, 14 Ib. 49; Tiernan v. Jackson, 5 Pet. 597; Duvall v. Craig, 2 Wheat. 56; Rathbone v. Stocking, 2 Barb. Sup. Ct. R. 185, and the cases referred to in the court's opinion.

The second instruction of the circuit court was correct, for the evidence showed that the surplus, after the redemption of the script, was all claimed by the Bank of Potomac and Chesapeake Bank.

McLaughlin was made a party to the proceeding in chancery and answered. The reservation avails nothing under the circumstances. This cause began in 1841, and was continued from term to term till 1851. He might have claimed the surplus in chancery. If he did not choose to assert his rights the decree must bind him.

Mr. Justice CURTIS delivered the opinion of the court.

This is a writ of error to the circuit court of the United States for the district of Maryland.

The plaintiff in error having recovered a judgment in that court against the Chesapeake and Ohio Canal Company, sued out a writ of foreign attachment against the lands and tenements, goods, chattels, and credits of that company, and on the 4th day of June, 1841, it was laid in the hands of James Swann and John S. Gittings. The garnishees having appeared and answered certain interrogatories, pleaded that at the time of laying the attachment they had not any goods, chattels, or credits of the company in their hands, and upon the trial a bill of exceptions was taken, from which it appears that the plaintiff offered evidence tending to prove, that, by an indenture, bearing date on the 15th day of April, 1840, between the company of the first part, and the garnishees, together with William Gunton, (who, residing out of the district, was not served with process,) of the second part, the party of the first part transferred to the party of the second part, two hundred and forty-eight bonds of the State of Maryland, each for two hundred and fifty pounds sterling, in trust to pay, from the proceeds thereof, such promissory notes of the company, described in a schedule annexed to the indenture, as should be presented to the trustees at the Chesapeake Bank in Baltimore, within six months from the date of the indenture; and at the end of the six months, to pay to the company any money, and to deliver to the company any of the bonds which might then remain in their hands, whether all the notes mentioned in the schedule should then be paid or not.

The plaintiff further offered evidence to prove, that Gittings, with the assent of the other trustees, sold the bonds prior to the 28th day of February, 1841, for the aggregate sum of $344,117$\frac{26}{100}$; and that the sums received by him for interest on the bonds amounted to $16,958$\frac{62}{100}$, amounting in the whole to the sum of $361,075$\frac{88}{100}$. The disbursements and payments made by the trustees in the execution of the trust, appeared to have been $324,825$\frac{18}{100}$, leaving a balance due from the trustees, after the complete execution of the trust declared in the indenture, of $36,250$\frac{70}{100}$.

Upon this state of facts, we think the plaintiff entitled to a verdict.

The trust was for the payment of specified debts, which should be presented to the trustees before a fixed day. The payments made, and the sums received in execution of the trust, were liquidated sums ascertained with entire precision. The trust was completely executed, and the balance remaining in the hands of the trustees was a sum certain.

Under these circumstances, an action at law for money had and received could be sustained by the canal company against the trustees, they not having sealed the deed.

In Case v. Roberts, (Holt's N. P. C. 500,) Burrough, J., states the rule on this subject to be: "If money is paid into the hands of a trustee for a specific purpose, it cannot be recovered in an action for money had and received, until that specific purpose is shown to be at an end. If the plaintiff show that the specific purpose has been satisfied, that it has absorbed a certain sum only, and left a balance, such balance (the trust being closed) becomes a clear and liquidated sum, for which an action will lie at law." This statement of the rule has been approved, and in conformity with it many cases decided. See, among others, English v. Blundell, 8 Car. & P. 332; Edwards v. Bates, 7 Man. & Gr. 590; Allen v. Impett, 8 Taunt. 263; Weston v. Barker, 12 Johns. R. 276.

This case, thus presented, comes within that rule; and as an action at law could have been sustained by the canal company to recover the liquidated balance remaining in the hands of the trustees, the plaintiff could subject that balance to the satisfaction of his judgment, by attaching it as a credit in the hands of the trustees.

But, in addition to the evidence above referred to, the bill of exceptions contains the following statement concerning evidence introduced by the defendants : —

"That on the 25th of June, 1841, a bill was filed in the court of chancery, in Maryland, against the said garnishees and the Chesapeake and Ohio Canal Company, and others, by the Bank of Potomac, claiming as assignee of the surplus which remained after satisfying the trusts under the deed of April, 1840, and praying an account and settlement of the trust, which bill is in the following words: It being agreed between the parties that the said bill and other portions of the pleadings or proceedings in that case, hereinafter mentioned to have been produced and read, shall be received in evidence and have the same effect as if the whole record was produced, and such pleadings or proceedings read from it."

Then follows a copy of the bill, of an opinion of the acting chancellor, and of the final decree in the cause. McLaughlin, the present plaintiff in error, is not made a party to this bill. How he came into the cause as a party does not appear. If by the amended bill, he ceased to be a party before the final decree, because that decree recites that the amended bill was dismissed by the complainants before the final submission of the cause to the chancellor. Nor does it appear for what purpose McLaughlin was made a party, or whether he at any time submitted his rights as an attaching creditor, by a process out of the circuit court of the United States, to a court of the State of Maryland, in a suit in equity, begun after his attachment was laid. But it does not appear to be material to consider either of these particulars, because the final decree concludes with this clause : —

"And it is further adjudged, ordered, and decreed, that this cause be, and the same is hereby dismissed as against the defendant, Patrick McLaughlin, and this decree is passed without prejudice to the rights of the said McLaughlin against any and every of the parties to this suit."

Either because the chancellor deemed it improper to pass on his rights acquired by an attachment under process of a court of the United States, or for some other reason, he has made a decree, which in express terms leaves McLaughlin in all respects unaffected by that suit.

We think, also, that so much of the record of the chancery suit as is in this record, though it was properly read in evidence to prove that such proceedings were had, and such decree made, is not evidence of any facts found by the chancellor, either in his opinion or in the decree.

The bill having been dismissed as against him, and all his rights, as against any and every of the parties, expressly saved,

19 *

there has been no matter tried or adjudicated as between him and any other party, and he stands, in all respects, as if he had never been a party to the suit.

It was insisted at the argument, that the stipulation already extracted from the bill of exceptions made the chancellor's opinion evidence, as against McLaughlin, of the facts it finds. This was denied by the plaintiff's counsel; and, however probable we may think the inference, that the chancellor's opinion was treated as evidence by the circuit court, with the consent of the plaintiff, yet we cannot say this appears to us judicially, by the bill of exceptions. The stipulation only extends so far as to make the parts of the record, which were read, have the same effect as if the whole record had been put in. The whole record might have properly been put in, to prove what was done and decreed in that suit, *valeat quantum.* But when it appeared that so far as respected the plaintiff and his rights, nothing was done or decreed, his rights in this suit could not be affected by anything appearing therein, or deducible therefrom. In our opinion, therefore, the case is presented to us upon the evidence, extraneous to the record of the state court. Upon that evidence, we think the jury would have been authorized and required to find for the plaintiff; and, consequently, that the instruction given in the court below, that their verdict must be for the defendants, was erroneous.

We express no opinion upon the defences supposed to arise out of the facts found in the opinion of the chancellor. If the facts, which may be proved in defence, on another trial, should amount to a legal defence to an action for money had and received, if brought by the Canal Company, they would also amount to a defence to this attachment. If they only show outstanding equities, in third persons, of such a character that a court of law cannot take notice of them, they must be availed of, if valid, by a bill brought by such third persons against McLaughlin, or by a bill of interpleader by the trustees. The attachment invests the plaintiff with the same right of action which belonged to the Canal Company; and no defence, which could not have been made at law to an action by the company, can be made to the attachment, which is but a substituted mode of pursuing the same right. Wanzer v. Truly, 17 How. 584. So far as respects equitable rights of set-off by the garnishee, a different rule has been followed in Massachusetts. Boston Type Co. v. Mortimer, 7 Pick. 166; Hathaway v. Russell, 16 Mass. 473; Green v. Nelson, 12 Met. 567. And, in the absence of an equitable jurisdiction in that State, there has been, until recently, no mode of giving effect to the equitable rights of the garnishee, or of third persons, save in the process of garnishment, or possibly by an action on the case in some instances. Foster *v.* Sinkler, 4 Mass. 450; Hawes *v.* Langton, 8 Pick. 67; Adams *v.* Cordis, 8 Pick. 260.

But, in other States, it has been held that only legal defences can be made to the attachment. Pennell *v.* Grubb, 13 Penn. R. 552; Taylor *v.* Gardner, 2 Wash. C. C. Rep. 488; Loftin *v.* Shackelford, 17 Alabama, 455; Edwards *v.* Delaplaine, 2 Harrington, 322; Watkins *v.* Field, 1 English, 891.

We are not aware that this subject has come under the examination of the courts of Maryland in any reported case. But in a State where the legal and equitable jurisdictions are distinct, and in a court of the United States, having full equity powers, we consider that a garnishee should stand as nearly as possible in the same position he would have occupied if sued at law by his creditor; and if he, or any third pers n, has equitable rights to the fund in his hands, they should be asserted in that jurisdiction which alone can suitably examine and completely protect them.

The judgment of the circuit court is to be reversed, and the cause remanded, with directions to issue a *venire facias de novo.*

THE STEAMBOAT NEW YORK, HER TACKLE, APPAREL, &C., THOMAS C. DURANT, CHARLES W. DURANT, AND SEPTIMUS LATHROP, CLAIMANTS AND APPELLANTS, *v.* ISAAC P. REA, OWNER OF THE BRIG SARAH JOHANNA.

Where a vessel was lying at anchor in the port of New York, and a steamboat came down the Hudson River with wind and tide in her favor, and also having several heavily loaded barges fastened on each side of her, and came into collision with the vessel which was lying at anchor, it was a gross fault in the steamboat to proceed, at night, on her way with a speed of from eight to ten miles per hour.

Moreover, the steamboat had not a sufficient look-out.

The statutes of the State of New York, regulating the light which the vessel lying at anchor was to show, have no binding force in the present case. The rule for the decision of the federal courts is derived from the general admiralty law.

Police regulations for the accommodation and safety of vessels in a harbor, may be enacted by the local authorities.

THIS was an appeal from the circuit court of the United States for the southern district of New York.

The district court decreed that the libellant should recover against the steamboat the sum of $ 3,875 and costs.

The circuit court affirmed this decree, and gave judgment for $ 4,174 and costs.

It was submitted upon printed arguments in this court by

Mr. Morton and *Mr. Cutting*, for the appellants, and *Mr. Betts*, for the appellee.

The arguments upon both sides consisted chiefly in comments upon the evidence.

Mr. Justice NELSON delivered the opinion of the court.

This is an appeal in admiralty from a decree of the circuit court of the United States for the southern district of New York.

The libel was filed by the owner of the brig Sarah Johanna against the steamboat, for a collision in the harbor of the city of New York. The brig was lying at anchor in the North River, off pier No. 6, nearer to the Jersey than the New York shore, her bow heading up the river, there being at the time a strong ebb-tide, and wind heavy from the northwest. The collision occurred between four and five o'clock in the morning of the 4th of November, 1850, — the river at this place being filled with vessels at anchor in the vicinity of the brig. The morning considerably dark.

The steamboat was passing down the North River to get round to her berth in the East River. She had in tow eleven heavily loaded barges and canal-boats, the first tier being three abreast on each side of her, the other boats astern, towed by lines attached to this first tier. The steamer, with the tows, occupied a breadth of some three hundred feet, and from three hundred and fifty to four hundred feet in length, her bows projecting some sixty feet ahead of the tows. She entered this thicket of vessels, at anchor in the river, at a rate of speed from eight to ten miles an hour, and, as we have seen, with a strong ebb-tide and heavy northwest wind; and, while passing through them, the centre tow-boat of the tier on the starboard side struck the bow of the brig, smashing her timbers, cut-water, and bowsprit, and otherwise doing great damage to the vessel.

The captain of the steamboat admits that he saw the brig from three to five hundred feet off before the collision, but, as he could not stop his boat in less than within ten or fifteen of her lengths, the collision was inevitable. He admits, also, that it would have required all her power to have stopped within that distance, as it would have depended upon the way the tow-boats were managed. The rear tows were not so fastened, he observes, as to prevent their swinging, and could not have been. He gave orders instantly, on discerning the brig, to starboard the helm, and passed the same order to the tow-boats. This was undoubtedly the proper order at the time, under the circumstances, but with the rate of speed of the steamer, and encumbered as she was with her tows, it was unavailing.

The Steamboat New York, &c., et al. v. Rea, &c.

Upon this statement of the facts in the case, it is manifest the steamer was grossly in fault in entering this crowd of vessels at anchor in the harbor, at the rate of speed with which she was moving, especially in the night time. A collision with some of them thus lying in her trail was the natural, if not inevitable, result. Lying at anchor, they were disabled from adopting any measure to get out of her way, and encumbered as she was with tows, she was not in a condition to adopt any prompt and effective manœuvre to avoid the danger. The continuance of the speed, therefore, under the circumstances of wind and tide, and encumbrance and embarrassment of the tows, was the grossest carelessness and neglect of duty, without the semblance of excuse. Indeed, the term carelessness hardly expresses the degree of fault; under the circumstances, it seems almost to have been wilful, or what, in degree, should be regarded as equally criminal.

The steamboat was also in fault in not having a look-out at the time, properly stationed. The captain admits that no person was stationed on the deck as a look-out. He claims to have been on that duty himself, although he stood upon the upper deck, some fifteen feet above the water, and sixty feet from the bow of the steamer, and was at the time engaged in giving directions for the management of her and her tows.

We have had occasion frequently to lay down the rule, that it is the duty of steamboats traversing waters where sailing vessels are often met with, to have a trustworthy and constant look-out, stationed at a part of the vessel best adapted for that purpose, and whose whole business was to discern vessels ahead, or approaching, so as to give the earliest notice to those in charge of the navigation of the vessel; and that the omission, in case of a collision, would be *primâ facie* evidence of fault on the part of the steamer. 12 How. 459; 10 Ib. 585.

It is insisted, however, on the part of the steamboat, that the brig was also in fault, in not showing a light while lying at anchor. We have looked carefully into the evidence on this branch of the case, and are satisfied that the clear weight of it is in favor of the libellants, and that a proper light was kept constantly in the fore-rigging, some seventeen feet above the deck.

Again, it is claimed that, admitting the brig had a light sufficient, within the requirements of the admiralty rule, still, she was in fault in not showing a light, in conformity with the statutes of New York, which required it should be suspended in the rigging, at least twenty feet above deck. 1 Rev. Stats. p. 685, § 12; also Sess. Laws, 1839, p. 322.

This is a rule of navigation prescribed by the laws of New York, and is doubtless binding upon her own courts, but cannot

The Steamboat New York, &c., et al. v. Rea, &c.

regulate the decisions of the federal courts, administering the general admiralty law. They can be governed only by the principles peculiar to that system, as generally recognized in maritime countries, modified by acts of congress independently of local legislation. The Johanna was a foreign ship, engaged in the general commerce of the country, not in the purely internal trade of a State. The Bark Chusan, 2 Story, 456.

We agree, an exception to this general principle is, the regulation of steamboats and other water-craft in the ports and harbors of the States, which is required for the accommodation and safety of vessels resorting thither in the pursuits of business and commerce. These are police regulations in aid and furtherance of commerce, enacted by the local authorities, who have a knowledge of the wants of the locality, and a deep interest in properly providing for them.

We are satisfied, the decree of the court below is right, and should be affirmed.

Mr. Justice DANIEL dissenting.

I dissent from the decision just pronounced. This record brings before us what the testimony shows to be a case of simple tort or trespass, alleged to have been committed in the harbor of New York, which might have been disposed of upon principles and under proceedings familiar to the habits of the people of the country, and at a greater economy of time and expense than is necessarily incident to proceedings like those just sanctioned. I should always be reluctant, were there no considerations other than those of mere convenience, or even of habit or prejudice involved, to interfere with the local institutions or customs of States or communities. It is proper to leave to these, wherever no paramount obligation forbids it, the adoption and practice of such local institutions, or local prejudices, if they may be so denominated. Much higher and stronger is the motive for forbearing such interference, where the latter cannot be clearly traced to an undoubted legitimate authority. I hold it as an axiom or postulate, that, by the admiralty jurisdiction vested by the constitution of the United States, a power has not been, nor was ever intended to be, delegated to those courts, to supersede or control the internal polity of the States in providing for the preservation of property, or for the regulation of order, or the security of personal rights. These subjects constitute a class, the control of which is inseparable from political or social existence in the States, every encroachment upon which is an instance of unwarrantable assumption in the federal government, and of progressive decline in the health and vigor in those of the States. Especially does it seem strange to me that there should anywhere exist a tendency to extend a system which, however attended with advantage when limited to the necessities in which it originated, must, almost in every instance, be attended with inconvenience, and not unfrequently with ruin to one side of the litigant parties, by operating the seizure and transmutation of property, and, of course, the suspension if not the destruction of all business in which that property formed a necessary instrument, — and this, too, before an adjudication upon the rights of litigants can possibly be had; and although such adjudication may be in favor of the person subjected to the consequences just mentioned. The guards which the wisdom and beneficence of the common law and equity jurisprudence of the country have thrown around the rights of property will tolerate no consequences like these; they require judgment before execution; and this single consideration, were there no other, should cause them to be cherished and maintained, rather than impugned or evaded.

The case before us furnishes a precedent, a pregnant precedent, for interference with the harbor regulations of every town in the Union, and this, too, under the ambitious and undefinable pretensions of a great system of maritime jurisprudence. Truly it may be said, that this pretension entirely reverses the maxim of that venerable, though neglected common law, *De minimis non curat lex;* a trespass in the harbor of New York would else be a quarry upon which it would disdain to stoop.

But, independently of the objection to the decision in this case, which, in my view of it, results from the absence of power under the constitution, upon the principles of justice and fairness, were there no restriction upon the powers of the court, its decision is altogether unwarranted.

The evidence, correctly compared, so far from fixing upon the steamboat the fault of the collision, shows that collision to have been very probably, if not certainly, the result of delinquency on the part of the brig. It seems to have become a favored doctrine, that, in all cases of collision between steamboats and sailing vessels, the burden of proof, either for excuse or exculpation, is to be placed on the steamboat, because it is said that she is in a great degree independent of the winds and the tide, and possesses entire control of her movements. This rule, when applied within the limits of reason and the bounds of unquestioned or obvious right as to all parties, is just, and should be enforced; but, if strained or perverted to the justification or toleration of wilful neglect, or caprice, or perverseness on the one side, and to the extension of penal infliction on those who have been involved, by the indulgence of such neglect or perverseness, the rule becomes the source of greater mischiefs than it professes to

prevent or cure. It imposes, upon an important class of interests
in society, conditions and burdens incompatible with the prosperity or even with the existence of those interests. By the
rule thus expounded — or if a steamer, merely because she is not
propelled by the winds or the tides, is, under all circumstances,
bound to avoid a vessel navigated by sails — it would follow, that
should a vessel of the latter description wantonly or designedly
place herself in the track of a steamer, or even put chase to her
with that object, the steamer would nevertheless be responsible
for the effects of a collision thus brought about.

Such an application of the rule cannot be correct. Steamers
have their rights upon the waters as certain and entire as can be
those of sailing vessels; and the exercise of those rights, under
the injunctions of integrity and discretion, is all that can justly
be demanded of them. There can be no sound reason why they
should be placed upon a ground of comparative disadvantage
with reference to others. Why should there be placed under a
species of judicial ban a mean of navigation and intercourse
which, in regard to commerce, science, literature, art, wealth,
comfort, and civilization, has, in a few years, advanced the world
by more than a thousand years, perhaps, beyond the point at
which the previous and ordinary modes of navigation would
possibly have attained? I am most unwilling to cripple or need-
lessly or unjustly to burden the means of such benefits to mankind by harsh and oppressive exactions.

The danger and injustice of such a course are, in my judgment, exemplified by the testimony in this case, and by the
conclusions deduced by the court from that testimony.

The witnesses examined in this case are of three classes or
descriptions: 1. Those who belonged to the crew of the brig.
2. Those who were engaged in the management of the steamer.
3. The owners or crews of the several barges then in tow by the
steamer.

It is admitted on all sides that the night on which the collision
occurred was dark, and that the brig was anchored in the much
frequented and even greatly thronged track of vessels of every
description, — in fact, in the very port of New York. And it is
equally shown, that, by the laws of the State of New York, and
by rules of the harbor, vessels thus situated are required to hoist
a light at the elevation of twenty feet above the deck. There
are no laws of the State, nor regulations of the port, inhibiting
ingress and egress into and from the harbor during the night, nor
prescribing the degree of speed at which these movements shall
be accomplished; and any such regulation would be inconven-
ient, and, to say the least of it, useless, where the precaution of
a light, such as that prescribed by the law and the regulation of

the port, was used. And it would seem to be as absurd and as vain to prescribe a given speed to a steam-vessel entering or leaving the harbor, as it would be to attempt the same thing as to sailing vessels, whose speed, at least, must depend upon the state of the wind at the time of her progress. Every necessity, every reasonable precaution, every guide, is supplied by a sufficient light, exhibited at the proper time and place.

The statements of the crew of the brig are vague, and by no means consistent, with respect to the precautions used on that vessel. They cannot state the precise time at which a light was displayed, nor that at which it was taken down to be used for other than the purposes of a signal; nor do they concur as to the hour at which the collision occurred, nor as to the lapse of time between the lowering of the signal-light, for the purpose of paying out chain, and the fact of collision. They do agree in stating the lowering, and in the use of the light for another purpose than that of a signal, shortly before the collision; and in the further important fact that the light, when up, was suspended several feet below the elevation required by the law and the harbor regulations.

It is an opinion frequently expressed, and which seems to have become trite with many persons, with reference to cases of collision, that the crews of the different vessels are almost certain to swear to such facts as will justify the conduct of their own vessel; or, in other words, will excuse or justify themselves, and cast the imputation of blame on the opposing vessel or party, even at the cost of perjury; and that, therefore, little or no faith can be given the oaths of the officers and crews of the respective vessels. With every proper allowance for the influence of selfishness, or alarm, or falsehood, it may be remarked that extreme opinions, like the one just stated, are themselves calculated to lead to error, and would often defeat the purpose which the diffidence or mistrust on which they rest would seek to attain. Collisions between vessels engaged in the navigation, either on the ocean or on rivers, rarely occur in the presence of spectators wholly detached from and indifferent to the events which really take place. The scene of such events is usually on the track of the ocean, the course of rivers, midst the darkness of night, where and when there are none to testify save those who participate in the catastrophe; and if such persons, under the influence of a foregone opinion, are to be set aside as unworthy of faith, decisions upon cases of collision will, and indeed must, become so entirely the result of conjecture, or of an arbitrary rule, as to challenge but a small share of public confidence; and what is of more importance, may be the instruments of injustice and oppression. The error and inconsistency of this rule is strikingly exemplified in the present instance, in which it is seen that the testimony on which the decision professes mainly to be founded is said to be that of the captain of the steamer, the party said to be in default — a source of evidence denounced by the rule as unworthy of belief. It so happens, however, by a conjuncture quite unusual, that the case before us is placed beyond the operation of the rule of evidence above adverted to. Of the fourteen witnesses who testify on behalf of the defendant in the libel, seven of them did not belong to the steamer. They were composed of the masters and crews of the barges then in tow of the former, and whose lives and property were imperilled by any misconduct of her conductors, with regard to whom there is no conceivable ground for bias or partiality on the part of these witnesses. Yet it is explicitly declared by them all — and they all appear to have been awake and in a situation to observe what was passing — that not one of them saw a light of any description or in any position displayed from the brig; that the latter was perceived as a dark spot upon the water, only when approached so closely as to be at the immediate point of collision. It is incomprehensible to my mind how this could have been the case had there been lights from the brig, and especially at the proper elevation prescribed by law. Such lights must have been in some degree perceptible, instead of the vessel being perceived only at the very point of contact, as a dark spot upon the water. But if in truth the brig had lights at all, provided they were placed in a situation to render them invisible, or on a place below that prescribed by law, she is as obnoxious to censure as if she displayed no lights. The steamer is proved to have been abundantly lighted. To excuse a departure from the law, either in failing to exhibit any lights, or displaying such as were insufficient or placed in an improper position, and still more to make such delinquency the ground of reclamation for injuries resulting therefrom, appears to me to be the award of a premium for a breach of duty, and an invitation to similar offences by others.

Without a further detail of the testimony in this case, I must say that the preponderance of that testimony is, in my judgment, against the libellant upon the merits. Independently, therefore, of the objection to the jurisdiction of the court, were I at liberty to disregard that objection, I think that the libel should not have been sustained. Upon the question of jurisdiction, it is my opinion that the libel should have been dismissed apart from the merits, and that the case should by this court be remanded to the circuit court, with directions to dismiss the libel, with costs.

THE SHIP HOWARD, HER TACKLE, &C., WILLIAM F. SCHMIDT AND GEORGE BELCHER, CLAIMANTS AND APPELLANTS, v. FREDERICK WISSMAN, LIBELLANT.

Where a cargo of potatoes was shipped at Hamburg to be delivered at New York, the evidence shows that they were in bad condition when shipped, and consequently the vessel is not responsible for their loss.

THIS was an appeal from the circuit court of the United States for the southern district of New York.

The facts are stated in the opinion of the court.

The case was argued by *Mr. Johnson*, for the appellants, upon which side there was also a brief filed by *Mr. Donohue*, and by *Mr. Betts*, for the appellees, upon which side there was also a brief filed by *Mr. Cutting*.

The points of law upon both sides were so connected with the testimony that they could not be explained without giving an abstract of the evidence.

Mr. Justice CATRON delivered the opinion of the court.

This is a proceeding *in rem*, against a foreign vessel, by libel; charging that the libellant shipped on her, at Hamburg, in Germany, 5,004 bushels of potatoes in good order and well conditioned for the purpose of shipping, and that, by the long and wilful delay of the vessel at Hamburg, and on her voyage to New York, (the port of destination,) and through the carelessness and misconduct of the master and owner, the potatoes became and were injured, decayed, and wholly lost to the libellant.

To this charge the respondents answer, that the decay of the potatoes was caused by their lying in port for some time before they were put on board; and that they were delivered to the vessel in a damp and wet state, and were not in a sound condition. The alleged negligence is denied generally.

On the foregoing issue the district court made an interlocutory decree, declaring that "the libellant recover in this action against the ship, the value of the potatoes at Hamburg at the time they were laden on board, together with charges and expenses, unless it be proved by the claimants that they were not then in a good, sound condition; or that they perished afterwards, in consequence of inherent disease or defects existing at the time of lading the same, and not from the prolonged detention in their transportation; and it is further ordered, that it be referred to a commissioner to ascertain and report the cause of the destruction and loss of the potatoes, and their value at the time of shipment."

The commissioner reported that he had heard the parties and their testimony, and found that the potatoes were in a sound condition, and that they did not perish afterwards in consequence of inherent disease or defects existing at the time of loading the same, but that the cause of their destruction and loss was the long and protracted voyage of one hundred and nine days; and that they were worth, when shipped, (including charges,) $2,256$\frac{77}{100}$.

This report was adopted by the district court, and a decree made accordingly.

An appeal was prosecuted by the claimants to the circuit court, where the decree below was affirmed.

The potatoes were shipped in bulk in the hold of the vessel, which mode of shipment was adopted at the instance of the libellants' agent, who superintended their stowage.

It appears that much rain fell during the time the potatoes were lying in lighters, awaiting an opportunity to ship them, being about a month; and it rained when they were alongside, and putting into the vessel; and in our opinion it is satisfactorily established, that the potatoes were wet to a considerable extent when delivered and stowed in the hold. Wulff, the stevedore, under whose immediate supervision they were stowed, deposes that they were wet, "and considering their condition, and their being shipped in bulk, he thinks they should not have been shipped across the Atlantic; for said potatoes began to steam before the sailing of the ship Howard."

The pilot of The Howard deposes, that he saw them steam out of the fore-hatch, during the passage down the river, before the vessel got outside.

Kumpel deposes, that he saw the potatoes in the lighters and on board, and that they were wet. So the other witnesses prove.

Kundsten, mate of The Howard, deposes that the potatoes began to have a bad smell when the vessel was fourteen days out. The captain says he smelt them when they were only eight days at sea.

It is proved by all the witnesses of both sides, that the potato crop of 1849 was much blighted and diseased, all over Germany; and several witnesses declare, that potatoes grown that year were generally unfit for shipment across the ocean.

The libellants' witness, Heidpriein, answers to cross interrogatories, that he purchased and sold that year 7,200,000 pounds of potatoes; that the crop was generally unsound, and would not stand being shipped in bulk for so long a voyage as from Hamburg to New York; says he shipped to Hamburg — about forty German miles, (160 of ours) — by water, and that no cargo arrived, after being on the way from four to fourteen days, without the potatoes being in a bad condition.   And respecting those shipped on The Howard, he states that Mr. Rawalle, Mr. Wissman's agent, applied to him to purchase potatoes; and he, having none to sell, told Mr. Rawalle of some for sale by Lehman and Cleve — which, not being sound, the deponent had refused to buy — and he understood Rawalle purchased them. Rawalle deposes that he got the potatoes he shipped of Deven and Lehman, but declares they were not sick or diseased.

Baalmann deposes that he saw the potatoes in the lighters; they were in a bad condition and diseased, he having made examination by cutting them with a knife, and found they were not in good shipping order; and he knows that potatoes of that year's growth, shipped in bulk to England, arrived there in a worthless state, and had to be thrown overboard.

Wulff, the stevedore, says, that when he stowed the potatoes he examined them, by breaking and cutting; they appeared to be unsound and diseased.

The master of The Howard deposes, that the ship Miles took a cargo of the potatoes purchased by Rawalle for Wissman, and what The Miles did not take were taken by The Howard; that he, the master, purchased some of the potatoes that were going to The Miles, for use on The Howard, which proved to be diseased and unfit for use on being cooked.

The mate declares that the potatoes looked well outside, but when cut open they had sickness in them; that the potatoes loaded on both vessels came from the same man.

Arianson, master of the bark Miles, deposes, that more potatoes were sent to The Miles, when loading at Hamburg, than he could take on board, and that the balance were sent to The Howard; that the potatoes that he brought rotted.   He discovered it five or six weeks after going to sea, by the smell, which was two or three weeks before arriving at New York.

The owner having been committed to the *primâ facie* facts of soundness and good condition by his contract of affreightment, it was properly imposed on him by the district court to establish the contrary by due proof; and our opinion is, that the proof produced by him does overcome the *primâ facie* presumption, and shows the potatoes of the libellant to have been unsound and unfit for shipment, and especially unfit to be shipped in bulk and wet, as was done by the libellants' agent.

Rawalle was examined for the libellant several times.   He deposes, that the potatoes were put on board in good order: that they were dry and sound; and in his opinion, if The Howard had sailed in due time, according to her advertisement, they would have arrived at New York in a sound condition.

As a dealer in this article, the witness had very small experience compared with various others examined; none of whom express the belief that this cargo, stowed in bulk, could have reached the port of destination uninjured. But what appears to us far more satisfactory than the speculations of witnesses is, that the cargo of The Miles was lost by decay, she being loaded at the same time and in the same manner as was The Howard, and with part of the potatoes taken from the same lighters—although The Miles made her voyage in due time.

Our conclusion is, that the libellant's case has no merits. It is therefore ordered, that the decree of the circuit court be reversed, and the cause remanded to that court, with directions to dismiss the libel with costs.

Mr. Justice DANIEL.

In the opinion just pronounced, so far as it goes to demonstrate the entire want of justice in the demand of the libellant, I entirely concur, the testimony in this case having satisfactorily ascertained that the loss of the cargo was inevitable from the character of the subject of which that cargo consisted, and that by no degree of diligence or care could it have been transported in good condition to its point of destination. But, independently of these considerations, and in advance of them, there is another which of itself, in my judgment, should have prevented the claim of the libellant from being established or entertained at all in the district and circuit courts, and which should operate with equal effect in preventing its being entertained here.

This case is one of contract between the owner of property and the master of a vessel to transport a cargo of potatoes from Hamburg and to deliver them in New York. It is nothing more than a contract between the owner of property and a carrier to convey a given subject for hire. It was a contract made upon land to be terminated and executed upon the land for a stipulated compensation, and not strictly or properly a maritime contract, in any sense beyond any other contract, in the performance of which a party or agent would be compellable to cross the ocean or even to pass a river. It did not begin and terminate on the sea. Upon this contract an action might have been instituted in a court of law either upon the charter-party or the bill of lading, in conformity with ancient and well-settled practice, and could have been as speedily and efficiently decided in such a court as it could be in the present form of proceeding, less familiar to the common understanding and habits of the country, dubious and undefined in its claims to power, and attended with expenses beyond those incident to the usual tribunals of the land.

My opinion is, that for want of jurisdiction in the case presented upon the face of the libel, that libel should have been dismissed by the circuit court, and that this court should now, for that cause, order it to be dismissed.

JOHN F. MCKINNEY, PLAINTIFF IN ERROR, *v.* MANUEL SAVIEGO, AND PILAR, HIS WIFE.

Where a person, who owned land in Texas whilst it was a part of Mexico, removed into Mexico prior to the declaration of independence by Texas, and continued to reside in Mexico until her death, her daughter, who was also a citizen of Mexico, could not, as heir, recover the land in Texas.

By the laws which governed Texas before the revolution, the proprietor of land must have resided within the jurisdiction of the Mexican government, and foreigners could not inherit land.

The constitution of Texas considered as aliens all those who did not reside there at the time of the declaration of independence, unless they were afterwards naturalized; and also decreed that no alien should hold land in Texas, except by titles emanating directly from the government of that republic.

The legislature of Texas had power to modify these rules, but did not change them in this respect when it introduced the common law by statute. Upon the death of the ancestor the estate was cast upon the State, without the necessity of an inquest of office.

The constitution and laws of Texas provide for the case of an alien heir who may inherit from a citizen, but not for an alien heir inheriting from an alien.

The treaty of Guadaloupe Hidalgo provides for those Mexicans who inhabited territories ceded to the United States, but had no relation to Texas.

THIS case was brought up, by writ of error, from the district court of the United States for the district of Texas.

The case is stated in the opinion of the court.

It was submitted on printed arguments by *Mr. Hale,* for the plaintiff in error, and by *Mr. Hughes,* for the defendants.

The arguments involved many points of the old Mexican law, but the principal one was thus stated by *Mr. Hale,* in his additional brief : —

The plaintiffs, in their petition, describe themselves as aliens, and in the thirteenth instruction which they requested, they assume that both the female plaintiff and her mother were aliens to the republic of Texas, and that the former is still an alien to the United States. It is evident, therefore, that at the time of the death of Gertrudis Barrera, the female plaintiff was, with respect to the land in Texas, the alien child of an alien, and the first question is, could she take the estate by inheritance ?

The tenth article of the general provisions of the constitution of the republic of Texas, Hart. Dig. p. 88, provides that " no alien shall hold land in Texas, except by titles emanating directly from the government of this republic. But if any citizen of this republic should die intestate or otherwise, his children or heirs shall inherit his estate, and aliens shall have a reasonable time to take possession and dispose of the same in a manner hereafter to be pointed out by law," &c. It is clear that the latter part of this provision, which gives to aliens a reasonable time to take possession and dispose of " the same," relates to the estate of a citizen of the republic, and not to that of an alien ; and that the power given to the congress of the republic to point out the manner in which this disposition should be made, authorizes only laws relating to the estates of citizens. The 14th section of the act of January 28, 1840, cited in the original brief, should, therefore, be restricted to this case ; and of this opinion were the supreme court of Texas, in the case of Cryer v. Andrews, 11 Texas, 181, where this clause of the constitution and this act are said to be " in relation to the alien heirs of a deceased citizen." The capacity of the alien children of an alien is thus left to be determined by the general prohibition of the constitution and by the principles of the common law, introduced into Texas, as a body, by the act of January 20, 1840, before the death of the plaintiff's ancestor. Hart. Dig. art. 127. And upon these, there can be no question that the female plaintiff, Pilar, being an alien, did not take the land in Texas, by descent, from her mother ; and that the district court erred in giving the thirteenth instruction requested by her counsel.

Mr. Hughes contended that Gertrudis Barrera did not lose her land by removing to Tamaulipas before the declaration of independence, because the 8th section of that instrument was prospective. " All persons who shall leave the country," &c. Hart. Dig. 37.

Even if the land were liable to forfeiture, the 13th article, § 4, declared that " the legislature shall, by law, provide a method for determining what lands may have been forfeited or escheated." Until this was done, the title remained as it was.

The articles 585, 600 (Hart. Dig.) allowed an alien to take by descent. The 38th article allowed the alien heirs of citizens a reasonable time to dispose of their property ; but this included alien heirs of an alien, because the section provides that it shall be no bar to a descent that one of the ancestors of the claimant was an alien.

Mr. Justice CAMPBELL delivered the opinion of the court.

The defendants (Saviego and wife) claimed, in the district court, two and one half leagues of land lying in the counties of Goliad and Refugio, in Texas, as an inheritance of Madame

Saviego, from her mother, Gertrudis Barrera, who died in Matamoros, in Mexico, in 1842.

Gertrudis Barrera acquired, in 1834, one league of the *locus in quo* by donation, and the remainder by purchase under the colonization laws of the State of Coahuila and Texas, while it formed a part of the republic of Mexico. She occupied and improved the land until the commencement of the revolutionary movements in Texas, in 1835, but prior to the declaration of independence in that year she emigrated and became a resident of Matamoros, where she continued until her death. The plaintiffs were also citizens of Coahuila and Texas, but abandoned their connection with Texas in company with their ancestress, and have retained their *status* as Mexican citizens.

They are described on the record as aliens and citizens, and residents of the city of Matamoros, in the State of Tamaulipas, in the republic of Mexico. The defendant claimed the land by virtue of locations and surveys of valid land certificates, which had been regularly returned to the general land-office, in Texas, before the 31st August, 1853.

A number of questions are presented in the bill of exceptions, but the opinion the court has formed upon the 12th, 13th, and 14th instructions, given at the instance of the plaintiffs, in the district court, renders it unnecessary for us to consider any others. These instructions are as follows :—

"12. If Gertrudis Barrera was a citizen of the republic of Mexico, domiciliated within the State of Coahuila and Texas when the land in question was granted to her, her abandonment of the State of Coahuila and Texas, and settlement in Matamoros, in the State of Tamaulipas, after the commencement of the revolution in Texas, and before the declaration of Texan independence, was not a forfeiture of the land so granted, nor did the land thereby become vacant; and after the close of the revolution in Texas, she would have been authorized to enforce her right, had she then been living.

"13. If Madame Barrera died in Tamaulipas, in 1842, then being a citizen of the said State of Tamaulipas, domiciliated there, and the female plaintiff was her only heir, she too being a citizen of, and domiciliated in Tamaulipas, said heir could and did take, by the law here, the land in contest, by descent, and had a right to enforce her title by descent, to the same extent that her ancestor could have done, but subject, as she is an alien, to forfeiture by proceedings on the part of the State.

"14. But if no proceedings were instituted and perfected before the late treaty between the United States and Mexico, the right in said heir becomes perfect, and not subject to forfeiture, by virtue of the 8th article of said treaty."

It is settled, in the jurisprudence of Texas, that the colonization laws of Coahuila and Texas annex, as an enduring and
peremptory condition, to all titles issued by their authority, that
the grantee, so long as he remains the proprietor, shall continue
his domicile within the republic of Mexico, of which that State
formed a part. A change of domicile operated to defeat the
estate of the grantee, and to restore the land without incumbrance to the public domain, so that, without a judicial or other
inquiry, it might be regranted. The same jurisprudence recognizes the prohibition upon foreigners to inherit lands in Mexico,
for the owners of lands were subject to charges and obligations
which citizens could alone perform. Halleman *v*. Peebles, 1
Texas, 673; Horton *v*. Brown, 2 ibid. 78; Yates *v*. James,
10 ibid. 168.

The conduct of Gertrudis Barrera and her children, the defendants in this suit, after the commencement of the revolutionary movements in Texas, and which separated that State from
Mexico, deprived them of all claim to political rights in the new
republic, and placed them under the civil disabilities of foreigners under its laws. The constitution of Texas, of 1836, identified
as citizens only such persons as were residing in Texas on the
day of the declaration of independence, or should be naturalized
according to its provisions. Hart. Dig. 35, 38; Inglis *v*. Trustees
of the Sailors' Snug Harbor, 3 Pet. 99. The same instrument
provided that "no alien shall hold land in Texas, except by titles
emanating directly from the government of this republic," (Hart.
Dig. 38, § 10,) and provided that congress should, as early as
practicable, introduce by statute the common law of England,
with such modifications as the circumstances of the State might
require. This duty was performed in 1840, by an enactment
that "the common law of England, so far as it is not inconsistent with the constitution or acts of congress now in force, shall,
together with such acts, be the rule of decision in this republic,
and shall continue in full force until altered or repealed by
congress." The common-law authorities clearly establish that
Madame Saviego, under the circumstances, is not deemed to be
an heir at law, having no inheritable blood, and, in the absence of
such heirs, the estate would be cast immediately upon the State,
without inquest of office. Orr *v*. Hodgson, 4 Wheat. 453;
Hardy *v*. De Leon, 5 Texas, 211, 242.

We shall now examine if there are other provisions in the
laws of Texas to relieve the defendants from the apparent disability.

The constitution of Texas, by way of exception to the general
inhibition upon aliens to "hold lands except by titles emanating
directly from the republic," declares, that "if any citizen should

die-intestate or otherwise, his children or heirs shall inherit his estate, and alien$ shall have a reasonable time to take possession of and dispose of the same in a manner hereafter to be pointed out by law." The 10th section of the law of distribution and descent, (Hart. Dig. art. 585,) provides: " In making title to land by descent, it shall be no bar to a party that any ancestor, through whom he derives his descent from the intestate, is or hath been an alien; and every alien to whom any land may be devised or may descend, shall have nine years to become a citizen of the republic and take possession of such land; or shall have nine years to sell the same, before it shall be declared forfeited, or before it shall escheat to the government." The first clause of this section is substantially a re-enactment of the statute of 11 and 12 William III. c. 6, and removes no other defect than the want of inheritable blood arising from the alienage of some person through whom the heir must deduce his claim. McCreery v. Somerville, 9 Wheat. 354.

The second clause modifies the existing laws which regulate the capacities of aliens to take or hold real property in the State, whether by devise or descent.

But the remedial effect of the act does not extend beyond the disability of an alien heir. It contains no enactment in favor of an alien who may have acquired possession or property in lands, whereby he could make a valid bequest or transmit it to his heirs, whether aliens or citizens by descent.

The act of which this section forms a part is framed for the disposal of the estates of those having " title to any estate in inheritance, and regulates its descent or distribution." The prohibition in the constitution upon aliens to hold lands in Texas, and the limited powers of congress to introduce favorable conditions in favor of alien heirs, must be remembered in ascertaining its meaning. The constitution had provided for the transmission of the estates of citizens to their children or heirs, (being citizens,) and then provides that congress shall legislate to give to aliens a reasonable time to take possession and to dispose of such an inheritance. Neither the language of the act nor the policy of the State, as it may be discovered from its constitutions and laws, authorizes the conclusion that an alien, claiming real property in Texas, can transmit it, by descent, to an heir who is also an alien.

The subject-matter to which these provisions all relate is the estates of citizens; and we cannot apply their conditions to the special and peculiar case of an inheritance claimed by an alien heir in the right of an alien intestate. The question has not arisen, so far as we can discover, in the courts of Texas; but in the case of Cryer v. Andrews, 11 Texas, 170. the court seems to assume that the act we have considered was a legislative com-

pliance with the constitutional guarantees in favor of the alien
heirs of deceased citizens; and that the alien heir must, within
nine years, sell the lands or become a citizen. In the present
instance, citizenship has not been acquired, which that court
seems to treat as a prerequisite to an entry on the inheritance.

The last question remaining for consideration arises on the
8th section of the treaty with the republic of Mexico of the 2d
February, 1848, (9 Stats. at Large, 923,) called the treaty of
Guadaloupe Hidalgo. The first clause of that article provides
" for the Mexicans now established in territories previously belonging to Mexico, and which remain for the future within the
limits of the United States." The second clause provides for
those who shall prefer to remain in the said territories, and they
are authorized to retain the title of Mexican citizens or acquire
the rights of citizens of the United States. The third clause
prescribes, " that in the said territories property of every kind,
now belonging to Mexicans not established there, shall be in-
violably respected. The present owners, the heirs of these, and
all Mexicans who may hereafter acquire said property by contract, shall enjoy with respect to it guarantees equally ample as
if the same belonged to citizens of the United States." To
what territories did the high contracting parties refer to in this
article? We think it clear that they did not refer to any portion
of the acknowledged limits of Texas. The territories alluded to
are those which had, previously to the treaty, belonged to Mexico, and which, after the treaty, should remain within the limits
of the United States. The republic of Texas had been many
years before acknowledged by the United States as existing separately and independently of Mexico; and as a separate and
independent State it had been admitted to the Union. The
government of the United States, by that act, had conferred
upon the population established there all the privileges within
their constitutional competency to grant.

The various stipulations contained in this article are wholly
inapplicable to the persons who, before the revolution in Texas,
had been citizens of Mexico, and who, by that revolution, had
been separated from it.

The right of property, to which this article of the treaty was
designed to afford a guarantee, extended to property of every
kind which, at its date, belonged to Mexican citizens, ("now belonging to Mexicans,") not established within the territories then
ceded to the United States. In the present instance, the republic of Texas had acquired title many years before, and the land
at the date formed a part of its public domain.

Our conclusion is, that the judgment of the district court
should be reversed, and the cause remanded to that court for
further proceedings.

THE UNITED STATES, PLAINTIFFS IN ERROR, v. THE MINNESOTA
AND NORTHWESTERN RAILROAD COMPANY.

12

Where the United States brought a case up to this court as plaintiffs in error, and
the attorney-general moved for a discontinuance upon the ground that he wished
other questions to be presented upon the record, which he deemed necessary for a
full elucidation of the case, the court, without expressing an opinion upon these
other questions, will grant the motion made by the legal representative of the government.

THIS was a motion by *Mr. Cushing*, (attorney-general,) to
withdraw the writ of error, and discontinue the appeal to this
court, to which the case had been brought up, by writ of error,
from the supreme court of the Territory of Minnesota.

The motion was argued by *Mr. Cushing*, and opposed by *Mr.
Barbour* and *Mr. Johnson*. Much matter of general interest
was introduced by both sides into the discussion, which it is
not deemed necessary to report, because the decision of the court
turned upon a single legal point.

Mr. Justice NELSON delivered the opinion of the court.

This is a writ of error to the supreme court of the Territory
of Minnesota.

An action of trespass was brought by the United States
against the defendants before the district court of the first district, in the county of Goodhue, in said Territory, for an alleged
trespass committed on section 8, in township No. 112 north, of
the public lands.

The defendants justified under an act of incorporation by
the legislature of the said Territory, passed March 4, 1854, and
by which they were empowered to construct a railroad from a
point on the northwest shore of Lake Superior, and near the
mouth of the St. Louis River, across the said Territory of Minnesota, by the way of St. Anthony and St. Paul, over the Mississippi at St. Paul, and to such point on the northern boundary
line of the State of Iowa, as the board of directors might designate, which point should be selected with reference to the best
route to the city of Dubuque, provided the location of the road
should conform in all respects to such route as might be designated in any act of congress granting lands for the construction
of a railroad through the Territory.

The act of incorporation also provided that any lands granted
to the Territory in aid of the construction of this road, should
be deemed vested in fee-simple in the company; and further, it
is alleged that by an act of congress, passed June 29, 1854, for
the purpose of aiding in the construction of the road, every al-
ternate section of land designated by odd numbers, for six sections

in width on each side of the road along the line, was granted to the Territory upon the terms and conditions specified in the said act; and also, that the said defendants caused a survey and location of the road as contemplated by the act of incorporation, and that said road includes the land upon which the trespass complained of was committed, and which is a portion of one of the sections granted to the Territory of Minnesota by the act of congress aforesaid.

The plaintiff to this defence set up, by way of replication, that before the trespasses complained of were committed, namely, on the 4th of August, 1854, an act was passed by congress repealing the act previously passed on the 29th of June, granting land in aid of the construction of said road.

To this replication the defendants demurred, and the plaintiff joined in the demurrer.

The district court gave judgment for the defendants on the demurrer.

An appeal was taken from this judgment to the supreme court of the Territory, where, after argument, the judgment was affirmed. From this judgment the plaintiff has appealed to this court by writ of error.

The writ of error was made returnable to this court on the fourth Monday of December, 1854, and the record was brought up by the defendants in error, and filed and docketed on the 21st of the same month.

The attorney-general now moves, on behalf of the United States, to withdraw his writ of error, and discontinue the appeal to this court, which motion is resisted by the counsel for the defendants.

After an appeal brought to the appellate court, the withdrawal or discontinuance of the same is not a matter of course, but, if the plaintiff finds it expedient to discontinue, he must first obtain leave of the court. 2 Daniel's Pr. 1644; 11 Pet. 55. The discontinuance is usually granted on the application, unless some special reason be shown by the defendant for retaining the case with a view to a determination on the merits. Usually, the courts will not allow it, if the party intend at some future time to bring a new appeal, as the allowance under such circumstances would be unjust to the defendant. There is no such ground of objection here, as the attorney-general disclaims trying the questions involved upon the present pleadings. These pleadings, with the exception of some questions arising upon the powers conferred upon the defendants under their act of incorporation, confine the issue to the effect and operation of the act of congress granting the lands in aid of the construction of the road, and of the subsequent repealing act. And these, doubtless, comprised all the questions which the counsel in the court below, representing the United States, supposed could be material. They are presented very fully and lawyer-like upon the record, and are involved in the judgment rendered in the court below,

The attorney-general, however, avers, that there are other questions than those appearing on the record, which he deems material to be brought to the consideration of the court in deciding upon the force and effect of these acts of congress referred to, and without which he is unwilling to submit the case to the final determination of this court; and asks, therefore, for a withdrawal of the appeal. Without expressing any opinion whether there may or may not be questions presented, other than those appearing upon this record, bearing upon the general matters involved in the litigation, the court are of opinion that the grounds stated by the attorney-general, and his opinion expressed as the legal representative of the government, are sufficient to justify us in granting leave for the discontinuance.

Some technical grounds have been presented, depending upon the rules and practice of the court for the dismissal of the case from the docket, and of the writ of error, which we have not deemed it important to notice, as we think the motion should be granted upon the general ground stated.

Motion to withdraw and discontinue the appeal by writ of error in this case granted.

JAMES L. CALCOTE, PLAINTIFF IN ERROR, v. FREDERICK STANTON AND HENRY S. BUCKNER.

This court has no jurisdiction, under the 25th section of the judiciary act, of a case like the following, namely: —

Where an assignee of some creditors of a person who had taken the benefit of the bankrupt act of the United States, filed a bill against the bankrupt to set aside the discharge as void upon the ground of fraud. The defendant demurred to the bill upon the ground of staleness, want of equity, and the statute of limitations.

It does not follow that the supreme court of the State, in dismissing the bill, placed any construction whatever upon the bankrupt act; and moreover, if they did, the decision must have been in favor of the privilege set up by the bankrupt and not against it.

THIS case was brought up from the high court of errors and appeals of the State of Mississippi, by a writ of error issued under the 25th section of the judiciary act.

Mr. Benjamin moved to dismiss it for want of jurisdiction, none of the cases provided for in the 25th section being applicable here. He then examined the provisions of the section, and contended that the construction placed by the court of appeals of Mississippi upon the fourth and fifth sections of the bankrupt act was not such as to give this court jurisdiction to review its decision. Besides, that court considered the claim to be barred by the statute of limitations.

The motion was opposed by *Mr. Day* and *Mr. Johnson*, who entered into an elaborate review of the judgment of the Mississippi court with a view of showing that, by necessary inference, that court must have decided against the right and title set up under the bankrupt act, because there was no other sufficient ground upon which to rest their judgment.

Mr. Justice GRIER delivered the opinion of the court.

This case comes before us on a motion to dismiss for want of jurisdiction. It is a writ of error to the high court of errors and appeals of the State of Mississippi.

The plaintiff in error, who was complainant in a bill in equity before the chancellor of that State, claims jurisdiction for this court to review the judgment of the court of appeals, under the 25th section of the judiciary act, because the title to his demand comes through a bankrupt assignee, and therefore from an authority exercised under an act of congress, and because the judgment of the state court was against his claim. He contends that his case is within the third clause of this section, which authorizes this court to review the decision of a state court "where is drawn in question the construction of any clause of the constitution, or of a treaty or statute, or commission held under the United States, and the decision is against the title, right, privilege, or exemption specially set up or claimed, &c."

It is not enough to give jurisdiction to this court, under this clause, that the decision of the state court was against a party claiming title under some statute of, or commission held under, the United States. The origin of the title may be but an accident of the controversy, and not the subject or substance of it. The suit must have drawn in question the construction of such statute or commission, and the judgment of the state court must have been adverse to the claim set up under them. "The record also must show, if not *ipsissimis verbis*, at least, by clear and necessary intendment, that such question of 'construction' was raised, and must have been decided in order to induce the judgment. It is not enough to show that the question might have arisen, and been applicable to the case, unless it is further shown on the record that it did arise, and was applied by the state court to the case." The cases which establish these principles are too numerous for quotation.

The record before us presents no evidence that such a question did arise, or could have been decided.

The bill shows that, twelve years after the defendants were discharged under the bankrupt act, the complainant got an assignment of certain claims against them from creditors who had received their dividends of the bankrupt's assets, without questioning the legality of their discharge; that being thus possessed, he set about "to ferret out the frauds, devices, combinations, priorities, preferences, &c., &c., practised, done, and given by the defendants"; and that he had discovered numerous instances of preferences given by the defendants to indorsers and other favored creditors previous to their bankruptcy, in consequence of which it was alleged that their certificate of discharge was void. The balances claimed under these assignments, with interest, would amount to near a million of dollars. The averment of the bill, that the assignments to the complainant were for "value received," would be satisfied by the consideration of a dollar or less. The respondents demurred to the bill, and set forth numerous causes of demurrer; the chief of which were a want of equity in the bill, and the bar of the statute of limitations, or the staleness of the demand. But in no one of them is any objection interposed which called for a construction of the bankrupt act, where the complainant claimed any title or exemption under it. The only "privilege or exemption" which could have been "drawn in question" under the act were those of the defendant, the validity of whose discharge under it was impugned. But as the decision was in their favor, the case is not brought within our jurisdiction. See Strader v. Baldwin, 9 How. 261.

The whole argument for plaintiff in error was expended in endeavoring to prove that the bill ought not to have been dismissed for want of equity or staleness; and, assuming this to be so, it was contended that the court could not have done so for these reasons, and consequently their decision must have been the result of some misconstruction of the bankrupt law as to the rights claimed by the complainant under it. But, as we have already shown, if the plaintiffs could successfully establish both their premises and conclusion it would not avail to give us jurisdiction. And we may add, moreover, that we see no reason, from anything that appears on this record, why the state court might not have dismissed the bill as devoid of equity, and as exhibiting a claim which, if not champertous, is on its face a litigious speculation in stale, abandoned, and, as to much the larger portion, wholly unfounded demands.

The writ of error is therefore dismissed for want of jurisdiction.

THE YORK AND CUMBERLAND RAILROAD COMPANY, PLAINTIFFS IN ERROR, *v.* JOHN G. MYERS.

An original writ has fulfilled its functions when the defendant is brought into court. If lost, the court can provide, in its discretion, for the filing of a copy.

The equity of the Statute of Westminster 2, allowing bills of exceptions, embraces all such judgments or opinions of the court that arise in the course of a cause, which are the subjects of revision by an appellate court, and which do not otherwise appear on the record.

But to present a question to this court, the subordinate tribunal must ascertain the facts upon which the judgment or opinion excepted to, is founded.

Therefore, where there was a reference in the circuit court, and the bill of exceptions set out the objections to the award together with the testimony of the arbitrator who was examined in open court, and that testimony showed the facts upon which the objections were founded, it was a sufficient exception.

If an arbitrator embraces in his award matter not submitted, and includes the result in a single conclusion, so as to render it impossible to separate the matters referred from those which have not been, the award is bad.

But in this case, the averments in the declaration and assignment of breaches in the covenant cover the ground upon which the arbitrator rested his award; and his conclusion is a final decision which this court cannot revise either upon the allegation of mistakes in law or mistakes in fact.

THIS case was brought up by writ of error from the circuit court of the United States for the District of Maine.

The case is stated in the opinion of the court.

It was argued by *Mr. Clifford* and *Mr. Shepley*, for the plaintiffs in error, and *Mr. Francis O. J. Smith*, for defendant.

With respect to the point that the bill of exceptions was well taken in this case, the counsel for the plaintiff in error laid down the following propositions :—

1. That the bill of exceptions in this case is within the intent if not within the very letter of the statute ; and therefore it is insisted that the legal questions herein presented are regularly within the revisory power of this court.

2. That if it is not strictly speaking a bill of exceptions, it is at least " an exception in the nature of a bill of exceptions," and therefore it is insisted that the legal questions are examinable on a writ of error.

3. That the rulings and determination of the circuit court, presented for revision are apparent in the record, inasmuch as they are incorporated into the record of the judgment together with the facts on which they were applied under the hand and seal of the circuit judge, and therefore it is insisted that the writ of error well lies.

In support of the first proposition, they cited and commented on 4 Bing. (N. C.) 83, (33 C. L. 288;) 6 Pet. 655 : Co. Litt. 288 *b;* 1 Arch. Prac. 530; 1 Bac. Abr. 529; 17 How. 6; 1 Halsted, 388 ; 7 Johns. 494.

DECEMBER TERM, 1855.   247

Y o r k a n d C u m b e r l a n d R . R . C o . *v.* M y e r s.

In support of the second: 16 Pet. 176; 7 How. 855, 866.

In support of the third: 7 Cranch, 596; 2 How. 894; 10 Ibid. 190, 329; 17 Ibid. 12; 4 Pet. 206.

They then referred to the course of proceeding in Maine, on awards of referees made under a rule of court, and cited a number of cases in that and other States.

Upon the main point in the case, they laid down the following propositions : —

1. A report or award of referees is wholly void if it includes damages for a matter not embraced in the submission, unless the amount improperly included can be ascertained and separated from the residue of the sum awarded. 5 Wheat. 394, and other cases.

2. Damages in lieu of the reserved stock, and at a valuation estimated by the referee, were included in the award; and the record affords no means whatever of ascertaining what that valuation was, or of ascertaining the amount so included.

3. No claim for the reserved stock, or for damages for non-delivery thereof, was embraced in the declaration, or sued for in the action; and, as the reference was one of the action merely, no such claim was submitted to the arbitrament of the referee.

These propositions led to a very minute examination of the facts and accounts in the case.

Mr. Smith, for defendant in error, made eleven points; but it is only necessary to state the one upon which the decision of the court rested : —

9. The several causes of complaint in the plaintiffs' bill of exceptions and assignment of errors, are in the nature and of the effect of a motion to set aside the award, and to grant a new trial, or to recommit the report of the referee; and, under the rule of court, are, as such, only fit matters to be addressed to the consideration and discretion of the circuit court to which the report was made returnable, and are not subject-matters for revision by this court, on a writ of error. Opinion of the circuit court of the United States for the district of Maine, annexed; Parsons *v.* Beford et al. 3 Pet. 445; Wright et al. *v.* Lessee of Hollingsworth et al. 1 Pet. 168; Cutler *v.* Grover, 15 Maine R. 159; Walker *v.* Sanborn, 8 Ibid. 288; Cumberland *v.* North Yarmouth, 4 Ibid. 459; Whitney *v.* Cook, 5 Mass. 143; Boardman *v.* England, 6 Mass. 70; Toland *v.* Sprague, 12 Pet. 331; Evans *v.* Phillips, 4 Wheat. 73; Henderson *v.* Moore, 5 Cranch, 11; Harker *v.* Ellicott et al. 7 Serg. & R. 285; Zeller's Lessee *v.* Eckert et al. 4 How. 289.

Mr. Justice CAMPBELL delivered the opinion of the court.

This is an action by the defendant in this court (Myers) against the railroad company, for the breach of the covenants in a contract made between these parties in August, 1850, by which the defendant agreed to perform certain work, incur charges and expenses, and supply equipments and materials in the construction of a railroad from the city of Portland, in Maine, to South Berwick, in New Hampshire; and also to fulfil the unexecuted engagements of certain contractors who had retired before completing their contract. Before the terms of the contract had been accomplished, the defendant was dismissed, as he alleges, without a sufficient cause; and the object of the suit is to recover such damages as he had sustained by the failure of the company to discharge the obligations they had assumed to him. The declaration recites at large the agreements of the parties, and contains a general averment that he entered upon the construction of the railroad, and the performance of all the matters and things upon his part to be done and performed, and had performed all the things required to be done and performed, until the 19th of August, 1852, and had nearly completed one of the sections of the road so as to be fit for use, and that it had been used; also, that he had expended large sums towards the engineering, surveys, construction, and grading of other parts of the road, until he was unlawfully dismissed, and hindered, and forbidden to prosecute the work any further.

The declaration then contains a general averment of the nonperformance by the plaintiffs (railroad company) of their obligations to suffer the work to proceed, to abide the decision of their engineer, or to pay the amounts that had become payable prior to his dismissal.

This averment is material, in connection with other parts of the case, and will be extracted hereafter.

The defendant (Myers) proceeds to take up the various stipulations of the railroad company, to describe their legal effect, and to denounce their breach by the company. None of these are of importance to the case here, save those that arise on the 8th and 9th articles of the contract. The first of these articles provides for the payments to be made on account of the first division of the road; and the other, for those on the three remaining sections into which it was divided. The 8th article provides that the corporation should pay to the defendant for the performance of his undertakings, and in full satisfaction of the obligations of the company on the prior contracts, $32,000 per mile for the first division of the work; that for all work done by the previous contractors, to the 1st of August, 1850, payments should be made according to their contracts, inclusive of the reserve fund; for all lands purchased by them, whether for cash, bonds, or stock, payments should be made in cash, bonds, or stock, according to the mode of the purchase; and for all such work on said first division, from the 1st of August, and as the same should progress, current payment should be made at the rate of fifty per cent in cash, twenty-five per cent in the six per cent bonds of the company, and twenty-five per cent in stock; one half of the latter to be reserved for an indemnity for the fulfilment of the contract, until said division of the road should be completed.

The 9th section of the agreement refers to the second, third, and fourth sections of the road. For the fulfilment of all its obligations, the company agreed to pay $27,500 per mile — thirty-three and one third per cent in cash, on the return and adjustment of each monthly estimate by the engineer; a like sum in the bonds of the company; and a like sum, reserving one half thereof for indemnity, in the stock certificates of the company. "The monthly estimates to be governed by the same gradation of actual expenditures as heretofore, and the payment to be made on such estimate of actual expenditures."

And it was provided, that, upon the completion of either of the second, third, or fourth sections, in work, material, station-houses, and equipments, the whole of the payments of cash, bonds, and certificates of stock, in corresponding amounts, equal to the sum aforesaid, should be made in complete discharge of said company upon all the contracts pertaining to that section of the road. The breaches laid in the declaration, applicable to the payments, are as follows: —

"And the said plaintiff in fact saith, that the said defendants, contrary to the covenants or agreements in the indenture aforesaid, did not abide by the decision of their engineer, as to the amount and quantity of the several kinds of work done, in and by said indenture contracted to be done by said plaintiff for said defendants, and which were done and performed by the plaintiff; nor did said defendants pay said plaintiff for the work done by him for them, according to said agreement; but, on the contrary, utterly refused to pay the plaintiff therefor, according to the estimate of their engineer; although the plaintiff avers that said engineer made to said defendants a return of the monthly estimates of the work and labor done by plaintiff upon said road."

The declaration recites the eighth article, and avers a breach in reference to the payments, as follows: "And the plaintiff avers that said defendants, in breach of their convenant aforesaid, did not, for all the work performed and material furnished up to said first of August, make a full settlement, as had been heretofore estimated, monthly, and pay the plaintiff therefor, in accordance with the covenants aforesaid; neither did said defendants, for all work on said division, as the same progressed, after said first of August, according to their convenants aforesaid, pay therefor fifty per cent in cash, twenty-five per cent in bonds, and twenty-five per cent in stock, one half being retained, as stipulated, for an indemnity; nor did said defendants pay the plaintiffs therefor, according to the monthly estimates of the engineer, as returned by him."

The breach of the covenants contained in the ninth article is averred in language similar to the above, with variances corresponding to the difference of the sums to be paid.

Before a trial, the parties agreed to refer the action to the determination of three persons, to be appointed by the court, whose report, or the report of any two, was to be made as soon as may be; and that judgment thereon was to be final, and execution to issue accordingly.

Afterwards, one of the persons appointed was authorized to act alone, and this person returned a decision in favor of the defendant, (Myers,) for an ascertained sum as damages.

Upon the return of the award to the court, the corporation submitted objections, and examined the arbitrator in support of them. These objections are as follows: —

"1. That the said Hale has acted and awarded upon, and included in said award, damages for a subject-matter not referred to him.

"2. That the said Hale has included in his said award damages for a claim not embraced in the plaintiff's writ and declaration, and not sued for in the above action, and not referred to his arbitration or decision.

"3. That, in and by his said award, he has awarded to the plaintiff in said action damages for the non-delivery of the reserved stock specified in said writ and declaration, and in the contracts therein set out and copied, although the said reserved stock is not sued for, nor is any allegation made in the said writ and declaration that the same had been demanded, nor was any proof of demand of the same offered at the hearing before said referee, nor was any claim for the same referred for his arbitration or decision.

"4. That the said Hale has awarded damages to the said plaintiff, in lieu of profits for work not performed by the plaintiff under his said contracts, contrary to law.

"5. That there having been no proof or claim that the defendants, in fraud of the plaintiff's rights under his said contract, had taken the contract from the plaintiff, and given to any other person at a lower rate, or taken it for the purpose of giving it to any other party at a lower rate, the referee has awarded a sum as damages to the plaintiff for prospective profits not earned by him, contrary to law.

" 6. That it does not appear in and by said award whether the said referee has credited or charged the plaintiff with an amount of bonds deposited in the hands of Levi Morrell, under the terms of the supplementary contract, dated February 6, 1851, and set out in said writ and declaration.

" 7. That it does not appear in and by said award what disposition was made by the referee of an amount of bonds in the hands of D. C. Emery, the treasurer of said corporation.

" 8. That it does not appear in and by said award whether the said referee charged the said plaintiff with an amount of bonds in his hands, purporting to have been issued by one Nathaniel J. Herrick, describing himself as treasurer *pro tempore* of said corporation."

The arbitrator testified that he had included the twelve and one half per cent of reserved stock in the award ; that he considered the demand for reserved stock as suspended by the proceeding, and that the plaintiff (Myers) was entitled to damages for not having received the stock previous to the breach of the contract. He says there was no distinct claim made before the referee for the reserved stock, but the account embraced it by way of debtor and creditor. The books showed he was entitled to reserved stock, but not as subject to his order, or that he had any opportunity to receive it. He said it was admitted that that amount of reserved stock would be due to him on settlement of his account, but not that he had at any time had it under his control, nor was there any evidence that he had demanded it.

This testimony, with more to the same effect, was elicited from the arbitrator upon his examination before the circuit court, upon the return of the award, and in support of the exceptions to it. The learned judge who presided received the evidence, but overruled the exceptions, and embodied the testimony and the decision in a bill of exceptions, reserving his opinion of the regularity of that mode of proceeding, and whether the judgment can be revised. We are of the opinion, that the equity of the statute allowing a bill of exceptions in courts of common law of original jurisdiction, embraces all such judgments or opinions of the court that arise in the course of a cause, which are the subjects of revision by an appellate court, and which do not otherwise appear on the record. Strother *v.* Hutchinson, 4 Bing. N. C. 83 ; Ford *v.* Potts, 1 Halst. 388 ; Nesbitt *v.* Dallam, 7 G. & J. 494 ; 9 Port. 136.

But to present a question to this court, the subordinate tribunal must ascertain the facts upon which the judgment, or opinion excepted to, is founded; for this court cannot determine the weight or effect of evidence, nor decide mixed questions of law and fact. Zeller v. Eckert, 4 How. 289.

The practice prevails in the courts, where rules of reference are in use, to examine the arbitrators as witnesses, to ascertain facts material to the validity of the award; and the appellate courts are accustomed to revise their decisions, and upon principle we see no objection to the introduction of the same practice into the courts of the United States under the limitations we have indicated. Thornton v. Carson, 7 Cranch, 597; Butler v. Mayor of N. Y. 7 Hill, 829; Lutz v. Linthicum, 8 Peters, 166; Sawyer v. Freeman, 35 Maine, 546; Ward v. American Bank, 7 Met. 486.

In the present instance we can collect from the evidence of the referee, as shown in the exceptions, the fact necessary to raise some of the questions contained in the objections to the award, without being involved in the dispute between the parties, as to the condition in which the reserved stock had been placed by the corporation.

The law is well settled, that by the reference of an action to the determination of an arbitrator, nothing is included in the submission but the subject-matter involved in it. Tidd's Pr. 822; 2 T. R. 645.

And if an arbitrator embraces in his award matter not submitted, and includes the result in a single conclusion, so as to render it impossible to separate the matters referred from those which have not been, the award is bad. Lyle v. Rodgers, 5 Wheat. 394; 33 Maine, 219; Sawyer v. Freeman, 35 Maine, 546.

The defendant contends that no claim for the reserved stock, or for damages for its non-delivery, was embraced in the declaration or sued for in the action; and, as the reference was one of the action merely, no such claim was submitted to the referee. This involves the construction of the declaration.

We have extracted the averments in the declaration that were designed to charge the corporation with the non-performance of the covenants, for the payment for work done before the dismissal of the contractor.

In one of those the charge is, that the corporation had neglected and refused to make any payments, and thus a total failure to fulfil its obligations in respect to payments is alleged. The assignments of the breaches of the 8th and 9th articles are made in the language of the covenants themselves, and the failure charged is coextensive with the obligations. If the corporation had created no reserved stock, or had made no appropriation for the contractor, according to the monthly estimates as the work progressed, and had finally dismissed him, so as to exclude his claim for the stock reserved when his contract had been fulfilled, there could have been no ground for affirming that a breach of the covenants had not been made by the corporation, and that damages were not due.

There would have been no argument to support the allegation, that the contractor was a corporator to the extent of the stock which should have been reserved. But, as we interpret the declaration, its averments have this scope and operation.

It was the duty of the arbitrator to ascertain the truth of these charges. They were the precise subject of the reference. The arbitrator has explained with clearness in his testimony his conclusion on the subject of this stock, that the contractor had no title to the shares; that is, that he had not been paid by the appropriation of so much reserved stock for his use. This conclusion of his is a final decision on the question, for this court cannot revise his mistakes, either of law or of fact, if such had been established. Burchell v. Marsh, 17 How. 344; Kleine v. Catara, 2 Gall. 61. The objections, we have noticed, include all that were insisted on in the argument.

The objection taken to the absence of an original writ, or to the supply of a copy, is not tenable. The original writ had fulfilled its function when the defendant had been brought into court, and its loss did not affect the action of the plaintiff; and, it was a matter resting in the discretion of the court, upon ascertaining the defective state of the record, to supply the deficiency.

Our conclusion is, there is no error in the record.

Judgment affirmed.

Mr. Justice DANIEL dissented.

JOHN G. SHIELDS, APPELLANT, v. ISAAC THOMAS, AND MARY, HIS WIFE, NANCY PIRTLE, JOHN B. GOLDSBURY, THOMAS STARKS, AND ELIZABETH, HIS WIFE, AND JAMES PICKETT, AND ANN, HIS WIFE.

Where there was an administration upon the estate of an intestate in Kentucky, the surety in the administration bond and a portion of the distributees residing there, the court of that place had jurisdiction over the subject-matter; and where the principal defendant, although residing out of the State, voluntarily appeared and answered a bill filed against him, the jurisdiction of the court was complete, and it had a right to pass a decree in the premises.

If several claimants of portions of an estate unite in filing a bill, this does not make it multifarious. The authorities upon this subject examined.

Shields v. Thomas et al.

In this case, this court has already decided the point. See 17 How. 4, 5.
The court in Kentucky having rendered a decree for the complainants, they had a right to file a bill in Iowa, to enforce this decree.

THIS was an appeal from the district court of the United States, for the northern District of Iowa.

The case is stated in the opinion of the court.

It was argued by *Mr. Gillett*, for the appellant, and *Mr. Platt Smith*, for appellees.

Mr. Gillett made nine points. Those which are touched upon in the opinion of the court were the following: —

2. The bill is multifarious, and therefore bad. 1 Dan. Ch. Pr. 384; Cooper's Eq. Pl. 182; Mitford, 146–7; 8 Peters, 123.

7. A judgment against persons not within the jurisdiction of the court, and who were not served with process, and who did not appear to the action, is null and void.

If a court in one State can render effective judgments against persons in other States, who are neither served with process nor appear to the action, there will be no security for the citizen. The mere shadow of claims might ripen into valid judgments, without the defendant having an opportunity to defend. No authoritative court has ever held such judgments valid. The following cases are conclusive upon this point. Ewer v. Coffin, 1 Cushing, 24; Hickey v. Smith, 1 Eng. 456; 3 id. 318, 324; Woodruff v. Taylor, 20 Vermont, 65; Davis v. Smith, 5 Geo. 274; Dunn v. Hall, 8 Blkf. 32, 335; 11 How. 165; 2 M'Lean 473; 8 J. J. Marshall, 600; 2 B. Monroe, 453; 8 B. Monroe, 218; 6 J. J. Marshall, 578; 8 B. Monroe, 137.

8. A judgment or decree void as to one or more of the parties is void as to all. 6 Pick. 232; 12 Johns, 434; 11 N. H. 299; 14 Ohio, 413.

Upon the principal points in the case, *Mr. Platt Smith* said:

We take the ground that the court in Kentucky had jurisdiction of the subject-matter, and of John G. Shields, and that consequently their decree cannot be inquired into, but full faith and credit are to be given to it, as is provided by the constitution and act of congress of the United States. Cons. U. S. art. 4, § 1; act con. 26th May, 1790; 1 U. S. Stat. at L., 122. That as to James Shields and Henry Yater, who were non residents, and proceeded against as such, the Kentucky decree would not be binding on them except in the State of Kentucky, for the courts of that State did not obtain jurisdiction over their persons. Story's Confl. of Laws, § 569; Williams v. Preston, 3 J. J. Marshall, 600; Cobb v. Haynes, 8 B. Monroe, 189. Still, that could not affect the validity of the decree as to John G. Shields, for the court had jurisdiction of his person and of the subject-matter, namely, the settlement of the estate of John Goldsbury, deceased; consequently their judgment or decree is not void, no matter whether it was right or wrong to join Henry Yater and James Shields in the rendition of the decree.

The present action is not multifarious. There is no mixture of different claims. Although the decree is virtually several, yet it is in fact only one thing, and grows out of one subject-matter; a trial of the question as to one complainant is a trial as to the whole.

The remedy at law is uncertain and would have caused a multiplicity of suits, for each complainant would, at law, have been obliged to bring a suit against John G. Shields; and to have sued at law would have raised the objection, first, that no action at law could be had on the decree of a court of equity; Hugh v. Higgs and wife, 8 Wheat. R. 697; Carpenter et al. v. Thornton, 3 B. & Al. 52; Elliott v. Ray, 2 Blackf. R. 31; and second, if the whole had been attempted in one suit, that there was no mutuality between the plaintiffs; Gould's Pl. 197; 2 Saund. R. 117, n. 2; and, third, if there had been several suits, then, that several distinct actions could not be brought on one decree.

The uncertainty, then, of an action or actions at law was sufficient ground for giving to a court of equity jurisdiction of the case; Story's Eq. Pl. § 478; and the avoidance of multiplicity of suits was another ground; 1 Story's Eq. Juris. § 64, k., also 67; Jesus College v. Bloom, 3 Atk. 263. ·

Mr. Justice DANIEL delivered the opinion of the court.

Upon an appeal from a decree in chancery by the district court of the northern district of Iowa.

This case, although upon the record a good deal extended in volume, is in effect narrowed to the questions of law arising upon the pleadings.

The facts of the case, so far as a statement of these is necessary to an accurate comprehension of the legal questions discussed and decided, were as follows: In the year 1839, a portion of the appellees, as heirs and distributees of John Goldsbury, by their bill filed in the circuit court for Grayson county, in the State of Kentucky, alleged that their ancestor died in Nelson county, in the State aforesaid, intestate, leaving a widow, Eleanor Goldsbury, and four children, — three daughters, Elizabeth, Nancy, and Mary, and one son, Bennett Goldsbury, — all these children infants at the time of their father's death. That John Goldsbury died possessed of one male and one female slave, and of other personal property, and perfectly free from debt. That the widow Eleanor Goldsbury, who was appointed the administratrix of her husband, and as such took possession of the estate within a year from the period of his death, intermarried with one James Shields, in conjunction with whom she had continued to hold the entire estate, and to apply it to their exclusive use, without having made any settlement or distribution thereof. The bill further charged, that Shields and wife, after enjoying the services and hires of the male slave for several years, had ultimately sold him, and that, in the year 1818, they removed from Kentucky to the State of Missouri, carrying with them the female slave belonging to the estate of John Goldsbury, together with her descendants, seven in number, and of great value; that upon application to said Shields and wife, for a surrender of those slaves, and for an account of the estate of John Goldsbury, so possessed and used by them, this request was refused, and that, by a fraudulent confederacy between Shields and wife, and John G. Shields, their son, and Henry Yates, their son-in-law, the slaves had by the son and son-in-law been secreted, carried off, and sold, in parts unknown to the complainants, and the other personal estate of John Goldsbury fraudulently disposed of in like manner. The bill also made defendants the representatives of the surety of Eleanor Goldsbury, in her bond given as administratrix of her first husband. The bill also made defendants, though not in an adversary interest, Isaac Thomas, and Mary, his wife, Elizabeth, John, and Ann Goldsbury, which said Elizabeth, John, and Ann are the infant children of Bennett Goldsbury, son of John Goldsbury, deceased.

After the filing of the bill in this case, it appearing to the satisfaction of the court that James Shields, and Eleanor, his wife, Elizabeth, John, and Ann Goldsbury, John Shields, and Henry Yates, were not inhabitants of the State of Kentucky, there was, on the 25th of December, 1839, under the authority of the statute of Kentucky with reference to absent defendants, issued by the court what is termed a warning order, by which the absent defendants were required to appear at the next April term of the court, and answer the complainants' bill.

Afterwards, namely, on the 28th of April, 1840, the absent defendants still not appearing, under the like authority of the law of the State, the clerk of the court, by its order, filed on behalf of those defendants a traverse denying the allegations of the complainants' bill.

Subsequently to this proceeding, namely, on the 30th of October, 1841, the said John G. Shields filed his answer to the complainants' bill, thereby recognizing as to himself personally the jurisdiction of the court.

Upon these pleadings, the cause after an examination of witnesses, and upon a report of the master, came to a hearing before the circuit court, and this tribunal decreed against the representative of the surety in the administration bond of Mrs. Goldsbury, (afterwards Mrs. Shields,) and against James Shields her husband, she having departed this life, John G. Shields, the son, and Henry Yates, the son-in-law, in favor of the heirs and distributees of John Goldsbury, the portions reported to be due to them respectively of the general effects of John Goldsbury, deceased, and of the values and hires of the slaves. Upon an appeal taken from this decree to the supreme court of Kentucky, it being the opinion of the latter that, under the circumstances, the surety in the administration bond should not be charged, and also that an amount equal to the price of the slave Mat, sold by the administratrix and her husband, and to the hires of the remaining slaves, had been properly applied to the dower of the widow and to the use of the heirs of John Goldsbury, it ordered the decree of the circuit court to be re-formed in conformity with the opinion of the supreme court. By a final decree of the circuit court of Grayson county, made on the 28th day of October, 1846, the bill as to the representative of the surety in the administration bond was dismissed, and the defendants, James Shields, John G. Shields, and Henry Yates, and each of them, who had, by fraudulent combination, secreted and carried off, and disposed of the descendants of the female slave, originally the property of John Goldsbury, were decreed and ordered to pay to the heirs of said John Goldsbury severally, the amounts ascertained to be due to them as their respective and separate portions of the value of the slaves thus fraudulently disposed of, without any allowance for the hires of those slaves.

To obtain the benefit of this last decree, the suit now before us was instituted in the names of the appellees, Isaac Thomas and Mary, his wife, Uriah Pirtle and Nancy, his wife, citizens of the State of Kentucky, and John B. Goldsbury, a citizen of the State of Missouri, the said Mary Thomas, and Nancy Pirtle, and John B. Goldsbury, being heirs and distributees of John Goldsbury, deceased, against John G. Shields, a citizen of the State of Iowa. The bill refers to the proceedings in the Kentucky suit, which proceedings are set forth *in extenso* as an exhibit in this cause; it further assigns as a reason for the non-joinder of a portion of the heirs of John Goldsbury as defendants, the fact that their residence precluded as to them the jurisdiction of the district court of Iowa. It sets out the sums of money severally and specifically decreed to the complainants by the circuit court of Grayson county, Kentucky, and prays that the defendant, John G. Shields, may be compelled to perform that decree by

22 *

the payment to the complainants respectively the sums so awarded them, and concludes with a prayer for general relief.

By an amendment to the original bill in this case, the several heirs and distributees of John Goldsbury, residing in the State of Missouri, beyond the jurisdiction of the district court of Iowa, and who, for that reason, were not made defendants by the original bill, were admitted as complainants in this suit, and united in the prayer for enforcing the decree in their favor, as rendered by the circuit court of Grayson county, Kentucky.

To the original and amended bills in this case, the defendant, John G. Shields, interposed a demurrer, which having been overruled, and the demurrant abiding by his demurrer, and declining to answer over, the district court for the district of Iowa, on the 17th day of January, 1854, adjudged and decreed to the complainants the sums respectively awarded to them by the circuit court of Grayson county, Kentucky, as against the defendant, John G. Shields, with interest upon those several sums from the 28th day of October, 1846, the date of the decree in the circuit court.

Upon an appeal from the district court of Iowa, several points arising upon the demurrer, and discussed and adjudged by that court, are presented for consideration here. Amongst the objections insisted upon, that which stands first in the natural order, is the alleged want of jurisdiction in the circuit court of Kentucky, either over the subject-matter or the parties embraced in the proceedings in that court.

In this objection no force is perceived. The subject-matter of the suit was the settlement of the estate of an intestate who lived and died within the limits of the court's authority, within which limits the qualification of the administratrix of the intestate, the appraisement of his estate, and the recording of that appraisement had taken place ; within which also was the residence of the surety in the administration bond, and of a portion of the distributees — both plaintiffs and defendants asserting before that court their interest in the estate. The court, as one vested with general equity powers, could act either *in personam* or *in rem*, as to persons or property within the State.

Under the laws and the practice in the State of Kentucky, already referred to, proceedings are authorized and prescribed in suits in equity against absent defendants; which proceedings, when regularly observed, are held within the State to be binding absolutely. With respect to absent defendants, such proceedings could be considered as binding beyond the limits of the State in instances only in which those defendants should have been legally and personally served with process, or in which they should have voluntarily submitted themselves as parties. In the suit in the state court, the subject-matter of the controversy, as well as a portion of the parties, both plaintiffs and defendants, being confessedly within its cognizance, no ground for exception to the jurisdiction could exist as to these. The defendant, John G. Shields, when he voluntarily entered his appearance, and answered the bill, placed himself in the same predicament with the other parties regularly before the court, and could not afterwards except to the jurisdiction upon the ground of his non-residence. The decree, therefore, so far as this exception is designed to affect it, cannot be impeached.

The objection which seems to follow next in order, is one levelled at the frame of the bill in the district court of the United States, irrespective of the justice or regularity of the proceedings in the state court. This objection is, that the bill filed in the district court of Iowa is multifarious, by embracing in one suit interests and causes of action in themselves separate and disconnected, and therefore such as it was improper to include in one bill.

There is, perhaps, no rule established for the conducting of equity pleadings, with reference to which (whilst as a rule it is universally admitted) there has existed less of certainty and uniformity in application, than has attended this relating to multifariousness. This effect, flowing, perhaps inevitably, from the variety of modes and degrees of right and interest entering into the transactions of life, seems to have led to a conclusion rendering the rule almost as much an exception as a rule, and that conclusion is, that each case must be determined by its peculiar features. Thus Daniel, in his work on Chancery Practice, vol. 1, p. 384, quoting from Lord Cottenham, says: "It is impossible, upon the authorities, to lay down any rule or abstract proposition, as to what constitutes multifariousness, which can be made universally applicable. The cases upon the subject are extremely various, and the court, in deciding upon them, seems to have considered what was convenient in particular cases, rather than to have attempted to lay down an absolute rule. The only way of reconciling the authorities upon the subject is, by adverting to the fact that, although the books speak generally of demurrers for multifariousness, yet in truth such demurrers may be divided into two distinct kinds. Frequently, the objection raised, though termed multifariousness, is in fact more properly misjoinder; that is to say, the cases or claims united in the bill are of so different a character that the court will not permit them to be litigated in one record. But what is more familiarly understood by the term multifariousness, as applied to a bill, is, where a party is able to say, he is brought as a defendant upon a record, with a large portion of which, and of the case made by which, he has no connection whatever."

Justice Story, in his compilation upon equity pleading, defines multifariousness in a bill to mean, "the improperly joining in one bill distinct and independent matters, and thereby confounding them." And the example by which he illustrates his definition is thus given : "The uniting in one bill several matters perfectly distinct and unconnected against one defendant, or the demand of several matters of a distinct and independent nature, against several defendants in the same bill." Sir Thomas Plumer, V. C., in allowing a demurrer which had been interposed by one of several defendants to a bill on the ground that it was multifarious, remarks, that "the court is always averse to multiplicity of suits, but certainly a defendant has the right to insist that he is not bound to answer a bill containing several distinct and separate matters relating to individuals with whom he has no connection." Brooks v. Lord Whitworth, 1 Mad. Ch. R. 57.

Justice Story closes his review of the authorities upon this defect in a bill with the following remark : "The conclusion to which a close survey of all the authorities will conduct us seems to be, that there is not any positive inflexible rule as to what, in the sense of a court of equity, constitutes multifariousness, which is fatal to a suit on demurrer." To bring the present case to the standard of the principles above stated, the appellees are seeking a subject their title to which is common to them all, founded in the relation they bear to a common ancestor. The different portions or shares into which the subject may be divisible amongst themselves can have no effect upon the nature or character of their title derived as above mentioned; and which in its character is an unit, and cannot be objected to for inconsistency or diversity of any kind. They seek an account and the recovery of a subject claimed by their common title, or an equivalent for that subject, against persons charged with having by fraudulent combination withheld and diverted that subject, and who, by such combination and diversion, rendered themselves equally, jointly, and severally liable therefor. Upon the face of this statement it would be consistent neither with justice nor convenience, nor consistent with the practice, to turn the appellees round to an action or actions at law, for any aliquot parts of each upon a division of this subject claimed under their common title, and which aliquot portions would have to be ascertained by an account which would not depend upon the question of liability of the defendants. The like principles and considerations would, in every case of equal responsibility in several persons, instead of condemning, commend, and in a court of equity would command, wherever practicable, a common proceeding against all to whom such responsibility extended.

But in truth, the question raised upon this point on the demurrer, seems to have been virtually, if not directly concluded by this court upon this very record. At the December term, 1854, of this court, a motion was made by a portion of the appellees to dismiss this appeal upon the following grounds: In the decree in favor of the distributees in Kentucky, the court having designated the shares of the whole amount recovered, which would belong to each distributee, and the district court of Iowa having adopted the same rate of distribution in enforcing the decree of the Kentucky court, by which rate it appeared that none of the distributable portions amounted to the sum of $2,000; those distributees, with the view, no doubt, of hastening the termination of this controversy, and of obtaining immediately the benefit of the decree in their favor, moved this court for a dismission of this cause, upon the ground that the sum in controversy between the appellant and the persons submitting that motion was less than $2,000, and, therefore, insufficient to give this court jurisdiction. The chief justice, in the opinion denying the motion to dismiss, uses this language: " The whole amount recovered against Shields in the proceeding in Iowa exceeds $2,000, but the sum allotted to each representative who joined in the bill was less; and the motion is made to dismiss, upon the ground that the sum due to each complainant is severally and specifically decreed to him; and that the amount thus decreed is the sum in controversy between each representative and the appellant, and not the whole amount for which he has been held liable. But the court think the matter in controversy in the Kentucky court was the sum due to the representatives of the deceased collectively, and not the particular sum to which each was entitled when the amount due was distributed among them according to the laws of the State. They all claimed under one and the same title. They had a common and undivided interest in the claim; and it was perfectly immaterial to the appellant how it was divided among them. He had no controversy with either of them on this point, and if there was any difficulty as to the proportions in which they were to share, the dispute was among themselves, and not with him." *Vide* 17 How. pp. 4, 5. This reasoning appears to be conclusive against the defect of multifariousness imputed to the claim of the appellees in this case; and we deem it equally so with respect to defendants sustaining an equal responsibility deducible from one and the same source.

The remaining objection arising upon the demurrer, which we deem it necessary to consider, is that urged against the right of the appellees to institute proceedings in equity in the State of Iowa, to enforce the decree rendered in their favor by the court in Kentucky. We can perceive no force in the effort to sustain this objection by citation of the 7th amendment of the Constitution of the United States, which provides, "that in suits at common law, where the value in controversy shall exceed twenty dollars, the right of trial by jury shall be preserved." This provision, correctly interpreted, cannot be made to embrace the established, exclusive jurisdiction of courts of equity, nor that which they have exercised as concurrent with courts of law; but should be understood as limited to rights and remedies peculiarly legal in their nature, and such as it was proper to assert in courts of law, and by the appropriate modes and proceedings of courts of law.

With respect to the character and effects of decrees in chancery, although they now rank in dignity upon an equality with judgments at law, it is well known that they were once regarded as not being matters of record; and that the final process incident to judgments at law was unknown to and not permitted in courts of equity; that where such process has been permitted to them, it has been the result of statutory enactments. But the extension to a court of equity of the power to avail itself of common-law process, cannot be regarded as implying any abridgment of the original constitutional powers or practice of the former; but as cumulative and ancillary, or as leaving those powers and that practice as they formerly existed, except as they should have been expressly restricted. Amongst the original and undoubted powers of a court of equity is that of entertaining a bill filed for enforcing and carrying into effect a decree of the same, or of a different court, as the exigencies of the case, or the interests of the parties may require. *Vide* Story's Equity Pleading, §§ 429, 430, 431, upon the authority of Mitford, Eq. Pl. 95, and of Cooper's Eq. Pl. 98, 99.

In the present case the appellees were, by the residence of the appellant in a different State, cut off from the benefit of final process upon the decree of the state court, which process would not run beyond the territorial jurisdiction of the State. They were left, therefore, to the alternative of instituting either an action or actions at law upon the decree in their favor, or of filing a bill for enforcing and carrying into effect that decree. Upon the former mode of proceeding, they would have been compelled to encounter circuity, and most probably the technical exceptions urged in argument here, founded upon the nature of the decree with respect to its unity or divisibility. The appellees have elected, as the remedy most beneficial for them, and as we think they had the right to do, the proceeding by bill in equity, to carry into execution the decree of the state court. We can perceive no just exception to the jurisdiction of the district court of Iowa in entertaining the bill of the appellants, nor to the measure of relief decreed, nor with respect to the party against whom that relief has been granted. We therefore order that the decree of the district court of Iowa be affirmed.

JOHN J. ORTON, APPELLANT, v. GEORGE SMITH.

Those only who have a clear, legal, and equitable title to land, connected with possession, have a right to claim the interference of a court of equity, to give them peace or dissipate a cloud on the title.

Therefore, where the complainant was the volunteer purchaser of a litigious claim; was the assignee of a secret equity for apparently a mere nominal consideration, and of the bare legal title for a like consideration, and this legal title assigned to him during the pendency of a suit in chancery in a State court, to ascertain the person justly entitled to it, it was error in the court below to grant to such complainant a perpetual injunction.

The courts of the United States should not entertain a bill of peace upon a title in litigation in a state court.

THIS was an appeal from the district court of the United States, for the district of Wisconsin.

The facts are stated in the opinion of the court.

It was argued by *Mr. Gillett* and *Mr. Lynde,* for the appellant, and *Mr. Brown,* for the appellee. There was also a brief filed on the same side by *Mr. Upham.*

The points made by the counsel were so interwoven with the facts, that they cannot be presented abstractedly.

Mr. Justice GRIER delivered the opinion of the court.

The bill, in this case, is in the nature of a "bill of peace," as authorized by the statutes of Wisconsin. Smith, the claimant below, claimed to be owner of certain lands, to which Orton claimed also to have some title. The bill prays an injunction against Orton, to prohibit him from setting up his claim, and thereby "casting a cloud" over the good legal title of complainant.

The facts of the case are somewhat complex, and its merits will be better apprehended by a succinct history of them, as elicited from the pleadings and evidence.

Hubbard had settled in Wisconsin, having escaped from his creditors, with some pecuniary means, which he thought it prudent to conceal. Hence, though he speculated in the purchase and sale of lands, the title to them was held by friends. He had contracted to sell certain lots in Milwaukie to Schram.

Orton *v.* Smith.

But Schram would not pay his money without a good legal title, or good security that it should be conveyed to him. Hubbard resided in the family of his friend Butler, and being addicted to idleness and intemperance, he confided the management of his affairs, in a great measure, to Butler. Schram would not pay his money on the security of Butler or the promise of Hubbard to obtain a title; and one Knab at length was prevailed on to enter into a bond with Butler, conditioned that a good legal title should be made to Schram for the lots. But Knab was unwilling to enter into this bond without security also. For this purpose the land in dispute in this suit was conveyed to him in fee by one Cyrus D. Davis, who held the legal title as friend and trustee of Hubbard. This deed was put on record by Knab, who, at the same time, gave his title-bond covenanting to convey the land to Butler, when the covenants of their bond to Schram would be satisfied or released. This title-bond was not given to Davis, because he claimed no beneficial interest in the land; nor to Hubbard, because his policy required him not to appear to have any title to property; but to Butler, the friend and active agent of Hubbard. Notwithstanding the testimony of Butler, that he paid Hubbard for the land, and did not hold as secret trustee for him, the fact may be considered doubtful; and it is not necessary to decide it, in our view of the present case. Hubbard is now deceased; but in his lifetime he assigned, for the consideration of one dollar, all his interest in the land in dispute to one Gruenhagen, (under whom Smith, the complainant, claims,) by deed dated in June, 1851.

On the 22d of February, 1851, Butler assigned to Orton, the defendant, the title-bond of Knab for the consideration of $2,100. This consideration has been pa without any knowledge or notice of any secret equity in Hubbard; and the covenants of the bond to Schram being fulfilled or released, Orton filed his bill in chancery on the 6th of August, 1851, against Knab, demanding from him a conveyance of the legal title according to the exigency of his bond.

During the pendency of this bill, which would settle the legal and equitable rights of all persons having any claim to the land in dispute, the complainant, Smith, becomes the purchaser of the real or supposed secret equity of Hubbard. And not only so, but he has obtained from Knab the transfer of the legal title for a nominal consideration; thereby substituting himself in the place of Knab in the contest pending in the state court. The charge of fraud made in the bill, because Knab's title-bond was made to Butler and not to Hubbard, is not substantiated. It was a matter of indifference to Knab whether Hubbard or Butler held the bond. He had no concern with the private arrangements or secret trusts between them. When the condition of his bond to Schram was released, Knab was bound to convey to Butler, by the exigency of his own contract, and could not make himself a judge of the equities between Butler and Hubbard. His assignment to Smith, under the circumstances, could have no effect but to substitute Smith in his own place, under the same liabilities.

On this state of the facts the court below decreed the title to the land to be in Smith.

" And further, that the said defendant, John J. Orton, be, and hereby is, perpetually enjoined and forever barred from setting up or asserting any claim in or right to said premises, by virtue of or upon said bond and assignment. But this injunction and decree are not in any way to affect or operate against him, the said John J. Orton, in the prosecution of a bill pending in the circuit court of Milwaukie county, in this State, wherein he is complainant, and David Knab is defendant; this court not intending to enjoin a proceeding in the state court."

We think the court erred in entering such a decree. Those only who have a clear, legal, and equitable title to land connected with possession, have any right to claim the interference of a court of equity to give them peace or dissipate a cloud on the title.

The complainant in this case is the volunteer purchaser of a litigious claim; he is the assignee of a secret equity for apparently a mere nominal consideration, and of the bare legal title for a like consideration. This legal title was improperly assigned to him, during the pendency of a suit in chancery to ascertain the person justly entitled to it.

Besides, the decree in this case demonstrates the impropriety of the interference of the court of the United States, and of its entertaining jurisdiction of a question of title then pending in the state court. It is true, if this were an ejectment in a court of law, the pendency of another ejectment between the same parties might not have afforded sufficient ground for a plea of *auter action pendent;* nor would the court have been bound, even by comity, to await the decision of the state court, or suffer the cause pending before them to be in any way affected by it. But a decree of a court of chancery, on a bill of peace, must necessarily operate by way of estoppel, as to the title of the land, and conclude all the parties to it, because it should put an end to all litigation between them. If they have suits pending in other courts, on the same question of title, they must cease. This bill acts by injunction, on the party — no injunction ever goes to the court having a concurrent jurisdiction of the question. The courts of the United States have no such power over suitors in a state court. But a decree on a bill of peace which does not put an end to litigation is a mere *brutum fulmen*. Unless the court can make a decree which it can execute, it is a sufficient reason for refusing to take cognizance of the case. It is a rule absolutely necessary to be observed by courts who have a concurrent jurisdiction, that in all cases " where the jurisdiction of a court and the right of a plaintiff to prosecute his suit in it have once attached, that right cannot be arrested or taken away by proceedings in another court." This rule, it is said, " has its foundation not merely in comity, but in necessity. If one may enjoin, the other may retort by injunction, and thus the parties be without remedy." See Peck *v.* Jenness, 7 How. 625 ; Taylor *v.* Royal Saxon, 1 Wall, 311.

If the decree in this case can be of any value whatever, let us look at the consequences which may possibly and probably will arise, in case it is enforced.

Orton, claiming as the *bonâ fide* assignee and purchaser of the title-bond given by Knab, has a bill pending in the state court to compel a transfer of the legal title. Pending this litigation, Knab assigns the legal title to a citizen of another State, who comes into the court of the United States praying an injunction against Orton from setting up his title. Suppose the state court decrees the title to be in Orton, and compels Knab and Smith, his assignee, to release the legal title to him ? Now the court below has made a decree that enjoins Orton from ever setting up his title against Smith. It is true the decree protests against interference with proceedings in a state court : but unless it is construed so as to be a perfect " *felo de se*," it must be enforced in favor of complainant somehow. When the sheriff puts Orton in possession under the decree of the state court, and expels Smith, the circuit court, by its officer, must replace Smith, or imprison Orton for a contempt. This would indeed be a humiliating spectacle. Such a disreputable collision of jurisdictions should be sedulously avoided. This can only be done by refusing to entertain a bill of peace for an injunction when the title is in litigation in a court of concurrent jurisdiction ; otherwise, the result of a bill of peace may be not peace, but war ; and, instead of dispelling a " cloud " from the title of either party, will doubly increase the darkness and difficulty with which it was environed.

Decree of the circuit court is therefore reversed, and the bill dismissed with costs —but without prejudice.

SAMUEL WARD, CLAIMANT OF THE BARK MOPANG, APPELLANT, v. WILLIAM M. PECK, JACOB BADGER, FREEMAN KINGSLEY, AND HUMPHREY DEVEREUX, LIBELLANTS.*

The courts of admiralty of the United States have jurisdiction of petitory as well as mere possessory actions.

The cases of The Tilton (5 Mason, 465,) and Taylor v. Royal Saxon, (1 Wall, 322,) confirmed.

The abandonment of a ship by her owners to the underwriters does not operate to ratify the title of one who claims her under an unauthorized sale by the master.

THIS was an appeal from the circuit court of the United States for the eastern district of Louisiana.

The circumstances of the case are stated in the opinion of the court.

It was submitted on the record by *Mr. Benjamin*, for the appellant, and argued by *Mr. Stanton*, for the appellees.

Mr. Stanton contended that the offer to abandon did not constitute a ratification of the sale by the master, and cited Phillips on Ins. § 1576; Abbott on Shipping, 19; 18 Pickering, 83; Phillips on Ins. § 1497; 2 Peck, 249; 5 Pet. 604; 15 Mass. 341; 9 Johns. 21; 1 Caines, 573; 18 Peck, 83.

Mr. Justice GRIER delivered the opinion of the court.

The pleadings in this case present but the single question of the title or ownership of the Bark Mopang.

Originally, the court of admiralty in England entertained jurisdiction of petitory as well as mere possessory actions. Since the Restoration, that court, through the jealous interference of courts of law, had ceased to pronounce directly on questions of ownership or property. Petitory suits were silently abandoned, and, if in a possessory action a question of mere property arose, especially of a more complicated nature, it declined to interfere.

This "submission to authority rather than reason" has continued till the statute of 3 and 4 Vict. c. 65, § 4, restored to the admiralty plenary jurisdiction of such questions. See case of The Aurora, 3 Rob. 133, 136, and the Warrior, 2 Dodson, 288, 2 Brown Civ. & Ad. 430.

In this country, where the courts of admiralty have not been subjected to such jealous restraints, the ancient jurisdiction over petitory suits or causes of property has been retained. In the

---

* Mr. Justice CATRON was absent on the trial of this cause.

case of The Tilton, (5 Mason, 465,) Mr. Justice Story has examined this question with his usual learning and ability. The authority of that case has never been questioned in our courts. See Taylor *v.* Royal Saxon, 1 Wall, 322. In the case of the New England Ins. Co. *v.* Brig Sarah Anne, 13 Pet. 387, in this court, the only question was the title or ownership of the brig, yet the cause was entertained without any expression of doubt as to jurisdiction.

The following agreed statement of facts presents the merits of this case:—

"That the libellants are the owners of the said Bark 'Mopang,' unless their title has been devested by the sale made by the master under the following circumstances: The bark sailed from New Orleans on or about the 29th November, 1846, for Tampico and other Mexican ports. That, on or about the 6th of December thereafter she struck aground, was abandoned by her officers and crew on the north breakers off the bar of Tampico; that she floated over the bar, and was boarded by one Clifton, who refused to deliver her to the master; that a claim for salvage was made; that by agreement between the master and Clifton, the vessel was sold to the claimant, Ward, on the ——. It is admitted that the sale to Ward was unauthorized by the circumstances in which the master was placed.

"The libellants had a valued policy upon the vessel taken out at New Orleans. On the 9th day of January, 1847, they gave notice of abandonment to the underwriters as for a total loss, who refused to accept the same. They were sued for a total loss by libellants. Judgment found for defendant."

This statement amounts to an admission of want of title in the claimant. The abandonment by her owners to the underwriters could not affect the title of the claimant, by way of ratification or estoppel. The insurance is but a wager between the parties to it, on the safety of the vessel. By the rule of the contract the ship may be abandoned, and the whole insurance claimed, when the damages exceed half the value.

Nothing but extreme necessity can justify the sale of the vessel by the master. The abandonment was based on the damage done to the vessel at the time of the accident. If accepted, the master became the agent of the insurer; and whether accepted or not, his act, without authority, can receive no ratification from allegations or admissions made by any party in a dispute on the contract of assurance, where the inquiry as to the act of the master was irrelevant. The defendant, having obtained possession unlawfully, was a trespasser, and can no more plead the abandonment as a confirmation of his title than if he had obtained it by theft or piracy, moreover, if the circumstances would have justified a sale by the master, no abandonment was necessary. It cannot, therefore, by any possible implication, amount to a confirmation of such sale.

The judgment of the circuit court is affirmed.

Mr. Justice DANIEL dissenting.

I dissent from the decision just pronounced: 1. On the ground that this case is not one regularly appertaining to a court of admiralty. 2. Because this decision professes to claim a power and jurisdiction admitted by the decision itself never to have been heretofore conceded to nor exerted by courts of admiralty in this country, whose power and jurisdiction in future are to be traced for their origin to this cause alone.

With respect to the objection first stated; this cause presents no example of a maritime contract or of a marine tort. It is simply a contest as to the right of property in a subject situated within the ordinary and settled jurisdiction of the courts of common law and equity of the State of Louisiana, and could have been there as effectively determined by an action of detinue or trover, or by a bill in equity if there was danger of an eloignment of the subject in controversy, as it could possibly be in admiralty: and this fact alone should have been a reason sufficient against an abandonment of the adequate and familiar modes of administering justice, and an unnecessary resort to a tribunal which in England, we are told by Lord Hale, was never established either by common law or by statute, but had grown up entirely by encroachment and sufferance.

It is true that the subject in controversy here is a vessel; but if that single fact could justify the interposition of the admiralty, it would equally imply the same power in that jurisdiction over any dispute concerning the right of property in a vessel, although she might still be upon the stocks, and although she had never reached the water, or might, by some casualty, never touch that element.

This was simply a question of property arising out of the extent of power in an agent to dispose of it, — a common and everyday question of law.

2. It is admitted that the jurisdiction now asserted for the first time in this court, — namely, the jurisdiction in petitory suits, — did not belong to the admiralty in England, or was not exercised by them for several hundred years at least; and that a recent statute in the present reign, had been enacted expressly to confer that jurisdiction. It has also been said, that the jurisdiction thus recently authorized had, in the olden time, existed in the admiralty, and had been restrained or forbidden only by the jealousy of the common lawyers. This appears to me to be an

argument not founded upon the judicial history of the country, and one which is neither logical nor tenable. A reference to others of the highest and most venerable authorities, which might be added to that of Lord Hale already cited, demolishes entirely the foundation on which this argument is based. The argument is in itself illogical and illusory; for had this jurisdiction been even legitimate in the admiralty, it might doubtless have been vindicated and maintained in despite of an illegal and unfounded jealousy of the common lawyers. It never could have been forced to yield to so baseless an opposition. No authority so potent as that of an express statute could have been required, to create what not only already had being, but which was established and venerable from justice and from lapse of time.

If the inhibition had been the mere creature of jealousy or prejudice, a returning sense of right and a conviction of public advantage, would, in this as in other instances falling within the power of the courts, have corrected previous errors. The very fact of the enactment of a statute, such as that referred to, is strong evidence to show that the jurisdiction it confers had no previous or rather no rightful existence.

But it is said that no jealousy like that once felt in England against the admiralty exists in this country; and, therefore, the inveterate powers ascribed to it formerly in England are free and unfettered for its exercise in this country. This course of argument naturally suggests with me the following inquiries: What fetters or limitations are recognized as placed upon the admiralty jurisdiction in the United States? Freed from the checks and restraints imposed upon such a jurisdiction in that country, from which the system was transferred to us, what are the checks imposed upon it here? Are there any such checks? Does it, either in theory or in practice, recognize any such, — how or where are they defined or ascertained? Has it any system at all, or is it left to the judgment or fancy of those who assume to exercise power under its name?

Too true does it seem to me the case, that the ambitious and undefined pretensions of this branch of jurisprudence have found greater favor here than, in my view, is compatible with civil liberty, with public policy, or private benefit; and hence I have been the more inclined to watch and prevent its dangerous encroachments, and in all sincerity can, in contemplating the favor extended to those encroachments exclaim, " *hinc illæ lachrymæ.* "

For the jurisdiction here claimed for the admiralty, we are referred to the treatise of Mr. Arthur Brown, professor of civil law in Ireland. I have no recollection of having before seen or heard the doctrines of this professor recognized as authority; and with respect to his theories, it may justly be remarked, that if these are to be adopted as law, there is no excess of extravagance to be found in the exploded notions of Sir Leoline Jenkins, or anywhere else, which will not find an apology, nay, a full justification, in the book of this civil-law doctor. If the theories of this professor are to be regarded as binding, his disciples may look forward at no distant day to an announcement from this bench, as there has been formerly from that of one of the circuits, of the doctrine, that a policy of insurance (a mere wager laid upon the safety of a vessel) is strictly and essentially a maritime contract, because, forsooth, the vessel had to navigate the ocean.

It seems somewhat singular, however, that Mr. Brown should be appealed to in support of the authority now claimed for the admiralty, when in truth his book again and again admits, that such jurisdiction had been utterly repudiated in England as a sheer usurpation, and may appropriately be styled a jeremiad over the lost authority and splendor of a system which he would exalt to the control of every other branch of jurisprudence.

I object, in all cases, to the decision of questions not strictly in point, or which have not been regularly discussed, and not only maturely but necessarily considered. If there is any one source of embarrassment more prolific than all others, it is this very practice. I cannot perceive the necessity nor the propriety of deciding matters in advance. The effect of such a practice is either the difficulty of getting clear of irregular and inapposite conclusions, or the sanction of them with the view of maintaining consistency whether right or wrong.

A great portion of the admiralty jurisdiction now permitted in this country may be traced to a *dictum* in argument in the case of The General Smith, 4 Wheat. p. 444, in the assertion of a doctrine which, if now for the first time discussed and examined, might not command the sanction of this tribunal.

It is that tendency of error once countenanced or tolerated to grow into precedent, which has ever enjoined it upon me as a sacred duty to resist its approaches before they have been matured into power; and even the conviction of an inability to accomplish this result, is with me no dispensation from the duty of resistance.

JOHN DEN, *ex dem.* JAMES B. MURRAY AND JOHN C. KAYSER, PLAINTIFFS, *v.* THE HOBOKEN LAND AND IMPROVEMENT COMPANY. JOHN DEN, *ex dem.* JAMES B. MURRAY ET AL. *v.* THE HOBOKEN LAND AND IMPROVEMENT COMPANY. JOHN DEN, *ex dem.* WILLIAM P. RATHBONE ET AL. *v.* RUTSEN SUCKLEY ET AL.

A distress warrant, issued by the solicitor of the treasury under the act of congress passed on the 15th May, 1820, (3 Stats. at Large, 592,) is not inconsistent with the constitution of the United States.

It was an exercise of executive and not of judicial power, according to the meaning of those words in the constitution ; and the privilege allowed to a collector to bring the question of his indebtedness before the courts of the United States, is merely the consent of congress to the suit, which is given in other classes of cases also.

Neither is it inconsistent with that part of the constitution which prohibits a citizen from being deprived of his liberty or property without due process of law. The historical and critical meaning of these words examined.

By the common law of England and the laws of many of the colonies before the revolution, and of States before the formation of the federal constitution, a summary process existed for the recovery of debts due to the government.

It does not necessarily follow that the adjustment of these balances is a controversy to which the United States is a party, within the meaning of the constitution.

Under the power of congress to collect taxes and the exercise of that power by the act above mentioned, the warrant of distress is conclusive evidence of the facts recited in it and of the authority to make the levy, so far as to justify the marshal in making it ; but the question of indebtedness may be the subject of a suit, congress having assented thereto, and the levy may provide security for the event of the suit.

The article of the constitution, requiring an oath or affirmation for a warrant, has no application to proceedings for the recovery of debts, where no search warrant is used.

The return of the marshal that he had levied on lands, by virtue of such a warrant, is, at least, *primâ facie* evidence that the levy was not irregular by reason of the existence of goods and chattels of the collector subject to his process.

THESE three cases came up from the circuit court of the United States for the district of New Jersey, upon a certificate of division in opinion between the judges thereof.

As the opinion of the court answers only the third question, it may be proper to say that the first two related to a mortgage executed by Henry Ogden, as the attorney in fact of Swartwout, to Henry D. Gilpin, solicitor of the treasury. It was necessary to the case of the plaintiffs to get rid of this mortgage in the first instance, and afterwards to avoid the sale under the distress warrant. If they failed in the last, the points raised in the first two questions became of no practical consequence, and, therefore, answers to them were not returned by this court.

The case is stated in the opinion of the court. The decision of one involved the two others, as they depended upon the same principles.

It was argued by *Mr. Van Winkle* and *Mr. Wood* for the plaintiffs, and by *Mr. Zabrinski, Mr. Gillett, Mr. Butler,* and *Mr. Bradley,* for the defendants.

The points relating to the power of attorney and the mortgage need not be noticed.

The counsel for the plaintiffs contended that the acts of congress, authorizing these proceedings under a distress warrant, were unconstitutional and void, because,—

The proceeding to establish this claim was, in its nature, a judicial proceeding, and could only be carried out under the judicial power. Const. U. S. art. 3, §§ 1, 2; 4 Devereux, 1, 13.

By the judicial power in the constitution, was meant that portion of such power which was recognized and understood to be such at the time of the adoption of the constitution. Federalist, No. 80; 2. Brock. 447.

This summary proceeding was considered and enforced as a judgment at law. 3 Wheat. 212, 222.

The warrant to sell and imprison is an execution issued upon a judgment. 9 Pet. 8.

The secretary of the treasury cannot be constituted a court for the exercise of judicial power. Const. U. S. art. 3, § 1.

The power of review of law and fact, given by the act to a court, does not change these views.

The proceeding in question took place without any hearing by the debtor and without a trial by jury, and is, therefore, unconstitutional and void. Article 7 of Amendments to Constitution; 5 Johns. 37.

As process, it was unconstitutional, because it changed the onus, and required the debtor to disprove the debt.

This process deprives of liberty and property without due process of law, contrary to the 5th article of amendments to the constitution.

This meant, by process of law, as then understood, charge, defence, judgment before and by a legally constituted court. Co. Lit. 2 Inst. 47, Magna Charta, chs. 8 and 29; 2 Kent's Com. (5th Ed.) 13; Story on the Const. § 1783; Sullivan's Lectures, chs. 39 and 40; Taylor v. Porter, 4 Hill, 146; Fletcher v. Peck, 6 Cranch, 138; Bank of Col. v. Oakley, 4 Pet. Cond. R. 443; 4 Cranch, 489; Van Zandt v. Waddell, 2 Yerger, 260; Jones's Heirs v. Perry et al. 10 ibid. 59; Bank of the State v. Charles Cooper et al. 2 ibid. 599; Lane v. Dorman, 3 Scam. 238, 241; White v. White, 5 Barbour's S. C. R. 481–483; Holden v. James, 11 Mass. 404.

No implied or express consent can make valid what is unconstitutional.

The distress warrant was not supported by oath or affirmation. Amendments to Constitution, article 4.

If the proceeding is constitutional, still, the statute must be strictly pursued. 6 Pet. 470 ; 3 ibid. 8 ; 1 Scam. 823 ; 6 Wheat. 119.

But it does not appear that there were no goods or chattels upon which to levy ; on the contrary, that the marshal levied upon some, but failed to sell them.

The counsel for the defendants contended : —

That these proceedings were not judicial acts. That they were the well-known proceeding by distress, established at common law, and regulated by statute in most of the States before the adoption of the federal constitution. 3 Black. Com. 3, 6.

Prior acts of congress regulated distress warrants. 3 Stats. at Large, 173, §§ 26, 14.

They have none of the characteristics of judicial proceedings. 1 Curt. Com. 99 ; 13 How. 40.

This court has laid down the distinction between the judicial power intended by the constitution, and this power conferred upon a particular officer. 8 Pet. 8 ; 6 ibid. 47 ; 13 How. 4, 52, note.

Mr. Justice CURTIS delivered the opinion of the court.

This case comes before us on a certificate of division of opinion of the judges of the circuit court of the United States for the district of New Jersey. It is an action of ejectment, in which both parties claim title under Samuel Swartwout, — the plaintiffs, under the levy of an execution on the 10th day of April, 1839, and the defendants, under a sale made by the marshal of the United States for the district of New Jersey, on the 1st day of June, 1839, — by virtue of what is denominated a distress warrant, issued by the solicitor of the treasury under the act of congress of May 15, 1820, entitled, " An act providing for the better organization of the treasury department." This act having provided, by its first section, that a lien for the amount due should exist on the lands of the debtor from the time of the levy and record thereof in the office of the district court of the United States for the proper district, and the date of that levy in this case being prior to the date of the judgment under which the plaintiffs' title was made, the question occurred in the circuit court, " whether the said warrant of distress in the special verdict mentioned, and the proceedings thereon and anterior thereto, under which the defendants claim title, are sufficient, under the constitution of the United States and the law of the land, to pass and transfer the title and estate of the said Swartwout in and to the premises in question, as against the lessors of the plaintiff." Upon this question, the judges being of opposite opinions, it was certified to this court, and has been argued by counsel.

No objection has been taken to the warrant on account of any defect or irregularity in the proceedings which preceded its issue. It is not denied that they were in conformity with the requirements of the act of congress. The special verdict finds that Swartwout was collector of the customs for the port of New York for eight years before the 29th of March, 1838: that, on the 10th of November, 1838, his account, as such collector, was audited by the first auditor, and certified by the first comptroller of the treasury; and for the balance thus found, amounting to the sum of $1,874,119$\frac{64}{100}$, the warrant in question was issued by the solicitor of the treasury. Its validity is denied by the plaintiffs, upon the ground that so much of the act of congress as authorized it is in conflict with the constitution of the United States.

In support of this position, the plaintiff relies on that part of the first section of the third article of the constitution which requires the judicial power of the United States to be vested in one supreme court and in such inferior courts as congress may, from time to time, ordain and establish; the judges whereof shall hold their offices during good behavior, and shall, at stated times, receive for their services a compensation, which shall not be diminished during their continuance in office. Also, on the second section of the same article, which declares that the judicial power shall extend to controversies to which the United States shall be a party.

It must be admitted that, if the auditing of this account, and the ascertainment of its balance, and the issuing of this process, was an exercise of the judicial power of the United States, the proceeding was void; for the officers who performed these acts could exercise no part of that judicial power. They neither constituted a court of the United States, nor were they, or either of them, so connected with any such court as to perform even any of the ministerial duties which arise out of judicial proceedings.

The question, whether these acts were an exercise of the judicial power of the United States, can best be considered under another inquiry, raised by the further objection of the plaintiff, that the effect of the proceedings authorized by the act in question is to deprive the party, against whom the warrant issues, of his liberty and property, "without due process of law"; and, therefore, is in conflict with the fifth article of the amendments of the constitution.

Taking these two objections together, they raise the questions, whether, under the constitution of the United States, a collector of the customs, from whom a balance of account has been found to be due by accounting officers of the treasury, designated for that purpose by law, can be deprived of his liberty, or property, in order to enforce payment of that balance, without the exercise of the judicial power of the United States, and yet by due process of law, within the meaning of those terms in the constitution; and if so, then, secondly, whether the warrant in question was such due process of law?

The words, "due process of law," were undoubtedly intended to convey the same meaning as the words, "by the law of the land," in *Magna Charta*. Lord Coke, in his commentary on those words, (2 Inst. 50,) says they mean due process of law. The constitutions which had been adopted by the several States before the formation of the federal constitution, following the language of the great charter more closely, generally contained the words, "but by the judgment of his peers, or the law of the land." The ordinance of congress of July 13, 1787, for the government of the territory of the United States northwest of the river Ohio, used the same words.

The constitution of the United States, as adopted, contained the provision, that "the trial of all crimes, except in cases of impeachment, shall be by jury." When the fifth article of amendment containing the words now in question was made, the trial by jury in criminal cases had thus already been provided for. By the sixth and seventh articles of amendment, further special provisions were separately made for that mode of trial in civil and criminal cases. To have followed, as in the state constitutions, and in the ordinance of 1787, the words of *Magna Charta*, and declared that no person shall be deprived of his life, liberty, or property but by the judgment of his peers or the law of the land, would have been in part superfluous and inappropriate. To have taken the clause, "law of the land," without its immediate context, might possibly have given rise to doubts, which would be effectually dispelled by using those words which the great commentator on *Magna Charta* had declared to be the true meaning of the phrase, "law of the land," in that instrument, and which were undoubtedly then received as their true meaning.

That the warrant now in question is legal process, is not denied. It was issued in conformity with an act of Congress. But is it "due process of law"? The constitution contains no description of those processes which it was intended to allow or forbid. It does not even declare what principles are to be applied to ascertain whether it be due process. It is manifest that it was not left to the legislative power to enact any process which might be devised. The article is a restraint on the legislative as well as on the executive and judicial powers of the government, and cannot be so construed as to leave congress free to make any process "due process of law," by its mere will. To what principles, then, are we to resort to ascertain whether this process, enacted by congress, is due process? To this the answer must be twofold. We must examine the constitution itself, to see whether this process be in conflict with any of its provisions. If not found to be so, we must look to those settled usages and modes of proceeding existing in the common and statue law of England, before the emigration of our ancestors, and which are shown not to have been unsuited to their civil and political condition by having been acted on by them after the settlement of this country. We apprehend there has been no period, since the establishment of the English monarchy, when there has not been, by the law of the land, a summary method for the recovery of debts due to the crown, and especially those due from receivers of the revenues. It is difficult, at this day, to trace with precision all the proceedings had for these purposes in the earliest ages in the common law. That they were summary and severe, and had been used for purposes of oppression, is inferable from the fact that one chapter of *Magna Charta* treats of their restraint. It declares: " We or our bailiffs shall not seize any land or rent for any debt as long as the present goods and chattles of the debtor do suffice to pay the debt, and the debtor himself be ready to satisfy therefor. Neither shall the pledges of the debtor be distrained, as long as the principal debtor is sufficient for the payment of the debt; and if the principal debtor fail in payment of the debt, having nothing wherewith to pay, or will not pay where he is able, the pledges shall answer for the debt. And if they will, they shall have the lands and rents of the debtor until they be satisfied of the debt which they before paid for him, except that the principal debtor can show himself to be acquitted against the said sureties."

By the common law, the body, lands, and goods of the king's debtor were liable to be levied on to obtain payment. In conformity with the above provision of *Magna Charta*, a conditional writ was framed, commanding the sheriff to inquire of the goods and chattels of the debtor, and, if they were insufficient, then to extend on the lands. 3 Co. 12 *b*; Com. Dig., Debt, G. 2; 2 Inst. 19. But it is said that since the statute 38 Hen. VIII. c. 39, the practice has been to issue the writ in an absolute form, without requiring any previous inquisition as to the goods. Gilbert's Exch. 127.

To authorize a writ of extent, however, the debt must be matter of record in the king's exchequer. The 33 Hen. VIII. c. 39, § 50, made all specialty debts due to the king of the same force and effect as debts by statute staple, thus giving to such debts the effect of debts of record. In regard to debts due upon simple contract, other than those due from collectors of the revenue and other accountants of the crown, the practice, from very ancient times, has been to issue a commission to inquire as to the existence of the debt.

This commission being returned, the debt found was thereby evidenced by a record, and an extent could issue thereon. No notice was required to be given to the alleged debtor of the execution of this commission, (2 Tidd's Pr. 1047,) though it seems that, in some cases, an order for notice might be obtained. 1 Ves. 269. Formerly, no witnesses were examined by the commission, (Chitty's Prerog. 267 ; West, 22 ;) the affidavit prepared to obtain an order for an immediate extent being the only evidence introduced. But this practice has been recently changed. 11 Price, 29. By the statute 13 Eliz. ch. 4, balances due from receivers of the revenue and all other accountants of the crown were placed on the same footing as debts acknowledged to be due by statute staple. These balances were found by auditors, the particular officers acting thereon having been from time to time varied by legislation and usage. The different methods of accounting in ancient and modern times are described in Mr. Price's Treatise on the Law and Practice of the Exchequer, ch. 9. Such balances, when found, were certified to what was called the pipe office, to be given in charge to the sheriffs for their levy. Price, 231.

If an accountant fail to render his accounts, a process was issued, termed a *capias nomine districtionis*, against the body, goods, and lands of the accountant. Price, 162, 233, note 8.

This brief sketch of the modes of proceeding to ascertain and enforce payment of balances due from receivers of the revenue in England, is sufficient to show that the methods of ascertaining the existence and amount of such debts, and compelling their payment, have varied widely from the usual course of the common law on other subjects ; and that, as respects such debts due from such officers, " the law of the land " authorized the employment of auditors, and an inquisition without notice, and a species of execution bearing a very close resemblance to what is termed a warrant of distress in the act of 1820, now in question.

It is certain that this diversity in " the law of the land " between public defaulters and ordinary debtors was understood in this country, and entered into the legislation of the colonies and provinces, and more especially of the States, after the declaration of independence and before the formation of the constitution of the United States. Not only was the process of distress in nearly or quite universal use for the collection of taxes, but what was generally termed a warrant of distress, running against the body, goods, and chattels of defaulting receivers of public money, was issued to some public officer, to whom was committed the power to ascertain the amount of the default, and by such warrant proceed to collect it. Without a wearisome repetition of details, it will be sufficient to give one section from the Massachusetts act of 1786 : " That if any constable or collector, to whom any tax or assessment shall be committed to collect, shall be remiss and negligent of his duty, in not levying and paying unto the treasurer and receiver-general such sum or sums of money as he shall from time to time have received, and as ought by him to have been paid within the respective time set and limited by the assessor's warrant, pursuant to law, the treasurer and receiver-general is hereby empowered, after the expiration of the time so set, by warrant under his hand and seal, directed to the sheriff or his deputy, to' cause such sum and sums of money to be levied by distress and sale of such deficient constable or collector's estate, real and personal, returning the overplus, if any there be ; and, for want of such estate, to take the body of such constable or collector, and imprison him until he shall pay the same ; which warrant the sheriff or his deputy is hereby empowered and required to execute accordingly." Then follows another provision, that if the deficient sum shall not be made by the first warrant, another shall issue against the town ; and if its proper authorities shall fail to take the prescribed means to raise and pay the same, a like warrant of distress shall go against the estates and bodies of the assessors of such town. Laws of Massachusetts, vol. i. p. 266. Provisions not distinguishable from these in principle may be found in the acts of Connecticut, (Revision of 1784, p. 198;) of Pennsylvania, 1782, (2 Laws of Penn. 13 ;) of South Carolina, 1788, (5 Stats.. of S. C. 55;) New York, 1788, (1 Jones & Varick's Laws, 34 ;) see also 1 Henning's Stats. of Virginia, 819, 848 ; 12 Ibid. 562 ; Laws of Vermont, (1797, 1800,) 340. Since the formation of the constitution of the United States, other States have passed similar laws. See 7 Louis. An. R. 192. Congress, from an early period, and in repeated instances, has legislated in a similar manner. By the fifteenth section of the "Act to lay and collect a direct tax within the United States," of July 14, 1798, the supervisor of each district was authorized and required to issue a warrant of distress against any delinquent collector and his sureties, to be levied upon the goods and chattels, and for want thereof upon the body of such collector ; and, failing of satisfaction thereby, upon the goods and chattels of the sureties. 1 Stats. at Large, 602. And again, in 1813, (3 Stats. at Large, 33, § 28,) and 1815, (3 Stats. at Large, 177, § 33,) the comptroller of the treasury was empowered to issue a similar warrant against collectors of the customs and their sureties. This legislative construction of the constitution, commencing so early in the government, when the first occasion for this manner of proceeding arose, con tinued throughout its existence, and repeatedly acted on by the judiciary and the executive, is entitled to no inconsiderable weight upon the question whether the proceeding adopted by it was "due process of law." Prigg *v.* Pennsylvania, 16 Pet. 621; United States *v.* Nourse, 9 Pet. 8; Randolph's case, 2 Brock. 447; Nourse's case, 4 Cranch, C. C. R. 151; Bullock's case, (cited 6 Pet. 485, note.)

Tested by the common and statute law of England prior to the emigration of our ancestors, and by the laws of many of the States at the time of the adoption of this amendment, the pro ceedings authorized by the act of 1820 cannot be denied to be due process of law, when applied to the ascertainment and re covery of balances due to the government from a collector of customs, unless there exists in the constitution some other pro vision which restrains congress from authorizing such proceed ings. For, though "due process of law" generally implies and includes *actor, reus, judex,* regular allegations, opportunity to answer, and a trial according to some settled course of judicial proceedings, (2 Inst. 47, 50; Hoke *v.* Henderson, 4 Dev. N. C. Rep. 15; Taylor *v.* Porter, 4 Hill, 146; Van Zandt *v.* Waddel, 2 Yerger, 260; State Bank *v.* Cooper, Ibid. 599; Jones's Heirs *v.* Perry, 10 Ibid. 59; Greene *v.* Briggs, 1 Curtis, 311,) yet, this is not universally true. There may be, and we have seen that there are cases, under the law of England after *Magna Charta,* and as it was brought to this country and acted on here, in which process, in its nature final, issues against the body, lands, and goods of certain public debtors without any such trial; and this brings us to the question, whether those provisions of the constitution which relate to the judicial power are incompatible with these proceedings?

That the auditing of the accounts of a receiver of public moneys may be, in an enlarged sense, a judicial act, must be admitted. So are all those administrative duties the perform ance of which involves an inquiry into the existence of facts and the application to them of rules of law. In this sense the act of the President in calling out the militia under the act of 1795, 12 Wheat. 19, or of a commissioner who makes a certifi cate for the extradition of a criminal, under a treaty, is judicial. But it is not sufficient to bring such matters under the judicial power, that they involve the exercise of judgment upon law and fact. United States *v.* Ferreira, 13 How. 40. It is necessary to go further, and show not only that the adjustment of the balances due from accounting officers may be, but from their nature must be, controversies to which the United States is a party, within the meaning of the second section of the third article of the

constitution. We do not doubt the power of congress to provide by law that such a question shall form the subject-matter
of a suit in which the judicial power can be exerted. The act
of 1820 makes such a provision for reviewing the decision of
the accounting officers of the treasury. But, until reviewed, it
is final and binding; and the question is, whether its subject-
matter is necessarily, and without regard to the consent of
congress, a judicial controversy. And we are of opinion it is
not.

Among the legislative powers of congress are the powers "to
lay and collect taxes, duties, imposts, and excises; to pay the
debts, and provide for the common defence and welfare of the
United States, to raise and support armies; to provide and
maintain a navy, and to make all laws which may be necessary
and proper for carrying into execution those powers." What
officers should be appointed to collect the revenue thus authorized to be raised, and to disburse it in payment of the debts of
the United States; what duties should be required of them;
when and how, and to whom they should account, and what
security they should furnish, and to what remedies they should
be subjected to enforce the proper discharge of their duties, congress was to determine. In the exercise of their powers, they
have required collectors of customs to be appointed; made it incumbent on them to account, from time to time, with certain
officers of the treasury department, and to furnish sureties, by
bond, for the payment of all balances of the public money which
may become due from them. And by the act of 1820, now in
question, they have undertaken to provide summary means to
compel these officers — and in case of their default, their sureties — to pay such balances of the public money as may be in their
hands.

The power to collect and disburse revenue, and to make all
laws which shall be necessary and proper for carrying that power
into effect, includes all known and appropriate means of effectually collecting and disbursing that revenue, unless some such
means should be forbidden in some other part of the constitution. The power has not been exhausted by the receipt of the
money by the collector. Its purpose is to raise money and use
it in payment of the debts of the government; and, whoever may
have possession of the public money, until it is actually disbursed,
the power to use those known and appropriate means to secure
its due application continues.

As we have already shown, the means provided by the act of
1820 do not differ in principle from those employed in England
from remote antiquity — and in many of the States, so far as we
know without objection — for this purpose, at the time the con-

stitution was formed.   It may be added, that probably there
are few governments which do or can permit their claims for
public taxes, either on the citizen or the officer employed for
their collection or disbursement, to become subjects of judicial
controversy, according to the course of the law of the land.
Imperative necessity has forced a distinction between such
claims and all others, which has sometimes been carried out by
summary methods of proceeding, and sometimes by systems of
fines and penalties, but always in some way observed and
yielded to. .

It is true that in England all these proceedings were had in
what is denominated the court of exchequer, in which Lord
Coke says, 4 Inst. 115, the barons are the sovereign auditors of
the kingdom.   But the barons exercise in person no judicial
power in auditing accounts, and it is necessary to remember that
the exchequer includes two distinct organizations, one of which
has charge of the revenues of the crown, and the other has long
been in fact, and now is for all purposes, one of the judicial
courts of the kingdom, whose proceedings are and have been
as distinct, in most respects, from those of the revenue side of
the exchequer, as the proceedings of the circuit court of this
district are from those of the treasury; and it would be an unwarrantable assumption to conclude that, because the accounts
of receivers of revenue were settled in what was denominated the
court of exchequer, they were judicial controversies between the
king and his subjects, according to the ordinary course of the
common law or equity.   The fact, as we have already seen, was
otherwise.

It was strongly urged by the plaintiff's counsel, that though
the government might have the rightful power to provide a
summary remedy for the recovery of its public dues, aside from
any exercise of the judicial power, yet it had not done so in this
instance.   That it had enabled the debtor to apply to the judicial
power, and having thus brought the subject-matter under its cognizance, it was not for the government to say that the subject-
matter was not within the judicial power.   That if it were not in
its nature a judicial controversy, congress could not make it
such, nor give jurisdiction over it to the district courts.   In
short, the argument is, that if this were not, in its nature, a judicial controversy, congress could not have conferred on the district court power to determine it upon a bill filed by the collector.
If it be such a controversy, then it is subject to the judicial power
alone; and the fact that congress has enabled the district court
to pass upon it, is conclusive evidence that it is a judicial controversy.

We cannot admit the correctness of the last position.   If we were of opinion that this subject-matter cannot be the subject of a judicial controversy, and that, consequently, it cannot be made a subject of judicial cognizance, the consequence would be, that the attempt to bring it under the jurisdiction of a court of the United States would be ineffectual. But the previous proceedings of the executive department would not necessarily be affected thereby. They might be final, instead of being subject to judicial review.

But the argument leaves out of view an essential element in the case, and also assumes something which cannot be admitted.

It assumes that the entire subject-matter is or is not, in every mode of presentation, a judicial controversy, essentially and in its own nature, aside from the will of congress to permit it to be so; and it leaves out of view the fact that the United States is a party.

It is necessary to take into view some settled rules.

Though, generally, both public and private wrongs are redressed through judicial action, there are more summary extrajudicial remedies for both. An instance of extrajudicial redress of a private wrong is, the recapture of goods by their lawful owner; of a public wrong, by a private person, is the abatement of a public nuisance; and the recovery of public dues by a summary process of distress, issued by some public officer authorized by law, is an instance of redress of a particular kind of public wrong, by the act of the public through its authorized agents. There is, however, an important distinction between these. Though a private person may retake his property, or abate a nuisance, he is directly responsible for his acts to the proper judicial tribunals. His authority to do these acts depends not merely on the law, but upon the existence of such facts as are, in point of law, sufficient to constitute that authority; and he may be required, by an action at law, to prove those facts; but a public agent, who acts pursuant to the command of a legal precept, can justify his act by the production of such precept. He cannot be made responsible in a judicial tribunal for obeying the lawful command of the government; and the government itself, which gave the command, cannot be sued without its own consent.

At the same time there can be no doubt that the mere question, whether a collector of the customs is indebted to the United States, may be one of judicial cognizance. It is competent for the United States to sue any of its debtors in a court of law. It is equally clear that the United States may consent to be sued, and may yield this consent upon such terms and under such restrictions as it may think just. Though both the marshal and the government are exempt from suit, for anything done by

the former in obedience to legal process, still, congress may provide by law, that both, or either, shall, in a particular class of
cases, and under such restrictions as they may think proper to
impose, come into a court of law or equity and abide by its determination. The United States may thus place the government
upon the same ground which is occupied by private persons who
proceed to take extrajudicial remedies for their wrongs, and they
may do so to such extent, and with such restrictions, as may be
thought fit.

When, therefore, the act of 1820 enacts, that after the levy
of the distress warrant has been begun, the collector may bring
before a district court the question, whether he is indebted as
recited in the warrant, it simply waives a privilege which belongs
to the government, and consents to make the legality of its
future proceedings dependent on the judgment of the court; as
we have already stated in case of a private person, every fact
upon which the legality of the extrajudicial remedy depends may
be drawn in question by a suit against him. The United States
consents that this fact of indebtedness may be drawn in question
by a suit against them. Though they might have withheld their
consent, we think that, by granting it, nothing which may not be
a subject of judicial cognizance is brought before the court.

To avoid misconstruction upon so grave a subject, we think it
proper to state that we do not consider congress can either withdraw from judicial cognizance any matter which, from its nature,
is the subject of a suit at the common law, or in equity, or admiralty; nor, on the other hand, can it bring under the judicial
power a matter which, from its nature, is not a subject for judicial determination. At the same time there are matters, involving public rights, which may be presented in such form that
the judicial power is capable of acting on them, and which are
susceptible of judicial determination, but which congress may
or may not bring within the cognizance of the courts of the
United States, as it may deem proper. Equitable claims to land
by the inhabitants of ceded territories form a striking instance
of such a class of cases; and as it depends upon the will of
congress whether a remedy in the courts shall be allowed at all,
in such cases, they may regulate it and prescribe such rules of
determination as they may think just and needful. Thus it has
been repeatedly decided in this class of cases, that upon their
trial the acts of executive officers, done under the authority of
congress, were conclusive, either upon particular facts involved
in the inquiry or upon the whole title. Foley v. Harrison, 15
How. 433; Burgess v. Gray, 16 How. 48; —— v. The Minnesota Mining Company at the present term.

It is true, also, that even in a suit between private persons to

Murray's Lessee et al. v. Hoboken Land and Improvement Co.

try a question of private right, the action of the executive power, upon a matter committed to its determination by the constitution and laws, is conclusive. Luther *v.* Borden, 7 How. 1; Doe *v.* Braden, 16 How. 635.

To apply these principles to the case before us, we say that, though a suit may be brought against the marshal for seizing property under such a warrant of distress, and he may be put to show his justification; yet the action of the executive power in issuing the warrant, pursuant to the act of 1820, passed under the powers to collect and disburse the revenue granted by the constitution, is conclusive evidence of the facts recited in it, and of the authority to make the levy; that though no suit can be brought against the United States without the consent of congress, yet congress may consent to have a suit brought, to try the question whether the collector be indebted, that being a subject capable of judicial determination, and may empower a court to act on that determination, and restrain the levy of the warrant of distress within the limits of the debt judicially found to exist.

It was further urged that, by thus subjecting the proceeding to the determination of a court, it did conclusively appear that there was no such necessity for a summary remedy, by the action of the executive power, as was essential to enable congress to authorize this mode of proceeding.

But it seems to us that the just inference from the entire law is, that there was such a necessity for the warrant and the commencement of the levy, but not for its completion, if the collector should interpose, and file his bill and give security. The provision that he may file his bill and give security, and thus arrest the summary proceedings, only proves that congress thought it not necessary to pursue them, after such security should be given, until a decision should be made by the court. It has no tendency to prove they were not, in the judgment of congress, of the highest necessity under all other circumstances; and of this necessity congress alone is the judge.

The remaining objection to this warrant is, that it was issued without the support of an oath or affirmation, and so was forbidden by the fourth article of the amendments of the constitution. But this article has no reference to civil proceedings for the recovery of debts, of which a search warrant is not made part. The process, in this case, is termed, in the act of congress, a warrant of distress. The name bestowed upon it cannot affect its constitutional validity. In substance, it is an extent authorizing a levy for the satisfaction of a debt; and as no other authority is conferred, to make searches or seizures, than is ordinarily embraced in every execution issued upon a recognizance, or a stipulation in the admiralty, we are of opinion it was not invalid for this cause.

Some objection was made to the proceedings of the marshal under the warrant, because he did not levy on certain shares of corporate stock belonging to Swartwout, and because it does not appear, by the return of the warrant, that he had not goods and chattels wherewith to satisfy the exigency of the warrant. In respect to the corporate stocks, they do not appear to have been goods or chattels, subject to such levy at the time it was made ; and the return of the marshal, that he had levied on the lands by virtue of the warrant, is, at least, *primâ facie* evidence that his levy was not irregular, by reason of the existence of goods and chattels of the collector subject to his process.

The third question is, therefore, to be answered in the affirmative.

This renders the other questions proposed immaterial, and no answer need be returned thereto.

The other two cases, — John Den, *ex dem.* James B. Murray et al. *v.* The Hoboken Land and Improvement Company. And John Den, *ex dem.* William P. Rathbone et al *v.* Rutsen Suckley et al., are disposed of by this opinion, the same questions having been certified therein.

WILLIAM D. NUTT, EXECUTOR OF ALEXANDER HUNTER, DECEASED, PLAINTIFF IN ERROR, *v.* PHILIP H. MINOR.

Where a case is brought up to this court upon an alleged error in a demurrer to evidence, inasmuch as the prayer to the court below was, that there was no evidence from which the jury could infer a certain promise ; and this court is of opinion that the court below judged rightly in thinking that there was such evidence, the judgment of the court below must be affirmed.

THIS case was brought up by·writ of error from the circuit court of the United States for the District of Columbia, holden in and for the county of Washington.

The facts are stated in the opinion of the court.

It was argued by *Mr. Davis* and *Mr. Bradley*, for the plaintiff in error, and by *Mr. Badger* and *Mr. Lawrence*, for the defendant.

Mr. Justice CATRON delivered the opinion of the court.

Minor sued Nutt as executor of Alexander Hunter, and sought to recover on a *quantum meruit* for services rendered as clerk for Hunter in the marshal's office for fourteen and a half years.

The defence is, that Minor entered on the service under a special agreement to receive four hundred dollars a year.

The bill of exceptions states, that "on the trial of this cause, the plaintiff, to maintain the issue on his part, gave evidence tending to prove that he had rendered the services mentioned in the declaration, during the period therein stated, and that the said services were faithful, valuable, and unremitting, during all the time aforesaid; and he further gave evidence by Daniel Minor, a competent witness, that the engagement under which the plaintiff commenced to serve as such clerk as aforesaid to the deceased, Hunter, was made verbally in the presence of the witness; that the witness was a surety in the official bond of the deceased, as marshal for the District of Columbia; that plaintiff is the brother of witness; that witness was the deputy marshal of Alexandria county from 1806 or 1807, down to 1826; and that the plaintiff was very familiar with the duties of clerk in the marshal's office, and that the said Hunter was wholly ignorant of the duties of said office; that the witness was desirous of having plaintiff employed as such clerk by said Hunter, and, with the plaintiff, went to the marshal's office and there met the said Hunter, and in said office, they there being present, they had a conversation about the employment of the plaintiff and the terms thereof; that witness told the said Hunter that he could find nobody who would suit the place better than the plaintiff; that Hunter said he did not know anything about the emoluments of the office, or the value of the plaintiff's services, but he would be willing to give him $250 per annum; that witness said that was out of the question, that plaintiff could not pay his board with it; the witness then said he would give $150, if Hunter would give $250, making the salary $400 for the first year; that said Hunter said he was willing to do that; that plaintiff was dissatisfied; that witness, then and there continuing the conversation, in the presence of the said Hunter, and speaking in the same tone as in the previous part of the conversation, and standing near to the said Hunter as before, told the plaintiff that he must try and get along with the $400 for the first year, and that afterwards, when Hunter should ascertain the value of the services, he would pay him accordingly; that said Hunter made no comment on the last statement; that said plaintiff thereupon acquiesced, and entered upon the duties of said clerkship. And further proved by another witness, that during the said first year, the plaintiff complained to the witness of the insufficiency of the salary; that witness thereupon saw and had a conversation with Hunter on the subject; that he could not recollect the language of said Hunter, but it was to the effect that if he gave plaintiff more now he would waste it; and other remarks which he could not distinctly repeat, but all which left the clear impression on the mind of the witness that after the said first year the plaintiff was to be better compensated; that the witness reported the conversation to the plaintiff. Another witness, Smith Minor, a brother of the plaintiff, deposed that the witness had a conversation with Hunter in the year 1843 or 1844, in which he told Hunter that the plaintiff had not been to see witness for ten years; that the plaintiff had given as a reason that he could not get enough money from said Hunter to hire a horse to ride to the country, where witness resided, in Fairfax county, Virginia. That said Hunter spoke in the highest terms of the plaintiff's services, and of his integrity and industry; said that he owed his fortune to the plaintiff, and that plaintiff had made him from 70 to $100,000, and other words to this effect; and said that he, Hunter, was keeping all he could back from the plaintiff for a rainy day, and to support him in his old age. And further proved by the evidence of Chief Judge CRANCH, of Marshal Wallach, Marshal Hoover, and John A. Smith, clerk, and others, that the plaintiff's services were well worth the amount claimed, (to wit, $800 per annum,) and by said ex-Marshal Wallach and Marshal Hoover, that they respectively paid plaintiff $1,000 per annum for similar services, and for the discharge of the same duties which he had rendered and discharged in the time of their said predecessor, Hunter. And further gave evidence tending to show that the said office of marshal, during the time the said Hunter had held the same, was very profitable, and that said Hunter had amassed a considerable fortune therefrom."

An account was also given in evidence by which it appeared that Minor, as clerk, had for the first year credited payments at the specific sum of 400 dollars; but that, afterwards, the credits were at irregular intervals, and usually of small sums — sometimes covering 400 dollars in the year; but often falling short of this amount. The account has the appearance of an open and running account.

The court was asked to charge the jury, on part of the defendant, that if they believed the plaintiff entered on the service upon an agreement for 400 dollars salary for that year, and continued in it from 1834 to 1848, and during all the time, from time to time, received from Hunter in full at that rate for the whole service, then the plaintiff is not entitled to recover. This instruction was given.

The principal instruction demanded and refused was, that there was no evidence legally competent from which the jury could infer that there was any agreement between Hunter and Minor, upon other terms than for the payment of the services at the rate of 400 dollars per annum.

Another instruction was asked and refused, assuming for the

defendant that Minor was bound to give Hunter notice that more than $400 was claimed after the expiration of the first year, before he could be allowed a higher rate of compensation.

As the case depended on proof of a promise, (arising by implication,) on the fact that Hunter assented to the proposition made by Daniel Minor to the plaintiff below, no proof of further notice could be required; so that the controversy must be limited to the instruction first refused.

This instruction, if given, would have taken the case from the jury by rejecting the entire evidence as legally incompetent, except such as established the special contract.

There was evidence from which the jury might infer a promise on part of Hunter to further compensate Minor; and it was the duty of the circuit court to leave the fact to the jury: indeed, the first instruction which was given went to the limit of the court's power in its bearing on the facts; the jury being told that if they found the plaintiff was to receive 400 dollars for the first year's service, and had received at that rate for the whole period, then the plaintiff was not entitled to recover.

It is ordered that the judgment of the circuit court be affirmed.

ISRAEL KINSMAN AND CALVIN L. GODDARD, APPELLANTS, *v.* STEPHEN R. PARKHURST.

Where there was an agreement between a patentee and an assignee that the latter should manufacture the machines for a certain time and upon certain terms, it is too late for him, when called upon in chancery for an account, to deny that the patentee was the original inventor of the thing patented.

Even if the patent were invalid, yet that does not so taint with illegality the sales of the machines by the assignee, as to affect the claim of the assignor to an account of the sales.

The agreement that one only of the parties should continue the manufacture was not void as being in restraint of trade.

The assignee could not legally purchase the outstanding claim of a third person, and set it up against the patentee with whom he had an existing agreement, in the nature of a copartnership.

If the assignee transfers his contract, the person to whom he tranfers it is bound by the same equities which existed between the original parties to the contract, having purchased with a full knowledge of the state of things.

If the report of the master was incorrect, exception should have been taken to it in the court below. It cannot be examined in this court; no exception having been taken.

THIS was an appeal from the circuit court of the United States for the southern district of New York.

The facts are stated in the opinion of the court.

It was argued by *Mr. Keller*, for the appellants, and *Mr. Gif-ford*, for the appellee.

Mr. Keller made ten points.

The first three assailed the validity of Parkhurst's patent. The others raised the following questions: —

4. Whether the agreement, preventing one of the parties from making the article and both from selling it under a certain price, was not void as being in restraint of trade and against public policy, if either or both of the parties knew that the patent was not valid.

The 5th, 6th, and 7th related to the responsibility of Goddard.

The 8th. Whether Kinsman and Goddard were responsible for bad debts, provided they were prevented from receiving the money by the interference of Parkhurst.

The 9th again attacked the patent.

The 10th. Whether Kinsman and Goddard were responsible, if the machines which they made did not, in law or fact, infringe the letters-patent.

Mr. Gifford made eleven points.

The first related to the propriety of entertaining the appeal at all.

The 2d, 3d, and 4th. That the agreements between the parties fixed their relation and prescribed their rights and obligations.

5. That Kinsman was estopped from denying the validity of the patent.

6. That Goddard, having come in under the agreement, was in the same situation as Kinsman.

7. That the machines made by Kinsman and Goddard were covered by the patent.

8. That Kinsman had made enough to reimburse himself and fraudulently refused to account for the surplus.

9. That Parkhurst was the inventor of the thing patented.

10. That he never obtained a single feature of his invention from any other person.

11. That he had always acted fairly.

Mr. Justice CURTIS delivered the opinion of the court.

This is an appeal from a decree of the circuit court of the United States for the southern district of New York, in a suit in equity brought by the appellee, Parkhurst, against the appellants. The bill states, and the proofs show, that Parkhurst, being the owner of letters-patent for improvements in the machine for ginning cotton and wool, on the 22d of May, 1845, entered into a written agreement with Kinsman, the substance of which was, that Parkhurst was to be the owner of two thirds, and Kinsman of one third, of the letters-patent; that the business of manufacturing and selling the patented machines should be carried on by the parties on their joint account, in the proportions of two thirds and one third, Kinsman giving his personal attention to the business, and advancing a sum not exceeding one thousand dollars for the purchase of machinery, stock, &c., for which advance he was to be repaid out of the first profits of the business. Kinsman was to pay Parkhurst two thousand dollars in cash, and give his note for one thousand dollars, payable in sixty days. Under this agreement, the manufacture and sales of the machines were begun and carried on until the 9th day of February, 1846, at which time the parties entered into a new agreement, the substantial part of which was as follows:—

"Whereas the party of the first part has advanced moneys, and become responsible for various sums of money which have been expended in getting up machinery, and tools, and stock, &c., for the manufacture of burning and carding machines, which were invented by the said Parkhurst; one third part of which he sold and assigned to the party of the first part: Now, therefore, the party of the first part, in consideration of one dollar in hand paid by the party of the second part, the receipt whereof is hereby acknowledged, hereby covenants and agrees, that, as soon as the profits which have accrued, and which may hereafter arise, from the manufacture and sale of the said machines, so invented by the party of the second part, and so made and sold by the party of the first part, shall be sufficient to pay all legal demands for the purchase of machinery, tools, &c., &c., and other expenses incurred by said party of the first part, then he, the said party of the first part, shall and will discontinue the manufacture and sale of said machines, invented as aforesaid, and that all machines which he shall manufacture and sell after this date should not be sold for a less profit than one hundred dollars each, and that he will be accountable for one hundred dollars profit on each and every machine made and sold from this day, unless he has the written consent of the party of the second part to sell at a less price."

"The party of the second part, in consideration of one dollar to him in hand paid by the party of the first part, the receipt whereof is hereby acknowledged, and also in consideration of the agreements aforesaid, hereby covenants and agrees with the party of the first part, that he will go on and manufacture the machines aforesaid as soon as the party of the first part discontinues the same, and that he will not sell any machine for a less profit than one hundred dollars, without the written consent of the party of the first part, and that he will pay over to the party of the first part one third part and share of the said profits upon all machines which he makes and sells hereafter, and that, for any machines which he may manufacture, or have manufactured, before the discontinuing of the building of the same by the party of the first part, shall be subject to the same restrictions of selling for at least one hundred dollars profit on each machine, one third of which shall be paid to the party of the first part."

The original and supplemental bills aver, that under this agreement Kinsman prosecuted the business, and not only reimbursed himself for the cost of the machinery, tools, &c., and all his other advances, but, in violation of his agreement, continued the manufacture and sale of the machines, so as to receive large profits, of which it prays an account, and also an injunction to restrain the further making or vending of the machines in violation of the agreement. A temporary injunction was applied for and obtained on the third day of July, 1847. On the 29th day of June, 1847, Kinsman made a transfer to the appellant, Goddard, who was then a clerk in his employment, of the tools, stock, &c., used in the manufacture; and, after Kinsman was enjoined, the business was carried on in Goddard's name. A supplemental bill was then filed, making Goddard a party, charging him with notice of all the complainant's rights at the time of the transfer to him, alleging the transfer itself to have been only colorable, and praying an account and decree as against him and Kinsman. The circuit court made an interlocutory decree, declaring Parkhurst's right to an account, referring the cause to a master, to take and state the accounts, directing the master, in taking the accounts, to ascertain and report the number of machines made and sold by Kinsman and Goddard, or either of them; the advances made by Kinsman and Goddard, or either of them; and charging a profit of one hundred dollars on each machine sold.

The master reported; and his report, not being excepted to was confirmed, and a final decree made, that Kinsman and Goddard should pay to the complainant the amount reported by the master to be due from them. From this decree the appeal now before us was taken.

The principal objection made by the appellants to the decree of the court below is that Parkhurst was not the original and first inventor of the thing patented. We are not satisfied that this is made out. But we have not found it necessary to come to a decided opinion upon this point, because we are all of opinion that, under the agreement of the ninth of February,

1846, the invalidity of the patent would not afford a bar to the complainant's right to an account. Having actually received profits from sales of the patented machine, which profits the defendants do not show have been or are in any way liable to be affected by the invalidity of the patent, its validity is immaterial. Moreover, we think the defendants are estopped from alleging that invalidity. They have made and sold these machines under the complainant's title and for his account; and they can no more be allowed to deny that title and retain the profits to their own use, than an agent, who has collected a debt for his principal, can insist on keeping the money, upon an allegation that the debt was not justly due.

The invalidity of the patent does not render the sales of the machine illegal, so as to taint with illegality the obligation of the defendants to account. Even where money has been received, either by an agent or a joint owner, by force of a contract which was illegal, the agent or joint owner cannot protect himself from accounting for what was so received, by setting up the illegality of the transaction in which it was paid to him. Thus where a vessel engaged in an illegal trade carried freight which came into the hands of one of the part owners, and on a bill filed by the other part owner for an account, the defendant relied on the illegality of the trade, but it was held to be no defence. Sharp v. Taylor, 2 Phil. Ch. R. 801. So in Tenant v. Elliot, 1 B. & P. 3, the defendant, an insurance broker, having effected an illegal insurance for the plaintiff, and received the amount of a loss, endeavored to defend against the claim of his principal by showing the illegality of the insurance, but the plaintiff recovered. See also McBlair v. Gibbes, 17 How. 236.

· Here, however, as already observed, there was no illegality; it is simply a question of failure of title, and as that does not appear in any manner to have affected the profits which the defendants received, there can be no ground to allow it to be shown in defence. Bartlett, ad'r, v. Holbrook, 1 Gray's R. 114 ; Wilder v. Adams, 2 Wood. & Minot, 329, are in point.

Similar views are decisive against the objection that this was a contract in restraint of trade. It was certainly competent for two persons, being joint owners of letters-patent, whether valid or invalid, to enter into a copartnership for the manufacture and sale of the patented machines, and to stipulate that one of them should alone conduct the business. This was a provision for the prosecution of the business in a particular mode, and not for its restraint. It is a very common and not an illegal stipulation in partnership articles, that neither partner shall carry on that business for which the partnership is formed, outside of the partnership and for his own account. Besides, if the contract

25 *

to refrain from the manufacture could not be enforced, as being against public policy, this would afford no answer to a claim for an account of profits actually realized by prosecuting the business, there being no connection between the illegal stipulation and the profits of the business.

It was insisted by the appellants that they did not act under the complainant's title, but under some right acquired from one Sargent. We are not satisfied that Sargent had even an inchoate right to a patent for the machines which the appellants made and sold. But even if he had, the defendant, Kinsman, could not secretly acquire the outstanding right of Sargent, if any, and set it up against his joint owner, Parkhurst, in derogation of his rights under the agreement of the 9th of February, which Kinsman entered into with knowledge of this alleged title of Sargent; and Goddard is bound by the same equities, for he not only purchased *pendente lite*, and with actual notice of the suit, but we are satisfied the sale to him was made to enable Kinsman to attempt to evade the injunction.

The appellant, Goddard, objects that he has been charged by the final decree, jointly with Kinsman, for the profits on sales of machines made before the transfer to him by Kinsman. If this be so, it arises from the report of the master, who was directed by the interlocutory decree to report the sales made by Kinsman and Goddard, or either of them, and the advances and expenditures of them, or either of them.

If his report was in this or any other particular erroneous, it was incumbent on the defendants to have pointed out the error by an exception filed pursuant to the rules of the court on that subject. But no exception was filed, the report was confirmed, and the final decree was drawn up and entered without objection by the appellant, Goddard, reciting that it appears by the report of the master that the sum of $23,220$\frac{78}{100}$ is due and owing by Kinsman and Goddard to Parkhurst, and thereupon proceeds to decree them to pay that sum. When a motion to dismiss the appeal was made at a former day, on the ground that the master's report not having been excepted to, and the appellants not having objected to the final decree, there was nothing open on this appeal, the appellant's counsel declared that the appeal was designed only to review the interlocutory decree which had decided the merits of the cause, and that, unless error was found therein, there was no ground for the appeal. The motion to dismiss the appeal was overruled, the court being of opinion that it was open to the appellants to review the decision made by the interlocutory decree. But the interlocutory decree does not direct the master to charge Goddard and Kinsman jointly with profits on sales made by Kinsman alone. If the master put such an interpretation on the decree, it was an erroneous interpretation, and should have been brought before the court below by an exception. It is too late to object to it here, for the first time.

The appellants also insist that they were charged with profits not actually received, by reason of the failure of the purchasers to pay, and other causes. But this was in accordance with the agreement of the 9th of February, which stipulates that Kinsman shall be accountable for one hundred dollars profit on each machine made and sold by him. By force of this stipulation, he and Goddard, who acted with him under this agreement, took the risk of bad debts. It appears, from the master's report, that evidence, tending to show that some of these losses were attributable to the interference of Parkhurst, was offered to the master and rejected by him. But, no exception having been taken to bring this point before the circuit court, it is not open here.

We have considered all the objections to the decree of the circuit court, and, finding them untenable, we order the decree to be affirmed, with damages and costs.

JAMES L. RANSOM, PLAINTIFF IN ERROR, v. WILLIAM WINN AND ISABELLA DAVIS, ADMINISTRATORS OF THOMAS J. DAVIS, DECEASED.

Where a petition is filed in a court of chancery by a creditor, praying to be admitted as a party complainant in a suit then existing, but the nature of the original suit is not made to appear, the proceeding is irregular, and cannot be sustained.

Where a chancery suit involves matters of account, the action of a master should be had in the inferior court, and the items admitted or rejected should be stated, so that exception may be taken to the particular items or class of items, and such a case should be brought before this court on the rulings of the exceptions by the circuit court.

THIS case was brought up by appeal from the circuit court of the United States for the District of Columbia, holden in and for the county of Washington.

Ransom filed a petition in a cause then pending in the circuit court of the District of Columbia, and all that the record exhibited with respect to said cause was its title, namely: —

William S. Herrman v. Isabella Davis and Thomas Winn, administrators, Ignatius T. Davis, Francis R. R. Davis et al., heirs at law of Thomas J. Davis, deceased. In chancery.

But upon what ground Herrman filed a bill against the administrators and heirs of Davis, the record did not show. The subsequent proceedings are stated in the opinion of the court.

It was argued by *Mr. W. S. Cox*, for the appellant, and *Mr. Davis*, for the appellees.

Mr. Justice McLEAN delivered the opinion of the court.

This is an appeal from the circuit court of the United States for the District of Columbia.

The proceedings on which the appeal was taken were had on a petition of the appellant, Ransom, in the circuit court of the District, stating that he was the creditor of the intestate for $8,113.48, a balance due on merchandise furnished, and other matters of account. An account was filed with the petition, showing the items charged, and he prayed to be made a party in a suit pending; and he adopts the allegations and prayers of the bill, and calls upon the defendants to answer, &c.

No answer was filed by the defendants, nor does any part of the original bill to which reference is made, or any proceeding in that suit, appear on the record.

An account is stated of the value of produce purchased by Ransom, and forwarded to Thomas J. Davis, and priced as of the 28th May, 1847, which, in the whole, amounted to $31,879.80. The entire expenditure in purchasing the produce, including losses, amounted to the sum of $21,280.43, leaving a profit of $10,599.37. A further account is stated in detail of purchases of grain amounting to a large sum. An auditor was appointed by the court, who, in a long report, states the correspondence between Ransom and Davis, which conduces to show that Ransom was engaged in purchasing wheat and other grain, to be forwarded to Davis, who owned a mill in Georgetown. Exceptions were taken to the report of the auditor, and the court ordered that the cause be again referred to him, with instructions to take such testimony as may be offered by Ransom, on the points mentioned in his affidavit filed in the cause; and that he report to this court, as soon as convenient, the substance of such testimony, and what changes, if any, such additional testimony may render proper in the report heretofore made by said auditor in reference to said claim.

The auditor returned the additional testimony which he took, but made no alteration in his former report. It was admitted in the argument that the estate of Davis was insolvent, and the object of Ransom seemed to be, to enforce his claim against the estate of Davis in preference to other creditors.

From the record, the nature of the suit, in which Ransom prayed to become a party, does not appear. It may have been a suit by other creditors, but no notice is taken of them in the subsequent proceeding, nor is there any pleading except the petition to be made a party. This proceeding is irregular, and cannot be sustained. The exceptions to the report of the auditor were overruled by the circuit court, and the petition of Ransom was dismissed.

Where a chancery suit involves matters of account, the action of a master should be had in the inferior court, and the items admitted or rejected should be stated, so that exception may be taken to the particular items or class of items, and such a case should be brought before this court on the rulings of the exceptions by the circuit court.

The bill is dismissed at the plaintiff's costs, without prejudice.

JOHN DOE, *ex dem.* JAMES B. MCCALL, HENRY V. MCCALL, AND MARY SIDNEY MCCALL, PLAINTIFFS IN ERROR *v.* WILLIARD CARPENTER AND JOHN A. REITZ.[*]

Where there was a decree of a court of chancery for the partition of real estate, an agreement to divide which had been previously made, but one of the parties to the agreement had conveyed all his interest in the estate to one of the complainants. and died before deeds of partition were executed, and the bill was filed against his heirs simply for partition, the decree of the court and deeds executed under it only operated upon the parties jointly interested in the property.

Two of the heirs were non-residents, and did not appear; the third was an infant.

Therefore, in an action of ejectment by the heirs, evidence was admissible to show that the deed from their ancestor had been obtained by fraud. The proceedings in chancery did not involve this question, nor was it adjudicated upon by the court.

Nor is the question of fraud appropriate to the proceeding in partition; if raised, the proceedings are usually suspended, and the question sent to a court of law.

The recitals in the deeds of partition have no binding force beyond what is derived from the decree.

The defendants were jointly interested with the complainants in one parcel embraced in the partition suit. The ancestor having conveyed away the property covered by the deed alleged to have been fraudulently obtained, the heirs had no interest in the partition of it.

These proceedings being *in rem,* only operated in respect to the title as against them, upon that part of the property in which they had a joint interest.

THIS case was brought up, by writ of error, from the circuit court of the United States for the district of Indiana.

It was an ejectment, brought by the McCalls against Carpenter and Reitz, to recover six blocks, seventy-two lots, and one half block, in Lamasco city, in the county of Vanderburgh, in the State of Indiana, of which blocks and lots Carpenter and Reitz were in possession.

The claim of the plaintiffs was founded upon the following circumstances : —

Prior to the 21st of March, 1840, certain persons were possessed of the city of Lamasco, and also of the southeast quarter of section 28, in town 6, south of range 11, west ; consisting of

---

[*] Mr. Justice CURTIS, apprehending that one of his connections was interested in the subject-matter of this case, did not sit therein.

160 acres. They owned this property in the following proportions, namely:—

John Law, ⅛; William H. Law, ¼; Boston and Indiana Land
Company, ⅛; Lucius H. Scott, ⅜; James B. McCall, ⅜.

On the 21st of March, 1840, the proprietors (the Boston Land
Company subsequently acquiescing) signed an agreement, under
seal, to divide the town lots and also the quarter section amongst
them. The town lots were divided into eight subdivisions,
whereof each proprietor of ⅜ had two, and the quarter section
was also divided into eight parts, allotted in the same proportion.

Before deeds of partition could be exchanged, McCall sold
and conveyed to Hugh Stewart all his undivided interest in the
town property, without including his share in the quarter section. This deed purported to be executed on 18th June, 1840.
It was not in the record, being offered in evidence upon the trial,
but rejected.

Shortly after the execution of this deed to Stewart, McCall
died, leaving three infant children, two of whom were non-residents of the State, the lessors of the plaintiff in error. These
children thus became the unquestioned heirs of their father's
interest in the quarter section, which was not included in the
deed to Stewart.

In order to bring about a partition, regularly, two bills ought
to have been filed: one for the partition of the town property, in
which the interest of the father of the infants appeared to be
held entirely by Stewart, they themselves having none; and the
other by their co-tenants in the quarter section in which Stewart
had no interest, and, therefore, should not have been a party.

It so happened, however, that at the March term, 1842, of the
Vanderburgh circuit court, a bill was filed by John Law, William H. Law, Lucius H. Scott, and Hugh Stewart, in their own
right, and also the trustees of the Boston Land Company. The
nature of the bill and the proceedings under it are stated in the
opinion of the court; as are also the proceedings in the ejectment which gave rise to the case now under consideration.

It was submitted on printed arguments by *Mr. Dunn*, for the
plaintiffs in error, and *Mr. Baker*, for the defendants.

Mr. Justice NELSON delivered the opinion of the court.

This is a writ of error to the circuit court of the United States
for the district of Indiana.

The suit in the court below was an action of ejectment by
the plaintiffs to recover the possession of certain town lots in
the city of Lamasco. They proved on the trial, that their father, James B. McCall, was the owner of an undivided fourth

of a certain part of said city, and had been in the possession of the same, and died in 1840; and that they were his heirs at law.

The defendants set up, in bar of the action, certain proceedings in partition, embracing the premises in question, in the circuit court of the fourth judicial district of Indiana.

The bill in partition was filed by the tenants in common of the town lots with McCall in his lifetime, against his children and heirs, the present plaintiffs. The two sons were non-residents of the State, at the time, and did not appear or answer to the bill. The daughter was a resident of the State, and was served personally with the subpœna. She and the younger brother were under age, for whom guardians *ad litem* were appointed by the court.

The bill, after setting out the interests of the respective tenants in common, and that partition had been agreed upon between them, describing particularly the manner in which the partition was to be made, and the portions assigned to each in the arrangement, charges, that after the agreement, J. B. McCall sold and conveyed all his undivided interest, to wit, one undivided fourth part of the town property, to Hugh Stewart for the sum of $11,500, and that shortly afterwards, and before he executed deeds of partition, according to the agreement, departed this life, leaving three children, his heirs at law, James B. McCall, non-resident of this State, and Henry McCall, also a non-resident, and Mary S. McCall, who are infants under the age of twenty-one years. The bill further charges, that the several proprietors, including Stewart, the grantee of McCall, had already interchanged deeds of partition, according to the agreement, or were ready to do so; and that they were ready to execute to the heirs deeds of all their right to subdivision No. 3 and 6 of the southeast quarter of section twenty-three, in town 6, and of all other portions to which the heirs were entitled; and then closes by stating, that, inasmuch as your orators are unable to obtain relief in the premises, except by an interposition of the court of chancery, they, for the purpose of perfecting their several titles to their respective portions of said property, pursuant to the agreement in partition, pray that the heirs be made defendants; that a guardian *ad litem* be appointed for the two infant heirs, that they may answer the bill; and if the same should be found true, that the court would appoint three commissioners to make deeds of partition, &c.

The bill was taken as confessed against the adult heir, and against the others upon the answer put in by the guardian; no proof, for aught that appears, having been given. The court decreed that the prayer of the complainants be granted; and that C. D. Bourne, C. Baker, and J. E. Blythe be commissioners to make deeds, &c., to the complainants, agreeably to the partition mentioned in the bill, and pursuant to, and agreeable with the said sale and conveyance made by James B. McCall, deceased, of his undivided interest in said town property, to the complainant, Hugh Stewart.

Deeds were executed in pursuance of the directions in the decree, and reported to the court and confirmed.

It appeared that McCall, besides being a joint owner in the town property which he had conveyed to Stewart, also owned, jointly with the complainants, (except Stewart,) one fourth of the southeast quarter of section No. 23, township 6, adjoining the town, and which descended to his heirs and was embraced in the bill of partition.

The counsel for the plaintiffs, when this record of partition was offered in evidence by the defendants, objected to the admission, on the ground that the decree was void for want of jurisdiction of the court; and also for fraud apparent on the face of the proceedings. The objection was overruled. It appeared that the defendants claim title from Stewart, the grantee of McCall.

They then rested, and the counsel for the plaintiffs then produced and read the conveyance from their father to Stewart mentioned in the bill of partition, and offered to prove that the conveyance was obtained by fraud on the part of Stewart, and also, that, at the time of its execution, their father was of unsound mind and incapable of making a valid contract; that said unsoundness was well known to Stewart, and that he took advantage of it in obtaining the deed; that the consideration of $11,500 mentioned was never paid, that $6,000 in depreciated state scrip was all that was ever paid or agreed to be paid, and that the defendants purchased of Stewart with full knowledge of all the facts; that the real estate purported to be conveyed by the deed was worth at the time at least $20,000.

To all which evidence the defendant's counsel objected, on the sole ground that the plaintiffs were barred by the record of the proceedings in partition, which objection was sustained by the court, and the evidence excluded.

The jury, under the direction of the court, rendered a verdict for the defendants.

We think the court erred in excluding this evidence.

The binding effect of the decree, in the chancery suit, is sought to be maintained upon the ground that the proceedings were instituted not only for the purpose of making partition, but also to quiet the title between the parties, and especially the title of Stewart under the conveyance from McCall, and that the children and heirs were made parties for this reason, and that the proceedings, in this aspect, being in the nature of proceedings *in rem*, would operate upon the title and bind the heirs, whether they appeared or not, if notice had been given in conformity with the statute or law of the State.

But we think the obvious answer to this view is, that the bill has not been framed in any such aspect, or for any such purpose, either in the body of it or in the prayer. There is no suggestion of any imperfection in the title of Stewart, under the deed of McCall, or of any imputation or questioning of the genuineness or validity of it; nor does the prayer ask for a decree to confirm the deed or the title to Stewart.

. The only pretext for the ground now taken to bind the heirs, is in the allegation as follows, namely: " As your orators are unable to obtain relief in the premises, except by the interposition of a court of chancery, they, for the purpose of perfecting their several titles to the respective portions of said property, agreeably with and in pursuance of said agreement of partition, would respectively pray," &c., and then follows the prayer for partition.

Now, it is manifest that this allegation refers simply to the subject of providing for the mutual releases or conveyances of the joint interest in the property, so that each might become vested, severally, with the title to his respective share, and nothing beyond this, as is further evinced by the prayer of the bill, which is, that if the allegations in the bill should be found true, not that Stewart should be quieted in his title under McCall, but that three commissioners be appointed to make the partition, &c. So in respect to the decree. It simply orders that the prayer of the bill of the complainants be granted, appoints the commissioners, and directs them to make the partition, by the execution of the deeds of conveyance, release, and partition to the complainants, according to their respective rights, &c.

The deeds of the commissioners have also been referred to as helping out the binding effect claimed for these proceedings.

The deed of the commissioners to Stewart may be taken as a sample of all of them. It recites their appointment, the object of it, to wit, execute the partition deeds, &c., and adds: " and to perfect the title of said Hugh Stewart to the interest heretofore conveyed to him in said property, by the said McCall in his lifetime," — they then go on and convey " all the right, title, and interest, claim and demand whatsoever of the said James B. McCall, deceased, at the time of his death, and of his heirs, naming the three defendants, since his decease, or at any other time, and of all or any other heirs or heir whatsoever, of the said

James B. McCall, deceased," &c.; seeking to bind those not made defendants as well as those who were.

The answer to all these recitals is, that they have no binding force or effect beyond what is derived from the decree of the court appointing the commissioners; and as that simply conferred authority on them to execute mutual conveyances and releases for the purpose of making partition between the parties, any recital going beyond this is nugatory. Neither should the simple confirmation of the deeds by the court be construed as intending to go beyond the terms and directions of the decree.

The case, then, is brought down to the question, so far as the effect and operation of the chancery suit are concerned, whether or not these defendants are estopped by the decree from impeaching the deed of their father to Stewart. And, in respect to this question, we may concede that, for the purposes of partition, the court, under the statute and law of Indiana, had jurisdiction of the subject-matter and were competent to make the partition.

The point is, whether or not the right of the plaintiffs to impeach this deed was involved in these proceedings, so as to be deemed *res judicata*, and all further examination or inquiry foreclosed.

As we have already seen, the question as to its validity was not presented upon the pleadings in that suit, nor did it become the subject of inquiry or examination in the course of the proceeding, nor did it enter into the decree of the court in the determination of the case. And the better opinion is, that no such question could have been raised by the defendants in that proceeding, if they had sought to invalidate the deed.. The most that the court would have been justified in doing, in the usual course of proceeding, would have been to have stayed the suit in partition till the question could have been settled at law. The proceedings in partition are not appropriate for a litigation between parties in respect to the title.

As to the binding effect of judgments or decrees, the general rule is, that the judgments of courts of concurrent jurisdiction are not admissible in a subsequent suit, unless they are upon the same matter, and directly on the point; when the same matter is directly in question, and the judgment in the former suit upon the point, it will then be as a plea, a bar, or as evidence, conclusive between the parties. 2 Phillips Ev. 13. So a judgment is conclusive upon a matter legitimately within the issue, and necessarily involved in the decision. 4 Cow. 559; 8 Wend. 9; C. & H. notes, part 2, note 22.

Testing the case by this principle, it seems quite clear that the proceedings in partition constituted no defence to this

Lessee of McCall et al. *v.* Carpenter et al.

action; no question was made upon the deed by the pleadings, nor any judgment given upon it; nor was any such question necessarily involved in the partition suit.

Besides, two of the defendants, plaintiffs here, were non-residents of the State, and neither appeared, nor were served personally with process. As to them, the proceedings were purely *in rem*, and the decree acted only upon the *res* or subject-matter. And, as to the subject-matter, the bill on its face shows, that these two plaintiffs had no interest in nor connection with the partition, except as respected the southeast quarter of section twenty-three. This tract was not included in the deed to Stewart, and of course descended to the heirs. Being tenants in common with the complainants, the decree of partition might operate upon it and bind them. But, as to the premises now in dispute it could have no effect, as it appears, by the averment of complainants themselves, the defendants had no interest in it. The title was in Stewart. The decree, therefore, operating simply *in rem*, could only operate upon such interest or estate of the defendant as was shown in the bill, and properly the subject of the partition against them. Beyond this, it was ineffectual, either as to its direct operation, or when in question collaterally.

Proceedings of this character are allowed to conclude the rights of the absent party, only as it respects property, whether real or personal, involved in the suit, the property of the party proceeded against. They act upon the thing, and bind the party in respect to it. Now, that in this case, so far as the two non-resident defendants were concerned, was their interest in the southeast quarter of section twenty-three? They were strangers as regarded any other piece or parcel of land involved in the proceedings.

Then, as to Mary, the daughter, the process was served personally upon her; she was an infant, and appeared by a guardian *ad litem*. But this was simply an appearance, as the representative of her interest in the undivided parcel which had descended to the heirs. The bill shows that she had no interest in the partition, except as to this; all the other parcels of which partition was sought belonged to other parties, and concerned them alone; as to these, John Doe might have been made a party with as much propriety as this defendant. It may be, as we have already said, that these proceedings conclude the question of partition from afterwards being agitated, a question which it is not now necessary to decide; but we think it clear that they cannot conclude the title even of a party to them, whom the proceedings themselves show had no interest or concern in the question of partition.

Upon the whole, after the best consideration we have been able to bestow upon the case, we think the court erred in excluding the evidence offered to impeach the deed of McCall to Stewart, and that the judgment below should be reversed, and a *venire de novo* awarded.

Mr. Justice DANIEL and Mr. Justice CAMPBELL dissented.

Mr. Justice CAMPBELL.

The circuit court of Vanderburgh county, Indiana, exercising chancery jurisdiction, in 1842, pronounced a decree, appointing three commissioners to make deeds of conveyance, release, and partition to the plaintiffs in the suit, of certain lots in the town of Lamasco, in that county, and which embrace the land included in this suit, according to an agreement for a partition made by a portion of the plaintiffs and James B. McCall, the ancestor of the lessors of the plaintiff in this cause, and also of a sale and conveyance by him to one Stewart of his undivided interest in the property, and directed that the deeds should convey the fee-simple to the complainants respectively.

The deeds were executed by the commissioners, were reported to the court, and were confirmed by an order.

This decree was rendered in a chancery cause, prosecuted by persons who had held in common the site of the town of Lamasco with McCall, and who had entered into the agreement, by which specified lots were set apart to each of the tenants, and for which mutual conveyances were to be made, and one Stewart, on whose behalf it was alleged that, after the agreement, and before deeds were made, McCall had sold and conveyed to him his entire undivided interest in the tract.

The object of the bill was to perfect in the complainants, according to the agreement of partition and the sale and conveyance to Stewart, their titles. One of the children of McCall was served with process, and two were called in by publication, and a guardian *ad litem* was appointed for the minors. The prayer of the bill was for the appointment of commissioners to make the conveyances according to the agreement and the sale.

The defendants claiming to hold the lands under these complainants, offered the record of the proceedings in evidence upon the trial in the circuit court, which was opposed, for the reason that the court had no jurisdiction, and for fraud, apparent on the face of the bill, the evidence was admitted as conclusive of the title, and an issue was formed on the bill of exceptions for this court.

The decree operates upon a title to lands within the county

and State where the circuit court, that rendered it, was held. That court possesses, under the constitution and laws of Indiana, a general chancery jurisdiction, and a special authority to appoint commissioners to execute decrees like the present. One of the defendants was before the court by process, and was defended by a guardian, and the others by publication, according to the authorized practice of that court. This being the state of the record — the jurisdiction of the court spreading over the subject-matter, and embracing the parties — the inquiry arises, on what principle can its authority be impeached in a collateral proceeding? It is said, that, it being apparent from the bill that James B. McCall had sold his entire interest in the town of Lamasco to Stewart, that Stewart might have completed his agreement for a partition, and that the heirs of McCall, having inherited no estate, were not proper parties to the bill, and that the deeds of conveyance, release, and partition, under the decree, did not conclude their rights. But who is to decide whether they were proper parties to the bill, and whether it was proper to terminate all contest upon the title, by requiring them to release their rights, whatever they might happen to be, to the plaintiffs? Upon whom was the duty devolved by the constitution and laws of Indiana, to determine whether the bill was framed according to the course of chancery practice, and the decree a proper expression of chancery jurisprudence? Certainly not this court, nor the circuit court of the United States for Indiana.

A court of the State of Indiana, with a plenary jurisdiction in chancery, having the subject-matter and parties within that jurisdiction, has pronounced the decree, from whence comes the power of this court to pronounce its jurisdiction usurped, and its decree a nullity? This court, of old, was accustomed to say, "that a judgment or execution irreversible by a superior court, cannot be declared a nullity by any authority of law, if it has been rendered by a court of competent jurisdiction of the parties and the subject-matter, with authority to use the process it has issued; it must remain the only test of the respective rights of the parties to it." And also, "the line which separates error in judgment from the usurpation of power is very definite, and is precisely that which denotes the cases where a judgment or decree is reversible only by an appellate court, or may be declared a nullity collaterally, when it is offered in evidence in an action concerning the matter adjudicated, or purporting to have been so. In the one case it is a record imputing absolute verity; in the other, mere waste paper. 10 Pet. 449.

We have only now to ascertain the extent of the jurisdiction of courts of chancery in the matters of partition, and to quiet title by removing dormant equities, and the effect of decrees in

26 *

such cases. The first branch of the inquiry is satisfactorily answered by Judge Story. "In all cases of partition," he says, "a court of equity does not act merely in a ministerial character and in obedience to the call of the parties who have a right to the partition, but it founds itself upon its general jurisdiction as a court of equity, and administers its relief *ex æquo et bono*, according to its own notions of general justice and equity between the parties. It will, therefore, by its decree, adjust all the equitable rights of the parties interested in the estate, and courts of equity, in making these adjustments, will not confine themselves to the mere legal rights of the original tenants in common, but will have regard to the legal and equitable rights of all other parties interested in the estate, which have been derived from any of the original tenants in common."

Such being the enlarged jurisdiction upon the subject-matter, the question arises as to the effect of the decrees upon the titles that are, or might have been, involved in a suit of that nature.

In Reese *v.* Holmes, 5 Rich. Eq. 531, the court determined that the parties to such a record were concluded by the decree from showing that they had a greater estate than, or one derived from a different source from, that set out in the proceedings and established by the decree.

The court said, "If any relievable fraud or mistake entered into the decree when it was pronounced, the party affected by it might have been heard, if he had come within a reasonable time, with a direct proceeding to set the proceeding aside; but while it stands, it is the standard to which every party taking under it must resort for the measure of his rights, and cannot be set aside or modified collaterally." In Stewart *v.* Migell, 8 Ind. Eq. 242, the court decide that a bill cannot be supported to set aside a decree formerly made between parties, though it be alleged that the facts found by the court did not exist; and that the decree was conclusive, in respect to the thing which the parties had, or admitted, or it was declared they had, and also in respect to the share to which each was entitled in severalty, and to the parcel so allotted. In Mills *v.* Witherington, 2 Dev. & B. 438, where land belonging to one in severalty was included in the petition as land held in common, and allotted to another in severalty, it was held, in an action of ejectment, that the lessor of the plaintiff, who had been a party to the judgment, "was concluded, bound, and estopped, to controvert anything contained in it." In Clapp *v.* Bromagham, 9 Cowen, 537, the court say, "that the judgment in partition, it is true, does not change the possession, but it establishes the title, and in an ejectment must be conclusive." 1 Md. Ch. Dec. 455; 14 Geo. 521; 17 Vesey, 355; 29 Maine, 128.

I do not consider it necessary to inquire, whether the fact of an absolute sale and a perfect conveyance by McCall to Stewart did not relieve the heirs from the duty of completing the agreement of their ancestor; nor do I consider it necessary to inquire whether, having such a sale and conveyance, Stewart had a good case to go into chancery to cut off possible but unpublished equities; nor do I consider it necessary to inquire whether there was sufficient or any evidence to support the 'decree. Those questions were all subject to the jurisdiction of the circuit court of Vanderburgh county, and might have been revised in the supreme court of Indiana.

Those courts had entire jurisdiction of the parties and the cause, and its decree cannot be collaterally impeached. I am authorized to say that Mr. Justice DANIEL concurs in this opinion.

Ex Parte: In the Matter of William Wells, on a Petition for a Writ of Habeas Corpus.

The second article of the Constitution of the United States, section two, contains this provision, namely: "The President shall have power to grant reprieves and pardons for offences against the United States, except in cases of impeachment."

Under this power, the President can grant a conditional pardon to a person under sentence of death, offering to commute that punishment into an imprisonment for life. If this is accepted by the convict, he has no right to contend that the pardon is absolute and the condition of it void. And the court below was justifiable in refusing to discharge the prisoner, when the application was placed upon that ground.

The language used in the Constitution as to the power of pardoning, must be construed by the exercise of that power in England prior to the Revolution, and in the States prior to the adoption of the Constitution.

The manner explained in which it was exercised in England and in many of the States.

The language of the Constitution is such that the power of the President to pardon conditionally is not one of inference, but is conferred in terms, that language being to "grant reprieves and pardons," which includes conditional as well as absolute pardons.

The acceptance, by the convict, of the condition, was not given under duress in the legal acceptation of that term.

THIS was a motion for a writ of *habeas corpus*, founded on a petition by Wells, setting forth the following circumstances, viz.: —

That Wells was convicted of murder, at the December term, 1851, of the criminal court for the county of Washington, District of Columbia, and was sentenced by said court to be hanged on the 28d of April, 1852, on which said 28d of April, Mr. Fillmore, then President of the United States, granted "a pardon of the offence of which he was convicted, upon condition that he be imprisoned during his natural life, that is, the sentence of death is hereby commuted to imprisonment for life in the penitentiary at Washington."

That while under the constraint of duress of imprisonment and *duress per minas* he subscribed an acceptance of the pardon with the condition annexed.

That on the 18th of April, 1855, he applied to the circuit court of the District of Columbia, for a writ of *habeas corpus*, which was granted, and that court proceeded to inquire into the cause of his imprisonment.

That the circuit court decided that the President had power to commute the punishment of death, and remanded him to the penitentiary, where he has ever since been confined.

He therefore prayed this court to issue a writ of *habeas corpus*.

In this case, as in the case of *ex parte* Watkins, (7 Pet. 571,) it was admitted that all the facts existing in the case had been laid before the court, exactly as they would appear if the *habeas corpus* had been duly awarded and returned; so that the judgment which the court were called upon to pronounce, was precisely that which ought to be pronounced upon a full hearing upon the return to the writ of *habeas corpus;* and it was accordingly so argued at the bar.

It will be seen also by a reference to that case that the court decided that the judgment which was pronounced upon the petition of Mr. Watkins, was an exercise of appellate and not of original jurisdiction.

The petition for a *habeas corpus* was sustained by *Mr. Charles Lee Jones*, for the petitioner, and opposed by *Mr. Cushing*, Attorney-General.

The subject is so fully discussed in the opinion of the court and the dissenting opinions of Mr. Justice McLean and Mr. Justice Curtis, that it is not thought necessary to give the arguments of counsel.

Mr. Justice WAYNE delivered the opinion of the court.

The petitioner was convicted of murder in the District of Columbia, and sentenced to be hung on the 23d of April, 1852. President Fillmore granted to him a conditional pardon. The material part of it is as follows: "For divers good and sufficient reasons I have granted, and do hereby grant unto him, the said William Wells, a pardon of the offence of which he was convicted — upon condition that he be imprisoned during his natural life; that is, the sentence of death is hereby commuted to imprisonment for life in the penitentiary of Washington." On the same day the pardon was accepted in these words: "I hereby accept the above and within pardon, with condition annexed."

An application was made by the petitioner to the circuit court of the District of Columbia, for a writ of *habeas corpus*. It was rejected, and is now before this court by way of appeal.

The second article of the constitution of the United States, section two, contains this provision: "The President shall have p wer to grant reprieves and pardons for offences against the United States, except in cases of impeachment."

Under this power, the President has granted reprieves and pardons since the commencement of the present government. Sundry provisions have been enacted, regulating its exercise for the army and navy, in virtue of the constitutional power of congress to make rules and regulations for the government of the army and navy. No statute has ever been passed regulating it in cases of conviction by the civil authorities. In such cases, the President has acted exclusively under the power as it is expressed in the constitution.

This case raises the question, whether the President can constitutionally grant a conditional pardon to a convicted murderer, sentenced to be hung, offering to change that punishment to imprisonment for life; and if he does, and it be accepted by the convict, whether it is not binding upon him; to justify a court to refuse him a writ of *habeas corpus*, applied for upon the ground that the pardon is absolute, and the condition of it void.

The counsel for the prisoner contends that the pardon is valid to remit entirely the sentence of the court for his execution, and that the condition annexed to the pardon, and accepted by the prisoner, is illegal. It is also said that a President granting such a pardon assumes a power not conferred by the constitution — that he legislates a new punishment into existence, and sentences the convict to suffer it; in this way violating the legislative and judicial powers of the government, it being the province of the first to enact laws for the punishment of offences against the United States, and that of the judiciary, to sentence convicts for violations of those laws according to them. It is said to be the exercise of prerogative, such as the king of England has in such cases; and that, under our system, there can be no other foundation, empowering a President of the United States to show the same clemency.

We think this is a mistake arising from the want of due consideration of the legal meaning of the word pardon. It is supposed that it was meant to be used exclusively with reference to an absolute pardon, exempting a criminal from the punishment which the law inflicts for a crime he has committed.

But such is not the sense or meaning of the word, either in common parlance or in law. In the first, it is forgiveness, release, remission. Forgiveness for an offence, whether it be one for which the person committing it is liable in law or otherwise.

Release from pecuniary obligation, as where it is said, I pardon you your debt. Or it is the remission of a penalty, to which one may have subjected himself by the non-performance of an undertaking or contract, or when a statutory penalty in money has been incurred, and it is remitted by a public functionary having power to remit it.

In the law it has different meanings, which were as well understood when the constitution was made as any other legal word in the constitution now is.

Such a thing is a pardon without a designation of its kind is not known in the law. Time out of mind, in the earliest books of the English law, every pardon has its particular denomination. They are general, special, or particular, conditional or absolute, statutory, not necessary in some cases, and in some grantable of course. Sometimes, though, an express pardon for one is a pardon for another, such as in approver and appellee, principal and accessary in certain cases, or where many are indicted for felony in the same indictment, because the felony is several in all of them, and not joint, and the pardon for one of them is a pardon for all, though they may not be mentioned in it; or it discharges sureties for a fine, payable at a certain day, and the king pardons the principal; or sureties for the peace, if the principal is pardoned, after forfeiture. We might mention other legal incidents of a pardon, but those mentioned are enough to illustrate the subject of pardon, and the extent or meaning of the President's power to grant reprieves and pardons. It meant that the power was to be used according to law; that is, as it had been used in England, and these States when they were colonies; not because it was a prerogative power, but as incidents of the power to pardon particularly when the circumstances of any case disclosed such uncertainties as made it doubtful if there should have been a conviction of the criminal, or when they are such as to show that there might be a mitigation of the punishment without lessening the obligation of vindicatory justice. Without such a power of clemency, to be exercised by some department or functionary of a government, it would be most imperfect and deficient in its political morality, and in that attribute of Deity whose judgments are always tempered with mercy. And it was with the fullest knowledge of the law upon the subject of pardons, and the philosophy of government in its bearing upon the constitution, when this court instructed Chief Justice Marshall to say, in the United States *v.* Wilson, 7 Pet. 162: "As the power has been exercised from time immemorial by the executive of that nation whose language is our language, and to whose judicial institutions ours bear a close resemblance, we adopt their principles respecting the operation and effect of a pardon, and look into their books for the rules prescribing the manner in which it is to be used by the person who would avail himself of it." We still think so, and that the language used in the constitution, conferring the power to grant reprieves and pardons, must be construed with reference to its meaning at the time of its adoption. At the time of our separation from Great Britain, that power had been exercised by the king, as the chief executive. Prior to the revolution, the colonies, being in effect under the laws of England, were accustomed to the exercise of it in the various forms, as they may be found in the English law books. They were, of course, to be applied as occasions occurred, and they constituted a part of the jurisprudence of Anglo-America. At the time of the adoption of the constitution, American statesmen were conversant with the laws of England, and familiar with the prerogatives exercised by the crown. Hence, when the words to grant pardons were used in the constitution, they conveyed to the mind the authority as exercised by the English crown, or by its representatives in the colonies. At that time both Englishmen and Americans attached the same meaning to the word pardon. In the convention which framed the constitution, no effort was made to define or change its meaning, although it was limited in cases of impeachment.

We must then give the word the same meaning as prevailed here and in England at the time it found a place in the constitution. This is in conformity with the principles laid down by this court in Cathcart *v.* Robinson, 5 Pet. 264, 280; and in Flavell's case, 8 Watts & Sargent, 197; Attorney-General's brief.

A pardon is said by Lord Coke to be a work of mercy, whereby the king, either before attainder, sentence, or conviction, or after, forgiveth any crime, offence, punishment, execution, right, title, debt, or duty, temporal or ecclesiastical, (3 Inst. 233.) And the king's coronation oath is, " that he will cause justice to be executed in mercy." It is frequently conditional, as he may extend his mercy upon what terms he pleases, and annex to his bounty a condition precedent or subsequent, on the performance of which the validity of the pardon will depend, (Co. Litt. 274, 276; 2 Hawkins Ch. 37, § 45; 4 Black. Com. 401.) And if the felon does not perform the condition of the pardon, it will be altogether void; and he may be brought to the bar and remanded, to suffer the punishment to which he was originally sentenced. Cole's case, Moore, 466; Bac. Abr., Pardon, E. In the case of Packer and others — Canadian prisoners — 5 Meeson & Welsby, 32, Lord Abinger decided for the court, if the condition upon which alone the pardon was granted be void, the pardon must also be void. If the condition were lawful, but the prisoner did not assent to it, nor submit to be transported, he cannot have the benefit of the pardon — or if, having assented to it, his assent be revocable, we must consider him to have retracted it by the application to be set at liberty, in which case he is equally unable to avail himself of the pardon.

But to the power of pardoning there are limitations. The king cannot, by any previous license, make an offence dispunishable which is *malum in se*, i. e. unlawful in itself, as being against the law of nature, or so far against the public good as to be indictable at common law. A grant of this kind would be against reason and the common good, and therefore void, (2 Hawk. C. 37, § 28.) So he cannot release a recognizance to keep the peace with another by name, and generally with other lieges of the king, because it is for the benefit and safety of all his subjects, (3 Inst. 238.) Nor, after suit has been brought in a popular action, can the king discharge the informer's part of the penalty, (3 Inst. 238;) and if the action be given to the party grieved, the king cannot discharge the same, (3 Inst. 237.) Nor can the king pardon for a common nuisance, because it would take away the means of compelling a redress of it, unless it be in a case where the fine is to the king, and not a forfeiture to the party grieved. Hawk. C. 37, § 33; 5 Chit. Burn. 2.

And this power to pardon has also been restrained by particular statutes. By the act of settlement, 12 & 13 Will. III. c. 2, Eng., no pardon under the great seal is pleadable to an impeachment by the Commons in Parliament, but after the articles of impeachment have been heard and determined, he may pardon. The provision in our constitution, excepting cases of impeachment out of the power of the President to pardon, was evidently taken from that statute, and is an improvement upon the same. Nor does the power to pardon in England extend to the *habeas corpus* act, 31 Car. II. c. 2, which makes it a *premunire* to send a subject to any prison out of England, &c., or beyond the seas, and further provides that any person so offending shall be incapable of the king's pardon. There are also pardons grantable as of common right, without any exercise of the king's discretion; as where a statute creating an offence, or enacting penalties for its future punishment, holds out a promise of immunity to accomplices to aid in the conviction of their associates. When accomplices do so voluntarily, they have a right absolutely to a pardon, 1 Chit. C. L. 766. Also, when, by the king's proclamation, they are promised immunity on discovering their accomplices and are the means of convicting them, Rudd's case Cowp. 334; 1 Leach, 118. But except in these cases, accomplices, though admitted according to the usual phrase to be

"king's evidence," have no absolute claim or legal right to a
pardon. But they have an equitable claim to pardon, if upon
the trial a full and fair disclosure of the joint guilt of one of
them and his associates is made. He cannot plead it in bar of
an indictment for such offence, but he may use it to put off the
trial, in order to give him time to apply for a pardon, (Rudd's
case, Cowp. 331; 1 Leach, 115.) So, conditional pardons by
the king do not permit transportation or exile as a commutable
punishment, unless the same has been provided for by legislation.
See 39 Eliz. c. 4 & 5 Geo. IV. c. 84, a consolidation of all the
laws regulating the transportation of offenders from Great
Britain.

Having shown, by the citation of many authorities, the king's
power to grant conditional pardons, with the restraints upon the
power, also when pardons for offences and crimes are grantable
of course, and when a party has an equitable right to apply for a
pardon, we now proceed to show, by the decisions of some of the
courts of the States of this Union, that they have expressed opinions coincident with what has been stated to be the law of England, and more particularly how the pardoning power may be
exercised in them by the governors of the States, whose constitutions have clauses giving to them the power to grant pardons, in
terms identical with those used in the constitution of the United
States.

In the constitution of the State of Pennsylvania, of 1790, it is
declared in the 2d article, section 9, that the governor shall have
power to remit fines and penalties, and grant reprieves and pardons, except in cases of impeachment.

Sargeant, Justice, said in Flavel's case, 8 Watts & Sergeant,
197, "several propositions were made in the convention which
formed the constitution of 1838, to limit and control the exercise
of the power of pardon by the executive, but they were overruled
and the provision left as it stood." "Now, no principle is better
settled than that for the definition of legal terms and construction of legal powers mentioned in our constitution and laws;
we must resort to the common law when no act of assembly,
or judicial interpretation, or settled usage, has altered their
meaning."

Then proceeding to show the nature and application of conditions, the learned judge remarks: "And so may the king make
a charter of pardon to a man of his life, upon condition. A
pardon, therefore, being an act of such a nature as that by the
common law it may be upon any condition, it has the same
nature and operation in Pennsylvania, and it follows that the
governor may annex to a pardon any condition, whether subsequent or precedent, not forbidden by law. And it lies upon the

grantee to perform the condition; or if the condition is not performed, the original sentence remains in full vigor and may be carried into effect."

To this case we add those of the State *v.* Smith, 1 Bailey's S. C. Rep. 283, 288; also Addington's case, in the 2d volume of the same reporter, p. 516; also Hunt, *ex parte;* also that of the People *v.* Potter, N. Y. Legal Observer, 177; S. C. 1 Parker Criminal Reports, 4; and the case of The United States *v.* Geo. Wilson, 7 Pet. 150,

But it was urged by the counsel who represents the petitioner, that the power to reprieve and pardon does not include the power to grant a conditional pardon, the latter not having been enumerated in the constitution as a distinct power. And he cited the constitutions of several of the States, the legislation of others, and two decisions, to show that when the power to commute punishment had not been given in terms, that legislation had authorized it; and that when that had not been done, that the courts had decided against the commutation by the governors of the States. And it was said, so far from the President having such a power, that, as the grant was not in the constitution, congress could not give it.

It not unfrequently happens in discussions upon the constitution, that an involuntary change is made in the words of it, or in their order, from which, as they are used, there may be a logical conclusion, though it be different from what the constitution is in fact. And even though the change may appear to be equivalent, it will be found upon reflection not to convey the full meaning of the words used in the constitution. This is an example of it. The power as given is not to reprieve and pardon, but that the President shall have power to grant reprieves and pardons for offences against the United States, except in cases of impeachment. The difference between the real language and that used in the argument is material. The first conveys only the idea of an absolute power as to the purpose or object for which it is given. The real language of the constitution is general, that is, common to the class of pardons, or extending the power to pardon to all kinds of pardons known in the law as such, whatever may be their denomination. We have shown that a conditional pardon is one of them. A single remark from the power to grant reprieves will illustrate the point. That is not only to be used to delay a judicial sentence when the President shall think the merits of the case, or some cause connected with the offender, may require it, but it extends also to cases *ex necessitate legis,* as where a female after conviction is found to be *enceinte,* or where a convict becomes insane, or is alleged to be so. Though the reprieve in either case produces delay in the execution of a sentence, the means to be used, to determine either of the two just mentioned, are clearly within the President's power to direct; and reprieves in such cases are different in their legal character, and different as to the causes which may induce the exercise of the power to reprieve.

In this view of the constitution, by giving to its words their proper meaning, the power to pardon conditionally is not one of inference at all, but one conferred in terms.

The mistake in the argument is, in considering an incident of the power to pardon the exercise of a new power, instead of its being a part of the power to pardon. We use the word incident as a legal term, meaning something appertaining to and necessarily depending upon another, which is termed the principal.

But admitting that to be so, it may be said, as the condition, when accepted, becomes a substitute for the sentence of the court, involving another punishment, the latter is substantially the exercise of a new power. But this is not so, for the power to offer a condition, without ability to enforce its acceptance, when accepted by the convict, is the substitution, by himself, of a lesser punishment than the law has imposed upon him, and he cannot complain if the law executes the choice he has made.

As to the suggestion that conditional pardons cannot be considered as being voluntarily accepted by convicts so as to be binding upon them, because they are made whilst under *duress per minas* and duress of imprisonment, it is only necessary to remark, that neither applies to this case, as the petitioner was legally in prison. "If a man be legally imprisoned, and either to procure his discharge, or on any other fair account, seal a bond or deed, this is not duress or imprisonment, and he is not at liberty to avoid it. And a man condemned to be hung cannot be permitted to escape the punishment altogether, by pleading that he had accepted his life by *duress per minas.*" And if it be further urged, as it was in the argument of this case, that no man can make himself a slave for life by convention, the answer is, that the petitioner had forfeited his life for crime, and had no liberty to part with.

We believe we have now noticed every point made in the argument by counsel on both sides, except that which deduces the President's power to grant a conditional pardon, from the local law of Maryland, of force in the District of Columbia. We do not think it necessary to discuss it, as we have shown that the President's power to do so exists under the constitution of the United States.

We are of opinion that the circuit court of the District of Columbia rightly refused the petitioner's application, and this court affirms it.

Mr. Justice Curtis and Mr. Justice Campbell dissented as to
the jurisdiction, and Mr. Justice M'Lean from the judgment of
the court.

Mr. Justice McLEAN dissenting.

William Wells was convicted of murder, in the District of
Columbia, and sentenced to be hung on the 23d of April, 1852;
on which day President Fillmore granted him a conditional
pardon, for his acceptance, as follows: "The sentence of death
is hereby commuted to imprisonment for life, in the penitentiary,
at Washington." On the same day this pardon was accepted,
as follows: "I hereby accept the above and within pardon, with
condition annexed." This acceptance was signed by Wells,
and witnessed by the jailer and warden. Wells now claims
that the pardon is absolute and the condition null and void,
and that, consequently, he is entitled to a discharge from imprisonment.

Application was made in this case to the circuit court of the
District of Columbia by petition for a *habeas corpus*, and on the
petition the following entry was made on the records of that
court: "William Wells, who was convicted, in the circuit court
of this District, of murder, and sentenced to be hung the 23d of
April, 1852, which sentence was on that day commuted, by the
President of the United States, to that of imprisonment for life
in the penitentiary of the District, having been brought before
that court on a writ of *habeas corpus*, the court, after hearing the
arguments of counsel, and mature deliberation being thereupon
had, do order that the said William Wells be remanded to the
penitentiary, the court being of opinion that the President of the
United States has the power to commute the sentence of death
to that of imprisonment for life, in the penitentiary."

A petition for a *habeas corpus* to this court has been presented,
and the case has been argued on its merits, and it is now before
us for consideration.

This case is brought here, not as an original application, but
in the nature of an appeal from the decision of the circuit court.
It is not an appeal in form, but in effect, as it brings the same
subject before us, with the decision of the circuit court on the
habeas corpus, that the principles laid down by it may be considered.

In *ex parte* Watkins, 7 Peters, 568, the court say: "Upon
this state of the facts several questions have arisen and been
argued at the bar; and one, which is preliminary in its nature,
at the suggestion of the court. This is, whether, under the circumstances of the case, the court possess jurisdiction to award
the writ; and upon full consideration, we are of opinion that

the court do possess jurisdiction. The question turns upon this, whether it is an exercise of original or appellate jurisdiction? If it be the former, then, as the present is not one of the cases in which the constitution allows this court to exercise original jurisdiction, the writ must be denied. Marbury v. Madison, 1 Cranch, 137; 1 Peters's Condensed Rep. 267. If the latter, then it may be awarded, since the judiciary act of 1789, sec. 14, has clearly authorized the court to issue it.

" This was decided in the case ex parte Hamilton, 8 Dall. 17; ex parte Bollman & Swartwout, 4 Cranch, 75; and ex parte Kearney, 7 Wheat. 38. The doubt was, whether, in the actual case before the court, the jurisdiction sought to be exercised was not original, since it brought into question, not the validity of the original process of capias ad satisfaciendum, but the present right of detainer of the prisoner under it. Upon further reflection, however, the doubt has been removed."

In that case, this court " considered Watkins in custody under process awarded by the circuit court, and that whether he was rightfully so was the very question before the court; and if the court should remand the prisoner, it would clearly be the exercise of an appellate jurisdiction." The same remark applies with equal force and effect to the case before us.

In this case the question is, whether Wells is rightfully detained, under the order of the circuit court, in virtue of the commutation of the original sentence by the President, and which the circuit court has held to be a legal detention.

It is not perceived that there is any difference, in principle, between this case and the case of Watkins. This court has no power to revise, in this form, the judgment of the circuit court under the law in a criminal case; but, as in the case of Watkins, we may decide whether the individual is held by a legal custody.

It is said the convict is now in prison under the original sentence of the court. So far as that sentence goes, the man is presumed to have been hung in April, 1852. But it is insisted the President had power to reprieve from the sentence of death. This is admitted; but no reprieve has been granted. On the contrary, an act has been done, entirely inconsistent with a reprieve, as that only suspends the punishment for a fixed period. The punishment of death has been commuted, for confinement to hard labor in the penitentiary during life. It is a perversion of the facts to say that Wells has been reprieved by the President; nor can it be said that he is now in confinement under a sentence of death. The sentence of death has been commuted for confinement. Since April, 1852, that sentence has been abrogated in effect; for if the President had power to commute the crime, the sentence is at an end. The culprit is detained in

27 *

prison under this commutation of the President, which the
circuit court held he had the power to do, and remanded the
prisoner on that ground; and whether this be legal, is the inquiry on the *habeas corpus*. It does not reach the original sentence of the court. That sentence is considered only as the
ground of the commutation; and, if the President had no power
to make it, the detention of Wells is illegal. Is not this a legitimate subject of inquiry on a *habeas corpus?* It has been held
to be a legal detention by the circuit court, and this opinion of
the circuit court is brought before us on the *habeas corpus*, as
the only cause of detention.

The second section of the second article of the constitution
of the United States declares, that "the President shall have
power to grant reprieves and pardons for offences against the
United States, except in cases of impeachments."

The meaning of the word pardon, as used in the constitution,
has never come before this court for decision. It has often been
decided in the States that the governor may grant conditional
pardons by commuting the punishment. But in these cases the
governor acted generally, if not uniformly, under special provisions in the constitution or laws of the State, or on the principles of the common law adopted by the State. This is the case
in New York, Maryland, Ohio, and many other States.

It is argued by the attorney-general that the word pardon
was used in the constitution, in reference to the construction
given to it in England, from whence was derived our system of
laws and practice; and that the powers exercised by the British
sovereign under the term pardon is a construction necessarily
adopted with the term. If this view be a sound one, it has the
merit of novelty. The executive office in England and that of
this country is so widely different, that doubts may be entertained whether it would be safe for a republican chief magistrate, who is the creature of the laws, to be influenced by the
exercise of any leading power of the British sovereign. Their
respective powers are as different in their origin as in their exercise. A safer rule of construction will be found in the nature
and principles of our own government. Whilst the prerogatives
of the crown are great, and occasionally, in English history, have
been more than a match for the parliament, the President has
no powers which are not given him by the constitution and
laws of the country; and all his acts beyond these limits are
null and void.

There is another consideration of paramount importance in
regard to this question. We have under the federal government no common-law offences, nor common-law powers to
punish in our courts; and the same may be said of our chief

magistrate. It would be strange indeed if our highest criminal courts should disclaim all common-law powers in the punishment of offences, whilst our President should claim and exercise such powers in pardoning convicts.

The power of commutation overrides the law and the judgments of courts. It substitutes a new, and, it may be, an undefined punishment for that which the law prescribes a specific penalty. It is, in fact, a suspension of the law, and substituting some other punishment which, to the executive, may seem to be more reasonable and proper. It is true the substituted punishment must be assented to by the convict; but the exercise of his judgment, under the circumstances, may be a very inadequate protection for his rights.

If the law controlled the exercise of this power, by authorizing solitary confinement for life, as a substitute for the punishment of death, and so of other offences, the power would be unobjectionable; the line of action would be certain, and abuses would be prevented. But where this power rests in the discretion of the executive, not only as to its exercise, but as to the degree and kind of punishment substituted, it does not seem to be a power fit to be exercised over a people subject only to the laws.

To speak of a contract, by a convict, to suffer a punishment not known to the law, nor authorized by it, is a strange language in a government of laws. Where the law sanctions such an arrangement, there can be no objection; but when the obligation to suffer arises only from the force of a contract, it is a singular instrument of executive power.

Who can foresee the excitements and convulsions which may arise in our future history? The struggle may be between a usurping executive and an incensed people. In such a struggle, this right, claimed by the executive, of substituting one punishment for another, under the pardoning power, may become dangerous to popular rights. It must be recollected that this power may be exercised, not only in capital cases, but also in misdemeanors, embracing all offences punished by the laws of congress. Banishment, or other modes of punishment, may be substituted and inflicted, at the discretion of the national executive. I cannot consent to the enlargement of executive power, acting upon the rights of individuals, which is not restrained and guided by positive law.

I have no doubt the President, under the power to pardon, may remit the penalty in part, but this consists in shortening the time of imprisonment, or reducing the amount of the fine, or in releasing entirely from the one or the other. This acts directly upon the sentence of the court, under the law, and is strictly an exercise of the pardoning power in lessening the degree of punishment, called for by mistaken facts on the trial, or new ones which have since become known.

The case of the United States v. Wilson, 7 Pet. 150, has been referred to by the attorney-general, as sanctioning conditional pardons. But the remarks of the court in that case arose on the pleadings, and not on the power of the President. He had pardoned Wilson, but that pardon had not been pleaded, or brought before the court by motion or otherwise, and the court held that the pardon could not be considered, unless it was brought judicially before it. In that case the chief justice said: "The constitution gives to the President, in general terms, the power to grant reprieves and pardons, for offences against the United States."

And he says, " as this power has been exercised from time immemorial by the executive of that nation whose language is our language, and to whose judicial institutions ours bear a close resemblance, we adopt their principles, respecting the operation and effect of a pardon, and look into their books for the rules prescribing the manner in which it is to be used by the person who would avail himself of it." And he goes on to show that a pardon, like any other defence, must be pleaded to enable the court to act upon it. There is nothing in the case which countenances the power of the President, as in this case is contended, to commute the punishment of death for confinement during life in the penitentiary. The chief justice said, " a pardon may be conditional," in reference to grants of pardon in England, and by governors of States.

There can be no doubt, where one punishment is substituted, under the laws of England, for another — as banishment for death — if the convict shall return, he may be arrested on the original offence ; and if he shall be found by a jury to be the identical person originally convicted, the penalty of death incurred by him may be inflicted. And the same thing may be done in regard to all offences where, in this country, the law authorizes the pardoning power to modify the punishment and give effect to the commutation.

In 4 Call. 85, in Virginia, a case is reported where the prisoner was indicted for felony. On motion of the attorney-general for an award of execution, the governor's pardon was pleaded, and urged as absolute, because the governor had no authority to annex the condition. The general court held that the condition was illegal, and therefore the pardon was absolute. Another case in North Carolina, reported in 4 Hawks. 193, the defendant was convicted of forgery, sentenced to the pillory, three years' imprisonment, thirty-nine lashes, and a fine of one thousand dollars; execution issued for fine and costs; conditional pardon by the governor. The judge said, the governor cannot add or commute a punishment — it was consistent with his power to remit."

We are told that when a term is used in our constitution or statutes which is known at the common law, we look to that system for its meaning. Pardon is a word familiar in common-law proceedings, but it is not a term peculiar to such proceedings. It applies to the ordinary intercourse of men, and it means remission, forgiveness. It is said, in a monarchy, the offence is against the monarch, and that, consequently, he is the only proper person to forgive.

Bacon says, the power of pardoning is irreparably incident to the crown, and is a high prerogative of the king. And Comyns, in his digest, says: "The king, by his prerogative, may grant his pardon to all offenders attainted or convicted of a crime; and that statutes do not restrain the king's prerogative, but they are a caution for using it well."

The power to pardon is a prerogative power of the monarch, which cannot, it seems, be restrained by statute. Is this the usage or the common-law meaning of the word pardon, to which we are to refer as a guide in the present case? If the President can exercise the pardoning power, as free from restraints as the Queen of England, his prerogative is much greater than has been supposed. Instead of looking into the nature of our government, for the true meaning of terms vesting powers in the executive, are we to be instructed by studying the regalia of the crown of England; not to ascertain the definition of the word pardon, but to be assured what powers are exercised under it by the monarch of England. This is a new rule of construction of the constitutional powers of the President. I had thought he was the mere instrument of the law, and that the flowers of the crown of England did not ornament his brow.

In his commentary on the constitution, Judge Story says, 346: "The whole structure of our government is so entirely different, and the elements of which it is composed are so dissimilar from that of England, that no argument can be drawn from the practice of the latter, to assist us in a just arrangement of the executive authority."

It is not the meaning of the word pardon that is objected to; but it is the prerogative powers of the crown which are exercised under that designation. The President is the executive power in this country, as the Queen holds the executive authority in England. Are we to be instructed as to the extent of the executive power in this country, by looking into the exercise of the same power in England?

In the act for the better government of the navy of the United States, passed the 23d April, 1800, (2 Stats. at Large, p. 51, art. 42,) it is declared: "The President of the United States, or, when the trial takes place out of the United States, the commander of the fleet or squadron, shall possess full power to pardon any offence committed against these articles, after conviction, or to mitigate the punishment decreed by a court-martial." If, in the opinion of congress, the power to pardon included the power to commute the punishment, this provision would seem to be unnecessary.

But admit that the power of the President to pardon is as great as are the prerogatives of the crown in England, still, the act before us is unsustainable. The Queen of England cannot do what the President has done in this instance. She has no power, except under statutes, to commute a punishment, to which the prisoner has been judicially sentenced, for any other punishment at her discretion.

By the act of George III. c. 140, it is provided, "that if his majesty shall be graciously pleased to extend his mercy to any offender liable to the punishment of death by the sentence of a naval court-martial, upon condition of transportation, or of transporting himself beyond seas, or upon condition of being imprisoned within any jail in Great Britain, or on condition of being kept to hard labor in any jail or house of correction, or penitentiary house, &c., it shall and may be lawful for any justice of the King's Bench, &c., upon such intention of mercy as aforesaid being notified in writing, to allow to such offender the benefit of such conditional pardon as shall be expressed in such notification. And the judge is required to make an order in regard to the punishment, which is declared to be as effectual as if such punishment had been inflicted by the sentence of the court; and the sentence of death was made to apply to such offender, should he escape."

And again, by the act of George IV. 21st June, 1824, it is provided, "when his majesty shall be pleased to extend his mercy, upon condition of transportation beyond seas, &c., one of his majesty's principal secretaries shall signify the same to the proper court, before which the offender has been convicted; such court shall allow to such offender the benefit of a conditional pardon, and make an order for the immediate transportation of such offender. And the act declares that any person found at large, who had been thus transported, should suffer death," &c.

Statute 28, 7 & 8 of George IV. § 18, declares that "when the king's majesty shall be pleased to extend his royal mercy to any offender, his royal sign-manual, countersigned by one of his principal secretaries of state, shall grant to such offender a free or a conditional pardon," &c.

In 54 Geo. III. c. 146, where there was a conviction for high treason, the king was authorized to change the punishment — that said person shall not be hanged by the neck — but that instead thereof such person should be beheaded, &c.

It is laid down in Coke's 3d Institute, vol. 6, p. 52: "Neither can the king by any warrant under the great seal alter the execution, otherwise than the judgment of the law doth direct." In the same book, p. 211, he says, "it is a maxim of law, that execution must be according to the judgment."

The sovereign of England, with all the prerogatives of the crown, in granting a conditional pardon, cannot substitute a punishment which the law does not authorize. The law authorizes the sovereign to transport, or inflict other punishments, for certain offences, and this being signified to some one or more of the judges, effect is given to the condition through his or their instrumentality. So that the punishment inflicted is matter of record. And should the offender return into England, after banishment, the law subjects him to punishment under the original conviction. Here is certainty in limiting on the one hand the discretion of the pardoning power, and on the other the rights of the culprit.

With very few, if any, exceptions, conditional pardons have not been granted by the governors of States, except where express authority has been given in the constitution or laws of the States. So early as the 12th of March, 1794, a law of New York provided "that it shall and may be lawful for the person administering the government of the State, for the time being, in all cases in which he is authorized by the constitution to grant pardons, to grant the same upon such conditions, and with such restrictions, and under such limitations, as he may think proper."

The distinguished attorney-general of the United States, Mr. Wirt, being called on for his opinion in a case differing from the present, but involving, to some extent, the same principles, in his letter of 4th January, 1820, to the Secretary of the Navy, says: "Your letter of the 80th ultimo submits, for my opinion, the power of the President to change the sentence of death, which has been passed by a general court-martial on William Bonsman, a private in the marine corps, into a sentence of "service and restraint for the space of one year, after which to cause him to be drummed from the marine corps as a disgrace to it."

He refers to the 42d article of the rules and regulations of the navy, which embrace the marine corps, and which declares that "the President of the United States shall possess full power to pardon any offence against these articles after conviction, or to mitigate the punishment decreed by a court-martial." And, he says, "the power of pardoning the offence does not, in my opinion, include the power of changing the punishment; but the 'power to mitigate the punishment,' decreed by a court-martial, cannot, I think, be fairly understood in any other sense than as meaning a power to substitute a milder punishment in the place of that decreed by the court-martial, in which sense it would justify the sentence which the President proposes to substitute, in the case under consideration."

The power of mitigation, he says, "in general terms, leaves the manner of performing this act of mercy to himself, and if it can be performed in no other way than by changing its species, the President has, in my opinion, the power of adopting this form of mitigation"; and he observes, "to deny him the power of changing the punishment in this instance, is to deny him the power of mitigating the severest of all punishments. Congress foresaw that there were cases in which the exercise of the power of entire pardon might be proper; they therefore, in the first branch of the article, gave him the power to pardon. But they foresaw also, that there would be cases in which it would be improper to pardon the offence entirely, in which there ought to be some punishment, but in which, nevertheless, it might be proper to inflict a milder punishment than that decreed by the court-martial; and hence, in another and distinct member of the article they give him, in general terms, the separate and distinct power of mitigation."

It will be seen that Mr. Wirt places the power of mitigation expressly under the article cited.

In a letter to the President on the power to pardon, dated 30th March, 1820, Mr. Wirt says: "The power of pardon, as given by the constitution, is the power of absolute and entire pardon. On the principle, however, that the greater power includes the less, I am of opinion that the power of pardoning absolutely includes the power of pardoning conditionally. There is, however," he says, "great danger lest a conditional pardon should operate as an absolute one, from the difficulty of enforcing the condition, or, in case of a breach of it, resorting to the original sentence of condemnation; which difficulty arises from the limited powers of the national government.

"But suppose," he remarks, "a pardon granted on a condition, to be executed by officers of the federal government, — as, for example, to work on a public fortification, — and suppose this condition violated by running away, where is the power of arrest, in these circumstances, given by any law of the United States? And suppose the arrest could be made, where is the clause in any of our judiciary acts that authorizes a court to proceed in such a state of things? And without some positive legislative regulation on the subject, I know that some of our federal judges would not feel themselves at liberty to proceed, *de novo*, on the original case. It is true the king of England grants such conditional pardons by the common law; but the same common law has provided the mode of proceeding for a breach of the condition on the part of the culprit. We have no common law here, however, and hence arises the difficulty." And he says, " If a condition can be devised whose execution would be certain, I have no doubt that the President may pardon on such condition. All conditions precedent would be of this character; e. g. pardon to a military officer under sentence of death, on the previous condition of resigning his commission."

In his letter to the President, dated 18th September, 1845, Mr. Attorney-General Mason says: " I cannot doubt the power of the President to mitigate a sentence of dismission from the service, by commuting it into a suspension for a term of years, without pay. A dismission is a perpetual suspension without pay; and the limited suspension without pay is the inferior degree of the same punishment. The minor is contained in the major." And he says: " The sentence of death for murder could be mitigated by substituting any punishment which the law would authorize the court to inflict for manslaughter. This is the inferior degree of the offence."

And again, in his letter to the Secretary of the Navy, dated 16th of October, 1845, Mr. Mason says: " Did this power to mitigate the sentence include the power to commute or substitute another and a milder punishment for that decreed by the court, (referring to a court-martial,) the mitigation," he says, " must be of the punishment adjudged, by reducing and modifying its severity, except as in sentences of death, where there is no degree." He says: " At the war department it has always been considered that the executive has not the power, by way of mitigation, to substitute a different punishment for that inflicted by sentence of a court-martial — the general rule being that the mitigated sentence must be a part of the punishment decreed." He further remarks, "that in 1820, Mr. Wirt gave an opinion recognizing this rule, but made a substitution of a different punishment for the sentence of death an exception; and he places it on the ground that capital punishment can only be mitigated by a change of punishment." Mr. Attorney-General should have said, that the power given in the article to mitigate was referred to by Mr. Wirt as authorizing the mitigation, and not the general power to pardon.

No higher authority than Mr. Wirt can be found, as coming

from the law officer of the government. It gives to the procedure now before us no countenance or support, but throws the weight of his great name against the exercise of the power assumed.

But it is said, that the power of commutation may be exercised by the President under the laws of Maryland, adopted by congress on the cession of the territory which now constitutes the District of Columbia.

The constitution of Maryland provides, that the governor "alone may exercise all other the executive powers of government, where the concurrence of council is not required according to the laws of the State, and grant reprieves or pardons for any crime, except in cases where the law shall otherwise direct." This, I suppose, no one will contend, can be applied to the President of the United States. The constitutional provision is made subject to the action of the legislature.

A statute of Maryland was passed in 1847, c. 17, to make conditional pardons effectual. This law can only tend to show that there was no prior law by which such pardons could be made effectual.

The first law of Maryland on the subject of pardon was enacted in 1787. The first section provided, "that the governor may, in his discretion, grant to any offender capitally convicted a pardon, on condition contained therein, and is and shall be effectual as a condition according to the intent thereof."

The second section provides, if the convict be a slave, he may be transported out of the State, and sold for the benefit of the State.

The 4th sect. declares, if a party who has been pardoned on condition of leaving the State shall return contrary thereto, he shall be arrested, and on being found by a jury to be the same person, the court shall pass such judgment as the law requires for the crime committed.

The second law on the same subject was enacted in 1795.

The 1st sect. requires the governor to issue a warrant to the sheriff, to carry the sentence of the court into effect. The 2d sect. that, in his discretion, the governor may commute or change any sentence or judgment of death into other punishment of such criminal of this State, upon such terms and conditions as he shall think expedient. And if a slave, he may be transported and sold for the benefit of the State.

By an act of congress of the 27th of February, 1801, it was declared, "that the laws of Maryland, as they now exist, shall be and continue in force in that part of the said district which was ceded by that State to the United States, and by them accepted." This provision covers what is now the District of Columbia.

That the general laws of Maryland for the punishment of offences, the practice of the courts, forms of actions, contracts, &c., come under the laws of Maryland, is undoubted. But the question is, whether the above laws which regulate pardons by the governor, apply to the President of the United States, in the exercise of the same power. After much reflection, I have come to the conclusion that they can neither justify nor control the exercise of the constitutional power of the President to grant a pardon, for the following reasons: —

1. Their language is inappropriate, and some of their provisions are inconsistent with the duties of the President. The governor is required to issue a warrant to execute the sentence of the court, and also to sell convicted slaves for the benefit of the State. Can the President do this?

2. For more than half a century these acts have not been applied to the President, although he has often granted pardons, until in the case now before us. Nor have either of the laws been referred to by any one of the attorneys-general who have been consulted on the subject, and who have given elaborate opinions, and particularly Mr. Wirt, who dwells upon the difficulty, if not impracticability, of carrying out the condition on which the pardon was granted, without specific legislation. No reference was made to these laws by the late attorney-general, on whose advice the punishment of death was commuted, in favor of Wells, to imprisonment for life.

3. Any regulation respecting the high prerogative power to pardon or commute the punishment of a convict, must be general, and extend as far as the federal jurisdiction extends, and cannot be restricted by any act of congress to any particular State or territory. The power is given in the constitution, and it may be exercised commensurate with that fundamental law; and any modification of the power, to be exercised at the discretion of the President, must be coextensive with the constitutional power.

The 8th section of the 1st article of the constitution declares, that congress shall have power "to make all laws which shall be necessary and proper for carrying into execution the foregoing powers, and all other powers vested by this constitution in the government of the United States, or in any department or officer thereof."

4. The above acts of Maryland can only operate in this case as acts of congress, and in that view they have been enacted more than fifty years, without being referred to or acted on during that period, although the subject of conditional pardon has been often discussed, and the want of provisions which they contain deeply felt and expressed. Under such circumstances,

is it possible to consider those acts, or either of them, as in force in this district since 1801? If this be so, it is the most extraordinary event that has occurred in the legal history of any country.

The laws adopted from Maryland were not specified by name; of course, those only which were local in their character, and were necessary in their nature to regulate local transactions, and the courts which settle controversies, were adopted. The laws which regulate the duty and powers of the governor, in regard to pardons granted to offenders, no more apply to the President than duties prescribed for the action of the governor in any other matter. This shows the reason why the above laws have been dormant, as if unknown, for more that fifty years. It is too late now to resuscitate them, however strongly the present exigency may call for them.

I am not opposed to commutation of punishment, where it may be called for by any great principle of justice or humanity; but the exercise of such power should be regulated by law, and not left to the discretion of the executive. As the law now stands, the punishment substituted, as well as the exercise of the power, rests upon discretion; and there is no legal mode of giving effect to the commutation; and this is an unanswerable objection to it. No court would execute the convict on the original sentence under such circumstances.

If the condition on which a pardon shall be granted be void, the pardon becomes absolute. This, I think, is a clear principle, although there may be found some opinions against it. The President has the power to pardon, and if he make the grant on an impossible condition — for a void condition may be considered of that character — the grant is valid.

The condition being void, I think Wells is illegally detained, and should be discharged.

Mr. Justice CURTIS dissenting.

In *Ex parte* Kaine, 14 How. 117, I examined, with care, the jurisdiction of this court to issue writs of *habeas corpus* to inquire into causes of commitment. I then came to the conclusion that the mere fact that a circuit court had examined the cause of commitment and refused to discharge the prisoner, did not enable this court, by a writ of *habeas corpus*, to re-examine the same cause of commitment. Though subsequent reflection has confirmed the opinion then formed, I should have acquiesced in the jurisdiction assumed in this case, if a majority of the court, in Kane's case had decided contrary to my opinion. But the question was then left undecided; and in this case, for the first time, in my judgment, has jurisdiction been assumed, on the ground, not that the cause of commitment was originally examinable here — for that would be an exercise of original jurisdiction — but that, though not thus originally examinable, yet, as the circuit court has had the prisoner before it, and has remanded him, this court, by a writ of *habeas corpus*, may examine that decision and see whether it be erroneous or not.

That this is the only ground on which the jurisdiction over this case can be rested, or that it cannot be considered to be an examination of the original cause of commitment, will clearly appear, if we attend to what that cause of commitment was. The petitioner was convicted capitally. His sentence is not brought before us in form, but we must infer that it ordered him to be imprisoned until the day which was by the court, or should be by the executive, fixed for his execution. He received a conditional pardon. Regularly, I consider, that he should have been brought before the circuit court upon a writ of *habeas corpus*, and have there pleaded his pardon, in bar of so much of his sentence as directed him to be hung; or, in bar of the entire sentence, if the condition requiring him to continue in imprisonment for life was inoperative. United States *v.* Wilson, 7 Peters, 150. If this had been done, the circuit court would have pronounced its judgment upon the validity of such plea; and in conformity with the decision which that court has made in this case, it must have entered a judgment vacating its former sentence, and sentencing the petitioner to imprisonment during life in the penitentiary of this District.

Over such a sentence this court could have exercised no control, either by writ of error or of *habeas corpus*. Not by writ of error, for none is allowed in criminal cases. Not by *habeas corpus*, for, as was held in *ex parte* Watkins, 3 Pet. 193, a writ of *habeas corpus* cannot issue from this court to examine a criminal sentence of the circuit court, even where the objection to the sentence is, that it appears on the face of the record, in the opinion of this court, that the circuit court had not jurisdiction, and its proceeding was merely void; because the circuit courts are the final judges of their own jurisdiction; and of all their proceedings in criminal cases. This court has no power to reverse one of their criminal judgments for any cause, and consequently no power to form any judicial opinion upon the correctness thereof.

In the case before us, so far as appears, the petitioner did not formally plead his pardon, nor did the circuit court, by an entry on its records, formally vacate the capital sentence, and sentence the prisoner anew. But that court, using its own final judgment as to the proper mode of proceeding in this criminal case, proceeded in such manner and form as it deemed to be accord-

ing to law. It remanded the prisoner, in execution of the
original sentence, so far as that directed his imprisonment.
After this had been done, the imprisonment may be viewed in
one of two aspects. It may be considered as continued under
the original sentence; the execution of that part of the sentence
which commanded him to be hung being postponed by the pardon, so long as there shall be no breach of the condition; or the
original sentence may be treated as modified by the proceedings
under the *habeas corpus* in the circuit court, and that part of
the sentence which commanded him to be hung, as annulled,
the residue remaining in force.

As I view this case, therefore, it stands thus: the petitioner
is imprisoned under a criminal sentence of the circuit court,
either as originally pronounced, or as modified by the order of
the circuit court made under the writ of *habeas corpus*. That
original or modified criminal sentence is the cause of his commitment. Though this court has no jurisdiction by writ of
error to revise such a sentence, and has deliberately decided, in
ex parte Watkins, that a writ of *habeas corpus* cannot be made
a writ of error for such a purpose, yet by a writ of *habeas corpus* we do revise such a sentence in this case.

It seems to me that the refusal of a writ of error in criminal
cases is not only idle, but mischievous, if a writ of *habeas corpus*,
which is certainly a very clumsy proceeding for the purpose,
may be resorted to, to bring the record of every criminal case,
of whatever kind, before this court.

With deference for the opinions of my brethren, in my judgment, it goes very little way towards avoiding the difficulty to
hold that, before one under a criminal sentence of a circuit court
can thus attack his sentence collaterally, in a court which cannot review it by any direct proceeding, he must first apply to
the circuit court for a writ of *habeas corpus*; and if the writ, or
his discharge under it, be refused, he may then bring into action
the appellate power of this court, and by a writ of *habeas corpus*
out of this court stop the execution of a sentence, which we have
no power to reverse. Few questions come before this court
which may affect the general course of justice more deeply than
questions of jurisdiction. This great remedial writ of *habeas
corpus*, so efficacious and prompt in its action, and so justly
valued in our country, may become an instrument to unsettle
the nicely adjusted lines of jurisdiction, and produce conflict and
disorder. If the true sphere of its action, and the precise limits
of the power to issue it, should become in any degree confused
or indistinct, serious consequences may follow — consequences
not only affecting the efficient administration of the criminal
laws of the United States, but the harmonious action of the

divided sovereignties by which our country is governed.   For these reasons, though sensible of the bias, which, I suppose, every one has in favor of this process, I have heretofore felt, and now feel, constrained to examine with care the question of our jurisdiction to issue it; and being of opinion that this court has not power to inquire into the validity of the cause of commitment stated in this petition, I think it should be dismissed for that reason.

In this opinion Mr. Justice CAMPBELL concurs.

GEORGE C. DODGE, APPELLANT, *v.* JOHN M. WOOLSEY.

A stockholder in a corporation has a remedy in chancery against the directors, to prevent them from doing acts which would amount to a violation of the charter, or to prevent any misapplication of their capital or profits which might lessen the value of the shares, if the acts intended to be done amount to what is called in law a breach of trust or duty.

So also a stockholder has a remedy against individuals, in whatever character they profess to act, if the subject of complaint is an imputed violation of a corporate franchise, or the denial of a right growing out of it, for which there is not an adequate remedy at law.

Therefore, where the directors of a bank refused to take the proper measures to resist the collection of a tax, which they themselves believed to have been imposed upon them in violation of their charter, this refusal amounted to what is termed in law a breach of trust, a stockholder had a right to file a bill in chancery asking for such a remedy as the case might require.

If the stockholder be a resident of another State than that in which the bank and persons attempting to violate its charter, or commit a breach of trust or duty have their domicile, he may file his bill in the courts of the United States.   He has this right under the constitution and laws of the United States.

The rights and duties of this court examined and explained, as an ultimate tribunal to determine whether laws enacted by congress, or by state legislatures or decisions of state courts are in conflict with the constitution of the United States.

Where the State of Ohio, chartered a bank in 1845, in which charter was stipulated the amount of tax which the bank should pay, in lieu of all taxes to which said company or the stockholders thereof, on account of stock owned therein, would otherwise be subject; and in 1852, the legislature passed an act levying taxes upon the bank to a greater amount and founded upon a different principle.   This act is in conflict with the constitution of the United States, as impairing the obligation of a contract, and therefore void.

The fact, that the people of the State had, in 1851, adopted a new constitution, in which it was declared that taxes should be imposed upon banks in the mode which the act of 1852 purported to carry out, cannot release the State from the obligations and duties imposed upon it by the constitution of the United States.

The case of the Piqua Branch of the State Bank of Ohio *v.* Knoop, 16 How. 369, again affirmed.

THIS was an appeal from the circuit court of the United States for the District of Ohio.

The circumstances of the case are fully stated in the opinion of the court.

It was argued by *Mr. Spalding* and *Mr. Pugh*, for the appellant, and by *Mr. Stanberry* and *Mr. Vinton*, for the appellee.

The points made by the counsel for the appellant, in this court, were substantially the same with the reasons assigned by Dodge, in the circuit court in support of a motion to dissolve the injunction.

They were the following, namely:—

1. The complainant cannot sustain a suit in equity against the defendant, George C. Dodge; for in the event of his making distress for the tax in said bill mentioned, the complainant will have "plain, adequate, and complete remedy at law."

2. The complainant, as one of the stockholders of said Commercial Branch Bank, has no right to call the directors of said bank to account, in a court of equity, for an error of judgment in respect to any matter confided to their discretion.

8. There is no allegation in the bill that the bank or its directors refuse, by collusion with this defendant, or with other persons, to prosecute a suit, or to take other measures to prevent the collection of said tax.

4. The complainant, in the character of a stockholder, has no right to call the bank to account in a court of equity for a breach of trust, as the relation of trustee and *cestui que trust* does not exist between the corporation and its several stockholders.

5. The said Commercial Branch Bank is the creature of the laws of Ohio, and has no corporate existence in any other State. In the law, such corporation is regarded in the light of a citizen and inhabitant of the State which creates and sustains it. The Commercial Branch Bank can have no right to institute a suit in the federal court against George C. Dodge, also a citizen and inhabitant of Ohio.

6. A stockholder of the Commercial Branch Bank is one of the component parts of the corporation. He has no distinct individuality, so far as it respects the interests of the bank, that will enable him to sue a citizen of Ohio in the federal court, although he may be a citizen and inhabitant of the State of Connecticut.

7. The complainant, in his bill, does not show himself entitled to the interposition of this honorable court, sitting as a court of equity.

8. The tax law of April 13, 1852, is a valid, constitutional enactment by the general assembly of the State of Ohio.

9. It is contrary to sound public policy, that the collection of the State revenue should be arrested by the instrumentality of a writ of injunction.

In support of the first, point it was alleged that the damages which the complainant estimated that he would sustain by the tax were not more than $500, whereas the answer of Dodge, showed him to be worth $80,000. Baldwin, C. C. R. 394.

In the case of Osborn v. The United States Bank, the whole franchise of the bank was in jeopardy, so far as it respected that State, 9 Wheat. 738.

The right called in question was the right of the bank, an artificial person, but having a legal existence within the State of Ohio, of which State, Dodge, the other party was a citizen. No suit could therefore be carried on between them in the circuit court of the United States.

2d, 3d, 4th, 5th, and 6th, points. A stockholder had no right to intervene for the protection of the bank. The persons specified in the charter, and they alone, are or can be the agents of the corporation. 1 Kyd on Corporations, 13 ; Angell & Ames, on Corporations, 259 ; 8 Sergeant & Rawle, 521 ; 6 Sergeant & Rawle, 508.

It is definitively settled, however, by a great weight of authority, that where the charter has invested the board of directors with power to manage the concerns of the corporation, no one stockholder, nor any number of stockholders, has a right to compel these, the charter agents of the body corporate, to do any act contrary to their own judgment exercised in good faith. The Commonwealth v. The Trustees of St. Mary's Church, 6 Sergeant & Rawle, 508 ; Hersey v. Veazie, 24 Maine, 9 ; Smith v. Hurd et al. 12 Metcalf, 371 ; State of Louisiana v. Bank of Louisiana, 6 Louisiana, 745 ; Scott v. Depeyster, 1 Edward's N. Y. Chan. Rep. 513 ; Robinson v. Smith, 3 Paige, Chan. Rep. 222 ; Baylies v. Orne et al. 1 Freeman's Chan. Rep. 161 ; Hodges v. New England Screw Co. 1 Rhode Island, 312 ; The Oswego Falls Bridge Co. v. Fish et al. 1 Barbour's Chan. Rep. 547 ; Forbes v. Whitlock, 3 Edward's Chan. Rep. 446 ; Russell v. McLellan, 14 Pickering, 69 ; Angell & Ames on Corporations, 565, § 560 ; 2 How. 461 ; 1 Phillips, 790 ; 11 Georgia, 556.

This bill is a contrivance to give jurisdiction to the federal courts, where none fairly exists, and must therefore be discountenanced. 4 Dallas, 330 ; 1 Wash. C. C. R. 83 ; 5 Cranch, 87.

8. The tax law of 1852, is a valid, constitutional enactment.

When the case of the Piqua Branch Bank was decided, 16 How. 369, it was with reference to this circumstance, namely, that the law imposing the additional tax was imposed by a legislature which was sitting under the same constitution as that which granted the charter of 1845 But this case is different in this respect.

The constitution of 1802, contained in article 8, § 1, this clause.

" For the great purpose of protecting their rights and liberties, and securing their independence, they (the people,) have at all times a complete power to alter, reform, or abolish their government whenever they may deem it necessary."

And in the mode prescribed by another article they altered their constitution in 1851, so far as to require that all property employed in banking, whether by banks then existing or thereafter to be created, should always bear a burden of taxation, equal to that imposed upon the property of individuals.

Therefore, the immunity granted to the banking companies of Ohio, by the 60th section of the act of February 24, 1845, was accepted by them with a tacit understanding that its efficacy might be impaired by the sovereignty of the State, upon the reformation of the government, and the adoption of a new constitution.

In McCullough v. The State of Maryland, 4 Wheat. p. 404, Mr. Chief Justice Marshall says: " It has been said that the people had already surrendered all their powers to the state sovereignties, and had nothing more to give. But, surely, the question whether they may resume and modify the powers granted to government does not remain to be settled in this country."

In Terrett v. Taylor, 9 Cranch, 43, Mr. Justice Story says: " Upon a change of government, too, it may be admitted that such exclusive privileges attached to a private corporation as are inconsistent with the new government, may be abolished."

In Mumma v. Potomac Company, 8 Peters, 281, the same learned justice remarks as follows: —

" A corporation, by the very terms and nature of its political existence, is subject to dissolution by a surrender of its corporate franchises, and by a forfeiture of them for wilful misuser and non-user.

" Every creditor must be presumed to understand the nature and incidents of such a body politic, and to contract with reference to them. And it would be a doctrine new in the law, that the existence of a private contract of the corporation should force upon it a perpetuity of existence contrary to public policy, and the nature and objects of its charter."

The counsel for the appellee contended that as the tax, for 1853, amounted to nine per cent upon the capital of the bank, the case was brought within Osborn v. United States Bank, 9 Wheat. 738; that there was danger of irreparable mischief to the franchise, and a necessity for protecting the moneys, and *choses in action* of the bank from sale, and alienation under the tax proceedings.

In the two cases cited on the other side, namely, 3 Ohio,

870, and the Mechanics' and Traders' Bank v. Debolt, the amount of tax would not have been destructive.

The next point is as to the right of the plaintiff to bring this bill.

He sues in the character of a stockholder, and makes the bank and the directors parties defendant. The case which he makes is, that an act is threatened to be done by Dodge, the tax collector, in violation of law, which, if not prevented, will result in irreparable mischief to the corporation, and to his interest as a stockholder; and that the directors of the bank refuse to take any step to prevent the threatened injury. It further appears, that although the directors have protested against the doing of the act as a violation of the charter of the bank, yet they did suffer the distraint to be made for the tax of 1852, and took no step to prevent the distraint for the tax of 1853, which was impending when the bill was filed. It appears that there was no time for delay; for the distraint was to be made on the 21st of December, and the injunction was not applied for until the day previous.

We claim that, under such circumstances, a stockholder has a clear right to intervene. 11 Georgia, 569; 3 Paige, 283; 1 Freeman, 173; 4 Russ. 575; Hodges v. New England Screw Co. 1 R. I. 312; 7 Ohio, Pt. 1, 218; 16 How. 288; Angell & Ames, on Corp. § 312.

Upon the other branch of the case, the counsel contended that the case of Piqua Branch Bank v. Knoop, 16 How. 369, decided that the 60th section of the charter was a contract, and therefore it was no longer an open question. The ground assumed by the other side, namely, that the adoption of a new constitution in 1851, gave validity to the act of 1852, cannot be sustained.

1. Because the constitution of every State must be made in subordination to the constitution of the United States; and that in this respect, the constitution of a State in no way differs from any other law, and such constitution can no more direct the legislature to pass a law impairing the obligation of a contract, than it can direct or authorize the State to make treaties, alliances, confederations, coin money, or to do any other of those acts which are prohibited to the States by the same clause where the one now in question is found.

2. Because the power to make treaties, alliances, confederations, coin money, pass *ex post facto* laws and laws impairing the obligation of contracts, &c., was surrendered by the States, and is no longer possessed by the people or by the legislatures of the States, and they cannot resume or exercise the power thus surrendered, by means of a State constitution, or in any other way short of an amendment of the constitution of the United States.

3. Because if this can be done, it not only annuls section 10 of the 1st article, but also that clause of article 6 of the constitution of the United States which declares that said constitution shall be the supreme law of the land; for if such State constitution be valid, it must put aside and override the constitution of the United States.

4. Because, thereby the constitution of the United States would virtually become in each State what the people of such State might choose to make it, without the consent of the States of the Union.

In the case of Briscoe *v.* Bank of Kentucky, 11 Pet. 257, the court say, a State cannot do that which the federal constitution declares it shall not do.

And it has even been held, that the stipulations of a treaty between the United States and a foreign nation are paramount to the provisions of the constitution of a particular State of the confederacy. Gordon *v.* Kerr, 1 Wash. Circuit Ct. Rep. 322.

Mr. Justice WAYNE delivered the opinion of the court.

It must often happen, under such a government as that of the United States, that constitutional questions will be brought to this court for decision, demanding extended investigation and its most careful judgment.

This is one of that kind; but fortunately it involves no new principles, nor any assertion of judicial action which has not been repeatedly declared to be within the constitutional and legislative jurisdiction of the courts of the United States, and by way of appeal or by writ of error, as the case may be, within that of the supreme court.

It is a suit in chancery, which was brought by John M. Woolsey, in the circuit court of the United States for the district of Ohio, seeking to enjoin the collection of a tax assessed by the State of Ohio on the Commercial Branch Bank of Cleveland, a branch of the State Bank of Ohio. He makes George C. Dodge, the tax collector, the directors of the bank, and the bank itself, defendants.

Woolsey avers that he is a citizen of the State of Connecticut, that he is the owner of thirty shares in the Branch Bank of Cleveland, that Dodge and the other defendants are all citizens of the State of Ohio, and that the Commercial Bank of Cleveland, is a corporation, and was made such, as a branch of the State Bank of Ohio, by an act of the general assembly of that State, passed the 24th of February, 1845, entitled "An act to incorporate the State Bank of Ohio and other banking companies." He alleges that the Commercial Bank has in all things complied with the requirements of its charter, and that, by the

60th section of the act, it is declared that each banking company organized under it and complying with its provisions, shall, semi-annually, on the 1st of May and 1st of November of each year, those being the days for declaring dividends, set off to the State of Ohio six per cent on the profits, deducting therefrom the expenses and ascertained losses of the company, for six months next preceding each dividend day; and that the sums so set off shall be in lieu of all taxes to which said company, or the stockholders thereof, on account of stock owned therein, would otherwise be subject; and that the cashier of such company shall, within ten days thereafter, inform the auditor of the State of Ohio of the amount set off, and shall pay the same to the treasurer of the State on the order of the auditor.

It is averred that the Bank of Cleveland had at all times complied with the requirements of the act. That, in the year 1853, it set off to the State six per cent on the two semi-annual dividends which had been made in that year, on the first day of May and the first day of November, which amounted in the aggregate to the sum of $3,206$\frac{65}{100}$. That the same had been notified to the auditor, and that the bank had always been ready to pay the same when demanded. The complainant then avers, that three years before bringing his suit, having full confidence that the State of Ohio would observe good faith towards the bank, in respect to its franchises and privileges conferred upon it by the act of incorporation, and that it would adhere with fidelity to the rule of taxation provided for in the charter, he had purchased thirty shares of the capital stock of the bank, and that he was then the owner of the same. He further states, after he had made such purchases, that on the 17th of June, 1851, a draft of a new constitution had been submitted to the electors of the State for their acceptance or rejection, which, if accepted by a majority of the electors who should vote, was to take effect as the constitution of the State, on the 1st of September, 1851. It is admitted that it was accepted, that it became and now is the constitution of the State of Ohio. It is provided in sections two and three of the 12th article of that constitution, that laws shall be passed, taxing by an uniform rule, all moneys, credits, investments in bonds, stock, joint-stock companies, or otherwise; and that the general assembly shall provide by law for taxing the notes and bills discounted or purchased, money loaned, and all other property, effects, or dues whatever, without deduction, of all banks now existing, or hereafter created, and of all bankers, so that all property employed in banking shall always bear a burden of taxation equal to that imposed on the property of individuals. And in the 4th section of the 18th article of the constitution of 1851, it is further de-

clared, that the property of corporations now existing, or hereafter created, shall be subject to taxation, as the property of
individuals.

It appears also by the bill, that the general assembly of the
State of Ohio passe an act on the 13th of April, 1852, for the
assessment and taxation of all property in the State, and for
levying taxes on the same according to its true value in money,
in which it is declared to be the duty of the president and
cashier of every bank, or banking company, "that shall have
been, or may hereafter be, incorporated by the laws of the State,
and having the right to issue bills for circulation as money, to
make and return, under oath, to the auditor of the county in
which such banks may be, in the month of May, annually, a
written statement containing, first, the average amount of notes
and bills discounted or purchased, which amount shall include
all the loans or discounts, whether originally made, or renewed
during the year, or at any time previous: whether made on bills
of exchange, notes, bonds, mortgages, or other evidence of indebtedness, at their actual cost value in money; whether due
previous to, during, or after the period aforesaid, and on which
said banking company has, at any time, recovered or received,
or is entitled to receive, any profit or other consideration whatever, either in the shape of interest, discount, exchange, or otherwise; and secondly, the average amount of all other moneys,
effects, or dues of every description, belonging to such bank, or
banking company, loaned, invested, or otherwise used or employed, with a view to profit, or upon which such bank, or
banking company receives, or is entitled to receive, interest.

The act then makes it the duty of the auditors, in the counties
in which a bank or banking companies may be, to receive from
them returns of notes and bills discounted, and all other moneys
and effects or dues, as provided for in the 19th section of the
act, to enter the same for taxation upon the grand duplicate of
the property of the county, and upon the city duplicate for city
taxes, in cases where the city tax is not returned upon the grand
duplicate, but is collected by city officers; which amounts so
returned and entered shall be taxed for the same purposes and
to the same extent that personal property is, or may be taxed,
in the place where such bank or banking company is situated.
It is then averred that the president and cashier of the Commercial Bank of Cleveland, fearing the penalty imposed by the
act for a refusal or neglect to make a return according to the
act, did, in the month of May, in the year 1852, make a return,
protesting against the right of the State to assess a tax upon
the bank, other than that which was provided for in the charter
of its incorporation, of the 24th February, 1845. But it appears

that the return so coerced from the president and directors of the bank had been assessed by the auditor, for the tax of 1852, at $10,197$\frac{55}{100}$, exceeding by $7,526$\frac{72}{100}$ the amount of tax for which the bank was liable under its charter, which George C. Dodge, as collector of taxes, seized and collected by distress on its moneys. It is also shown by the bill, that there has been another entry of taxation against the bank for the year 1853, of $14,771$\frac{87}{100}$, exceeding the sum to which it is liable under its charter by $11,665$\frac{22}{100}$ for that year.

It is against the collection of this tax that John M. Woolsey, as a stockholder in the bank, has brought this suit, claiming an exemption from it as a stockholder, upon the ground that the act of the general assembly of the State of Ohio, and the tax assessed under it upon the bank, are in violation of the 10th section of the 1st article of the constitution of the United States, which declares that no State shall pass any law impairing the obligation of contracts. And he seeks the aid of the circuit court to enjoin Dodge, the defendant, from collecting the same from the bank, as collector of taxes, as he had threatened to do by distress, and as he had done for the assessed tax for the year 1852.

The complainant gives a further aspect to his suit which it is also proper to notice. It is, if the taxes are permitted to be assessed and collected from the bank, under the act of the 13th of April, 1852, it will virtually destroy and annul the contract between the State and the bank, in respect to the tax which the State imposed upon it by the charter of its incorporation, in lieu of all other taxes upon the bank or the stockholders thereof, on account of stock owned therein; that his stock will be thereby lessened in value, his dividends diminished; and that the tax is so onerous upon the bank, that it will compel a suspension and final cessation of its business. He finally declares that as a stockholder, on his own behalf, he had requested the directors of the bank to take measures, by suit or otherwise, to assert the franchises of the bank against the collection of what he believes to be an unconstitutional tax, and that they had refused to do so.

To this bill the defendant, George C. Dodge, filed an answer. The other defendants did not answer. He admits the material allegations of the bill, except the allegation that the tax law of April 13, 1852, is unconstitutional; says that the act is in conformity with the constitution of Ohio, which took effect September 1, 1851, and that it is in harmony with the constitution of the United States. He denies that any application was made by Woolsey to the directors of the bank, to take measures, by suit or otherwise, to prevent the collection of the tax, and insists that this averment was inserted merely for the purpose of giving color to a proceeding in chancery. That the complainant would not have sustained an irreparable injury even if he had, as treasurer, proceeded to distrain for the tax; for that the bank would have had a remedy at law against him for all damages which might have been sustained in consequence of such distress, as he is worth, at a reasonable estimate, eighty thousand dollars after the payment of all his debts. And he insists that the complainant had not exhibited such a case as entitled him to the interposition of a court of equity. To this answer a general replication was filed. But it was agreed by the counsel in the cause, that the complainant had, by his attorney, addressed a letter to the Commercial Bank of Cleveland, to institute proper proceedings to prevent the collection of the tax by Dodge, in the same manner as had been done by the attorney of a stockholder in the Canal Bank of Cleveland, for a tax assessed upon it under the same act, and that the action of the board of the Commercial Bank, in answer to Woolsey's application, was the same as had been given by the directors of the Canal Bank. That resolution was in these words: "Resolved, that we fully concur in the views expressed in said letter as to the illegality of the tax therein named, and believe it to be in no way binding upon the bank; but, in consideration of the many obstacles in the way of testing the law in the courts of the State, we cannot consent to take the action which we are called upon to take, but must leave the said Kleman to pursue such measures as he may deem best in the premises."

Upon the foregoing pleadings and admission, the circuit court rendered a final decree for the complainant, perpetually enjoining the treasurer against the collection of the tax, under the act of the 13th February, 1852, and subjecting the defendant, Dodge, to the payment of the costs of the suit. From that decision the defendant, Dodge, has appealed to this court.

His counsel have relied upon the following points to sustain the appeal:—

1. The complainant does not show himself to be entitled to relief in a court of chancery, because the charter of the bank provides, that its affairs shall be managed by a board of directors, and that they are not amenable to the stockholders for an error of judgment merely. And that in order to make them so, it should have been averred that they were in collusion with the tax collector in their refusal to take legal steps to test the validity of the tax.

2. It was urged that this suit had been improperly brought in the circuit court of the United States for the district of Ohio, because it is a contrivance to create a jurisdiction, where none

fairly exists, by substituting an individual stockholder in place of the Commercial Bank as complainant, and making the directors defendants; the stockholder being made complainant, because he is a citizen of the State of Connecticut, and the directors being made defendants to give countenance to his suit.

3d. It was said, if the foregoing points were not available to defeat the action, that it might be contended that the defendant was in the discharge of his official duty when interrupted by the mandate of the circuit court, and that the tax had been properly assessed by a law of the State, in conformity with its constitution, of the 1st September, 1851.

We will consider the points in their order. The first comprehends two propositions, namely: that courts of equity have no jurisdiction over corporations, as such, at the suit of a stockholder for violations of charters, and none for the errors of judgment of those who manage their business ordinarily.

There has been a conflict of judicial authority in both. Still, it has been found necessary, for prevention of injuries for which common-law courts were inadequate, to entertain in equity such a jurisdiction in the progressive development of the powers and effects of private corporations upon all the business and interests of society.

It is now no longer doubted, either in England or the United States, that courts of equity, in both, have a jurisdiction over corporations, at the instance of one or more of their members; to apply preventive remedies by injunction, to restrain those who administer them from doing acts which would amount to a violation of charters, or to prevent any misapplication of their capitals or profits, which might result in lessening the dividends of stockholders, or the value of their shares, as either may be protected by the franchises of a corporation, if the acts intended to be done create what is in the law denominated a breach of trust. And the jurisdiction extends to inquire into, and to enjoin, as the case may require that to be done, any proceedings by individuals, in whatever character they may profess to act, if the subject of complaint is an imputed violation of a corporate franchise, or the denial of a right growing out of it, for which there is not an adequate remedy at law. 2 Russ. & Mylne Ch. R., Cunliffe v. Manchester and Bolton Canal Company, 480, n.; Ware v. Grand Junction Water Company, 2 Russ. & Mylne, 470; Bagshaw v. Eastern Counties Railway Company, 7 Hare Ch. R. 114; Angell & Ames, 4th ed. 424, and the other cases there cited.

It was ruled in the case of Cunliffe v. The Manchester and Bolton Canal Company, 2 Russ. & Mylne Ch. R. 481, that where the legal remedy against a corporation is inadequate, a court of

29 *

equity will interfere, and that there were cases in which a bill in equity will lie against a corporation by one of its members. "It is a breach of trust towards a shareholder in a joint-stock incorporated company, established for certain definite purposes prescribed by its charter, if the funds or credit of the company are, without his consent, diverted from such purpose, though the misapplication be sanctioned by the votes of a majority; and, therefore, he may file a bill in equity against the company in his own behalf, to restrain the company by injunction from any such diversion or misapplication. In the case of Ware v. Grand Junction Water Company, 2 Russell & Mylne, a bill filed by a member of the company against it, Lord Brougham said: "It is said this is an attempt on the part of the company to do acts which they are not empowered to do by the acts of parliament," meaning the charter of the company; "so far I restrain them by injunction." "Indeed, an investment in the stock of a corporation must, by every one, be considered a wild speculation, if it exposed the owners of the stock to all sorts of risk in support of plausible projects not set forth and authorized by the act of incorporation, and which may possibly lead to extraordinary losses. The same jurisdiction was invoked and applied in the case of Bagshaw v. The Eastern Counties Railway Company; so, also, in Coleman v. The same company, 10 Beavan's Ch. Reports, 1. It appeared in that case that the directors of the company, for the purpose of increasing their traffic, proposed to guarantee certain profits, and to secure the capital of an intended steam-packet company, which was to act in connection with the railway. It was held, such a transaction was not within the scope of their powers, and they were restrained by injunction. And in the second place, that in such a case one of the shareholders in the railway company was entitled to sue in behalf of himself and all the other shareholders, except the directors, who were defendants, although some of the shareholders had taken shares in the steam-packet company. It was contended in this case that the corporation might pledge, without limit, the funds of the company for the encouragement of other transactions, however various and extensive, provided the object of that liability was to increase the traffic upon the railway, and thereby increase the traffic to the shareholders. But the master of the rolls, Lord Langdale, said, "there was no authority for anything of that kind."

But further, it is not only illegal for a corporation to apply its capital to objects not contemplated by its charter, but also to apply its profits. And therefore a shareholder may maintain a bill in equity against the directors and compel the company to refund any of the profits thus improperly applied. It is an improper application for a railway company to invest the profits of the company in the purchase of shares in another company. The dividend (says Lord Langdale, in Solamons *v.* Laing, 14 Jurist for December, 1850) which belongs to the shareholders, and is divisible among them, may be applied severally as their own property; but the company itself or the directors, or any number of shareholders, at a meeting or otherwise, have no right to dispose of his shares of the general dividends, which belong to the particular shareholder, in any manner contrary to the will, or without the consent or authority of, that particular shareholder.

We do not mean to say that the jurisdiction in equity over corporations at the suit of a shareholder has not been contested. The cases cited in this argument show it to have been otherwise; but when the case of Hodges *v.* The New England Screw Company et al. was cited against it,—(we may say the best argued and judicially considered case which we know upon the point, both upon the original hearing and rehearing of that cause,)—the counsel could not have been aware of the fact that, upon the rehearing of it, the learned court, which had decided that courts of equity have no jurisdiction over corporations as such at the suit of a stockholder for violations of charter, reviewed and recalled that conclusion. The language of the court is: " We have thought it our duty to review in this general form this new and unsettled jurisdiction, and to say, in view of the novelty and importance of the subject, and the additional light which has been thrown upon it since the trial, we consider the jurisdiction of this court over corporations for breaches of charter, at the suit of shareholders, and how far it shall be extended, and subject to what limits, is still an open question in this court. 1 Rhode Island Reports, 812 — rehearing of the case September term, 1853."

The result of the cases is well stated in Angell & Ames, paragraphs 391, 393. " In cases where the legal remedy against a corporation is inadequate, a court of equity will interfere, is well settled, and there are cases in which a bill in equity will lie against a corporation by one of its members." " Though the result of the authorities clearly is, that in a corporation, when acting within the scope of and in obedience to the provisions of its constitution, the will of the majority, duly expressed at a legally constituted meeting, must govern; yet beyond the limits of the act of incorporation, the will of the majority cannot make an act valid; and the powers of a court of equity may be put in motion at the instance of a single shareholder, if he can show that the corporation are employing their statutory powers for the accomplishment of purposes not within the scope of their institution. Yet it is to be observed, that there is an important

Dodge *v.* Woolsey.

distinction between this class of cases and those in which ther is no breach of trust, but only error and misapprehension, o simple negligence on the part of the directors." *

We have then the rule and its limitation. It is contende that this case is within the limitation; or that the directors of the Commercial Bank of Cleveland, in their action in respect the tax assessed upon it, under the act of April 18, 1852, and in their refusal to take proper measures for testing its validity, hav committed an "error of judgment merely."

It is obvious, from the rule, that the circumstances of each ca must determine the jurisdiction of a court of equity to give th relief sought. That the pleadings must be relied upon to collec what they are, to ascertain in what character, and to what end shareholder invokes the interposition of a court of equity, on account of the mismanagement of a board of directors. Whethe such acts are out of or beyond the limits of the act of incorpora tion, either of commission contrary thereto, or of negligence not doing what it may be their chartered duty to do.

This brings us to the inquiry, as to what the directors hav done in this case, and what they refused to do upon the applica tion of their co-corporator, John M. Woolsey. After a full sta ment of his case, comprehending all of his rights and theirs also alleging in his bill that his object was to test the validity of tax upon the ground that it was unconstitutional, because it im paired the obligation of a contract made by the State of Ohi

---

* So it has been repeatedly decided, that a private corporation may be sued at la by one of its own members. The text upon this subject is so well expressed, wi authorities to support it, that we will extract the paragraph 390 from Angell & Am entire. A private corporation may be sued by one of its own members. This poin came directly before the court, in the State of South Carolina in an action of assum sit against the Catawba Company. The plea in abatement was, that the plainti himself was a member of that company, and therefore could maintain no actio against it in his individual capacity. The court, after hearing argument, overrul the plea as containing principles subversive of justice; and they moreover said, th the point had been settled by two former cases, wherein certain officers were allow to maintain actions for their salaries due by the company. In this respect, the ca of incorporated companies are entirely dissimilar from those of ordinary copartner ships, or unincorporated joint-stock companies. In the former, the individual mem bers of the company are entirely distinct from the artificial body endowed with co porate powers. A member of a corporation who is a creditor, has the same right any other creditor to secure the payment of his demands, by attachment or by lev upon the property of the corporation, although he may be personally liable by statu to satisfy other judgments against the corporation. An action was maintained agains a corporation on a bond securing a certain sum to the plaintiff, a member of the co poration, the member being deemed by the court a stranger. Pierce & Partridge 3 Met. Mass. 44; so of notes and bonds, accounts and rights to dividends. Hill *v* Manchester and Salford Water-works, 5 Adol. & Ellis, 866; Dunston *v.* Imperia Glass Company, 3 B. & Adol. 125; Geer *v.* School District, 6 Vermont, 187; Me dist Episcopal Society, 18 Ib. 405; Rogers *v.* Danby Universalist Society, 19 Ib 187.

with the Commercial Bank of Cleveland, and the stockholders thereof; he represents in his own behalf, as a stockholder, that he had applied to the directors, requesting them to take measures, by suit or otherwise, to prevent the collection of the tax by the treasurer, and that they refused to do so, accompanying, however, their refusal with the declaration that they fully concurred with Woolsey in his views as to the illegality of the tax; that they believed it in no way binding upon the bank, but that, in consideration of the many obstacles in the way of resisting the collection of the tax in the courts of the State, they could not consent to take legal measures for testing it. Besides this refusal, the papers in the case disclose the fact that the directors had previously made two protests against the constitutionality of the tax, because it was repugnant to the constitution of the United States, and to that of Ohio also, both concluding with a resolution that they would not, as then advised, pay the tax, unless compelled by law to do so, and that they were determined to rely upon the constitutional and legal rights of the bank under its charter. Now, in our view, the refusal upon the part of the directors, by their own showing, partakes more of disregard of duty, than of an error of judgment. It was a non-performance of a confessed official obligation, amounting to what the law considers a breach of trust, though it may not involve intentional moral delinquency. It was a mistake, it is true, of what their duty required from them, according to their own sense of it, but, being a duty by their own confession, their refusal was an act outside of the obligation which the charter imposed upon them to protect what they conscientiously believed to be the franchises of the bank. A sense of duty and conduct contrary to it, is not " an error of judgment merely," and cannot be so called in any case. It amounted to an illegal application of the profits due to the stockholders of the bank, into which a court of equity will inquire to prevent its being made.

Thinking, as we do, that the action of the board of directors was not " an error of judgment merely," but a breach of duty, it is our opinion that they were properly made parties to the bill, and that the jurisdiction of a court of equity reaches such a case to give such a remedy as its circumstances may require. This conclusion makes it unnecessary for us to notice further the point made by the counsel that the suit should have been brought in the name of the corporation, in support of which they cited the case of the Bank of the United States v. Osborn. The obvious difference between this case and that is, that the Bank of the United States brought a bill in the circuit court of the United States for the district of Ohio, to resist a tax assessed under an act of that State, and executed by its auditor, and here the

directors of the Commercial Bank of Cleveland, by refusing to
do what they had declared it to be their duty to do, have forced
one of its corporators, in self-defence, to sue. If the directors
had done so in a state court of Ohio, and put their case upon
the unconstitutionality of the tax act, because it impaired the
obligation of a contract, and had the decision been against such
· claim, the judgment of the state court could have been re-examined, in that particular, in the supreme court of the United
States, under the same authority or jurisdiction by which it reversed the judgment of the supreme court of Ohio, in the case
of the Piqua Branch of the State Bank of Ohio v. Jacob Knoop,
treasurer of Miami county, 16 How. 369.

But it was said in the argument, that this suit had been improperly brought in the circuit court of the United States, because it was a contrivance by Woolsey, or between him and the
directors of the bank, to give that court jurisdiction, on account
of their residence and citizenship being in different States.
That the subject-matter of the suit was within the exclusive
jurisdiction of the state courts, and that, if the jurisdiction in
the courts of the United States was sustained, it would make
inoperative to a great extent the 7th amendment of the constitution of the United States and the 16th section of the Judiciary
Act of 1789, this last being a declaratory act, settling the law,
as to cases of equity jurisdiction, in the nature of a proviso, limitation, or exception to its exercise. And further, that it would
make the judiciary of the United States paramount to that of
the individual States, and the legislative and executive departments of the federal government paramount to the same departments of the individual States.

We first remark as to the imputation of contrivance, that it is
the assertion of a fact which does not appear in the case, one
which the defendants should have proved if they meant to rely
upon it to abate or defeat the complainant's suit, and that, not
having done so, as they might have attempted to do, we cannot
presume its existence. Mr. Woolsey's right, as a citizen of the
State of Connecticut, to sue citizens of the State of Ohio in the
courts of the United States, for that State, cannot be questioned.
The papers in the case also show, that the directors and himself
occupy antagonist grounds in respect to the controversy which
their refusal to sue forced him to take in defence of his rights as
a shareholder in the bank. Nor can the counsel for the defendant assume the existence of such a fact in the argument of their
case in this court, in the absence of any attempt on their part to
prove it in the circuit court.

We remark, as to the subject-matter of the suit being within
the exclusive jurisdiction of the State courts, that the courts of

the United States and the courts of the States have concurrent jurisdiction in all cases between citizens of different States, whatever may be the matter in controversy, if it be one for judicial cognizance. Such is the constitution of the United States, and the legislation to congress "in pursuance thereof." And when it was urged that the jurisdiction of the case belonged exclusively to the state courts of Ohio, under the 7th article of the amendments to the constitution, and the 16th section of the judiciary act of 1789 was invoked to sustain the position, it seems it was forgotten that this court and other courts of the United States had repeatedly decided that the equity jurisdiction of the courts of the United States is independent of the local law of any State, and is the same in nature and extent as the equity jurisdiction of England, from which it is derived, and that it is no objection to this jurisdiction, that there is a remedy under the local law. Gordon v. Hobart, 2 Sumner, C. C. Rep. 401.

It was also said by both of the counsel for the defendant, and argued with some zeal, that if the court sustained the jurisdiction in this case, it would be difficult to determine whether anything, and how much of state sovereignty may hereafter exist. We shall give to this observation our particular consideration, regretting that it should be necessary, but not doubting that such a jurisdiction exists at the suit of a shareholder, and that the appellate jurisdiction of this court may be exercised in the matter, not only without taking away any of the rights of the States, but, by doing so, giving additional securities for their preservation, to the great benefit of the people of the United States. If it does not exist and was not exercised, we should indeed have a very imperfect national government, altogether unworthy of the wisdom and foresight of those who framed it; incompetent, too, to secure for the future those advantages hitherto secured by it to the people of the United States, and which were in their contemplation, when, by their conventions in the several States, the constitution was ratified.

Impelled then by a sense of duty to the constitution, and the administration of so much of it as has been assigned to the judiciary, we proceed with the discussion.

The departments of the government are legislative, executive, and judicial. They are co-ordinate in degree to the extent of the powers delegated to each of them. Each, in the exercise of its powers, is independent of the other, but all, rightfully done by either, is binding upon the others. The constitution is supreme over all of them, because the people who ratified it have made it so; consequently, anything which may be done unauthorized by it is unlawful. But it is not only over the departments of the government that the constitution is supreme. It is so, to the extent of its delegated powers, over all who made themselves parties to it; States as well as persons, within those concessions of sovereign powers yielded by the people of the States, when they accepted the constitution in their conventions. Nor does its supremacy end there. It is supreme over the people of the United States, aggregately and in their separate sovereignties, because they have excluded themselves from any direct or immediate agency in making amendments to it, and have directed that amendments should be made representatively for them, by the congress of the United States, when two thirds of both houses shall propose them; or where the legislatures of two thirds of the several States shall call a convention for proposing amendments, which, in either case, become valid, to all intents and purposes, as a part of the constitution, when ratified by the legislatures of three fourths of the several States, or by conventions in three fourths of them, as one or the other mode of ratification may be proposed by congress. The same article declares that no amendment, which might be made prior to the year 1808, should, in any manner, affect the first and fourth clauses in the ninth section of the first article, and that no State, without its consent, shall be deprived of its equal suffrage in the senate. The first being a temporary disability to amend, and the other two permanent and unalterable exceptions to the power of amendment.

Now, whether such a supremacy of the constitution, with its limitations in the particulars just mentioned, and with the further restriction laid by the people upon themselves, and for themselves, as to the modes of amendment, be right or wrong politically, no one can deny that the constitution is supreme, as has been stated, and that the statement is in exact conformity with it.

Further, the constitution is not only supreme in the sense we have said it was, for the people in the ratification of it have chosen to add that "this constitution and the laws of the United States which shall be made in pursuance thereof; and all treaties made, or which shall be made, under the authority of the United States, shall be the supreme law of the land, and the judges in every State shall be bound thereby, anything in the constitution or laws of any State to the contrary notwithstanding." And, in that connection, to make its supremacy more complete, impressive, and practical, that there should be no escape from its operation, and that its binding force upon the States and the members of congress should be unmistakable, it is declared that "the senators and representatives, before mentioned, and the members of the state legislatures, and all executive and judicial officers, both of the United States and of the several States, shall be bound by an oath or affirmation to support this constitution.

Having stated, not by way of argument or inference, but in the words of the constitution, the particulars in which it is declared to be supreme, we proceed to show that it contains an interpreter, or has given directions for determining what is its meaning and operation, what "laws are made in pursuance thereof," and to fix the meaning of treaties which had been made, or which shall be made, under the authority of the United States, when either the constitution, the laws of congress, or a treaty, are brought judicially in question, in which a State, or a citizen of the United States, or a foreigner, shall claim rights before the courts of the United States, or in the courts of the States, either under the constitution or the laws of the United States, or from a treaty.

All legislative powers in the constitution are vested in a congress of the United States, which shall consist of a senate and house of representatives. Then stating of whom the house shall be composed, how they shall be chosen by the people of the several States, the qualification of electors, the age of representatives, the time of their citizenship, and their inhabitancy in the State in which they shall be chosen; how representatives and direct taxes shall be apportioned, how the senate shall be composed, with sundry other provisions relating to the house and the senate, the powers of congress are enumerated affirmatively. The 9th section then declares what the congress shall not have power to do, and it is followed by the 10th, consisting of three paragraphs, all of them prohibitions upon the States from doing the particulars expressed in them.

Our first suggestion now is, as all the legislative powers are concessions of sovereignty from the people of the States, and the prohibitions upon them in the 10th section are likewise so, both raise an obligation upon the States not to legislate upon either; each, however, conferring rights, according to what may be the constitutional legislation of congress upon the first; and the second giving rights of equal force, without legislation in respect to such of them as execute themselves, on account of their being prohibitions of what the States shall not do. For instance, no legislation by congress is wanted to make more binding upon the States what they have bound themselves in absolute terms not to do. As where it is said "no State shall enter into any treaty, alliance, or confederation, grant letters of marque and reprisal, coin money, emit bills of credit, make anything but gold and silver coin a tender in payment of debts, pass any bill of attainder, *ex post facto* law, or law impairing the obligation of contracts, or grant any title of nobility."

Our next suggestion is, that the grants of legislative powers, and the negation of the exercise of other powers by the States, some of them being declarations that they would not legislate upon those matters which had been exclusively given up for the legislation of congress, do not imply that the States would be wilfully disregardful of the obligations solemnly placed upon them by their people; but that there might be interferences from their legislation in some of those particulars, either with the constitution, or between their enactments and those of congress. But this apprehension (not without cause) was founded upon the legislation of some of the States during the continuance of the articles of confederation, affecting the rights and interests of persons in their contracts, from which they could get no relief, unless it was granted by the same State legislatures which passed the acts. This suggested the necessity, or rather made it obvious, that our national union would be incomplete and altogether insufficient for the great ends contemplated, unless a constitutional arbiter was provided to give certainty and uniformity, in all of the States, to the interpretation of the constitution and the legislation of congress; with powers also to declare judicially what acts of the legislatures of the States might be in conflict with either. Had this not been done, there would have been no mutuality of constitutional obligation between the States, either in respect to the constitution or the laws of congress, and each of them would have determined for itself the operation of both, either by legislation or judicial action. In either way, exempting itself and its citizens from engagements which it had not made by itself, but in common with other States of the Union, equally sovereign; by which they bound their sovereignties to each other, that neither of them should assume to settle a principle or interest for itself, in a matter which was the common interest of all of them. Such is certainly the common-sense view of the people, when any number of them enter into a contract for their mutual benefit, in the same proportions of interest. In such a case, neither should assume the right to bind his compeers by his judgment, as to the stipulations of their contract. If one of them did so, any other of them might call in the aid of the law to settle their differences, and its judgment would terminate the controversy. It must not be said that the illustration is inappropriate, because individuals have no other mode to settle their disputes, and that States and nations, from their equal sovereignty, have no tribunal to terminate authoritatively their differences, each having the right to judge and do so for itself.

But ours is not such a government. The States, or rather the people forming it, though sovereign as to the powers not delegated to the United States by the constitution, nor prohibited by it to the States, are not independent of each other, in respect to the powers ceded in the constitution.

Their union, by the constitution, was made by each of them conceding portions of their equal sovereignties for all of them, and it acts upon the States conjunctively and separately, and in the same manner upon their citizens, aggregately in some things, and in others individually, in many of their relations of business, and also upon their civil conduct, so far as their obedience to the laws of congress is concerned.

In such a union, the States are bound by all of those principles of justice which bind individuals to their contracts. They are bound by their mutual acquiescence in the powers of the constitution, that neither of them should be the judge, or should be allowed to be the final judge of the powers of the constitution, or of the interpretation of the laws of congress. This is not so, because their sovereignty is impaired; but the exercise of it is diminished in quantity, because they have, in certain respects, put restraints upon that exercise, in virtue of voluntary engagements. (Vattel, Ch. 1, section 10.)

We will now give two illustrations — one from the constitution, and the other from one of the cases decided in this court, upon a tax act of the State of Ohio — to show that the framers of the constitution, and the conventions which ratified it, were fully aware of the necessity for and meant to make a department of it, to which was to be confided the final decision judicially of the powers of that instrument, the conformity of laws with it, which either congress or the legislatures of the States may enact, and to review the judgments of the state courts, in which a right is decided against, which has been claimed in virtue of the constitution or the laws of congress.

The third clause of the 2d section of the 1st article of the constitution is, " that representatives and direct taxes shall be apportioned among the several States, according to their respective numbers, which shall be determined by adding to the whole number of free persons, including those bound to service for a term of years, and excluding Indians not taxed, three fifths of all other persons." We will suppose that congress shall again impose a direct tax, and that a citizen liable to assessment should dispute its application to a kind of his property, alleging it not to be a direct tax, in the sense of that provision of the constitution; and that he should apply to a state court for relief from an execution which had been levied upon his property for its collection, making the United States collector of the tax a party to his suit; and that the court should enjoin him from further proceedings to collect the tax. It is plain, if such a judgment was final, and could not be reviewed by any other court, or by the supreme court of the United States, in virtue of its appellate jurisdiction, as that has been given by the act of congress, the result would be, that the citizens of the State in which the judgment was given, would be exempted from the payment of a tax which had been intended by congress to be apportioned upon the property of all of the citizens of the United States, in conformity with the constitution. This would practically defeat the rule of apportionment if it was acquiesced in by the government of the United States, and the constitutional collection of the tax could not be made in any State according to the act. We do not mean that the officers of the United States could not collect the tax in those States in which no such judgment had been given; but if the judgment could not be reviewed, that the constitutional rule for the imposition of direct taxes could not be executed by any legislation of congress which a State legislature or a state court might not say was unconstitutional. We should not then have a more perfect union than we had under the articles of confederation. Each State then paid the requisition of congress, when it pleased to do so. Had it been continued, the union would be more feeble for all national purposes than it had been. Then the States only disregarded their obligations to suit their convenience. Had it not been corrected, as it has been done in the constitution, we have no reason to believe that there would not be like results, or that the courts of the States would not be resorted to, to determine the constitutionality of taxes laid by congress. This was certainly not meant by the framers of the constitution, nor can its disallowance be brought under the 10th article of its amendments, which declares "that the powers not delegated to the United States by the constitution, nor prohibited by it to the States, are reserved to the States respectively, or to the people."

The illustration given, and its results, have been drawn from the constitution of the United States, also from what might be the action of the state legislatures and state courts, which could not be prevented unless the supreme court of the United States had the power to review the action of the state courts upon a matter exclusively of national interest, made so by the legislation of congress.

Hitherto, no such case as we have supposed has happened, but a reference to the case of Hylton v. The United States, 3 Dallas, 171, in which an attempt was made to test the constitutionality of a tax assessed by the United States, will show that a case of the kind is not unlikely to occur, when congress shall impose a tax apportioning representation and direct taxation; or, under the general declaration in the 8th section of the 1st article of the constitution, that "congress shall have power to lay and collect taxes, duties, imposts, and excises, but that all duties shall be uniform throughout the United States." Let it be understood, too, that the power is not only to impose duties and taxes, but to collect them, and from the power to collect must necessarily be inferred the disability of the legislatures of the States, or of the courts of the States, in any way to interfere with its execution, as that may be directed by congress. If the courts of the States, or their legislatures, could finally determine against the constitutionality of a tax laid by congress, there would be no certainty or uniformity of taxation upon the citizens of the United States, or of the apportionment of representation and direct taxation according to the constitution.

Other illustrations of the propriety and necessity for a judicial tribunal of the United States to settle such questions finally, might be made from other clauses of the constitution. We will, however, cite but one of them in addition to such as have been already mentioned. It is the power of congress to regulate commerce, and we refer to the case of Brown v. The State of Maryland, as an instance of the attempt of that State to lay a tax upon imports, which this court pronounced to be unconstitutional.

We will now give other illustrations, in which the rights of property are involved, to show the cautious wisdom of that provision of the constitution which secures to the citizens of the different States a right to sue in the courts of the United States, and to claim either in them, or in the courts of the States, the protection either of the constitution or of the laws of congress.

The legislature of Ohio passed an act in 1803, incorporating the proprietors of the half-million of acres of land south of Lake Erie called the "Sufferers' Land." This act required the appointment of directors, who were authorized to extinguish the Indian title, to survey the land into townships, or otherwise make partition among the owners; and, among other things provided, "that, to defray all necessary expenses of the company in purchasing and extinguishing the Indian claim of title to the land, surveying, locating, and making partition, and all other necessary expenses of said company, power is hereby vested in the said directors, and their successors in office, to levy a tax or taxes on said land, and enforce the collection thereof." It was also provided that the directors should have power and authority to do whatever it shall appear to them to be necessary and proper to be done for the well-ordering and interest of the proprietors, not contrary to the laws of the State. Subsequently, the legislature of Ohio imposed a tax upon these lands as a part of the revenue to be raised for the State. The directors assessed a tax upon the share of each proprietor, to pay the tax to the State. A sale of a part of the land was made for that purpose, and the question subsequently raised in the circuit court of the United States for the district of Ohio, in a suit at the instance of the heirs of one of the proprietors whose land had been sold, was, whether the sale conveyed a title to the land to the purchaser. It was determined by this court, that it did not, because the directors had not power to make an assessment upon the lands to pay the state tax, and that the tax, as laid by the State, had been done in violation of the corporate powers given to the directors. In this case the plaintiffs sought protection against the tax laid by Ohio, and acquiesced in by the directors of the corporation, because that tax was contrary to the contract which the State had made with the corporation for the benefit of the proprietors of the land. The State, without being a party to the record, was interested in the question. It was a suit between citizens of different States, brought by the plaintiffs in the United States circuit court for Ohio; and the motive for seeking that tribunal was, that his rights might be tried in one not subject either to State or local influences. It placed both parties upon an equality, in fact and in appearances; and whatever might have been the result, neither could complain of the disinterestedness of the court which adjudged their rights. Beatty v. The Lessee of Knowles, 4 Peters, 152.

The foundation of the right of citizens of different States to sue each other in the courts of the United States, is not an unworthy jealousy of the impartiality of the state tribunals. It has a higher aim and purpose. It is to make the people think and feel, though residing in different States of the Union, that their relations to each other were protected by the strictest justice, administered in courts independent of all local control or connection with the subject-matter of the controversy between the parties to a suit.

Men unite in civil society, expecting to enjoy peaceably what belongs to them, and that they may regain it by the law when wrongfully withheld. That can only be accomplished by good laws, with suitable provisions for the establishment of courts of justice, and for the enforcement of their decisions. The right to establish them flows from the same source which determines the extent of the legislative and executive powers of government. Experience has shown that the object cannot be attained without a supreme tribunal, as one of the departments of the government, with defined powers in its organic structure, and the mode for exercising them to be provided legislatively. This has been done in the constitution of the United States. Its framers were well aware of their responsibilities to secure justice to the people;

and well knew, as the object of all trials in courts was to determine the suits between citizens, that it could not be done satisfactorily to them, unless they had the privilege to appeal from the first tribunal which had jurisdiction of a suit to another which should have authority to pronounce definitively upon its merits. (Vattel, 9th chapter, on justice and polity.) Without such a court the citizens of each State could not have enjoyed all the privileges and immunities of citizens in the several States, as they were intended to be secured by the second section of the 4th article of the constitution. Nor would the judicial power have been extended in fact to "all cases in law and equity arising under the constitution, the laws of the United States, and treaties made or which shall be made under their authority, to all cases affecting ambassadors and other public ministers and consuls; to all cases of admiralty and maritime jurisdiction; to controversies to which the United States shall be a party; to controversies between two or more States; to those between citizens of different States, or between citizens of the same State, claiming lands under grants of different States; and between a State and the citizens thereof and foreign States, citizens or subjects." Article 3d, section 1st.

Without the supreme court, as it has been constitutionally and legislatively constituted, neither the constitution nor the laws of congress passed in pursuance of it, nor treaties, would be in practice or in fact the supreme law of the land, and the injunction that the judges in every State should be bound thereby, anything in the constitution or laws of any State to the contrary notwithstanding, would be useless, if the judges of state courts, in any one of the States, could finally determine what was the meaning and operation of the constitution and laws of congress, or the extent of the obligation of treaties.

But let it be remembered, that the appellate jurisdiction of the supreme court, as it is, is one of perfect equality between the States and the United States. It acts upon the constitution and laws of both, in the same way, to the same extent, for the same purposes, and with the same final result. Neither the dignity nor the independence of either are lessened by its organization or action.

The same electors choose the members of the house of representatives who choose the members of the most popular branch of the state legislatures. The senators of the United States are chosen by the legislatures of the States. The senate and house of representatives of the United States exercise their legislative powers independently of each other, their concurrence being necessary to pass laws. The States are represented in the one, the people in the other and in both. But as it was thought that they and the state legislatures might pass laws conflicting with the letter or the spirit of the constitution under which they legislated, it became necessary to make a judicial department for the United States, with a jurisdiction best suited to preserve harmony between the States, severally and collectively, with the national government, and which would give the people of all of the States that confidence and security under it anticipated by them when they announced "that we, the people of the United States, in order to form a more perfect union, establish justice and domestic tranquillity, provide for the common defence, and promote the general welfare, and secure the blessings of liberty to ourselves and our posterity, do ordain this constitution for the United States." Without a judicial department, just such as it is, neither the powers of the constitution nor the purposes for which they were given could have been attained.

We do not know a case more appropriate to show the necessity for such a jurisdiction than that before us.

A citizen of the United States, residing in Connecticut, having a large pecuniary interest in a bank in Ohio, with a board of directors opposed, in fact, to the only course which could be taken to test the constitutional validity of a law of that State bearing upon the franchises of their corporation, is told by the directors, that though they fully concur with him in believing the tax law of Ohio unconstitutional and in no way binding upon the bank, they will not institute legal proceedings to prevent the collection of the tax, "in consideration of the many obstacles in the way of resisting the tax in the state courts." Without partaking, ourselves, in their uncertainty of relief in the courts of Ohio, it must be admitted their declaration was calculated to diminish this suitor's confidence in such a result, and to induce him to resort to the only other tribunal which there was to take cognizance of his cause. Besides, it was not his interest alone which would be affected by the result. Hundreds, citizens of the State of Ohio and citizens of other States, are concerned in the question. Millions of money in that State, and millions upon millions of banking capital in the other States, are to be affected by its judicial decision; all depending upon the assertion, in opposition to the claim of the complainant, that a new constitution of a State supersedes every legislative enactment touching its own internal policy, and bearing upon the interest of persons, which may have been the subject of legislation under a preceding constitution. In the words of the counsel for the defendant, that all such legislation must give way when found to contravene the will of the sovereign people, subsequently expressed in a new state constitution. The assertion may be met and confuted, without further argument, by what was said by Mr. Madison, in the 48d number of The Federalist, upon the 6th article of the constitution, which is: " All debts and engagements entered into before the adoption of this constitution shall be as valid against the United States under this constitution as under the confederation." His remark is, " This can only be considered as a declaratory proposition, and may have been inserted, among other reasons, for the satisfaction of foreign creditors, who cannot be strangers to the pretended doctrine, that a change in the political form of civil society has the magical effect of dissolving its moral obligations."

And here we will cite another passage from the writings of that great statesman, and venerated man by every citizen of the United States who knows how much his political wisdom contributed to the establishment of our American popular institutions. He says, in the 22d number of The Federalist: " A circumstance which shows the defects of the confederation remains to be mentioned, — the want of a judiciary power. Laws are a dead letter without courts to expound and define their true meaning and operation. The treaties of the United States, to have any force at all, must be considered as a part of the law of the land. Their true import, as regards individuals, must, like all other laws, be ascertained by judicial determinations. To produce uniformity in these determinations, they ought to be submitted to a supreme tribunal; and this tribunal ought to be instituted under the same authorities which form the treaties themselves. These ingredients are both indispensable. If there is in each State a court of final jurisdiction, there may be as many different final determinations on the same point as there are courts. There are endless diversities in the opinions of men. We often see not only different courts, but the judges of the same court, differing from each other. To avoid the confusion which would unavoidably result from the contradictory decisions of a number of independent judicatures, all nations have found it necessary to establish one tribunal paramount to the rest, possessing a general superintendence, and authorized to settle and declare in the last resort a uniform rule of civil justice. This is the more necessary where the frame of the government is so compounded that the laws of the whole are in danger of being contravened by the laws of the parts. In this case, if the particular tribunals are invested with a right of ultimate decision, besides the contradictions to be expected from difference of opinion, there will be much to fear from the bias of local views and prejudices, and from the interference of local institutions. As often as such an interference should happen, there would be reason to apprehend that the provisions of the particular laws might be preferred to those of the general laws, from the deference with which men in office naturally look up to that authority to which they owe their official existence."

Hitherto we have shown from the constitution itself that the framers of it meant to provide a jurisdiction for its final interpretation, and for the laws passed by Congress, to give them an equal operation in all of the States.

But there are considerations out of the constitution which contribute to show it, which we will briefly mention. Without such a judicial tribunal there are no means provided by which the conflicting legislation of the States with the constitution and the laws of congress may be terminated, so as to give to either a national operation in each of the States. In such an event no means have been provided for an amicable accommodation; none for a compromise; none for mediation; none for arbitration; none for a congress of the States as a mode of conciliation. The consequence of which would be a permanent diversity of the operation of the constitution in the States, as well in matters exclusively of public concern as in those which secure individual rights. Fortunately it is not so. A supreme tribunal has been provided, which has hitherto, by its decisions, settled all differences which have arisen between the authorities of the States and those of the United States. The legislation under which its appellate power is exercised has been of sixty-seven years' duration, without any countenanced attempt to repeal it. It is rather late to question it; and in continuing to exercise it, this court complies with the decisions of its predecessors, believing, after the fullest examination, that its appellate jurisdiction is given in conformity with the constitution.

The last position taken by the counsel for the defendant, now the appellant here, is, that George C. Dodge was in the discharge of his official duty as treasurer of Cuyahoga county in the State of Ohio, when interrupted by the mandate of the circuit court; that the tax in his hands for collection against the bank was regularly assessed under a valid law of the State, passed April 18, 1852, in conformity with the requisitions of the constitution, adopted June 17, 1851, which took effect 1st September, 1851.

It was admitted, in the argument of it, that the only difference between this case and that of the Piqua Branch of the State of Ohio v. Jacob Knoop, 16 Howard, 369, is, that the latter was a claim for a tax under a law of Ohio, of March 21, 1851, under the former constitution of Ohio, of 1802; and that the tax now claimed is assessed under the act of April 18, 1852, under the new constitution of Ohio.

Both acts, in effect, are the same in their operation upon the charter of the bank, as that was passed by the general assembly of Ohio, in the year 1845. Each of them is intended to collect, by way of tax, a larger sum than the bank was liable to pay, under the charter of 1845. This is admitted. It is not denied, the record shows that the tax assessed for the year 1853 exceeds the sum to which it was liable, under its charter, $11,565$\frac{22}{100}$. The tax assessed is $14,771$\frac{87}{100}$. The tax which it would have paid, under the act of 1845, would have been $8,206$\frac{65}{100}$.

The fact raises the question whether the tax now claimed has not been assessed in violation of the 10th section of the 1st article of the constitution, which declares that no State shall pass any law impairing the obligation of contracts.

The law of 1845 was an agreement with the bank, *quasi ex contractu*, — and also an agreement separately with the share-holders, *quasi ex contractu*, — that neither the bank as such, nor the shareholders as such, should be liable to any other tax larger than that which was to be levied under the 60th section of the act of 1845.

That 60th section is, " that each banking company under the act, on accepting thereof and complying with its provisions, shall semiannually, on the days designated for declaring dividends, set off to the State six per cent on the profits, deducting therefrom the expenses and ascertained losses of the company for the six months next preceding, which sum or amount so set off shall be in lieu of all taxes to which the company, or the stockholders therein, would otherwise be subject. The sum so set off to be paid to the treasurer, on the order of the auditor of the State." The act under which the tax of 1853 has been assessed is: " That the president and cashier of every bank and banking company that shall have been, or may hereafter be, incorporated by the laws of this State, and having the right to issue bills of circulation as money, shall make and return, under oath, to the auditor of the county in which such bank or banking company may be situated, in the month of May annually, a written statement containing, first, the average amount of notes and bills discounted or purchased, which amount shall include all the loans or discounts, whether originally made or renewed during the year aforesaid, or at any previous time, whether made on bills of exchange, notes, bonds, or mortgages, or any other evidence of indebtedness, at their actual cost value in money, whether due previous to, during, or after the period aforesaid, and on which such banking company has at any time reserved or received, or is entitled to receive, any profit or other consideration whatever; and, secondly, the average amount of all other moneys, effects, or dues of every description belonging to the bank or banking company, loaned, invested, or otherwise used with a view to profit, or upon which the bank, &c., receives, or is entitled to receive, interest."

The two acts have been put in connection, that the difference between the modes of taxation may be more obvious; and it will be readily seen, that the second is not intended to tax the profits of the bank, but its entire business, capital, circulation, credits, and debts due to it, being professed to be intended to equalize the tax to be paid by the bank with that required to be paid upon personal property. A careful examination of the two acts, and of the tabular returns annexed to this opinion, will prove that such equality of taxation has not been attained. It will show that the bank is taxed more than three times the number of mills upon the dollars that is assessed upon personal property, whatever may be comprehended under that denomination by the act of the 13th April, 1852. But if it did not, it could make no difference in our conclusion. For the tax to be paid by the bank under the act of 24th February, 1824, is a legislative contract, equally operative upon the State and upon the bank, and the stockholders of the bank, until the expiration of its charter, which will be in 1866. No critical examination of the words, " that on the days designated for declaring dividends, to wit, on the first Monday in May and November of each year, the bank shall set off to the said State of Ohio six per cent on the profits, deducting therefrom the expenses and ascertained losses of said company for six months next preceding each dividend day, and that the sums or amounts so set off shall be in lieu of all taxes to which said company or the stockholders thereof on account of stock owned therein would otherwise be subject," could make them more exact in meaning than they are. The words "would otherwise be subject," relate to the legislative power to tax, and is a relinquishment of it, binding upon that legislature which passed the act, and upon succeeding legislatures as a contract not to tax the bank during its continuance with more than six per cent upon its semiannual profits. A change of constitution cannot release a State from contracts made under a constitution which permits them to be made. The inquiry is, Is the contract permitted by the existing constitution? If so, and that cannot be denied in this case, the sovereignty which ratified it in 1802 was the same sovereignty which made the constitution of 1851, neither having more power than the other to impair a contract made by the state legislature with individuals. The moral obligations never die. If broken by states and nations, though the terms of reproach are not the same with which we are accustomed to designate the faithlessness of individuals, the violation of justice is not the less.

This case is coincident with that of the Piqua Branch of the State Bank of Ohio v. Knoop, 16 How. 369, decided by this court in the year 1853. It rules this in every particular; and to the opinion then given we have nothing to add, nor anything to take away. We affirm the decree of the circuit court, and direct a mandate accordingly.

Mr. Justice CATRON, Mr. Justice DANIEL, and Mr. Justice CAMPBELL dissented.

(No. 1.)

Statement of the Commercial Branch Bank, Cleveland, made to the Auditor of Cuyahoga County, May 25, 1853.

1st. The average amount of notes and bills discounted and purchased by the Commercial Branch Bank of Cleveland, including all loans or discounts whether made or renewed during the year, from May 1st, 1852, to May 1st, 1853, inclusive, is $582,735

2d. The average amount of all other moneys, effects, or dues of every description belonging to said Commercial Branch Bank, loaned, invested, or otherwise used or employed with a view to profit, or upon which said bank received, or was entitled to receive, interest during the above period, was 88,714

Total $671,449

W. A. OTIS, *President.*

F. P. HANDY, *Cashier.*

STATE OF OHIO, *Cuyahoga county, ss.*

CLEVELAND, *May 25,* 1853.

Personally appeared William A. Otis, President, and Freeman P. Handy, Cashier of the Commercial Branch Bank of Cleveland, and made oath that the aforesaid statement is true and correct, according to their best knowledge and belief.

Before me, witness my hand. JOHN T. NEWTON, *Notary Public.*

The following resolutions have been adopted by the directors of this bank : —

Resolved, That in the opinion of the directors of the Commercial Branch Bank of Cleveland, that the act for the assessment and taxation of all property in this State, and for levying taxes thereon according to its true value in money, passed April 13, 1852, so far as it imposes a tax on this bank or banking company, or the listing or valuing of its property different from that required by its charter, without the consent of the corporators, is unconstitutional and void, and is also repugnant to the constitution of the State of Ohio, — which declares that all laws shall be passed taxing by uniform rule all investments in stock or otherwise, and that property employed in banking shall bear a burden of taxation equal to that imposed on the property of individuals; and, again, — that the property of corporations now existing or hereafter created, shall be forever subject to taxation the same as the property of individuals, and therefore creates no legal liability against this bank, and that this bank will not, as at present advised, pay such additional tax unless compelled by law, and hereby enters its protest against its imposition and collection.

Resolved, That the cashier attach a copy of these resolutions, signed by the president and cashier of this bank, to the return of this bank, made under said law. Also file a copy so attested with the treasurer of this county, and transmit a like copy to the

Dodge *v.* Woolsey.

auditor of state, as an evidence of the dissent of this bank from all the provisions of said law, and its determination to rely upon the constitution and legal rights of this bank under its charter.

F. P. HANDY, *Cashier.*

W. A. OTIS, *President.*

COMMERCIAL BRANCH BANK, *Cleveland, May 25,* 1853.

AUDITOR's OFFICE, CUYAHOGA COUNTY,
Cleveland, February 22, 1856.

I hereby certify, that the foregoing is a true copy of the statement of the Commercial Branch Bank, made to the Auditor of Cuyahoga county, May 25, 1853.

WILLIAM FULLER, *County Auditor.*

(No. 2.)

AUDITOR's OFFICE, CUYAHOGA COUNTY,
Cleveland, February 22, 1856.

I hereby certify, that there was entered upon the tax duplicate of this county, for the year 1853, for taxation, in the name of the Commercial Branch Bank of Cleveland, the sum of six hundred seventy-one thousand four hundred and forty-nine dollars, in accordance with the statement of said bank, made to the auditor of said county, May 25, 1853.

And that the amount of taxes assessed thereon in said year, for State, county, city, and road purposes, is fourteen thousand seven hundred and seventy-one dollars eighty seven cents and seven mills, ($14,771 87 7,) as follows.

WILLIAM FULLER, *County Auditor.*

Owners' Names.	Personal property.	Value.— Dolls.	Total taxes on duplicate.	State, county, and city taxes.	Road Tax.
			Dolls. Cts. Ma.	Dolls. Cts. Ma.	Dolls. Cts. M.
Commercial Branch Bank	. . . .	671,449	14,771 87 7	14,234 71 8	537 15 9

Mr. Justice CAMPBELL dissenting.

The following case is made upon the record of this cause:—

The Commercial Bank of Cleveland, Ohio, was organized in 1845, according to the act of the general assembly of February, 1845, for the incorporation of the State Bank of Ohio and other companies, with a capital which was increased in 1848 to $175,000, and placed under the management of five directors.

From its organization until 1851 the taxes of the bank were determined by the 60th section of the act aforesaid, which required the banks semiannually to set off to the State six per cent of the net profits for the six months next preceding, and the sum so set off the act declared should be " in lieu of all taxes to which such company or the stockholders thereof on account of stock owned therein would otherwise be subject." In the year 1851, the general assembly of Ohio altered this rule of taxation, and required that the capital stock, surplus and contingent funds of the banks should be listed for taxation at their money value, and should be assessed for the same purposes and to the same extent that personal property might be in the place of their location.

During the same year the people of Ohio, in the mode prescribed in their fundamental law, adopted a new constitution. One of the articles (art. 12, § 3) requires "the general assembly to provide by law for taxing the notes and bills discounted or purchased, and all other property, effects, dues of every description (without deduction) of all banks now existing or hereafter created, and of all bankers, so that all property employed in banking shall always bear a burden of taxation equal to that imposed on the property of individuals." In 1852, the general assembly fulfilled this direction by a law which required the banks to disclose the average amount of all bills, notes discounted or purchased, and the average amount of their moneys, dues and effects, so as to afford a basis for taxation : and by the same act taxes were directed to be laid upon these amounts without deduction.

The directors, stockholders, and officers of this bank have disputed the validity of these changes in the rule of taxation, as violating a right derived by contract, obligatory on the State, and contained in the 60th section of the act first mentioned, and no voluntary obedience has been rendered to them ; but, on the contrary, the successive measures taken for the collection of these taxes have met with opposition from the corporation, and submission has always been accompanied with a protest on the part of the directors, in which their determination was expressed to rely upon the constitutional and legal rights of the bank.

The taxes for the year 1852 were collected in current bank bills, and the packages were prepared and placed within the reach of the treasurer, who held the duplicate for collection, by the officers of the bank, and immediately after they were assigned by the bank to one Deshler, who replevied the same by a writ from the circuit court of the United States for Ohio, and thus made a case which subsequently came to this court. Deshler *v.* Dodge, 16 How. 622.

In December, 1853, some five days before the taxes were payable, John M. Woolsey, a stockholder of the bank for thirty shares, at the par value of $100 each, addressed the directors of the bank a letter, requiring them "to institute the proper legal proceedings to prevent the collection" of the assessment for that year, averring that the bank was not bound to pay them. The board of directors replied, " that they considered the tax to have been illegally assessed, but in consideration of the many obstacles in the way of resisting said tax in the courts of Ohio they could not take the action they were called upon in the letter to take," but must leave to Mr. Woolsey to take such a course as he might be advised. It sufficiently appears that the treasurer is able to pay any damages which the bank might sustain, and no evidence exists of any indisposition of the directors to meet all the obligations of their station, except what is found in the letter I have described.

This bill was filed by Woolsey, as a stockholder of the bank, against the treasurer of the county of Cuyahoga, the five directors of the bank, and the corporation itself, alleging his apprehensions that the treasurer would proceed to make the collection of the excess above the tax due under the 60th section, and that it would impair the credit of the bank, invade its franchise, and ultimately compel its dissolution; and that the directors had refused to take measures to prevent its collection, on his requisition, and prays for an injunction on the officer to restrain his further proceedings. The circuit court affirmed the bill so as to restrain the collection of all taxes assessed upon the bank, except such as were laid under the act of 1845.

The first inquiry that arises is, Has this court a jurisdiction of the parties to the suit? The case is one of a stockholder of a corporation, bringing the corporation before the courts of United States to redress a corporate wrong in which both are similarly interested. The early decisions of this court on this question would be conclusive against the bill. They require that the plaintiff should be from a State different from all the individual members of the corporation. The chief justice said, that invisible, intangible, and artificial being, that mere legal entity — a corporation aggregate — is certainly not a citizen ; and consequently cannot sue or be sued in the courts of the United States, unless the rights of the members in this respect can be exercised in their corporate name. 5 Cranch, 57, 61, 78; 6 Wheat. 450; 14 Pet. 60.

These cases required that the citizenship of all the corporators should appear on the record, so that the court might be sure that the controversy had arisen between citizens of different States, or citizens of a State and foreign states, citizens or subjects. In Marshall v. Baltimore and Ohio Railroad Co. 16 How. 814, the court relaxed its strictness in reference to this averment, and was satisfied by an allegation of the habitat of the corporation, but still intimated that the national character of the corporators was an essential subject of inquiry in a question of jurisdiction.

The court says: "The persons who act under these faculties and use the corporate name, may be justly presumed to be resident in the State which is the necessary habitat of the corporation, and where alone they can be made subject to suit, and should be estopped in equity from averring a different domicile as against those who are compelled to seek them there, and nowhere else." And again: "The presumption arising from the habitat of a corporation being conclusive of those who use the corporate name and exercise the faculties of it."

This case is one of a corporator suing the corporation of which he is a member, and is the first instance of such a case in the court. He cannot aver against the manifest truth, that all the corporators, himself included, are of a different State from himself, to give the court jurisdiction upon the principle of the earlier cases. And if the doctrine of an equitable estoppel can be applied to a subject where facts, and not arbitrary presumptions, were the only objects of consideration; and if, indeed, the character of the corporator, as a matter of law, is to be assumed to be that of the *situs* of the corporation, then all the corporators, plaintiffs as well as defendants, stand upon this record as citizens of the same State, and this suit cannot be maintained. But if no inquiry into the citizenship of stockholders may be made; if a foreign stockholder, upon the real or affected indifference of a board of directors, or on some imaginary or actual obstacle to relief, arising in the state of opinion in the courts of the State, can draw questions of equitable cognizance into the courts of the United States, in which corporate rights are involved, or evils are threatened or inflicted on corporate property, making the corporation and its managers parties, then a very compendious method of bringing into the courts of the United States all questions in which these artificial beings are concerned has been invented, and the most morbid appetite for jurisdiction among all their various members will be gratified, and upon a class of cases where grave doubts exist whether those who made the constitution ever intended to confer any jurisdiction whatever. Nor can this jurisdiction be supported by affirming that the corporation is not a necessary party to the bill. The subject of the bill is the title of the corporation to an exemption under the act of incorporation, and its object is the protection of corporate franchises and property. The being of the corporation is charged to be an issue involved in the prayer for relief, and the inaction of the directors affords the motive for the suit.

The conduct of the directors was determined in the course of their duty as the governing body of the corporation, under the law of their organization. Their measures and judgments were the acts of the corporation. Whether these were conclusive

31 *

upon the corporators, or whether they might be impeached at
the suit of a single dissenting shareholder; whether the relations
between the State and the corporation were to be settled in a
suit between them or in this suit, are the matters in issue, and
the corporation was an essential party to their adjudication.
The principle of the bill is, that in declining to take effective
measures of prevention — that is, refusing to apply for an injunction — the directors abdicated their controlling powers, and any
stockholder became entitled to intervene for the interests of himself and his associates.   The decree in this cause is not a decree
for the relief of this corporator, but is a decree for the corporation, and does not differ from a decree proper to a case of the
corporation against the treasurer.   It is clear, therefore, that the
corporation was a necessary party to the bill, and so are the adjudged cases.   Bagshaw v. East. Union R. R. Co. 7 Hare, 114;
Cunningham v. Pell, 5 Paige, 607; Rumney v. Monce, Finch R.
334, 336; 1 Danl. Ch. Pr. 251; Charles. Ins. & T. Co. v. Sebring,
5 Rich. Eq. R. 342.

The case is one between a corporator and the corporation, and
the jurisdiction cannot be affirmed unless the court is prepared
to answer the question whether a mere legal entity, an artificial
person, invisible, intangible, can be a citizen of the United States
in the sense in which that word is used in the constitution; and
relying upon the case of Marshall v. The Baltimore and Ohio
Railroad Company, with a long list of antecessors, I am forced
to conclude that it cannot be.

The court has assumed this jurisdiction, and I am therefore
called to inquire whether a court of chancery can take cognizance
of the bill?   The act of incorporation of the bank charges the
board of directors with the care of the corporate affairs, subject
to an annual responsibility to the stockholders.   The principle of
a court of chancery is, to decline any interference with the discretion of such directors, or to regulate their conduct or management in respect to the duties committed to them.

The business of that court is to redress grievances illegally inflicted or threatened, not to supply the prudence, knowledge, or
forecast requisite to successful corporate management.   The facts
of this case involve, in my opinion, merely a question of discretion in the performance of an official duty.   In 1852, the taxes
were withdrawn from the treasurer of Cuyahoga county, by an
assignee of the bank, and were never passed into the State
treasury.   The supreme court of Ohio, subsequently to this,
pronounced the taxes to be legally assessed upon these banks,
and that there was no contract between the State and the banks,
and there was no exemption from the tax by anything apparent
in the act of 1845.   Some of these judgments were pending in

this court upon writs of error then undecided, no judgment having been given contrary to that of the authorities, legislative, executive, and judicial, as well as by the people of Ohio. It was under these conditions that this stockholder, who purchased stock after the controversy had arisen in Ohio, some five days before the taxes were payable, addressed the directors of the Commercial Bank to take preventive measures — that is, I suppose, to file a bill for an injunction instantly — and, upon their suggestion of difficulties, proceeds to take charge of the corporate rights of the bank by this suit, in the circuit court of the United States. The directors were elected annually; they were, collectively, owners of one tenth of the stock of the bank, and no evidence is shown that any other stockholder supposed that "preventive measures," under the circumstances, could be sustained. There is no charge of fraud, collusion, neglect of duty, or of indifference by the directors, save this omission to take some undefined "preventive measures," which the plaintiff affected to suppose might be proper.

I understand the rule of chancery, in reference to such a case, to be that no suit can be maintained by an individual stockholder for a wrong done, or threatened, to such a corporation, unless it appears that the plaintiff has no means of procuring a suit to be instituted in the name of the corporation; and that the rule is universal, applicable, as well to the cases where the acts which afford the ground for complaint were either such as a majority might sanction, or whether it belonged to the category of those acts by which no stockholder could be bound except by his own consent. This principle has the highest sanction in the decisions of that court. (Foss v. Harbottle, 2 Hare, 461 — affirmed 1 Phil. 790; 2 Phil. 740; 7 Hare, 130.) The principle is an obvious consequence from the relations between the officers and members of a chartered corporation, and the corporation itself. These are explained in Smith v. Hurd, 12 Met. 371. The court says: "There is no legal privity, relation, or immediate connection between the holders of shares in a bank in their individual capacity, on the one side, and the directors of the bank on the other. The directors are not the bailers, the factors, agents, or trustees of such individual stockholders. The bank is a corporation and body politic having a separate existence, as a distinct person in law, in whom the whole stock and property of the bank are vested, and to whom all agents, debtors, officers, and servants are responsible for all contracts, express or implied, made in reference to such capital; and for all torts and injuries, diminishing or impairing it." The corporation, therefore, must vindicate its own wrongs, and assert its own rights, in the modes pointed out by law.

I do not say that a court of chancery will never permit an individual stockholder to come before it to assert a right of the corporation in which he is a shareholder, where there is an obstacle of such a nature that the name of the corporation cannot be employed before legitimate tribunals in their regular modes of proceeding, but the burden is thrown upon the plaintiff to establish the existence of an urgent necessity for such a suit.

The consideration of analogous cases will strengthen this conclusion; cases where courts of chancery are more free to intervene, from the fiduciary relations between the parties and the extent of its general jurisdiction over them. Such are cases of danger to the interests of a creditor of an estate from the collusion of an executor with the debtor of the estate, or the insolvency of the executor; or where an executor wrongfully fails to make a settlement with a surviving partner, and a residuary legatee seeks one entire settlement of the estate against the executor and partner; or where a decedent in his life has fraudulently conveyed assets, and his executor is estopped to impute fraud, and there are creditors; or where the managers of a joint-stock company have been guilty of fraud, illegality, waste, and their stockholders desire relief. In all these cases the court of chancery will suffer a party remotely interested to institute the suit which his trustee, or other representative, should have brought, and will grant the relief on that suit which would have been appropriate to the case of him who should have commenced it. Sir John Romilly, in a late case belonging to one of these categories, says:

"To support such a bill as this it is not sufficient to prove that it may be an unpleasant duty to the executors and trustees to take the necessary steps for protecting the property intrusted to them. It is not sufficient to show that it will be for their interests not to take such steps. It is necessary to show that they prefer their own interests to their duty, and that they intend to neglect the performance of the obligation incidental to the office imposed upon them, and which they assumed to perform; or, as said in Travis v. Mylne, that a substantial impediment to the prosecution by the executors of the rights of the parties interested in the estate against the surviving partner exists." Stainton v. Carron Co. 23 L. & Eq. 815; Travis v. Mylne, 9 Hare, 141; Hersey v. Veazie, 11 Shep. 1; Colquitt v. Howard, 11 Geo. 556.

These cases afford no support to this suit. The Cleveland Bank has betrayed no purpose to abandon its corporate duty. The interests and obligations of the directors coincide to support its pretensions. There is no supineness in their past conduct, nor indifference to the existing peril. The evidence, at the most, convicts them only of a present disinclination to commence suits, which were likely to be unproductive, at the request of a single shareholder. The answer shows that the taxes for 1852 had not been recovered by the State, but had been retaken by an assignee of the bank. Nor does the correspondence show that the directors had decided to abandon the contest. The case here does not at all fulfil the conditions on which the interposition of a shareholder is allowable. Elmslie v. McAulay, 3 Bro. C. C. 224, 1 Phil. 790; Law v. Law, 2 Coll. 41; Walker v. Trott, 4 Ed. Ch. R. 38.

But the evidence does not allow me to conclude that any impediment whatever existed to a suit in the name of the corporation, from any disposition of the directors to resist the claims of the State. Their protest appears at every successive stage of the action of the fiscal officers. This suit is evidently maintained with their consent; there has been no appearance either by the directors or the corporation, but they abide the case of the stockholder. The decree is for the benefit of the corporation. The question then is, can a corporation belonging to a State, and whose officers are citizens, upon some hope or assurance that the opinions of the courts of the United States are more favorable to their pretensions, by any combination, contrivance, or agreement with a non-resident shareholder, devolve upon him the right to seek for the redress of corporate grievances, which are the subjects of equitable cognizance in the courts of the United States, by a suit in his own name. In my opinion, there should be but one answer to the question.

I come now to the merits of the case made by the bill.

In the suit of the Piqua Bank v. Knoop, 16 How. 369, I gave the opinion that the act of February, 1845, did not contain a contract obligatory between the State of Ohio and the banking corporations which might be originated by it, in reference to the rule of taxation to be applied to their capital or business. That the act imposed no limit upon the power of the general assembly of the State, but that the rate of taxation established in that act was alterable at their pleasure. To that opinion I now adhere.

But assuming a contract to be collected from the indeterminate expressions of the 60th section of the act, as interpreted by its general objects and the supposed policy of the State, the question is presented, what consequence did the reconstitution of the political system of the State by the people in 1851, and their direction to the legislature to adopt equality as the rule of assessment of taxes upon corporate property, accomplish to the claims of these corporations?

Certainly no greater question — none involving a more elemental or important principle — has ever been submitted to a judicial

tribunal. It involves the operation and efficiency of the fundamental principles on which the American constitutions have
been supposed to rest.

The proposition of this confederacy of some fifty banking corporations, having one fortieth of the property of the State, is,
that by the law of their organization for the whole term of their
corporate being, there exists no power in the government nor
people of Ohio to impair the concessions contained in the act
of 1845, particularly that determining the amount of their contribution to the public revenue. This proposition does not depend for its truth upon the limitation of time imposed upon the
corporate existence of the banks. It would not affect the proposition if the charters were for a century, or in perpetuity. Nor
does the proposition derive strength from the fact that the statute applies only to banking corporations, or corporations confined to a single form of commercial dealing. The proposition
would have had the same degree of accuracy if the act had been
universal, applicable to all private corporations, whether for
manufactures, trade, intercourse, mining, morals, or religion. It
is said by a competent authority, that in the State of Massachusetts there are near twenty-five hundred trading corporations, and
that more than seven tenths of the real and personal property of
that State is held by corporations. The proportion between the
property of corporations and individuals is greater there than in
other States, but the property held by corporations in other States
is large enough to awaken the most earnest attention. A concession of the kind contained in this act, by a careless or a corrupt legislature, for a term or in perpetuity, would impair in
many States their resources to an alarming extent.

Writers upon the condition of the Turkish empire say, that
three fourths of the landed property of the empire is held in
mortmain, as vakuf by mosques or charitable institutions, for
their own use, or in trust for their owners. This property ceases
to contribute to the public revenues, except in a specific form of
certain objectionable taxes on produce, and is inalienable. If held
in trust, it is exempt from forced sales and confiscations, and, on
the death of the owner without children, passes to the mosque
or other charitable trustee. In that empire, the ecclesiastical and
judicial is the dominant interest, for the Ulemas are both priests
and lawyers, just as the corporate moneyed interest is dominant
in Ohio, and in either country that interest claims exemption
from the usual burdens and ordinary legislation of the State.
The judgment of this court would establish the permanent existence of such an incubus upon the resources and growth of that
country, if that interest should have taken their privileges in the
form of a contract, and had such a constitution as ours. Yet the

first step for the regeneration of Turkey, according to the wisest statesmanship, is to abolish the vakuf.

Bentham, treating upon constitutional provisions in favor of contracts, says: "If all contracts were to be observed, all misdeeds would be to be committed, for there is no misdeed the committal of which may not be made the subject of a contract; and to establish in favor of themselves, or of any other person or persons, an absolute despotism, a set of legislators would have no more to do than to enter into any engagement — say with a foreign despot, say with a member of their own community — for this purpose." And were this to happen, should it be that a State of this Union had become the victim of vicious legislation, its property alienated, its powers of taxation renounced in favor of chartered associations, and the resources of the body politic cut off, what remedy has the people against the misgovernment? Under the doctrines of this court none is to be found in the government, and none exists in the inherent powers of the people, if the wrong has taken the form of a contract. The most deliberate and solemn acts of the people would not serve to redress the injustice, and the overreaching speculator upon the facility or corruption of their legislature would be protected by the powers of this court in the profits of his bargain. Where would the people find a remedy? Let the case before us form an illustration. Congress cannot limit the term nor abolish the privileges of these corporations; they are corporations of Ohio, and beyond her limits they have no legal existence; they live in the contemplation of her laws and dwell in the place of their creation. (13 Pet. 512; 16 How. 314.) Nor can congress enlarge the subjects for state taxation, nor interfere in the support of the state government. They could not empower the State to collect taxes from these corporations. Were the resources of the State oppressed with the burden of a Turkish vakuf, congress could not afford relief.

The faculties of the judicial department are even more fatal to the State than the impotence of congress. The courts cannot look to the corruption, the blindness, nor mischievous effects of state legislation, to determine its binding operation. (Fletcher v. Peck, 6 Cr. 87.) The court, therefore, becomes the patron of such legislation, by furnishing motives of incalculable power to the corporations to stimulate it, and affording stability and security to the successful effort. Where, then, is the remedy for the people? They have none in their state government nor in themselves, and the federal government is enlisted by their adversary. It may be that an amendment of the constitution of the United States, by the proposal of two thirds of congress and the ratification of the legislatures of three fourths of the States, might enable the people of Ohio to assess taxes for the support of their government, upon terms of equality among her citizens.

The first observation to be made upon this is, that these extraordinary pretensions of corporations are not unfamiliar to an inquirer into their nature and history. The steady aim of the most thoroughly organized and powerful of the corporate establishments of Europe has ever been to place themselves under the protection of an external authority, superior to the government and people where they dwell — an authority sufficiently powerful to shield them from responsibility and to secure their privileges from question. I do not refer to the claim of kings to passive obedience under a divine title. Ecclesiastical corporations, acknowledging the supremacy of the Pope, afford a case parallel to that before us. I find their principles compendiously declared in an allocution of a minister of Rome to the court of Sardinia, in reference to taxes on church property there. I find that " religious corporations, forming a portion of the ecclesiastical family at large, are by their very nature, under the guardianship and authority of the church; and, consequently, no measure or laws can be adopted with respect to them, except by the spiritual power, or through its agency, especially in what touches their existence or their conduct in the institutions to which they respectively belong; nor can any other rule be recognized, even in matters that concern their property. It is, in truth, beyond dispute that the property possessed by ecclesiastical or religious foundations belongs to the general category of property of the church, and constitutes a true and proper portion of its patrimony. In consequence whereof, as the property of the church is inviolable, so are the possessions of such foundations." Nor was the doctrine of the inviolableness of contracts foreign to these controversies. The sagacious and far-sighted members of the ecclesiastical interests fortified themselves with concordats, and these concordats were affirmed to be " contracts," and, like these, " entail obligations"; and " if the bond of a bargain is to be respected in private life," so they declared " it is sacred and inviolable in the life of States." A slight change of expression will demonstrate that the principle of corporate policy, the dictate of corporate ambition, which has predominated in the contests in Europe, leading to desolating wars, is the same which this court is required to sanction in favor of corporations in the United States. The allocution of the Ohio banks to this court may be thus stated: " That the charters of incorporation granted by the state governments are in their essence and nature ' contracts,' which ' entail obligations '; that, consequently, they are finally under the guardianship and protection of the judiciary establishment of the United States; that no acts of the state legislature which conferred them, in whatever touches their existence, methods of proceeding, or corporate privilege, are binding on them; that, as the state legislatures are agents of the people, whatever they have done in these respects is obligatory upon them, and irrevocable by them, in any form of their action, or in the exercise of any of their sovereign authority; and as the judiciary establishment of the Union is charged with the duty of holding the States and people to their limited orbits, and to afford redress for violated contracts, and to prevent serious resulting damage; and as these corporations cannot sue in the courts of the United States, it is the duty of the court to suffer the corporate wrongs to be redressed in the suit and at the solicitation of any of their stockholders who can appear there — for the state of opinion in the state courts will not allow the hope of redress from them."

The allowance of this plea interposes this court between these corporations and the government and people of Ohio, to which they owe their existence, and by whose laws they derive all their faculties. It will establish on the soil of every State a caste made up of combinations of men for the most part under the most favorable conditions in society, who will habitually look beyond the institutions and the authorities of the State to the central government for the strength and support necessary to maintain them in the enjoyment of their special privileges and exemptions. The consequence will be a new element of alienation and discord between the different classes of society, and the introduction of a fresh cause of disturbance in our distracted political and social system. In the end, the doctrine of this decision may lead to a violent overturn of the whole system of corporate combinations.

Having thus examined the proportions of the doctrine contained in the judgment of the court, I oppose to it a deliberate and earnest dissent.

And, first, as to the claim made for the court to be the final arbiter of these questions of political power, I can imagine no pretension more likely to be fatal to the constitution of the court itself. If this court is to have an office so transcendent as to decide finally the powers of the people over persons and things within the State, a much closer connection and a much more direct responsibility of its members to the people is a necessary condition for the safety of the popular rights. Justice Woodbury, in Luther v. Borden, 7 How. 52, has exposed this danger with great discrimination and force. He said: " Another evil, alarming and little foreseen, involved in regarding these as questions for the final arbitrament of judges, would be, that in such an event all political privileges and rights would in a dispute among the people depend on our decision finally. We would possess the power to decide against them, as well as for them; and, under a prejudiced or arbitrary judiciary, the public liberties or popular privileges might thus be much perverted, if not entirely prostrated. And if the people, in the distribution of powers under the constitution, should ever think of making judges supreme arbiters in political controversies, when not selected by nor amenable to them, nor at liberty to follow the various considerations that belong to political questions in their judgments, they will dethrone themselves, and lose one of their invaluable birthrights, — building up in this way slowly, but surely, a new sovereign power in this republic in most respects irresponsible, unchangeable for life, and one, in theory at least, more dangerous than the worst elective monarchy in the worst of times."

The inquiry recurs, have the people of Ohio deposited with this tribunal the authority to overrule their own judgment upon the extent of their own powers over institutions created by their own government and commorant within the State? The fundamental principle of American constitutions, it seems to me, is, that to the people of the several States belongs the resolution of all questions, whether of regulation, compact, or punitive justice, arising out of the action of their municipal government upon their citizens, or depending upon their constitutions and laws, and are judges of the validity of all acts done by their municipal authorities in the exercise of their sovereign rights, in either case without responsibility or control from any department of the federal government. This I understand to be the import of the municipal sovereignty of the people within the State.

In 1802, the inhabitants of Ohio were released from their pupilage to the federal authority, placed in full possession of their rights to self-government, and were invited to adapt their institutions to the federal system, of which the State, when formed, was authorized to become a member.

The people of Ohio, by their state constitution, reserved to themselves "complete power" to "alter, reform, and abolish their government"; "to petition for redress of grievances"; and to "recur, as often as might be necessary, to the first principles of government." It was by a constitution adopted according to established forms, and expressive of the sovereign will of the body politic, that the rule of taxation complained of in this suit was prescribed.

The inquiry arises, to what did the authority of the people extend? It was their right to ameliorate every vicious institution, and to do whatever an enlightened statesmanship might prescribe for the advancement of their own happiness; and for this end, persons and things in the State were submitted to their authority. A material distinction has always been acknowledged to exist as to the degrees of the authority that a people could legitimately exert over persons and corporations. Individuals are not the creatures of the State, but constitute it. They come into society with rights, which cannot be invaded without injustice. But corporations derive their existence from the society, are the offspring of transitory conditions of the State; and, with faculties for good in such conditions, combine durable dispositions for evil. They display a love of power, a preference for corporate interests to moral or political principles or public duties, and an antagonism to individual freedom, which have marked them as objects of jealousy in every epoch of their history. Therefore, the power has been exercised, in all civilized States, to limit their privileges, or to suppress their existence, under the exigencies either of public policy or political necessity.

Sir James McIntosh says: " Property is indeed, in some sense, created by act of the public will, but it is by one of those fundamental acts which constitute society. Theory proves it to be essential to the social state. Experience proves that it has, in some degree, existed in every age and nation of the world. But those public acts, which form and endow corporations, are subsequent and subordinate. They are only ordinary expedients of legislation. The property of individuals is established on a general principle, which seems coeval with civil society itself. But bodies are instruments fabricated by the legislature for a specific purpose, which ought to be preserved while they are beneficial, amended when they are impaired, and rejected when they become useless or injurious." Vind. Gal. 48, note.

Who, in the United States, is to determine when the public interests demand the suppression of bodies whose existence or modes of action are contrary to the well-being of the state?

If the powers of the people of a State are inadequate to this object, then their grave and solemn declarations of their rights and their authority over their governments, and of the ends for which their governments and the institutions of their governments were framed, and the responsibility of rulers and magistrates to themselves, are nothing but " great swelling words of vanity."

But not only is the jurisdiction of Ohio " complete " over the public institutions of her government, but the subject-matter upon which their will was expressed in their constitution was independently of their control over the corporations, one over which their jurisdiction was plenary. They declared in what manner property held within the State by these artificial bodies should contribute to the public support, in the form of regular and apportioned taxation. When the constitution of the United States was before the people of the States for their ratification, they were told, that, with the exception of duties on exports and imports, the States retained " an independent and uncontrollable authority " to " raise their own revenue in the most absolute and unqualified sense "; and that any attempt, on the part of the federal government, to abridge them in the exercise of it, would be " a violent assumption of power unwarranted by any clause of the constitution." (Fed. 168, by Hamilton.) And the opinions of this court are filled with disclaimers on the same subject. 4 Wheat. 429.

The true principle, therefore, would seem to be, that if there was any conflict in the tax laws of the State, and a supposed contract of its legislative or executive agents with one of its citizens, it would be for the State to harmonize the two upon principles of general equity; but in no condition of facts for the judiciary department to interfere with state affairs by writs of replevin or injunction. The acknowledgment of such a power would be to establish the alarming doctrine that the empire of Ohio, and the remaining States of the Union, over their revenues, is not to be found in their people, but in the numerical majority of the judges of this court.

In the opinion I gave in the case of the Piqua Bank, I exhibited evidence that the care of the public domain, whether consisting of crown lands or of taxes on property, belonged to the sovereign power of the State, and that improvident alienations by the crown were, from time to time, set aside by the parliament of Great Britain under the dictates of a public policy. Twelve acts of parliament are cited by Sir William Davenant of this character, and having this object. Davenant, Grants and Res. 244.

A similar condition existed in France. The kings were bound, by their coronation oath, " to maintain and preserve the public domain with all their power," and it was an inviolable maxim, that it could not be alienated, except in specified cases determined in the fundamental laws of the monarchy. This legal result was declared by the national assembly in 1790, to the effect that the public domain, with all its accretions, belonged to the nation; that this property is the most perfect that can be imagined, since there exists no superior power that can restrain or modify it; that the power to alienate — the essential attribute of property — exists in the nation; that every appropriation of the public domain is essentially revocable, if made without the consent of the nation; that it preserves over the property alienated the same right and authority as if it had remained under its control; and that this principle was one which no lapse of time nor legal formality could evade. All grants, therefore, of the public rights, and especially those partaking of the nature of taxes, or subsidies, such as fines, confiscations, and stamps, were revoked, because the subject was not alienable. 8 Merlin Rep., tit. Dom. Pub.; 1 Proud., Dom. Pub. 62.

If the power to review the illegal or improvident acts of a monarch, by which the domain and patrimony of the crown (one of the principal sinews of the state, as they are termed in the ordinances) was dilapidated or impoverished, in the nearly absolute monarchies of Europe, was reserved to the nation, it would seem to follow that in the American States, where so little has been conceded to the government, and whose "complete power" to amend or abrogate is so distinctly reserved that no inference nor implication can arise, that the same has been relinquished or abdicated. My conclusion is, that the constitution of Ohio, whether it is to be regarded as the expression of the sovereign will of the people, that the extraordinary exemptions granted to these corporations, by which they contribute unequally to the public support, is contrary to the genius of their institutions; or whether they are inconsistent with a just apportionment of the public burdens; or whether, as a declaration of the exigency of the State, requiring an additional contribution from them to its revenue; or a judgment of condemnation of the former government for an abuse of the powers it enjoyed; that it is above and beyond the supervision or control of the judiciary department of this government.

Nor does the opinion, that this department can exert such an empire over the people of Ohio, derive support, in my opinion, from the clause in the constitution on the subject of the obligation of contracts, nor the decisions of this court upon that clause of the constitution.

That the people of the States should have released their powers over the artificial bodies which originate under the legislation of their representatives, or over the improvident charges or concessions imposed by them upon its revenues, or over the acts of their own functionaries, is not to be assumed. Such a surrender was not essential to any policy of the Union, nor required by any confederate obligation. Such an abandonment could have served no other interest than that of the corporations, or individuals who might profit by the legislative acts themselves. Combinations of classes in society, united by the bond of a corporate spirit, for the accumulation of power, influence, or wealth, by the control of intercourse or trade, or the spiritual or moral concerns of society, unquestionably desire limitations upon the sovereignty

32 *

of the people, and the existence of an authority upon which they can repose in security and confidence. But the framers of the constitution were imbued with no desire to call into existence such combinations, nor dread of the sovereignty of the people. They denied to congress the power to create, (3 Mad. Deb. 1576,) and the most salutary jealousy was expressed in reference to them. The people of the States, during the existence of the confederation, suffered from the violation of private property by their governments. In reconstituting their political system, they abstained from delegating to the United States the powers to emit bills of credit; to make anything but gold and silver a tender in the payment of debts; to pass any bill of attainder or *ex post facto* law, or law to impair the obligation of contracts, except so far as necessary to a uniform law of bankruptcy; while they protected property from unreasonable searches and seizures, and the title from detriment, except in the due course of legal proceeding.

The state governments were prohibited from any corresponding legislation, either by their federal or state constitutions.

The power to interfere with private contracts is one of the most delicate and difficult, in its exercise, of any belonging to the social system, and one which there is constant temptation to abuse. That its exercise is sometimes necessary is proved by the history of every civilized State. Its judicious exercise constitutes the titles of Solon and Sully to fame, and has been vindicated by the most enlightened statesmen. But the people reserved to themselves to determine the exigencies which should call it into existence. The prohibition is a limitation upon the ordinary government, and not upon the popular sovereignty. In Fletcher v. Peck, 6 Cr. 87, the chief justice doubted whether the repeal of a grant, issued under a legislative act by the executive of a State, was within the competence of the legislative authority; and notices the distinction between acts of legislation and sovereignty, and treats the clause of the constitution under consideration as an inhibition on legislation. In Dartmouth College v. Woodward, 4 Wheat. 518, 558, Mr. Webster presents the distinction with prominence in his argument. He says: "It is not too much to assert that the legislature of New Hampshire would not have been competent to pass the acts in question, and make them binding on the plaintiffs, without their assent, even if there had been in the constitution of the United States, or of New Hampshire, no special restriction on their power, because these acts are not the exercise of a power properly legislative. . . . . The British Parliament could not have annulled or revoked this grant as an ordinary act of legislation. If it had done it at all, it could only have been in virtue of that sovereign power called omnipotent, which does not belong to any legislature of the United States. The legislature of New Hampshire has the same power over the charter which belonged to the king who granted it, and no more. By the law of England, the power to grant corporations is a part of the royal prerogative. By the revolution, this power may be considered as having devolved on the legislature of the State, and it has been accordingly exercised by the legislature. But the king cannot abolish a corporation, or new-model it, or alter its powers, without its assent." . . . .

Chief Justice Marshall, in describing the jurisdiction of the court over such contracts, says, it belongs to it "the duty of protecting from legislative violation those contracts which the constitution of the country has placed beyond legislative control." And, in defining the object and extent of the prohibition, he says: "Before the formation of the constitution, a course of legislation had prevailed in many, if not in all the States, which weakened the confidence of man in man, and embarrassed all transactions between individuals by dispensing with a faithful performance of engagements. To correct this mischief by restraining the power which produced it, the state legislatures were forbidden to pass any law impairing the obligation of contracts; that is, of contracts respecting property under which some individual could claim a right to something beneficial to himself." These selections from opinions delivered in this court, which have carried the prerogative jurisdiction of the court to its farthest limit, and portions of which are not easily reconciled with a long series of cases subsequently decided, (Satterlee v. Matthewson, 2 Pet. 380; Charles River Bridge, 11 Pet. 420; West River Bridge v. Dix, 6 How. 507, 8 How. 569, 10 How. 511,) show with clearness that this court has not, till now, impugned the sovereignty of the people of a State over these artificial bodies called into existence by their own legislatures.

I have thus given the reasons for the opinion that the constitution of Ohio and the acts of her government, done by its special authority and direction, are valid dispositions. It is no part of my jurisdiction to inquire whether these public acts of the people and the State were just or equitable. Those questions belong entirely to themselves.

It may be that the people may abuse the powers with which they are invested, and, even in correcting the abuses of their government, may not in every case act with wisdom and circumspection.

But, for my part, when I consider the justice, moderation, the restraints upon arbitrary power, the stability of social order, the security of personal rights, and general harmony which existed in the country before the sovereignty of governments was asserted, and when the sovereignty of the people was a living and operative principle, and governments were administered subject to the limitations and with reference to the specific ends for which they were organized, and their members recognized their responsibility and dependence, I feel no anxiety nor apprehension in leaving to the people of Ohio a "complete power" over their government, and all the institutions and establishments it has called into existence. My conclusion is, that the decree of the circuit court of Ohio is erroneous, and that the judgment of this court should be to reverse that decree and to dismiss the bill of the plaintiff.

Mr. Justice DANIEL:

"I concur entirely in the preceding opinion of my brother Campbell."

Mr. Justice CATRON:

"I also dissent, and concur with the conclusions of the opinion just read."

THE MECHANICS' AND TRADERS' BANK, BRANCH OF THE STATE BANK OF OHIO, PLAINTIFFS IN ERROR, *v.* HENRY DEBOLT, LATE TREASURER OF HAMILTON COUNTY.

The decision in the preceding case of Dodge *v.* Woolsey again affirmed.

THIS case was brought up from the supreme court of the State of Ohio, by a writ of error, issued under the 25th section of the judiciary act.

It originated in the court of common pleas in the county of Hamilton and State of Ohio, and was an action brought by the bank against Debolt, the nature of which is explained in the following agreed case.

The parties above named hereby agree upon the following facts, upon which a controversy depends between them, and submit the case to the court of common pleas for determination and judgment, in pursuance of section four hundred and ninety-five of the code of civil procedure:—

It is agreed that the plaintiff is a duly authorized banking company, under the act passed by the general assembly of the State of Ohio, on the 24th day of February, 1845, entitled, "An Act to incorporate the State Bank of Ohio, and other banking companies," which act is made a part of this case; that at the foundation thereof, on the 30th day of June, 1845, it assumed to itself a capital of $100,000, and elected to be a branch of the State Bank of Ohio, and, as such branch, has, from the said time of its organization under said act to the present time, carried on the business of banking in the city of Cincinnati.

It is further agreed that the sixtieth section of the said act is in the words following, namely: "Each banking company organized under this act, or accepting thereof and complying with its provisions, shall, semiannually, on the days designated in the fifty-ninth section for declaring dividends, set off to the State six per centum on the profits, deducting therefrom the expenses and ascertained losses of the company for the six months next preceding, which sum or amount so set off shall be in lieu of all taxes to which said company, or the stockholders thereof, on account of stock owned therein, could otherwise be subject; and the cashier shall, within ten days thereafter, inform the auditor of state of the amount so set off, and shall pay the same to the treasurer of state on the order of said auditor; but in computing the profits of the company, for the purposes aforesaid, the interest received on the funded debt of this State, held by the company, or deposited with and transferred to the treasurer of State, or to the board of control, by such company, shall not be taken into account"; and it is further agreed, that the days named in the fifty-ninth section of said act, and referred to in the said sixtieth section, are the first Monday in May and the first Monday in November.

It is further agreed, that on the first Monday in May, 1851, the said bank did set off to the State, according to the provisions of said section, the sum of $195.65; and on the first Monday in November of the same year, the further sum of $241.72; and it is agreed that the said sums so set off were in fact six per centum upon the profits of said bank during the half years then respectively expiring, after deducting, according to the provisions of said sixtieth section, the expenses and ascertained losses of the said company for the said periods respectively.

It is further agreed, that the auditor of State did, subsequently, direct the said amounts to be paid to the treasurer of State, and that the said order was presented to and paid by the plaintiff on the twenty-fifth day of November, in the year 1851.

It is further agreed, that subsequent to the said payment to the treasurer of State, upon said order of the auditor of State, the auditor of Hamilton County proceeded to list the capital stock of said bank, and its surplus and contingent fund, upon the tax-list of said county, at the sum of $102,462, and added to the said assessment a penalty of fifty per centum, and charged upon the said sums, amounting in all to $158,092, a tax of $2,296.88, being at the rate of   mills on the dollar.

It is further agreed, that on the 22d day of March, 1854, the said Henry Debolt, treasurer aforesaid, did forcibly, and against the consent and protest of the plaintiff, take from the plaintiff the said tax of $2,296.88, together with the further sum of $114.82, being a penalty of five per centum thereon, making in all the sum of $2,411.20.

It is further agreed, that the said proceedings of said treasurer of Hamilton County, and of said county auditor, were taken in accordance with the provisions of an act of the general assembly of the State of Ohio, passed on the 21st day of March, in the year 1851, entitled "An Act to tax banks and bank and other stocks, the same as other property is now taxable by the laws of this State"; and it is agreed, that the first section of the said act is in the words following, namely: —

"That it shall be the duty of the president and cashier of each and every banking institution incorporated by the laws of this State, and having the right to issue bills or notes for circulation, at the time for listing personal property under the laws of this State, to list the capital stock of such banking institution, under oath, at its true value in money, and return the same, with the amount of surplus and contingent fund belonging to said banking institution, to the assessor of the township or ward in which such banking institution is located, and the amount so returned shall be placed on the grand duplicate of the proper county, and upon the city duplicate for city taxes, in cases where such city tax does not go upon the grand duplicate, but is collected by the city officers, and taxed for the same purposes and to the same extent that personal property is or may be required to be taxed in the place where such bank is located; and such tax shall be collected and paid over in the same manner that taxes on other personal property are required by law to be collected and paid over. Provided, however, that the capital stock of any bank shall not be returned or taxed for a less amount than its capital stock paid in."

It is further agreed that the plaintiff, the said Mechanics' and Traders' Bank, has never accepted the said act, nor any part of the said act passed on the twenty-first day of March, 1851, as an amendment to the charter of said bank, nor in any way assented to the same as a valid law, so far as the said act related to the said bank, and to the listing of the capital stock and surplus, and contingent fund of said bank, and to the payment of any tax thereon, different from the tax provided for in the said sixtieth section of the said act passed on the 24th day of February, 1845; and it is agreed that the said first section of the said act passed on the 21st day of March, 1851, does provide for a tax different from the tax prescribed by the said sixtieth section of the act passed on the 24th of February, 1845.

The controversy between the parties depends upon the following questions, namely: whether the act passed on the 21st day of March, in the year 1851, entitled "An Act to tax banks and bank and other stocks, the same as other property is now taxable by the laws of this State," is contrary to the constitution of the United States, so far as the said act relates to the said Mechanics' and Traders' Bank, imposes upon the said bank any tax. If the court shall determine this question in the affirmative, then judgment is to be entered in favor of the plaintiff against the said defendant, for the sum of $ 2,411.20, with interest from the 22d day of March, in the year 1854. If the court shall decide the said question in the negative, then judgment is to be entered against the plaintiff for costs. It is agreed that all other questions are waived, and that the judgment to be entered herein shall be subject to review and reversal as in other cases.

Upon this state of facts, the court of common pleas rendered a judgment in favor of the defendant, and gave a certificate that the controversy depended upon the question whether the act passed by the general assembly of Ohio on the 21st of March, 1851, was contrary to the constitution of the United States, so far as the said act related to the Mechanics' and Traders' Bank. The certificate further stated that the supreme court of Ohio decided the said act to be valid, and not contrary to the constitution.

A writ of error brought this judgment before this court for review.

Mr. Stanberry, for the plaintiff in error, and *Mr. Pugh*, for the defendant in error, considered that all the questions which arose in this case had been fully argued in the preceding case of Woolsey v. Dodge.

Mr. Perry filed a brief for the plaintiff in error, entering into an elaborate examination of the points in the case.

Mr. Justice WAYNE delivered the opinion of the court.

Upon our examination of the agreed statement in this case, we find that it is ruled by the cases of The Piqua Branch of the State Bank of Ohio v. Knoop, 16 How. 369, and that of Dodge v. Woolsey, decided at this term. We therefore reverse the decree of the supreme court, and direct a mandate to issue accordingly.

Mr. Justice CATRON, Mr. Justice DANIEL, and Mr. Justice CAMPBELL, dissented.

THE MECHANICS' AND TRADERS' BANK, BRANCH OF THE STATE
BANK OF OHIO, PLAINTIFF IN ERROR, v. CHARLES THOMAS,
TREASURER OF HAMILTON COUNTY.

The decision in the preceding case of Woolsey v. Dodge, again affirmed.

THIS case, like the preceding, was brought up from the supreme court of the State of Ohio, by a writ of error, issued under
the 25th section of the judiciary act.

It originated in the court of common pleas for Hamilton
County, and contained an agreed statement of facts similar to
that in the preceding case, with the following exceptions, after
stating the profits of the bank as follows, namely: —

	Profits.	Tax under § 60.
From May, 1852, to Nov., 1852,	$4,476.08	$268.46
" Nov., 1852, to May, 1858,	5,861.52	321.69
" May, 1858, to Nov., 1858,	4,860.19	291.61

The auditor of Hamilton County listed the bank for taxation as
follows: —

	Assessment.	Tax.
September 1, 1852,	$414,088	$6,832.45 $\frac{2}{10}$.
September 1, 1853,	712,315	13,177.32 $\frac{3}{10}$.

The agreed statement of facts contained also the following: —

If the court shall determine this question in the affirmative,
then judgment is to be entered in favor of the plaintiff against
the said defendant, for the sum of twenty thousand one hundred
and twenty-eight dollars and thirty cents, (20,128 $\frac{30}{100}$ dols.,)
with interest from the twenty-second day of March, in the year
eighteen hundred and fifty-four.

If the court shall decide the said question in the negative, then
judgment is to be entered against the plaintiff for costs.

It is agreed that all other questions are waived, and that the
judgment to be entered herein, in the court of common pleas,
shall be subject to review and reversal as in other cases.

MECHANICS' AND TRADERS' BANK,
By C. E. NOURSE, Cashier.
CHARLES THOMAS, Treas. Hamilton Co.

The court of common pleas gave judgment for the defendant,
which was affirmed by the supreme court of Ohio.

This case involved a question which did not exist in the preceding one; namely, whether the constitution adopted by Ohio

in September, 1851, had any legal effect upon the contract between the State and the bank contained in the sixtieth section of the Bank Law of February, 1845.

Mr. Stanberry, for the plaintiff in error, and *Mr. Pugh*, for the defendant in error, considered that all the questions which arose in this case were fully argued in the case of Woolsey *v.* Dodge. Mr. Perry filed a brief for the plaintiff in error.

Mr. Justice WAYNE delivered the opinion of the court.

We find upon the agreed statement of facts in this case, that it is ruled by the decision of the court in the cases of the Piqua Branch of the State Bank of Ohio *v.* Knoop, 16 Howard, 369, and that of Dodge *v.* Woolsey, decided at this term. We therefore reverse the decision of the supreme court of Ohio, and direct a mandate to be issued accordingly.

Mr. Justice CATRON, Mr. Justice DANIEL, and Mr. Justice CAMPBELL dissented.

JOSEPH WILKINS, TENANT, AND FRANCIS G. BAILEY, JOSEPH PEACOCK, AND SAMUEL BAILEY, EXECUTORS OF MICHAEL ALLEN, DECEASED, PLAINTIFFS IN ERROR, *v.* DAVID ALLEN, MARTHA ALLEN, CATHERINE ALLEN, AND ISABELLA ALLEN.

Where a testator, in Pennsylvania, gave to his wife a life estate in the homestead and two lots, and charged upon his goods and lands an annuity to her, but did not mention his lands in any other part of the will, and then, after sundry legacies bequeathed the surplus to be applied to the purposes of the Presbyterian church, this surplus does not relate to his lands, which his heirs will take.

By the law of Pennsylvania, heirs must take, unless they are disinherited by express words or necessary implication.

Evidence of extrinsic circumstances, such as the amount and condition of the estate, &c., cannot be received to control the interpretation of the will. It is only admissible to explain ambiguities arising out of extrinsic circumstances.

THIS case was brought up, by writ of error, from the circuit court of the United States for the western district of Pennsylvania.

It was an ejectment brought by the Allens, who were aliens and subjects of the Queen of Great Britain and Ireland, to recover four undivided fifth parts of one undivided half of a lot in Pittsburg. They were heirs of Michael Allen, and the question was, whether Allen, the testator, had devised the property in question by his will.

The substance of the will is given in the opinion of the court, as are also the rulings of the circuit court.

It was argued by *Mr. Williams*, for the plaintiffs in error, and by *Mr. Loomis* and *Mr. Stanton*, for the defendants.

The points made by *Mr. Williams* are thus stated in his brief: The case presents two questions only: —

1st. Whether the terms of the will are sufficient, *proprio vigore*, and interpreting the same by the context, to carry the real estate to the executors; and,

2d. Whether the interpretation thereof may not be aided, if necessary, by extrinsic circumstances, to wit: memoranda, declarations, and the actual amount and condition of the estate, as offered to be shown by the defendants.

On the first of these questions, and for the purpose of showing that the intention (which is only another name for the will) of the testator, is the great point of inquiry, and must be collected from the whole writing, and every word and sentence thereof; and that to serve it, words may be used either in the technical or general sense, and even supplied, transposed, or changed, the counsel for the plaintiffs in error will refer to the cases of Ruston *v.* Ruston, 2 Dall. 244; Findlay *v.* Riddle, 3 Binn. 149; Lynn *v.* Downes, 1 Yeates, 518; Beltzhoover *v.* Costen, 7 Barr, 16; Turbett *v.* Turbett, 3 Yeates, 187; Hunter's estate, 6 Barr, 97; Earp's Will, 1 Par. 457; Den *v.* Blackwell, 3 Green, 386; Den *v.* McMurtrie, Ib. 276; 1 Jarman on Wills, chap. xvii., and cases there cited.

That, as a consequence of the foregoing rules, real estate may pass under a devise by any form of expression not properly and technically descriptive thereof, if such an intent can be collected from the context — that general expressions may be restrained and special expressions enlarged, and the same words sometimes understood in one sense, and sometimes in another, will be shown in the cases of Huxtep *v.* Brooman, 1 Brown C. C. 437; Taylor *v.* Webb, 2 Sid. 75; Pitman *v.* Stevens, 15 East, 505; Wilce *v.* Wilce, 5 Moore & Payne, 682; Tolar *v.* Tolar, 3 Hawks, 74; Hope *v.* Taylor, 1 Bur. 268; Doe *v.* White, 1 East, 33; Den *v.* Trout, 15 East, 394; King *v.* Shrives, 4 Moore & Scott, 149; Anon. 3 Dale, 477; Jackson *v.* Housel, 17 Johns. 281; Ferguson *v.* Zepp. 4 W. C. C. R. 645; Hogan *v.* Jackson, Cowper, 299; Marchant *v.* Twisden, Gilb. Eq. Ca. 30; Wilkinson *v.* Merryland, Cro. Car. 447, 449; Cliffe *v.* Gibbons, 2 Ld. Raym. 1324; Bullard *v.* Goffe, 20 Pick. 252; Doe *v.* Rout, 7 Taunt. 79; Woolham *v.* Kenworthy, 9 Ves. 137; Timewell *v.* Perkins, 2 Atk. 102; Roe *v.* Yeud, 2 B. & P. (N. R.) 214.

That the circumstance of a previous specific devise of land, always favors the extension of the subsequent general words to property of the same description, although even the absence of that circumstamce is not considered as conclusive against it, even when the subsequent terms are associated with words descriptive of personal property only. 1 Jarman on Wills, 575.

That the word "surplus" and its equivalents, without more, may operate by reference, to carry either realty or personalty, or both, he will refer particularly to the cases of Bebb v. Penoyre, 11 East, 160; and Dewey v. Morgan, 18 Pick. 295.

That the interpretation of the testator's language is to be made with reference to the law and usages of the place of his actual domicile, 2 Greenl. Ev. § 671; Story's Confl. of Laws, § 479, f.; Harrison v. Nixon, 9 Pet. 483; and that, by the law of Pennsylvania, the whole interest of a testator passes without words of inheritance or perpetuity, unless a different intent appear; act of 8th April, 1833, § 9 (Ph. L. 249;) Purdon's Dig. 844; that real estate is assets for the payment of debts and legacies are chargeable on lands where the personalty is insufficient to meet them; Nichols v. Postlethwaite, 2 Dall. 131; English v. Harvey, 2 Rawle, 309; and that, therefore, the habit of treating both as equally a fund to pay any demand, would n t probably be forgotten by a testator when making his will. Ib.

On the second and last of the questions proposed, namely, whether the construction may be aided by proof of extrinsic circumstances, the counsel for the plaintiff,

To show that the court may and ought to put themselves in the place of the testator, by looking into the state of his property, and the circumstances by which he was actually surrounded, will refer to 1 Greenl. Ev. §§ 287, 288, 289, & 290, and notes; Ruston v. Ruston, *Supra* (2 Dall. 244); Brownfield v. Brownfield, 8 Har. 59; Root v. Stuyvesant, 18 Wend. 257; Jarvis v. Buttrick, 1 Met. 480; Morton v. Perry, Ib. 446; Fox v. Phelps, 17 Wend. 393; Wigram on Wills, 5th proposition, page 5, and cases cited in illustration thereof.

That when words, used in their strict and primary sense, are insensible, with reference to extrinsic circumstances, the court may look to those circumstances to see whether the meaning would be sensible in any popular or secondary sense, of which, with reference to those circumstances, they are capable, (third proposition, Wigram on Wills,) and that even without reference to such distinction, the court may look into the facts, where the construction claimed would render the devise or bequest inoperative. Smith v. Smith, 1 Edw. Ch. 189; Whilden v. Whilden, Riley's Ch. 205; Trustees v. Peaslee, 15 N. H. 317; Kinsey v. Rhem, 2 Iredell, 192; Ayres v. Weed, 16 Conn. 291; Hand v.

Hoffman, 3 Halstead, 71; Allen *v.* Lyons, 2 Wash. C. C. R. 475, and cases cited of misnomer and misdescription generally. And that even the declarations of the testator, to prove a fact collateral to the question of intention in aid of the interpretation of words, may be admitted in evidence. 1 Greenl. Ev. § 291 and note; Trustees *v.* Peaslee, 15 N. H. 317; Ryerss *v.* Wheeler, 22 Wend. 148.

The plaintiffs' counsel will, moreover, in aid of the offer of evidence to show the inadequacy of the personal estate to satisfy the previous legacies, insist on the assertion of the substantive fact of a "considerable surplus," by the testator himself, which was only true upon the hypothesis that he did include real estate, in his estimate and devise, as necessitating a reference to the actual condition of his affairs at the time of making his will, for the purpose of showing that there was no such property as he is supposed to have intended by the word "surplus," while there was property answering the description of a surplus upon which the will might operate.

In further support of the proposition that the construction of the will in question may be aided and controlled by the proof of extrinsic facts and circumstances, the counsel for the plaintiffs in error will refer also to 1 Jarm. on Wills, 355, and note 1; Wilde's case, 6 Rep. 17; Roper, 60, 67 (3d ed.); Cartwright *v.* Vawdry, 5 Ves. 530; Lord Woodhouselee *v.* Dalrymple, 2 Mer. 419; Rose *v.* Bartlett, Cro. Car. 293; Davis *v.* Gibbs, 8 P. Wms. 26; Knottsford *v.* Gardiner, 2 Atk. 450; Thompson *v.* Lawley, 2 B. & P. 403; Day *v.* Trig, 1 P. Wms. 286; Fonnereau *v.* Poyntz, 1 Bro. C. C. 472; Druce *v.* Dennison, 6 Ves. 397; Finch *v.* Inglis, 3 Bro. C. C. 420; Attorney-General *v.* Grote, 3 Mer. 316; Colpoys *v.* Colpoys, Jac. 463; Smith *v.* d. Doe Jersey, 2 Brod. & Bingh. 553; Jeacock *v.* Falconer, 1 Bro. C. C. 296; Selwood *v.* Mildmay, 3 Ves. 306; Doe d. Belasyse *v.* Lucan, 9 East, 488; Attorney-General *v.* Vigor, 8 Ves. 256; Standen *v.* Standen, 2 Ves. 589; 3 Kent, 384, 385; Lowe *v.* Lord Huntingtower, 4 Russ. 532; 8 Rep. 155; Rewalt *v.* Ulrich, 11 Har. 388.

The points made by *Mr. Loomis* and *Mr. Stanton* were the following :—

1. In the disposition, by the will of Michael Allen, of the surplus remaining after the payment of all claims and bequests, there is neither doubt, uncertainty, nor ambiguity.

2. If that disposition be doubtful or uncertain, it must receive appropriate construction from the words of the will itself, and no parol proof or declaration ought to be admitted out of the will to ascertain it. Bradford *v.* Bradford, 6 Wharton, 244;

Weatherhead's Lessee *v.* Baskerville et al. 11 How. 357, 358, 359; Murrell *v.* Livermore, 7 Eng. Com. Law, 9; 5 Barn. & Ald. 18.

8. In determining such construction, the heir at law is not, and especially those standing in the place of the common-law heir are not, to be disinherited, except by express devise, or by implication so inevitable that an intention to the contrary cannot be supposed. 1 Powell on Devises, 199; French *v.* M'Ilhenny, 2 Binney's Rep. 20; Clayton *v.* Clayton, 3 Binney's Rep. 484; Brown *v.* Dysinger et al. 1 Rawle, 415; Finley *v.* King's Lessee, 3 Pet. 379; Bradford *v.* Bradford, 6 Wharton, 244; Doe on dem. Spearing *v.* Buckner, 6 Term Rep. 611, 612, 613; Hayden *v.* Stoughton, 5 Pick. 536; Roosevelt *v.* Heirs of Fulton, 7 Cowen, 79, 187; Roper on Wills, 352, 358.

4. The application of the principles embraced in the last two points to the construction of the disposition before mentioned, will show clearly and conclusively that the title of the heirs of the testator to the real estate, of which he died seised, has not been thereby devested.

5. Parol evidence cannot be adduced to contradict, add to, or explain the contents of a will. Parol evidence of the actual intention of a testator is inadmissible for the purpose of controlling or influencing the construction of the written will. No word or phrase in the will can be diverted from its appropriate subject or object by extrinsic evidence. Wigram on Wills, 1st and 2d Rules; Ib. 24, 27, 80, 81, 82, 88–92, 96, 130; 1 Jarman on Wills, c. 14, pp. 349, 358; 11 How. 357, 358, 359; Farrar *v.* Ayres, 5 Pick. 409; Barrett *v.* Wright, 13 Pick. 48; Mann *v.* Mann, 14 Johns. 9, 14; S. C. 1 Johns. Ch. 231.

6. There is but one case in which parol evidence of intention can properly be admitted, and that is where the meaning of the testator's words is neither ambiguous nor obscure, and where the devise is, on the face of it, perfect and intelligible; but from some of the circumstances admitted in proof, an ambiguity arises as to which of the two or more things, or which of the two or more persons, (each answering the words in the will,) the testator intended to express. 1 Greenl. Ev. § 289; Hiscocks *v.* Hiscocks, 5 Mee. & Wels. 363, 367; Atkinson's Lessee *v.* Cummins, 9 How. 486; Miller *v.* Travers, 8 Bingh. Rep. 244; 21 Eng. Com. Law Rep. 290; Aspden Estate, 2 Wallace's Rep. 448.

7. A testator's parol declarations are not admissible to control the construction of his will, nor his evidence, as to the state of his property, admissible for that purpose. Ryeres *v.* Wheeler, 22 Wend. 151; Fonnereau *v.* Poyntz, 1 Bro. Ch. R. 472; Roberts on Wills, 24, 34; Brown *v.* Selwyn, Cases Temp.

33 *

Talbot, 240 ; Attorney-General v. Grote, 3 Mer. 316 ; 10 Wheat. 229 ; 3 Halsted, 71.

Mr. Justice CATRON delivered the opinion of the court.

Michael Allen, of the city of Pittsburg, made his will in 1849, by which he bequeathed to his wife, for life, his dwelling-house in said city, with two lots of ground occupied by him and her as a garden. He also gave her the household furniture and library. "And still furthermore," he declares, "that, first and foremost, there shall be secured to my dear wife, on my real and personal estate, an annuity of twelve hundred dollars a year, to be punctually paid semiannually during her lifetime, and that my executors pay all the taxes on the premises occupied by my dear wife during her lifetime."

The testator then bequeathes : 1st. To the five children of Dr. Robert Wray, five hundred dollars each. 2d. To the managers of the orphan asylums of the cities of Pittsburg and Alleghany, two thousand dollars each. 3d. To the pastor and sessions of the First Presbyterian Church, two thousand dollars. 4th. To the general assembly of the Presbyterian church, ten thousand dollars. 5th. To the trustees of the board of sessions of said general assembly, four thousand dollars. 6th. To the Foreign Evangelical Society, located in New York, three thousand dollars. 7th, 8th, and 9th, he gave for the use of the Presbyterian church, eleven thousand dollars. 10th. To the American Bible Society, six thousand dollars. 11th. To the American Tract Society, four thousand dollars. 12th. For the use of the Sunday School Union, situate in Philadelphia, four thousand dollars.

He next declares : " As to my debts, they will amount to very little ; but, and after paying all claims and bequests, there will remain a considerable surplus, which I give and bequeath in trust to my executors, be the same more or less, to be applied to the religious and benevolent purposes of the several institutions of the general assembly of the Presbyterian church in the United States of America, as before mentioned " ; and then constitutes and appoints his executors (who are the plaintiffs in error) to carry out the provisions of the will.

The defendants in error are the heirs at law of Michael Allen. They sued his executors in ejectment to recover a portion of the lands situate in the city of Pittsburg, of which he died seised, insisting that the lands did not pass by the will.

The residuary clause was supposed to be of doubtful meaning and obscure. To remove the alleged obscurity, the defendants below offered to prove on the trial, " from memoranda made by the testator at the time of the execution of said last will and testament, and upon the basis of which the same was prepared by him, and also by declarations made by him at and about the same time, what was his real meaning in the employment of the word 'surplus' in the residuary clause of said will, and that the same was intended to comprehend his whole remaining estate, as well real as personal."

"And further, to show by other evidence, besides the said memoranda, the actual amount and condition of the personal estate at the time of the execution of the said last will and testament, as well as at the period of the testator's death, and that the same was entirely insufficient, at either of the said periods, to pay the specific and pecuniary legacies provided therein; and this, for the purpose of explaining the meaning of the testator in the said residuary clause, and the employment of the said word 'surplus' therein, by showing that, if the same did not embrace the real estate, the said residuary clause would be entirely inoperative, for the reason that there was, in point of fact, under such construction, at neither of said periods, any surplus whatever, as supposed and declared by the testator himself."

On motion of the plaintiffs, the court rejected the evidence, and instructed the jury that no title vested in the executors by the residuary clause.

On this state of facts, the first question presented for our consideration is, whether the terms of the will are sufficient in themselves, when interpreted by their context, to carry the real estate to the executors?

As, in this instance, the testator's language must be construed with reference to the laws and policy of the country of his domicile, it is our duty to ascertain what the laws and policy of Pennsylvania are, so far as they may have a controlling influence in the construction of this will.

In the first place, Pennsylvania has only so far altered the English common law as to substitute all the children for the sole heir, carrying out this rule of descent through the collateral branches. This is the will the law makes in case of intestacy, and is the policy of the State. Under the law, the heirs must take, unless they are "disinherited by express words, or necessary implication." "Conjecture, nor uncertainty, shall never disinherit him." Such was the ground assumed by counsel in the case of Clayton v. Clayton, 3 Binney, 481, and which assumption was sustained by the court; ib. 486. Chief Justice Tilghman says: "The rule of law gives the estate to the heir, unless the will takes it from him: and, in order to take it from him, it must give it to some other person. Thus we are brought back to the question, are there any words in the will sufficient to convey more than an estate for life to the devisees. I can find none."

In the case referred to, the testator devised a homestead to his niece, Sarah Evans, and her children, without adding the word heirs. That he intended to give an estate in fee was hardly open to controversy; but the words of the will did not carry the fee, and the court refused to follow a doubtful intention. It there came fairly up to the rule laid down in the English case of Mudge v. Blight et ux. Cowp. 855, that "where there are no words of limitation, the court must determine in the case of a devise affecting real estate, that the devisee has only an estate for life, because the principle is fully settled and established, and no conjecture of a private imagination can shake a rule of law. If the intention of the testator is doubtful, the rule of law must take place; and so if the court cannot find words in the will sufficient to carry a fee. Though they should themselves be satisfied beyond the possibility of a doubt, as to what the intention of the party was, they must adhere to the rule of law."

This decision was made in 1811, and the principles then laid down have since been adhered to with uncommon care and strictness.

In speaking of expressions in a will necessary to disinherit the heir, Chief Justice Gibson, in delivering the opinion of the court in the case of Bradford v. Bradford, 6 Wharton, 244, says: "The intention must be manifest, and rest on something more certain than conjecture. The court must proceed on known principles and established rules, not on loose conjectural interpretations, nor considering what a man may be imagined to do in the testator's circumstances. The principle is applicable in all its force in a case like the present, in which the question goes to the birthright of those who, standing in place of the common-law heir, are not to be disinherited except by express devise, or, as is said in 1 Powell on Devises, 199, by implication so inevitable that an intention to the contrary cannot be supposed."

It is there admitted that when the testator provided that "all his worldly goods of all sorts and kinds" should be vested in trust and held as one fund, for a hundred years, and his children and their descendants should receive the rents and profits, that he most probably intended to include his lands. This, however, (the court declares,) is no more than a confident conjecture, and that it must come at last to an analysis of the testator's language to ascertain the legal meaning of the will.

Now, testing the will before us by these rules, and where can any provision be found in it showing a plain intention to disinherit the heirs? The lands are never named except where the wife is given a life estate in the homestead, and two lots, and, secondly, where her annuity of twelve hundred dollars is imposed on the goods and lands as a charge.

But as the residuary clause is mainly relied on, as carrying the real estate to the executors, it is proper that some further notice should be taken of its import. The testator declared that his debts amounted to very little, and that, after paying all claims and bequests, there would remain a considerable surplus, and this he bequeathed to his executors, to be applied to religious and benevolent purposes. He did not indicate any new fund, nor a surplus arising from the sale of lands, in the concluding clause of the will more than in any previous clause, where he provided for the support of the Presbyterian church.

The terms of the will, *proprio vigore*, being insufficient to disinherit the heirs, the next question is, whether the interpretation thereof may not be aided by extrinsic circumstances, namely, memoranda, declaration, and the actual amount and condition of the estate, as offered to be shown by the defendants below.

That the court may put itself in the place of the testator, by looking into the state of his property, and the circumstances by which he was surrounded when he made the will, is not only true as a general proposition, but without such information it must often happen that the will could not be sensibly construed. Wigram (10, 60) lays down the rule with much distinctness. Such evidence, however, is only admissible to explain ambiguities arising out of extrinsic circumstances, as to persons provided for, objects of disposition, and the like. For instance, if the testator gave to his grandson, J. S., a plantation, and he had two grandsons of that name; or he devised his son J. his plantation on a certain river, and he had two plantations there, — in each case proof might be heard to show the person or thing intended. But evidence cannot be heard to show a different intention in the testator from that which the will discloses.

Such is the established doctrine of this court, as was held in the case of Weatherhead v. Barksdale, 11 How. 857.

The only English case we will refer to is that of Miller v. Traverse, 8 Bingh. 248. There the testator devised and vested in trust " all his freehold and real estates whatsoever in the county of Limerick, and the city of Limerick." At the time of making the will, he had no real estate in the county of Limerick, but had a small estate in the city of Limerick, and considerable real estate in the county of Clare; and the question was whether the devisees could be admitted to have an issue and trial at law on the ground that they offered to prove that, by the original draft of the will, the estates in Clare were included, and the county left out by oversight or mistake; and also that the testator so expressed himself.

The lord chancellor was assisted by the chief justice of the common pleas and the chief baron, and they all concurred in holding that the evidence offered could not be heard to change the import of the will, and refused the issue. And so it is manifest here, that if the evidence were to show all that is assumed for it, yet it could not be heard to affect this will.

It is ordered that the judgment of the circuit court be affirmed.

MARY ANN CONNOR, ALIAS MARY ANN VAN NESS, TENANT, &C., PLAINTIFF IN ERROR, v. SAMUEL A. PEUGH'S LESSEE.

Where a declaration in ejectment was served on the 15th of the month and the court met on the 27th, it was ten days before the commencement of the term.
Judgment being entered against the casual ejector, the tenant having neglected to make herself a party, cannot bring a writ of error to the judgment.
A motion to set the judgment aside was an application to the sound discretion of the court below. No appeal lies from its decision, nor is it the subject of a bill of exceptions or writ of error.

THIS case was brought up by writ of error from the circuit court of the United States for the District of Columbia, holden in and for the county of Washington.

The counsel for the defendant in error moved to dismiss the writ of error under the following circumstances: —

An action of ejectment was brought by Peugh's lessee to recover the eastern half part of lot number seven, in the square or reservation marked B in the city of Washington. A copy of the declaration was served on Mrs. Connor, on the 15th March, 1854, the court being about to meet on the 27th, and the rules requiring the service to be made at least ten days before court. At the term of March, there being no appearance for the defendant, a motion was made by the plaintiffs' counsel for judgment against the casual ejector, which was postponed till next term.

At October term, 1854, judgment was entered against the casual ejector, and also against Mary Ann Connor, the tenant in possession.

On the 24th of March, 1855, a writ of *habere facias possessionem* was sued out, which was returned, "came to hand too late for service."

On the 23d of May, 1855, an alias writ was issued, returnable on third Monday of October thereafter.

Before the return day of this writ, namely, on the 5th of June, 1855, Mrs. Connor appeared in court by her counsel and moved to set aside the judgment and also to quash the writ of *hab. fac. poss.*, upon the ground that a copy of the declaration was not served upon her ten days before the meeting of the court at

March term, 1854. In which case no judgment by default ought to have been rendered against her until March term, 1855.

At October term, 1855, this motion was overruled and the petition was dismissed. Whereupon Mrs. Connor prayed an appeal to the supreme court of the United States, which was granted.

A writ of error brought the whole proceedings up to this court.

The motion to dismiss upon the ground that the ruling of the court below in dismissing the petition was a matter within the sound discretion of the court, and not the subject of a writ of error, was argued by *Mr. Bradley* and *Mr. Lawrence* in support of it, and opposed by *Mr. Brent.*

Mr. Justice GRIER delivered the opinion of the court.

Defendant in error moves to dismiss the writ of error in this case. It is an action of ejectment brought in the circuit court of this district in the usual form, by serving a declaration on the tenant in possession with notice. The declaration and notice were served by the marshal, more than ten days before March term, 1854. The tenant did not appear and have herself made defendant in place of the casual ejector, according to the exigency of the notice; and at October term a judgment was entered against the casual ejector, in the usual and proper form. On the 5th of June, 1855, the tenant in possession came into court for the first time, and moved to set aside the judgment and execution issued thereon, and to be allowed to defend the suit, for reasons set forth in her affidavit. The court refused to grant this motion, " whereupon the said Mary Ann Connor prayed an appeal," &c.

The tenant in possession having neglected to appear and have herself made defendant, and confess lease, entry, and ouster, the judgment was properly entered against the casual ejector. No one but a party to the suit can bring a writ of error. The tenant having neglected to have herself made such, cannot have a writ of error to the judgment against the casual ejector.

The motion afterwards made to have the judgment set aside, and for leave to intervene, was an application to the sound discretion of the court. To the action of the court on such a motion no appeal lies, nor is it the subject of a bill of exceptions or writ of error.

Writ of error dismissed.

DANIEL SOUTH, JOHN W. STOUFFER, JACOB FIERY, DANIEL MIDDLEKAUFF, SENIOR, AND JOHN A. K. BREWER, PLAINTIFFS IN ERROR, *v.* THE STATE OF MARYLAND, USE OF JONATHAN W. POTTLE.

5-8

Where, in an action upon a sheriff's bond, the declaration did not charge the sheriff with a breach of his duty in the execution of any writ or process in which the real plaintiff was personally interested; but with a neglect or refusal to preserve the public peace, in consequence of which the plaintiff suffered great wrong and injury from the unlawful violence of a mob; the declaration did not set forth a sufficient cause of action against the sheriff and his sureties.

The powers and duties of a sheriff explained; and the difference pointed out between his ministerial and judicial functions.

It is only for a breach of his duty in the execution of the former, that the sheriff and his sureties are liable upon his bond, and the declaration in this case does not set out such a breach.

THIS case came up by writ of error from the circuit court of the United States for the District of Maryland, having been tried in that court by the late Judge Glenn, district judge.

It was an action brought in the name of the State of Maryland by Pottle upon a sheriffs' bond given by South with the other plaintiffs in error as sureties. Under the instructions of the court below, the verdict and judgment were for the plaintiff. Being brought to this court, by writ of error, it was argued at a former term, and was ordered to be reargued and the following questions suggested for discussion : —

1. Whether or not, the declaration contains a cause of action entitling the plaintiff (Pottle) to recover against the sheriff and his sureties within the condition of the official bond, according to the laws of the State of Maryland?

2. Whether or not, the sheriff, as conservator of the public peace, is liable to a civil action for an injury to the person or property of an individual, from a riotous assembly or mob, according to any law of the State of Maryland, if it should appear said sheriff unreasonably omitted or neglected to exert his authority to suppress it?

3. Whether or not the sheriff, as conservator of the public peace, is liable to the plaintiff in an execution, attending personally upon the levy or sale under it, for an injury to his person or property from a riotous assembly or mob, according to any law of the State of Maryland, if it should appear that said sheriff unreasonably omitted or neglected to exert his authority to suppress it?

4. Whether or not, on the case last stated, the sheriff would be liable to the plaintiff in the execution, if he desisted in good faith from the exertion of his authority at the instance and request of said plaintiff, while in the hands of the mob, from an

apprehension of greater bodily injury if an effort should be made to suppress it?

It was again argued at this term by *Mr. Nelson*, for the plaintiffs in error, and by *Mr. Dobbin* and *Mr. Johnson*, for the defendant.

As the case turned upon the sufficiency of the declaration, which sets out the case, it is thought proper to insert it, viz:—

Narr.

UNITED STATES OF AMERICA,
       District of Maryland, sct.

Daniel South, John W. Stouffer, Jacob Fierey, Daniel Middlekauff, senior, and John A. K. Brewer, late of said district, citizens of the State of Maryland, were summoned to answer unto the State of Maryland, of a plea that they render unto the said State the sum of twenty-six thousand six hundred and sixty-six dollars and sixty-six and two third cents, which to the said State they owe, and from the said State unjustly detain: And whereupon the said State, by Dobbin and Talbott, its attorneys, complains that whereas the said defendants, on the seventeenth day of December, in the year eighteen hundred and forty-nine, at the district aforesaid, by their certain writing obligatory, sealed with their seals, and to the court now here shown, whose date is the day and year aforesaid, acknowledged themselves to be held and firmly bound to the said plaintiff in the just and full sum of twenty-six thousand six hundred and sixty-six dollars and sixty-six and two third cents, to be paid to the said plaintiff whenever afterwards they, the said defendants, should be thereto required, which said writing was and is subject to a certain condition thereunder written, to wit: That if the said Daniel South, as sheriff of Washington county, did and should well and faithfully execute the same office in all things appertaining thereto, and should also render to the several officers within the said State a just and true account of all fees placed in his hands for collection within the times limited by law, and should also well and truly pay all sums of money received by him, and also collect and pay all public dues, fines, and forfeitures, which are due or belonging to the State, and should also well and faithfully execute and return all writs, process, and warrants, to him directed and delivered, and should also pay and deliver to the person or persons entitled to receive the same all sum or sums of money, tobacco, goods, chattels, or property by him levied, seized, or taken, agreeably to the directions of the writ, process, or warrant under which the same should be levied and seized; and should also detain and keep in his custody all and every person and persons committed to his custody, or by him taken in execution, or who should be committed for the want of bail, without suffering them or any of them to escape or depart from his custody; and should also pay and satisfy all judgments which should or might be rendered against him as sheriff, and should also well and truly execute and perform the several duties required of and imposed upon him by the laws of said State, then the said obligation was to be void and of none effect, otherwise to remain in full force and virtue in law.

And the said plaintiff further saith, that the said Daniel South, at the time of making the writing obligatory aforesaid mentioned, and long before and thereafter, and at the time of, and after the committing the wrongs hereinafter complained of, was sheriff of Washington county, in the State aforesaid, duly elected, commissioned, and qualified, and by the duty of his office of sheriff aforesaid, and according to the tenor and effect of the condition of the writing obligatory aforesaid, ought to have preserved and maintained the peace of the State of Maryland, in the county of Washington aforesaid.

And the said plaintiff further saith, that a certain Jonathan W. Pottle, a citizen of the State of Massachusetts, in the indorsement of the writ original in this cause mentioned, at whose instance and for whose use the same is instituted, was, after the making of said writing obligatory, and during the time within which said Daniel was sheriff as aforesaid, to wit, on the twelfth day of June, in the year eighteen hundred and fifty, lawfully present in Washington county aforesaid, and engaged in and about his lawful business; and the said Daniel South, sheriff as aforesaid, was then and there also present with the said Jonathan W. Pottle, when certain evil-disposed persons came about the said Jonathan W. Pottle, and by force and arms hindered and prevented him in the execution of his lawful business, and threatened the life and personal safety of the said Jonathan W. Pottle, and with force and arms demanded of said Jonathan W. Pottle a large sum of money, the property of the said Jonathan W. Pottle, to wit, the sum of twenty-five hundred dollars, and then and there unlawfully and injuriously, and against the will of the said Jonathan W. Pottle, and also against the laws of the said State, and without any legal warrant, authority, or legal or justifiable cause whatsoever, did imprison, and detain so imprisoned there the said Jonathan W. Pottle for a long space of time, to wit, for the space of four days then next ensuing, and until he, the said Jonathan W. Pottle, had paid to the said evil-disposed persons the sum of two thousand five hundred dollars for his enlargement, and other wrongs to the said Jonathan W.

Pottle then and there did, to the great damage of the said Jonathan W. Pottle, and against the peace of the State of Maryland.

And the said Jonathan W. Pottle then and there applied to the said Daniel South, sheriff as aforesaid, then and there present, to protect and defend him, the said Jonathan, from the said unlawful conduct and threatened violence of the said evil-disposed persons, and to preserve and keep the peace of the State of Maryland, in Washington county aforesaid, the said Daniel South, sheriff as aforesaid, then and there having the power and authority so to do. But the said Daniel South, sheriff as aforesaid, did then and there neglect and refuse to protect and defend the said Jonathan from the said unlawful conduct and threatened violence of the said evil-disposed persons, and to preserve and keep the peace of the State of Maryland, in Washington county aforesaid; and so the said plaintiff saith that the said Daniel South did not well and faithfully execute the office of sheriff of Washington county, in all things appertaining thereto according to the form and effect of the condition aforesaid, to wit, at the district aforesaid, whereby the said writing obligatory became forfeited, by reason whereof an action hath accrued to the said plaintiff to demand and have of and from the said defendants the said sum of twenty-six thousand six hundred and sixty-six dollars and sixty-six and two third cents.

Nevertheless, the said defendants, although often requested, have not, nor hath either of them paid the said sum of money above demanded of them, or any part thereof, but so to do have hitherto wholly refused, and still do refuse, to the damage of the said plaintiff twenty thousand dollars; and thereupon it brings suit, &c.

DOBBIN AND TALBOTT,
For plaintiff.

Mr. Nelson, for the plaintiffs in error, made the following points, viz:—

1. That the declaration contains no cause of action entitling the plaintiff to recover against the sheriff and his sureties within the condition of the official bond, according to the laws of the State of Maryland.

2. That the sheriff, as conservator of the public peace, is not liable to a civil action for an injury to the person or property of an individual from a riotous assembly, or mob, according to any law of the State of Maryland, even if it should appear that said sheriff unreasonably omitted or neglected to exert his authority to suppress it. 1 Thomas's Coke, 81, 82; Comyn's Dig. tit. Viscount — authority of a sheriff (c. 1.); Watson's sheriff, 2, 8; 1 Perry & Davidson, 297; Pitcher v. King, 2 Barnewall & Ald. 478;

Hilary *v.* Breare and Holmes, 1 Moody & Malkin, 52; Tensley *v.* Nassau, 7 State Trials, 442; 6 Howell, 1094; Soames *v.* Barrardister; 12 Coke, 24.

8. That the sheriff, as conservator of the public peace is not liable to the plaintiff in an execution attending personally upon the levy or sale under it for an injury to his person or property from a riotous assembly or mob, according to any law of the State of Maryland, even if it should appear that said sheriff unreasonably omitted or neglected to exert his authority to suppress it.

4. That in the case last stated the sheriff would not be liable to the plaintiff in the execution, if he desisted in good faith from the exertion of his authority at the instance and request of said plaintiff, while in the hands of the mob from an apprehension of greater bodily injury if an effort should be made to suppress it. 6 Barn. & Cress. 789, Cook and others *v.* Palmer; 8 Barn. & Cress. 598; 7 Missouri, 536; 18 Ibid. 487.

5. That however true it may be as a general proposition, that the sheriff is responsible for the acts and omissions of his deputy, yet that in this case no such responsibility exists, because, by his declaration, the plaintiff charged no such acts or omissions.

6. That there was error in the instruction given by the court below; because it took from the jury the inquiry whether the omission of the sheriff to exert his authority to suppress the riot, was unreasonable or otherwise.

Mr. Dobbin and *Mr. Johnson*, for the defendant in error, made the following points, viz:—

1. That the sheriff, South, was *virtute officii*, the conservator of the peace of the State. Dalton on Sheriff, 26; Com. Dig. Sheriff, C. a, C. 1, C. 2; 2 Hawk, P. C. c. 8, § 4; Cro. Car. 27; 8 Bac. Abr. 689, tit. Sheriff, L.

2. That, as sheriff, he was responsible for the acts and omissions of his deputies; and that, whether so or not, South, the high sheriff, having been present during two days of the riot, became responsible for all omissions of his official duty after such presence. Dalton, 176; 8 Bac. Abr. 675; 2 McLean, 193; 6 Shep. 277; 2 App. 93.

8. That the sheriff's official bond, which is here the subject of suit, is liable for every failure on his part to faithfully execute his office of sheriff in any thing appertaining thereto, and that his failure to protect and relieve Pottle was a breach of the condition of the bond, upon which a right of action accrued to Pottle against the sheriff and his sureties. 1 Pet. 46; 12 Pick. 808; 6 Wend. 454.

4. That the sheriff, having permitted the said unlawful duress

of imprisonment to be made and continued, is not discharged from liability therefor by any declaration made by Pottle during such duress.

Mr. Justice GRIER delivered the opinion of the court.

In this case a verdict was rendered for the plaintiff in the court below, and the defendant moved, in arrest of judgment, "that the matters set out in the declaration of the plaintiff are not sufficient, in law, to support the action." If it be found that the court erred in overruling this motion and in entering judgment on the verdict, a consideration of the other points raised on the trial will be unnecessary.

The action is brought on the official bond of South, as sheriff of Washington county. The declaration sets forth the condition of the bond at length. The breach alleged is, in substance, "that while Pottle was engaged about his lawful business, certain evil-disposed persons came about him, hindered and prevented him, threatened his life, with force of arms demanded of him a large sum of money, and imprisoned and detained him for the space of four days, and until he paid them the sum of $2,500 for his enlargement."

That South, the sheriff, being present, the plaintiff, Pottle, applied to him for protection, and requested him to keep the peace of the State of Maryland, he, the said sheriff, having power and authority so to do. That the sheriff neglected and refused to protect and defend the plaintiff, and to keep the peace, wherefore, it is charged, "the sheriff did not well and truly execute and perform the duties required of him by the laws of said State"; and thereby the said writing obligatory became forfeited, and action accrued to the plaintiff.

This declaration does not charge the sheriff with a breach of his duty in the execution of any writ or process in which Pottle, the real plaintiff in this case, was personally interested, but a neglect or refusal to preserve the public peace, in consequence of which the plaintiff suffered great wrong and injury from the unlawful violence of a mob. It assumes as a postulate, that every breach or neglect of a public duty subjects the officer to a civil suit by any individual who, in consequence thereof, has suffered loss or injury; and consequently, that the sheriff and his sureties are liable to this suit on his bond, because he has not "executed and performed all the duties required of and imposed on him by the laws of the State."

The powers and duties of the sheriff are usually arranged under four distinct classes: —

1. In his judicial capacity, he formerly held the sheriff's tourn, or county courts, and performed other functions which need not be enumerated.

34 *

2. As king's bailiff, he seized to the king's use all escheats, forfeitures, waifs, wrecks, estrays, &c.

8. As conservator of the peace in his county or bailiwick, he is the representative of the king, or sovereign power of the State for that purpose. He has the care of the county, and, though forbidden by *magna charta* to act as a justice of the peace in trial of criminal cases, he exercises all the authority of that office where the public peace was concerned. He may upon view, without writ or process, commit to prison all persons who break the peace or attempt to break it; he may award process of the peace, and bind any one in recognizance to keep it. He is bound, *ex officio*, to pursue and take all traitors, murderers, felons, and other misdoers, and commit them to jail for safe custody. For these purposes he may command the *posse comitatus* or power of the country; and this summons, every one over the age of fifteen years is bound to obey, under pain of fine and imprisonment.

4. In his ministerial capacity he is bound to execute all processes issuing from the courts of justice. He is keeper of the county jail, and answerable for the safe-keeping of prisoners. He summons and returns juries, arrests, imprisons, and executes the sentence of the court, &c., &c. 1 Black. Com. 848; 2 Hawk, P. C. C. 8, § 4, &c., &c.

Originally, the office of sheriff could be held by none but men of large estate, who were able to support the retinue of followers which the dignity of his office required, and to answer in damages to those who were injured by his neglect of duty in the performance of his ministerial functions. In more modern times, a bond with sureties supplies the place of personal wealth. The object of these bonds is security, not the imposition of liabilities upon the sheriff, to which he was not subject at common law. The specific enumeration of duties in the bond in this case includes none but those that are classed as ministerial. The general expression, in conclusion, should be construed to include only such other duties of the same kind as were not specially enumerated. To entitle a citizen to sue on this bond to his own use, he must show such a default as would entitle him to recover against the sheriff in an action on the case. When the sheriff is punishable by indictment as for a misdemeanor, in cases of a breach of some public duty, his sureties are not bound to suffer in his place, or to indemnify individuals for the consequences of such a criminal neglect.

It is an undisputed principle of the common law, that for a breach of a public duty, an officer is punishable by indictment; but where he acts ministerially, and is bound to render certain services to individuals, for a compensation in fees or salary, he is liable for acts of misfeasance or non-feasance to the party who is injured by them.

The powers and duties of conservator of the peace exercised by the sheriff are not strictly judicial; but he may be said to act as the chief magistrate of his county, wielding the executive power for the preservation of the public peace. It is a public duty, for neglect of which he is amenable to the public, and punishable by indictment only.

The history of the law for centuries proves this to be the case. Actions against the sheriff for a breach of his ministerial duties in the execution of process are to be found in almost every book of reports. But no instance can be found where a civil action has been sustained against him for his default or misbehavior as conservator of the peace by those who have suffered injury to their property or persons through the violence of mobs, riots, or insurrections.

In the case of Entick v. Carrington, State Trials, vol. 19, page 1062, Lord Camden remarks: "No man ever heard of an action against a conservator of the peace, as such."

The case of Ashby v. White, 2 Lord Raym. 938, has been often quoted to show that a sheriff may be liable to a civil action where he has acted in a judicial rather than a ministerial capacity. This was an action brought by a citizen entitled to vote for member of parliament, against the sheriff for refusing his vote at an election. Gould, Justice, thought the action would not lie, because the sheriff acted as a judge. Powis, because, though not strictly a judge, he acted *quasi* judicially. But Holt, C. J., decided that the action would lie: 1. "Because the plaintiff had a right or privilege. 2. That, by the act of the officer, he was hindered from the enjoyment of it." 3. By the finding of the jury the act was done maliciously. The later cases all concur in the doctrine, that where the officer is held liable to a civil action for acts not simply ministerial, the plaintiff must allege and prove each of these propositions. See Cullen v. Morris, 2 Starkie, N. P. C.; Harman v. Tappenden, 1 East, 555, &c., &c.

The declaration in the case before us is clearly not within the principles of these decisions. It alleges no special individual right, privilege, or franchise in the plaintiff, from the enjoyment of which he has been restrained or hindered by the malicious act of the sheriff; nor does it charge him with any misfeasance or non-feasance in his ministerial capacity, in the execution of any process in which the plaintiff was concerned. Consequently, we are of opinion that the declaration sets forth no sufficient cause of action.

The judgment of the circuit court is therefore reversed.

THE LAFAYETTE INSURANCE COMPANY, PLAINTIFF IN ERROR, v.
MAYNARD FRENCH, EDWARD K. STRONG, AND THOMAS B.
FINE.

Where a corporation is sued, it is not enough, in order to give jurisdiction, to say that
the corporation is a citizen of the State where the suit is brought. But an averment
is sufficient, when admitted by a demurrer, that the corporation was created by the
laws of the State, and had its principal place of business there.

Where a corporation, chartered by the State of Indiana, was allowed by a law of Ohio
to transact business in the latter State upon the condition that service of process upon
the agent of the corporation should be considered as service upon the corporation
itself, a judgment against the corporation, obtained by means of such process, ought
to have been received in Indiana with the same faith and credit that it was entitled
to in Ohio.

The State of Ohio had a right to impose such a condition; and when the company
sent its agent into the State, it must be presumed to have assented to the rule.

If the judgment was recovered in Ohio against the company by an erroneous name,
but the suit upon the judgment was brought in Indiana against the company using
its chartered name correctly, accompanied with an averment that it was the same
company, this mistake is no ground of error; it could only be taken advantage of
by a plea in abatement, in the suit in which the first judgment was recovered.

THIS case was brought up, by a writ of error, from the circuit
court of the United States for the district of Indiana.

In 1836, the legislature of Indiana chartered the Lafayette
Insurance Company with the usual powers of a company to insure against losses by fire. Their principal office or place of
business was at Lafayette, in Indiana, but they also had an
office at Cincinnati, in the county of Hamilton and State of
Ohio. At the latter place the agent issued a policy to the defendants in error, to insure certain property against fire, which
was afterwards consumed. An action was brought upon the
policy in Ohio, the process being served upon the agent, and a
judgment was entered against the company. Upon a record of
this judgment, an action was brought in the circuit court of the
United States, in Indiana, and judgment again entered against
the company.

Upon the trial the plaintiffs offered in evidence a copy of the
record of the case, as tried in Ohio, to the introduction of which
the defendant objected for the following reasons, namely: —

1. Because said judgment record shows and evidences a judgment recovered against "The President, Directors, and Company
of the Lafayette Insurance Company," and does not show or evidence the recovery of a judgment against this defendant.

2. Because said judgment record does not show or evidence
the service of process upon this defendant as required by law,
nor the appearance of this defendant by attorney, or otherwise
in said action or suit in said commercial court, and that said
judgment, as a judgment, is therefore a nullity.

8. Because the said judgment record does not evidence the existence or rendition of a judgment *in personam* against said defendant.

But the court admitted the evidence. Some of the counts in the declaration being upon the policy as well as the record, the plaintiffs then introduced evidence to show the loss, value, &c., of the property insured. Judgment was rendered against the defendants for $2,817.11.

It was argued in this court by *Mr. Gillett*, for the plaintiff in error, and submitted upon a printed argument by *Mr. O. H. Smith*, for the defendants.

Pending the argument a copy of a law of Ohio was produced (Ohio General Laws, vol. 45, p. 17) entitled "An Act to authorize suits upon contracts of insurance to be brought in the county in which the contract may be made," the third section of which provided for the service of process, as in this case.

Mr. Justice CURTIS delivered the opinion of the court.

This is a writ of error to the circuit court of the United States for the district of Indiana, in an action of debt on a judgment recovered in the commercial court of Cincinnati, in the State of Ohio. In the declaration, the plaintiffs are averred to be citizens of Ohio; and they "complain of the Lafayette Insurance Company, a citizen of the State of Indiana." This averment is not sufficient to show jurisdiction. It does not appear from it that the Lafayette Insurance Company is a corporation; or, if it be such, by the law of what State it was created. The averment, that the company is a citizen of the State of Indiana, can have no sensible meaning attached to it. This court does not hold, that either a voluntary association of persons, or an association into a body politic, created by law, is a citizen of a State within the meaning of the constitution. And, therefore, if the defective averment in the declaration had not been otherwise supplied, the suit must have been dismissed. But the plaintiff's replication alleges that the defendants are a corporation, created under the laws of the State of Indiana, having its principal place of business in that State. These allegations are confessed by the demurrer; and they bring the case within the decision of this court in Marshall v. The Baltimore and Ohio Railroad Company, 16 How. 314, and the previous decisions therein referred to.

Upon the merits, it was objected that the judgment declared on was rendered by the commercial court of Cincinnati, without jurisdiction over the person sued; and the argument was, that as this corporation was created by a law of the State of Indiana, it could have no existence out of that State, and, consequently, could not be sued in Ohio.

The precise facts upon which this objection depends are, that this corporation was created by a law of the State of Indiana, and had its principal office for business within that State. It had also an agent authorized to contract for insurance who resided in the State of Ohio. The contract on which the judgment in question was recovered was made in Ohio, and was to be there performed; because it was a contract with the citizens of Ohio to insure property within that State. A statute of Ohio makes special provision for suits against foreign corporations, founded on contracts of insurance there made by them with citizens of that State; and one of its provisions is, that service of process on such resident agent of the foreign corporation shall be "as effectual as though the same were served on the principal."

The question is, whether a judgment recovered in Ohio against the Indiana corporation, upon a contract made by that corporation in Ohio with citizens of that State to insure property there, after the law above mentioned was enacted, — service of process having been made on such resident agent, — is a judgment entitled to the same faith and credit in the State of Indiana as in the State of Ohio, under the constitution and laws of the United States.

No question has been made that this judgment would be held binding in the State of Ohio, and would there be satisfied out of any property of the defendants existing in that State.

The act of May 26, 1790, (1 Stats. at Large, 122,) gives to a judgment rendered in any State such faith and credit as it had in the courts of the State where it was recovered. But this provision, though general in its terms, does not extend to judgments rendered against persons not amenable to the jurisdiction rendering the judgments. D'Arcy v. Ketchum, 11 How. 165. And, consequently, notwithstanding the act of congress, whenever an action is brought in one State on a judgment recovered in another, it is not enough to show it to be valid in the State where it was rendered; it must also appear that the defendant was either personally within the jurisdiction of the State, or had legal notice of the suit, and was in some way subject to its laws, so as to be bound to appear and contest the suit, or suffer a judgment by default. In more general terms, the doctrine of this court, as well as of the courts of many of the States, is, that this act of Congress was not designed to displace that principle of natural justice which requires a person to have notice of a suit before he can be conclusively bound by its result; nor those rules of public law which protect persons and property within one State from the exercise of jurisdiction over them by another.

This corporation, existing only by virtue of a law of Indiana, cannot be deemed to pass personally beyond the limits of that State. Bank of Augusta *v.* Earle, 13 Pet. 519. But it does not necessarily follow that a valid judgment could be recovered against it only in that State. A corporation may sue in a foreign state, by its attorney there; and if it fails in the suit, be subject to a judgment for costs. And so if a corporation, though in Indiana, should appoint an attorney to appear, in an action brought in Ohio, and the attorney should appear, the court would have jurisdiction to render a judgment, in all respects as obligatory as if the defendant were within the State. The inquiry is, not whether the defendant was personally within the State, but whether he, or some one authorized to act for him in reference to the suit, had notice and appeared; or, if he did not appear, whether he was bound to appear or suffer a judgment by default.

And the true question in this case is, whether this corporation had such notice of the suit, and was so far subject to the jurisdiction and laws of Ohio, that it was bound to appear, or take the consequences of non-appearance.

A corporation created by Indiana can transact business in Ohio only with the consent, express or implied, of the latter State. 13 Pet. 519. This consent may be accompanied by such conditions as Ohio may think fit to impose; and these conditions must be deemed valid and effectual by other States, and by this court, provided they are not repugnant to the constitution or laws of the United States, or inconsistent with those rules of public law which secure the jurisdiction and authority of each State from encroachment by all others, or that principle of natural justice which forbids condemnation without opportunity for defence.

In this instance, one of the conditions imposed by Ohio was, in effect, that the agent who should reside in Ohio and enter into contracts of insurance there in behalf of the foreign corporation, should also be deemed its agent to receive service of process in suits founded on such contracts. We find nothing in this provision either unreasonable in itself, or in conflict with any principle of public law. It cannot be deemed unreasonable that the State of Ohio should endeavor to secure to its citizens a remedy, in their domestic forum, upon this important class of contracts made and to be performed within that State, and fully subject to its laws; nor that proper means should be used to compel foreign corporations, transacting this business of insurance within the State, for their benefit and profit, to answer there for the breach of their contracts of insurance there made and to be performed.

Nor do we think the means adopted to effect this object are open to the objection, that it is an attempt improperly to extend the jurisdiction of the State beyond its own limits to a person in another State. Process can be served on a corporation only by making service thereof on some one or more of its agents. The law may, and ordinarily does, designate the agent or officer on whom process is to be served. For the purpose of receiving such service, and being bound by it, the corporation is identified with such agent or officer. The corporate power to receive and act on such service, so far as to make it known to the corporation, is thus vested in such officer or agent. Now, when this corporation sent its agent into Ohio, with authority to make contracts of insurance there, the corporation must be taken to assent to the condition upon which alone such business could be there trans acted by them; that condition being, that an agent, to make contracts, should also be the agent of the corporation to receive service of process in suits on such contracts; and, in legal contemplation, the appointment of such an agent clothed him with power to receive notice, for and on behalf of the corporation, as effectually as if he were designated in the charter as the officer on whom process was to be served; or, as if he had received from the president and directors a power of attorney to that effect. The process was served within the limits and jurisdiction of Ohio, upon a person qualified by law to represent the corporation there in respect to such service; and notice to him was notice to the corporation which he there represented, and for whom he was empowered to take notice.

We consider this foreign corporation, entering into contracts made and to be performed in Ohio, was under an obligation to attend, by its duly authorized attorney, on the courts of that State, in suits founded on such contracts, whereof notice should be given by due process of law, served on the agent of the corporation resident in Ohio, and qualified by the law of Ohio and the presumed assent of the corporation to receive and act on such notice; that this obligation is well founded in policy and morals, and not inconsistent with any principle of public law; and that when so sued on such contracts in Ohio, the corporation was personally amenable to that jurisdiction; and we hold such a judgment, recovered after such notice, to be as valid as if the corporation had had its *habitat* within the State; that is, entitled to the same faith and credit in Indiana as in Ohio, under the constitution and laws of the United States.

We limit our decision to the case of a corporation acting in a State foreign to its creation, under a law of that State which recognized its existence, for the purposes of making contracts there and being sued on them, through notice to its contracting agents. The case of natural persons, and of other foreign corporations, is attended with other considerations, which might or might not distinguish it; upon this we give no opinion.

This decision renders it unnecessary to consider the questions arising under the counts on the policy.

It was objected that the judgment recovered in the commercial court was against "the president, directors, and company of the Lafayette Insurance Company," while this action is against the "Lafayette Insurance Company"; but the declaration describes the judgment correctly, and then avers that the judgment was recovered against the defendants by that other name. We must assume that this fact was proved; and the only question open here is, whether, if a mistake be made in the name of a defendant, and he fails to plead it in abatement, the judgment binds him, though called by a wrong name. Of this we have no doubt. Evidence that it was an erroneous name of the same person must, therefore, be admissible; otherwise, a mistake in the defendant's name, instead of being available only by a plea in abatement, would render a judgment wholly inoperative.

In the case of the Medway Cotton Manufactory v. Adams, 10 Mass. 360, the plaintiffs, a corporation, declared on a promissory note made to Richardson, Metcalf, and Co., and averred that the maker promised the corporation by that name. The defendant demurred to the declaration, and assigned, in argument, the same cause which has been relied on at the bar in this case, — that it was not competent to prove by parol evidence that the promisee of the note was the corporation, the name not being the same. The court held otherwise, and overruled the demurrer.

A similar decision was made in an action of debt on bond by the supreme court of New York, in the case of New York African Society v. Varick et al. 13 Johns. 88. See, also, Inhabitants, &c. v. String, 5 Halst. 323; and the authorities cited in the cases in New York and Massachusetts.

The decision of the circuit court is affirmed.

Mr. Justice CAMPBELL dissented.

JOSHUA R. STANFORD, PLAINTIFF IN ERROR, v. CLAY TAYLOR.

Where an imperfect Spanish title to land in Missouri was confirmed by the commissioners, but the claim required a survey to ascertain its limits and boundaries, evidence cannot be received that the survey was erroneously made, by showing pos-

Stanford v. Taylor.

session, by the confirmee, of land in a different place than that where the survey placed his land.

THIS case was brought up, by writ of error, from the circuit court of the United States for the district of Missouri.

The case is stated in the opinion of the court.

It was argued by *Mr. Lawrence* and *Mr. Johnson* for the plaintiff in error, and by *Mr. Williams*, for the defendant.

Mr. Lawrence made the following points, namely: —

This survey was entirely erroneous, as plaintiff claims and offered to show, for reasons:

1. That the location was such that it did not include the possession as required by the commissioners' certificate.

2. It did not adjoin Robert in any way, but was put three arpens west of it.

8. It was made upon the grant to Mad. Papin, long before surveyed and patented to her representatives, and held by them.

4. It was in violation of the instructions of the surveyor-general.

This survey was, therefore, void in every respect that could affect the plaintiff's rights under the confirmation. A survey, if necessary at all, is not final or unalterable. If wrong, it may (most certainly should) be corrected by the courts.

Kittridge *v.* Landry, 2 Rob., Lou. 72; Latiolais *v.* Richard, 6 Mar. Lou. (N. S.) 218; Fay *v.* Chambers, 4 Lou. An. R. 481.

It may be conceded that a survey by a government officer, made in a case of a confirmation for land, of which there had been no possession, and which is undefined and floating, should possess something of the nature of conclusiveness. But where there has been possession, and that possession is shown, and the land confirmed is for a definite location " conformable " to that possession, no act of survey ought to affect the rights of the confirmee. To say that it could, would be to place every man's titles at the mercy of an executive officer.

The act of surveying is merely ministerial in its character, and if performed in open violation of facts and law — as it was in this case — it goes for naught, and should be disregarded entirely.

The true effect and force of a survey is properly declared in the fourth instruction of circuit court of Missouri, in the case of West *v.* Cochran, when it is stated to be *primâ facie* evidence of its conformity to the confirmation. The strong reason why this should be its only effect is, that it is made the duty of government to survey the land of a confirmee, and to so survey it that it shall agree with the decision of the board. The land surveyed should be the same as that possessed originally.

The survey is intended only as an official designation of the land confirmed, for the purpose of obtaining patent evidence of title. When it violates the description in the concession, and is at variance with the decision of the commissioners, it is no survey; and the courts should at once proceed to correct that which the executive department has done under mistake, and in violation of a right confirmed by law. This case differs from that of West *v.* Cochran, 17 How. 403.

In that case, it is shown by the record, that Brazeau (through whom the plaintiff claimed) had never been in possession of the ground claimed by him. Nor had he, or any assignee or representative of his, ever had proper registry of the claim; nor did any one come before the board of commissioners as a claimant under the act of 1807.

The proofs and offers of proofs by plaintiff made out a good *primâ facie* case in ejectment.

Defendant showed no title in himself, and plaintiff ought to have been allowed to show the erroneous character of the surveys produced by the defendant. 9 Pet. 171; 10 Ib. 326, 340; United States *v.* Levy, 13 Pet. 83; 15 Ib. 172; 16 Ib. 146, 228; 8 How. 295; 10 Ib. 541; 11 Ib. 115.

Mr. Justice CATRON delivered the opinion of the court.

The plaintiff, Stanford, sued Taylor in ejectment, claiming title to the land in dispute under a concession from " Don Francisco Cruzat, lieutenant-governor, dated in 1785, who decreed as follows: —

" In view of what is set forth in the present memorial, presented by Angela Chovin, widow of the deceased Miguel Bolica, of this town of St. Louis, under date of the sixth of May of the current year, I have granted to her, in proprietary title, for her, her heirs, and others who may represent her right, forty arpens front of land upon forty in depth, along the river called *De los Padres*, (Des Pères,) from the north to the south, which is bounded on the one side by the lands of Louis Robert, and on the other by the domain of the king," &c.

This claim was confirmed in general terms to Jean F. Perry, as assignee, by the board of commissioners sitting at St. Louis, in 1811, for 1,600 arpens, " situate in the district of St. Louis, on the River Des Pères," and ordered to be surveyed " conformably to the possession, by virtue of a concession, or order of survey, from Francis Cruzat, lieutenant-general."

The plaintiff derives title under Perry.

The survey directed to be made by the board of commissioners was not executed till 1834, when the surveyor-general ordered the land to be located west of Louis Robert's tract, and on both sides of the River Des Pères. But the plaintiff insists that the land granted and confirmed adjoins Robert's tract on the east, and that the location is so plainly apparent on the face of the concession as not to require a survey; and, furthermore, he offered to show by proof that the possession of Perry, the confirmee, was part of a tract of land east of the tract of Louis Robert, of seven by forty arpens, and adjoining it; and, if located there, would include the premises in controversy. The court rejected the evidence offered, and permitted the defendant to give in evidence the official survey of the tract of 1,600 arpens; to overcome the effect of which, the plaintiff offered to prove that the official survey was improperly made west of Robert's tract, and not adjoining it; whereas it should have been made east of the same. This evidence was also rejected, when the court instructed the jury as follows: " The parties agreeing that the official survey of confirmation, under which the plaintiff claims the land in dispute, does not include the premises sued for, the jury ought to find for the defendant."

To the rejection of the parol evidence, and to the charge of the court, the plaintiff excepted.

The law is settled, that where there is a specific tract of land confirmed according to ascertained boundaries, the confirmee takes a title on which he may sue in ejectment. The case of Bissell v. Penrose, 8 How. 317, lays down the true rule.

But where the claim has no certain limits, and the judgment of confirmation carries along with it the condition that the land shall be surveyed, and severed from the public domain and the lands of others, then it is not open to controversy, that the title attaches to no land; nor has a court of justice any authority in law to ascertain and establish its boundaries, this being reserved to the executive department. The case of West v. Cochran, 17 How. 403, need only be referred to as settling this point. And the question here is, whether the concession to Perry is indefinite and vague, and subject to be located at different places.

It is to be forty by forty arpens in extent; it is to lie along the River Des Pères, from the north to the south; and to be bounded on the one side by the lands of Louis Robert, and on the other by the domain of the king. On which side of Robert's land it is to lie we are not informed, further than that it is to lie along the river from north to south. The record shows, that if surveyed west of Robert's tract, the forty by forty arpens includes the River Des Pères; but, if surveyed east of Robert's land, it will not include the river. The uncertainty of out-boundary in this instance is too manifest, in our opinion, to require discussion to show that a public survey is required to attach the concession to any land.

JAMES C. CONVERSE, ADMINISTRATOR OF PHILIP GREELY, DECEASED, PLAINTIFF IN ERROR, *v.* BENJAMIN BURGESS, NATHAN B. GIBBS, AND BENJAMIN T. BURGESS, COPARTNERS, UNDER THE FIRM OF BENJAMIN BURGESS AND SON.

Where merchant appraisers were appointed, under the tariff acts of 1842 and 1846, to review the decision of the public appraisers, it was a question of fact for the jury to decide, whether the examination of samples drawn, some weeks before their appraisement, was a substantial compliance with the law which required them to examine one package, at least, of every ten packages of goods, wares, and merchandise.

Being a question of fact for the jury, evidence was admissible tending to show that they had not complied with the law.

The protest being "that the goods were not fairly and faithfully examined by the appraisers" was a sufficient notice of the grounds upon which the importers contended that the appraisement was unlawful. It was not necessary to set forth, specifically, the reasons upon which the charge was founded.

THIS case was brought up, by writ of error, from the circuit court of the United States for the district of Massachusetts.

The facts of the case are stated in the opinion of the court. It is only necessary to add the protest and evidence offered as they were stated in the bill of exceptions, namely: —

"I this day pay to Philip Greely, jr., collector of this port, on behalf of Messrs. B. Burgess and Sons, the sum of sixteen hundred forty-three dollars and $\frac{48}{100}$, more or less, claimed by him as due to the United States from them, on merchandise imported by them in the brig Eliza Burgess, under protest, with the intention of reclaiming the same or any part thereof, as may be found to have been illegally paid by them. Said sum is claimed by advance of value on the merchandise by the appraisers, thereby increasing the duties and assessing a penalty, — all of which we protest against on the ground of fair valuation in the invoice, and that the goods were not fairly and faithfully examined by the appraisers.

"N. B. GIBBS."

The plaintiffs further offered to prove, under said protest, that the merchant appraisers did not examine or see any of the original packages of the merchandise in question, and only saw samples which had been taken on the 26th of April, 1850, from one in ten of the packages described in the invoice, and that such

35 *

samples, so drawn and exposed to the air, would not afford a fair criterion by which to judge of the importation, and claimed the right to go behind the return of the said merchant appraisers, on the ground that they had not examined the sugars, as required by law, and to put it as a question of fact to the jury without alleging fraud.

The defendant objected to the admission of such evidence to go to the jury in the absence of fraud on the part of the appraisers, and claimed that their decision was in the nature of an award, and final under the statute, and not open under this protest. But this court ruled that the evidence was admissible, and that the plaintiffs might go to the jury on the facts, whether the examination made by the merchant appraisers was, in substance and effect, equivalent to an examination of one package in ten of the importation, and if it was not, that the appraisement was void. Whereupon the counsel for the defendant did then and there except to the said rulings of the court, and thereupon the jury returned a verdict for the plaintiffs for $2,127.68.

The case was submitted, on printed arguments, by *Mr. Cushing*, (attorney-general,) for the plaintiff in error, and *Mr. Andros*, for the defendants.

Mr. Justice CAMPBELL delivered the opinion of the court.

The intestate of the plaintiff is charged in this judgment for an excess of duties collected by him in his capacity of collector of customs at the port of Boston, under color of a law of the United States.

The defendants in April, 1850, imported into Boston an invoice of sugars from the Island of Cuba, and made entry as in case of goods purchased, by the production of the invoice and an oath that it exhibited a just and faithful account of the actual cost and all charges thereon, &c. The public appraisers advanced the valuation of the merchandise contained in the invoice ten per cent above the invoice price, and made their return to the collector accordingly, the 14th May, 1850. From this valuation the defendants appealed, and merchant appraisers were appointed to make a new appraisement. These returned their report the 4th June, to the effect that the sugars could not have been purchased at the time of exportation for less than the sum assessed by the appraisers, at the principal markets of Cuba.

Duties were levied according to this appraisement, and also an additional duty of 20 per cent under the 8th section of the act of 30th July, 1846. These duties were paid 4th June, 1850, under a protest, by the defendants, with the declared " intention of reclaiming the same or any part thereof as may be found to have been illegally paid by them"; and affirm as the ground of their protest the "fair valuation in the invoice, and that the goods were not fairly and faithfully examined by the appraisers."

Upon the trial of the cause the importers (defendants) offered to prove that the merchant appraisers did not examine nor see any of the original packages of the merchandise in question, but only saw samples which had been taken on the 26th April, 1850, from one in ten of the packages described in the invoice; and that such samples so drawn and exposed to the air would not afford a true criterion by which to judge of the importation; and claimed the right to go behind the return of the said merchant appraisers, on the ground that they had not examined the sugars as required by law, and to put that as a question of fact to the jury, without alleging fraud.

The collector (plaintiff's intestate) objected to this evidence, and claimed that the decision of the appraisers was in the nature of an award, and final under the statute, and not open under this protest, in the absence of fraud, to review.

The circuit court admitted this evidence, and decided that the importers (defendants) might go to the jury on the facts, whether the examination made by the merchant appraisers was in substance and effect equivalent to an examination of one package in ten of the importation, and if it was not, that the appraisement was void.

A verdict and judgment were rendered in favor of the importers, and these decisions of the circuit court have been assigned for error in this court.

The right of an importer, who has paid money, under a valid protest, to a collector of the customs, for duties illegally assessed, to maintain an action for its return has been acknowledged by congress and in this court. 5 Stats. at Large, 727, c. 22; Greely v. Thompson, 10 How. 225. The only inquiries in such an action are, whether the duties have been legally charged, and does the protest conform to the act of congress above cited? The ascertainment of the value of imports, upon which the assessment of duties is made, is confided in the first instance to officers of the government, and, in the case of dissatisfaction of the importer with their assessment, to discreet and experienced merchants familiar with the character and value of the goods in question, whose decision is final, provided it is made in pursuance of law.

They are required by all reasonable ways or means in their power to ascertain, estimate, and appraise "the true and actual market value and wholesale price of the import," at the time and place or places specified in the statutes, "any invoice or affidavit thereto to the contrary notwithstanding"; they are authorized " to call before them and examine upon oath or affirmation any owner, importer, consignee, or other person, touching any matter or thing they may deem material in ascertaining the true market value or wholesale price of any merchandise imported, and to require the production, on oath or affirmation, of any letters, accounts, or invoices in his possession relating to the same." It is the duty of the collector to designate on the invoice at least one package of every invoice, and one package at least of every ten packages of goods, wares, and merchandise, and a greater number, should he, or either of the appraisers, deem it necessary, to be opened, examined, and appraised, and shall order the package or packages so designated to the public stores for examination. 5 Stats. at Large, 563–565, §§ 16, 17, 21. The appraisers take an oath diligently and faithfully to examine and inspect such goods, wares, and merchandise as the collector may direct, and truly to report, to the best of their knowledge and belief, the true value thereof. 8 Stats. at Large, 735, § 16.

These acts of congress provide for the appointment, regulate the duties, and impose the limitations on the authority of the appraisers, and determine the conditions on which the validity of their assessment depends. All their powers are derived from these acts, and it is their duty to observe the restrictions, and to obey the directions they contain. In the present instance, there was a neglect of the positive mandate " to open, examine, and appraise one package of every invoice, and one package, at least, of every ten packages of goods, wares, and merchandise"; and the jury have found, that the inquiry they made was not, in substance nor in effect, an equivalent for such an examination.

We are, therefore, of the opinion that the importer was not precluded by their return from disputing the sufficiency or accuracy of their assessment. But to enable the importer to do this, he must, before making payment of the duties, enter " a protest," in writing, signed by him, setting forth, " distinctly and specifically, the grounds of objection" to the payment of the duties. In the present instance there was a protest, to which there is no objection, except that its statement was not sufficiently distinct and specific. The ground of objection stated in the protest is, " that the goods were not fairly and faithfully examined by the appraisers."

And the proof offered was, that the appraisers did not examine nor see any of the original packages of the merchandise, and only saw samples which had been taken several weeks before, and which would not afford a true criterion by which to judge of the importation.

This statute was designed for practical use by men engaged

in active commercial pursuits, and was intended to superinduce a prompt and amicable settlement of differences between the government and the importer. The officers of the government on the one part, and the importer or his agent on the other, are brought into communication and intercourse by the act of entry of the import, and opportunities for explanation easily occur for every difference that may arise. We are not, therefore, disposed to exact any nice precision, nor to apply any strict rule of construction upon the notices required under this statute. It is sufficient if the importer indicates distinctly and definitely the source of his complaint, and his design to make it the foundation for a claim against the government.

In the present instance, he asserts that the goods were not fairly and faithfully examined by the appraisers. This, we think, was sufficient, without disclosing the grounds upon which he contended that the appraisement was unfair or unfaithful.

In Jones v. Bird, 5 B. & A. 887, which arose under a local act of parliament relating to the commissioners of sewers for Westminster, which provides that no plaintiff should recover in any action for anything done under certain acts of parliament, unless notice was given to the defendants, specifying the cause of action, Chief Justice Abbott said: " I think the notice sufficient, and that it ought not to be construed with great strictness, its object being merely to inform the defendant substantially of the ground of the complaint, but not of the mode or manner in which the injury has been sustained." And Justice Bayley said: " A notice of this sort does not require the same precision as a declaration. It is quite sufficient if it calls the attention of the defendants to the general nature of the injury, so that they may go to the premises and see what the ground of complaint is."

Under the act of 24 George II. c. 44, which required a notice to justices of the peace which should contain, " clearly and explicitly, the course of action which the party hath, or claimeth to have," the court of exchequer held a notice sufficient, although it was in the form of a declaration, and comprised not only the specific complaint, but all the redundancy and general averments which the experience of pleaders has led them to introduce into that description of pleadings, "for it could not have misled nor imposed any difficulty on the defendants, as to the tender of the amends they might have thought fit to make, and is, therefore, sufficient." Gimbert v. Coyney, McClelland & Y. 469.

These authorities disclose a sound principle of interpretation in regard to such notices, and support the principle we have announced in respect to that under consideration.

Upon the whole case, we think there is no error in the record, and judgment is affirmed.

Mr. Chief Justice TANEY, Mr. Justice DANIEL, and Mr. Justice NELSON dissented.

Mr. Chief Justice TANEY. I dissent from the opinion of the court, being of opinion that the grounds of objection are not "distinctly and specifically" set forth in the protest, within the meaning of the act of Congress, and that the protest did not apprise the collector of the particular objection taken at the trial, and which could easily have been removed by another appraisement if it had been brought to the notice of the collector in the pootest.

Mr. Justice DANIEL and Mr. Justice NELSON concurred with the Chief Justice.

RICHARD C. STOCKTON, APPELLANT, v. JAMES C. FORD.

In the case of Stockton v. Ford, reported in 11 Howard, 232, this court decided the
following propositions, namely : —
"Where there was a judgment which had been recorded under the laws of Louisiana
and thus made equivalent to a mortgage upon the property of the debtor, and the
plaintiff assigned this judgment, and was then himself sued and had an execution
issued against him, his rights under this recorded judgment could not be sold under
this execution, because he had previously transferred all those rights.
"The attorney who had recovered the judgment which was thus recovered and assigned, and who stood as attorney to the assignee, was not at liberty to purchase it
at the sale on execution, for his own benefit. The purchase enured to the benefit
of the client."
And in the report of the case it is stated at page 234, that the assignment was made,
inter alia, to cover the attorney's fees and other costs.
The court now decides,
1. That the present plaintiff being the same, the validity of the assignment, as to him,
was decided in the former case.
2. The question, under the assignment, for attorney's fees was necessarily involved,
and should have been made in the former trial. The former suit, therefore, constitutes a bar to the present.
3. The evidence now shows that no censure could be properly attributed to the attorney for his share in the transaction.

THIS was an appeal from the circuit court of the United States for the eastern district of Louisiana.

A full history of the transactions which led to the dispute is given in the report of the case of Stockton v. Ford, 11 How. 232.

It was submitted, on printed arguments, by *Mr. Stockton* and *Mr. Johnson*, for appellant, and by *Mr. Duncan*, for appellee.

The arguments were so connected with the facts of the case, that it is impossible to give the points by themselves.

Stockton v. Ford.

Mr. Justice NELSON delivered the opinion of the court.

This is an appeal from a decree of the circuit court of the United States for the eastern district of Louisiana.

The bill was filed by the plaintiff to charge the plantation and slaves of the defendant with a judicial mortgage, originally obtained by one Prior, against the firm of N. and E. Ford and Co. The plaintiff claims an interest in this mortgage, first, by purchase on execution against Prior; and second, by a trust created in the assignment of the same by Prior, under which the defendant derived title to it. The bill sets out the sale of the mortgage and purchase by the plaintiff, and also the assignment of the same by Prior to Jones, and by him to the defendant. The assignment to Jones provided for the payment first of the attorney's fees and all other costs out of the proceeds of the judgment, and the balance to be applied to the debts of Prior for which Jones was responsible, and the surplus, if any, to the assignor.

The plaintiff prayed that the defendant might be decreed to pay the attorney's fees and costs on obtaining the judicial mortgage, according to the condition of the assignment; and, also, any balance that might be found due after satisfying the debts for which Jones was responsible.

The defendant, among other defences, set up a former suit in bar.

A previous bill had been filed by the plaintiff against the defendant, seeking to foreclose this judicial mortgage, in which the same title as in this case under the execution and sale against Prior was relied on. And among other defences to that suit, the defendant set up the assignment of the mortgage by Prior to Jones previous to the said sale on execution, and by Jones to the defendant.

This right of the plaintiff to the judicial mortgage under the sale on execution, and of the defendant under the assignments, were directly involved in that suit, and presented the principal questions in the case. The validity of the assignments over the claim of the plaintiff was maintained by the judgment of the court below, and which was affirmed on appeal to this court. 11 How. 232. This court, after a full examination of the pleadings and proof, say, " that in any view, therefore, that can be properly taken of the case, the plaintiff has shown no right or interest in the judicial mortgage, which he seeks to enforce against the plantation and slaves in question. The whole interest is in the defendant.

The court also observed, " that the assignment (to Jones) was made upon full consideration, without any concealment, or, for aught that appears, intent to hinder and delay creditors; and was well known to the plaintiff long before he became the purchaser at the sheriff's sale. It passed the legal interest in the judicial mortgage out of Prior, and vested it in Jones, as early as the 12th of March, 1840, and we are wholly unable to perceive any ground of equity in the plaintiff, or of those under whom he holds, for disturbing it through a judgment against the assignor, rendered nearly two years afterwards. The sheriff's sale, therefore, could not operate to pass any interest in it to the plaintiff."

. One of the questions now sought to be agitated again is precisely the same as this one in the previous suit; namely, the right of the plaintiff to the judicial mortgage under the execution and sale against Prior. The other is somewhat varied; namely, the equitable right or interest in the mortgage of the plaintiff, as the attorney of Prior, for the fees and costs provided for in the assignment to Jones. But this question was properly involved in the former case, and might have been there raised and determined. The neglect of the plaintiff to avail himself of it, even if it were tenable, furnishes no reason for another litigation. The right of the respective parties to the judicial mortgage was the main question in the former suit. That issue, of course, involved the whole or any partial interest in the mortgage. We are satisfied, therefore, that the former suit constitutes a complete bar to the present.

The court, in the former suit, also expressed the opinion that the plaintiff was not in a situation to maintain his claim of title to the mortgage under the execution and sale against Prior; as it appeared in that case that he was the attorney of Prior in the judicial mortgage, and stood in that relation to Jones at the time of the purchase, and, for aught that appears, had made the purchase without his knowledge or consent; and that, under such circumstances, the purchase would enure to the benefit of the client and those holding under him.

It is due to the plaintiff to say, that the evidence in this case, explanatory of the point in the former, shows that he did not stand in the relation of attorney to Jones at the time of the sale; or, at least, had no reason to suppose that he stood in that relation; and that no just ground for censure exists in the transaction against him: the explanatory evidence has fully removed it.

We think the decree below is right, and should be affirmed.

THE STATE OF PENNSYLVANIA v. THE WHEELING AND BELMONT BRIDGE COMPANY ET AL.

The power of congress to regulate commerce, includes the regulation of intercourse and navigation, and consequently the power to determine what shall or shall not be deemed, in judgment of law, an obstruction of navigation.

The provisions of the act of congress passed August 31, 1852, (10 Stats. at Large, 112,) in its 6th and 7th sections declaring the bridges over the Ohio River at Wheeling and Bridgeport to be lawful structures at their then height and position, and requiring the officers and crews of vessels navigating the Ohio River to regulate their vessels so as not to interfere with the elevation and construction of said bridges, are within the legitimate exercise, by congress, of its constitutional power to regulate commerce.

The said sections of the aforesaid act of congress are not invalid by reason of the compact, in respect to the free navigation of the Ohio River, made between the States of Virginia and Kentucky, with the sanction of congress at the time the latter State was admitted into the Union.

Neither are they in conflict with the provision of the constitution of the United States providing that "no preference shall be given by any regulation of commerce or revenue to the ports of one State over those of another."

As a general proposition it is true, that an act of congress cannot annul a judgment of the supreme court of the United States, or impair the rights determined thereby, especially as respects adjudications upon the private rights of parties; and hence the decree of this court heretofore rendered in this case, so far as it respects the costs adjudged to the complainant, is unaffected by the act of congress referred to.

But that portion of the decree of this court at the May term, 1852, in the case of the State of Pennsylvania v. The Wheeling and Belmont Bridge Company, which relates to the abatement of the bridge, proceeded upon the ground that the bridge was in conflict with the then existing regulations of commerce by congress, and was executory, depending upon the bridge continuing to be an unlawful obstruction to the public right of free navigation; and that right having since been modified by congress in the exercise of its constitutional power to regulate commerce so that the bridge is no longer an unlawful obstruction, the decree cannot now be enforced.

After the passage of the act of congress referred to, the bridge no longer being an unlawful interference with a public right, the defendant's authority to maintain it, in its then position and height, existed from the moment of the enactment; for their authority then combined the concurrent powers of both governments, state and federal, and if these are not sufficient, none can be found in our system.

The complainant's motions for a writ of assistance to execute the decree of the 27th of May, 1852, by the abatement of the bridge and for a sequestration against the corporation and attachment against its officers for disobeying said decree are therefore refused; and the motions to punish the contempt of the corporation and its officers in disobeying the injunction granted by Mr. Justice Grier, on the 27th of June, 1854, are also overruled, and the injunction is dissolved.

The decree for costs being unaffected by the act of congress, the motion for taxation and award of execution for their collection is granted.

THIS case was one of original jurisdiction in this court, upon the equity side; and may be said to be a continuation of the suit between the same parties reported in 18 How. 518.

By turning to that case, the reader will perceive that at page 627, a day was given to the plaintiffs to move the court on the subject of the decree. It is now proposed to continue the narrative from that time.

The motion made by the complainant and the motion made by the defendants to dismiss the suit, need not be particularly stated.

In the summer of 1854, the bridge was blown down by a violent storm, and the company were preparing to rebuild it according to the original plan, when the next step in the history of the case was taken.

On the 26th day of June, 1854, in vacation of the supreme court, the State of Pennsylvania, by her attorney-general and her counsel, Edwin M. Stanton, pursuant to previous notice served on the Wheeling and Belmont Bridge Company, appeared before the Honorable R. C. Grier, one of the justices of the supreme court of the United States, at chambers, and moved for an injunction as prayed for in a supplemental bill then exhibited. The substance and object of the bill is stated in the subjoined order.

On hearing the bill and affidavits, the following order was made and injunction granted.

"*In the Supreme Court of the United States.*

THE STATE OF PENNSYLVANIA
v.
THE WHEELING AND BELMONT BRIDGE COMPANY. } In Equity.

Before the Honorable R. C. GRIER, one of the judges of the supreme court of the United States.

"Whereas, on the 26th day of June, 1854, at the United States court-room in the city of Philadelphia, the State of Pennsylvania, by her attorney-general and counsel, exhibited before me, R. C. Grier, one of the justices of the supreme court of the United States, her bill of complaint in equity against the Wheeling and Belmont Bridge Company, setting forth, among other things, that the said Wheeling and Belmont Bridge Company is about to erect and construct a bridge over and across the eastern channel of the Ohio River at Wheeling, between Zane's Island and the main Virginia shore, at a less elevation than is prescribed by the decree of the supreme court of the United States heretofore rendered against said company on complaint of said State, whereby the navigation of the Ohio River by steamboats of the largest class will be obstructed, to the injury of the said State; and in the vacation of the supreme court the said complainant hath applied to me for an injunction as prayed for in said bill against the said Wheeling and Belmont Bridge Company, and its president, managers, officers, engineers, agents, contractors, and servants, to enjoin them from erecting and constructing a bridge at the place aforesaid at a less elevation than is prescribed by the decree aforesaid, and from doing any act or thing to obstruct the navigation of the Ohio River, as prayed in said bill:

" And reasonable notice of said application having been given unto the said Wheeling and Belmont Bridge Company to appear before me, to resist said application, and the proofs and arguments of counsel being heard, it is considered and adjudged that an injunction, as prayed for in the said bill, be, and the same is hereby, allowed. And it is ordered that the writ of injunction of the United States of America be forthwith issued by the clerk of the supreme court of the United States, under the seal of the said court, against the said Wheeling and Belmont Bridge Company, its president, managers, officers, engineers, agents, contractors, and servants, and all persons acting by their instigation, authority, or procurement, or otherwise, commanding and requiring them, and every of them, under the penalty of the law, that they do forthwith and absolutely desist and abstain from erecting and constructing, or causing to be erected or constructed, any bridge, structure, or device, in, over, or across the eastern channel of the Ohio River, at Wheeling, between Zane's Island and the main Virginia shore, at a less elevation than is prescribed by the decree aforesaid of the supreme court of the United States against said bridge company, entered at the adjourned term in May, 1852, and from stretching, suspending, or placing, or causing to be stretched, suspended, or placed, any iron cables, ropes, wires, or chains, or any timber, structure, material, or thing whatsoever, in, over, or across the said channel, at a less elevation than is prescribed by the decree aforesaid, and from keeping and maintaining any cable, rope, wire, chain, timber, or thing whatsoever, suspended in, over, or across the said channel, at a less elevation than is prescribed by the decree aforesaid, and from doing, or causing to be done, any act or thing to obstruct the free navigation of said channel of the Ohio River."

" It is ordered that the marshal of the District of Columbia do forthwith serve said writ."

And the clerk of the supreme court of the United States is directed to file the bill of complainant on which the aforesaid application and allowance are made, and enter this order and issue the writ of injunction above allowed ; and also, that he issue the writ of subpœna in chancery, to be served by said marshal, requiring said Wheeling and Belmont Bridge Company to appear, plead, answer, or demur to said bill within ninety days from the service of said writ.

Given under my hand, at Philadelphia, this 26th day of June, 1854. R. C. GRIER,
Associate Justice Sup. Court U. S.

The preceding order having been filed in the office of the clerk of the supreme court on the 27th day of June, a writ of injunction, with a certified copy of the decree of the supreme court, entered at May term, 1852, annexed thereto, was issued and delivered to the marshal of the District of Columbia, as follows: —

THE UNITED STATES OF AMERICA.

In the Supreme Court of the United States, ss.

The President of the United States of America, to the Wheeling and Belmont Bridge Company, its president, managers, officers, engineers, agents, contractors, and servants, and to each and every of them, and to all persons whomsoever, greeting:

Whereas, the State of Pennsylvania hath made application before the Honorable R. C. Grier, one of the justices of the supreme court of the United States, for an injunction as prayed for in her bill of complaint exhibited before said justice, and filed in the supreme court of the United States:

And whereas, upon hearing of said application, the following order was made: —

[In the injunction, the preceding order was recited.]

We, therefore, having regard to the matter aforesaid, do strictly enjoin and command the said Wheeling and Belmont Bridge Company, its pres ent, managers, officers, engineers, agents, contractors, and servants, and all persons acting by their instigation, authority, advice, procurement, or otherwise, to observe and obey the aforesaid order and injunction.

Hereof fail not, under the full penalty of the law thence ensuing.

Witness the Honorable Roger B. Taney, chief justice of the supreme court of the United States, this 28th day of June, A. D. 1854.

Attest,   WM. THOMAS CARROLL,
          Clerk of the Supreme Court of the United States.

The writs of injunction being served upon the company by leaving a copy at its office and with its president and secretary, and also upon the managers of the company, they proceeded to erect the bridge notwithstanding the injunction, and it was completed in November.

At December term, 1854, the complainant, by her counsel, having given previous notice to the company, filed a motion for a sequestration against the company, for a contempt of court in disobeying the injunction, and a motion for an attachment against the officers personally for their contempt in disobeying the injunction. The motions were as follows:—

Motion for Sequestration.

And now, to wit, at the December term, 1854, comes the State of Pennsylvania, by her attorney-general, and moves the court to order and direct a writ to be issued against the Wheeling and Belmont Bridge Company, to sequestrate its estate, real, personal, and mixed, and the rents, issues, and profits thereof, its privileges and franchises, goods, chattels, rights, credits, moneys, and effects, for a contempt of court, by breach of and disobedience to the lawful writ, process, orders, decree, and commands of the supreme court of the United States.

The breaches and disobedience to said writ, process, orders, decree, and commands aforesaid are stated and charged specifically as follows:—

1. That after service upon the Wheeling and Belmont Bridge Company, by the marshal of the District of Columbia, of a copy of a writ of injunction issued out of said court, pursuant to an order of allowance made on the 26th day of June, 1854, by the Honorable R. C. Grier, one of the judges of the said supreme court, the said company have disobeyed said writ of injunction, and are engaged in doing and performing acts, and have caused and procured acts to be done, in disobedience of said injunction and of the process and authority of said court.

2. That after service upon said company by the marshal aforesaid, of a copy of the decree entered by said supreme court at the adjourned term of May, 1852, in the case of The State of Pennsylvania *v.* The Wheeling and Belmont Bridge Company and others, said company have disobeyed said decree.

8. That since the service of the writ of injunction and decree as aforesaid upon said company, said company have stretched, suspended, and placed, and caused and procured to be stretched, suspended, and placed, iron cables, ropes, wires, or chains, over and across the eastern channel of the Ohio River, between Zane's Island and the main Virginia shore, at Wheeling, in disobedience of said injunction; and have erected and constructed, and are engaged in erecting and constructing, and in causing and procuring to be erected and constructed, a bridge over and across the said channel, at a less elevation than is prescribed by the said decree of the supreme court of the United States, entered as aforesaid, at the adjourned term of May, 1852, and in disobedience of said writ of injunction; and have kept and maintained, and are keeping and maintaining, cables, wires, chains,

36 *

timbers, and planks suspended in, over, and across the said channel, at a less elevation than is prescribed by the decree aforesaid.

4. That since the service of said writ and decree as aforesaid, the said company have obstructed the free navigation of the said channel of the Ohio River, and have caused and procured the same to be obstructed, and are now keeping the same obstructed, in breach and disobedience of said writ of injunction and decree.　　　　　　　　　　　F. W. HUGHES,
Attorney-General of Pennsylvania.

Motion for Attachment.

And now, to wit, at the December term, 1854, comes the State of Pennsylvania, by her attorney-general, and moves the court for an order that Charles Ellet, Jr., James Baker, and E. H. Fitzhugh stand committed to the jail of the District of Columbia, for a contempt of court, by breach of and disobedience to the lawful writ, process, order, decree, and commands of the supreme court of the United States.

[The breaches set out were the same as above.]

A motion for a writ of assistance to execute the decree of this court made in May, 1852, was also filed, praying the court to order and direct such a writ to the marshal of the District of Columbia.

A motion was also made for an award of execution for the costs decreed in May, 1852.

The defendants appeared by their counsel, and resisted the foregoing motions under the 6th and 7th sections of the act of congress, (10 Stat. at Large, 112,) entitled

"An act making appropriations for the service of The Post-Office Department during the fiscal year ending the thirtieth of June, one thousand eight hundred and fifty-three, and for other purposes.

SEC. 6. And be it further enacted that the bridges across the Ohio River at Wheeling, in the State of Virginia, and at Bridgeport, in the State of Ohio, abutting on Zane's Island, in said river, are hereby declared to be lawful structures, in their present position and elevation, and shall be so held and taken to be, anything in any law or laws of the United States to the contrary notwithstanding.

SEC. 7. And be it further enacted, that the said bridges are declared to be and are established post-roads for the passage of the mails of the United States, and that the Wheeling and Belmont Bridge Company are authorized to have and maintain their said bridges at their present site and elevation, and the officers and crews of all vessels and boats navigating said river are required to regulate the use of their said vessels and boats, and of any pipes or chimneys belonging thereto, so as not to interfere with the elevation and construction of said bridges.

The defendants also moved to dissolve the injunction granted by Mr. Justice Grier.

At December term, 1854, these several motions came on to be heard, and were argued by *Mr. Edwin M. Stanton*, for the State of Pennsylvania and by *Mr. Johnson* and *Mr. Charles M. Russell*, for the defendants.

Mr. Stanton, for the complainant, made the following points, viz. : —

1. That at the date of the passage of the act of congress legalizing the Wheeling Bridge, the State of Pennsylvania had by the judgment of the supreme court of the United States, " a just and legal right to have the navigation of the Ohio River made free by the removal of the bridge, or by its alteration," in conformity with the decree entered in May, 1852.

2. That this right is not taken away by congress declaring the bridge to be a " lawful structure," because congress has no judicial authority to review or reverse the judgment of the supreme court, and such declaration is not within the scope of the legislative authority of congress.

3. It is not taken away by the bridge being " established as a post-road," because under the power to establish post-roads, congress has no authority to construct or maintain a road within a State to the injury of private property or individual right.

4. It is not taken away by the requirements of the act imposing on vessels the duty " not to interfere with the construction and elevation of the bridge," because those requirements are imposed for an object not intrusted to the general government, nor in execution of its commercial power ; and they operate to tax the exports of a State, and give a preference by a regulation of commerce to the ports of one State, over the ports of another.

5. It could not be taken away by any power of congress without just compensation, and none is rendered.

6. It was the duty of the defendants to obey the command of the court, by removing or altering their bridge as required by the decree ; and for their disobedience, they are in contempt, and they are in further contempt by rebuilding the bridge in defiance of the decree, and of the injunction issued on the 27th of June, 1854, and should be dealt with accordingly by sequestration and attachment.

7. The decree of the court remains now in force, and the complainant is entitled to have it executed by writ of assistance and

to have process to compel the payment of the costs awarded by the decree.

The counsel for the defendants made the following points, viz.:

I. On the motion to dissolve the injunction.

1. The injunction was awarded without "reasonable notice of the time and place" of the application. Act of March 2, 1798, § 5.

2. It was awarded by a judge of a different circuit from that in which it was to operate. Laws U. S. Courts, p. 34, note.

8. It was awarded without requiring bond and security to indemnify the defendant.

4. It was awarded on a bill filed either to carry on the proceedings in a pending suit, or to carry into effect a decree made in a former suit; and this bill does not lie, nor is it in proper form for either purpose. Story's Eq. Plead. § 352, 429; Adams v. Dowdings, 2 Madd, 58.

5. Congress has legalized the Wheeling Bridge; act of August 31, 1852; and had constitutional power to legalize it. See the opinions formerly delivered in the Wheeling Bridge case. The act may be sustained under the power to regulate commerce; Gibbons v. Ogden, 9 Wheat. 1; United States v. Coombs, 12 Pet. 72, (op. 78;) or under the power to establish postroads; or under both powers. And this, notwithstanding the compact between Virginia and Kentucky; Pollard's Lessee v. Hagam, 3 How. 212, (op. 229, 230;) The Society for propagating the Gospel v. Wheeler, 2 Gallis, C. C. R. 138; Evans v. Easton, 1 Pet. C. C. R. 322. But that compact does not apply.

6. A motion was offered to make absolute the decree in said bill mentioned, and was dismissed by this court for want of prosecution on the 15th day of December, 1858.

II. Against the motion for the writ of assistance.

The same authorities as above and hereafter cited.

III. Against motions for attachment and sequestration.

1. The evidence offered does not show that the parties have been guilty of contempt.

2. The injunction was, and is a nullity, because awarded without notice, without requiring bond, and by a judge having no jurisdiction.

8. The injunction was not regularly issued, or served by proper officers.

4. The injunction did not point out the duties it required of the defendants with adequate certainty. In effect it commanded the defendants to observe the requirements of a decree which "required" nothing such as the order of injunction vaguely

seemed to assume that it did acquire. That decree was on its face interlocutory and left open the questions which the injunction may assume to have been decided. Birchett v. Bollings, 5 Munf. 442.

5. The court has no power to inflict summary punishment for disobedience to any mere order of a judge at chambers. Such disobedience can only be punished, if at all, by indictment. Act of 1831, c. 99, 4 Stats. at Large, 487.

Mr. Justice NELSON delivered the opinion of the court.

The motion in this case is founded upon a bill filed to carry into execution a decree of the court, rendered against the defendants at the adjourned term in May, 1852, which decree declared the bridge erected by them across the Ohio River, between Wheeling and Zane's Island, to be an obstruction of the free navigation of the said river, and thereby occasioned a special damage to the plaintiff, for which there was not an adequate remedy at law, and directed that the obstruction be removed, either by elevating the bridge to a height designated, or by abatement.

Since the rendition of this decree, and on the 31st August, 1852, an act of congress has been passed as follows: "That the bridges across the Ohio River at Wheeling, in the State of Virginia, and at Bridgeport, in the State of Ohio, abutting on Zane's Island, in said river, are hereby declared to be lawful structures in their present positions and elevations, and shall be so held and taken to be, anything in the law or laws of the United States to the contrary notwithstanding."

And further: "That the said bridges be declared to be and are established post-roads for the passage of the mails of the United States, and that the Wheeling and Belmont Bridge Company are authorized to have and maintain their bridges at their present site and elevation; and the officers and crews of all vessels and boats navigating said river are required to regulate the use of their said vessels, and of any pipes or chimneys belonging thereto, so as not to interfere with the elevation and construction of said bridges."

The defendants rely upon this act of congress as furnishing authority for the continuance of the bridge as constructed, and as superseding the effect and operation of the decree of the court previously rendered, declaring it an obstruction to the navigation.

On the part of the plaintiff, it is insisted that the act is unconstitutional and void, which raises the principal question in the case.

In order to a proper understanding of this question it is material to recur to the ground and principles upon which the majority of the court proceeded in rendering the decree now sought to be enforced.

The bridge had been constructed under an act of the legislature of the State of Virginia; and it was admitted that act conferred full authority upon the defendants for the erection, subject only to the power of congress in the regulation of commerce. It was claimed, however, that congress had acted upon the subject and had regulated the navigation of the Ohio River, and had thereby secured to the public, by virtue of its authority, the free and unobstructed use of the same; and that the erection of the bridge, so far as it interfered with the enjoyment of this use, was inconsistent with and in violation of the acts of congress, and destructive of the right derived under them; and that, to the extent of this interference with the free navigation of the river, the act of the legislature of Virginia afforded no authority or justification. It was in conflict with the acts of congress, which were the paramount law.

This being the view of the case taken by a majority of the court, they found no difficulty in arriving at the conclusion, that the obstruction of the navigation of the river, by the bridge, was a violation of the right secured to the public by the constitution and laws of congress, nor in applying the appropriate remedy in behalf of the plaintiff. The ground and principles upon which the court proceeded will be found reported in 13 How. 518.

Since, however, the rendition of this decree, the acts of congress, already referred to, have been passed, by which the bridge is made a post-road for the passage of the mails of the United States, and the defendants are authorized to have and maintain it at its present site and elevation, and requiring all persons navigating the river to regulate such navigation so as not to interfere with it.

So far, therefore, as this bridge created an obstruction to the free navigation of the river, in view of the previous acts of congress, they are to be regarded as modified by this subsequent legislation; and, although it still may be an obstruction in fact, is not so in the contemplation of law. We have already said, and the principle is undoubted, that the act of the legislature of Virginia conferred full authority to erect and maintain the bridge, subject to the exercise of the power of congress to regulate the navigation of the river. That body having in the exercise of this power, regulated the navigation consistent with its preservation and continuation, the authority to maintain it would seem to be complete. That authority combines the concurrent powers of both governments, state and federal, which, if not sufficient, certainly none can be found in our system of government.

We do not enter upon the question, whether or not congress possess the power, under the authority in the constitution, " to establish post-offices and post-roads," to legalize this bridge; for, conceding that no such powers can be derived from this clause, it must be admitted that it is, at least, necessarily included in the power conferred to regulate commerce among the several States. The regulation of commerce includes intercourse and navigation, and, of course, the power to determine what shall or shall not be deemed in judgment of law an obstruction to navigation; and that power, as we have seen, has been exercised consistent with the continuance of the bridge.

But it is urged, that the act of congress cannot have the effect and operation to annul the judgment of the court already rendered, or the rights determined thereby in favor of the plaintiff. This, as a general proposition, is certainly not to be denied, especially as it respects adjudication upon the private rights of parties. When they have passed into judgment the right becomes absolute, and it is the duty of the court to enforce it.

The case before us, however, is distinguishable from this class of cases, so far as it respects that portion of the decree directing the abatement of the bridge. Its interference with the free navigation of the river constituted an obstruction of a public right secured by acts of congress.

But, although this right of navigation be a public right common to all, yet, a private party sustaining special damage by the obstruction may, as has been held in this case, maintain an action at law against the party creating it, to recover his damages; or, to prevent irreparable injury, file a bill in chancery for the purpose of removing the obstruction. In both cases, the private right to damages, or to the removal, arises out of the unlawful interference with the enjoyment of the public right, which, as we have seen, is under the regulation of congress. Now, we agree, if the remedy in this case had been an action at law, and a judgment rendered in favor of the plaintiff for damages, the right to these would have passed beyond the reach of the power of congress. It would have depended, not upon the public right of the free navigation of the river, but upon the judgment of the court. The decree before us, so far as it respect the costs adjudged, stands upon the same principles, and is unaffected by the subsequent law. But that part of the decree, directing the abatement of the obstruction, is executory, a continuing decree, which requires not only the removal of the bridge, but enjoins the defendants against any reconstruction or continuance. Now, whether it is a future existing or continuing obstruction depends upon the question whether or not it interferes with the right of navigation. If, in the mean time, since the decree, this right has been modified by the competent authority, so that the bridge is no longer an unlawful obstruction, it is quite plain the decree of the court cannot be enforced. There is no longer any interference with the enjoyment of the public right inconsistent with law, no more than there would be where the plaintiff himself had consented to it, after the rendition of the decree. Suppose the decree had been executed, and after that the assage of the law in question, can it be doubted but that the defendants would have had a right to reconstruct it? And is it not equally clear that the right to maintain it, if not abated, existed from the moment of the enactment?

A class of cases that have frequently occurred in the state courts contain principles analogous to those involved in the present case. The purely internal streams of a State which are navigable belong to the riparian owners to the thread of the stream, and, as such, they have a right to use the waters and bed beneath, for their own private emolument, subject only to the public right of navigation. They may construct wharves or dams or canals for the purpose of subjecting the stream to the various uses to which it may be applied, subject to this public easement. But, if these structures materially interfere with the public right, the obstruction may be removed or abated as a public nuisance.

In respect to these purely internal streams of a State, the public right of navigation is exclusively under the control and regulation of the state legislature; and in cases where these erections or obstructions to the navigation are constructed under a law of the State, or sanctioned by legislative authority, they are neither a public nuisance subject to abatement, nor is the individual who may have sustained special damage from their interference with the public use entitled to any remedy for his loss. So far as the public use of the stream is concerned, the legislature having the power to control and regulate it, the statute authorizing the structure, though it may be a real impediment to the navigation, makes it lawful. 5 Wend. 448, 449; 15 Ib. 118; 17 T. R. 195; 20 Ib. 90, 101; 5 Cow. 165.

It is also urged that this act of congress is void, for the reason that it is inconsistent with the compact between the States of Virginia and Kentucky, at the time of the admission of the latter into the Union, by which it was agreed, "that the use and navigation of the river Ohio, so far as the territory of the proposed, or the territory that shall remain within the limits of this commonwealth, lies thereon, shall be free and common to the citizens of the United States," and which compact was assented to by congress at the time of the admission of the State.

This court held, in the case of Green et al. v. Biddle, 2 Wheat.

1, that an act of the legislature of Kentucky in contravention of the compact was null and void, within the provision of the constitution forbidding a State to pass any law impairing the obligation of contracts. But that is not the question here. The question here is, whether or not the compact can operate as a restriction upon the power of congress under the constitution to regulate commerce among the several States? Clearly not. Otherwise congress and two States would possess the power to modify and alter the constitution itself.

This is so plain that it is unnecessary to pursue the argument further. But we may refer to the case of Wilson v. Mason, 1 Cranch, 88, 92, where it was held that this compact, which stipulated that rights acquired under the commonwealth of Virginia shall be decided according to the then existing laws, could not deprive congress of the power to regulate the appellate jurisdiction of this court, and prevent a review where none was given in the state law existing at the time of the compact. Again, it is insisted that the act of congress is void, as being inconsistent with the clause in the ninth section of article first of the constitution, which declares that "no preference shall be given by any regulation of commerce or revenue to the ports of one State over those of another; nor shall vessels bound to or from one State be obliged to enter, clear, or pay duties in another."

It is urged that the interruption of the navigation of the steamboats engaged in commerce and conveyance of passengers upon the Ohio River at Wheeling from the erection of the bridge, and the delay and expense arising therefrom, virtually operate to give a preference to this port over that of Pittsburg; that the vessels to and from Pittsburg navigating the Ohio and Mississippi rivers are not only subjected to this delay and expense in the course of the voyage, but that the obstruction will necessarily have the effect to stop the trade and business at Wheeling, or divert the same in some other direction or channel of commerce. Conceding all this to be true, a majority of the court are of opinion that the act of congress is not inconsistent with the clause of the constitution referred to — in other words, that is not giving a preference to the ports of one State over those of another, within the true meaning of that provision. There are many acts of congress passed in the exercise of this power to regulate commerce, providing for a special advantage to the port or ports of one State, and which very advantage may incidentally operate to the prejudice of the ports in a neighboring State, which have never been supposed to conflict with this limitation upon its power. The improvement of rivers and harbors, the erection of light-houses, and other facilities of commerce, may be referred to as examples. It will not do to say that the exercise of an admitted power of congress conferred by the constitution is to be withheld, if it appears, or can be shown, that the effect and operation of the law may incidentally extend beyond the limitation of the power. Upon any such interpretation, the principal object of the framers of the instrument in conferring the power would be sacrificed to the subordinate consequences resulting from its exercise. These consequences and incidents are very proper considerations to be urged upon congress for the purpose of dissuading that body from its exercise, but afford no ground for denying the power itself, or the right to exercise it.

The court are also of opinion that, according to the true exposition of this prohibition upon the power of congress, the law in question cannot be regarded as in conflict with it.

The propositions originally introduced into the convention, from which this clause in the constitution was derived, declared that congress shall not have power to compel vessels belonging to citizens or foreigners to enter or pay duties or imposts in any other State than that to which they were bound, nor to clear from any other than that in which their cargoes were laden. Nor shall any privilege or immunity be granted to any vessels on entering or clearing out, or paying duties or imposts, in one State in preference to another. Also, that congress shall not have power to fix or establish the particular ports for collecting the duties or imposts in any State, unless the State should neglect to fix them upon notice. I give merely the substance of the several propositions.

Luther Martin, in his letter to the legislature of Maryland, says that these propositions were introduced into the convention by the Maryland delegation; and that without them, he observes, it would have been in the power of congress to compel ships sailing in or out of the Chesapeake to clear or enter at Norfolk, or some port in Virginia — a regulation that would be injurious to the commerce of Maryland. It appears also, from the reports of the convention, that several of the delegates from that State expressed apprehensions that under the power to regulate commerce congress might favor ports of particular States, by requiring vessels destined to other States to enter and clear at the ports of the favored ones, as a vessel bound for Baltimore to enter and clear at Norfolk

These several propositions finally took the form of the clause in question, namely: No preference shall be given by any regulation of commerce or revenue to the ports of one State over those of another; nor shall vessels bound to or from one State be obliged to enter or clear or pay duties in another." 1 Elliot's Deb. 266, 270, 279, 280, 311, 375; 5 Ib. 478, 483, 502, 545.

The power to establish their ports of entry and clearance by the States was given up, and left to congress. But the rights of the States were secured, by the exemption of vessels from the necessity of entering or paying duties in the ports of any State other than that to which they were bound, or to obtain a clearance from any port other than at the home port, or that from which they sailed. And, also, by the provision that no preference should be given, by any regulation of commerce or revenue, to the ports of one State over those of another. So far as the regulation of revenue is concerned, the prohibition in the clause does not seem to have been very important, as, in a previous section, (8,) it was declared, that "all duties, imposts, and excises shall be uniform throughout the United States"; and, as to a preference by a regulation of commerce, the history of the provision, as well as its language, looks to a prohibition against granting privileges or immunities to vessels entering or clearing from the ports of one State over those of another. That these privileges and immunities, whatever they may be in the judgment of congress, shall be common and equal in all the ports of the several States. Thus much is undoubtedly embraced in the prohibition; and it may, certainly, also embrace any other description of legislation looking to a direct privilege or preference of the ports of any particular State over those of another. Indeed, the clause, in terms, seems to import a prohibition against some positive legislation by congress to this effect, and not against any incidental advantages that might possibly result from the legislation of congress upon other subjects connected with commerce, and confessedly within its power.

Besides, it is a mistake to assume that congress is forbidden to give a preference to a port in one State over a port in another. Such preference is given in every instance where it makes a port in one State a port of entry, and refuses to make another port in another State a port of entry. No greater preference, in one sense, can be more directly given than in this way; and yet, the power of congress to give such preference has never been questioned. Nor can it be without asserting that the moment congress makes a port in one State a port of entry, it is bound, at the same time, to make all other ports in all other States ports of entry. The truth seems to be, that what is forbidden is, not discrimination between individual ports within the same or different States, but discrimination between States; and if so, in order to bring this case within the prohibition, it is necessary to show, not merely discrimination between Pittsburg and Wheeling, but discrimination between the ports of Virginia and those of Pennsylvania.

Upon the whole, without pursuing the examination further, our conclusion is, that, so far as respects that portion of the decree which directs the alteration or abatement of the bridge, it cannot be carried into execution since the act of congress which regulates the navigation of the Ohio River, consistent with the existence and continuance of the bridge; and that this part of the motion, in behalf of the plaintiff, must be denied. But that, so far as respects that portion of the decree which directs the costs to be paid by the defendants, the motion must be granted.

A motion has also been made, on behalf of the plaintiff, for attachments against the president of the Bridge Company and others, for disobedience of an injunction issued by Mr. Justice Grier, in vacation, on the 27th June, 1854.

It appears that since the rendition of the decree of this court and the passage of the act of congress, and before any proceedings taken to enforce the execution of the decree, notwithstanding this act, the bridge was broken down, in a gale of wind, leaving only some of the cables suspended from the towers across the river. Upon the happening of this event, a bill was filed by the plaintiff, and an application for the injunction above mentioned was made, which was granted, enjoining the defendants, their officers and agents, against a reconstruction of the bridge, unless in conformity with the requirements of the previous decree in the case. The object of the injunction was to suspend the work, together with the great expenses attending it, until the determination of the question by this court as to the force and effect of the act of congress, in respect to the execution of the decree. The defendants did not appear upon the notice given of the motion for the injunction, and it was, consequently, granted without opposition.

After the writ was served, it was disobeyed, the defendants proceeding in the reconstruction of the bridge, which they had already begun before the issuing or service of the process.

A motion is now made for attachments against the persons mentioned for this disobedience and contempt.

A majority of the court are of opinion, inasmuch as we have arrived at the conclusion that the act of congress afforded full authority to the defendants to reconstruct the bridge, and the decree directing its alteration or abatement could not, therefore, be carried into execution after the enactment of this law, and inasmuch as the granting of an attachment for the disobedience is a question resting in the discretion of the court, that, under all the circumstances of the case, the motion should be denied.

Some of the judges also entertain doubts as to the regularity of the proceedings in pursuance of which the injunction was issued.

Mr. Justice WAYNE, Mr. Justice GRIER, and Mr. Justice CURTIS are of opinion that, upon the case presented, the attachment for contempt should issue, and in which opinion I concur.

The motion for the attachment is denied, and the injunction dissolved.

Mr. Justice McLEAN, dissenting.

A motion was made, at the last term, for process of contempt against the bridge company, for not complying with the decree of this court to elevate or abate the suspension bridge, or open a draw in the bridge over the western branch of the Ohio; so as to afford a safe channel for steamboats when the water is too high for them to pass under the suspension bridge; and also for not obeying the injunction granted, &c.

In opposition to this motion the act of congress of the 31st of August, 1852, is set up, which purports to legalize both bridges.

The 6th section of the above act provides "that the bridges across the Ohio River at Wheeling, in the State of Virginia, and at Bridgeport, in the State of Ohio, abutting on Zane's Island, in said river, are hereby declared to be lawful structures in their present position and elevation, and shall be so held and taken to be, anything in any law or laws of the United States to the contrary notwithstanding."

7th section. "And be it further enacted, that the said bridges are declared to be and are established post-roads for the passage of the mails of the United States, and that the Wheeling and Belmont Bridge Company are authorized to have and maintain their said bridges at their present site and elevation; and the officers and crews of all vessels and boats navigating said river are required to regulate the use of their said vessels and boats, and of any pipes or chimneys belonging thereto, so as not to interfere with the elevation and construction of said bridges."

This court, in the exercise of its judicial functions, with the approbation of seven of its members, which included all the judges present, with but one exception, took jurisdiction of a complaint made by the State of Pennsylvania against the Wheeling Bridge Company, which was charged with having constructed its bridge so low as to cause a material obstruction to the commerce of the Ohio River; and which was especially injurious to the State of Pennsylvania, which had expended several millions of dollars in the construction of lines of improvement from Philadelphia to Pittsburg — such as turnpike roads, railroads, canals, and slackwater navigation — over which more than fifty millions' worth of property were transported annually, in connection with the Ohio River; and that any material obstruction to the navigation of the river by the bridge would be injurious to that State, by lessening the transportation of passengers and freight on the above lines.

After a very tedious and minute investigation of the facts of

37 *

the case, which embraced the reports of practical engineers, depositions from the most experienced river men, statements of the stages of water in the river throughout the year, and also after a full consideration of the legal principles applicable to the matter in controversy, six of the members of this tribunal, two only dissenting, were brought to the conclusion that the bridge was a material obstruction to the navigation of the river, at seasons of the year and under circumstances which rendered its navigation most important to the public and to the complainant, and that there was no adequate remedy for it by an action at common law.

From the facts developed in the course of the investigation, it appeared that the seven passenger packets, which plied between Cincinnati and Pittsburg, whose progress was obstructed by the bridge, conveyed about one half of the goods, in value, which were transported on the river, and three fourths of the passengers between the above cities. That each packet transported annually thirty thousand nine hundred and sixty tons of freight, and twelve thousand passengers.

It appeared that a steamboat drawing five feet water, and whose chimneys were seventy-nine feet six inches high, could never pass under the apex of the bridge, at any stage of the water, without lowering its chimneys. And the court found by lowering the chimneys, including the expense of machinery, and delay of time, without an estimate as to the dangers incurred by the operation, that a tax was imposed upon the seven packets, annually, of $5,598.00, which sum was exacted from the owners, for the accommodation of the crossing public and the bridge proprietors.

The court also found that the cost of each packet, per running hour, was eight dollars and thirty-three cents; and, as was estimated, if the chimney should be made shorter, so as to pass under the bridge at an ordinary stage of water, it would cause the average loss of four hours in each trip between Cincinnati and Pittsburg, which would amount to the sum of thirty-three dollars and thirty-two cents, which, being multiplied by sixty, the average number of trips each season, would amount to the sum of $1,999.20; and this, being multiplied by seven, would make the sum of $18,994.40, which would be an annual loss by the owners of these packets.

The court also found, that from the great weight of the chimneys of the packets, and other boats of that class, they could not be lowered by hinges at the tops; that they could only be let down at the hurricane deck by means of a derrick. The average weight of the chimneys, which must be lowered upon each of the large boats, was about four tons; and if this enormous weight, hanging over the cabin, or rather over the berths of the passengers, in the process of lowering, should come down by the run, their weight would crush the hurricane deck, break through the berths of the cabin, and be arrested, probably, only by the cargo or the lower flooring of the vessel.

For these reasons, and others contained in the opinion of the court, they came to the decision that the bridge obstructed the navigation of the Ohio, and to the irremediable injury at law of the public works of Pennsylvania. But, to avoid any greater hardship on the bridge owners than would be required by the maintenance of the commercial right, this court decreed that if the defendant would open a draw in the western channel which would admit the passage of boats, when, from the high water, they could not pass under the suspension bridge, that it would remove all reasonable ground of complaint by the plaintiffs. But this it refused to do, and invoked the legislation of congress successfully, in procuring the passage of the act above cited.

That congress have a constitutional power to regulate commerce among the States, as with foreign nations, must be admitted. And where the constitution imposes no restriction on this power, it is exercised at discretion; and the correction of impolicy, or abuse, is only through the ballot-box. During the existence of the embargo, in the year 1808, it was contended that, under the commercial power, an embargo could not be imposed, as it destroyed commerce. But it was held otherwise; so that the constitutionality of a regulation of commerce by congress does not depend upon the policy and justice of such an act, but generally upon its discretion.

An embargo is a temporary regulation, and is designed for the protection of commerce, though, for a time, it may suspend it. There are, however, limitations on the exercise of the commercial power by congress. As stated in the opinion of the court, congress had regulated the commerce of the Ohio River. But all such regulations, before the passage of the above act, were of a general character, and tended to the security of transportation, whether of freight or passengers.

The decree in the Wheeling bridge case was the result of a judicial investigation, founded upon facts ascertained in the course of the hearing. It was strictly a judicial question. The complaint was an obstruction of commerce, by the bridge, to the injury of the complainant, and the court found the fact to be as alleged in the bill. It was said by Chief Justice Marshall, many years ago, that congress could do many things, but that it could not alter a fact. This it has attempted to do in the above act. An obstruction to the navigation of the river was, technically, a nuisance, and, in their decree, this court so pronounced.

The compact between Virginia and Kentucky, which "declared, that the use and navigation of the river Ohio should be free and common to the citizens of the United States," was incorporated into the Kentucky constitution of 1791, and received the sanction of congress in the admission of that State into the Union. This compact bound both parties; and this court held, that a violation of it by a law of Kentucky, called the occupying claimant law, was void, as it impaired the obligation of the compact. Virginia, no more than Kentucky, could violate any of its provisions, although they extended to citizens of the Union.

The effect that the act of congress shall have upon the decree of the court, I will now consider. This subject can be treated only with the profoundest respect for the legislative action of the nation, and with a sincere desire to give to it all the effect which such an expression should have.

The congress and the court constitute co-ordinate branches of the government; their duties are distinct and of a different character. The judicial power cannot legislate, nor can the legislative power act judicially. The constitution has declared, that the judicial power shall extend to all cases in law and equity arising under the constitution, the laws of the United States, and treaties, &c. All legislative powers are vested in congress. While these functionaries are limited to their appropriate duties as vested, there can be little or no conflict of jurisdiction.

From the organization of the legislative power, it is unfitted for the discharge of judicial duties; and the same may be said of this court in regard to legislation. It may therefore happen, that, when either trenches upon the appropriate powers of the other, their acts are inoperative and void.

The judicial power is exercised in the decision of cases; the legislative, in making general regulations by the enactment of laws. The latter acts from considerations of public policy; the former by the pleadings and evidence in a case. From this view it is at once seen, that congress could not undertake to hear the complaint of Pennsylvania in this case, take testimony or cause it to be taken, examine the surveys and reports of engineers, decide the questions of law which arise on the admission of the testimony, and give the proper and legal effect to the evidence in the final decree. To do this is the appropriate duty of the judicial power. And this is what was done by this court, before the above act of congress was passed. The court held, that the bridge obstructed the navigation of the Ohio River, and that, consequently, it was a nuisance. The act declared the bridge to be a legal structure, and, consequently, that it was not a nuisance. Now, is this a legislative or a judicial act? Whether it be a nuisance or not, depends upon the fact of obstruction; and this would seem to be strictly a judicial question, to be decided on evidence produced by the parties in a case.

We do not speak of a public commercial right, but of an obstruction to it, by which an individual wrong is done, that at law is irremediable. A regulation of the public right belongs exclusively to congress. It is a question of policy, which seldom, if ever, comes within the range of judicial action. All such questions belong to the legislative power.

The words of the seventh section of the act are, "that the said bridges are declared to be and are established post-roads for the passage of the mails of the United States; and that the Wheeling and Belmont Bridge Company are authorized to have and maintain their said bridges, at their present site and elevation; and the officers and crews of all vessels and boats navigating the river are required to regulate the use of their said vessels and boats, and of any pipes or chimneys belonging thereto, so as not to interfere with the elevation and construction of said bridges."

The provisions of this section are: 1. The bridges are declared to be post-roads; and, 2. The pipes and chimneys of the boats are required to be cut down, so as not to interfere with said bridges.

And, first, as to the effect of making the bridges post-roads: —

By the act of the 7th July, 1838, all railroads are declared to be post-roads; and, for more than twenty years, all navigable waters on which steamboats regularly ply are established as post-roads.

The policy of extending the lines of post-roads on all railroads and navigable waters was to require, under a penalty, all boats and railroad cars to deposit in post-offices all letters which they may carry, so that the postage may be charged. It gives to the government no rights on these lines of communication, except where the mail may be carried under a contract, which, if obstructed, subjects the offender to prosecution. It gives to the government no other interest in or control over the road.

The railroad may be changed at the will of the proprietors, and the mail will not be carried in the cars, except by contract, for which a compensation is paid. The same principle applies to a turnpike road on which the mail is carried. Even an ordinary road, though a post-road, may be altered or vacated at the will of the local authority.

It is difficult to perceive what benefit can result to the public from these bridges being declared a post-road. It cannot use the bridges without paying toll the same as for the use of a turnpike road or railroad. It does not prevent the Bridge Compan from pulling down the bridge or altering it in any respect. They are under no obligation by reason of this use to keep up the bridge or repair it. They may abandon it, and if it should be again prostrated by the winds, they are not obliged to rebuild it.

The idea that making the bridge a post-road would exempt it from the consequence of being a nuisance, is wholly unsustainable. Should the contractor to carry the mail refuse or neglect to pay the customary tolls, he would be liable to a suit for the amount. If one of the Pittsburg packets carry the mail under a contract with the post-office department, and the bridge should obstruct the boat, such an obstruction would make the bridge company liable, unless the above act, which gives a preference to the crossing mail, applies a different rule to the mail boat; and it would seem that no such preference can arise under the law declaring the bridge to be a post-road.

But is there a power in congress to legalize a bridge over a navigable water within the jurisdiction of any State or States? It has the power to regulate commerce among the several States, requiring two or more States to authorize the regulation. But this does not necessarily include the power to construct bridges which may obstruct commerce, but can never increase its facilities on a navigable water. Any power which congress may have in regard to such a structure is indirect, and results from a commercial regulation. It may, under this power, declare that no bridge shall be built which shall be an obstruction to the use of a navigable water. And this, it would seem, is as far as the commercial power by congress can be exercised.

The same power that would enable congress to build a bridge over a navigable stream would authorize it to construct a railroad or turnpike road through the States of the Union, as it might deem expedient. This power may have been asserted in regard to post-roads, but the settled opinion now seems to be, that to establish post-roads within the meaning of the constitution is to designate them. In this sense congress may establish post-roads extending over bridges, but it can neither build them nor exercise any control over them, except the mere use for the conveyance of the mail on paying toll.

It has often been held, that in throwing a bridge across a navigable river or arm of a lake, or the sea, the sovereign power of the State in some form may authorize it, under such restrictions and conditions as may be considered best for the public. But this power must always be so exercised as not materially to obstruct navigation. Over this public right congress exercises exclusive legislation, except where the constitution restricts it; and the judicial power can never interpose, except in regard to private injuries. It would be otherwise if congress should authorize an indictment for obstructing the public right of navigation on the Ohio, or generally. If, under the commercial power, congress may make bridges over navigable waters, it would be difficult to find any limitation of such a power. Turnpike roads, railroads, and canals might on the same principle be built by congress. And if this be a constitutional power, it cannot be restricted or interfered with by any state regulation. So extravagant and absorbing a federal power as this has rarely, if ever, been claimed by any one. It would, in a great degree, supersede the state governments by the tremendous authority and patronage it would exercise. But if the power be found in the constitution, no principle is perceived by which it can be practically restricted. This dilemma leads us to the conclusion that it is not a constitutional power. Having arrived at this point, it only remains to say, that the act of congress declaring the bridge to be a legal structure, being the exercise of a judicial and an appellate power, is unconstitutional, and consequently inoperative. It is what it purports to be, a reversal of the decree of this court, in effect, if not in terms.

Under the commercial power, congress may declare what shall constitute an obstruction of commerce, on a navigable water; and so far as the public right is concerned, there is no limitation to the exercise of this power, unless it be found in the constitution.

It must be admitted that the provision in the 7th section in regard to the length of the pipes and chimneys of the boats which ply on the Ohio from and to Pittsburg is a commercial regulation. Congress have required the boilers of steamboats to be inspected, and that an iron chain should be used as a tiller-rope on all steamboats, and this has been required with a view to the safety of the boat, its passengers and cargo. In the event of fire the rope is generally burnt, and the boat becomes unmanageable. This is as far as congress has legislated, in regard to the tackle of the boat. No attempt has before been made to regulate the height of the chimneys.

From facts above stated, it appears the speed of the seven packets, by cutting down the chimney, would be reduced four hours, on an average, each, on a trip between Pittsburg and Cincinnati. This, as the statement shows, would increase the expense of the owners of the seven packets, in addition to the loss of time, $13,994.40 per annum. Such a regulation would seem to be the more objectionable, as the loss arises from the preference given to the bridge, which the public accommodation does not require.

But there is another objection, of a more serious nature. In

the 9th section of the 2d article of the constitution, it is declared
" that no preference shall be given, by any regulation of commerce
or revenue, to the ports of one State over those of another." This
can have no relation to " duties and imposts," as, in the 8th section, it is declared " they shall be uniform throughout the United
States." The clause must refer to some other regulation, and it
applies, of course, to all regulations affecting commerce.

It was said in the late argument of this case, that the Pittsburg packets had done a larger business in transportation the
last year, than within the same time at any former period. If
this be so, the injury by cutting down the chimneys of all the
boats to and from Pittsburg must amount to a larger sum than
above stated. Nothing could more forcibly illustrate the propriety of the above provision in the constitution, that no port in
one State shall have a preference over those of another.

Practical knowledge in regard to steamboat and railroad
transportation of freight is better than theory. Notwithstanding the lines of railroad from Pittsburg to Cincinnati, and to
St. Louis, by the way of Chicago, for the past year have been
in operation, the business on the steamboat lines has greatly
increased in freight; and from published prices it would seem
that the water transportation is three times cheaper than the
railroad, and, on account of the frequent detention of freight cars,
is much more expeditious.

But it is said many regulations of commerce, from local circumstances, cannot operate equally on all ports. As, for instance, a breakwater may be more beneficial to one port than
another; and the same inequality may exist from the establishment of light-houses and the improvement of harbors. But
these are incidental and not direct consequences, resulting from
the exercise of the legislative power, and no prudence can,
effectually, guard against them. As near as may be, equal
facilities should be given to ports of equal importance; this
however, is a matter for the decision of congress, and does not
belong to the judiciary. But where a prohibition is imposed on
congress in the exercise of the commercial power, and it is not
regarded, it is a judicial question, and this is the only check to
be relied on against such unconstitutional legislation.

It is objected that the court cannot determine what degree of
preference shall be given to one port over another, to make the
regulation come within the prohibition. If this be so, then is
the constitutional prohibition a dead letter; but this is not the
practical view which this court have uniformly taken of the
constitution. The restrictions on state powers stand upon the
same footing, and no insuperable difficulty has been found in
giving effect to them.

"No State shall coin money; emit bills of credit; make any thing but gold and silver coin a tender in payments of debts; pass any bill of attainder, *ex post facto* law, or law impairing the obligation of contracts." To determine the unconstitutionality of a law under some of these prohibitions would be attended with as much, if not more, difficulty than to say whether a commercial regulation gives a preference to one port over another.

In the case of McCulloch v. The State of Maryland, 4 Wheat. 431, the court say, "that the power to tax 'the Bank of the United States' involves the power to destroy," and on this ground the tax on the bank by the legislature of Maryland was declared to be unconstitutional and void. If this rule be applied to the point under consideration, no doubt could exist. Congress are prohibited from giving a preference to one port over another in different States, and consequently, if any such preference be given, the regulation is void. Not an incidental preference, but a regulation which necessarily acts injuriously and oppressively on one to the exclusion of other ports.

Suppose congress had declared by law that all steamboats plying to and from Pittsburg should not use chimneys more than forty feet high, which would essentially retard their progress, and consequently injure their business, would any court hesitate to pronounce such a regulation unconstitutional, as giving a preference to all other ports on the river over that of Pittsburg. This congress has in effect done, and the only justification for it must be found, if any exist, in the regulated height of the bridge. But the bridge, at a very small expense comparatively, could have been elevated as our decree required, and as the charter under which it was built also required. Less than this: if a draw had been made in the bridge over the western channel, so as to enable boats to pass up and down the river when they could not pass under the suspension bridge, nothing more was required. The expense of the draw, it is believed, would not exceed twenty-five thousand dollars, — a sum less, as it would seem, than the annual injury inflicted on the commerce of Pittsburg by the bridge.

If the regulation of the chimneys of steamboats, as in the law to protect the bridge, would be unconstitutional without the bridge, it is not perceived how the bridge could make it consti tutional. The right to cross the river by a bridge, and to navigate it, is admitted; but these public rights are not incompatible. They can both be enjoyed without any material interference of the one with the other. This being the case, congress, it would seem, cannot restrict the right to navigate the river for the benefit of the bridge. It cannot violate the constitutional inhibition in giving a preference to other ports over that of Pittsburg, by declaring the Wheeling bridge formed no obstruction to navigation. The constitution declares congress shall not give a pref erence to one port over another ; the act, if done, is not constitutional, though done under the power to regulate com merce.

The equality which such a regulation was intended to secure is a matter intimately connected with the commercial prosperity of the country. For a wrong thus done by congress there is no remedy, except through the exercise of the judicial power. This court is sworn to support the constitution, and in every iufraction of that instrument by congress or state legislatures, where individual injury is inflicted, redress may be obtained by action in court. Congress is prohibited from laying a duty on exports, except for port charges. Can a duty be imposed on exports beyond this under the commercial power ? The commercial power is limited in this and in other cases, and if the limit be exceeded the act is void. The federal government in all its forms exercises enumerated and limited powers. But if the limitation depends upon the discretion of congress, there is neither limitation nor protection. This is neither the theory nor the practical operation of the government. Congress has power to regulate commerce, but it has no power in such regulation to give a preference to one port in a State over another port in a different State. If it may do this to an extent materially injurious, it may equally disregard every other restriction in the constitution. The regulation of the height of the chimneys of steamboats which ply to and from Pittsburg, by the present elevation of the bridge, is the same in effect and in principle as if the act had required such steamers to cut down their chimneys without reference to the bridge. The bridge affords no justification or excuse for an unconstitutional regulation.

But it is said there is great difficulty in ascertaining the fact, that a regulation gives a preference to one or more ports in a State over those of another, and it is intimated that a jury should be called to ascertain the fact. This argument was used in regard to the fact of obstruction complained of by Pennsylvania; but this court very properly determined that a court of chancery, having jurisdiction, could inquire whether the bridge constituted such an obstruction to commerce as materially to injure the public works of Pennsylvania, and on such a finding by this court the late decree was entered for the removal of the obstruction.

What fact beyond this is necessary to determine the fact of preference of one port over another ? The chimneys of the steamboats which ply to and from Pittsburg are required to be cut down, so as to pass under the bridge. By this the rights of the port of Pittsburg are measured by the Wheeling bridge, and that bridge, this court have held, is so material an obstruction to commerce as to be a nuisance to the State of Pennsylvania.

This obstruction or nuisance consists in the necessity, when a boat passes under the bridge, of lowering its chimneys or cutting them down, so as to pass under it; and if this be a material injury to the commerce of the State of Pennsylvania, on its lines of improvement, how much greater the injury to the port of Pittsburg, from and to which one hundred millions' worth of property is transported annually? Can any one fail to see that the proof of preference to the port of Wheeling, and those below it, is given by the regulation complained of, over the port of Pittsburg and others above the bridge? The proof of this important fact, as found by the decision of the court already pronounced, is more conclusive to show the preference than to establish the claim of Pennsylvania.

Can it be urged that this preference is limited to a mere entry of the port? Had the Wheeling bridge been constructed over the Ohio River, a short distance below Pittsburg, it would have been far less injurious to that port than it now is; the boats, with their propelling power undiminished, could have approached near to that port, where their cargoes are discharged and received.

It is contended that the commerce across the river required the consideration of congress equally with that which floated upon its surface. There is no ground for such an argument. Some twenty-five or thirty thousand dollars, under the decree, would open a passage in the western channel so as to remove the obstruction. The annual injury to the commerce of the port of Pittsburg by the bridge is believed to exceed that sum.

Had the act of congress required all steamboats which ply upon the Ohio River to cut down their chimneys, so as to pass under the Wheeling bridge, the regulation, being general, however injurious, would not have given a preference to one port over another. It would have been the exercise of the commercial power, within the constitution.

The principle involved in this case is of the deepest interest to the commerce of the West. The Mississippi River and its tributaries water a country unsurpassed, if equalled, in the world, in extent and fertility. But if the obstruction of the Wheeling bridge may be repeated wherever the crossing public shall think proper to build a bridge, one third of the internal commerce of the Union will be materially obstructed. The injury of such a regulation would be very limited in the Atlantic

States, as there the rivers are short, and navigation is generally limited to the ebb and flow of the tide. If the Wheeling bridge be a legal structure, hundreds of bridges on the same principle may be thrown over the Mississippi and its navigable tributaries, to the great and remediless injury of western commerce.

That commerce is rapidly increasing, and at this time it probably amounts to four hundred millions of dollars annually; and if the Father of Waters and his tributaries shall have the same regulation extended to them as is now applied to the Wheeling bridge, it will impose a tax upon western commerce of several hundred thousand dollars annually; and this will be, not for the advancement of commerce over those waters, as it will greatly obstruct it, but to save a few thousand dollars in the structure of each bridge.

In regard to the motion for process of contempt against the bridge company, we must, I think, be governed by matters which appear upon the record. Shortly after the first decree was entered, the defendants made application to congress for relief. The object of the bridge company in making this application, was to counteract and annul the decision of this court. It is not supposed, however, that such was the intention of congress in passing the law. The two sections referred to were moved as an amendment to an act making appropriations for the service of the post-office department, on the 31st of August, 1852, at the close of that session. But little time was afforded for investigation of the important questions involved in the act. This fact is not stated to impair the force and effect of the act, but I think it is fit to be considered on this motion, in regard to the conduct of the bridge company.

The court may pr er consider, if they are not bound to do so, that the defendants, in making application to congress, and in procuring the passage of the act, as having acted in good faith. And although the law, if it has been passed in violation of the constitution, cannot be held valid, yet it may save the defendants from the contempt charged. On its face, it gave to the bridge company all that it could desire or ask against the decree of this court. It legalized what the court held to be illegal; and it required all steamboats, running to and from Pittsburg, from any point below Wheeling, to regulate their chimneys so as to pass under the bridge. It was the exercise of a judicial power without an examination of the principles of law applicable, and without a knowledge of the facts on which the decree was founded. No imputation is cast upon that honorable body, but the fact must be known to every one that the senate and house of representatives, however distinguished for their high ability and legal learning, could not discharge, to the public advantage, the duties of an appellate court.

I have no doubt that the learned judge had power to grant the injunction. The 5th section of the act of the 2d of March, 1793, (1 Stats. at Large, 384,) declares " that writs of *ne exeat* and of injunction may be granted by any judge of the supreme court, in cases where they might be granted by the supreme or circuit court." The 14th section of the judiciary act of 1789 declares that " the courts of the United States shall have power to issue writs of *scire facias, habeas corpus,* and all other writs not specially provided for by statute, which may be necessary for the exercise of their respective jurisdictions, and agreeable to the principles and usages of law."

Six of my brethren now hold that the act of congress arrested the progress of the court in carrying their decree into effect, and gave the defendants a right to rebuild their bridge. The injunction prohibited them from reconstructing it; can the defendants be punished for contempt, for doing that which the law authorized? This view shows that the injunction ought not to have been granted, as it was against law. And is not this a sufficient excuse for the contempt charged? My view is, that the law was unconstitutional and void, and yet I consider it as excusing the defendants' contempt. I cannot punish defendants, by fine or imprisonment, for doing that which the law authorized them to do.

There was no opposition made when the injunction was applied for; and it was granted, as a matter of course, on the face of the bill. Had the act of congress been set up against the allowance of the injunction, the motion, in all probability, would have been referred to the supreme court by the judge.

Having come to the conclusion, for the reasons above stated, that the act of congress is inoperative and void, although it may excuse the contempt, it can afford no excuse for a further refusal to perform the decree. I would, therefore, order that the final decree, heretofore made, be carried into effect according to its true intent, by the first day of October next, and that the defendants pay the costs.

Mr. Justice GRIER.

I concur with the majority of this court, that in cases where this court has original jurisdiction, an interlocutory or preliminary injunction may be awarded, in vacation, by any judge of the court. I differ with the majority in declining to punish a wanton contempt of the process of the court.

I concur with my brother McLean, that congress cannot annul or vacate any decree of this court; that the assumption of such a power is without precedent, and, as a precedent for the future, it is of dangerous example.

38 *

Mr. Justice WAYNE.

I concur with Mr. Justices Nelson, Grier, and Curtis, in thinking that the attachment for contempt should have been granted by this court.

I concur with the majority of the court in the view taken by them of the liability of the defendants for the costs of this suit.

I dissent from the majority of the court in the opinion given, that the 6th and 7th sections of the act of the 31st August, 1852, (10 Stats. at Large, 112,) relieve the defendants from the operation of the judgment of this court in behalf of the plaintiff. That judgment was for the abatement of a nuisance of which the plaintiff complained. This court decided it was a nuisance, causing injury and great pecuniary loss, inasmuch as it prevented the State of Pennsylvania from navigating the Ohio River at all stages of its waters, to the uninterrupted navigation of which they had a right under the constitution of the United States. I know of no power in congress to interfere with such a judgment, under the pretence of a power to legalize the structure of bridges over the public navigable rivers of the United States, either within the States, or dividing States from each other, or under the commercial power of congress to regulate commerce among the States. Nor does the power of congress to establish post-offices and post-roads give any power to congress to do more between the States, or within the States, than to declare the routes for carrying the mails upon roads already existing, and to designate the localities upon those roads where post-offices shall be kept for the delivery and transmission of letters, and other things or parcels which congress may declare to be mailable. Whatever congress may have intended by the act of August, 1852, I do not think it admits of the interpretation given to it by the majority of the court; and if it does, then my opinion is that the act would be unconstitutional.

I concur with many of the views taken by Mr. Justice McLean in his dissenting opinion; but I shall take another opportunity to express my opinion fully upon the action of this court and of congress in this case.

Mr. Justice DANIEL.

In the decision of the court dissolving the injunction and refusing the coercive measures asked for in this case, I entirely concur. But as, in the argument by which the court have proceeded to their conclusions, important questions of constitutional law appear to me to have been, some of them, passed over without consideration, and others inaccurately expounded, convictions of duty impel me to express my own interpretation of those questions. The correctness or incorrectness of that interpretation is left to the judgment of those whom curiosity or interest may incline to its examination; but whether examined, or approved, or condemned, or otherwise, it has been given because commanded by a sense of obligation, from obedience to which I hold that no one is or can be absolved.

When the controversy now revived before us was, in January, 1850, for the first time brought to our attention, there suggested themselves to my mind serious difficulties with respect both to the authority and the mode by which it was attempted to place that controversy within the cognizance of this tribunal.

I was unable to perceive by what warrant a judge of a circuit court, circumscribed in his jurisdiction both as to parties and to subjects-matter of litigation within specified limits, could claim cognizance as to parties and subjects-matter confessedly beyond the prescribed bounds of his jurisdiction. Still less could I comprehend by what warrant a circuit judge could, by an interlocutory order at chambers, relative to rights of person and property beyond the bounds of his jurisdiction, transfer a controversy affecting subjects thus situated to the supreme court of the United States.

An attempt to avoid these difficulties (for they were not directly met) was essayed, by the assumption that the application to the circuit court might be adopted here, as the commencement of an original suit by the State of Pennsylvania, that State possessing the right to institute an action in the supreme court, under the provision in the constitution which defines the original jurisdiction of that court. Accordingly, this case was received and treated as one authorized by the constitution, in virtue of the original jurisdiction vested exclusively in the supreme court, — a jurisdiction which an inferior court, or a judge of an inferior court, could have no power to exert.

However irregular and unauthorized the first proceeding in this case appeared to me, the granting of the second injunction, and the measures directed for enforcing it, I am constrained to regard as still more irregular, — a much wider departure from precedent or legitimate authority.

This second proceeding brings to our notice the following state of facts: An application to a circuit judge at chambers, to control by compulsory process persons and property, both of them situated beyond and without the bounds of his legitimate power. This application is granted at chambers, and not by a proceeding in court at all; and the order of the judge so made, and the mandate directed by him singly for the execution of his order, are entitled as a proceeding in and before the supreme court, and as an act of the supreme court; and the peculiar and appropriate officer of this tribunal is ordered to carry that mandate into effect.

According to my interpretation of the constitution of the United States, the supreme court is a distinct, aggregate, collective body, — one which can act collectively, and in term or in united session only. It cannot delegate its functions, nor can it impose its duties upon any number of the body less than a quorum, constituted of a majority of its members. Much less can a single judge be clothed with its joint powers, to be wielded by him at any time or in any place, or to any extent to which his individual discretion may point. Yet, in the case before us, we have a proceeding begun, prosecuted, and consummated in the name of the supreme court, — nay, denominated their proper act, when eight of the nine judges constituting this tribunal had no participation in that proceeding, perhaps never even suspected its existence. It may very well be inquired whether a majority of the judges, either acting individually or collectively in court, would, on principles of power or of justice, have sanctioned the course pursued in this case? For one, I can answer that by him it would have been unhesitatingly rejected.

Yet this course it is now attempted to justify and sustain, under the 5th section of the act of congress of the 2d of March, 1793, (1 Stats. at Large, 334,) which provides that " writs of *ne exeat* and injunction may be granted by any judge of the supreme court in cases where they might be granted by the supreme court or a circuit court."

The inference sought to be drawn from the provision just cited I propose cursorily to examine, with the view of showing its incorrectness as a deduction from the language or the purposes of that provision, and especially with the view of exposing the total inapplicability of the attempted conclusion to the facts developed by the record before us.

The subjects embraced within the proposed inquiry, namely, the distribution and exercise of power in the different divisions of the federal judiciary — the definition and establishment of the distinctive boundaries within which those several divisions should revolve, are matters of an importance much too grave to be incidentally or lightly disposed of. They are matters inseparable alike from the order and harmony and stability of public authority, and from the safety and enjoyment of private right.

By the act of congress establishing the judicial courts of the United States, (1 Stats. at Large, 81,) no power was conferred upon the judges of the courts of the United States to grant writs of injunction ; nor was the power to grant an injunction *eo nomine* conferred upon any of the courts. This authority was, however, as to the courts, given by implication in the 14th section of the statute, which authorized the courts thereinbefore enumerated, to grant writs of *scire facias*, *habeas corpus*, and all other writs not specially provided for by statute, which may be necessary for the exercise of their respective jurisdictions.

The feature of this provision proper for consideration here is this: that the power was conferred upon the courts, and not upon the judges, and was given in cases only in which it was necessary for the exercise of the jurisdiction of those courts. What was the jurisdiction of the circuit courts, as to persons or property, or both? With respect to proceedings *in rem*, as the process of the court could not run beyond the prescribed limits of its appropriate district, the jurisdiction or power of the court could be coextensive only with those limits, and was consequently impotent and null as to any direct control of the subject-matter when situated beyond them. And with respect to the jurisdiction over persons or parties, we find it declared by the 11th section of the judiciary act, that "no civil suit shall be brought before either of the said courts, against an inhabitant of the United States, in any other district than that whereof he is an inhabitant, or in which he shall be found at the time of serving the writ"; and so careful have been the authors of this restriction to insure its effectual observance, that in the same section of the statute they have prohibited every transfer of the interests or rights of parties made with the view of evading its operation. An interpretation of the 11th section of the judiciary act—one conclusive upon the jurisdiction of the circuit courts —has been declared in repeated decisions by this court, as may be seen amongst other instances which might be adduced, in the cases of M'Micken *v.* Webb, 11 Pet. 86; of Toland *v.* Sprague, 12 Pet. p. 300; and of Keary *v.* The Farmers' and Mechanics' Bank of Memphis, 16 Pet. p. 89. In the second of the cases just cited, the effect of the statute in defining the jurisdiction of the circuit courts is examined with much minuteness and particularity.

It follows, then, by necessary induction, both from the language of the judiciary act and from the interpretation thereof by this court, that the jurisdiction—as auxiliary to which, and as a means of enforcing its exercise, the power to grant injunctions was conferred upon the circuit courts—is that jurisdiction restricted to persons and property found within the prescribed local bounds assigned to those courts.

But it has been argued, that whilst the restrictions above mentioned may be imposed upon the courts as such, in the most solemn and deliberate exercise of their functions, the judges individually, out of court, and distinguished as they are by the language of the law from the courts, have been released from the same or similar restraints, and have been clothed with power separately to exert this extraordinary jurisdiction over persons and property residing or situated anywhere and everywhere within the United States. Nothing more is required, according to this argument, to overstep the fixed and designated boundary of the courts' authority than the *sic jubeo* of the individual judge.

In considering the interpretation now placed upon the 5th section of the act of March 2, 1793, the mind is impressed with the irregularity and inconsistency which this interpretation implies; and with the inutility and inefficiency for any beneficial object, of the power it is said to have created. It is certainly a novelty, and an anomaly in jurisprudence, to allege in a judicial officer acting out of court, and as it were *in pais*, the existence of a jurisdiction over persons and property with respect to which he has no power to adjudicate in court, and his acts in relation to which he possesses no authority to reverse or modify or even to revise. Yet this is precisely the attitude which the circuit courts and the judges of those courts are made to occupy in relation to each other, by the interpretation now attempted.

In the next place, so far as usefulness or efficiency may be supposed to have been the objects of the statute, much of these are taken away by denying to the courts the power claimed for the judges out of court to act upon persons or property beyond the bounds of the respective circuits. The same necessity which would dictate a resort to one, requiring equally a resort to both or either.

Some obscurity and difficulty is perceived and felt as arising from that portion of § 5 of the act of March 2, 1793, which permits the judges of the circuit courts to grant injunctions in cases wherein they might be granted by the supreme court; but this language it is thought, when correctly understood, operates no change, or extension, or enlargement of the powers and jurisdiction of the circuit courts, or of the judges of those courts. If indeed it should be contended that this section of the statute was designed to confer, or by its terms purported to confer upon the circuit courts, or upon the judges thereof, the jurisdiction and functions of the supreme court, then must that section, so far at least, be rejected as absolutely void, being in violation of the constitution.

The supreme court of the United States is the creature of the constitution. By this instrument its powers and jurisdiction, original and appellate, are conferred and defined; these are peculiar and exclusive, and by no legislation can they be enlarged or diminished, much less can they either in whole or in part, be delegated to other tribunals or officers of any grade or description.

I am clearly of the opinion, therefore, that by the 5th section

State of Pennsylvania v. Wheeling and Belmont Bridge Co.

of the act of 1798, no power to exercise authority or jurisdiction appertaining to the supreme court was, or could have been, conferred either upon the circuit courts or upon the judges thereof; but that this section must be understood as simply conferring upon the judges a power previously confined to the courts alone, — namely, the power to grant injunctions, and this subject to every limitation by which the circuit courts were controlled.

But the interpretation of the act of 1798 now contended for, broad as it is, still is not wide enough to cover the proceeding which it is now used to shield and protect. To accomplish this end, it must be stretched still more ; and until it can be made to comprise an identification of a single judge of the supreme court with the entire court itself, and the transformation of an act by an individual judge — an act performed without the accustomed formalities of a regular court — into a proceeding by the supreme court in the exercise of its constitutional and only legitimate functions.

The order granting the second injunction in this case, were it obnoxious to no other objection, appears to me to be unwarranted and void, for the reason that it assumes to contravene and overrule in effect, if not in terms, an existing decree of this court, between these same parties and upon the same subject-matter.

The decree of this court, first pronounced in February, 1852, decided that the suspension bridge at Wheeling was an obstruction to the passage of steamboats on the Ohio River, and that unless it should be elevated to the height of one hundred and eleven feet above low-water mark, before the 1st day of February next following this decree, it should be abated. Upon a subsequent day of the same term, the decree was so modified as to substitute for the requirement of increased elevation, or of the alternative of an abatement, permission to the proprietors of the suspension bridge to construct in the permanent wooden bridge, which spans the western channel of the river, a draw of a capacity sufficient for the passage of steamboats of the largest class ; the additional distance or the short delay (of a few minutes only) incident to this arrangement constituting, as expressed in the language of this court, "no appreciable injury to commerce." Liberty was reserved by this decree to either party to "move the court in relation to this matter on the 1st Monday of February ensuing." *Vide* 13 How. 625.

In obedience to a notice from the complainant, under the liberty reserved in the decree, the defendants appeared on the regular return day by counsel in court ; but the complainant failing to prosecute this motion, it was permitted to be discontinued. To a second notice to the defendants they again appeared, but the complainant again making default, was formally called, and the motion was dismissed.

From this failure or refusal on the part of those who were authorized to move in the case, this court, for aught that could be judicially known to them, might have been justified in the conclusion, that everything they had ordered had been complied with, or had been arranged to the mutual satisfaction of the parties. Certainly up to this period, there was no fact regularly and formally before them, on which to found or justify process for contempt. Under this state of things, the suspension bridge at Wheeling remained, and was authorized to remain.

This court had prescribed the conditions, according to which it was to stand or to be abated, and had designated the parties by whom, the modes by which, and the extent to which, the decree might be carried into effect.

In this attitude of the case, a mandate is issued from a judge at chambers, superseding the mode pointed out by this court for the execution of its decree, and wholly irrespective of any condition according to which that decree had been, by its own terms, modified, as above mentioned.

The above mandate assumes to order, in the name of this court, that no bridge of an elevation less than that prescribed by this order, shall be thrown across the Ohio from Zane's Island to Wheeling, regardless altogether of any facility, however complete, which might be provided for the passage of steamboats by the western channel of the river.

This mandate, therefore, was itself a palpable violation of the decree of this court, and of rights reserved to the defendants by that decree, — rights which they twice evinced their readiness to vindicate before this court, in opposition to the reiterated, but subsequently abandoned attempts by the complainant to assail them.

Can contempt, then, be affirmed or imputed with reference to a readiness to yield obedience to the regular authority of the court, or with reference to an unwillingness to comply with a proceeding not merely void in itself, but one also in manifest violation of the constitution and the law?

To which it may be asked, were the defendants bound to conform to the authority of this court, deliberately announced upon a question regularly before them as a court, or to an order from a single judge, obviously in contravention of the former, assuming to exercise an authority belonging only to the court as an aggregate body, and by which assumption this court is placed in an attitude adversary to its own decree?

There is still another view of this case, which, to my mind, is conclusive against the proceedings on the part of the circuit judge, and equally so against every motion now urged before us as founded thereon, or on either the principal or modified decree heretofore pronounced in this cause.

Previously to the application for the second injunction, the congress of the United States, by a formal statutory enactment, declared the bridges which had been erected over the Ohio at Wheeling in Virginia, and at Bridgeport in the State of Ohio, abutting on Zane's Island, to be lawful structures in their present position and elevation, "anything in any law or laws of the United States to the contrary notwithstanding." And they further enacted, "that the officers and crews of all vessels and boats navigating the said river, are required to regulate the use of their said vessels and boats, and any pipes, or chimney, or chimneys belonging thereto, so as not to interfere with the elevation and structure of the said bridges." *Vide* 10 Stats. at Large, 112.

Against the effect of these very explicit enactments, it has been contended that they are void, because, as it is said, they reverse a decision of this court, which congress has no power to do. In answer to this argument, it may be conceded that the position assumed by it might be true with reference to the adjustment or security of private rights vested under previously existing laws or adjudications; but such a position is wholly inapplicable to measures of public policy falling appropriately within the legislative competency, and much less can it have any influence to warrant in any other department of the government the exercise of powers vested exclusively in the national legislature.

It is impossible to read either the original or the modified decree, by the majority of the court in this cause, without perceiving that both these decrees, as well as the entire argument in support of them, were based upon the single assumption that the erection of the suspension bridge at Wheeling was an interference with the right to regulate commerce vested in congress by the constitution. It is equally manifest, from the arguments and opinions of the minority of the court, that the right in congress to regulate commerce is not only conceded by the minority, but the exclusiveness of that power in congress is insisted upon. These later opinions maintain the doctrine that congress alone are competent to exercise this right or power, and can neither be controlled nor anticipated with respect to it by the judicial department, upon any fancied necessity, nor upon any supposed neglect, or omission, or incompetency, which the latter may impute to congress, and may imagine the judicial department called upon to remedy.

In these views are seen essentially, nay explicitly, the diversity existing in the opinions of the majority and minority of the judges, as declared in this case.

Congress have, by statute already referred to, undertaken to regulate the commerce upon the Ohio River, so far as the matters involved in this controversy are concerned. And who shall question their power to do this? Does it belong to this court, under any article or clause of the constitution, or of any statute, to assume such a superiority? Congress have ordained that the vehicles of commerce on the Ohio, the steamboats, shall so graduate the height of their chimneys, as not to interfere with the bridges at Wheeling, as existing at the date of the statute. By this they have at least declared that these bridges are deemed by them no invasion either of the power or the policy of congress with reference to the commerce of the Ohio River. They have regulated this matter upon a scale by them conceived to be just and impartial, with reference to that commerce which pursues the course of the river, and to that which traverses its channel, and is broadly diffused through the country.

They have at the same time by what they have done, secured to the government, and to the public at large, the essential advantage of a safe and certain transit over the Ohio, — an advantage which, previously to the erection of the Wheeling bridge, was greatly desired, but never attained.

In what has been done by congress, I can have no doubt that they have acted wisely, justly, and strictly within their constitutional competency. By their action they have completely overthrown every foundation upon which the decrees of this court, the orders of the circuit judge, and every motion purporting to be based upon these or either of them, could rest. I am, therefore, of the opinion that each and every motion submitted by the complainant under color of the decrees heretofore pronounced in this cause, or of the injunction awarded by the judge of the circuit court, should be overruled; that the injunction awarded as aforesaid should be dissolved, and the bill praying for that injunction should be dismissed; and that in each instance the defendants should be decreed their costs.

Order — in the original case.

This court at a prior term, to wit, on 27th May, 1852, having declared that the bridge of the respondents was an obstruction to the navigation of the Ohio River, and that it did a special damage to the complainant, and having decreed that the same should be altered as thereby directed, or removed by the respondents, and the complainant having subsequently moved this court for writs of assistance, of sequestration and of attachment against the said respondents, and also for a taxation of the costs decreed by this court, and for the process of this court to enforce the payment thereof by the said respondents, and the congress of the United States having by an act passed on the 31st of August, 1852, entitled "An Act making appropriations for the service of the Post-Office Department, during the fiscal year ending the 30th of June, 1853, and for other purposes," provided for the navigation of the Ohio River, and so regulated the navigation of the said river as to be consistent with the maintenance of the said bridge. And the respective parties having been fully heard by counsel, and after mature deliberation thereupon had by this court, it is now here considered and decreed by this court that the said motion for writs of assistance, sequestration, and attachment be and the same is hereby overruled, and that the said writs be and they are hereby denied. And it is further considered and decreed by the court that the said complainant do have and recover from the said respondents the costs of the said complainant as decreed by this court on the aforesaid 27th day of May, A. D. 1852, to be taxed by the clerk, and that the said respondents do pay the same to the complainant within ninety days from this date; and that in default of such payment, that execution do issue therefor to be directed to the marshal of the United States for the District of Columbia to enforce the same.

Order—with respect to the bill filed before Mr. Justice Grier and injunction issued by his order.

This cause came on to be heard upon the bill of complaint, an order by the Honorable R. C. Grier, an associate justice of this court, on the 26th day of June, 1854, granting an injunction as prayed for in the said bill, and upon the motion by the complainant for writs of assistance, of sequestration, and of attachment against the said respondent, and upon a motion by the respondent to dissolve the said injunction, and was fully argued by counsel on both sides; upon consideration whereof, and after mature deliberation thereupon had, it is now here ordered and decreed by this court that the said motion by the said complainant for writs of assistance, of sequestration, and of attachment be and the same is hereby overruled, and that the said injunction, so as aforesaid granted, be and the same is hereby dissolved.

THE STATE OF PENNSYLVANIA, COMPLAINANT, *v.* THE WHEELING
    AND BELMONT BRIDGE COMPANY.

This court has power, in a case of original jurisdiction, to award costs against either
    of the parties.

The statutes of the United States upon the subject of costs, examined.

Moreover, this court has equity jurisdiction in certain cases, under the constitution of
    the United States ; and in those cases, it is guided by the rules and principles of the
    court of chancery in England, as they existed when our constitution was formed
    That court had power to award costs and this court must have the same power.

The bill of costs in this case was taxed by the clerk under the order of this court.
    Either party had leave to file exceptions, but both parties, by a written agreement,
    waived all exceptions, and the court confirmed the report. After this, it is too
    late to object.

A motion to file a bill of review upon the subject of costs, and also for a re-taxation
    of them, is, therefore, overruled.

THIS was a case of original jurisdiction upon the equity side
of this court, and was a sequel to the preceding case between
the same parties.

Mr. Charles W. Russell, as the solicitor for the Bridge Company, filed a petition praying leave to file a bill of review of an
order of this court, made at the December term, 1851, respecting
the costs, in the original case between the parties. The petition
set forth that this court had no power to condemn either party
to a suit originally brought in this court to pay the costs of the
suit ; or if it had the power, then the amount of costs must be
regulated by some previous act of congress or rule of this court.
It also set forth that the report of the clerk, which was confirmed by an order, was liable to objection, and prayed that the
report might be reopened.

Mr. Justice NELSON delivered the opinion of the court.
This is an application made on the part of the defendants,
for leave to file a bill of review, so far as respects the orders
and decrees for costs heretofore rendered in the above case
against them.

The court have already determined that the decree rendered
for costs against the defendants was unaffected by the act of
congress passed August 31, 1852, and with which determination it is entirely satisfied.

It is suggested, however, on the part of the applicant, that
there is no act of congress expressly conferring power upon this
court in the case of original jurisdiction, to award costs against
either of the parties. This may be true, but it is equally true
in respect to the circuit courts of the United States, and yet no
one has doubted the power in those courts since their first organ-

ization; 1 Blatchford R. 652; and the grounds upon which that power rests apply with equal force to the supreme court in the cases mentioned. In the distribution of original jurisdiction between the supreme and circuit courts, there is nothing peculiar in the nature or character of that conferred upon the former to distinguish it specially from the latter. Indeed, a large portion of this jurisdiction is concurrent with that of the circuit courts. It is exclusive only in a few cases having regard to the sovereign character of the party to the suit, or in cases where the interests of our foreign relations may be concerned, and principles of international law involved.

In the nature of the jurisdiction, therefore, or in the character of the suits in this court of original jurisdiction, we perceive nothing that should lead us to distinguish, on the question of costs, between this court and the circuit courts. And, as we have already said, the grounds for the exercise of the power — namely, the repeated recognition by acts of congress of the right of the prevailing party to costs — is as applicable to the one court as the other.

It would be an endless task to refer to the various acts of congress passed from time to time recognizing the right of the party to costs in proceedings in the courts of the United States, and, of course, including this court. It will be sufficient to say, that they will be found in the laws of congress, running through its entire legislation on the subject of judicial proceedings, and regulation of the power and authority of the federal courts and its officers. Among the first acts is that of May 9, 1792, "An Act for regulating processes in the courts of the United States, and providing compensations for the officers of the said courts and for jurors and witnesses." 1 Stats. at Large, 275. The compensation here provided for, on behalf of officers and persons concerned in the administration of justice, not payable out of the treasury of the United States, was recoverable as costs of the suit. § 6, p. 278.

The act of July 22, 1813, (2 Stats. at Large, 19,) "An Act concerning suits and costs in courts of the United States," provided, (§ 1,) that where several actions against persons who might be joined in one action touching a demand in any court of the United States, if judgment be given for the plaintiff, such party shall not recover the costs of more than one action, &c. And the 3d section provided, that where causes of like nature, &c., shall be pending before a court of the United States, it is made the duty of the court to make rules or orders to avoid unnecessary costs, and consolidate the causes. It is also provided that if any attorney or person admitted to conduct causes in a court of the United States shall appear to have multiplied proceedings

39 *

in any cause, so as to increase costs vexatiously, such person may be required to satisfy any excess of costs so incurred. But we shall not pursue this inquiry. We could multiply instances of similar recognition of the right of the party to costs, and power of the court to award them, to almost any extent. The instances we have referred to are but samples, and, we think, sufficient for the purpose designed.

But, independent of this, the constitution provides that the judicial power of the United States shall extend to all cases in equity between a State and the citizens of another State; and that, in cases in which a State shall be a party, this court shall have original jurisdiction. There is thus conferred by the constitution on this court original jurisdiction over "cases in equity" between a State and citizens of another State; and this is the jurisdiction we have exercised in the matter now before us.

Original jurisdiction in equity, in a particular class of cases, conferred by the constitution on this court, has been interpreted to impose the duty to adjudicate according to such rules and principles as governed the action of the court of chancery in England, which administered equity at the time of the emigration of our ancestors, and down to the period when our constitution was formed. And when the constitution of the United States conferred that jurisdiction on this court, it cannot be construed to exclude the power possessed and constantly exercised by every court of equity then known, to use its discretion to award or refuse costs, as its judgment of the right of the case, in that particular, might require. The court entertains no doubt of its power to award costs, and deny the application to file a bill of review.

Then as to the bill of costs taxed by the clerk. It is sufficient to say, that the bill as we understand it, consists entirely of the expenses attending the taking of testimony in the case, and of the surveys, examinations, and reports of the engineer, preparatory to the final hearing of the case, and which services were performed under the special order and direction of the court, together with the fees for the services of the officers of the court. And, further, that the bill of costs has been referred to the clerk of the court, with directions to examine witnesses, and resort to such other proofs for the purpose of ascertaining the proper compensation to be allowed the commissioners, and to the engineers and clerks employed by him, and also to ascertain the whole amount of expenses incurred by said commissioner, and the amount advanced by the respective parties, and report on the same; and that either party have leave to except to the report, in writing, as to any of the items or sums of money allowed by the clerk.

This report was duly made in conformity with the order, and the counsel for the respective parties filed at the time a written declaration waiving all exceptions to any part of said account or vouchers, and stating that they do not mean to except to said report, nor desire any further time to examine or except to it; whereupon the report was confirmed by this court.

It can hardly be expected, after this deliberate proceeding by the court to ascertain the costs and expenses attending the trial and hearing of the case, and the opportunity of the counsel for the respective parties at the time to scrutinize the several items of the account, their attendance before the master, and, after the proper scrutiny, entering into and filing an express written waiver of exceptions to the taxation and solemn recognition of its justice and propriety, that the court will open the question for a re-examination, or can desire any further inquiry into or review of the matter thus disposed of. There must be an end of litigation. We are not only satisfied that the party applicant for a review of the question has already had full opportunity to present his objections to the bill of costs, and, indeed, has already availed himself of the benefit of it, but are also satisfied with the order and judgment of the court heretofore given in the premises.

The motion for bill of review, and also for re-taxation of costs, is denied.

JAMES W. GOSLEE, DUNCAN B. FRIERSON, HANNIBAL S. BLOOD, AND JOHN GOODRICH, OWNERS OF THE STEAMBOAT AUTOCRAT, LIBELLANTS AND APPELLANTS, v. THEODORE SHUTE, EXECUTOR OF MARIA SHUTE, DECEASED, AND MARY A. SHUTE, OWNERS AND CLAIMAMTS OF THE STEAMER MAGNOLIA.

In a collision which occurred upon the Mississippi River between an ascending and descending steamboat, whereby the former was destroyed, the collision was chiefly owing to the neglect, by the ascending boat, of the rule which requires the ascending boat to keep near the right bank and the descending one to keep near the middle of the river.

Moreover, the ascending boat had not a sufficient watch, and in other respects its officers were to blame.

THIS was an appeal from the circuit court of the United States for the eastern district of Louisiana.

The facts of the case are stated in the opinion of the court.

The district court held that both boats were in fault, and divided the damages, and ordered judgment to be entered against The Magnolia for $17,900.

From this decision both parties appealed to the circuit court, where the judgment of the district court was reversed, and the libel dismissed with costs. The libellants, who were owners of The Autocrat, appealed to this court.

It was argued by Mr. Sargent and Mr. Crittenden, for the appellants, on whose side was also filed an argument by Mr. Pike. For the appellees, it was argued by Mr. Benjamin.

Mr. Justice McLEAN delivered the opinion of the court.

This is an appeal in admiralty, from the circuit court for the eastern district of Louisiana.

The libellant charges, that on a trip from New Orleans to Memphis in the steamer Autocrat, with a full cargo and a great number of passengers, The Magnolia ran into her, forward of the wheel on her larboard side, which caused her to sink in less than ten minutes; by which the boat and cargo were lost, and the lives of several passengers.

On the hearing in the district court, it was held that both boats were in fault; and, under the well-established rule of the admiralty, the damage was divided. From that decision an appeal was taken to the circuit court, which reversed the decree of the district court. The appeal now before us is from the circuit court.

As usual, in collision cases, there is some conflict among the witnesses in regard to the facts of the case, as well as to matters of opinion.

On the 9th of February, 1852, the steamboat Magnolia, descending the Mississippi River, one hundred miles above New Orleans, about five o'clock in the morning, landed to wood, on the left bank of the river, at a place called Col. Robinson's wood-yard. Before the boat left the wood-yard, when the pilot was on deck and about to take the helm, his attention was called to an ascending boat, which was near Bayou Goula, a mile and a half or two miles below. When first seen, the ascending boat was running to the right bank of the river.

There is a bar on the left side of the river about a mile below the wood-yard. The course of ascending boats is to cross into the bend, just above Bayou Goula, and keep up the right shore some six or seven miles. This course was taken by The Autocrat, averaging, generally, less than one hundred yards from the right shore.

On leaving the wood-yard, The Magnolia backed out on both wheels, her bow being fast on the shore; as she came off both engines were stopped, and then the boat went ahead on both wheels to check her up. As soon as this was done, her stern being opposite the wood-yard, the larboard engine was stopped,

to let her come round by the action of the starboard wheel. The
Autocrat continued up the right bank until she came opposite,
or nearly opposite, to Col. Butler's residence.   At this place she
was within less than one hundred yards of the shore, when she
changed her course to the left shore, nearly in the direction of
the wood-yard which had a few minutes before been left by The
Magnolia.   The river at this place is about three quarters of a
mile wide.

In rounding, The Magnolia passed the middle of the river, but
as her bow was thrown down the stream, The Autocrat, turning
suddenly to the right, approached her with a speed of some ten
or twelve miles an hour.   As The Autocrat approached, by a tap
of the bell she signified her intention to cross to the left bank,
and before the bow of The Magnolia, whose bell was rung two
taps, indicating the same direction. Seeing the imminent danger,
The Magnolia rang her bells to back ; and it is stated by her pilot,
that when the collision happened she lay upon the water, not
having a descending movement of more than at the rate of a
mile or a mile and a half to the hour.   The Autocrat struck her
with so much force as to turn her bow up the stream.   In less
than ten minutes The Autocrat sunk in deep water.   It was not
more than five minutes after The Magnolia left the wood-yard,
until the collision occurred.   The pilot says The Magnolia was
brought round, as soon as could be done, by the action of her
starboard wheel.

The nose of The Magnolia struck The Autocrat's guard near
the forward part of the cylinder, on the larboard side, and the
hull, at the other end of the cylinder, and brought up in her
wheel.   The collision took place not far from the middle of the
river, somewhat nearer to the right bank than to the left.   After
the boats were separated, the machinery of The Autocrat continued to work for a few minutes, her course being directed to
the right bank, on reaching which, she went down.

Entire accuracy of witnesses as to the direction and position
of the boats in a case of collision at night, is not to be expected.
The peril is too great and absorbing to note and detail the events
as they transpired, by the officers and hands of either boat.   The
leading facts being ascertained by the weight of the testimony,
when properly considered, will lead to a more just result than by
a minute examination of the evidence.

What was the duty of the respective boats, when they first
came within view of each other ? The Magnolia was at the wood-
yard on the left bank of the river; The Autocrat was near Bayou
Goula, crossing over to the right bank of the river, about a mile
and a half below the wood-yard.

Although there is some contrariety of evidence in regard to

the usage which should govern the respective boats, occupying the positions above stated, yet the weight of the evidence clearly establishes the rule, that the ascending boat should keep near the right bank and the descending one about in the middle of the river. Each boat was bound to keep a vigilant and competent watch, and to slacken the speed of the boat and stop it, as the danger becomes imminent. This is dictated by a common prudence of a qualified pilot.

The principal fact relied on to show fault in The Magnolia is, that she left the wood-yard, and described too large a circle in rounding; that the larboard wheel should have made backwater, which would have reduced the circle and have thrown the bow down the stream in less time.

After a misfortune has happened, it is easy to see how it might have been avoided. If The Magnolia had remained at the wood-yard some eight or ten minutes longer, there could have been no collision. But this is not a fair mode of trying the case. Had the officers of The Magnolia a right to expect that The Autocrat would not depart from her course; and if she had not done so, could the boats have come in contact? It is clear, if the ascending boat had continued near the right bank of the river, there would have been no collision. This is an important fact. Admit that The Magnolia passed the middle of the stream in rounding, still ample space was left for the ascending boat. One third or even one fourth of the river, the water being deep, was sufficient for this purpose. The testimony shows that at least one third of the river, along the right bank, was open for The Autocrat.

But it is said that the pilot of The Autocrat, seeing The Magnolia was rounding off from the wood-yard, had a right to conclude that it intended to cross over to the right bank. This was a little after five o'clock in the morning; daylight was breaking, but the stars had not disappeared.

Being acquainted with the locality of the wood-yard, and the general course of the river, the pilot of The Autocrat must be presumed to know that a large boat could not round in a narrow circle. His inference would naturally be, that the boat was rounding from the wood-yard, and not to cross the stream. But admit that the direction of The Magnolia was doubtful — it was the duty of the officers of The Autocrat to slacken her speed, and even to stop her engines, until those doubts were removed. No such precautions were used. The Autocrat, by a great pressure of steam, was propelled onward, changing her course; and in attempting to pass the bow of The Magnolia, came in contact with her. Her pilot had hoped, it seems, to pass her stern; but to any prudent man, either attempt would have been considered a dangerous experiment. His great error, however, consisted in leaving the way established by usage; such to him would have been the way of safety. Every deviation from it, in meeting a boat, is always hazardous, and often fatal.

There was another defect, in not having an efficient watch on The Autocrat. This is indispensable, especially in navigating our western rivers. The captain was asleep; the watchman did not occupy the proper position; there, in fact, was no watch to direct or advise the pilot; he seems to have been left to the exercise of his own judgment, unaided by suggestions or facts from any quarter. This is enough to charge The Autocrat with fault.

Leaving the wood-yard by The Magnolia, under the circumstances, was not charged as a fault in the libel, nor was it so stated in the protest. The Magnolia had an efficient watch at the proper place for observation, and an experienced pilot. She rounded in the ordinary way. While the pilot of The Autocrat was a mile from The Magnolia, he ascertained that she was a descending boat. Still under the impression that she intended to run down the right bank, the course of The Autocrat was so changed across the river, in the direction of the wood-yard as to bring the boats in conflict. Had the pilot of The Autocrat designed to produce a collision, he could not have taken a different course from the one he did take. From intimidation, or some other cause, he showed a culpable defect of judgment, and a disregard of the established usage.

The Magnolia seems to have taken every precaution she was required to take to avoid the collision. She was in her proper place, near the middle of the river, moving down the stream with less force than the current. If The Autocrat had met the crisis with the same precaution, a collision could have caused little or no damage.

The decree of the circuit court is affirmed.

Mr. Chief Justice TANEY, Mr. Justice WAYNE, and Mr. Justice DANIEL dissented.

RICHARD D. WOOD, JOHN YARROW, JAMES ABBOTT, AND JOSEPH BACON, COPARTNERS UNDER THE NAME AND STYLE OF WOOD, ABBOTT, AND COMPANY, APPELLANTS, v. ALEXANDER C. DAVIS.

Where a bill in chancery was filed in a state court, by a citizen of that State, against parties, some of whom resided in that State and some in another State, and the latter removed the cause into the circuit court of the United States; and that court, after answer filed, remanded it to the state court, this order was, under the circumstances of the case, erroneous.

The real parties in interest were those who resided out of the State. The circumstance that other and formal parties were joined with them in the bill, cannot oust the federal courts of jurisdiction.

THIS was an appeal from the circuit court of the United States for the northern district of Illinois.

The case is stated in the opinion of the court.

It was argued by *Mr. St. George T. Campbell* and *Mr. Browning*, for the appellants, and *Mr. Carlisle*, for the defendant.

The argument turned chiefly upon the point, whether Foster and Stohl, who held the deed, and Hooper and Campbell, who held the note, were real or nominal parties in the cause.

Mr. Justice NELSON delivered the opinion of the court.

This is an appeal from a decree of the circuit court of the United States for the northern district of Illinois.

Davis, a citizen resident of Illinois, filed a bill in the 14th judicial circuit of that State, in chancery, against the appellants, citizens and residents of Pennsylvania, and four other persons who will be more particularly noticed hereafter, setting out various dealings and business transactions between the complainant and the appellants, under the firm of Wood, Abbott, and Co., from the year 1843 down to the year 1849. That in October of the latter year, the firm, claiming to be largely in advance to the complainant, sent one of the partners to his place of business for the purpose of procuring a settlement of the accounts, and security for the balance of indebtedness. The balance was ascertained to be some $29,000, the payment of which was eventually secured by the conveyance of certain parcels of real estate; the firm, at the same time, entering into an agreement to resell and reconvey the same for the amount of the debt and interest, in one, two, three, and four years. The complainant also gave his notes for the amount for the purchase-money. All the notes have been paid, and parcels of the land reconveyed from time to time, except the last note of $6,000, and the parcels of land retained as security for its payment.

This note having become due, the firm of Wood, Abbott, and Co., the appellants, transmitted it and a deed of the land to Foster and Stohl, with directions to collect the money, and on receipt of the same to deliver the deed to the complainant. The note having been presented for payment, it was refused, upon which they placed it in the hands of Hooper and Campbell, attorneys at law, for collection. The bill in this case was filed against Wood, Abbott, and Co., the appellants, Stohl and Foster, the agents, and Hooper and Campbell, the attorneys, setting out the facts substantially as above stated, together with the additional charges that the account presented by the firm of Wood, Abbott, and Co. was overcharged and fraudulently made up, and that a much less balance was due to them than the amount secured upon a fair and equitable adjustment. The bill avers that Stohl and Foster had no interest in the transaction except to receive the money on the note, and to deliver the deed as agents of Wood, Abbott, and Co.; and that Hooper and Campbell have no interest, except as attorneys for the collection of the note. There is a prayer for subpœna against all the defendants, and for answers; also, that an account be taken between the complainant and Wood, Abbot, and Co.; and that the note be given up, and the deed be delivered to complainant; that an injunction be issued, enjoining Stohl and Foster, and Hooper and Campbell, from delivering over the note to the appellants.

The firm of Wood, Abbott, and Co. entered their appearance at November term, 1853, and petitioned the court, under the 12th section of the judiciary act, for a removal of the cause to the circuit court of the United States, on the ground that they were citizens and residents of the State of Pennsylvania, which application was granted.

The appellants, afterwards, in April, 1854, filed an answer to the bill in the circuit court of the United States; and on the 29th of June, 1855, that court ordered the cause to be remanded back to the state court from which it was sent.

The case is now here on an appeal from that order.

The ground upon which the cause was remanded is, that four of the defendants were citizens of the State of Illinois — namely, Stohl and Foster, and Hooper and Campbell — the same State of which the complainant was a citizen. And this presents the question whether or not these defendants were parties in interest in the subject of litigation, or, in other words, were proper or necessary parties in the suit. It has been repeatedly decided by this court, that formal parties, or nominal parties, or parties without interest, united with the real parties to the litigation, cannot oust the federal courts of jurisdiction, if the citizenship, or character of the real parties, be such as to confer it within the 11th section of the judiciary act. 7 Cranch, 98; 3 Ib. 267; 8 Wheat. 421; 5 Cranch, 303.

It would be difficult to state a case of parties more destitute of interest, or in which they were used merely as formal parties, than in the case of these defendants. Stohl and Foster were simply agents of Wood, Abbott, and Co., with special instructions in which the complainant had no participation, and which could be recalled at any time before carried into execution ; and, until carried into execution, the complainant certainly could set up no right under them, much less a right in disregard and defiance of them.   Even if the state court had gone on and decreed against these defendants, and compelled a surrender of the note, or a delivery of the deed in the absence of the principals, it could not have extinguished the note, or have transferred the title to the land, as the decree could have had no binding effect upon them.   Before the surrender could extinguish the note, or the delivery could have the effect to pass the estate in the land, the decree must operate upon the principals, the real parties in interest, and coerce them to make such surrender or delivery. The agents had no authority to represent them in the litigation. Nor had they any interest of their own in the subject in controversy.   This is not the case of a stakeholder, or holder of a deed as an escrow, where a trust has been created by the parties which is sought to be enforced by one of them.   In all such cases the trustee may be a proper party, as he has a duty to perform, and which the court may enforce if improperly neglected or refused.

The above view applies with equal if not greater force to the case of the attorneys.

Even if there could be any doubt about the correctness of the view above taken, after the real parties in interest appeared and took upon themselves the defence, the defendants, Stohl and Foster, and Hooper and Campbell, were no longer parties in interest, or necessary parties, as the possession of the note and of the deed by the agents and the attorneys, was, in judgment of law, the possession of the principals and clients, and any decree or injunction against them would bind the agents or attorneys.   6 Ves. 143 ; 1 Mer. 123 ; 1 Daniel's Pr. 843 ; 7 Hare, 428 ; Story Eq. Pl. §§ 229, 231, 232.

We are satisfied that the decision of the court below was erroneous, and that the order remanding the cause to the state court must be reversed, and the cause restored to its place in the circuit court of the United States.

EUPHROSINE FOUVERGNE ET AL. APPELLANTS, v. THE MUNICIPALITY NO. 2, OF THE CITY OF NEW ORLEANS ET AL.

Where a will was established in New Orleans, in 1792, by order of the alcalde, an officer who had jurisdiction over the subject-matter, his decree must be considered as a judicial act, not now to be called into question.

The courts of the United States have no probate jurisdiction, and must receive the sentences of the courts to which the jurisdiction over testamentary matters is committed, as conclusive of the validity and contents of a will. An original bill cannot be sustained upon an allegation that the probate of a will is contrary to law.
Moreover, the fraud charged in this case, is not established by the evidence.

THIS was an appeal from the circuit court of the United States for the eastern district of Louisiana, sitting as a court of equity.

The principal circumstances of the case, which furnished the basis of the judgment of this court, are set forth in the opinion.

The entire case was one which covered a vast deal of ground. For the appellants there was a brief filed by Mr. S. Paul, of nearly 150 pages, which was adopted by Mr. Taylor, and one by Mr. Taylor himself, of the same size. On the part of the appellees, the brief of Mr. Janin was only 30 pages. These papers contained a vast deal of research into the civil law upon many points of the case which were not noticed in the opinion of the court, whose judgment rested upon a single point as disposing of the case. It is not necessary, therefore, to report them.

The case was argued by *Mr. Taylor* and *Mr. Lewis* for the appellants, and by *Mr. Janin*, for the appellees.

Mr. Justice CAMPBELL delivered the opinion of the court.

The plaintiff filed her bill in chancery to recover a share of the succession of Marie Josepha Deslondes, (wife of Bertrand Gravier,) who died at New Orleans, in November, 1792, without lineal heirs, she claiming to be one of the heirs at law of said decedent. After the death of his wife, Bertrand Gravier placed a petition before the first alcalde of New Orleans, stating that his wife had made a will before a notary and three assisting witnesses; that the testamentary dispositions, as set down, conformed to her instructions, and were given while she was of a sound mind, but she had lost her consciousness before she had signed the paper; and prayed that the assisting witnesses might be examined to prove the will, and that the same might be declared valid in all its parts, in the same manner as if she had signed it. An order was made by the alcalde on this petition, with the approbation of the assessor of the intendancy, and the sanction of the governor and intendant-general, directing the notary to take the examination of the witnesses, as the petitioner had solicited. The witnesses, on their examination, testified that the notary had drawn the will in accordance with the directions of the testatrix, and they were given when her mind and memory were sound; but that before the formal writing was finished she had lost her consciousness, and did not therefore sign the same. Upon the return of the depositions to the alcalde, he entered the following decree:—

Decree.

Under advisement, [*vistos.*] The will, proved by a legalized notarial act to have been made by Dona Maria Josefa Deslondes, who was the lawful wife of Don Bertrand Gravier, is declared valid and subsisting; let it be kept and executed in all its parts; and in order that this declaration, relative to said will, may remain permanent, there shall be placed on the notarial register, and on the original will, a note referring to the proceedings, giving to the parties interested certified copies of both documents, whenever they may ask for them. And whereas the said Don Bertrand Gravier, sole heir, has attained the years of majority, and that the property is notoriously large, there is, for this reason, no necessity for judicial proceedings; and for security for payment of the six thousand dollars to the absent heirs, he (Gravier) will immediately mortgage the plantation until final payment, or till otherwise agreed to by the parties. Whereupon, these proceedings terminated, let the costs be taxed by D'n Louis Liotaud, after acceptance and oath, and let them be paid by the heir, twenty-four reals having been received as the assessor's fee.

(Signed)   PEDRO DE MARIGNY,
                 LICENTIATE MANUEL SERRANO.

Thus decreed by D'n Pedro de Marigny, knight of the order of St. Louis, and first alcalde for his majesty, having original jurisdiction in this city and its judicial precincts, with the approbatory opinion of D'n Manuel Serrano, assessor-general of this intendancy, and he signed the same in the city of New Orleans, the 21st November, 1792.

(Signed)   PEDRO PEDESCLAUX,
                                        Not. Pub.

By this will, the testatrix bestowed legacies in favor of a number of her relations, and instituted her husband for her sole and universal heir, in order that after her death he should inherit the remainder of her property. The defendants claim the property described in the bill under titles derived from this heir.

The bill charges that Bertrand Gravier fraudulently induced the notary to prepare a will for his wife, and witnesses to attest the act, and, although the legal formalities were wanting which were necessary to its validity, a "sham decree" of probate was procured from the alcalde by the corrupt agency of the said instituted heir. The defendants deny these allegations, and they have not been supported by testimony. The will has remained without contestation for above a half century. The alcalde, assessor, notary, and witnesses maintained during their lives a good reputation for probity. The property of the testatrix was distributed without opposition, according to the provisions of the will, and is now held, under titles derived from the instituted heir. This evidence disposes of the allegations of the bill, except those which impugn the sufficiency of the act as a legal instrument.

That question, in our opinion, is closed by the decree of the alcalde. That decree declares the will to be valid and subsisting, and directs its execution. We are obliged to treat the decree as the judicial act of a court of competent jurisdiction. In fact, it was the only judicial authority in the province of Louisiana, except that exercised by the governor.

This decree remains in full force, never having been impeached, except in this collateral way. The courts of the United States have no probate jurisdiction, and must receive the sentences of the courts to which the jurisdiction over testamentary matters is committed, as conclusive of the validity and contents of a will; an original bill cannot be sustained upon an allegation that the probate of a will is contrary to law. If any error was committed in allowing the probate, the remedy is in the state courts, according to their appropriate modes of proceeding; such was the decision of this court in Tarver v. Tarver, 9 Pet. 174.

The decision of this question is sufficient to dispose of the case, and we decline any inquiry in reference to any other which was discussed at the hearing.

Decree of the circuit court affirmed.

AMARON LEDOUX, ALPHONSE MILTENBERGER, AND GEORGE O. HALL, PLAINTIFFS IN ERROR, v. JOHN BLACK, JOHN HAGAN, JR., JOHN HAGAN, SR., FRANCIS WREN, J. M. SMILEY, AND EPHRAIM McLEAN.

In the case of an imperfect Spanish title to land in Louisiana, a confirmation by congress is inoperative, unless the title or survey under it will enable the court to ascertain the specific boundaries of the land.

If, before a survey, in such a case, an entry is made and a patent taken out for land, which conflicts with a subsequent survey of the confirmed concession, the patentee has the better title.

THIS case was brought up from the supreme court of Louis-
40 *

iana by a writ of error, issued under the 25th section of the judiciary act.

The case is stated in the opinion of the court.

It was argued by *Mr. Carlisle* and *Mr. Badger*, for the plaintiffs in error, and by *Mr. Benjamin*, for the defendants.

Mr. Justice CATRON delivered the opinion of the court.

This cause is brought here from the supreme court of Louisiana, by writ of error, under the 25th section of the judiciary act of 1789. The only question presented for our consideration is, which party has the better right to the land in dispute? The defendant, Black, claims title under an entry made in 1808, and a patent founded on the entry, dated in 1810, in the name of General Lafayette, for a thousand acres. The validity of this title as against the United States is not denied; but the plaintiffs claim to have an elder title, by virtue of a concession to Ursino Bouligny, of forty arpens front by forty arpens in depth, dated January 10, 1796, of which the plaintiffs are assignees. They allege that under an act of congress of February, 1813, Bouligny prosecuted his claim to the proper register and receiver, who reported in its favor on the 20th of November, 1816; that their report was confirmed by act of congress, the 11th of May, 1820, and that claim was regularly surveyed by order of the surveyor-general of Louisiana, in 1843, and the survey approved in 1844.

To show the point made and decided on these facts, by the supreme court of Louisiana, we give an extract of their opinion, which is found in the record:—

"Conceding," (says the court,) "for the sake of argument, that the claim of the plaintiffs was filed in the land-office in the manner required by law, before the issuing of the patent to General Lafayette; that it has been confirmed by the act of congress of the 11th of May, 1820, and that the confirmation should be made to refer back to the date of the original title, unless that title or a survey made under it by the Spanish surveyor, in compliance with the order of the governor, will enable the court to ascertain the specific boundaries of the land granted, the location of the warrant under which the patent issued to General Lafayette cannot be disturbed. We have uniformly adhered to the rule laid down by our predecessors in the cases of Lefebvre *v.* Cameau, 11 L. R. 823; Slack *v.* Orillon, 11 L. R. 587; Lott et al. *v.* Prudhomme et al. 3 R. R. 298; Metoyer *v.* Larenaudière, 6 R. R. 189.

"In the case of Lott, the court say, referring to the other two: 'We then held, that when the boundaries of a confirmed claim are vague and uncertain, and are to be fixed by the operations of the surveying department, or such confirmation is only the recognition of a pre-existing right or claim, and before the survey and location the government sells a part of the land not necessarily embraced within the tract confirmed, the title of the purchaser will prevail.' Let us test the title of the plaintiffs by that rule, and ascertain whether the land now claimed is necessarily embraced within the tract confirmed to them, supposing that such a confirmation had taken place.

" There was no survey under the Spanish government, and no possession by the grantee. The boundaries are to be ascertained exclusively by the calls of the *requête*, and of the order of the governor upon it. Both described the land as a tract of forty arpens front by forty deep, in the district of Point Coupée, *en el parage*, called the Lagoon of the Raccourci. It is not stated whether the land is to front upon the Lagoon, or upon the Mississippi River; and as one location would answer the calls as well as the other, the description is, perhaps, on that ground alone defective. Lafayette *v.* Blanc, 3 Annual R. 59.

" But supposing that the front was intended to be upon the river, where is it to begin, how is it to run, and where is it to end? Whether the words of description used mean at the place called the Lagoon, or in the vicinity of the Lagoon, the starting-point of the survey is alike uncertain, and the designation of it by the surveyor who located the grant purely abitrary, so far at least as it affects the rights of the defendants."

Until the confirmation took place, (supposing the act of 1820 did confirm Bouligny's claim,) no valid title as against the United States was vested in the grantee to any specific tract of land. We need only to refer to the case of De Vilemont *v.* The United States, 13 How. 266, for authority to this effect. The cases are alike in all their features.

Nor did the mere act of confirmation tend to locate the claim, and sever the land from the public domain; this could only be done by a public survey, and which was not done till 1844. Up to that date the government could sell and convey a legal title to General Lafayette, regardless of the fact that Bouligny's concession existed, and might be surveyed on the land previously granted. This question was settled by the decision in the case of Menard's Heirs *v.* Massey, 8 How. 301, and is not now open to controversy.

We order that the judgment of the supreme court of Louisiana be affirmed.

IN THE MATTER OF THE UNITED STATES *v.* SHERMAN M. BOOTH. STEPHEN V. R. ABLEMAN, PLAINTIFF IN ERROR, *v.* SHERMAM M. BOOTH.

Where the clerk of the supreme court of a state neglects or refuses to make a return to a writ of error issued under the 25th section of the judiciary act, this court will lay a rule upon him to make return on or before the first day of the next term, or show cause why such return has not been made in conformity to law.

And where there is another case upon the docket involving the same questions the court will direct it to be continued, in order that both cases may be argued together.

THESE two cases will be reported together, although in some respects they were dissimilar. In both, however, writs of error had been issued by this court directed to the supreme court of Wisconsin. In the first case, viz. The United States *v.* Booth, the writ was not returned, and Mr. Cushing (attorney-general) filed a copy of the record and moved the court to docket the case, and set it down for argument at the next term. In the other case, viz. Ableman *v.* Booth, the writ was returned, accompanied by a certified copy of the record, and the case stood regularly upon the trial docket.

In the case of the United States *v.* Booth the motion of the attorney-general was as follows:—

And now the attorney-general comes into court and says that, to the writ of error in the present case to the supreme court of the State of Wisconsin, issued by the chief justice of the United States, no return has been made; whereupon he moves that an authentic copy of the record of the said supreme court of the State of Wisconsin in the case, and of the writ of error, with certificate of other proceedings since had, may be filed, and the case entered, and proceed to final judgment on the said copies.

The other proceedings, mentioned in the above motion were comprised in the following certificates, &c.

1. A petition of the attorney-general, reciting the facts stated in the opinion of the court, and praying for a writ of error to remove the case from the supreme court of Wisconsin to this court.

2. The allowance of the writ on the 21st of April, 1855. On the 5th of September, 1855, John R. Sharpstein, district attorney of the United States, made oath before Judge Miller, judge of the district court, that he delivered the writ of error to Lafayette Kellogg, Esq., clerk of the supreme court of Wisconsin, at his office in Madison, on the 30th of May, 1855.

8. The citation to Booth and the service of it by Ableman, the marshal.

4. The following affidavit by Sharpstein:—

I, John R. Sharpstein, attorney of the United States for said district, do solemnly swear, that I have been informed by Lafayette Kellogg, Esq., clerk of the supreme court of the State of Wisconsin, and also by Abram D. Smith, an associate justice of said court, that the said court directed the said clerk to make no return to the writ of error issued out of the supreme court of the United States, in the above entitled cause, and by this deponent served, according to law and the rules of the said last-mentioned court, and that the said supreme court of the State of Wisconsin further directed the said clerk to enter no order upon the journal or records of said court concerning the same, and further deponent says not.

J. R. SHARPSTEIN.

5. A copy of the record.

In the Matter of The United States v. Sherman M. Booth.

Mr. Chief Justice TANEY delivered the opinion of the court.

The court proceed to dispose of the motion made by the attorney-general to docket the case of The United States v. Booth, to stand for argument in this court at the next term.

In support of this motion he has produced a copy of the record of the proceedings in the supreme court of Wisconsin in the above-mentioned case, certified by the clerk under the seal of the court, by which it appears that Booth was indicted in the district court of the United States for the district of Wisconsin, for aiding a fugitive slave to escape from the custody of the marshal, — the marshal having the said slave at that time legally in his custody; and that upon that indictment the said Booth was tried and found guilty, and sentenced by the court to be imprisoned for one month, and to pay a fine of one thousand dollars. That while he was thus imprisoned he obtained a writ of *habeas corpus* from the state court; and, upon a hearing in the supreme court of the State, was discharged from imprisonment by that court, upon the ground that the imprisonment under the sentence of the district court of the United States was illegal.

It further appears, that a writ of error afterwards issued from this court, at the instance of the attorney-general in behalf of the United States, returnable to the present term, and directed to the judges of the supreme court of the State of Wisconsin in order to bring the said proceedings and judgment here for revision, according to the provisions of the 25th section of the act of congress of 1789, ch. 20. But no return has been made to the writ; and it appears by the affidavit of the district attorney, filed with the motion, that the writ of error was duly served on the clerk of the supreme court of the State, and that he was informed by the said clerk that the court had directed him to make no return to the writ of error.

Upon this state of facts the attorney-general has made the motion above mentioned.

The writ of error, without doubt, was rightfully issued from this court, to carry into execution the appellate powers confided to it by the constitution and laws of the United States; and it was the duty of the clerk to obey it, and to send a transcript of the record and proceedings therein mentioned, together with the writ of error, to this court at the present term. And certainly the order of no other tribunal will justify an officer in disobeying the process of this court lawfully issued.

The refusal of the clerk, however, cannot prevent the exercise of the appellate powers of this court; and the court will take such order in the case, as will enable it to fulfil the duties imposed upon it.

But in a matter of so much gravity and importance, we deem it proper, before any other proceeding is had, to lay a rule upon the clerk to make the return required by the writ of error, on or before the first day of the next term of this court; or to show cause, if any he hath, to excuse or justify his neglect or refusal to obey the writ.

The motion to docket the case is, therefore, continued over to the next term, and the court will make the following order: —

Rule.

It having been suggested and shown to this court by the attorney-general of the United States, that the writ of error heretofore allowed and awarded by the chief justice of the supreme court of the United States, and which issued out of this court, pursuant to the several acts of congress in such case made and provided, directed to the supreme court of the State of Wisconsin, requiring the record and proceedings of the said supreme court of the State of Wisconsin in the matter of Sherman M. Booth, for a writ of *habeas corpus* and to be discharged from imprisonment, to be sent to this court, has not been returned pursuant to the exigency of the said writ: —

It is thereupon ordered, that the clerk of said supreme court of the State of Wisconsin do make due return of the said writ of error, pursuant to the mandate therein contained, and according to the laws of the United States in that behalf, on or before the first day of the term of this court next to be holden at the city of Washington, on the first Monday of December, in the year of our Lord one thousand eight hundred and fifty-six, or then and there show cause why such return has not been made in conformity to law. And it is further ordered that a copy of this rule be served on the said clerk on or before the first day of August next.

STEPHEN V. R. ABLEMAN, PLFF. IN ER.,   No. 85.—In error to the
v.   supreme court of the
SHERMAN M. BOOTH.   State of Wisconsin.

Mr. Chief Justice TANEY delivered the opinion of the court.

Upon looking into the transcript in this case, we find that the questions of constitutional law which it involves arose in a preliminary proceeding in the case between the same parties, of which we have just spoken. In that case, the whole subject was disposed of in the state court, and the principal question in it is precisely the same with that which is presented in this, which the attorney-general proposes to argue. The two cases ought to be argued together. It would hardly be proper for the court, where questions of so much interest are concerned, to hear a portion of them at one term and a portion of them at another. All of the questions which are involved in the two cases have grown out of one transaction, and depend upon the same facts, and it is impossible to decide one without disposing of the principal question in the other. The court, therefore, will not hear the argument in these cases separately. They must be argued together. And as the principal case is not before the court in a form that will enable the court to hear it at the present term, this preliminary portion of it must be continued until the next term, to be argued when the whole subject is ready for hearing.

JOHN BACON AND THOMAS ROBINS, SURVIVING TRUSTEES OF THE
BANK OF THE UNITED STATES, WILLIAM R. WHITE AND
JOHN HOOPER, CITIZENS OF PENNSYLVANIA, LEWIS PHŒNIX
AND JOHN D. BEERS, CITIZENS OF NEW YORK, STOCKHOLDERS
OF THE LATE COMMERCIAL BANK OF NATCHEZ, WHO SUE ON BE-
HALF OF THEMSELVES AND ALL OTHER STOCKHOLDERS OF SAID
LATE COMMERCIAL BANK OF NATCHEZ, WHO ARE CITIZENS OF
OTHER STATES THAN MISSISSIPPI, WHO SHALL COME IN AND SEEK
RELIEF BY, AND CONTRIBUTE TO THE EXPENSES OF THIS SUIT,
COMPLAINANTS AND APPELLANTS, v. WILLIAM ROBERTSON,
PHILIP HOGGATT, HENRY CHOTARD, AND JOHN F. GILLESPIE,
AND OTHERS, (NAMES UNKNOWN,) STOCKHOLDERS OF THE LATE
COMMERCIAL BANK OF NATCHEZ, AND CITIZENS OF THE STATE
OF MISSISSIPPI.

In the State of Mississippi, a judgment of forfeiture was rendered against the Commercial Bank of Natchez, and a trustee was appointed to take charge of the books
and assets of the bank.
Under the laws of Mississippi and the general principles of equity jurisprudence, the
surplus of the assets which may remain after the payment of debts and expenses,
belongs to the stockholders of the bank.
The early and late English cases examined, as to what becomes of the property of a
corporation whose charter has been forfeited by a judicial sentence.
The modern rules of the English courts have been adopted in the United States, extending the protection of chancery over the civil rights of members of moneyed corporations, and recognizing the existence of distinct and individual rights in their
capital and business.
The trustee is estopped from denying the title of the stockholders to a distribution.
The courts of the United States have jurisdiction over the case, and a bill can be
maintained, filed by a number of stockholders owning one fifth part of the capital
stock, suing for themselves and such of the stockholders as were not citizens of
Mississippi, nor defendants in the bill.

THIS was an appeal from the circuit court of the United States
for the southern district of Mississippi.

The transaction to which the suit relates was partly and incidentally brought before the notice of this court in 16 How. 106.

The facts are stated in the opinion of the court.

It was argued by *Mr. Wharton* and *Mr. Yerger*, for the appellants, and *Mr. Lawrence*, for the appellees.

Mr. Justice CAMPBELL delivered the opinion of the court.

This bill was filed in the circuit court against William Robertson, a trustee, appointed to liquidate the affairs of the late
Commercial Bank of Natchez, Mississippi, and such of the stockholders of the bank as are citizens of that State, and is prosecuted
by a number of stockholders, owning one fifth part of the capital
stock, for themselves, and such of the stockholders as are not
citizens of Mississippi, or defendants in the bill.

The Commercial Bank was incorporated and organized under enactments of the legislature in 1836, with a capital of $3,050,-000, divided into shares of $100 each, which are now distributed among two hundred and eighty persons.

The corporation carried on the business of banking through the agency of presidents, directors, cashiers, and other officers, at Natchez, and four other towns of Mississippi, for a number of years. During this time there was a temporary suspension of specie payments, which the bill avers to have been accidental, and to have formed the only ground for the proceedings taken against the corporation. In June, 1845, the circuit court of Adams county rendered a judgment against the bank, upon an information in the nature of a *quo warranto* preferred pursuant to the act of the legislature of July, 1843. By this judgment the bank was " prejudged and excluded from further holding or exercising the liberties, privileges, and franchises granted by the said charter "; " the liberties, privileges, and franchises granted to the bank were seized " by the State ; the " property, books, and assets of the bank " were adjudged to be seized and delivered to a trustee, who might have execution therefor. William Robertson was appointed that trustee " to take charge of the books and assets of the bank." His duties are declared, conformably to the act of 1843, which will be considered in another part of this opinion.

The bank appealed from this judgment, and in the spring session of the high court of errors and appeals, in 1846, it was affirmed. William Robertson entered upon the office of trustee in July, 1846. He took possession of money, stocks, evidences of debt, and real estate having a nominal value of near four millions of dollars, and continues to hold them, except in so far as he has applied them to the payment of the charges of the trust, and the debts of the corporation. The bill alleges that all the debts have been paid, and that only a small sum is due for costs, and that property of great value, consisting of money, stocks, evidences of debt, bonds, and personality, remains with the trustee, who refuses to account for them to the stockholders. The object of the bill is to establish the title of the stockholders to this surplus, and to obtain the ratable shares of such of them as are able and willing to join as plaintiffs in this suit. The bill names a number of the stockholders as parties, and is fitted to embrace all by the representation of these.

The defendants joined in a general demurrer to the bill; a decree of dismissal was rendered at the hearing at the circuit, and, by appeal, was taken up to this court to revise that decision.

When the defendant, Robertson, assumed the office of trustee, his duties were defined by two acts of the legislature of Mississippi. The act of July, 1843, directed the institution of suits against such of the banking corporations of the State as had violated their charters in such a manner as to incur their forfeiture, and prescribed the form of the suits for the enforcement of that forfeiture. It enacted "that upon a judgment of forfeiture against any bank, the debtors of the bank shall not be released from their debts and liabilities to the same; but it was made the duty of the circuit court, rendering the said judgment, to appoint one or more trustees to take charge of the books and assets of the banks; who should sue for and collect all debts due such bank, and sell and dispose of all property owned by it, or held by others for its use; and the proceeds of the debts, when collected, and of the property when sold, to apply, as may hereafter be directed by law, to the payment of the debts of such bank. The trustee was made subject to a criminal prosecution for embezzlement, conversion of the trust property, as a failure to account for it according to law; and both acts prescribed a bond to be given to secure the faithful performance of his duty. The act of February, 1846, amended and enlarged the scope of the act of 1843, and was applicable to all trustees appointed under either.

This act provided a summary remedy in favor of the trustee to obtain the control of the corporate property; for an inventory to be made to the first court, after his appointment; for an order of sale of all the corporate property at auction, for cash, after a notice of ninety days, at specified places; for commissioners to audit the claims against the banks, and for their presentation to these commissioners; for early decisions upon the exceptions to their report; for a final decree of distribution, first, in the payment of expenses, then public dues, costs, and fees, the debts reported, and, lastly, "the surplus, if any shall be ratably distributed among the stockholders." There was a provision that the bills of the bank should be receivable for debts, and that the debtor might redeem from any purchaser of his debt or obligation, (so sold,) during two years, by paying the purchase-money, all costs, and twelve and a half per cent interest. The object of the two statutes can hardly be misconceived. They are parts of a system, the latter act being auxiliary to, and adopted in aid of, the provisions of the earlier act of 1843, — the two acts containing the full expression of the will of the legislature. The circumstances of the legislature enabled it to defer the promulgation of its entire policy until the year 1846. The exigencies of the State were entirely answered by the directions given in 1843 to the executive officers to take initiatory measures for placing these corporations under restraint, and for the security of their property. To effectuate these, involved delay and litigation, and the legislature might well await their issue, before unfolding their whole plan of liquidation and settlement. The two statutes which embody it have formed the subject of much discussion in the courts of Mississippi, and difficulty has been experienced there in carrying them into execution. No suit has been instituted there by the stockholders, though their rights have been incidentally debated, both at the bar and by the supreme appellate court. To comprehend the import of this legislation, we must consider the mischiefs it was designed to prevent or remove, and the mode adopted to accomplish the end; for the legislation is of a character wholly remedial. The common law of Great Britain was deficient in supplying the instrumentalities for a speedy and just settlement of the affairs of an insolvent corporation whose charter had been forfeited by a judicial sentence. The opinion usually expressed as to the effect of such a sentence was unsatisfactory and questioned. There had been instances in Great Britain of the dissolution of public or ecclesiastical corporations by the exertion of the public authority, or as a consequence of the death of their members, and parliament and the courts had affirmed in these instances that the endowments they had received from the prince or pious founders would revert in such a case. Stat. de terris Templariorum, 17 Edw. II.; Dean and Canons of Windsor, Godb. 211; Johnson *v.* Norway, Winch. 37; Owen, 73; 6 Vin. Abr. 280. What was to become of their personal estate and of their debts and credits had not been settled in any adjudged case, and as was said by Pollexfen in the argument of the *quo warranto* against the city of London, was perhaps "*non definitur in jure.*" Solicitor Finch, who argued for the crown in that cause, admitted, "I do not find any judgment in a *quo warranto* of a corporation being forfeited." Treby, on behalf of the city, said, "the dissolving a corporation by a judgment in law, as is here sought, I believe is a thing that never came within the compass of any man's imagination till now; no, not so much as in the putting of a case. For in all my search, (and upon this occasion I have bestowed a great deal of time in searching,) I cannot find that it ever so much as entered into the conception of any man before; and I am the more confirmed in it because so learned a gentleman as Mr. Solicitor has not cited any one such case wherein it has been (I do not say adjudged but) even so much as questioned or attempted; and, therefore, I may very boldly call this a case *primæ impressionis.*" The argument of Pollexfen was equally positive. The power of courts to adjudge a forfeiture so as to dissolve a corporation was affirmed in that case, but the effect of that judgment was not illustrated by any execution, and the courts were relieved from their embarrassment by an act of parliament annulling it. Smith's case, 4 Mod. 58; Skin. 310; 8 St. Tri. 1042, 1057, 1288. Nor have the discussions since the Revolution extended our knowledge upon this intricate subject. The case of Rex v. The Amery, 2 D. & E. 515, has exerted much influence upon text writers. The questions were, whether a judgment of seizure *quousque* upon a default was final, and if so, whether the king's grant of pardon and restitution would overreach and defeat a charter granting to a new body of men the same liberties intermediate the seizure and the pardon. The king's bench, relying upon the Year-book of 15 Edw. IV., declared the judgment to be final and the new charter irrepealable. But the House of Lords reversed the judgment. The judges, upon an examination of the original roll of the case in the Year-book, discovered that it did not support the conclusion drawn from it, and Chief Baron Eyre says, " that Lord Coke had adopted the doctrine too hastily." The discussions upon this case show how much the knowledge of the writ of *quo warranto* as it had been used and applied under the Plantagenets and Tudors, had gone from the memories of courts and lawyers. 4 D. & E. 122, Tan. on Quo Warranto, 24. In Colchester v. Seaber, 3 Bur. 1866, where the suit was upon a bond, and the defence was, that certain facts had occurred to dissolve the corporation, and that the creditor's claim was extinguished on the bond, Lord Mansfield said, " Without an express authority, so strong as not to be gotten over, we ought not to determine a case so much against reason as that parliament should be obliged to interfere." The question occurs here, Could parliament interfere? And the answer would be by their authorizing a suit to be brought notwithstanding the dissolution. These are all cases of municipal corporations where the corporations had no rights in the property of the corporation in severalty. The courts of Westminster have found much difficulty in applying the principles settled in regard to such, to the commercial and trading corporations that have come into existence during this century. The courts there within the last twelve months have been troubled to discuss whether a commercial corporation could recover damages for the breach of a parole contract, or whether the contract should have had a seal to make it valid. Austra. R. M. N. Co. v. Marzetti, 82 L. & E. 572; 8 Ib. 420. It may be admitted that the courts of law could not give any relief to the shareholders of a corporation disfranchised by a judicial sentence in respect to a corporate right. Their modes of proceeding do not provide for the case as they have not for many others. 1 Plow. 276, 277;

Richards *v*. Richards, 2 B. & Adol. 447; Will. Ex. 1129. But this concession does not involve an acknowledgment that the rights of the corporations are extinguished. Courts of chancery have been forced into a closer contact with these associations, and have formed a more rational conception of their constitution and a more accurate estimate of their importance to the industrial relations of society. Those courts have evinced a spirit of accommodation of their modes of proceeding so as to adapt them to the changing exigencies of society. Lord Cottenham, in Wallworth *v*. Holt, 4 M. & C. 635, in reference to the conduct of suits in which similar associations were concerned, said: "I think it is the duty of this court to adapt its practice and course of proceeding to the existing state of society, and not, by too strict an adherence to rules and forms established under different circumstances, to decline to administer justice and to enforce rights for which there is no other remedy." In the same spirit, Sir James Wigram, V. C., observes: "Corporations of this kind are in truth little more than private partnerships; and in cases which may be easily suggested, it would be too much to hold that a society of private persons associated together in undertakings which, though certainly beneficial to the public, are nevertheless matters of private property, are to be deprived of their civil rights *inter se*, because, in order to make their common objects more attainable, the crown or legislature have conferred upon them the benefit of a corporate character." Foss *v*. Harbottle, 2 Hare, 491. These just views which have afforded to wise chancellors a sufficient motive to enlarge the scope and relax the rigor of the rules of chancery proceeding, so as to bring the civil rights of individuals in whatever form they may exist, or however complicated or ramified, under the protection of legitimate judicial administration, have been adopted in the United States, not simply for the improvement of methods of proceeding, but also for the adjustment of rights and the assertion of responsibilities among the members of such associations. In the Bank of the United States *v*. Deveaux, 5 Cr. 61, this court held "that the technical definition of a corporation does not uniformly circumscribe its capacities, but that courts for legitimate purposes will contemplate it more substantially; and the court in that case allowed the corporation to use its corporate name for the purposes of suit in the courts of the United States to represent the civil capacities of the persons who composed it. So the court has held that corporate acts need not to be evinced by writing, nor corporate contracts by a common seal; that corporations are liable on contracts made or defaults or torts committed by their officers or agents in the course of their employment. 12 Wheat.

40; Ib. 64; 6 How. 344; 14 Ib. 468. In Lennox v. Roberts, 2 Wheat. 378, the court gave effect to a general assignment of a corporation of its *choses in action* made in anticipation of the expiration of its charter, and which was designed to preserve to the corporators their rights of property. In the Mumma v. Potomac Company, 8 Pet. 281, it held that the assignment of all the property of a corporation and the surrender and cancellation of its charter with the consent of the legislature, did not defeat the right of the judgment creditor to satisfaction out of the property which had belonged to it. The power of courts of equity in cases like these was recognized as adequate to maintain the rights of the parties beneficially interested, and this doctrine was repeated and developed in Curran v. Arkansas, 15 How. 304.

The tendency of the discussions and judgments of the court of chancery in Great Britain, and of the courts of this country, is to concede the existence of a distinct and positive right of property in the individuals composing the corporation, in its capital and business, which is subject in the main to the management and control of the corporation itself; but that cases may arise where the corporators may assert not only their own rights, but the rights of the corporate body. And no reason can be given why the dissolution of a corporation, whether by judicial sentence or otherwise, whose capital was contributed by shareholders, for a lawful and perhaps laudable enterprise, with the consent of the legislature, should suspend the operation of these principles, or hinder the effective interference of the court of chancery for the preservation of individual rights of property in such a case. The withdrawal of the charter — that is, the right to use the corporate name for the purposes of suits before the ordinary tribunals — is such a substantial impediment to the prosecution of the rights of the parties interested, whether creditors or debtors, as would authorize equitable interposition in their behalf, within the doctrine of chancery precedents. Stainton v. The Carron Company, 28 L. and E. 315; Travis v. Milne, 9 Hare, 141; 2 Ib. 491. For the sentence of forfeiture does not attain the rights of property of the corporators or corporation, for then the State would appropriate it. If those rights are put an end to, it would seem to be rather from a careless disregard, or hardened and reckless indifference to consequences, on the part of the public authority, than from any preconceived plan or purpose. For, according to the doctrine of the text writers on this subject, the consequences are visited without any discrimination; the losses are imposed upon those who are not blameworthy, and the benefits are accumulated upon those who are without desert. The effects of a dissolution of a corporation are usually described to be, the reversion of the lands to those who had granted them; the extinguishment of the debts, either to or from the corporate body, so that they are not a charge nor a benefit to the members. The instances which support the *dictum* in reference to the lands, consist of the statutes and judgments which followed the suppression of the military and religious orders of knights, and whose lands returned to those who had granted them, and did not fall to the king as an escheat; or of cases of dissolution of monasteries and other ecclesiastical foundations, upon the death of all their members; or of donations to public bodies, such as a mayor and commonalty. But such cases afford no analogy to that before us. The acquisitions of real property by a trading corporation are commonly made upon a bargain and sale, for a full consideration, and without conditions in the deed; and no conditions are implied in law in reference to such conveyances. The vendor has no interest in the appropriation of the property to any specific object, nor any reversion, where the succession fails. If the statement of the consequences of a dissolution upon the debts and credits of the corporation is literally taken, there can be no objection to it. The members cannot recover nor be charged with them, in their natural capacities, in a court of law. But this does not solve the difficulty. The question is, has the *bonâ fide* and just creditor of a corporation, dissolved under a judicial sentence for a breach in its charter, any claim upon the corporate property for the satisfaction of his debt, apart from the reservation in the act of the legislature which directed the prosecution? Can the lands be resumed in disregard of their rights by vendors, who have received a full payment of their price, and executed an absolute conveyance? Can the careless, improvident, or faithless debtor, plead the extinction of his debt, or of the creditor's claim, and thus receive protection in his delinquency? The creditor is blameless, — he has not participated in the corporate mismanagement, nor procured the judicial sentence; he has trusted upon visible property acquired by the corporation, in virtue of its legislative sanction. How can the vendors of the lands or the delinquent debtors resist the might of his equity? But, if the claims of the creditor are irresistible, those of the stockholder are not inferior, at least against the parties who claim to hold the corporate property. The money, evidences of debt, lands, and personalty acquired by the corporation were purchased with the capital they lawfully contributed to a legitimate enterprise, conducted under the legislative authority. The enterprise has failed under circumstances, it may well be, which entitle the State to withdraw its special support and encouragement; but the State does not affirm that any cause for the confiscation of the property, or for the infliction of a heavier penalty, has arisen. It is a case, therefore, in which courts of chancery, upon their well-settled principles, would aid the parties to realize the property belonging to the corporation, and compel its application to the satisfaction of the demands which legitimately rest upon it.

In our view of the equity of this bill we have the support and sanction of the legislature of Mississippi. Their legislation excludes all the consequences which have been imputed as necessary to a sentence of dissolution on a civil corporation. From the plenitude of their powers, for the amelioration of the condition of the body politic, and the supply of defects in their system of remedial laws, they have afforded a plan for the liquidation and settlement of the business of these corporations in which the equities of the creditors and shareholders respectively are recognized, as attaching to all the corporate property of whatever description. And the inquiry arises, who is authorized to obstruct the enforcement of these equities in so far as the stockholders of the Commercial Bank of Natchez are concerned? The creditors have been satisfied. The defendant in the present suit is the trustee appointed under these legislative enactments. His demurrer confesses that he has received money, stocks, evidences of debt, lands, and personal property, which he refuses to distribute. He claims that the stockholders have no rights since the dissolution of the corporation, and if any, they must be looked for in the circuit court of Adams county, Mississippi. But the trustee cannot deny the title of the stockholders to a distribution. To collect and distribute the property of the corporation among the creditors and stockholders, is his commission, — for this end he was placed in the possession of the property, and was armed with all the powers he has exercised.

His title is in subordination to theirs, and his duties are to maintain their rights and to consult their advantage. Pearson v. Lindley, 2 Ju. 758; 8 Pet. 48; 4 Bligh. 1; Willis Trus. 125, 172, 178. He is estopped from making the defence of a want of title in the stockholders. Nor is the objection to the jurisdiction of this court tenable. Ten years have nearly elapsed since this trust was created. The acts of the legislature contemplated a prompt and speedy settlement. They direct the reduction of all the property into ready money, and an early distribution among the parties concerned. The trustee confesses that he has not sold the lands nor personal estate, and that he has refused to distribute the money. He has committed a palpable breach of trust according to the case made by the bill and as confessed by the demurrer. All the other trusts having been fulfilled, the stockholders are entitled to such an administration as will be most beneficial to them, or to a sale of the trust property in the manner prescribed by the statute of Mississippi. Nor is the objection to the form of the suit tenable. If the trust estate had been liquidated and the interests of the stockholders ascertained, any stockholder might have maintained a suit for his aliquot share without including any other stockholder. Smith *v.* Snow, 3 Mad. C. R. 310. But the trust estate has not been sold, nor are the names of all the stockholders ascertained, the trustee is called on to account, and the bill asks for the collection and disposal of the remaining property under the authority of the court of chancery.

The stockholders are interested in these questions, and are then proper parties to the bill. The number of the parties renders it impracticable to bring all before the court, and therefore the suit may be prosecuted in the form which has been employed in this suit. This court sustained such a bill in the case of Smith *v.* Swormstedt, 16 How. 288.

We do not intend to decide any of the questions of the cause which may arise as to the mode of administering the relief prayed for in this bill. Our opinion is that the plaintiffs have shown a proper case for equitable interposition by the circuit court, and that the decree of that court dismissing the bill is erroneous.

Decree reversed, and cause remanded.

SOLOMON S. MASTERS AND WILLIAM K. MASTERS, TRADING AS PARTNERS UNDER THE FIRM AND STYLE OF S. S. MASTERS AND SON, PLAINTIFFS IN ERROR, *v.* FREDERICK L. BARREDA AND PHILLIPPE BARREDA, TRADING AS PARTNERS UNDER THE FIRM OF F. L. BARREDA AND BROTHER.

When there is a dealing between merchants, for successive cargoes of merchandise upon time, for which notes of hand were to be given, payable from the date of the ascertainment of the quantity of each cargo, and an arrangement is afterwards made for the substitution of an interest account for the notes which were to be given; and, in that arrangement, the seller stipulates that the allowance of the interest account should depend upon the continuance of the original time of credit, and that the buyer's balance on account should always be under a certain sum; and the buyer exceeds that amount and refuses to make a remittance or payment, upon the call of the seller, to bring the account within that sum, the seller may arrest the further delivery of any cargo or cargoes, though the same was in the course of being delivered to the buyer upon the seller's indorsement of the invoices and bills of lading of such cargoes.

In the absence of all understanding between the buyer and seller, that any cargo which had been delivered and not actually paid for, though notes of hand had been given for the same, was not to be considered within the new arrangement, such cargo must be taken into the computation in ascertaining whether the balance due by the buyer exceeds the amount of credit allowed to him.

In this case, the true construction of the new arrangement is, that the existing notes of hand are to be counted as making a part of the limit which the buyer was not to exceed.

THIS case was brought up, by writ of error, from the circuit court of the United States for the eastern district of Virginia.

The facts of the case are stated in the opinion of the court.

Upon the trial in the circuit court, the counsel for the plaintiffs (the Barredas) and defendants offered several prayers to the court as instructions to the jury, which the court declined to grant, and instructed the jury as follows: —

"1. Under the contract made by the letters of the 9th, 10th, and 11th of March, the amount for the cargo of The Lucy Elizabeth, and for which notes had been given, must be taken into the calculation, and charged against the defendants, in determining whether the balance against them amounted to $40,000.

"2. If, in this mode of computation, the balance against the defendants for guano previously sold and delivered amounted to $40,000 at the time when the further delivery of the cargoes of The Beatrice and The Ailsa was refused by the plaintiffs, the refusal was justifiable under the contract. They were not bound, in such a state of the account, to deliver these cargoes on credit. And, if they offered to deliver them to the payment of the money or satisfactory security, and the defendants refused to comply with these terms, the plaintiffs had a right to stop the delivery, notwithstanding the previous indorsement and delivery of the bill of lading to the defendants; and the refusal as stated in the testimony is no breach of contract on the part of the plaintiffs, and is not a bar to the recovery in this action of the amount due for the guano actually received by the defendants."

To which instructions the counsel for the defendants excepted and the jury found a verdict for the plaintiffs for $74,636.18, with interest from 12th of September, 1854, till paid.

The case was argued in this court by *Mr. Johnson*, for the plaintiffs in error, and by *Mr. Carlisle* and *Mr. Bradley*, with whom was *Mr. F. L. Smith*, for defendants.

Mr. Justice WAYNE delivered the opinion of the court.

This is an action of *assumpsit* brought in the circuit court of the United States for the eastern district of Virginia, by the defendants in error, against Masters and Son, to recover from them a balance of $77,966.18 arising from the sales of guano, as stated in the bill of particulars, at pages three and four of the record.

The transactions out of which this dispute arose commenced on the 21st of January, 1854.

Barreda and Brother, residing in the city of Baltimore, were largely engaged in the importation of guano into the United States. Masters and Son were shipping and commission merchants in Alexandria, Virginia. Barreda and Brother had found it necessary in conducting their business to establish a limit of credit, both as to time and amount for purchases made by those who dealt with them. For any excess above that credit, purchasers had to pay cash, or give satisfactory paper, with their indorsement. The uncontradicted statement of the Barredas, in their letter to Masters and Son of the 15th May, 1854, corroborated by other circumstances, shows, that in the year 1852, this limit of credit was $25,000; and that their dealings with the Masters from that time, up to the sale of two cargoes of guano on the 21st January, 1854, and afterwards, until changed by the letters between them of the 9th and 10th March, 1854, had been regulated accordingly.

The sale of the two cargoes of guano, just mentioned, is as follows: —

"We have sold to Messrs. S. S. Masters and Son two cargoes of Peruvian guano, — from vessels Lucy Elizabeth three hundred and thirty-five tons, and Giaour two hundred and seventy-one, — both on their way from Peru. The said guano to be delivered in the port of Alexandria, in Virginia, when the vessels may arrive. Messrs. Masters and Son will act as our agents to receive the cargo and attend to the vessels, free of any charge, and to pay the value of the guano they may receive, at the price of $47.50 per ton in bulk, in notes payable in Baltimore, four months after date. "F. BARREDA AND BROTHER.

"*Baltimore*, 21st January, 1854."

Subsequently to that date, (the precise time when does not appear from the record,) Masters and Son purchased from the Barredas another cargo of the ship Princess Alice, and on the 18th February a fourth, — that of the ship Ailsa.

The Lucy Elizabeth arrived with her cargo at Alexandria on the 1st February. The Giaour, with hers, about the 10th of the same month. Masters and Son attended to unlading the cargoes of both vessels, and sent to the Barredas a certificate of the cargo received from The Lucy Elizabeth, on the 2d March, namely, 485.21.4 tons of No. 1 guano, (in bulk at $47.50 per ton,) and 25.1.21 tons of No. 2 guano in bulk, for which they were charged $24,108.64; the quantity of No. 2 being charged to them at $42.50. They remitted to the Barredas on the 6th March, three notes of hand payable on the 2d and 5th of July; two of them for $8,000, and a third for $8,108.64; amounting to $24,108.64. Up to this time, the cargoes of The Giaour and The Princess Alice had not been ascertained, though both ships were then being unladed under the agency of Masters and Son, according to the arrangement in the memorandum of sale of the 21st January. And the correspondence shows that then there had not been any extension by the Barredas of the amount of credit, which had hitherto been allowed to Masters and Son upon their previous purchases. In this state of their dealing Masters and Son wrote to the Barredas on the 9th March: "As our purchases are likely to be pretty large this year, and we noticed, some time ago, that one of our mutual friends (H. W. Fry) had arranged with you to keep an interest account with him, at six per cent, and we, for the same reason, prefer not to give notes. Further, as it is at times an advantage to have it in our power to make payments when the local exchange is most favorable, we will be obliged, if you will allow us also this accommodation, giving us an average credit of four months on these other cargoes." To this letter Barreda and Brother reply on the 10th March. They state, "we will keep an interest account with you, at six per cent, to facilitate your payments, provided that you will never exceed an average time of four months for the payment of each cargo; and that the balance on account against you will always be under forty thousand dollars, being the largest credit we use to allow." The Masters' reply in a letter of the 11th March: "Your acceptance of our proposition, made with the view of our not having to pay the whole value of our purchases in notes, &c., is also duly appreciated,—and we note the conditions regarding the open account."

At the date of this arrangement, there was charged to Masters and Son on the books of Barreda and Brother $24,108.64, the value of The Lucy Elizabeth's cargo, for which the Masters had given three notes, payable on the 2d and 5th July. Eighteen days after this arrangement the Masters send to the Barredas a certificate of Giaour's cargo, amounting to $17,094.84, and remit a payment on account of it of $6,000. The next item in the account is the value of the cargo of The Princess Alice, amounting to $38,029.92. But they had written to the Barredas on the 30th March, saying: "The Ailsa cannot now reach this too soon for us, and we prefer not relinquishing our purchase of the said cargo; and, further, we believe we are selling by considerable the bulk of the guano applied for here, (we wish it was at a better profit,) and find the demand good. From present prospects we shall want a cargo each ensuing month. With your present unprecedentedly large importations, we suppose we can make our calculations to get this supply from you without having to look far ahead." The Barredas answer: "For the present, we have no cargo to offer you in the time you mention." But on the 18th April they write: "We will send you The Beatrice, reply immediately." Masters and Son write on the same day: "We will take The Beatrice"; and the Barredas rejoin: "Ship Beatrice will be ordered to you, provided she arrives before the end of May next." She arrived on the 24th April, and was ordered to Masters and Son. On the same day the Barredas ask in another letter: "Will you take the Ailsa if she arrives here?" The Masters answer: "Send The Ailsa if she comes as heretofore concluded upon." She arrived early in May, and was ordered to Alexandria. Thus, in the whole, five cargoes were bought by the Masters from the Barredas. Each of them upon a credit of four months, notes having been given for that of The Lucy Elizabeth, with the understanding by both parties that notes were not to be given for the other purchases, the quantities of which had not been ascertained when the arrangement of the 10th March was made, and that they were to be paid for according to that arrangement. But the value of three of the cargoes had been ascertained, amounting, according to the returns of Masters and Son to Barreda and Brother, to $79,232.90. Payments had been made to the amount of $29,000. On the 12th May the Barredas wrote, calling the attention of Masters and Son to the state of the account, and requesting them to make a remittance of $10,232.90, "as our limit in your account is $40,000, and it being then beyond the limit of the credit in the amount of the remittance asked for." In a postscript to the letter, they say: "Of course the value of The Beatrice and Ailsa cargoes must be paid cash. 2 P. C. off." To this letter the Masters reply without making the remittance, and say: "On the 9th March last, we had purchased from you four cargoes of guano, about 2,500 tons, or $120,000 worth, at four months,—no other terms mentioned, (and to this moment we have never heard of any other,) three of the said cargoes were received and being received, and the fourth was daily expected. On the above-named date we asked you to allow us to keep an interest or open account with you, as we did not like to pay the whole value of our purchases in notes; to this you had no objection to the value of $40,000; the balance, as we had to infer, we must settle for agreeably to the original bill of purchase." To this letter the Barredas reply: "Yours of the 18th instant has been received. When we first went into business with you, we mentioned to you that our limit for credit was

$25,000, we making to you the sales of three, or four, or twenty cargoes, our impression would have been, as was in that case, that we were to accept your paper for $25,000, and the balance that you might owe in satisfactory paper with your indorsement. Certainly, you could never have expected us to accept your notes for such an amount as our sales, though your responsibility may be superior to it. Afterwards, when you proposed to open with us an account, with interest, to facilitate your payments, we agreed to it; provided, that you would never exceed an average time of four months for the payment of each cargo, and that the balance on account against you will always be under $40,000,—this being the largest credit we use to allow. You also understood in the same way our conditions, and took good care to make a remittance of $6,000, together with the return of The Giaour's cargo, to keep yourselves within the limits of your credit with us." In a few days after writing their letter of the 17th, Barreda and Brother made an effort through the agency of Mr. Coyle, to have an amicable settlement with Masters and Son, offering to them either of the following propositions: That they would deliver to Mr. Coyle all the guano received from The Beatrice and Ailsa, and such a portion of the cargo of The Princess Alice as may be necessary to cover the $10,234.90 of excess of their account,—or settle their values in cash, less two per cent,—or give satisfactory paper with their indorsement, payable in New York or Baltimore, at four months from the day when the offer was made, that being the 22d of May.

Neither of these propositions were accepted, and this suit was brought to recover the balance on account against Masters and Son, including the value of all the guano they had received from The Lucy Elizabeth, The Giaour, Princess Alice, Beatrice, and Ailsa, after having given to them credit for payments made. There is no dispute concerning either the debit or credit side of the account, but the controversy arose from the different view entertained by the parties as to their respective rights under the arrangement made for an interest account and the limit of credit mentioned in it, and whether, in the actual state of the account and under the course pursued by the Barredas, they were justified in arresting the delivery of the undischarged portions of the cargoes of The Beatrice and Ailsa, on account of the neglect and refusal of Masters and Son to make the required remittance to reduce the account against them to $40,000.

Our first objection to the construction of that arrangement as given by Masters and Son, is its variance from the terms used by them in their letter of the 9th of March, asking for the substitution of an interest account, instead of giving notes for their purchases, and from their language in their letter of the 11th March, in reply to the letter of the Barredas of the 10th, granting their request upon the conditions mentioned in it. They preface their application by saying, " as our purchases will be very large this year, we prefer not to give notes, and will be obliged if you will allow us an interest account, giving us an average credit of four months on these other cargoes ; and in their letter of the 11th say, your acceptance of our proposition, made with the view of our not having to pay the whole value of our purchases in notes, &c., is also duly appreciated, and we note the conditions regarding the open account." If from the first an application may be made that it was their intention that the favor asked by them was to be applied to future purchases, and not to include purchases which they had made and which had not been paid for, there can be no doubt that their understanding of the arrangement was, 'that it was to include both, when in thanking the Barredas for their acceptance of their proposition, they state it was made with the view of their not having to pay the whole value of their purchases in notes. Besides having applied the arrangement to their purchases of the cargoes of The Giaour and Princess Alice, both of which had been bought, but neither of which had been ascertained when they asked for an interest account, and when it was granted, they could not afterwards give to the arrangement an exclusive application to cargoes to be thereafter bought; and when they say their request for an interest or open account had been made with the view of not having to pay the whole value of their purchases in notes, and afterwards say, " we note the conditions regarding the open account," one of them being that the balance on account against them shall never be larger than $40,000, it is conclusive that they then understood that amount to be the extent of their credit for all of their purchases, according to the account as it then stood on the books of the Barredas, or as it might be enlarged.

But it was urged that the limit of the amount of their credit was not to exceed at the time when the Barredas wrote their letter of the 12th May. It was said that the amount then still due for the cargo of The Lucy Elizabeth should not have been taken into the computation in ascertaining whether the balance due by the Masters amounted to more than $40,000, because that cargo had been sold under a different contract, in no way connected with the other purchases. Such, however, was not the fact, for The Giaour's cargo was bought under the same memorandum of sale ; and the cargo of The Princess Alice had been bought before the cargo of The Giaour had been ascertained; and the Masters, after the arrangement had been made for an interest account, applied it to both, when their cargoes were ascertained, by not giving notes for either, and transmitting their certificates of the quantity of each, without any direction that a new and separate account of their cost should be made of them distinct from the debit against them in the books of the Barredas for the cargo of The Lucy Elizabeth. Had it been intended otherwise, they should have given such a direction; and not have said, we note the conditions regarding the open account, the limitation of the credit to be allowed being one of them, expressed in language so plain that it cannot be doubted that the Barredas never meant to give to Masters and Son a larger credit upon their purchases than $40,000; and that, when their account exceeded it, they were to have the right to call for payments to reduce it to that amount. When they called for the remittance of $10,282.90, the account against Masters and Son exceeded it by that amount. They failed to make the payment, and continuing to refuse to do so, we are of the opinion that the Barredas had a right to arrest the delivery of the cargoes of The Beatrice and Ailsa, notwithstanding the indorsement and delivery of the bills of lading to Masters and Son, and that their refusal to deliver the same, as stated in the testimony, is no breach of contract, and is not a bar to the recovery in this action of the amount due for the guano actually received by Masters and Son. Such was the instruction given by the court upon the trial of the case in the circuit court; and, having expressed our concurrence with that view, we will only add, that when there is a dealing between merchants for successive cargoes of merchandise upon time, for which notes of hand were to be given, payable from the date of the ascertainment of the quantity of each cargo, and an arrangement is afterwards made for the substitution of an interest account for the notes which were to be given; and, in that arrangement, the seller stipulates that the allowance of the interest account should depend upon the continuance of the original time of credit; and that the buyer's balance on account should always be under a certain sum; and the buyer exceeds that amount, and refuses to make a remittance or payment, upon the call of the seller, to bring the account within that sum, the seller may arrest the further delivery of any cargo or cargoes, though the same was in the course of being delivered to the buyer upon the seller's indorsement of the invoices and bills of lading of such cargoes.

In the absence of all understanding between the buyer and seller that any cargo which had been delivered and not actually paid for, though notes of hand had been given for the same, was not to be considered within the new arrangement, such cargo must be taken into the computation in ascertaining whether the balance due by the buyer exceeds the amount of credit allowed to him.

Judgment of the circuit court is affirmed.

GUSTAVUS T. BEAUREGARD, HEIR AND EXECUTOR OF MADAM EMILIE T. POULTNEY, COMPLAINANT AND APPELLANT, v. THE CITY OF NEW ORLEANS, WILLIAM H. LAYTON, AND OTHERS.

The habit of this court has been to defer to the decisions of the judicial tribunals of the States, upon questions arising out of the common law of the State, especially when applied to the title of lands.

Therefore, where the supreme court of Louisiana has decided questions relating to the jurisdiction of the district court of the first judicial district of the State, over the succession of a debtor who was enjoying a respite from the claims of his creditors, for a certain time and died before the time expired; to the mode in which that jurisdiction should be exercised; to the propriety of collaterally attacking a sale made by its authority; to the point whether or not the death of the party transferred the proceedings to the court of probate, and to the mode in which the court of probate should exercise its jurisdiction; this court will adopt these decisions, and especially where many of them concur with the judgments of this court upon the same or similar points.

The Louisiana cases and those of this court examined.

THIS was an appeal from the circuit court of the United States, for the eastern district of Louisiana.

It was a bill filed by Madam Emilie Poultney, in her lifetime, against the city of New Orleans, and about eight hundred and fifty other parties, some of whom included a number of persons, such as the Presbyterian Church, Bank of the United States, &c., &c.

The facts in the case are stated in the opinion of the court.

In November, 1854, the circuit court dismissed the bill, and the complainant appealed to this court.

It was argued by *Mr. Henderson*, for the appellants, and *Mr. Taylor*, for the appellees.

Mr. Justice CAMPBELL delivered the opinion of the court.

The plaintiff's testatrix filed this bill in the circuit court to annul a sale of a portion of the succession of John Poultney, deceased, which had been made under the authority of decrees in the first district court of New Orleans, and of the court of probate of that city, alleging a defect of jurisdiction in the courts, and fraud and irregularity in the proceedings.

42 *

Her title to the succession is as heir at law of the children, and heirs of John Poultney, of whom she was the mother.

In May, 1818, John Poultney, a merchant of New Orleans, purchased of Mad. Rousseau, her plantation lying on the Mississippi River, a short distance above New Orleans, and which is now included within the corporate limits.

The price agreed to was $100,000, one fifth of which was paid at the time, and notes with the indorsement of Harrod and Ogdens, (a firm composed of Charles Harrod, Peter V. Ogden, and George M. Ogden,) payable in five annual instalments, and secured by a mortgage on the property, were given for the remainder. The mortgage contains a stipulation that, in the event the indorsers should pay either of the notes, they should be subrogated to the rights of the vendor and holder of the mortgage for indemnity. In April, 1819, Poultney acknowledged in a petition to the first district court that his affairs were embarrassed, and that he could not meet his engagements; he made a statement of his property and debts, showing a surplus in his favor, and prayed the court to convene his creditors that they might deliberate upon his proposition for a respite of one, two, and three years.

The court made the order, the creditors were convened, the requisite number agreed to the proposition, and an order was accordingly entered the 28th June, 1819, for a respite of one, two, and three years.

Harrod and Ogdens appeared at this meeting,—claimed to have paid the first instalment on the purchase of the Rousseau plantation, and assented to the action of the creditors, reserving their mortgage security.

In October, 1819, John Poultney died. His widow, the plaintiff's testatrix, in January thereafter renounced her right as partner in community, and failed to qualify as tutrix of her two children, one aged five, and the other seven years, who were the heirs at law of John Poultney, and did not until eight years after the sales referred to, take any concern about the succession.

The representation made by John Poultney of his affairs at the time his petition for a respite was exhibited, implies a hopeless state of insolvency. His debts are acknowledged to be $235,000, while his property is rated at $266,000,—but from its nature affording but little prospect that such an amount could be realized. By the renunciation of his widow of her title as partner in community, and her failure to interpose on behalf of her children, the succession was unrepresented, and was what is termed in the Louisiana code a vacant estate. In February, 1820, a portion of the creditors of Poultney informed the district court that this succession was insolvent,—had no representative, nor claimant — and prayed that measures might be taken for the appointment of a syndic to represent and administer it for the benefit of all concerned. A meeting of the creditors was ordered by the court — and took place — resulting in the appointment of three syndics, (one of whom was Peter V. Ogden,) who were recognized by the court. On the 9th of May, 1820, Harrod and Ogden represented in a petition to the district court the facts of the purchase by Poultney of the Rousseau plantation, their payment of the first instalment of the purchase-money, and their liability to pay another then shortly after to become due; that the succession of Poultney was insolvent, and was in the hands of syndics; and prayed that the plantation might be seized and sold for the satisfaction of their debt and the instalments yet unpaid on the mortgage, and for a citation to the syndics. The usual order of seizure was made by the district judge, and a citation was served on one of the syndics. On the 29th May the syndics agreed in court to the terms of sale and waived the appraisement, and the property was sold on the 13th June by the sheriff on the writ of seizure for the payment of the money then due, the purchaser agreeing to assume the mortgage.

At this sale, George M. Ogden, one of the firm of Harrod and Ogden, was the purchaser, and a deed was subsequently executed to him by the sheriff under the order of the court.

Some time after the close of these transactions, a conviction seems to have been impressed on the minds of Harrod and Ogden that the proceedings in the district court were inoperative; and in 1824, Harrod and the representative of Ogden commenced a suit in the court of probate, having for its object to obtain a satisfaction of the same debt, by the sale of the same property. They sought a seizure and sale of the property, without taking any notice of what had been done in the district court, and prayed a citation to Mad. Poultney as tutrix of her children. No citation appears in the record, but there is evidence of a seizure, judgment, and sale.

The purchasers were Charles Harrod and Francis B. Ogden, who are charged to be the representatives of the first purchaser, G. M. Ogden. These purchasers afterwards, in 1824, represented to the district court that the debt to Mad. Rousseau had been paid, and that the mortgage of George M. Ogden, given, in 1820, to secure the unpaid instalments, was not operative, for that the district court had no jurisdiction to make the sale, and asked that it might be raised from the property. The sheriff admitted all the facts, and the court granted the petition.

These were the last proceedings which had any relation to the case.

The defendants, by plea and answer, affirm that these proceedings were conformable to law, and vested the purchasers with all the title which John Poultney ever acquired in the property, and that the plaintiff never had any right therein; that they had no participation in, nor knowledge of, any fraud, but that they have translative titles from these purchasers, and rely upon their sufficiency.

In 1832, Mad. Poultney assumed the office of tutrix of her minor children, and commenced, immediately after, suits in the state courts of Louisiana for the recovery of portions of this plantation. Three of these suits were decided in the supreme court in 1835, after elaborate and learned arguments, and a patient investigation by the court. Poultney's Heirs v. Cecil, 8th La. R. 322; v. Ogden, 8 La. 428; v. Barrett, 8 La. 441. These decisions were made upon a state of facts similar to that presented in this record; and the discussion in those cases has diminished the care and responsibility of this court. For it is apparent that the questions presented to us relate exclusively to the local jurisprudence of Louisiana. When the controversy arose all the parties were citizens of that State, while the subject of the suit is the validity of titles passed under decrees of its courts, and in the course of duty, by their executive officers.

The material inquiries are, whether the first district court had a jurisdiction competent to the legal transfer of the succession of a debtor, who was enjoying a respite from the claims of his creditors for an unexpired term, at the time of his death and before any default had arisen in the fulfilment of the conditions of the respite as to payment. 2. Whether this jurisdiction could be exerted without any citation to the natural heirs, or any measures taken to secure their interests in the succession? 3. Were the modes prescribed for the disposal of the estates of insolvent debtors, or of minors, essential constituents of a valid exercise of the jurisdiction, and for the neglect of these may the sale be collaterally attacked? 4. Did the death of Poultney determine the jurisdiction of the district court, and remove to the court of probate the administration and settlement of the succession, and were all the proceedings in the district court *coram non judice?* 5. Was a citation to the heirs necessary to a valid decree of sale in the court of probate? An important share of the attention of all courts of a limited jurisdiction is engrossed in ascertaining the causes over which they may legitimately claim cognizance, and the administration of an involved or insolvent succession, from the number of the parties in interest, and the variety of conflicting and complicated claims that are oftentimes exhibited, frequently affords difficult questions of this description.

The supreme court of Louisiana treat the questions arising

upon the records now before us, as difficult and embarrassing, calling for undivided and anxious attention, and much care was employed in deciding them, so as to maintain in that State an accordant system of jurisprudence. The claim of an embarrassed debtor to exhibit the condition of his affairs to a court with a view to obtain its assistance to convoke his creditors, that they may deliberate upon a proposition to grant him a delay or respite, and to bind the minority to the conclusions of a consenting majority, is one which has no recognition in the common law. It was derived in Louisiana from the continental codes of Europe, upon which the legal institutions of that State are founded. The supreme court of Louisiana, upon an investigation of those codes, determined that the death of Poultney in a state of insolvency, without heirs who were willing to accept his succession unconditionally, and thereby to afford security for the fulfilment of the conditions of the decree of respite which the debtor had assumed, relieved his creditors from their obligations to respect it, and empowered them to proceed, *in rem*, against the estate of their debtor in the hands of a syndic.

The same tribunal, (supreme court of Louisiana,) after tracing the sources of the jurisdiction of the district court, extending, as it did, to "all civil cases," determined that it was not without jurisdiction *ratione materiæ* of a suit against such an estate, and that judgments rendered in that court were not radically null. They say, "The undisputed exercise of such a jurisdiction for a long series of years, the general acquiescence of the legal profession, the universal understanding among the people, as well as the courts and bar, form together such contemporaneous interpretations of the laws relating to conflicting jurisdictions, that, however doubtful it may appear on a close analysis, it cannot now be disturbed without the greatest injustice, and inflicting incalculable mischiefs on the country." And in Robinett *v.* Compton, 2 Ann, R. 847, 855, the same court says, "That, previous to the passage of the act of the 18th March, 1820, fixing the jurisdiction of the courts of probate in this State, it seems to have been settled by various decisions of this court that the district courts were not deprived of jurisdiction *ratione materiæ* in such cases. The practice was universal to bring suits against successions in the district court, and we are not prepared to say it was erroneous." And, since the act of 1820, (which, however, was not promulgated so as to be in force when this sale was made,) the court say, "that such judgments in that court might be erroneous, but were not mere nullities." The jurisdiction of the district court to render the judgment being admitted, the further question arises, Was the jurisdiction so exercised as to be operative? The supreme court, in the case of Cecil above cited, determine " that the rules which apply to the sale of minors' property as such, when the title is fully vested in them, are not strictly applicable to a case like the present, where the rights of minors were contingent and residuary, subject to the undoubted claims of creditors *deducto ære alieno*, and who, in this very case, appear as beneficiary heirs claiming property already alienated for the payment of debts," &c. And in McCullough *v.* Minor, 2 Ann, 466, the same court affirm " that in cases like this, the purchaser is not bound to look beyond the decree."

The jurisdiction of the court was undoubted, and the jurisprudence of the State has long since been settled that a *bona fide* purchaser at a judicial sale is protected by the decree. 11 Louisa. 68; 13 Louisa. 482; 16 Louisa. 440; 8 Rob. 122. The judgments of the supreme court of Louisiana upon the validity of the sales impugned in this bill were given more than twenty years ago. They have formed the foundation upon which the expectations and conduct of the inhabitants of that State have been regulated. They have quieted apprehensions and doubts respecting a title to an important portion of a large and growing city. They have invited a multitude of transactions and engagements in which the well-being of hundreds, perhaps thousands, of the citizens of that State depend. In this bill there are several hundreds of defendants.

The constitution of this court requires it to follow the laws of the several States as rules of decision wherever they properly apply. And the habit of the court has been to defer to the decisions of their judicial tribunals upon questions arising out of the common law of the State, especially when applied to the title of lands.

No other course could be adopted with any regard to propriety. Upon cases like the present the relation of the courts of the United States to a State is the same as that of its own tribunals. They administer the laws of the State, and to fulfil that duty, they must find them as they exist in the habits of the people, and in the exposition of their constituted authorities. Without this, the peculiar organization of the judicial tribunals of the States and the Union would be productive of the greatest mischief and confusion. Jackson *v.* Chew, 12 Wheat. 158.

But, if we were required to depart from that jurisprudence to find a solution of these difficult and embarrassing questions, we should not have to leave the precedents afforded by this court for the support of many of their conclusions. This court has contributed its share to that stability which results from a respect for things adjudicated: *Status reipublicæ maximé judicatis rebus continetur.*" It is the settled doctrine of the court, that when the proceedings of a court of justice are collaterally drawn in question, and it appears upon the face of them that the subject-matter was within its jurisdiction, they cannot be impeached for error or irregularity; that, if a court has jurisdiction, its decision upon all the questions that arise regularly in the cause are binding upon all other courts until they are reversed. 2 Pet. 157; 1 Ib. 840. And when the object is to sell the real estate of an insolvent or embarrassed succession, the settled doctrine is, there are no adversary parties,—the proceeding is *in rem*,—the administrator represents the land. They are analogous to proceedings in admiralty, where the only question of jurisdiction is the power of the court over the thing,—the subject-matter before them,—without regard to the parties who may have an interest in it. All the world are parties. In the orphans' court, and all the courts which have power to sell the estates of decedents, their action operates on the estate, not on the heirs of the intestate. A purchaser claims not their title, but one paramount. The estate passes by operation of law. 2 How. 819; 11 S. & R. 426; 6 Port. 219, 249.

The identity of the principles applied by the supreme court of Louisiana, in ascertaining the effect of the judgments of their courts, and those accepted as true by this court, leaves no question resting upon the authority of the State tribunals, except that of the nature and extent of the jurisdiction of their courts under the organic law of the State. And no principle would authorize this court to dissent from their conclusion on that subject, when the land disposed of was within their borders, and the parties in interest were citizens belonging to their community.

Our opinion is, that the pleas of the defendants afford a complete answer to the bill; and that the decree of the circuit court must be affirmed.

THE PRESIDENT, DIRECTORS, AND COMPANY OF THE UNION BANK OF TENNESSEE, APPELLANTS, *v.* MICAJAH J. VAIDEN AND JOHN H. KEITH, ADMINISTRATORS OF WILLIAM JOLLY, DECEASED.

Where a suit was brought in the United States court by citizens of another State against a citizen of Mississippi, who appeared to the suit, pleaded and then died, after which the suit was revived against his administrators, and judgment obtained against them, the following proceedings of the probate court afford no bar to the recovery of the claim:—

1. A declaration by the probate court that the estate was insolvent, and a reference of the matter to a commissioner in insolvency

2. A publication notifying the creditors of the estate to appear and file their claims, or be forever barred of their demands.

3. A report by the commissioner, leaving out the claim in question, which report was confirmed by the court.

Where the estate turned out not to be insolvent, but a fund remained in hand for distributees, the creditors can recover by a bill in chancery against the administrators, notwithstanding the proceedings in the probate court.

The law of a State, limiting the remedies of its citizens in its own courts, cannot be applied to prevent the citizens of other States from suing in the courts of the United States in that State, for the recovery of any property or money there, to which they may be legally or equitably entitled.

THIS was an appeal from the district court of the United States for the northern district of Mississippi.

The facts of the case are stated in the opinion of the court.

It was argued by *Mr. Coxe*, for the appellants, and *Mr. Stanton*, for the appellees.

Mr. Justice WAYNE delivered the opinion of the court.

This is an appeal from the district court for the northern district of Mississippi.

The appellants filed a bill in December on the equity side of the district court against the appellees.

"The bill charges that in November, 1846, the bank instituted a suit on the law side of the same district court against William Jolly, as indorser of a bill of exchange held by plaintiffs. Jolly appeared to the suit, and filed his plea. He died in March, 1847, and appellees were appointed his administrators by the Panola court of probate, in Mississippi. The suit against Jolly was revived against his administrators, the appellees, and in June, 1851, the same came on for trial on the issue joined on the single plea of *non assumpsit*, and a judgment was rendered in favor of plaintiff for $5,041.33 with costs. Upon this judgment execution was issued, which was returned by the marshal *nulla bona*. The judgment remains wholly unpaid, and there is no visible property in the hands of the administrators upon which a levy could be made.

"The bill proceeds to charge, that pending the said suit against the administrators in April, 1848, they represented to the said probate court of Panola county, that the estate of their intestate was insolvent, and procured a declaration to be made by said court to that effect, whereas the bill charges that said estate was not and is not insolvent, and that the assets in the hands of the administrators are more than sufficient to pay all the liabilities of the estate. That the administrators have converted the assets into cash to the amount of upwards of $20,000, and have fully paid all the debts of intestate, with the single exception of that due to complainant. The debts they have paid amount to about $11,000, and the administrators have upwards of $9,000 in cash or available assets belonging to the estate, which is not required for the payment of any other debt, but refuse to apply any part thereof to the payment of complainant's debt, and will shortly pay the same over to the heirs at law of Jolly, unless prevented by the interposition of the court.

"The defendants pretend that complainants have no right to require payment of their judgment out of said assets, because they have not established the claims upon which the judgment is founded before the probate court of Panola county, and had the same allowed by said court, but complainants are advised and insist that such allowance by said probate court is not necessary.

"Sundry special interrogatories are appended to the bill.

"In June, 1852, defendants filed their answer. The principal averments in the bill are admitted,—it is admitted that they have received assets to the amount of $20,000; that they have paid all the debts which have been legally established against the estate to the amount of more than $13,000, and have in their hands assets to the value of $6,500, and that if complainants' claim is disallowed, the estate will be worth to the heirs about $6,000. They are advised that complainants' judgment is barred, and if they were to pay it, they would pay it in their own wrong.

"They deny that they did illegally or fraudulently procure the estate to be declared insolvent. When they took charge of the estate as administrators, it was appraised at $18,090.76¼, and debts or claims against it were brought to the notice of respondents $18,597.40. Respondents, looking to probable results, believed it might prove and would probably prove insolvent; under these circumstances they procured the declaration. The clerk was appointed commissioner of insolvency, and publication was made for the period of twelve months, warning all creditors of Jolly to present their claims to the commissioner for allowance. In April, 1849, the commissioner made his report, and an order was passed requiring all persons interested to appear and except to the report at July term, 1849,—at July term respondents alone excepted to the report, they excepted to two claims which had been allowed, one of these claims was allowed, the other disallowed; and in October term, 1849, the report was approved and confirmed—p. 8. Respondents append a transcript to these proceedings, and rely upon the same as a bar to complainants' claim."

To the answer of the defendants a general replication was filed, and, on the hearing of the cause, the court decreed a dismissal of the complainants' bill.

In the argument of the case in this court, the counsel of the defendants urged the following grounds against the right of the complainants to recover: —

" If the complainants' demand is not barred by their failure to present it in the probate court, their remedy is at law, and not in equity. The defendants admit that they have $6,000 in their hands, belonging to the estate of their intestate. If they are bound to pay this to the complainants, and refuse to do so, they are guilty of a *devastavit*, and are liable to an action on their bond. In their answer, they expressly deny that complainant (the bank) has made out a cause entitling it to relief in the premises, and that this court has jurisdiction thereof.

" But the complainants are entitled to no relief, either in equity or at law.

" The defendants cannot be prejudiced by suffering judgment to go against them on the plea of *non assumpsit*. Hutchison's Code, 657, § 57 ; Hemphill v. Fortner, 11 Sm. & Mar. 844.

" The decrees of probate courts, in case of estates reported insolvent, cannot be questioned or set aside, unless by a regular appeal taken, or on account of fraud. Hutchison's Code, 667, 668, 673, 683, 684; Chewning v. Peck, 6 How. Mi. Rep. 524; Smith v. Berry, 1 Sm. & Mar. 321; Addison v. Eldridge, 1 Ib. 510; Herrings v. Wellons, 5 Ib. 354; Dalgren v. Duncan et al. 7 Ib. 280.

" Insolvency may be declared when the debts appear to be greater than the probable value of all the real and personal property. The court has a discretion, which, when exercised, is conclusive, unless a direct appeal be taken. Saunders's Admr. v. Planter's Bank, 2 Sm. & Mar. 304.

" As to the responsibility of an administrator who pays debts, when the estate subsequently becomes insolvent, see Woodward v. Fisher et al. 11 Sm. & Mar. 304 ; Bramblet v. Webb et al. 11 Ib. 488.

" Creditors whose claims have not been presented to the commissioner, are forever barred, even when the estate proves not to be insolvent. Allen and Apperson v. Keith and Vaiden, 26 Miss. Rep. 232 ; Anderson v. Tindall, 26 Miss. Rep. 832.

" The creditor must present his claim to the commissioner of insolvency, though he have a suit pending against the administrator. Trezevant et al. v. McQueen, 13 Sm. & Mar. 811.

" And when a commission of insolvency has been regularly opened and closed, it will not be reopened, even at the instance of a judgment creditor, whose judgment bears date since the closing of the commission. Harrison v. Motz et al. 5 Sm. & Mar. 578.

" The foregoing authorities must be deemed conclusive against the appellants, unless the rendition of a judgment by a federal court can be held to take away from the probate courts their exclusive jurisdiction, in the administration of the assets of deceased insolvents. But there can be no doubt that the laws of the State, from which the executor or administrator derives his authority to act, must prevail, as well in the federal as in the state tribunals.   Citizens of other States, possibly, cannot be prevented from suing in the federal courts in order to establish their demands; yet the effect of the judgment, its lien, or other operation upon the assets of the deceased, must be absolutely controlled by the local law; otherwise the conflict of jurisdictions would be irreconcilable and disastrous.   And such it is believed is the well-established doctrine of this and all other courts.   Story's Conflict of Laws, 3d ed. § 521.   Williams *v.* Benedict, 8 How. Sup. C. R. 107.   McGill *v.* Armour, 11 How. Sup. C. R. 142."

But we do not deem it necessary to discuss them in detail, for the law of a State limiting the remedies of its citizens in its own courts cannot be applied to prevent the citizens of other States from suing in the courts of the United States in that State for the recovery of any property or money there, to which they may be legally or equitably entitled.   This principle was fully discussed, and decided by this court in the case of Suydam *v.* Brodnax, and others, 14 Pet. 67.   We refer to the reasoning in support of it given in that case without repeating it, or thinking it necessary to add anything on this occasion.   It concludes this case.

And it is our opinion, under the circumstances and the testimony in this case, that the surplus in the hands of the defendants must be applied to the payment of the judgment of the complainant in preference to any claim which has been asserted to it for the heirs at law or distributees of the intestate, Jolly.   We reverse the decree of the court below, and shall remand the case with directions to that court for further proceedings in conformity with this opinion.

CHARLES MCMICKEN, APPELLANT, *v.* FRANKLIN PERIN.

A purchase of an interest in property by an attorney, made after judgment has been obtained, is not forbidden by the laws of Louisiana.

And where money is borrowed to make the purchase, the lender of the money is estopped from pleading illegality in the purchase, and thus retaining the property which had been conveyed to himself as security for the loan.

In the contract between him and the borrower there was no illegality.

No objections to a master's report can be made which were not taken before the master; nor after a decree pro confesso can a defendant go before the master without a special order, but the accounts are to be taken *ex parte*.

An appeal will not lie from the refusal of a court to open a former decree, nor have the circuit courts power to set aside their decrees in equity, on motion, after the term at which they were rendered.

THIS was an appeal from the circuit court of the United States for the eastern district of Louisiana.

The facts in the case are stated in the opinion of the court.

It was argued by *Mr. Henderson*, for the appellant, and *Mr. Smiley*, for the appellee.

Mr. Henderson made the following points: —

1. That the decree validates a void purchase of a litigions right.

2. That the complainant's alleged title was void by the Louisiana statute of champerty.

3. That no loan of money and no resulting trust is shown.

4. There is no express trust in writing shown, though such trust is averred.

5. That the amount admitted by the bill and exhibits to be due to the defendant on the purchase was not allowed him in the decree.

6. That Mary Perin was not made a party to the bill, though her interest in one half of the property in controversy was shown.

Mr. Justice CAMPBELL delivered the opinion of the court.

The appellee (Perin) filed his bill in the circuit court, alleging that he had been employed to institute suits in the courts of Louisiana, on behalf of certain persons claiming to be the heirs of James Fletcher, for which service he was to receive fifty per cent on the money value, or a fee equal to one half the net value of the property, real or personal, in controversy. Pending the suits his clients offered to sell their interest to him for $5,000, or to other persons for $10,000. There were some negotiations upon this subject, but nothing seems to have been concluded until after the final judgment had been rendered; after that time, the bill proceeds to state as follows: —

"That, upon the said proposition being renewed, the complainant addressed divers letters to the defendant, asking for a loan of $5,000 for the purpose of purchasing the said interest of the Fletchers in and to the said property; and that, in reply to the complainant's said letters, the defendant answered in writing, giving a promise of said loan," as will appear by the exhibits C and D; one of which was written by the defendant on the 8th of September, 1848, nearly three months after the judgment for the land had become final and executory.

"And your orator further shows unto your honors that, relying on the promises and the honesty of the defendant, and upon the understanding and agreement with him, the complainant purchased the said property of the said Fletcher, on the 19th of October, 1848, while the defendant was absent in Cincinnati; and in order to secure the said McMicken in the loan of the said \$5,000, the complainant caused the title of the said property to be made out in the name of the defendant, with the express condition that the purchase was made in the name of the defendant for the use and benefit of the complainant, all of which will appear by reference to the act of sale, marked exhibit F; to the letter of the complainant to the defendant, dated on the 19th of October, 1848, accompanying a copy of the act of sale sent to the defendant, marked exhibit G, and other proofs to be hereafter exhibited. That said defendant accepted the said sale, &c., took the said property, &c., and held the same in trust for the use of complainant, and upon no other condition or understanding, subject only to the repayment of the money advanced for the purchase thereof."

The bill avers that the plaintiff being thus invested with all the legal and equitable rights of the heirs of Fletcher, he tendered to the defendant (McMicken) immediately after his ratification of the sale, the sum of five thousand and fifty dollars, with the proper interest due thereon, and demanded a conveyance of all the said property and rights so purchased and held in trust, which the defendant refused.

The bill charges certain fraudulent pretexts on the part of McMicken for withholding the deed according to his agreement, denies their validity, and affirms that the plaintiff has been forced into a court of chancery in consequence of the repeated refusals of the defendant to deliver up his property and convey the same to him.

The bill prays that the defendant may by the order and decree of the court, be required to convey the said property to the plaintiff upon the payment or tender to the said defendant of the amount of his advances, and for general relief.

A decree *pro confesso* was entered at the spring term of the circuit court, 1853, and at the same term of the court in 1854 a decree was rendered requiring the defendant to convey the property specified in the bill to the plaintiff, upon the payment to the said defendant of the debt reported to be due within six months after the date of the decree.

It is objected in this court that the arrangement between the heirs of Fletcher and his attorney, (Perin,) by which the latter became the purchaser of their interest in the subject of the litigation he had been conducting in their behalf, was illegal, and he could take no benefit from his contract. The articles of the code of Louisiana affecting this question are as follows: art. 2623, "a right is said to be litigious whenever there exists a suit and contestation about the same": art. 3522, No. 22,

13 *

"litigious rights are those which cannot be exercised without undergoing a lawsuit"; art. 2624, "public officers connected with courts of justice, such as judges, advocates, attorneys, clerks, and sheriffs, cannot purchase litigious rights which fall under the jurisdiction of the tribunal in which they exercise their functions, under penalty of nullity and of having to defray all costs, damages, and interest."

The courts of Louisiana have decided "that where a judgment has been rendered litigation has ceased." Marshall *v.* McRae, 2 Ann. 79. And when the thing ceded is not contested and is not the subject of a suit at the time of cession, the thing is not litigious. Provost *v.* Johnson, 9 Mart. 184. The bill charges that the purchase was made after a final judgment had been rendered, declaring the property to belong to the heirs of Fletcher. The subject of the sale was ascertained, the title recognized, and consequently none of the mischiefs which occasioned these articles could then follow. Such is the conclusion of the commentators and courts of France upon the corresponding articles in the code Napoleon. Trop. de Vente, § 201; 39 Dall. part 2, 196.

But upon well-established principles the appellant is estopped from contesting the title of the appellee. The case made is that the appellee borrowed of the appellant a sum of money to complete his purchase, and that the title was placed in the name of the appellant to secure the repayment of that advance. The latter cannot be heard to object that there was illegality in the contract between Fletcher's heirs and the appellee, nor to appropriate to himself the fruit of that contract. The contract between the appellee and appellant is uninfected by any illegality.

The consideration was a loan of money upon a security. The contract between Fletcher's heirs and the appellee is completed and closed, and will not be disturbed by anything which the court may decree in this case. McBlair *v.* Gibbes, 17 How. 232.

The appellant further objects that his debt was not accurately ascertained by the master upon the decree of reference. In Story *v.* Livingston, 13 Pet. 359, this court decided that no objections to a master's report can be made which were not taken before the master; the object being to save time, and to give him an opportunity to correct his errors and reconsider his opinion. And in Heyn *v.* Heyn, 4 Jacob. 47, it was decided that after a decree *pro confesso*, the defendant is not at liberty to go before the master without a special order, but the accounts are to be taken *ex parte*. This court will not review a master's report upon objections taken here for the first time.

Our conclusion is, there is no error in the final decree, rendered in the circuit court.

At a subsequent term, the appellant filed a petition in the circuit court, alleging that he had been deceived by the appellee in reference to the prosecution of the bill, and had consequently failed to make any appearance or answer, and that he had a meritorious defence.

He prayed the court to set aside the decree, and to allow him to file an answer to the bill. This petition was dismissed. We concur in the judgment of the circuit court as to the propriety of this course. This court, in Brockett v. Brockett, 2 How. 238, determined that an appeal would not lie from the refusal of a court to open a former decree, though the petition in that case was filed during the term at which the decree was entered. In Cameron v. McRoberts, 3 Wheat. 591, it decided that the circuit courts have no power to set aside their decrees in equity on motion after the term at which they were rendered.

These decisions are conclusive of the questions raised upon the order dismissing the petition.

The decrees of the circuit court are affirmed, with costs.

JOSHUA MAXWELL AND HENRY N. WALKER, PLAINTIFFS IN ERROR, v. ALEXANDER H. NEWBOLD AND OTHERS.

In order to give jurisdiction to this court, under the 25th section of the judiciary act of 1789, it must appear by the record that one of the questions stated in the section did arise, and was decided in the state court; and it is not sufficient that it might have arisen or been applicable; it must appear that it did arise, and was applied.

This rule was established in the case of Crowell v. Randall, 10 Pet. 368, and has been since adhered to.

Hence an allegation that "the charge of the court, the verdict of the jury, and the judgment below are each against, and in conflict with, the constitution and laws of the United States, and therefore erroneous," is too general and indefinite to come within the provisions of the act of congress or the decisions of this court.

The clause in the constitution and the law of congress should have been specified by the plaintiffs in error in the state court, in order that this court might see what was the right claimed by them, and whether it was denied to them by the decision of the state court.

THIS case was brought up from the supreme court of the State of Michigan, by a writ of error, issued under the 25th section of the judiciary act.

The facts are fully set forth in the opinion of the court.

It was argued by *Mr. Lawrence* and *Mr. Haven*, for the

plaintiffs in error, and *Mr. Cushing*, (attorney-general,) for the defendants.

Mr. Chief Justice TANEY delivered the opinion of the court.

This case comes before the court upon a writ of error to the supreme court of the State of Michigan.

The facts in the case, so far as they are material to the decision of this court, are as follows: —

The steamboat Globe was built in the State of Michigan, and by the laws of that State the persons who furnish materials for her construction had a lien upon her, and had a right to enforce their claims by a proceeding *in rem* against the vessel. Before these claims were discharged she was removed to Cleveland, in the State of Ohio, where she received her machinery and was fitted out; and for the debts thus incurred the Ohio creditors, like those in Michigan, had a lien on the vessel, and were authorized to proceed against her by attachment and seizure.

Afterwards, when the steamboat was in the port of Cleveland, the Ohio creditors obtained process against her, and she was seized, condemned, and sold, according to the laws of that State, to satisfy these liens. A certain E. S. Sterling became the purchaser at this sale, and afterwards sold her to Maxwell, one of the plaintiffs in error.

After these proceedings, the steamboat returned to Michigan, and was there seized by virtue of the prior lien created by the laws of that State, as above mentioned. The party at whose instance and for whose benefit the proceeding was instituted under the Michigan lien, had filed his claim in the previous proceedings in Ohio, but was permitted by the court to withdraw it without prejudice.

The plaintiffs in error, who were the owners, or had an interest in the steamboat, appeared in the Michigan court to defend her against this claim. And the principal ground of defence appears to have been, that the sale in Ohio was not made subject to the prior liens in Michigan; that it was an absolute and unconditional sale, made by competent judicial authority, and vested the property in the purchaser, free and discharged from all previous liens and incumbrances.

The record contains the pleadings, evidence, and admissions of the parties in relation to these transactions, and the proceedings in the state courts. But it is unnecessary to state them at large, as the above summary is sufficient to show the matter in controversy in the state courts, and how the questions raised in the state courts were brought before them.

At the trial in the circuit court of Michigan, the defendants in error, who were plaintiffs in that court, prayed the court to give the following instructions to the jury : —

" 1. That if the jury should find, from the evidence adduced in this cause, that the steamboat Globe, mentioned in the declaration, has been constructed and built in this State, and was used in navigating the waters thereof, and that the debt, claim, or demand for which she was attached by the plaintiff has been contracted in this State by the owners, joint-owner, or agent thereof, on account of supplies furnished by said plaintiff for the use of said boat, or on account of work done or materials furnished by said plaintiffs in or about the building, fitting, furnishing, or equipping of said boat in said State ; that then said plaintiff acquired and had a lien on said boat for said debt, claim, or demand, under and by virtue of the law of this State.

" 2. That if the jury should be of the opinion, from said evidence, that said claim or demand of said plaintiff constituted a lien on said boat, which had been acquired as aforesaid, and that the contracting parties were then citizens of this State, then that such lien had not been displaced or affected by the legal proceedings resorted to in the court of Ohio, exemplifications of which were introduced in evidence by the defendants ; that if any title was acquired under the same, or the laws of Ohio, such title is subordinate to the lien acquired by the plaintiff in this State, by virtue of the laws thereof ; that such proceedings do not constitute a valid defence to this action, and that said boat, on coming within the jurisdiction of this court, was subject to be attached for said claim."

And the plaintiffs in error asked for the following instructions on their part : —

" 1. That the facts contained in the notice of defendants, and which are admitted as true by the plaintiffs, constitute in law a defence to the plaintiffs' action. 2. That the sale under the laws of Ohio, if fair and *bonâ fide*, constitutes a defence to a purchaser under such laws to a prosecution by a creditor under the laws of this State, such as the plaintiffs in this case have shown themselves to be. 3. That defendant Maxwell's title is good against the lien or claim of the plaintiff Wight in this cause, even if that of Sterling was not. 4. That the filing of the plaintiff's claim in the Ohio court precludes him from raising the objection that such court had no jurisdiction of his rights so as to devest his lien by a sale in that State. 5. That a lien under the statutes of this State, though valid in its inception, cannot be enforced against a purchaser in good faith under a sale under the laws of the State of Ohio, so given in evidence."

Whereupon the court gave the instructions asked for by the

defendants in error, and refused those requested by the plaintiffs, who, thereupon, excepted to these opinions, and the verdict and judgment in that court being against them, they removed the case to the supreme court of the State, and assigned there the following errors, for which they prayed that the judgment of the circuit court might be reversed:—

"1. The court erred in charging the jury, as requested by the plaintiffs below, and upon the points and to the effect stated more fully in the bill of exceptions filed herein, and to which reference is hereby had.

"2. The court erred in refusing to charge the jury as requested by the defendants below, upon the points and to the effect stated in the bill of exceptions filed herein, and to which, for fuller particularity, reference is hereby had.

"8. The charge of the court, the verdict of the jury, and the judgment below, are each against and in conflict with the constitution and laws of the United States, and therefore erroneous.

"4. By the record aforesaid, it appears that the judgment was given against the plaintiffs in error, whereas, by the law of the land, the said judgment should have been in favor of the plaintiffs in error, and against the defendants in error."

But the supreme court, it appears, concurred in opinion with the circuit court, and affirmed its judgment; and the plaintiffs in error have now brought the case before this court by writ of error, and have assigned here the following errors:—

"1. By the record aforesaid it appears that judgment was given against the plaintiffs in error; whereas, by the law of the land, and under the evidence appearing in the bill of exceptions, the judgment should have been rendered in favor of the plaintiffs in error.

"2. There was drawn in question in this suit, as appears by the said record, a statute of the United States; and the decision and judgment of the said supreme court of the State of Michigan was against the validity of such statute.

"8. The said supreme court of the State of Michigan erred in deciding that the said proceedings, judgment, and sale had in the State of Ohio was not a bar to the claim prosecuted in this suit.

"4. The said supreme court erred, in that it did not give to the said records of judicial proceedings and sale of the steamboat Globe, had in the State of Ohio, the same faith and credit as they have by law in the said State of Ohio."

Upon these proceedings, as they appear in the record before us, the first question to be considered is, whether any point appears to have been decided in the supreme court of the State, which will authorize this court to affirm or reverse its judgment, under the 25th section of the act of congress of 1789. The error alleged here is, that it did not give to the records of the judicial proceedings and sale of the steamboat, had in Ohio, the same faith and credit that they have by law in that State. But to bring that question for decision in this court, it is not sufficient to raise the objection here, and to show that it was involved in the controversy in the state court, and might, and ought, to have been considered by it when making its decision. It must appear on the face of the record that it was in fact raised; that the judicial mind of the court was exercised upon it; and their decision against the right claimed under it.

It is true, that in some of the earlier cases, when writs of error to state courts were comparatively new in this court, a broader and more comprehensive rule was sometimes recognized. And in the case of Miller v. Nicholls, 4 Wheat. 311, it was said to be sufficient, to give jurisdiction, that an act of congress was applicable to the case. But experience showed that this rule was not a safe one; and that it might sometimes happen, that although in one view of the subject an act of congress or a clause of the constitution might be applicable to a case, yet the state court, upon a different view of the case, might have decided upon principles of state law altogether independent of any provision in the constitution or laws of the United States, and in no wise in conflict with either. And if this court reversed the judgment, upon the assumption that a right claimed under the constitution or laws of the United States, and to which the party was entitled, had been denied to him, the reversal would sometimes be for a supposed error which the state court had not committed, and upon a point which the state court had not decided. Other cases might be referred to, in which expressions are used in the opinion of the court that might seem in some measure to sanction the doctrine in Miller v. Nicholls; but the general current of the decisions, from the earliest period of the court, will be found to maintain the rule which we have hereinbefore stated. And as this want of harmony in the decisions and language of the court was calculated to mislead and embarrass counsel in the prosecution of writs of error to state courts, this court, at the January term of 1836, when the subject was again brought before it, in the case of Crowell v. Randall, 10 Pet. 368, determined to give the subject a careful and deliberate examination, in order to remove any doubts which might have arisen from previous decisions. Accordingly, all of the preceding cases are reviewed and commented on in the opinion delivered by the court in that case, and the doctrine clearly announced, that, in order to give jurisdiction to this court, it must appear by the record that one of the questions stated in the 25th section of the act of 1789 did arise, and was decided in the state court; and that it was not sufficient that it might have arisen or been applicable, — it must appear that it did arise and was applied. This rule has been uniformly adhered to since the decision of that case. We think it the true one, and the only one, consistent with the spirit and language of the section referred to, which so carefully and plainly limits the authority which it confers upon this court over the judgments of state tribunals.

Applying this principle to the case before us, the writ of error cannot be maintained. The questions raised and decided in the state circuit court, point altogether for their solution to the laws of the State, and make no reference whatever to the constitution or laws of the United States. Undoubtedly, this did not preclude the plaintiffs in error from raising the point in the supreme court of the State, if it was involved in the case as presented to that court. And whether a writ of error from this court will lie or not, depends upon the questions raised and decided in that court. But neither of the questions made there by the errors assigned refer in any manner to the constitution or laws of the United States, except the third, and the language of that is too general and indefinite to come within the provisions of the act of congress, or the decisions of this court. It alleges that the charge of the court was against, and in conflict with, the constitution and laws of the United States. But what right did he claim under the constitution of the United States which was denied him by the state court? Under what clause of the constitution did he make his claim? And what right did he claim under an act of congress? And under what act, in the wide range of our statutes, did he claim it? The record does not show, — nor can this court undertake to determine that the question as to the faith and credit due to the record and judicial proceedings in Ohio was made or determined in the state court, or that that court ever gave any opinion on the question. For aught that appears in the record, some other clause in the constitution, or some law of congress may have been relied on, and the mind of the court never called to the clause of the constitution now assigned as error in this court.

This case cannot be distinguished from the case of Lawler v. Walker and others, 14 How. 149. In that case the state court certified that there was drawn in question the validity of statutes of the State of Ohio, &c., without saying what statutes. And in the opinion of this court dismissing the case for want of jurisdiction, they say: " The statutes complained of in this case should have been stated ; without that, the court cannot apply them to the subject-matter of ligitation to determine whether or not they violated the constitution of the United States." So in the case before us, the clause in the constitution and the law of congress should have been specified by the plaintiffs in error in the state court, in order that this court might see what was the right claimed by them, and whether it was denied to them by the decision of the state court.

Upon these grounds we think this writ of error cannot be maintained, and therefore dismiss it for want of jurisdiction.

MATTHEW WATSON, PLAINTIFF IN ERROR, v. COLIN S. TARPLEY.

The regularity and legality of the proceedings which take place as to protest and notice upon a dishonored bill of exchange, is a question of law for the court to decide, and not a question to be left to the jury.

By the general rules of commercial law, the payee or indorsee of a bill, upon its presentment and upon refusal by the drawee to accept, has the right to immediate recourse against the drawer. He is not bound to wait to see whether or not the bill will be paid at maturity.

A statute of a State, which forbids a suit from being brought in such a case until after the maturity of the bill, can have no effect upon suits brought in the courts of the United States. So also, if the statute seeks to make the right of recovery in a suit brought in case of non-acceptance, dependent upon proof of subsequent presentment, protest, and notice for non-payment.

The decisions of this court upon these points, examined.

THIS case came up, by writ of error, from the circuit court of the United States for the southern district of Mississippi.

The facts are stated in the opinion of the court.

It was argued by *Mr. Badger*, for the plaintiff in error, no counsel appearing for the defendant.

Mr. Justice DANIEL delivered the opinion of the court.

On the 29th April, 1850, the pant ff in error, a citizen of Tennessee, brought this action of *hisuimpsit* against the defendant, a citizen of Mississippi, in the circuit court of the United States for the southern district of Mississippi, upon a bill of exchange, dated 4th April, 1850, drawn by the defendant upon Messrs. McKee, Bulkely, and Co., of New Orleans, Louisiana, for $2,827.49, payable twelve months after date, in favor of James Bankhead, and by him indorsed to the plaintiff, and declared in two counts, — one on the non-acceptance and the other on the non-payment of the said bill. Pr. Rec., p. 4. The defendant pleaded " *non assumpsit*," and on this plea issue was joined, (page six,) and the action tried on the 11th of January, 1855, when a verdict was found for the defendant. On the trial, a bill of exceptions was taken by the plaintiff in error, from which it appears that the plaintiff read in evidence the bill of exchange, and proved the presentment thereof to the drawers, at their office in New Orleans, for acceptance on the 27th of April, 1850, the due protest thereof for non-acceptance, and a notification of its dishonor given the same day by letter addressed to the defendant at his residence in Mississippi. See Notarial Protest and Depositions, 17 – 22..

The plaintiff also proved the presentment of the said bill for payment on the 7th April, 1851, the refusal of payment, the due protest thereof, and notice to the defendant. See Notarial Protest and Depositions of H. B. Cenas, A. Commandeur, and Charles F. Barry, 7 – 15.

The defendant then offered to read in evidence a certificate, set out on the 23d page of the Record ; and which being read, after objection taken thereto by the plaintiff, the judge instructed the jury. Record, 23.

" That the plaintiff was not entitled to recover on the count in the declaration on the protest of the bill for non-acceptance, unless due and regular notice was proved of the protest of the bill for non-payment, though the jury might be satisfied from the proof, that the bill had been regularly protested for non-acceptance, and due notice thereof given to the defendant ; that to entitle the plaintiff to recover, notwithstanding the proof of protest for non-acceptance and due notice thereof, the plaintiff must prove protest for non-payment and due notice thereof, to the defendant ; and that the jury were the judges of the testimony, and could give to the witnesses such credit as they thought them entitled to, looking to all the circumstances of the case."

The material questions involved in this case are comprised within a comparatively narrow compass, and present themselves prominently out upon the face of the record. On each of the questions thus deemed material, we think that the circuit court has erred.

Upon the relevancy or effect of the certificate of H. B. Cenas, under date of the 7th of April, 1851, and which was under an exception by the plaintiff permitted to be read in evidence with the view of impairing the previous statement of this witness as to the regularity of his proceedings upon the dishonor of the bill, we do not think it necessary to express an opinion. Our views of the law of this case as applicable to the instruction given by the circuit court, are in no degree affected by the character of the statements in that certificate.

We think that the instruction of the court was erroneous in

committing it to the jury to determine whether the proceedings as to protest and notice upon the dishonor of the bill for non-payment were regular and legal. This is a matter which must, upon the facts given in evidence, be determined by the court as a question of law, and which cannot be regularly submitted to the jury. Such is the doctrine uniformly ruled by this court; we mention the cases of the Bank of Columbia v. Lawrence, 1 Pet. 578; Dickins v. Beale, 10 Ib. 572; Rhett v. Poe, 2 How. 457; Camden v. Doremus et al. 8 Ib. 515; Harris v. Robinson, 4 Ib. 336; Lambert v. Ghiselin, 9 Ib. 552. To the same point might be cited the several English decisions referred to in the case of Rhett v. Poe, already mentioned.

We also hold to be erroneous the instruction of the court declaring that after presentment of the bill for acceptance, and after regular protest and notice for non-acceptance, an action could not be maintained by the payee or indorsee until after the maturity of the bill, and then only upon proof of demand for payment, and of a regular protest and notice founded upon the refusal to pay.

It is a rule of commercial law, too familiarly known to require the citation of authorities, or to admit of question, that the payee or indorsee of a bill upon its presentment and upon refusal by the drawee to accept, has the right to immediate recourse against the drawer. Upon no principle of reason or justice can he be required to await the maturity of the bill, by the dishonor of which he has been assured that it will not be paid, and with which the drawee has disclaimed all connection. Justice to the drawer, with the view of enabling him to guard himself from injury, imposes upon the holder the obligation of protest and notice upon non-acceptance; but beyond this, he sustains no connection with the drawee of the bill, and is under no obligation afterwards to present the latter for payment; of course, he cannot be rightfully held to protest and notice for non-payment.

In the several compilations of the law of bills and notes by Kyd, Bayley, Chitty, Byles, and Story, are collected the decisions by which this doctrine has been settled.

It has been suggested that the instruction by the judge at circuit, may have been founded upon a provision in a statute of the State of Mississippi of 1836, contained in a collection of the laws of that state by Howard and Hutchinson, pp. 375, 376, § 18, by which, amongst other enactments, it is declared that " no action or suit shall be sustained or commenced on any bill of exchange, until after the maturity thereof"; and this prohibition or postponement of the right of action it is thought may have been interpreted by the judge as requiring after presentment for acceptance, and, after protest and notice upon non-acceptance, a like presentment and demand for payment upon the maturity of the bill; and upon refusal to pay, a like protest and notice in order to authorize a recovery.

The answer to the above suggestion is this: that if such be a just interpretation of the statute of Mississippi, that interpretation, and the consequences deducible therefrom, we must regard as wholly inadmissible.

Whilst it will not be denied, that the laws of the several States are of binding authority upon their domestic tribunals, and upon persons and property within their appropriate jurisdiction, it is equally clear that those laws cannot affect, either by enlargement or diminution, the jurisdiction of the courts of the United States as vested and prescribed by the constitution and laws of the United States, nor destroy or control the rights of parties litigant to whom the right of resort to these courts has been secured by the laws and constitution. This is a position which has been frequently affirmed by this court, and would seem to compel the general assent upon its simple enunciation.

In the case of Swift v. Tyson, 16 Pet. 1, this court in giving a construction to the 34th section of the judiciary act, which declares " that the laws of the several States, except where the constitution, treaties, or statutes of the United States shall otherwise require or provide, shall be regarded as rules of decision in trials at common law in the courts of the United States, in cases where they apply," has said: " It never has been supposed by us, that this section did apply, or was intended to apply, to questions of a more general nature, not at all dependent upon local statutes or local usages of a fixed and permanent operation; as, for example, to the construction of ordinary contracts or other written instruments, and especially to questions of general commercial law, where the state tribunals are called upon to perform the like functions as ourselves; that is, to ascertain upon general reasoning and legal analogies, what is the true exposition of the contract, or what is the just rule furnished by the principles of commercial law to govern the case." Again, in the same case it is said by this court: " The law respecting negotiable instruments may be truly declared, in the language of Cicero, adopted by Lord Mansfield in Luke v. Lyde, 2 Burr, 883, 887, to be in a great measure not the law of a single country only, but of the commercial world."

In the cases of Keary v. The Farmers and Merchants of Memphis, 16 Pet. 89, and of Dromgoole v. The Farmer's Bank, 2 How. 241, it was ruled by this court, that the courts of the United States themselves, can have no authority to adopt any provisions of state laws which are repugnant to or incompatible with the positive enactments of congress, upon the jurisdiction or practice, or proceedings of such courts.

The general commercial law being circumscribed within no local limits, nor committed for its administration to any peculiar jurisdiction, and the constitution and laws of the United States having conferred upon the citizens of the several States, and upon aliens, the power or privilege of litigating and enforcing their rights acquired under and defined by that general commercial law, before the judicial tribunals of the United States, it must follow by regular consequence, that any state law or regulation, the effect of which would be to impair the rights thus secured, or to devest the federal courts of cognizance thereof, in their fullest acceptation under the commercial law, must be nugatory and unavailing. The statute of Mississippi, so far as it may be understood to deny, or in any degree to impair the right of a non-resident holder of a bill of exchange, immediately after presentment to, and refusal to accept by the drawee, and after protest and notice, to resort forthwith to the courts of the United States by suit upon such bill, must be regarded as wholly without authority and inoperative. The same want of authority may be affirmed of a provision in the statute which would seek to render the right of recovery by the holder, after regular presentment and protest, and notice for non-acceptance, dependent upon proof of subsequent presentment, protest, and notice for non-payment.

A requisition like this would be a violation of the general commercial law, which a State would have no power to impose, and which the courts of the United States would be bound to disregard.

We think that the instruction given by the circuit court in this case was erroneous; that its decision should be, as it is hereby reversed; and the cause is remanded to the circuit court, to be proceeded in upon a *venire de novo*, in conformity with the principles above ruled.

WILLIAM STAIRS AND ANOTHER, PLAINTIFFS, *v.* CHARLES H. PEASLEE.

The tariff act of March 3, 1851, (9 Stats. at Large, 629,) repealed so much of the former laws as provided that merchandise, when imported from a country other than that of production or manufacture, should be appraised at the market value of similar articles at the principal markets of the country of production or manufacture, at the period of the exportation to the United States.

44 *

It must be appraised according to the value of the goods in the principal markets of the country from which they are exported.

Therefore cutch, which is a product of the East Indies only, and the great market for which, there, is Calcutta, must be appraised, not according to its value there, but at London and Liverpool, which are the principal markets of Great Britain, exclusive of India; and not at Halifax, from which place it was brought into the United States.

The word "country," mentioned above, embraces all the possessions of a foreign state, however widely separated, which are subject to the same supreme executive and legislative control.

It is for the merchant appraisers to decide what markets in these dominions are the principal ones for the goods in question, and their decision is final.

The penal duty of twenty per centum exacted by the 8th section of the tariff act of July 30, 1846, (9 Stats. at Large, 43,) is properly levied upon goods entered at their invoice value, if it is found to be ten per cent below the dutiable value, as well as those goods where the importer makes an addition to the invoice value.

The case of Bartlett v. Kane, 16 How. 263, commented upon.

THIS case came up, on a certificate of division in opinion between the judges of the circuit court of the United States for the district of Massachusetts.

The facts are stated in the opinion of the court.

It was argued by *Mr. Griswold,* for the plaintiffs, and *Mr. Gillet,* for the defendant.

Mr. Griswold's first and fourth points were as follows: —

1. The tariff act of March 3, 1851, did not repeal so much of former laws as provided that merchandise, when imported from a country other than that of production or manufacture, should be appraised at the market value of similar articles at the principal markets of the country of production or manufacture, at the period of the exportation to the United States. But that the provision in the 16th section of the tariff act of 1842 is still in force. Act Aug. 30, 1842, c. 270, § 16, 5 Stats. at Large, 564; Act March 3, 1851, c. 38, § 1, 9 Ib. 629; Act July 30, 1846, c. 74, § 8, 9 Ib. 48.

(*a*) Because congress in passing the tariff act of March 3, 1851, did not intend to repeal or modify the proviso in the 16th section of the tariff act of August 30, 1842. But only so much of the main body of the section as provided that merchandise, when imported from the country of production or manufacture, should be liable to duty on the appraised value at the time when purchased.

And the intention, if it can be ascertained, must govern in the interpretation of these statutes. Greely v. Thompson et al. 10 How. 225; Norcross v. Greely, 1 Curtis, 116; Barnard et al. v. Morton, Ib. 409.

(*b*) Because the act of March 3, 1851, was passed in consequence of the decision by this court in the case of Greely v. Thompson et al. 10 How. 225, and Maxwell v. Griswold, Ib. 242, to the effect that by the 16th section of the tariff act of

August 80, 1842, merchandise, when imported from the country of production or manufacture, was liable to duty on the appraised value thereof at the time when purchased, and not at the period of the exportation, as had been claimed by the secretary of the treasury.

And the intention of congress was simply to change the time with reference to which the value should be appraised, from the time when purchased, to the period of the exportation. Greely v. Thompson et al. 10 How. 225 ; Maxwell v. Griswold et al. 10 Ib. 242 ; Norcross v. Greely, 1 Curtis, 116 ; Barnard et al. v. Morton, Ib. 409 ; 1 Kent's Com. 462 ; Act March 3, 1851, c. 38, § 1, 9 Stats. at Large, 629 ; Act July 80, 1846, c. 74, § 8, 9 Ib. 48 ; Act Aug. 30, 1842, c. 270, § 16, 5 Ib. 564 ; Act March 1, 1828, c. 21, § 5, 8 Ib. 733 ; Act May 19, 1828, c. 55, §§ 8, 9, 4 Ib. 274 ; Act July 14, 1832, c. 227, § 7, 4 Ib. 592.

(c) Because sect. 1 of the tariff act of March 3, 1851, is not repugnant to, or inconsistent with, the proviso in the 16th section of the tariff act of August 80, 1842, but is cumulative, and should be construed with it, *in pari materia*. United States v. Sixty-seven Packages of Dry Goods, 17 How. 93 ; Wood v. United States, 16 Pet. 364 ; United States v. Freeman, 8 How. 564 ; Daviess et al. v. Fairbairn et al. Ib. 646 ; Morlot v. Lawrence, 1 Blatch, 612 ; Saving Institution v. Makin, 28 Maine, 860.

4. If the court shall hold that the appraisements of the cutch were legally made, still the additional duty of twenty per centum under the 8th section of the act of 1846 was wrongfully exacted by the defendant.

(a) Because the additional duty provided by the 8th section of the act of 1846 applies only in cases where the importer or consignee, on entry of merchandise, has voluntarily added to the invoice value. Act 1846, c. 74, § 8, 9 Stats. at Large, 48 ; Kreisler v. Morton, 1 Curtis, 415.

(b) Because the 17th section of the act of 1842 is still in force, and this imposes on merchandise which has been procured by purchase, an additional duty of fifty per cent of the duty prescribed by law, in case the appraised value thereof exceeds by ten per cent, or more, the invoice value ; and this section embraces and applies to all cases of purchased goods, where the owner, importer, or consignee has not, on entry thereof, voluntarily added to the invoice value. Kreisler v. Morton, 1 Curtis, 415 ; Act 1846, § 8, 9 Stats. at Large, 48.

(c) Because the 8th section of the act of 1846 secures to owners, importers, and consignees of imports which have been actually purchased, the right of making such additions to the invoices on entry thereof, as shall, in their opinion, raise the same to the true market value of such imports in the principal markets, &c., &c., — (a privilege not enjoyed under the 17th section of the act of 1842 ;) — and it also provides that if the owner, importer, or consignee, having availed himself of this privilege, fails to make a sufficient addition to his invoice, he shall pay an additional duty of twenty per cent on the appraised value, — a severer penalty than is inflicted by the 17th section of the act of 1842.

(*d*) Because the additional duty provided by the 17th section of the act of 1842 is not inconsistent with, or repugnant to, that in the 8th section of the act of 1846 ; because the latter is only applicable to cases of declarations of increased values voluntarily made by the owner, consignee, or agent on entry.

(*e*) Because the basis of appraisement by the two sections are entirely different.

By the 17th section of the act of 1842, if the appraised value exceed by ten per cent or more, the invoice value, then fifty per cent of the duty prescribed by law is to be added ; while by the 8th section of the act of 1846, if the appraised value exceed by ten per cent or more, the value declared in the entry, then an additional duty of twenty per cent on the appraised value shall be assessed.

Mr. Chief Justice TANEY delivered the opinion of the court.

This case comes before the court upon a certificate of division in opinion between the judges of the circuit court of the United States for the district of Massachusetts.

It is an action for money had and received, brought by the plaintiffs, who are merchants, resident and doing business at Halifax, Nova Scotia, to recover of the defendant, the collector of customs for the port of Boston, money alleged to have been illegally exacted on payment of duties on fifty bags of cutch, shipped by the plaintiffs at Halifax, consigned to Messrs. Clark, Jones, and Co., of Boston.

The invoice was dated at Halifax, November 10, 1853, and the cutch was entered at the custom-house, Boston, on the 16th of the same month, at the invoice value.

The value of the cutch, as appraised by the United States appraisers, exceeded by ten per centum the invoice value ; and the plaintiff appealed, and a reappraisement was had by two merchant's appraisers, and their appraisement also exceeded by ten per centum the invoice value ; whereupon the defendant assessed a duty of ten per centum *ad valorem* on the appraised value, and also an additional duty or penalty of twenty per centum on the same value, under the 8th section of the tariff act of July 30, 1846.

It was proved that the cutch was the product of the East Indies only, and that Calcutta was the great market of the country of production. And it appeared on the trial that this fact was known to the appraisers when the appraisement was made. It was also proved that London and Liverpool were the principal markets of Great Britain, exclusive of India, for said article ; and, so far as appeared at the trial, this cargo was the only one known to have been sold in, or exported from, Halifax.

It was also proved that the appraisers appraised the cutch at its market value in London and Liverpool, and not at Halifax or Calcutta, at the period of its exportation from the port of Halifax to the United States.

The case coming on to be tried, it occurred as a question : —

1. Whether the tariff act of March 3, 1851, repealed so much of all former laws as provided that merchandise, when imported from a country other than that of production or manufacture, should be appraised at the market value of similar articles at the principal markets of the country of production or manufacture, at the period of the exportation to the United States.

On which question the opinions of the judges were opposed.

2. Whether in estimating the dutiable value of the cutch, the appraisers should have taken the value at the market of Calcutta, or London and Liverpool, or Halifax, at the period of the exportation from Halifax.

On which question the opinions of the judges were also opposed.

3. Whether if the appraisements were legally made, the additional duty of twenty per centum, under the 8th section of the tariff act of July 30, 1846, was rightfully exacted by the defendant.

On which question the opinions of the judges were opposed.

Wherefore, upon the motion of the plaintiffs, the points were certified to this court for final decision.

The first question certified by the circuit court depends altogether upon the construction of the act of 1851, 9 Stats. at Large, 629.

The language of this act of congress is general, and embraces all importations of goods that are subject to an *ad valorem* duty ; and directs that their value shall be estimated and ascertained by the wholesale price at the period of exportation to the United States, in the principal markets of the country from which they are imported. The time and the place to which the appraisers are required to look, when making their appraisement, are both distinctly specified in the law, --the time being the period of exportation, and the place the country from which they were imported into the United States. It makes no reference to their value in the country of production, or the time of purchase. And as there is no ambiguity in the language of the act, and it embraces all goods subject to an *ad valorem* duty, the court would hardly be justified in giving a construction to it narrower than its words fairly import.

It is true, as urged by the counsel for the plaintiff, that in the previous laws upon the same subject, the country of production or manufacture was the place to which the appraisers were referred in order to ascertain their value. And undoubtedly the previous acts of congress, and the policy which they indicate, are proper to be considered in interpreting the act of 1851, and might influence its construction if its language was found to be ambiguous. But that is not the case in the present instance. The law taken by itself will admit of but one construction, — and that is, the appraisement must be made, by the value of the goods in the principal markets of the country from which they are exported, at the time of such exportation to the United States. And, so far as these provisions are inconsistent with the provisions of previous laws, they show that congress had changed its policy in this respect, and intended to repeal the laws by which it had been established.

As regards the second point certified, the word country in the revenue laws of the United States has always been construed to embrace all the possessions of a foreign State however widely separated, which are subject to the same supreme executive and legislative control. The question was brought before the treasury department in 1817 ; and, on the 29th of September in that year, instructions were issued by the department, in a circular addressed to the different collectors, in which the construction above stated is given to the word. The practice of the government has ever since conformed to this construction ; and it must be presumed that congress, in its subsequent legislation on the subject, used the word according to its known and established interpretation.

Apart, however, from this consideration, we regard the construction of the treasury department as the true one. Congress certainly could not have intended to refer to mere localities or geographical divisions, without regard to the state or nation to which they belonged. For, if the word country were used in that sense, the law furnishes no certain and fixed limits to guide the appraisers in determining what are its principal markets ; and it would often be difficult to decide whether the market selected by appraisers, to regulate the value, was actually within the limits of the country from which the exportation was made. And, moreover, if the construction contended for by the plaintiff could be maintained, it would soon be found that goods would not generally be exported directly to the United States, from the principal market where they were procured, but sent to some other place where they were not in demand, to be shipped to this country, and invoiced far below their real value. The case before us shows what may be done to evade the payment of the just amount of duty; and neither the words of any revenue law, nor any policy of the government, would justify a construction alike injurious to the public and to the fair and honest importer.

It follows, therefore, as the cutch in question was shipped and invoiced from Halifax, that it was the duty of the appraisers to estimate and appraise it according to its value in the principal markets of the British dominions. What markets within these dominions were the principal ones for an article of this description was a question of fact, not of law, and to be decided by the appraisers, and not by the court. They, it appears, determined that London and Liverpool were the principal markets in Great Britain for the goods in question, and appraised the cutch according to its value in these markets. And as the appraisers are by law the tribunal appointed to determine this question, their decision is conclusive upon the importer as well as the government.

The third point presents a question of more difficulty.

By the act of congress of 1842, (5 Stats. at Large, 563,) it was provided that in cases where goods purchased were subject to an *ad valorem* duty, if the appraisement exceeded the value at which they were invoiced by ten per cent, or more, then in addition to the duty imposed by law on the same, there should be levied and collected on the same goods, wares, and merchandise, fifty per cent of the duty imposed on the same when fairly invoiced.

It would seem, however, that this provision was found by experience to operate, in some instances, unjustly upon the importer; and that it sometimes happened that, under favorable opportunities of time or place, goods were purchased in a foreign country for ten per cent less than their market value in the principal markets of the country from which they were imported into the United States. And if they were so invoiced, the importer was liable for the above-mentioned penal duty, although he was willing and offered to make the entry at their dutiable value. The fact that the invoice value was ten per cent below the standard of value fixed by law, subjected him to the penal duty; and he had no means of escaping from it.

The 8th section of the tariff act of 1846 was obviously intended to relieve the importer from this hardship. It provides that the owner, consignee, or agents of imports which have been actually purchased, may, on entry of the same, make such addition in the entry, to the cost or value given in the invoice, as, in his opinion, may raise the same to the true market value of such imports in the principal markets of the country whence the importation shall have been made, or in which the goods imported shall have been originally manufactured or produced, as the case may be; and to add thereto all the costs and charges which, under existing laws, would form a part of the true value, at the port where the same may be entered, upon which the duties should be assessed. And the section further provides that if the appraised value shall exceed by ten per cent, or more, the value so declared on the entry, then, in addition to the duties imposed by law, there should be levied a duty of twenty per centum *ad valorem* on such appraised value, — with a proviso that in no case should the duty be assessed upon an amount less than the invoice value.

The difficulty has arisen upon the construction of this act. It appears that the goods in question were entered at the value stated in the invoice, without any addition by the importer. That value, upon the appraisement, was found to be more than ten per cent below their dutiable value. And it has been argued, on behalf of the plaintiff, that the penal duty imposed by this law is incurred in those cases only, in which the importer makes an addition to the invoice value; and that this provision does not embrace cases in which the goods are entered at the invoice cost or value, although that value should be more than ten per cent below the appraisement.

We think this construction cannot be maintained. It is the duty of the importer to enter his goods at their dutiable value, — ascertaining it according to the rules and regulations prescribed by law. The entry required is not a mere list of the articles imported. It must also state their value. And if he enters them at the value stated in the invoice, it is a declaration on his part that such and no more is the amount upon which the *ad valorem* duty is to be paid. It is the value declared on the entry, as much so as if he had availed himself of the privilege conferred by this act of congress, and entered them at a higher value. He is, consequently, subject to the penal duty, if the value declared in the invoice is ten per cent below the appraisement. And this construction is strengthened by the proviso in the same section, which directs that in no case should the duty be assessed upon a less amount than the invoice value. This provision, it would seem, was introduced upon the principle that the party having admitted the value in the invoice which he produces, (and which he is bound to produce when he makes the entry,) shall not be permitted to deny the truth of the declaration he thus makes, and enter them at a lower value.

Indeed, the plain object and policy of the law would be defeated by the construction contended for. It was evidently the purpose of this section of the act of 1846 to relieve the importer from the hardship to which he was exposed by the act of 1842, where the undervaluation in the invoice arose from error, or from ignorance of the mode of valuation prescribed by the revenue laws of the United States. For, while it gives him the privilege of relieving himself from the penal duty, by entering them at their true dutiable valuation, it would, according to the construction claimed by the plaintiff, hold out to him, at the same time, the strongest temptation not to avail himself of it,—as a much higher penal duty would be exacted, when he added to the value in the invoice, if he still fell ten per cent below the appraisement, than if he had stood upon the invoice itself. For, in the former case, he would be subject to a penal duty of twenty per cent on the dutiable value of the goods, and, in the latter, would be liable to only fifty per cent on the amount of duty which he would be required to pay. It would be difficult to assign a reason for such a distinction; and we think none such is made by the law, and that the importer is liable to the penal duty of twenty per cent wherever the goods are undervalued in the entry; and it matters not whether this undervaluation is found in an entry made according to the value in the invoice, or in an entry at a higher valuation by the importer.

The treasury department in carrying into execution the act of 1846, has given to it the same construction that the court now place upon it; and the penal duty of twenty per cent has been constantly exacted for an undervaluation in cases where the entry was according to the value stated in the invoice, as well as in cases where an addition had been made by the importer.

In the case of Bartlett v. Kane, (reported in 16 How. 268,) the entry was at the invoice price, and as that was found by the appraisers to be ten per cent below its dutiable value, the penal duty was exacted by the government officers. A portion of the goods were warehoused, and afterwards entered for exportation. And the owner demanded a return of the twenty per cent as a portion of the duty he had paid, and which he was entitled to have refunded upon the exportation of the goods. The demand being refused, the suit above mentioned was brought against the collector to recover it. But this court held that this penal duty was legally levied by the collector, and legally retained, and the plaintiff failed to recover.

It will be observed that the right of the collector to demand and retain this penal duty for an undervaluation in the invoice, was directly in question in that suit; and if the act of 1846 does not embrace cases of that description, the plaintiff was undoubtedly entitled to recover. But the point now made was not suggested in the argument, nor noticed in the opinion of the court, nor was any distinction in this respect taken between an undervaluation, in an entry at the invoice value, and an undervaluation where the importer added to the value.

We do not refer to this case as a judicial decision of the question before us; because, although it was in the case, the attention of the court was not called to it. But it certainly may fairly be inferred from it that in 1858, when this case was decided, no doubt had been suggested as to the construction of the act of 1846, and that the mercantile community, and the members of the bar to whom their interests were confided, concurred with the secretary in his construction of the law. And after that construction had been thus sanctioned, impliedly, in a judicial proceeding in this court, and acted on for so many years by all the parties interested, the court think it ought to be regarded as settled, and that what has been done under it ought not to be disturbed, even if this construction was far more doubtful than it is. We shall therefore certify to the circuit court: —

1. That the tariff act of March 3, 1851, repealed so much of the former laws as provided that merchandise, when imported from a country other than that of production or manufacture, should be appraised at the market value of similar articles at the principal markets of the country of production or manufacture at the period of the exportation to the United States.

2. That in estimating the value of the cutch, it was the duty of the appraisers to determine what were the principal markets of the country from which it was exported into the United States, and their decision that London and Liverpool were the principal markets for that article is conclusive.

3. The appraisement appearing to have been legally made, the additional duty of twenty per cent, under the 8th section of the tariff act of July 30, 1846, was rightfully exacted by the defendant.

ROBERT HUDGINS ET AL., APPELLANTS, v. WYNDHAM KEMP, ASSIGNEE IN BANKRUPTCY OF JOHN L. HUDGINS. ELLIOTT W. HUDGINS ET AL., APPELLANTS, v. WYNDHAM KEMP, ASSIGNEE IN BANKRUPTCY OF JOHN L. HUDGINS.

Where the record, certified by the clerk of the circuit court, states that an appeal from a decree in chancery was taken in open court, no evidence *dehors* the record can be received to impeach its verity, on a motion to dismiss the appeal for want of jurisdiction upon the ground that the case has not been regularly brought up.

If the record is defective, the errors can be corrected in several modes.

The distinction pointed out between appeals which operate as a *supersedeas* and those which do not.

If the evidence offered were received, it would not furnish a sufficient reason for dismissing the appeal.

The appeal being taken orally in open court, an omission of the clerk to enter it in the order book could not devest the party of the enjoyment of his legal right to appeal.

The mode of removing a case from an inferior to an appellate court is regulated by acts of congress, and does not depend on the laws or practice of the State in which the court may happen to be held.

An appeal bond may be approved of by the judge out of court.

THESE two cases were appeals from the circuit court of the United States for the eastern district of Virginia. Being exactly alike, it will only be necessary to state the first.

A motion was made to dismiss the first case upon the following grounds, and was argued by *Mr. Robinson* and *Mr. Pallon* in support thereof, and opposed by *Mr. Johnson* and *Mr. Lyons*.

The counsel for the motion filed the following certificate : —

I, Philip Mayo, clerk of the United States court for the fourth circuit and eastern district of Virginia, do certify that, in a suit in chancery in the said court between Wyndham Kemp, assignee in bankruptcy of John L. Hudgins, a bankrupt plaintiff, and Elliott W. Hudgins and John L. Hudgins, defendants, a final decree was rendered on the twenty-seventh day of June, 1855 ; that the term of the court at which the same was rendered ended on the twenty-eighth day of that month; that afterwards in the vacation of the said court, to wit, on the 16th of October, 1855, there was filed in my office, a writing under the hand of R. B. Taney, judge of the said court, bearing date on the thirteenth of that month, whereby it was "ordered that the appeal in this case, which was taken in open court when the decree was pronounced, be entered accordingly on the order book of the court of the last term, to wit: of May term, 1855 " ; that, in view of this order, the clerk on its being so filed wrote on the order book of the court, at the foot of the decree of the 27th of June, 1855, the following words: "And from the foregoing decree the defendants prayed an appeal, which was granted them on giving bond and security to be approved by the court in double the amount of said decree, conditioned for their prosecuting the said appeal " ; and that at the time of filing the said vacation order of the judge, there was also filed in the clerk's office, bond and security approved by the said judge in double the amount of said decree, conditioned for their prosecuting the said appeal. Given under my hand this 21st day of April, 1856.

P. MAYO, *Clerk.*

And then made the following points for dismissal : —

I. It cannot take jurisdiction of the appeals as having been allowed by the court, when the record as it stood at the end of the term, and as it was then signed by the presiding judge, shows no allowance of such appeals. In Burch, &c. *v.* White, 3 Rand, 104, cited in 1 Rob. Pract. 642, (old edit.,) it appeared that at the preceding term the appeal was prayed and bond and security then given; but the clerk of the court had omitted to enter on the records thereof the appeal so granted. The supreme court of appeals of Virginia decided that this omission could not be remedied by an amendment of the record made after the term had ended ; and the appeal was therefore dismissed. Though the appeal bond was filed with the clerk, it was considered there was nothing in the record to amend by. *A fortiori,* it must be so in these cases, when no appeal bond was given during the term; and there was nothing whatever to amend by.

II. If the appeal had been duly allowed, the appeal bond has not been properly given.

Under the act of congress of March 3, 1803, (2 Story, 905,) appeals are "subject to the same rules, regulations, and restrictions as are prescribed in law in cases of writs of error." One of the rules as to a writ of error is, that it "shall be a *supersedeas* and stay execution in cases only where the writ of error is served, by a copy thereof being lodged for the adverse party in the clerk's office, where the record remains, within ten days, Sundays exclusive, after rendering the judgment or passing the decree complained of." 1 Story, 61, § 23 ; Wallen *v.* Williams, 7 Cranch, 278. Now it is well established that an appeal in chancery cannot operate as a *supersedeas*, unless the appeal be perfected by giving an appeal bond within the ten days. Adams, &c. *v.* Law, 16 How. 148. And it is clear that we are entitled to process to carry these decrees into effect. S. C. 17 How. 417. But perhaps it may be said that in other cases — in cases where there is no *supersedeas* — the mode of taking the security, and the bond for perfecting it, are matters of discretion to be regulated by the court granting the appeal; and that when its order is complied with, the whole has relation back to the time when the appeal was prayed. The Dos Hermanos, 10 Wheat. 306. Still, if we are to take the regulation of the court granting the appeal from its order on the record book of the court, even as it now appears, since the alteration of the record, that order has not been complied with ; for according to that order, the appeal was granted on giving bond and security, to be approved by the court, and the bond and security given have not been approved by the court in term, but only by the judge in vacation.

III. If the appeals could be allowed in vacation, and could in these cases be regarded as so allowed, still, the appeals would be defective for want of citation and notice. *Ex parte* Crenshaw, 15 Pet. 119; Villabolos *v.* United States, 6 How. 90; Hogan *v.* Ross, 9 Ib. 602.

The propriety of the rules above insisted on, is strikingly illustrated by what in fact took place in these cases; for here the assignee, immediately after the term was ended, procured copies of the decrees; there was nothing either in these copies or in the record itself to inform him of there being appeals, no such information was afterwards obtained by means of citation or notice, and he proceeded to make sale according to the decrees.

The counsel, in opposition to the motion to dismiss, filed the following certificates: —

I, P. Mayo, clerk of the United States court for the fourth circuit and eastern district of Virginia, hereby certify that in the case of Wyndham Kemp, assignee in bankruptcy of John L. Hudgins, against Robert Hudgins, John L. Hudgins, Elliott W. Hudgins, and Albert G. Hudgins, lately decided in the said court, an appeal was granted the defendants from the decree entered against them on the 27th of June, 1855, and that their said appeal was entered among the minutes of the proceedings of that day, but was omitted to be entered in the order book, by the inadvertence of the clerk; but was subsequently entered therein, as of the date when entered in the minutes; by the order of Chief Justice Taney, to wit, Wednesday, June 27, 1855.

Given under my hand this 23d day of April, 1856.

P. MAYO, *Clerk.*

Filed, 2d May.

Nos. 239 and 240.

In the clerk's office of the circuit court of the United States for the fourth circuit and eastern district of Virginia.

I, P. Mayo, clerk of the circuit court of the United States for the fourth circuit and eastern district of Virginia do hereby certify that the term of the said circuit court at which the cases of Kemp, assignee, *v.* Hudgins were decided, adjourned the next day after the decrees in those cases were entered, until the next term of the court, and that the district judge, the Hon. James D. Halyburton, had previously declined to sit in those cases because

45 *

he was a party interested in them. And I do further certify that the bonds, required to be given on the appeals granted in those cases, were filed in this office on the 16th day of October, 1855.

Given under my hand this 29th day of April, 1856.

P. MAYO, *Clerk.*

Filed, 2d May.

Mr. Chief Justice TANEY delivered the opinion of the court.

This case has been brought up to this court by appeal from the decree of the circuit court of the United States, from the district of Virginia; and a motion is made on behalf of the appellee to dismiss it, upon the ground that it has not been removed in the manner the law requires, and that therefore we have no jurisdiction over it. And certificates and statements of the clerk, outside of the record, and given since it was certified and transmitted to this court, have been filed as evidence of the irregularity of the removal.

This evidence is not admissible upon the present motion. The record transmitted to this court, certified by the clerk of the circuit court, states that the appeal was taken in open court. This is sufficient evidence of that fact. And upon a motion to dismiss, as well as on the hearing on the merits, no evidence *dehors* the record, as certified and returned by the clerk of the circuit court, can be received here to impeach its verity, or to show that the certificate ought not to have been given. The case, as therein set forth, is the case before this court. And if from inadvertence or mistake of the clerk of the court below, or from any other cause, the record transmitted in this case is defective or incorrect, the errors or omissions should have been suggested in this court, and a *certiorari* moved to bring up a correct and true transcript of the proceedings.

It is true an amendment may be made here by consent, as was done in the case of Fletcher *v.* Peck, 6 Cranch, 87. And so also, where it appeared by the certificate of the clerk that he had committed a clerical error in the transcript, in the form in which he had entered a judgment, in ejectment, and it was evident, from the declaration, that it was a mere clerical error, the court suffered it to be amended here, without sending a *certiorari* to the circuit court to have it corrected. Woodward *v.* Brown, 13 Pet. 1.

But in the case before us, there is no consent to amend, and the errors alleged are of a very different character, from the mere formal error in the case of Woodward *v.* Brown. And if it were otherwise, still, there should have been a motion to amend, by inserting in the transcript the certificates above mentioned of the clerk, before the motion was made to dismiss. But no such motion has been made, and the transcript now before the court is the one originally certified, without any amendment here by consent or by order of the court. And the motion is made to dismiss the case, not for any irregularity apparent in the record, but by testimony *aliunde*, offered to show that the transcript is incorrect. It is very clear that such testimony cannot be received to support this motion. And the record, as it stands when the motion is heard, presents the case which this court is called upon to decide; and nothing outside of it can be introduced to affect the decision.

Neither is it of any importance as concerns this motion whether the appeal does or does not operate as a *supersedeas*. A writ of error or appeal does not operate as a *supersedeas* under the act of congress, unless security is given sufficient to cover the amount recovered within ten days after the judgment or decree is rendered. But yet, if the party does not give the bond within the ten days, he may, nevertheless, sue out his writ of error or take his appeal, as the case may be, at any time within five years from the date of the decree or judgment, upon giving security sufficient to cover the costs that may be awarded against him in the appellate court. And his omission to give the security in ten days is no ground for dismissing the appeal.

In this case, certainly, the appeal did not operate as a *supersedeas*. The security was given and approved long after the time limited by the act of congress. Nor was any *supersedeas* moved for, or awarded by the circuit court, or the judge of the supreme court who approved the bonds. Nor could any have been awarded by any court or judge. And, upon the expiration of the ten days, the plaintiff had a right to proceed on his decree and carry it into execution, notwithstanding the pendency of the appeal in this court.

But if a *supersedeas* had been awarded, this motion could not be sustained. The motion should have been to discharge the order, not to dismiss the appeal. And the propriety or impropriety of an order granting a *supersedeas* could not be considered on a motion to dismiss. The order for the *supersedeas* might be discharged, and the appeal still maintained.

The decision of these points disposes of the motion. But in order to avoid any further controversy on the subject, it is proper to add that if the facts offered in evidence were inserted in the record, they would furnish no ground for dismissing the appeal. They are substantially as follows : —

The district judge had an interest in the issue of the case, and withdrew from the bench, and the chief justice of the supreme court sat alone at the trial. The decree was passed on the 27th of June, 1855, and the appellant on the same day, in open court, appealed to this court, and his appeal was entered by the clerk among the minutes of the proceedings of that day, by order of the court; and on the next day, June 28, the court closed its session and adjourned to the next term.

It is the practice in the state courts of Virginia, for the clerk to make written minutes of the proceedings in court as they occur during the day; and after the court adjourns for the day, they are all written out in full in what is called the order book, and presented to the court when it meets next morning, and read; and if found to be correct, is signed by the presiding judge, as evidence that the proceedings are therein correctly stated. This practice has been followed by the circuit court of the United States when sitting in Virginia; and according to this practice, it seems the clerk supposed that the appeal ought to have been entered in the order book, but omitted it through inadvertence; and did not discover the omission until after the term had closed. The fact was brought to the attention of the chief justice, by a certificate from the clerk, when the appeal bonds were presented for approval, which was in October, 1855; and when he approved the bonds, he at the same time sent a written direction to the clerk to enter the appeal in the order book, as having been made in open court; and as of the day when it was actually made and entered in the minutes. It may be proper to say, that the penalty of the appeal bond presented for approval was much larger than necessary; because, as the appeal could not then operate as a *supersedeas*, the act of congress required such security only as would cover the costs of the appellee in case the decree should be affirmed. But it certainly could be no ground of objection when the bond was offered for approval, that the penalty was larger than it need have been.

These are the material facts, as they appear in the certificates of the clerk, produced and relied on in the argument. And the appellees contend that the order book is the only record of the proceedings of the court; that this record could not lawfully be amended by the order of the judge after the term was over; that the entry of the appeal made by his direction, is not legally a record; and that as there is no record of an appeal in open court on the 27th of June, 1855, the clerk had no legal authority for certifying that such an appeal was made; that his certificate on that account is erroneous; and the case, therefore, is not removed to, and is not in this court, according to law.

The counsel for the appellee, in support of these objections, has referred to a decision of the court of appeals of Virginia, and to the practice in the courts of that State in cases of appeal. The answer, however, to this argument is obvious. The power of making amendments, and the mode of removing a case from an inferior to an appellate court of the United States, are regulated by acts of congress, and do not depend upon the laws or practice of the State in which the court may happen to be held. The decisions or practice of the courts of Virginia, cannot therefore have any influence in deciding the motion before us.

Neither is it necessary to inquire, whether the entry made in the order book is to be regarded as a part of the record, — or merely a memorandum to preserve the history of the case, by entering the appeal in the book where it is usually found, and would naturally be looked for by the party interested. In either view this entry was not necessary to give validity to the appeal. In making the appeal the party exercised a legal right. It was made in open court, and the clerk had official knowledge of the fact. And it would have been his duty, even if no written memorandum of it had been made, to certify it to this court, when the security was approved by the judge and the appeal allowed. And his certificate of the fact is all that is required in the appellate tribunal. He does not certify it as a copy from the record. The appeal is made orally, and the entry usually made on the minutes or in the order book, is to preserve the evidence of the act, and is not necessary to give it validity.

The act of congress does not require an appeal to be made in open court — or to be in writing — or entered on the minutes of the court — or to be recorded. It is often made before a judge in vacation, when it cannot be recorded in the order book as a part of the proceedings of the court. And the law makes no difference, as to the form in which it is to be made, whether it be taken in court or out of court before a judge. In either case it may be made orally or in writing. And the only difference is, that this court has decided that where the appeal is made in open court, during the term at which the decree is passed, no citation is necessary to the adverse party. He is presumed to be in court, and therefore to have notice. But when the appeal is taken out of court, the citation is necessary to give him notice. In all other respects the same rules apply to either mode of taking an appeal. Reilly v. Lamar, 2 Cranch, 344; Yestor v. Lenox, 7 Pet. 220.

The act of March 3, 1803, which authorizes the appeals, provides that they shall be subject to the same rules, regulations, and restrictions as are prescribed by law in cases of writs of error. And in the case of Innerarity v. Byrne, 5 How. 295, where the record transmitted to this court did not show that a citation had been issued and served, it was held to be no ground for dismissing the case, and that the fact might be proved *aliunde*. It is not necessary that all of the steps required to give this court jurisdiction should even be on file in the court below, and certainly need not appear to be of record in that court. Masten v. Hunter, 1 Wheat. 304.

We think it evident, therefore, that the want of record evidence in the circuit court that the appeal was prayed, would be no ground of dismissal; and the certificate of the clerk that it was so prayed, is all that is required in this court.

The objection that the entry on the minutes, and also in the order book, required that the bond should be approved by the court, and that the approval by the judge out of court is therefore not sufficient, is equally untenable.

No copy of the order of the judge directing the entry in the order book has been produced. But the clerk states in his certificate that the order directed him to enter the appeal as of the day on which the decree passed; and without doubt he states it correctly. And in executing that order he appears to have followed the form he had adopted in his entry on the minutes. The same form may perhaps be used in other circuits, and is in some cases probably borrowed from the formulas used in like cases in the state courts. But the appellant had legal rights, and he cannot be deprived of them by any irregularity in a clerical entry. Strictly speaking, nothing ought to have been entered either in the minutes or on the order book as of the day the decree was passed, except the appeal itself. And this, indeed, would appear to have been all the judge ordered. For the appeal could not have been allowed on that day, because an order of a court, or a judge allowing an appeal, is in effect nothing more than an order to send the transcript of the record to the appellate court. It is the clerk's authority for making the return to the superior court. And that order could not be legally given until the security required by law was offered and approved. But, when the appeal was taken, the approval of the court could not be made the only condition upon which it should be allowed. He had a right by law to carry up his appeal, if the security he offered was approved by the judge, out of court, in vacation; and no entry of the clerk, and indeed no order of the court, could deprive him of this right. Neither could the amount of the security be then prescribed. For he had a right to produce his security within the ten days, if he desired to do so, and thereby supersede the judgment, until the decision of this court was had in the premises. And in order to obtain the *supersedeas*, the law requires that the security given shall be sufficient to cover the whole amount of the sum recovered against him. But, if he preferred carrying up his case without superseding, the law does not exact security to the amount recovered. Security is required in that case for no greater amount than will cover the costs that may be recovered against him in the superior court. Such were the legal rights of the appellant when he made his appeal; and he cannot be deprived of them by the form adopted by the clerk in entering it. The approval of the security by the judge, as it appears in the certificates offered in evidence, is sufficient, and the objection that it was not approved by the court cannot be maintained.

Upon the whole, we see no ground for dismissing the appeal; and the motion to dismiss is overruled.

ELLIOTT W. HUDGINS ET AL., APPELLANTS, *v.* WINDHAM KEMP, ASSIGNEE IN BANKRUPTCY OF JOHN L. HUDGINS.

THIS case is in all respects the same with that of Robert Hudgins *v.* Kemp, above decided; and for the reasons stated in that case, the motion in this to dismiss is overruled.

MARIA DE LA SOLIDAD DE ARGUELLO ET AL., CLAIMANTS AND APPELLANTS, *v.* THE UNITED STATES. THE UNITED STATES, APPELLANTS, *v.* MARIA DE LA SOLIDAD DE ARGUELLO ET AL.

The title of the family of Arguello confirmed to the following described tract of land in California, namely, bounded on the south by the Arroyo, or Creek of San Fran-cisquito, on the north by the Creek San Mateo, on the east by the Esteras, or waters of the bay of San Francisco, and on the west by the eastern borders of the valley known as the Cañada de Raymundo.

On the 26th of November, 1835, the governor of California gave an order that the petitioner should have a tract of land without specifying the boundaries, which was done by an order, having the formalities of a definitive title on the 27th. This latter document must govern the case. No good title is shown which can include the valley on the west.

The testimony upon this point examined.

The decree of 1824 and regulations of 1828 forbid the colonization of territory compre-hended within twenty leagues of the boundaries of any foreign state, and within ten leagues of the sea-coast, without the consent of the supreme executive power.

But this restriction only included grants to empresarios, who intended to introduce large colonies of foreigners. It did not prohibit grants of land within those limits to natives of the country.

THESE were appeals from the district court of the United States for the northern district of California.

The facts are stated in the opinion of the court.

They were argued by *Mr. Jones*, with whom were *Mr. Benton* and *Mr. Strode*, for the claimants, and by *Mr. Gillett*, for the United States, upon which side there was also a brief filed by *Mr. Cushing*, (attorney-general.)

Mr. Justice GRIER delivered the opinion of the court.

The claimants in this case presented their petition to the commissioners for settling private land claims in California, praying to have their title confirmed " to a certain tract of land called the ' Rancho de las Pulgas.' " They allege that this tract contains twelve square leagues of land, having a front on the bay of San Francisco of four leagues, bounded southerly by a creek called San Francisquito, and northerly by the San Mateo, and extending back from the bay some three leagues to the sierra or range of mountains, so as to include the valley, or Cañada de Raymundo.

The commissioners confirmed the claim to the extent of four leagues in length between said creeks, and one league in breadth, excluding the valley Raymundo, and bounded by it on the west. This decision of the commissioners was confirmed by the district court, and both parties have appealed to this court.

We shall first consider the appeal of the claimants.

Have they shown a title to more than the four leagues confirmed to them by the commissioners and the court below?

The appellants represent the heirs of Don Luis Arguello, who died about the year 1830.

1. They allege that Don José Dario Arguello, father of Don Luis, being one of the founders of the country, and in its military service as commandanté of the Presideo at San Francisco, was the owner of a tract called " Las Pulgas," by virtue of some title or license derived from Don Diego Borica, then governor of the province, who was in possession of it as early as 1795 ; that this early title has been lost, and remains only in tradition.

2. That, in 1820 or 1821, Don Pablo Vincenté de Sola made a new title to Don Luis Arguello, who had succeeded his father, Don José, in the possession.

3. That after the death of Don Luis, in 1830, his family re mained in possession ; that in August, 1835, one Alvisu petitioned the governor for a grant of the " Cañada de Raymundo," and, it being found that the heirs of Arguello claimed that valley to be within the bounds of their rancho Pulgas, notice was ordered to be given to the widow and heirs, of Alvisu's petition. That they appeared by their attorney, Estrada, before the governor, and protested against the grant to Alvisu ; and that the governor on inquiry, acknowledged the justice of the claim of the Arguello, and refused to grant the valley to Alvisu.

4. That in October, 1835, Estrada, the executor of Luis Arguello, and acting as agent for the family, made application to the governor, setting forth their long possession and praying a corresponding title to be issued in their names; and that the governor, after examining into the justice of their claim, issued a decree of concession dated 26th of November, 1835, which was approved by the territorial assembly on the 10th of December following.

This last-mentioned decree or grant thus approved is the only documentary evidence of title exhibited by the claimants. If it includes within its boundaries the "Cañada de Raymundo," as part of "Las Pulgas," it will follow that the claimants have shown a complete title thereto; and our inquiry would end here. Therefore, though last in order in the claimants' deraignment of their title, we shall consider it first.

On the 27th of October, 1835, Don José Estrada, executor of Don Luis Arguello, presented his petition on behalf of the widow and heirs, to Don José Castro, the governor, praying for a grant of the "rancho of Las Pulgas," and describing its boundaries as "from the Creek of San Matteo to the Creek of San Francesquito, and from the Estheros, (the estuary or bay,) to the Sierra, or mountains." The petition alleged also that the Arguellos had "been in possession of the same since 1800, as is publicly and notoriously known, but the papers of possession had been mislaid."

The rough draft (diseno) accompanying this petition represents a range of hills designated as "Lomeria baja," and parallel to these a range of loftier character marked "Sierra"; between these ranges is a cañada, or valley; this is the Valley Raymundo. The claim of the petition is evidently intended to include it.

On the 26th of October, 1835, the governor made the usual order requiring the alcaldé of San Francisco de Assiz to take information as to the land, and make return of the expediente. The alcaldé made a report, accompanied by the testimony of three witnesses, who proved an occupancy of the rancho of Las Pulgas by the Arguellos for many years as a cattle range. One describes it as extending from east to west (evidently a mistake for north to south) four leagues, and from the estuary to the hills (lomas) situate at the west of Monte Redondo and Cañada "Raymundo." This would include the valley now claimed. But the second witness describes it as "about four leagues" from creek to creek, and "one league from the estuary to the mountains covered with trees." The third as "four leagues from creek to creek and one league from the estuary to the mountains covered with trees, of the Cañada Raymundo."

The petitioner did not exhibit any documentary evidence of a prior grant of any given quantity of land, or setting forth any certain boundary, nor did the witnesses pretend to have ever seen any.

When the report was returned to the governor, he made the following order, dated 26th November, 1835:—

"Monterey, November 26, 1835.

"In view of the petition with which this espediente begins, and the information of three competent witnesses, and in conformity with the laws and regulations of the subject, the minor orphans of the deceased citizen, Don Louis Arguello, at the petition of José Estrada, citizen, are declared the owners in property of the tract known under the name of 'Las Pulgas'; reserving the approval of the M. E. territorial deputation, to which this espediente shall be sent, the corresponding patent to be signed, and recorded in the corresponding book, delivering it to the interested parties for its suitable uses. Senor Don José Castro, senior member (vocal) of the M. E. territorial deputation, and political chief, *ad interim*, of Upper California, thus ordered, decreed, and signed; to which I certify."

On the next day (27th of November, 1835,) the governor executed the following document to serve as a title or letters-patent. It is signed by the governor and secretary, and recorded in the archives.

"Whereas, citizen José Estrada has petitioned in the name of his wards, José Ramon and Luis Arguello, and the girls M'a Concepcion and M'a Josefa, minors and legitimate children of the deceased citizen, Luis Arguello, having previously taken the deposition of proper witnesses, and they having declared the land called 'Las Pulgas' to have been their property of the deceased ever since the year of 1800, whereof the limits are on the south, the Arrogo of San Francisquito, on the north, that of San Matteo, on the east the estuaries, and on the west the Cañada de Raymundo; and using the faculties which are conferred on me by decree of this day, and in the name of the Mexican nation, I have come to declare him the owner thereof by the present letters, this grant being understood as made in entire conformity with the disposition of the laws with the reservation of the approval of the most excellent territorial deputation. The land herein mentioned is four leagues in latitude and one in longitude. In consequence, I order that the present, serving as a title to him, and to be held as firm and valid, be recorded in the book thereto corresponding, and be delivered to the petitioner for his security and other purposes."

The claimants rely upon the first document, dated November 26, which gives no definite boundary or quantity; and argue that, the grant being thus approved by the assembly, the power of the governor over it ceased, and, consequently, that the document, dated on the 27th, which defines the boundaries and quantity of the concession, is not the definitive grant described in the rules and regulations of 1828. But a glance at these rules and at the contents of these documents will show the fallacy of this assumption.

The first section of these regulations gives the authority to governors (*gefé politico*) to grant vacant lands. The second directs the form and manner in which those who solicit such grant shall address the governor. The third requires the governor to obtain the necessary information required by the laws of 1824, and consult the municipal authorities, whether there are any objections to making such concession. By the 4th section, the governor being thus informed may "accede or not" to the prayer of the petition. This was done in two ways, — sometimes he expressed his consent by merely writing the word "concedo" at the bottom of the expediente; at other times it was expressed with more formality, as in the present case. But it seldom specified the boundaries, extent, or conditions of the grant. It is intended merely to show that the governor has "acceded" to the request of the applicant, and as an order for a patent or definitive title in due form to be drawn out for execution. It is not itself such a document as is required by the 8th section, which directs "that the definitive grant asked for being made, a document signed by the governor shall be given to serve as a title to the parties interested."

The document of the 26th has none of the characteristics of a definitive grant. It shows only that the governor assents that the petitioner shall have a grant of a tract of land called "Las Pulgas." It describes no boundary, and ascertains no quantity. It contemplates a "corresponding patent," and does not purport itself to be such document.

On the contrary, the document of the 27th has all the formalities of a definitive title, and purports on its face to be made for that purpose. It gives the boundaries of the tract known as "Las Pulgas," namely: "On the south the creek San Francisquito, on the north the San Matteo, on the east the estuary, on the west the Cañada de Raymundo, four leagues in length and one in breadth."

The Mexican authorities have themselves given a construction to this grant in 1840, when they granted the Cañada de Raymundo to Coppinger, calling for "Las Pulgas" as its eastern boundary. Moreover, juridical possession was given to the Arguellos, establishing the western boundary of the

Las Pulgas, one league west of the estuary or bay of San Francisco.

The commissioners and the court below having confirmed the claim of the appellants to the extent of this legal title, the question on their appeal is, whether they have shown any title to the valley of Raymundo, or for any land west of the boundary adjudged to Las Pulgas by the Mexican authorities, so many years ago. In support of their claim the appellants rely upon a supposed grant from Governor Borrica to Don José Arguello, at an early day, and a regrant or new title to Don Luis Arguello in 1820 or 1821, by De Sola.

Much parol testimony, and some historical documents, have been introduced on this subject. The value and effect of this evidence has been very fully discussed by the commissioners and the court below. We fully concur in their conclusions on this subject, but do not think it necessary to indicate our opinion by a special and particular examination of it. It will be sufficient to state the results at which we arrived after a careful consideration.

1. There is no sufficient evidence to satisfy our minds that any grant was ever made by Governor Borrica, or by De Sola. The archives of government show no trace of evidence of such a grant from either of them. They have not proved the existence of it by the testimony of any one who had seen it; they assume the existence and loss of the documents, from the fact that none can now be found.

Without stopping to inquire, whether, by the Spanish law, a subject could claim against the king by prescription, we will assume, for the purposes of this case, that as a presumption of fact, the court would be justified in presuming a grant on proof of fifty years' continuous, notorious, adverse possession of a tract of land having certain admitted and well-defined boundaries; and inquire whether we have such evidence as regards this valley of Raymundo, and the eight additional leagues of land now claimed to belong to the ranches of Las Pulgas.

Don José Arguello was, for many years, commandant of the Presidio of San Francisco; after his death he was succeeded in the command by his son Don Luis. As early as 1797, the king's horses were pastured and herded on this rancho. As early as 1804, soldiers, under the command of Don José, resided in huts on the land included in the grant made to appellants in 1835, and had charge of cattle said to belong to the commandant Don José. The sheep of the neighboring mission of Santa Clara were sometimes pastured on it. The king's cattle, as well as those of the commandant, were pastured on it as late as 1821. After the death of Don José, his son and successor in office,

Don Luis, continued the occupation of it, by his herds and herdsmen. The cattle on this rancho, at some seasons, wandered over the valley of Raymundo, and to the foot of the western sierra. Don Luis also cut timber at one time on the hills west of said valley.

About 1821, Governor Sola had the king's cattle removed, and permitted Don Luis to remain in possession of the rancho, which he continued to claim as his own up to the time of his death; though he took no steps towards obtaining a definitive title. As to the extent of his claim; his eastern, northern, and southern boundaries by the creek and the estuary were well known and ascertained. The western, though said to be the hills, or mountains, and, in one sense, a fixed boundary, was very uncertain. It might be at one league from the bay to the first range of woody hills, or four leagues to the highest summit of the main ridge of the sierra. Not one of the witnesses who attempt to establish this title by tradition can state what number of square leagues it contained.

No inference of an adverse claim or grant can be drawn from the fact that the commandant of a post pastured his own cattle with those of the king, or that the son and successor in office should continue in possession of the rancho by permission of the governor after the king's cattle were removed. The fact that the cattle of Arguello wandered to the mountains and over this valley affords no necessary presumption that he claimed it or owned it. And in a frontier country the cutting of timber is very equivocal evidence of even a claim of ownership of the land. The evidence shows also an unequivocal denial of Don Luis that his claim extended beyond the bounds of the grant since made to his heirs, or included the Cañada Raymundo.

The fact that the governor, in 1835, refused to grant this valley to Alvisu, because it belonged or was claimed by the heirs of Arguello, cannot operate to give a title to them by way of estoppel. The only inferences that can be drawn from these proceedings are: 1. That Alvisu applied for the land. 2. That the Arguellos claimed it. 3. That the governor refused, for that reason, to grant it to Alvisu. It has always been the wise and just policy of the Mexican government to avoid granting litigious titles. Hence the caution shown in refusing to grant to Alvisu till the true extent of the Arguello claim was established. Estrada, who acted on that occasion for the widow and heirs, reserved to himself the right "to further develop their claim." This was immediately done by his application to the governor for a title, and the proceedings thereon in 1835, which have been already noticed. This proceeding was instituted for the purpose of having a direct adjudication

46 *

on the claim of the Arguellos, and the extent and boundaries of
Las Pulgas, which they then occupied as a rancho. Here we
have the first proceeding which can operate as an estoppel on
either party. The king may be estopped by his deed, and the
appellants by accepting as a definitive title to the Las Pulgas a
deed excluding the valley of Raymundo, are estopped from
asserting that it is included in their grant. Here, for the first
time, we have a juridical investigation to ascertain and fix the
boundaries of Las Pulgas. A name which represented heretofore an unknown quantity has been reduced to certainty. This
grant has been registered among the public archives, accepted
by the claimants, and possession delivered accordingly. Having
thus, by a regular juridical proceeding, ascertained the boundaries and quantity of land represented by the name of Las
Pulgas, the valley of Raymundo, being without the boundary so
fixed, is, in 1840, granted as public land to Coppinger.

There is no evidence to show either fraud or mistake in these
proceedings. The appellants have got Las Pulgas by a valid
title, according to the boundaries ascertained by the proper
public authorities, and cannot now be permitted to recur to
vague tradition of a vague and uncertain boundary, to unsettle
the titles to a large territory since granted to others.

The case of the United States v. Roselius, 15 How. 31, bears
a strong resemblance to the present. There it was decided,
that "when a part of the land claimed under a Spanish title
was granted to and accepted by the claimant, without any saving of his claim, this must be taken to have satisfied his whole
claim upon the equity of the government." It is, say the court,
in the nature of a compromise, and conclusive as to the rights
of the claimant.

In the case before us, the equity of the claimant was adjudicated after an investigation of the claim, and an ascertainment
of its boundary and quantity. But, whether it be treated as
res judicata or as a compromise, it is equally conclusive as to
the claims of the appellant on the equity of the government.

2. We come now to the consideration of the appeal entered
on behalf of the United States.

The authenticity of the patent or concession to the claimants
for Las Pulgas, in 1835, is not disputed; but it is contended
that it is void, "because, under the regulations of 1824, lands
lying within the littoral leagues could not be granted by territorial governors, but only by the supreme government."

On the contrary, it is contended by the counsel for the claimants, "that this clause in the colonization laws is not intended as
a general prohibition of grants of land within those boundaries,
but refers only to foreign colonization; and is applicable to
States only, and not to the Territories of the republic."

It is evident from an inspection of this act of 1824, and consequent regulations of 1828, that they contemplate two distinct species of grants. 1. Grants to *impresarios*, or contractors, sometimes called *pobladores*, who engaged to introduce a body of foreign settlers. 2. The distribution of lands to Mexican citizens, " families or single persons."

While these countries were under the dominion of Spain, the governors had authority to make grants of the latter description, while those of the former required the sanction of the king. As examples of such colonization contracts in Louisiana, those of the Marquis of Maison Rouge and the Baron de Bastrop may be referred to. They came under the consideration of this court in the cases of the United States *v.* King and Coxe, 7 How. 833, and the United States *v.* Philadelphia, 11 How. 609. These contracts were executory. They designated a certain tract of country, which was "appropriated" to be gratuitously distributed among the colonists, but did not confer an absolute or immediate title to the whole tract to be colonized by the contractor. " As the object of these grants was to obtain a body of foreign agriculturists, who would settle together under one common leader, in whom the government could confide, liberal terms were offered. A body of such colonists, besides opening, cultivating, and improving, the wild lands, served as a protection against the Indians, and created inducements to others of their countrymen to join them, and thus promote the early settlement of the province."

The same policy was pursued by the Mexican government. Besides the desire of fortifying themselves against apprehended attempts at subjugation by Spain, they had before their eyes the prosperous growth of the United States consequent on the liberal encouragement of European immigration. But, while anxious to encourage immigration of foreigners, they nevertheless entertained some jealousy, well founded, perhaps, that in case of conflict with a powerful neighbor, their sympathies and allegiance might not be safely relied on.

Hence, the caution exhibited in requiring the approval of the supreme government " to grants made to impresarios " for them to " colonize with many families." But while a judicious policy might forbid the settlement of large bodies of foreigners on the boundaries and sea-coast, we cannot impute to them the weakness, or folly, of confining their native citizens to the interior, and thus leaving their sea-coast a wilderness without population. On the contrary, the same considerations of policy which excluded foreigners, would encourage the settlement of natives within those bounds. The statute books of Mexico abound in acts offering every inducement to Mexican families to settle on the

frontiers; proffering gratuitous grants of land and of agricul-
tural implements, — expenses of their voyage, — maintenance for
a year, — and leave to import certain articles free of duty. The
military posts in the territory were on the sea-coast; and it
would be strange policy indeed which would isolate the posts
intended for the protection of settlers, and compel them to dwell
among the savages without protection. Numerous enactments,
also, exhibit their cautious jealousy with respect to foreigners,
and especially their coterminous neighbors on the north. An
act of 1828 directs all Spaniards living on the coast of the
Mexican gulf to retire twenty leagues from it. Another, of
1830, prohibits settlements of foreigners from coterminous
nations on any part of their border states.

A careful examination of this decree of 1824, and regulations
of 1828, will show that their letter conforms to this policy, pursued with so much solicitude. The title to the decree shows its
subject to be "colonization." The term colonization implies
immigration in numbers. The first section speaks of the subjects of such colonization as "foreigners." It guarantees to them
security of person and property. The second and third describe
the lands open to such colonists, and require the states to make
rules and regulations for colonization within their limits. The
fourth (whose construction is now under consideration) forbids
the colonization of the territory comprehended within twenty
leagues of the boundaries of any foreign state, and within ten
leagues of the sea-coast, without the consent of the supreme
executive power. The sixth section provides that no duties shall
be imposed on the entrance of "foreigners." The seventh
forbids the immigration of "foreigners" to be prohibited prior
to 1840, except of some particular nation, and under peculiar
circumstances. The seventh indicates the possibility that the
government may find it necessary to take measures of precaution for the security of the federation with respect to foreigners
who come to colonize.

These are all the sections of the act which refer directly to
colonization. The subjects of it are called "foreigners" throughout. They are the only persons to whom the fourth section has
any reference or application.

The 9th section first speaks of the "distribution of lands" to
individuals and families, as distinguished from colonists, and
provides that Mexican citizens should be preferred, without distinction of classes, except as to those who have rendered special
service to their country.

Thus we have seen that the first eight sections apply wholly
to colonists and foreigners. It would be contrary to every canon
of construction to apply the provisions made for them to the

subject introduced for the first time in the 9th section, or to select the 4th section as applicable to native citizens, while the other seven are confined by their terms to "foreigners."

The regulations of 1828, made for the purpose of carrying into execution the law of 1824, evidently give this construction to that act. It makes a clear distinction between *empresario* contracts for colonization, and grants to Mexican citizens. In conformity with the 4th section of that act, it requires grants to *empresarios* to have the sanction of the supreme government, while those made to individuals or families need only the approval of the territorial deputation. This may be said to be a legislative construction of the act of 1824, and demonstrates that this restraint of grants within the lateral leagues had no application except to colonies of foreigners.

If anything further were wanted to fortify this construction, the uniform practice of the territorial governors to make grants to individuals and families within those bounds would be conclusive.

The petition of Jimeno in 1840, praying the governor to apply to the supreme government for a confirmation of these grants, confirms the views we have taken. It shows what had been the antecedent practice on the subject, and that, although Jimeno had doubts about its legality, others had not.

On the whole, we are of opinion that the judgment of the district court is correct, and it is adjudged that the said claim of the petitioners is valid as to that portion of the land described in the petition, which is bounded as follows, to wit: On the south by the Arrogo, or creek of San Francisquito, on the north by the creek San Matteo, on the east by the Esteras, or waters of the bay of San Francisco, and on the west by the eastern borders of the valley known as the "Cañada de Raymundo," said land being of the extent of four leagues in length and one in breadth, be the same more or less, and it is therefore hereby decreed that the said land be, and the same is hereby confirmed to them ; and it is further adjudged and decreed that the said petitioners have and hold the same under this confirmation in the following shares or proportions, to wit: Maria de la Solidad Ortega Arguello, one equal undivided half thereof; José Ramon Arguello, one equal undivided fourth part thereof ; Luis Antonio Arguello, one equal undivided tenth part thereof ; and S. M. Mezes three equal undivided twentieth parts of said premises.

And as to the portion of the premises described in said petition, which is not included within the boundaries above mentioned, the claim of the petitioners is adjudged not to be valid.

No. 77. ARGUELLO et al. v. THE UNITED STATES.
No. 78. THE UNITED STATES v. ARGUELLO et al.
No. 92. THE UNITED STATES v. CERVANTES.
No. 94. THE UNITED STATES v. VACA AND PENA.
No. 99. THE UNITED STATES v. LARKIN AND MISSROON.

Mr. Justice DANIEL, dissenting.

From the decision of the court in each of these causes, (as I have done in that of the United States v. Reading, during the present term, and as I should have done in those of the United States v. Ritchie, 17 How. 525, and of the United States v. Fremont, 17 Ib. 542, had I set in the causes last mentioned,) I am constrained to declare my dissent.

The decisions in all the causes above enumerated have, according to my apprehension, been made in violation of the acknowledged laws and authority of that government which should have controlled those decisions and the subjects to which they relate; are subversive alike of justice and of the rights and the policy of the United States in the distribution and seating of the public lands, — of the welfare of the people of California, by inciting and pampering a corrupt and grasping spirit of speculation and monopoly, — subversive, likewise, of rules and principles of adjudication heretofore asserted by this court in relation to claims to lands within the acquired domain of the United States.

It has by this court been repeatedly and expressly ruled, with respect to the territories acquired by the United States, either by purchase or conquest, that the laws and institutions in force within those territories at the time of the acquisition, were not from thence to be regarded as foreign laws, and in that aspect to be proved as matters of fact, but that the courts of the United States were authorized and bound to take the same judicial cognizance and notice of these laws which they were authorized and bound to extend to the laws of the several States. This doctrine has been ruled after much consideration and reconsideration, as will be seen in the cases of The United States v. King and Coxe, 7 How. 833; The United States v. The cities of Philadelphia and New Orleans, 11 Ib. 609; and The United States v. Turner et al. 11 Ib. 663.

It is conceded that at the times at which the claims now sanctioned by this court came into being, and from a period anterior to the origin of those claims, down to the transfer of the country to the United States, there existed laws and regulations enacted by the Mexican government with respect to the granting of lands within the republic, prescribing the modes in which, and the agents by whom, all grants should be made, and prescribing also the limitations and exceptions to which the power of making grants was subjected.

Amongst the laws and ordinances here referred to, are those by which the authority of the provincial commanders or governors to originate the titles to lands was conferred and limited. The prerequisites indispensable for the consummation of titles; the immunity from the power of the provincial governors, or from grants or alienations by them, of lands belonging to the Missions; the prohibition of colonization and settlement within twenty leagues of a foreign territory, and within what have been denominated the littoral leagues, or ten leagues from the sea-coast; and the necessity for a sanction by the departmental assemblies to give validity to private or individual titles, were all, by the same system or body of laws, established and proclaimed.

With the wisdom or justice of those laws and ordinances, it is conceived that this court can have no legitimate concernment; much less can it exercise the power to dispense with them, or to modify them in any degree whatsoever. Its province and its duty are confined to inquiries as to the existence of such laws, and to their just effect upon the pretensions of claimants necessarily dependent upon and subordinate to those laws; and to the protection of the United States, the successors and possessors of that authority by which those laws were ordained.

Whenever these inquiries shall lead to the conclusion that such pretensions are unfounded in law, the right to the subjects to which they relate devolves necessarily upon the United States as succeeding to the sovereignty of the Mexican government; succeeding, also, to the high obligation of so disposing of these subjects as shall render them conducive to the national revenue; shall baffle and defeat the schemes of corrupt and corrupting avarice and monopoly; and shall maintain and secure an equality of privilege and benefit to all the citizens of the nation.

That the laws and ordinances above referred to were solemnly, formally, and legitimately established and proclaimed by the government of Mexico, is not denied, nor is it pretended that they have ever been expressly or openly repealed by the government of the republic. An attempt is made, however, to escape from the authority and effect of those public laws by setting up a practice in violation of them, and, from the proof of this practice, to establish a different code or system by which the former, regularly adopted and promulged, and never directly repealed, has been abrogated and disannulled. The results of this attempt, if successful, (and by this court it has been thus far rendered unsuccessful,) are these, that the laws and institutions of the

republic of Mexico, inscribed in her archives, are not to be
received and judicially noticed by this court; but they are to
be sought for in the existence of machinations and abuses which
have at different times obtained, in defiance of the established
or regular government, — proofs to be collected from sources
however impure or liable to improper influences ; — in other
words the laws of Mexico are to be extracted from statements
varying or contradictory as they may be, and resting on the mere
assertion of individuals, all of them perhaps interested.

How a proceeding like this is to be reconciled with the
decisions of this court already cited, or how indeed it can be
reconciled with uniformity or with the safety either of property
or person, passes my comprehension to conceive. It can hardly
admit of a rational doubt in the mind of any man who considers the character of much of the population of the late
Spanish dominions in America, — sunk in ignorance, and marked
by the traits which tyranny and degradation, political and moral,
naturally and usually engender, — that proofs, or rather statements, might be obtained, as to any fact or circumstance which
it might be deemed desirable or profitable to establish. And it
will very probably be developed in the progress of the struggle
or scramble for monopoly of the public domain, that many of
the witnesses upon whose testimony the novel and sturdy Mexican code of practice or seizure is to be established, in abroga-
tion of the written law, are directly or intermediately interested
in the success of a monopoly by which, under the countenance
of this court, PRINCIPALITIES are won by AN AFFIDAVIT, and conferred upon the unscrupulous few, to the exclusion and detriment
of the many, and by the sacrifice of the sovereign rights of the
United States.

A transient view of the circumstances under which these
enormous pretensions have been originated is sufficient, if not
for their absolute condemnation, at least, to subject them to a
most vigilant scrutiny.

If we look at the condition of the country at the time, we
find it in a state of almost incessant agitation, disorder, and
revolution, — controlled in rapid succession by men either themselves directly and violently seizing upon power, or becoming
the instruments of those who had practised such irregularities,
— men whose position was created or maintained by no regular
or constitutional authority, but simply by force, and continuing
only until overthrown by superior violence. Turning our attention next to the grants themselves, they are, without an exception,
--- deficient in the requisites prescribed by the established written laws of the country, as indispensable to impart to them
validity, -- but rest solely upon the circumstances (and boldly

challenging countenance and support here upon those circumstances) that they have originated in practical and temporary usurpations of power; and that, amidst scenes of violence and disorder, have been either maintained or acquiesced in, in defiance of the known public law.

Yet, these avowals with respect to the origin and growth of these claims — avowals which infect and taint their entire being and character, and which ought to consign them to the sternest reprobation — constitute the merits by which they commend themselves to the countenance and support of a tribunal whose highest function is the assertion of law, justice, integrity, order, — the dispensation of right equally to all.

Upon such a foundation, such a pretence, or rather such a defiance of authority, I will not, by an abuse of language, call it even a pretence of right. I cannot consent to impair or destroy the sovereign rights and the financial interests of the United States in the public domain. I can perceive no merit, no claim whatsoever, to favor, on the part of the grasping and unscrupulous speculator and monopolist; no propriety in retarding, for his advantage or profit, the settlement and population of new States, by excluding therefrom the honest citizen of small means, by whose presence and industry the improvement and wealth, and social and moral health, and advancement of the country are always sure to be promoted.

THE UNITED STATES, APPELLANTS, v. CRUZ CERVANTES.

The court again decides (as in United States v. Reading, page 1) that it was the duty of the governor of California, and not that of the grantee, to submit a grant of land to the departmental assembly.

And, moreover, when the case was submitted, and a committee reported in favor of the grant, but no final action appeared to have been had upon the matter, the grantee should have the benefit of the presumption of a decision in his favor.

It again decides, as in the preceding case of Arguello v. The United States, that the ten littoral leagues spoken of in the regulations of 1824 and 1828, do not mean prohibition of grants of land to native citizens for their own use.

The title to lands held by the missions of California, was never vested in the church, which had only an usufruct in them; and in the present case, the mission assented to the grant in question.

The 17th section of the regulations of 1828 has no application to the present case.

Also, in 1833 and 1834, the government of Mexico passed laws to secularize the missions.

THIS was an appeal from the district court of the United States for the northern district of California.

The nature of the claim is stated in the opinion of the court.

The decree of the district court was as follows:—

　This cause came on to be heard at the above-stated court, on the transcript and evidence and the arguments of counsel for the United States, and for the claimant Cruz Cervantes being. It is hereby ordered, adjudged, and decreed, that the decision and decree of the board of commissioners, for the ascertainment and settlement of private land claims in claim of the appellant, Cruz Cervantes, be and the same is hereby confirmed, to the extent of two square leagues or sitios de ganado mayor, and for no more; being the same land described in the grant and expediente referred to therein, and of which judicial possession was given to him, as appears by the evidence; provided that the said quantity to him granted and now to him confirmed, be contained within the boundaries called for in said grant, and map to which the grant refers, and, if there be less than two square leagues, or sitios de ganado mayor, within the said bounds, then there is confirmed to him the said less quantity.

M. H. M'ALLISTER, Circuit Judge.
OGDEN HOFFMAN, JR., District Judge.

From this decree, the United States appealed to this court.

It was argued by *Mr. Cushing*, (attorney-general,) for the United States, and by *Mr. Jones*, for the appellee.

Mr. Justice GRIER delivered the opinion of the court.

The appellee, Cruz Cervantes, having complied with the provisions required by law, obtained a grant from Nicholas Guterriez, then governor of California, "of a parcel of land known by the name of San Joaquin, bounded on the north by San Felipe, on the south by Santa, on the west by the plain of San Juan, and on the east by the hills of the same name," containing the quantity of two leagues.

This concession, dated April 1, 1836, was presented to the departmental assembly for confirmation. The committee reported in favor of the grant,—"on the 12th of July it was returned to the committee for its reformation." This concludes the expediente as certified from the archives. It does not appear whether any further action was taken on the subject by the assembly; nor do the books exist among the archives from which any further facts can be ascertained.

The land granted was reported to be within the ten littoral leagues, and as having at one time appertained to the mission of San Juan Bautista,—on a reference of the expediente made to the steward of the mission, their consent was certified, that "the place to be adjudicated to the petitioner so far as the hills, without touching the oak grove," &c.

Within the space of two years Cervantes entered on the land, built on it, and cultivated it, and continues so to do. On the 10th of February, 1841, juridical possession was delivered to him by metes and bounds with the customary formalities.

The objections to the validity of this grant are: 1. That it was not approved by the departmental assembly. 2. That the land is within the ten littoral leagues. 8. That it belonged to a mission, and it was therefore unlawful to grant it.

1. The first objection, if true in fact, has been disposed of by this court in the case of United States v. Reading, decided at this term. Besides, so far as the archives show any action of the assembly on this grant, it is an approval of it; and as there is no evidence that it was rejected or annulled, or any further report made on it, the grantee should have the benefit of the presumption of a decision in his favor.

2. The objection that the land lies within the ten littoral leagues, has just been disposed of, in the case of The United States v. Arguello.

8. As to the objection that the land had belonged to the mission.

The large tracts of land appurtenant to the mission establishments, were never vested in the church, or any other corporation or individual, by any grant of a legal title. The missionaries and Indians had an usufruct or occupancy of the land, at the will of the sovereign. The record shows, that though the lands now in question had formerly been occupied by the mission, they were not so at the time this grant was made. It was made, also, with the assent of the mission, who set up no claim to further occupancy.

The 17th section of the regulations of 1828 forbids lands "occupied" by missions from being made the subject of "colonization grants for the present," &c., and can therefore have no application to lands not so occupied, and not made the subject of "colonization." Besides, in 1833 and 1834, the government of Mexico passed laws to secularize the missions; since which time, the public authorities have granted these lands to individuals in the same manner as other public lands; as has been decided by this court in the case of United States v. Ritchie, 17 How. 525.

The judgment of the district court is, therefore, affirmed.

Mr. Justice DANIEL dissented.

For the reasons of his dissent see the preceding case of Arguello v. The United States.

THE UNITED STATES, APPELLANTS, *v.* JUAN MANUEL VACA AND
JUAN FELIPE PENA.

Where there was a grant of land in California in 1843, with three boundaries and the
quantity stated; and in 1845 a new grant was made which was approved by the
departmental assembly, subject to the condition, that within four months a map of
the land should be made; this was a condition subsequent, the non-compliance with
which did not work a forfeiture of the grant, but only left the land liable to be
denounced.
Moreover, the disturbed state of the country was a sufficient reason for not making the
survey.

THIS was an appeal from the district court of the United
States for the northern district of California.
The facts are stated in the opinion of the court.

It was argued by *Mr. Cushing,* (attorney-general,) for the
United States, and by *Mr. Jones,* with whom was *Mr. Strode,* for
the appellees.

Mr. Justice GRIER delivered the opinion of the court.
On the 27th January, 1843, the claimants and appellees in this
case, Juan Manuel Vaca and José Phelipe Peña, (the latter
under the name of Armijo,) received a grant of land from Micheltorena, then governor; the boundaries of which, as stated in the
grant, are the Sacramento River on the east, on the west the
Sierra of Napa; at the north, the Creek of Lihuaytos, (which was
also given as the name by which the tract should be designated,)
and the extent ten sitios de ganado mayor. Prior to this grant,
a sketch or map was furnished, according to the law, as is shown
in the recitals of the grant.
The grant was made, as expressed in it, subject to " the meas-
urements to be made of contiguous ranchos," and the juridical
possession to be given after the confirmation of the grant.
Among the contiguous ranchos, on the same creek or river, and
which had not been measured, was that of William Wolfskill.
Between the claimants and Wolfskill a dispute of boundary
arose, which prevented the lands of either from being measured,
which continued till 1845.
In 1845, the dispute was settled by proceedings had before the
proper authorities, in which it was agreed that Wolfskill should
remain with the lands that he claimed on the upper part of the
creek, and Vaca and Peña should take theirs adjoining his on
the east.
Vaca and Peña petitioned to Governor Pico for a new grant,
corresponding to the agreement, and producing the former grant
as a foundation for it.

The governor made the grant according to the agreement, bounding the rancho by the eastern limits of Wolfskill, and subject to the measurement to be made of the contiguous ranchos previously conceded.

The prior proceedings and decree of concession were passed to the departmental assembly, and the concession was approved, under the condition that within four months they should put in the hands of the governor a proper map of the land.

The grant by Pico designated the tract as " Los Putos." The stream of Los Putos is the same called in the former grant " Lihuaytos."

It is not worth while to inquire whether the departmental assembly had any authority to annex new conditions to the grant thus approved by them. It is a condition subsequent, which, at the worst, only left the title of the grantee open to be denounced. But as the claimant was hindered from performing it by the revolutionary state of the country, the non-fulfilment of it will not work a forfeiture of his title.

The chief objection urged to this grant, is the want of a survey, and that there is no sufficient designation of boundaries to sever it from the public domain. It is a sufficient answer to this, — that the quantity is defined and the general locality. The claimant had been in possession before applying for the grant under a license from Vallejo; the tract was known by the designation of " Los Putos," or " Lihuaytos." It was to be located on the eastern boundary of Wolfskill, and on the margin of the river.

The district court confirmed the grant on the authority of the case of Fremont v. United States, 17 How. 542. As that case is directly in point and overrules the objections made to this grant, we do not think it necessary to pursue the subject further.

The decree of the district court is affirmed.

Mr. Justice DANIEL dissented.

For the reasons of his dissent see the preceding case of Arguello v. The United States.

THE UNITED STATES, APPELLANTS, v. THOMAS O. LARKIN AND JOHN S. MISSROON.

Where there was a grant of land in California made by the governor to the secretary of the government, and neither the petition nor the patent stated the quantity, but the concession and direction by the governor to the proper officer to issue the patent, limited the quantity to eleven square leagues, this concession and direction

47 *

constitute a part of the evidence of title, and are sufficient to make a good grant for that amount.

The petition to the governor was accompanied with a sketch or map giving the location and boundaries of the tract. The patent refers to this sketch, and by it the land can be located.

The fraudulent nature of the grant was not made a question in the court below and therefore cannot be made here. Moreover, there is no evidence of fraud.

The objections that the case was not submitted to the departmental assembly, and that judicial possession was not taken of the land, are overruled by the case of United States *v.* Fremont, 17 How. 542.

Neither the act of the Mexican congress of 1824, nor the regulations of 1828, prescribe any particular form of grants or patents of the public lands. And there is no uniformity with respect to the conditions imposed upon the grantee, either in those which relate to the cultivation or taking possession of the land. The absence of the condition of settlement within a limited time will not avoid the grant in this case.

THIS was an appeal from the district court of the United States for the northern district of California.

The facts are stated in the opinion of the court.

It was argued by *Mr. Cushing,* (attorney-general,) for the United States, and by *Mr. Lawrence,* with whom was *Mr. Goold,* for the appellees.

Mr. Justice NELSON delivered the opinion of the court.

This is an appeal from. a decree of the district court of the United States for the northern district of California, in which a land claim was confirmed to the appellees, and which had been previously confirmed by the board of commissioners.

The grant was made to Manuel Jimeno, who was at the time secretary of the government of California, by Governor Micheltorena, on the 4th November, 1844.

The petition for the same is as follows : —

" EXCELLENT SIR GOVERNOR:

" I, Manuel Jimeno Cassarin, a resident of this department, represent before Y. E., with due respect, that, inasmuch as it suits my interests to establish a rancho about (port) the Sacramento River, according to the accompanying sketch, I entreat Y. E. to be pleased to grant to me, since it lies completely unoccupied, and nobody has petitioned for it, the land, as it is made apparent by the general map, formed this year by the Land Surveyor Bidwell. By which grace I will receive mercy from Y. E.

(Signed)						" MANUEL JIMENO.

" Monterey, November the 1st, 1844."

And on the same day the governor made the following memorandum : —

" Monterey, November 1, 1844.

" The party concerned not being able to report, on account of his being at a time concerned, party and secretary of government, I order that, whatever it may be convenient to have in mind, for the purpose of coming to a determination, be brought to my knowledge.

(Signed) " MICHELTORENA."

And on the next day directions were given for the issuing of the patent, as follows : —

"Monterey, November the 2d, 1844.

" After having seen the petition at the head of this record of proceedings, the uncultivated state in which the land petitioned for lies, according to the general map which has been formed of the Sacramento River, and whatever else it was found convenient to attend to, in conformity with the laws and regulations on the subject, I declare Don Manuel Jimeno .the owner of eleven square leagues (" Sitios de Ganado Mayor ") between Sacramento River, the ranch which the children of Senor Larkin have applied for, and the vacant lands lying south, as the respective sketch shows. Let the corresponding patent be issued ; let it be entered in the respective book ; and let it be delivered to the party concerned, for his security, and other ends.

(Signed) " MICHELTORENA."

And on the 4th November the patent was issued, in the following terms : —

" [L. S.] The citizen Manuel Micheltorena, general [Maritime Custom House, of brigade of the Mexican army, adjutant-Monterey.] general of the staff of the same, governor, commandant-general, and inspector of the department of Californias.

" [L. S.] Whereas Don Manuel Jimeno has peti- [Govern't of the depart- tioned for his personal benefit for the tract ment of the Californias.] of land which is unoccupied between the ranch which has been granted to the children of Don Tomas O. Larkin, the River Sacramento, and the uncultivated lands which are on the side of the south, entirely in conformity with the showing in the corresponding plan. The necessary preliminaries and investigations having been gone through with, as directed by the laws and regulations on the subject; exercising the authority in me vested, in the name of the Mexican nation, I have just granted to him the said land, subject to the following conditions : —

" 1. He may inclose it without prejudice to the cross-ways, roads, and right of way ; he shall enjoy it freely and exclusively, destining it to the use and cultivation which best suits him.

" 2. He shall solicit the proper judge to give him juridical possession of it, in virtue of this grant, for the which boundaries thereof shall be marked out, within the limits of which, besides the usual landmarks, he shall plant some fruit-bearing or some forest trees of some utility.

"8. If he shall contravene these conditions he will lose his right to the land.

"Wherefore, I order this title, being of itself duly firm and valid. Record thereof shall be taken in the proper book, and that it be delivered to the party interested for his security, and for other purposes.

"Given in Monterey, this fourth day of November, one thousand eight hundred and forty-four.

(Sg'd)   "MAN'L MICHELT'A.

(Sg'd)   FRANC'O ARCE,

First Official.

"The record of this grant has been taken in the proper book, folio.

"FRANC'O ARCE."

On the 21st April, 1846, Jimeno made application to the departmental assembly for a confirmation of his grant.

"To the excellent departmental assembly : —

"I, Manuel Jimeno, represent before Y. E., with all due respect, that by the adjoined title is proved the grant, made in my favor, of a tract of land on the margins of the Sacramento ('corresponde') River, and, inasmuch as it pertains (correspond) to Y. E., to give Y. E. approval.

"I beg Y. E. to deign to grant it to me, whereby I will receive grace and mercy. I swear so ; and Y. E. will be pleased to excuse my usage of common paper, there being none of the corresponding paper.

(Signed)   "MANUEL JIMENO.

"Monterey, April the 21st, 1846."

And on the 8d June, the same year, that body acted upon the application of which we have the following record : —

"Angeles, June the 3d, 1846.

"Account having been given in to-day's session to the excellent departmental assembly, with this instancy, it was ordered to be referred, together with the respective record of proceedings, to the committee on vacant lands.

(Signed)   "AUGUSTIN OLIVERA."

Jimeno and his wife conveyed all their interest in the land to the appellees on the 30th August, 1847; soon after which the grantees took actual possession, and have occupied and possessed the same ever since.

The petition to the governor was accompanied with a sketch or map giving the location, and boundaries of the tract solicited, and referred, also, to a general map of the valley of the Sacramento River, made by Bidwell, a land surveyor, the same year. The quantity of land was not specifically designated in the petition. Neither does the patent itself designate the quantity, but refers to the sketch accompanying the petition. But the concession and direction by the governor to the proper officer to issue the patent, limits the quantity to eleven square leagues, and which concession and direction constitute a part of the evidence of the title, or, according to the Mexican vocabulary, a part of the "expediente," and therefore may well qualify and limit the quantity to this number, even if the number of leagues within the boundaries, as given by the rough sketch, exceeded it; especially should this construction be given as the power of the governor to grant to a single person was limited so as not to exceed this quantity, according to the 12th section of the decree of the Mexican congress of the 18th August, 1824.

The decree of the commissioners, and also of the district court, very properly limited the confirmation to the extent only of eleven square leagues, provided the quantity should be contained within the sketch called for by the patent, and if there should be less than that quantity, then no more than this lesser quantity is confirmed.

No question appears to have been made as to the practicability of locating the grant in the tribunals below; nor do we see any ground upon which such a question could have been properly raised in the case.

The plan or sketch found in the expediente in connection with the description given in the grant furnishes all the materials essential to determine the boundaries. Three sides are given, and the quantity will guide the surveyor in closing the lines by running the fourth.

It has been suggested on the argument here, that this grant is a fictitious one, made by the governor to the secretary of the territory according to the forms of law, for the purpose of defrauding the United States. One answer to the suggestion is, that no objection as to the *bona fides* of the grant was taken before either of the tribunals below, where it should have been made, if relied on by the government, so as to have given the claimants an opportunity to have met it. To permit it to be taken in the appellate court for the first time, where there is no opportunity for explanation, would be a surprise upon them, of which they might justly complain. The commissioners say, " the grant is fully proven, and we find no cause to doubt its genuineness." And the judges of the district court observe, " that the grant is fully proved ; nor is its genuineness called in question."

Besides this answer to the suggestion, even were we to entertain the question, we see nothing in the record to justify the imputation. The grant was made 4th November, 1844, at a time when California was in the full possession of the Mexican authorities, and more than a year previous to any hostile entry of the forces of the United States, and more than three years before the cession of the country to this government. The fact that seems most to be relied on to maintain the suggestion is, that Jimeno, the grantee, was the secretary of the territory at the time, and hence the grant an act of favoritism. But there is nothing in the decree of 18th August, 1824, of the Mexican congress, or in the regulations of the 21st November, 1828, forbidding such grants. On the contrary, it is known to be the usual mode of remuneration to an officer of the government for meritorious public services. A preference is given to such officers in the distribution of the public lands by the 9th article of decree of 1824, above referred to.

It is also objected that the grant does not contain the condition of confirmation by the departmental assembly ; and also that there has been no confirmation by that body.

The 5th regulation of November, 1828, provides, that grants to individuals or families shall not be definitively valid without the previous approbation of the departmental assembly to which the respective " expedientes " shall be referred. There is nothing in this or any other regulation that requires this condition to be inserted in the patent.

It appears from the records in the case, that the grant was submitted to this body by Jimeno on the 21st April, 1846 ; and that that body, on the 3d June following, referred it to the committee on vacant lands ; but, for aught that appears, no further action was had upon it. The expediente, however, which was before this body, seems afterwards to have been returned to the appropriate office for the keeping of these records, and was found in the government archives.

The 6th regulation of 1828 provides that, " if the governor does not obtain the approval of the departmental assembly, he shall report the same to the supreme government," together with the " expediente," for its decision. Inasmuch as the record of the title was found returned by the governor to the government archives, and not forwarded to the supreme government, it is insisted, on behalf of the claimants, that the fair presumption is, that the grant had been approved ; otherwise, it would not have been returned to government archives.

However this may be, it is not important to determine, as it was settled, after full consideration, in the case of Fremont *v.* United States, 17 How. 542, 563, that the omission to procure the confirmation under circumstances existing similar to those attending this case did not operate to defeat or avoid the title.

The grant, in that case, to Alvarado, was made by the same governor, and in the same year of the present grant, and, we may add that the grantee was a military officer of the government at the time ; the present grantee was a civil officer.

The same case also furnishes a full answer to the objections, that judicial possession was not taken of the land. We refer to the grounds there stated without repeating them, as the facts in this case fully warrant the view there presented.

It is also objected that the grant does not contain the usual condition of cultivation and habitation within the year. Neither the act of the Mexican congress of 1824 nor the regulations of 1828 prescribe any particular form of grants or patents of the public lands. And there appears to have been no uniformity in the conditions annexed in those issued by the different political chiefs, nor even as it respects those issued by the same individual. Great latitude seems to have been exercised in prescribing these conditions, both as to the number and the nature of them ; also, in respect to the time within which the possession was to be taken when inserted as a condition. It is understood that the condition was usually dispensed with in cases where the grantee was in actual possession at the time of the grant. It was probably dispensed with in the present case ; as the grantee was the secretary of the territory, and his services required at the seat of government ; especially, as it appears that a civil disturbance had broken out between the political authorities, and which continued down until possession was taken of the country by the United States in 1846 and 1847.

We think it would be going further than required by any of the provisions of the law of 1824, or regulations of 1828, to hold the grant void for the want of this condition of possession within a limited time ; more especially, as it appears that actual possession was taken of the land as soon as the state and condition of the country would admit, and which has been held ever since. And we are the more bound to hold this construction in respect to this particular condition, as the court have already held, after the fullest consideration, that even in cases where the condition is contained in the grant, the non-compliance with its terms will not necessarily have the effect to avoid the title. Circumstances may excuse the omission.

Upon the whole, we are satisfied that the judgment of the court below was right, and should be affirmed.

Mr. Justice DANIEL and Mr. Justice CAMPBELL dissented. For the reasons of Mr. Justice Daniel's dissent, see the preceding case of Arguello *v.* The United States.

Mr. Justice CAMPBELL, dissenting.

In exercising the jurisdiction conferred by the act of congress of the 3d March, 1851, in reference to claims for lands in California, it seems to me this court should be satisfied that the claimant has received a title from the governor who was a legal representative of the Mexican nation, and that no credit should attach to the acts of the usurpers who from time to time occasioned anarchy and civil war in that territory; that the grant should be, in spirit and effect, a colonization grant, in accordance with the Mexican laws; that it should describe the lands so that they can be identified; and that the conditions of improvement and occupancy should be substantially fulfilled. The case before us is a claim for eleven leagues of land lying on the Sacramento River, with that length and of a league in width. The papers purport to have been made during the four first days of November, 1844, by the governor of the territory, in favor of one Jimeno, the secretary of the government. The usual inquiries could not be made, for the party interested was charged with the performance of that duty; though the governor recites that, in making the grant, he had conformed to the regulations. The patent issued the 4th November, 1844, subject to the conditions that juridical possession should be taken, and the proper boundaries marked out, and that the grantee should plant fruit-bearing, or forest trees of some utility; and if he failed to perform the conditions he should lose the land. No act was done by this person during 1844 or 1845, or the early part of 1846, which indicates any claim on his part to this land. There is a petition entered by himself on the expediente, directed to the departmental assembly, dated 21st April, 1846, asking for a confirmation and a certificate of one Olivera, dated 3d June, 1846, that it had been presented and referred to the committee of public lands. Here the connection of Jimeno terminates. The preparation of these papers is the whole extent of that connection. In August, 1847, the petitioner, Larkin, consul of the United States at Monterey, purchases from Jimeno this claim for one thousand dollars, or rather, that is the price recited in the deed of Jimeno to him. The American flag had been raised at Monterey twelve months before, and the whole country was then in the possession of General Kearney.

We have some unsatisfactory evidence that Larkin, either in 1847 or 1848 sent a Spaniard to enter upon this land ; a camp, in which he might find a shelter and some conveniences for collecting cattle, form the facts of this settlement.

Neither Jimeno nor Larkin entered upon or occupied the land. This evidence merely shows that Larkin was laying the foundations for a claim upon the United States, and was wholly unconnected with the Mexican regulations. The evidence satisfies me that this claim was fabricated after the difficulties between the United States and Mexico had occurred, with a view to enable the American consul at Monterey to profit from it, in the event of the cession of the country to the United States. I lay no stress upon the fact that the papers are found in the archives. I presume Jimeno was the keeper of those archives. I dissent from the judgment of the court confirming this claim.

ALEXANDER DENNISTOUN, JOHN DENNISTOUN, WILLIAM MYLINE, AND WILLIAM WOOD, PARTNERS, UNDER THE STYLE OF A. DENNISTOUN AND CO., PLAINTIFFS, v. ROGER STEWART.

Where questions are certified up to this court, in consequence of a division in opinion between the judges of the circuit court, they must be questions of law and not questions of fact; not such as involve or imply conclusions or judgment by the judges, upon the weight or effect of testimony or facts, adduced in the cause.
The questions must also be distinctly and particularly stated with reference to that part of the case upon which such questions shall have arisen.
The points stated must be single, and must not bring up the whole case for decision.

THIS case came up from the circuit court of the United States for the southern district of Alabama, upon a certificate of division in opinion between the judges thereof.

The case was before the court at the preceding term, and is reported in 17 How. 606.

The certificate of division commenced as follows, namely : —

Certificate of Division of Opinion.

CIRCUIT COURT OF THE U. S.,
  Southern Dist. of Ala.

A. DENNISTOUN AND CO. ⎫
   v.   ⎬
JAMES REID AND CO. ⎭

Upon the trial of this cause in the circuit court aforesaid, the defendant, among other defences to the case of the plaintiffs, insisted that the plaintiffs had surrendered, to one Byrne, a bill of lading for ten hundred and fifty-eight bales of cotton on The

Windsor Castle, whereby the said Byrne was enabled to dispose of the said cotton, and apply the proceeds otherwise than
for the payment of the bill upon which this suit was brought,
against the rights and interests of the said defendant, whereby
he was injured to the whole amount of the bill. And upon the
point of this defence the depositions of Joseph Bramwell, Robert Barrett, Robert Winthrop, A. E. Byrne, Orlando Jones,
Andrew Stewart, Charles Livingston, Moses Joynson, T. D.
Anderson, and Wm. Moreland, which are hereunto attached,
were read to the jury, and formed the testimony relied on by
the parties in reference to such defence. And upon the instructions proper to be given to the jury upon the said defence, the
following questions arose, and upon which the members of the
court were opposed and divided in opinion : —

(Then followed the questions as they are stated in the opinion
of the court.)

The case was argued by *Mr. Phillips*, for the plaintiffs, and
submitted on a printed argument by *Mr. Stewart*, for himself.

Mr. Justice DANIEL delivered the opinion of the court.

This cause comes before us upon a certificate of division in
opinion between the judges of the circuit court of the United
States for the 5th circuit and southern district of Alabama.

The evidence before the circuit court on which the division in
opinion arose was of the following character : —

The defendant, on the 9th day of September, 1850, at Mobile,
in the names of James Reid and Co., of which firm the defendant was a member, drew a bill on Henry Goa Booth, at Liverpool, for the sum of forty-four hundred and seventeen pounds
fourteen shillings and eleven pence sterling, payable at sixty
days' sight, to the order of the drawers in London, on account of
1,058 bales of cotton, shipped by the drawers to the drawee by
the ship Windsor Castle.

This bill was indorsed by the defendant, by the name and
style of his firm, to the plaintiffs, and, after acceptance, having
been returned protested for non-payment, an action of *assumpsit*
was brought for the amount of the bill and charges by the indorsees against the defendant as drawer.

Upon the trial before the circuit court there were introduced
and read the testimony of sundry witnesses, examined on the
part both of the plaintiffs and the defendant.

The object of the plaintiffs was to sustain their right of
recovery upon the bill, by showing that this right had not been
lost or impaired by any irregularity or delinquency of the plaintiffs as indorsees and holders of the bill for value.

By the evidence adduced by the defendant it was designed to show that, previously to the purchase of the 1,058 bales of cotton, and as a part of the agreement on which the purchase was to be made, the defendant, or the person or persons by whom the funds for that purchase should be advanced, should hold the bill of lading of the cargo as security for such advances; that this agreement was adopted by the plaintiffs, who required and received the bill of lading as a precedent condition to their purchase of the bills drawn on Booth by the defendant; that the bill of lading thus received as a security, was transmitted by the plaintiffs to a branch of their firm in Liverpool, and by the Liverpool branch, with the knowledge and in violation of that agreement, was surrendered to one Byrne, a creditor of Booth, and thus diverted from the purposes it was intended to secure.

Upon the instructions prayed from the court to the jury, the court were divided in opinion upon the following questions: —

1. Whether the firm of Dennistoun, Wood, and Co., of New York, or the plaintiffs, were bound to hold the said bill of lading for the shipment on the said Windsor Castle as a security for the bill of exchange described in the declaration, and whether any amount of loss arising to the said defendant from their failure to hold the said bill for the purpose of securing the proceeds of the cotton specified therein, for the payment of the bill of exchange described in the declaration, can be used as a defence against the bill, or any part thereof.

2. Whether the said Dennistoun and Co. were required to hold the said bill of lading as a security for any bill of exchange drawn by the defendant or his agents upon the said shipment of cotton, other than those to which the same was attached, or of which they, the said plaintiffs, had specific and direct notice at the time of the settlement with Byrne in the manner stated in the depositions; and whether notice to Dennistoun, Wood, and Co., in New York, was operative as a notice to the plaintiffs in Liverpool, though no notice was received by the house in Liverpool of such outstanding bill before said settlement.

3. Whether, if the plaintiffs surrendered the said bill of lading to the said Byrne, under a promise from him that the proceeds of the cotton should be applied to the payment of bills that might come forward, and that this bill should subsequently come forward; and that the plaintiffs have failed to sue said Byrne, or to take any other legal proceeding against him, and that the said Byrne has the proceeds of the cotton more than sufficient to pay the bill, these facts or any other facts in connection therewith that are contained in the said testimony, offer any defence against the case of the plaintiffs.

4. Whether any view of the evidence introduced upon the said trial and hereto attached, would warrant the jury in finding for the defendant, upon this point of the defence to the case of the plaintiffs.

5. And the further question arose, whether the statute of Alabama regulating the damages upon bills of exchange like the present, returned under protest, regulates the rate of damage in this case.

We think that our jurisdiction of the questions certified on the record of this cause is forbidden by previous decisions of this court, bearing upon those questions considered separately, as well as upon the case as presented by them in an aggregate point of view.

In the interpretations by this court of the act of congress of April 29, 1802, authorizing divisions of opinion at circuit to be certified, the following requisites have been prescribed as indispensable to the jurisdiction of this court over questions upon which the judges shall have been opposed in opinion.

1. They must be questions of law and not questions of fact, — not such as involve or imply conclusions or judgment by the judges upon the weight or effect of testimony or facts adduced in the cause. *Vide* Wilson *v.* Barnum, 8 How. 258. And the question or questions upon which the judges were opposed in opinion must be distinctly and particularly stated with reference to that part of the case upon which such question or questions shall have arisen. *Vide* The United States *v.* Briggs, 5 How. 208. It is said by the chief justice in delivering the opinion of the court in this case, "we are not authorized to decide in such cases unless the particular point upon which the judges differed is stated"; again he says: "the difference of opinion is indeed stated to have been on the point whether the demurrer should be sustained. But such a question can hardly be called a point in the case within the meaning of the act of congress, for it does not show whether the difficulty arose upon the construction of the act of congress on which the indictment was founded, or upon the form of proceeding adopted to inflict the punishment or upon any supposed defect in the counts in the indictment. On the contrary, the whole case is ordered to be certified upon the indictment, demurrer, and joinder, leaving this court to look into the record to determine for itself, whether any sufficient objection can be made in bar of the prosecution.

2. The points stated must be single, and must not bring up the whole case for decision.

In the establishment of this position, the rulings of this court have been reiterated, and most explicit.

Beginning with the case of the United States *v.* John Bailey,

9 Pet. 257, it is in that case declared by the late chief justice, that "the language of the 6th section of the act to amend the judicial system of the United States, shows conclusively, that congress intended to provide for a division of opinion on single points which frequently occur in the trial of a cause; not to enable a circuit court to transfer an entire cause into this court before a final judgment; a construction which would authorize such a transfer would counteract the policy which forbids writs of error or appeals until the judgment or decree be final." To the same effect, and enunciated in language equally if not even more explicit, will be found the decisions of Adams and Co. *v.* Jones, 12 Pet. 207; of White *v.* Turk et al. Ib. 238; of Nesmith *v.* Sheldon et al. 6 How. 41; of Webster *v.* Cooper, 10 Ib. 54.

Upon the trial in the circuit court the examination of witnesses was introduced and relied on both by plaintiffs and defendant to show the nature of the agreement upon which the cargo of The Windsor Castle was purchased, and upon which the plaintiffs consented to purchase and did purchase the bills drawn by the defendant upon Booth; the character of the security proffered and said to have been accepted in the bill of lading for the indemnity of the plaintiffs in purchasing the bills drawn upon Booth, and the obligation of the same plaintiffs not to surrender that security, nor to use it to the detriment of the defendant. The case was not placed before the judges upon any general or settled principle of the law-merchant, nor was their opposition in opinion founded upon a case moulded and governed simply by that law, but they have divided upon a case which was or might have been affected by facts heard in evidence, the influence of which facts, as controlling the acts and obligations of the parties, fell peculiarly and properly within the province of the jury.

Again, we do not think that the certificate of the judges of the circuit court conforms to the settled interpretation of the act of congress as expounded by the cases cited, in presenting to this court any single or specific question of law arising in the progress of the cause, but that it refers to this court the entire law of the case as it might arise upon all the facts supposed by the court, and which have not been found by the jury. We are therefore of the opinion that this court cannot take jurisdiction of this case as certified from the circuit court, but that it should be remanded to that court to be proceeded in according to law.

48 *

THE STEAMER OREGON, ROGER A. HEIRN, MASTER AND PART-
OWNER, APPELLANT, *v.* JOSEPH AND FRANCIS ROCCA. THE
STEAMER OREGON, ROGER A. HEIRN, MASTER AND PART-
OWNER, APPELLANT, *v.* ROBERT TURNER AND WILLIAM
TWIFORD.

Where a decree in admiralty was rendered in the circuit court upon an appeal from
the district court, said decree being given *pro forma* because the presiding judge
had been of counsel for one of the parties, this court has jurisdiction to try and
determine the case.
Where a collision took place in the bay of Mobile between a schooner and a steamer,
the latter was in fault.
The rule of this court is, when a steamer approaches a sailing vessel, the steamer is
required to exercise the necessary precaution to avoid a collision ; and if this be not
done, *primâ facie*, the steamer is chargeable with fault.
Whether this rule be regarded or the weight of the testimony, the steamer must, in the
present case, be considered in the wrong.

THESE were appeals from the circuit court of the United States
for the southern district of Alabama.

In the first case, a libel was filed in the district court of the
United States for the southern district of Alabama claiming
damages resulting from a collision between the schooner William Ozman and the steamer Oregon, in the bay of Mobile, on
the 8th of September, 1849, whereby one hundred and forty
bales of cotton on board said schooner were injured and in part
destroyed.

In the second, a like libel was filed by Turner and Twiford as
the owners of the schooner, claiming damages for injuries done
to the vessel.

In January, 1851, the district judge decreed in favor of the
libellants, in the first-named case for $6,599.64, and in the second
for $1,989.47.

From these decrees the owners of the steamer appealed to the
circuit court.

On the 21st of April, 1855, the circuit court passed an order
in each case reciting that " the said cause being submitted to
the court, a decree is rendered *pro forma*, the presiding judge
having been of counsel for the defendants, affirming the judgment that was rendered in this case," namely, &c., &c.

An appeal from these decrees brought the cases up to this
court.

The attention of the court having been called to this state of
affairs, after consultation, the following order was passed in each
case.

Order.

It is now here considered by the court that although it appears
from the record that the decree of the circuit court in this cause

was entered *pro forma*, yet that this court has jurisdiction to try and determine the case. Whereupon it is now here ordered by the court that this cause be and the same is hereby set down for argument next after the case fixed for to-day.

Dissenting-Justices, DANIEL and CATRON.

The cases were argued by *Mr. Johnson*, a brief being also filed by *Mr. Nelson*, for the appellants, and by *Mr. Phillips*, for the appellee.

Mr. Justice McLEAN delivered the opinion of the court.

These are appeals in admiralty, from the circuit court for the southern district of Alabama.

The first case is an appeal from the decree of the circuit court for damages resulting from a collision between the schooner William Ozman and the steamer Oregon, in the bay of Mobile, on the 8th of September, 1849, whereby one hundred and forty bales of cotton on board said schooner, alleged to belong to the appellees, were injured, and in part destroyed.

A similar libel was filed by the appellees as the owners of the schooner, claiming damages for the injuries done to the vessel. The libels are substantially the same, and they both rest on the same evidence.

The collision took place in the bay of Mobile, where it is eleven miles wide, and sufficient depth of water for the navigation of vessels. The schooner was sailing down the bay before the wind at the rate of six miles an hour. The Oregon was on her passage from New Orleans to Mobile, and was running at the rate of eight miles per hour. It was a starlight night, and the moon also shone. The collision occurred before daylight; but the vessels in approaching each other were seen from a mile and a half to two miles. Under such circumstances, it is extraordinary that they should come in contact.

The witnesses on board The Oregon say, that as the vessels approached each other, the schooner suddenly changed her course, which caused the collision; whilst the witnesses on board the schooner state, it was occasioned by a change of her course by the steamer. In such a conflict of testimony, where the vessels were both steamers or sailing vessels, and there were no leading facts for discrimination, fault would be chargeable to both vessels. But in the case before us the vessels, in regard to a collision, occupy a very different relation to each other. The steamer, having the propelling power, is under the control of her pilot. Her course may be changed, and her progress checked or arrested. Having this power to avoid a collision with a vessel propelled by the wind, she is generally chargeable with fault, when such an occurrence happens. The exception to this rule must be clearly established by strong circumstances, to excuse the steamer.

The vessels in question saw each other at the distance of more than a mile, probably a mile and a half to two miles. The Oregon was steering near a due north course; the course of the schooner was south. Both vessels continued their course until they came within one hundred and fifty yards of each other. As evidence that the steamer changed her course the fact is relied on that the schooner ran into the steamer, a little forward of midships, with her bow. This result might, possibly, have followed a change of course by the schooner. But, as the movement of the steamer was more rapid than the schooner, such an occurrence would not be so likely to happen, as an attempt by the steamboat to pass the bow of the schooner.

Several experts were examined on both sides to show that the theory of each is wrong, judging from the injury received by The Oregon. The witnesses give their opinions without reserve on this subject. We derive but little light from this part of the examination.

In St. John v. Paine, 10 How. 557, this court say: "As a general rule, therefore, when meeting a sailing vessel, whether closehauled or with the wind free, the latter has a right to keep her course, and it is the duty of the steamer to adopt such precautions as will avoid her." Practically, when a rule for this purpose is laid down, it is rendered ineffectual by admitting exceptions to it. The mind begins to waver as soon as the danger arises, and the exception, rather than the rule, becomes a subject of solicitude with the masters of both boats; and this, practically, annuls the rule, and causes the movements of both vessels to be uncertain. If the rule were absolute, and an insuperable difficulty should prevent one of the boats from observing it, it would be safer and better to slow the vessel or stop it, until the danger shall be past. This would occur so seldom as to be inappreciable, when compared to the safety it would secure. The rule adopted by the Trinity masters, and sanctioned by this court, is the safe one, that when two vessels on opposite tacks are approaching each other, each should turn to the right, passing each other on the larboard side. This rule is too simple to be misunderstood, and if observed, collisions would not occur between moving boats, whether propelled by sails or steam. The rule once established, every deviation from it should be chargeable as a fault.

The rule of this court is, when a steamer approaches a sailing vessel, the steamer is required to exercise the necessary precau-

The Steamer Oregon et al. *v.* Rocca et al.

tion to avoid a collision; and if this be not done, *primâ facie* the steamer is chargeable with fault. Whether this rule be regarded or the weight of the testimony, we think, in the present case, The Oregon was in the wrong. The decrees of the circuit court are, therefore, affirmed.

Mr. Justice CATRON and Mr. Justice DANIEL dissented.

Mr. Justice DANIEL.

I am constrained by a sense of duty to differ with the court in their determination to take cognizance of these causes.

It is my deliberate opinion that these causes, in the form in which they are presented to our consideration, fall within no one of the categories, either in the constitution or the laws of the United States, by which the jurisdiction of this court or that of the circuit courts have been conferred or prescribed.

The first thing to be observed with reference to these cases, is the fact that they are cases in which confessedly no decision has been made, no opinion formed or expressed, nor any judicial action had by the circuit court, in which the judges by their certificate declare, that they have forborne to mature or declare any judgment upon their character, and which they have sent to this court in effect to be moulded and settled *ab origine* by this court.

The true inquiry as to such a proceeding is, can this be done in conformity with the letter, the spirit, or the beneficial ends and design of the constitution and laws?

In article 8, sect. 2, of the constitution, the jurisdiction of this court, both original and appellate, is defined. The former is limited to cases affecting ambassadors, other public ministers and consuls. In all the other cases enumerated in this article the jurisdiction of this court is appellate.

To my mind it would involve a solecism too gross for a moment's consideration, to suppose that by any distortion the language or objects of this article of the constitution could be so interpreted as to invest this court with an appellate power over its own decisions; and yet it is not less an extravagance and a solecism to contend that this court can by any direct or indirect agency shape the original decision of any and every case which may be pending in a circuit court, and then recall such decision into this forum for a mere reiteration of what they had already determined and done, under the mere show of an appellate or revising jurisdiction. The framers of the constitution too well understood the nature of human frailty, the influence of prepossession or vanity to believe that, by such a proceeding, either wisdom or impartiality, or the safety of private right would be promoted.

They have authorized no such proceeding, and the expositions of the constitution given in the organization of the courts by the acts of congress conclusively show the conviction of the legislature as to the importance of restricting the several courts to that sphere within which their functions could be exercised wisely, impartially, and without the danger of bias or disturbance from foregone conclusions.

Thus, in the "Act to establish the judicial courts of the United States," it is provided by the 22d section of that act, that final judgments and decrees in civil actions and suits in equity in a circuit court may be re-examined and reversed or affirmed in the supreme court.

In the construction of this section the inquiry first suggests itself, what is it which the act of congress permits to be affirmed or reversed? The answer is, a judgment or decree. What is a judgment or decree? It is an act or conclusion of the mind, founded upon a view of all the facts and circumstances surrounding the subject as to which that conclusion is formed; and it is to be a final judgment, showing still more clearly that all the facts and circumstances have been weighed and appreciated. Such a judgment, it is provided by the statute, may be re-examined by this court. Can it be rationally contended that such a judgment as the statute describes can be affirmed of a proceeding which on its face declares that no conclusion upon any fact or circumstance, nor on any question of law connected with it, has been formed? That all that has occurred is a mere formality, and nothing more, and has been adopted expressly to avoid a judgment. How can that be said to be re-examined, as to which it is admitted there has been no previous examination?

Turning, in the next place, to the law by which divisions of opinion are authorized to be certified to this court, we find the language of the law to be thus. Act of April 29, 1802, § 6, 2 Stats. at Large, 159, "That whenever any question shall occur before a circuit court, upon which the opinions of the judges shall be opposed, the point upon which the disagreement shall happen shall, during the same term, upon the request of either party or their counsel, be stated under the direction of the judges, and certified under the seal of the court to the supreme court." Here then is the sole authority by which certificates of division in opinion are permitted or directed; and what does that authority explicitly require? That there shall be pending in the circuit court a question or questions upon which the opinions of the judges shall be opposed; that there must be a disagreement between the judges, and that only the point upon which such disagreement shall happen shall be certified. Can language be possibly plainer than this? I will not so far offend against common sense as to attempt an argument to show that opposition in opinion or disagreement has not existed between persons as to a matter with reference to which they have formed or expressed no opinion whatsoever, and with regard to which they declare that such is the truth of the case.

The cases before us comprise no one requisite prescribed by the constitution and act of congress. Let us for an instant look to the consequences likely to ensue, which indeed must inevitably ensue, from the doctrine now promulged from this court? There are at this time, it is believed, thirty-one States in this Union, besides several territories; and of these territories it has been recently stated on the floor of congress there is space sufficient for the formation of sixty additional States. In a majority of the existing States there have been created more than one district court, invested with circuit court jurisdiction. If this privilege of forcing upon the supreme court the original decision of causes instituted in the circuit courts be legitimate, it appertains to every court possessing circuit court jurisdiction existing in the States already members of the confederacy, and must appertain equally to any number, however augmented. It cannot be extended to a portion of the courts and denied to the residue.

To those who already feel the burden of the litigation of this extended country, when restricted within the narrowest limits prescribed by the constitution and laws, it need not be shown what are to be the effects of throwing upon them the entire mass of circuit court duty and cognizance; but beyond those who more immediately experience those effects, it becomes a subject of gravest reflection to every one interested in the regular and effectual administration of the law in the federal courts.

But it has been said that the practice sanctioned by the decision in this case is warranted by the authority of precedent in this court. It is undeniably true, that instances like the present, without having their nature or tendencies brought by argument to the test of examination, have several times occurred. But can the simple fact that such instances have occurred affect their justification in violation of the constitution and law, and to the absolute destruction of everything like efficiency in the federal courts?

I am fully impressed with the importance of precedent, and would never attempt to impair its influence within the sphere of its legitimate authority; but I can never yield to it my support, much less implicit obedience, when invoked for the purpose either of introducing or of hallowing abuses. If the mere existence or the prevalence of these can impart to them either authority or sanctity, the cause of justice or morals would indeed be desperate; there could never be reformation. There has perhaps never been a time in which many abuses in politics, law, morals, and religion have not obtained currency; indeed, the human imagination can hardly picture an error, a folly, a vice, or a crime, which has not had its prototype. But the decision cannot invoke the weight or authority of established precedent in its support. On the contrary, the more recent and well-considered cases determined by this tribunal are in direct opposition thereto. Without entering upon them at large, the cases of White v. Turk et al. 12 Pet. 238, of The United States v. Stone, 14 Pet. 524, of Nesmith v. Sheldon et al. 6 How. 41, and of Webster v. Cooper, 10 How. 54, are confidently appealed to in support of this position. These cases, so well considered, and so recently ruled, are now in effect reversed, for the purpose of reviving a practice unauthorized by the constitution or by the legislation of congress; a practice necessarily fruitful of great mischief.

I object, in fine, to the decision in this case, because to me it seems calculated to impair, if not to destroy, that satisfaction and confidence which it is so desirable should everywhere prevail with reference to the proceedings of this tribunal.

With private persons, or in governments, or in public bodies of any description, there is no experiment or course of action more pregnant with danger than is the exercise or the effort to exercise forbidden or even doubtful powers. Such an assumption rarely fails to react, or to operate reflectively upon those by whom it is essayed; never, indeed, except in instances in which it can be sustained by a power absolute and irresponsible enough to repress opposition, or to silence the expression of public sentiment. In such instances, but in those only, the act or the attempt can be safe. But under our system of polity no immunity was ever designed, much less has one been provided for anything of this kind. With whatever deference and to whatever extent, therefore, the opinions of this tribunal may be recognized, (and by no one will they within their proper bounds be maintained with truer loyalty than by myself,) yet when challenged to obedience to those opinions, I am bound to remember that the constitution is above all and over all, and that public opinion conveyed through its legitimate channel, the legislation of the country, will cause itself to be heard and respected.

ADAM OGILVIE ET AL. COMPLAINANTS, *v.* THE KNOX INSURANCE COMPANY ET AL.

Where questions are certified up to this court in consequence of a division in opinion between the judges of the circuit court, which questions involve the consequences of fraud by an agent of a company and no facts are set forth showing the connection of the agent with the company, the questions are too general and abstract for this court to answer.
The cause must, therefore, be dismissed.

THIS case came up from the circuit court of the United States for the district of Indiana, upon a certificate of division in opinion between the judges thereof.

As the record was very short, it is thought proper to insert the whole of it.

Be it remembered, that amongst the records of the United States circuit court for the seventh judicial circuit and district of Indiana, begun, continued, and holden at Indianapolis, in said district, on the first day of June, in the year of our Lord 1855, — that being the eleventh day of said term of said court, — before the Honorable John McLean and the Honorable Elisha M. Huntington, judges of said circuit and district, is the following order, to wit:

ADAM OGILVIE et al.
v.   } Chancery. — No. 3.
THE KNOX INSURANCE COMPANY et al.

Now at this time come the parties, and the judges of this court being opposed in opinion on certain questions arising in this cause, they order and direct that the following statement of the matters and questions upon which the opinions of the judges are so opposed be entered upon the record of this court, and that the same be certified under the seal of this court to the supreme court of the United States, to be finally decided.

OGILVIE and others, complainants,
v.   }
THE KNOX INSURANCE Co., Cullom and others, defendants.

The complainants are the several creditors of the Knox Insurance Company, holding judgments and executions returned "no property," &c., against the company. Cullom and the other defendants, twenty-five in number, are charged as stockholders in default in the payment of their several stock subscriptions.

The bill charges substantially as follows: —

1. That some time before the 12th of February, 1850, the

company was duly organized under its charter, and had authority to receive further subscriptions of stock; and that afterwards, at various times, between that time and the first of June, 1850, Cullom and the other defendants, severally became subscribers for stock, and either paid in cash or secured by note or bill of exchange ten per cent of the amounts severally subscribed, and for the balance made their notes or bills; and that the bills of exchange made for the ten per cent were renewed by other bills of exchange drawn in September and October, 1850, and the bill sets out all the securities remaining due and unpaid.

2. That the complainants are creditors of the company by reason of losses on policies issued by the company, at various times, after the subscriptions of the defendants, and the judgments and executions are stated.

3. That the company is destitute of property subject to execution.

4. That the company has neglected to enforce the collection of the money due from the defendants.

5. That the defendants refuse to pay, on the pretence that their subscriptions were procured by means of certain false representations concerning the situation, prospects, and actual business of the company.

7. And that the complainants are advised that it is not material to them or to others who have dealt with the company, how or why the defendants became stockholders; that, by becoming such, the defendants gave credit to the company, by means whereof the complainants were induced to deal with it.

8. That of the defendants, Battorff, Cullom, Hughes, Sparkes, and Savitz, and one Kegwin, a debtor, subscriber not made a party because a citizen of Kentucky, acted as officers of the company throughout the year 1850.

9. And that the defendants, nor any of them, did not, at any time in any manner, attempt to inform the public of the alleged facts now set up in defence.

The prayer is that the defendants pay, &c., and for general relief. The Knox Insurance Company answered, and admitted generally the facts stated in the bill, &c. Cullom and the other defendants severally answered. The answers admit the execution of the securities by the defendants on account of the stock subscribed by them, and set up as a defence substantially the following: That Robert N. Carnan was an agent of the company to procure subscriptions of stock, and as such, in February, 1850, made to defendants certain false representations, by which they were induced to subscribe for said stock, and give their said notes and bills. Their representations were as to the amount of stock then subscribed and secured at Vincennes, and as to the amount of funds on hand; and that defendants had not at that time any means of knowing the accuracy of these representations.

The depositions of Cullom, Savitz, and Schwartz (three of the defendants) were taken and offered to be read in evidence in behalf of the other defendants, but not in behalf of themselves, to prove the allegations of fraud set out in the answers. The complainants objected to the competency of said witnesses, because they were parties to this action, and the objections by consent of parties were reserved to the hearing.

At the May term, 1854, this cause was submitted to the court on the bill, the answers, and the depositions, including the depositions of Cullom, Savitz, and Schwartz, which were then read, subject to the objections above mentioned; and after argument, the said cause was continued under advisement to the November term following.

At the November term, 1854, the cause was continued to the May term, 1855, under advisement.

And now, at the May term, 1855, under the pleadings and on the state of facts above set forth, the following questions occurred:

1. Are the depositions of said Cullom, Savitz, and Schwartz, under the circumstances of this case, and to the effect above stated, competent as evidence for their co-defendants? And, on this question, the opinions of the judges were opposed.

2. Will the fraud of the agent of the Knox Insurance Company, in procuring said subscriptions, notes, and bills, if sufficient to avoid said subscriptions, notes, and bills, as against said Insurance Company, be a defence against the complainants in this suit.

And on this question the opinions of the judges were opposed.

Whereupon, it is ordered, according to the request of the complainants, and to the law in that case provided, that the foregoing statement of the pleadings and facts, which is made under the directions of the judges, be certified under the seal of this court to the supreme court to be finally decided.

I, Horace Bassett, clerk of said court, do hereby certify, that the above and foregoing is a true and correct copy from the records now in my office.

In witness whereof, I have hereto set my hand and affixed the seal of said court, on this sixth June, in the year of our [L. S.] Lord one thousand eight hundred and fifty-five.

H. BASSETT, *Clerk.*

Mr. Justice DANIEL delivered the opinion of the court.

The complainants, by bill in equity, claim an indemnity for losses upon policies issued to them by the company. They allege that the company by its charter, were authorized after their organization, to increase the amount of their stock by further subscriptions thereto. That in virtue of the authority of this permission, several individuals who are made defendants to the bill, did in June, 1850, subscribe for shares in the company; that they had paid in cash a portion of those shares, and had executed for the residue securities which were still unpaid. The bill further alleges, that the company are destitute of funds or property which can be reached by execution, and prays that the amounts subscribed by the individual defendants as stockholders, and which are still unpaid, may be applied to the satisfaction of the demand of the complainants.

The answer of the company, which is not made a part of this record, is stated to contain a general admission of the charges in the bill. The individual defendants, whilst they do not deny their subscription to the stock of the company, nor their execution of the securities for the payment of that subscription, deny their liability to payment thereof upon the ground that their subscription, and the execution of those securities, were obtained from them by fraudulent representations by the agent of the company, as to the amount of the stock actually subscribed, and as to the funds possessed by the company. The depositions of three of the individual defendants were offered in evidence on behalf of others, who were co-defendants, to prove the fraud in the agent of the company alleged in the answers, and were excepted to as incompetent evidence. But the facts stated by these witnesses are not set forth in the record. At the hearing the following order was made by the court, viz.: And now at the May term, 1855, under the pleadings and on the facts above set forth, the following questions occurred:—

1. Are the depositions of the defendants, Savitz, Cullom, and Schwartz, under the circumstances of this case and to the effect above stated, competent as evidence for their co-defendants?

2. Will the fraud of the agent of the Knox Insurance Company in procuring said subscriptions, notes, and bills, if sufficient to avoid the said subscriptions, notes, and bills, as against the said insurance company, be a defence against the complainants in this suit?

Upon the first question propounded by the certificate in this case, we deem it unnecessary to express an opinion, because, whatever might be the opinion of this court as to the degree of interest which shall disqualify a witness, we consider the solution of any such question as irrelevant, under the considerations by which our opinion upon this case as presented to us must be controlled.

The foundation of the case certified is, first the assumption of fraud practised by the agent of the insurance company; and, secondly, an inquiry as to the liability of the company resulting from the connection of the company as principal with their agent, and from the character of the fraud assumed as above.

The question of fraud or no fraud, is one necessarily compounded of fact and of law; and without a correct and precise knowledge of the facts from which the legal conclusion should be deduced, it is not easy to perceive how any legal conclusion can be reached.

In this case, as certified, there is no fact shown by which the precise connection of this alleged agent with the company is established; or the character or extent of any representations said to have been made by him, and upon which it is assumed that the company may be bound. There is nothing then before us upon which this court could deduce any inference or conclusion properly applicable to the case as it really exists. The question propounded, therefore, appears to be one that is entirely general and abstract, and which can admit of no answer but one which is equally abstract and general, and which may in truth have no application to the case. We therefore think that this certificate admits of no other answer than an order that the case be remanded to the circuit court to be proceeded in according to law.

JONATHAN CROCKETT, ARCHIBALD C. SPALDING, JOHN GREGORY, CHRISTOPHER DYER, AND NATHANIEL DYER, LIBELLANTS AND APPELLANTS, *v.* THE STEAMBOAT ISAAC NEWTON, HER TACKLE, &c., ISAAC NEWTON, CLAIMANT. AUGUSTUS LORD, LIBELLANT AND APPELLANT, *v.* THE STEAMBOAT ISAAC NEWTON, HER TACKLE, &c., DANIEL DREW, CLAIMANT.

The general rule is, for a sailing vessel meeting a steamer, to keep her course, while the steamer takes the necessary measures to avoid a collision.

And though this rule should not be observed when the circumstances are such that it is apparent its observance must occasion a collision, while a departure from it will prevent one, yet it must be a strong case which puts the sailing vessel in the wrong for obeying the rule.

The present is not such a strong case, and therefore the steamer must be condemned in the damages and costs resulting from a collision between herself and a sailing vessel.

THESE two cases were appeals from the circuit court of the United States for the southern district of New York.

In the first case, the libellants were owners of the schooner

49 *

Hero, of Maine, and in the second case, Lord was the owner of a cargo of corn and flour laden on board of The Hero, bound from New York to Portsmouth, New Hampshire.

The circumstances of the collision are set forth in the opinion of the court.

The district court dismissed the libels with costs, which decree was affirmed in the circuit court.

The case was argued in this court by *Mr. Benedict*, for the appellants, and by *Mr. Cowles*, for the appellees.

Mr. Justice CURTIS delivered the opinion of the court.

This is an appeal from a decree of the circuit court of the United States for the southern district of New York, in a cause of collision, prosecuted by the owners of the schooner Hero, against the steamer Isaac Newton.

On the sixteenth of July, 1850, the schooner Hero, of the burden of 100 tons, which had been lying at pier No. 15 on the North River, in the city of New York, hauled out of the dock, soon after sunrise got up her mainsail and both jibs, and pushed off into the stream. The tide was about half ebb, setting to the southward and eastward, and the wind was about southeast, but so light that very little way could be made. A brig was at anchor in the river, a little below pier No. 15, about one hundred and fifty yards from the piers; and immediately below the brig, at the distance of about 300 feet, two ships were also anchored. When The Hero had got within a short distance of the brig, and was nearly between the brig and the town, and while her crew were in the act of hoisting the peak of the foresail, the body of the sail being up, the steamer Isaac Newton came down the river, and seeing no clear passage to her dock at pier No. 16, except that of about 300 feet between the brig and the ships at anchor, swung round, passed between those vessels at anchor, straightened up alongside the brig for her dock, and then, for the first time, discovered The Hero directly in her course. The two ships being at anchor astern of the steamer, the latter could not back, without the certainty of injuring herself and one of the ships; she kept on her course, struck The Hero on the starboard bow, which was stove, and the schooner almost immediately filled.

It is pleaded that The Hero was in fault, because her helm was not put hard down and kept there, when the danger was first discovered. The distance between the steamer and the schooner, when the latter straightened up and headed for the former, was only about 400 feet, as testified by the pilot in charge of the steamer. The opportunity for the schooner to make any manœuvre was consequently very small; and though some of the witnesses say there was breeze enough at the moment to give the schooner steerage way, others deny this. It must be remembered that the general rule is, for a sailing vessel, meeting a steamer, to keep her course, while the steamer takes the necessary measures to avoid a collision. And though this rule should not be observed when the circumstances are such that it is apparent its observance must occasion a collision, while a departure from it will prevent one, yet it must be a strong case which puts the sailing vessel in the wrong for obeying the rule. The court must clearly see, not only that a deviation from the rule would have prevented collision, but that the commander of the sailing vessel was guilty of negligence or a culpable want of seamanship, in not perceiving the necessity for a departure from the rule, and acting accordingly.

We do not think this was such a case. Besides, the master of the schooner testifies, that the helm of the schooner had been put hard down by him, and fastened there in a becket, as soon as he saw the steamer, and before hailed from the latter. In this he is corroborated by his mate and crew. Other witnesses say they saw a man run aft, when hailed, and put the helm first up and then down. This apparent discrepancy may be accounted for by the fact mentioned by those on board the schooner; that, after the master had left the helm hard down in a becket, and just before the collision, the mate ran aft. Perhaps he went to the helm, and he may have changed it. But we do not think what he did could have influenced the result. Fault was also attributed to the schooner, in the argument at the bar, because she left her dock when the wind was so light and baffling that she was not really manageable. But we think there was no impropriety in her being where she was at the time of the collision, with her sails hoisted, waiting for a wind to get out of the harbor, any more than in her being at anchor there. It is true she would have no right to endanger other vessels by drifting afoul of them. This she was bound to avoid, by coming to anchor. But till there was danger of this, and none such appears in the case, she had a right to wait for a wind there in daylight, with her sails hoisted.

We hold the schooner to have been free from fault.

After a careful consideration of the evidence we cannot think the steamer did all that could reasonably be required to avoid the collision. After the schooner was seen from the steamer, we have no doubt a collision, either with the schooner, or with one of the ships at anchor, was inevitable; and that the steamer chose that alternative least dangerous to herself, and ran down the schooner. But the fault was, in not discerning the schooner before getting into that position. Though the brig was at anchor between the steamer and the schooner when the former was sweeping across the river and heading for the opening between the brig and the ships, yet the sails of the schooner were hoisted, and must have been visible over the hull of the brig. The steamer, therefore, made for this passage, not only without first ascertaining it to be clear, but without discovering the sails of the schooner which might and ought to have been seen, and which, if seen, would have warned those managing her that the passage there was not clear. We hold this attempt of the steamer to come to her landing between the vessels at anchor, without first ascertaining that the track was clear, to have been culpable, and, accordingly, that she must be condemned in the damages and costs.

The decree of the circuit court is reversed, and the cause remanded to be proceeded with according to law. .

Mr. Justice DANIEL dissented in both cases.

AUGUSTUS LORD, LIBELLANT AND APPELLANT, *v.* THE STEAMBOAT ISAAC NEWTON, HER TACKLE, &C., DANIEL DREW, CLAIMANT.

THIS being a libel by the owner of the cargo on board The Hero at the time of the collision, is disposed of by the opinion in the case of the libel by the owners of the vessel. It was argued with the other case. Depends on the same evidence, and the decree must, in like manner, be reversed and the cause remanded.

WILLIAM B. CULBERTSON, APPELLANT, *v.* THE STEAMER SOUTHERN BELLE; HENRY B. SHAW, WILLIAM M. SHAW, ELAM BOWMAN, SIDNEY A. LACOSTE, AND JOHN DE SEBASTIAN, CLAIMANTS.

Where a regulation was made in one of the harbors of the Mississippi River, assigning their positions to different species of boats, if the regulation was generally known, it was the duty of all persons to conform to it.

Where a flat-boat was moored at the place designated for flat-boats, and a steamboat, in attempting to land, came into collision with and sunk the flat-boat, the steamboat must be liable for the damage done.

When a steamer is about to enter a harbor, great caution is required   Ordinary care, under such circumstances, will not excuse a steamer for a wrong done.

THIS was an appeal from the circuit court of the United States for the eastern district of Louisiana.

The facts of the case are stated in the opinion of the court.

It was argued by *Mr. Benjamin* and *Mr. Vinton*, for the appellant, and by *Mr. Crittenden*, for the appellees, upon which side there was also an argument filed by *Mr. Pike*.

Mr. Justice McLEAN delivered the opinion of the court.

This is an appeal, in admiralty, from the decree of the circuit court, for the eastern district of Louisiana.

The libel states that the libellant was the owner of a flat-boat, called The Rainbow, with a cargo of the value of three thousand dollars and upwards; that the said boat, with its cargo, being a stanch vessel of its kind, with an efficient crew, on a voyage down the Mississippi River, was moored, at night, at Grand Gulf, in the proper and usual place for flat-boats, and securely tied to the bank of the river; that while so fastened, close to the shore, the steamer Southern Belle, a regular packet on said river, in attempting to land at the town of Grand Gulf, run into and sunk the flat-boat, which caused the total loss of the boat and cargo; that the steamer was out of its place and carelessly managed, by reason of which the collision occurred. The libellant claims damages, &c.

The owners of the steamboat, in their answer, allege that she plied as a regular packet between New Orleans and Milliken's Bend, in Louisiana; that in ascending the river on the 3d of January, 1853, shortly before daybreak, she approached the town of Grand Gulf; that, in drawing near the wharf-boat, used as a landing, it was discovered that another steamer was fastened to the wharf; that as the wind was high toward the shore it was deemed unsafe to make fast to the steamer; The Southern Belle, therefore, dropped down, with the intention of coming in astern of the steamer, and below the wharf-boat; that in making this change, the flat-boat was first seen lying close under the high bank of the river, about thirty yards below the wharf-boat; that an attempt was immediately made to back out and avoid the collision, which could not be done, as the wind blew strongly; that the place occupied by the flat-boat was known to be the cotton landing, where The Southern Belle regularly landed every trip to take cotton on board; that the place appropriated for flat-boats was about three hundred yards above the wharf-boat; that the master of the flat-boat was notified before the collision; that his boat was not moored in its proper place, and that he neglected to keep a light, &c.; that the collision was caused, not by any negligence or want of skill on the part of the crew and officers of The Southern Belle, but in consequence of the negligence of the master and crew of the flat-boat, &c.

The district court decreed in favor of the libellant, for the amount of the damage sustained, which decree was reversed on an appeal to the circuit court. The latter decree is now before us on an appeal.

An ordinance of the town of Grand Gulf, passed in 1838, was given in evidence, relating to the division of the landings for different kinds of boats. In this ordinance, the landings for steamboats, keel-boats, and flat-boats were designated and the duties of the harbor-master were defined. An objection by the respondent being made, that no sufficient proof had been offered as to the power of the town to pass the ordinance, the objection was obviated by the fact in the record, which showed that the respondent had introduced the ordinance as evidence. It was then insisted that the ordinance had fallen into disuse by common consent, and could not be considered as evidence of a usage or law. But from the evidence it would seem that the duties of the harbor-master were performed, and that the places of landing for the different boats were generally understood.

Whether a rule on this subject be established by an ordinance or general usage is immaterial, if the regulation has been so made as to be generally known; and this seems to have been the case at Grand Gulf, in regard to the ordinance in question.

The Rainbow arrived, and was moored within the ground designated for flat-boats, and was fastened to the bank the evening which preceded the morning of the collision. The Southern Belle, in ascending the river, arrived at Grand Gulf about daylight, — some of the witnesses say a little before, others a little after. It appears that the moon was shining, and that, in passing the flat-boat, it was light enough to read from it the name of The Southern Belle, on her wheel-house, some hundred yards from the shore. The pilot of the steamer intended to land at the steamboat wharf, three hundred and thirty feet above the place where the flat-boat was fastened. But, in approaching the wharf, he discovered The Atlantic steamer, with cattle on board, occupied it; and the wind being high, he was afraid that an attempt to land, so as to fasten to The Atlantic, might do damage, at least, to the cattle on board of that boat. To avoid this, orders were given to back the boat, and land below the wharf. In doing this, the control of the boat was lost, and the wind to the shore being high, The Southern Belle was thrown against the flat-boat, which immediately sunk her. As the steamer was falling back, it is alleged the flat-boat, for the first time, was discovered; but it was too late, under an adverse wind, to avoid the collision. George W. Smith says, The Southern Belle, by keeping on her steam, might have landed above the wharf-boat. That landing, for three hundred yards, is as good as the landing below.

At the time the steamer passed within one hundred yards of the flat-boat, it could be seen two hundred yards or more. A witness states at the time, he could distinctly see across the river. It appears from some of the witnesses, that there was space enough to land the steamer below the wharf-boat, and above the flat-boat.

Some time during Monday night, a floating log struck the bow of The Rainbow, so as to break a hole through it, but the damage in a short time was repaired. The bow was turned down the stream to avoid the force of the current.

It is objected that the flat-boat had no lights. She had a light on deck, as proved by her captain and another witness, fifteen minutes before the collision, and at the time it occurred; but as she was fastened to the shore, and from the weight of evidence was in her right place, a light was not necessary. Where a boat is anchored in the path of vessels, a light is indispensable; but it is not required where the boat is fastened to the shore, especially at a place set apart for such boats.

When a steamer is about to enter a harbor, great caution is required. There being no usage as to an open way, the vigilance is thrown upon the entering vessel. Ordinary care, under such circumstances, will not excuse a steamer for a wrong done. A vessel tied to the shore is helpless. No movement can be made by it to avoid an entering boat; therefore, the whole responsibility rests on such boat.

It is admitted that where a collision occurs, as the result of uncontrollable circumstances, no responsibility attaches to either party; but this cannot be said of the respondent. The evidence shows no fault in the flat-boat, but there was fault in the steamer. The wind was high when she approached the landing, — this should have produced in her officers the utmost vigilance. That they were sensible of this, was shown by their not attempting to fasten to The Atlantic.' But they were highly culpable in not keeping up the steam, so as to have the control of their boat. The river was open, so that, had the steam power been kept up, the boat might have been turned against the wind, and made a safe landing. But her headway had been lost by backing, so that she became as a log driven by the winds and waves, and in this manner was thrown upon the flat-boat.

The evidence authorizes the inference that the flat-boat was seen from on board the steamer as she passed it in running up to the wharf. It is inconceivable that others should be able to see the opposite shore of the river, and for a hundred and fifty yards plainly discern the flat-boat from the steamboat wharf, while the officers of the steamer, in passing so near the shore, should not have observed it.   The responsible officers of a steamer, when about to land, are not presumed to close their eyes ; on the contrary, all experience requires an exercise of uncommon vigilance.   Landing a boat, especially when the wind is high, is always attended with more or less danger.   After making due allowance for the lights of the steamer, which enabled persons from the flat-boat or wharf to see the steamer, and read her name while passing, the vision of those on board the steamer could not have been so defective, or blinded by her lights, as not to perceive the flat-boat.   The captain of the steamer was not sworn, and from this a strong presumption arises that his evidence would have been against his owners.   He must have been on the alert in landing, as his duty required, and indeed as the evidence shows he was.

There is no ground of suspicion that the officers of The Southern Belle designed to injure The Rainbow, — on the contrary, when it was too late, they endeavored to avoid the collision. Their fault consisted in not landing above the wharf-boat, or in not keeping up the steam, so as to give them the control of the boat.   The flat-boat was plainly discernible from the wharf-boat; and if the officers of the steamer did not see it, it was because they were wanting in vigilance.   But whether they saw it, or not, the respondents are liable for the damage done.   The decree of the circuit court is reversed.

THE UNITED STATES, PLAINTIFFS, *v.* WILLIAM G. SHACKLEFORD.

The act of congress, passed on the 20th of July, 1840, (5 Stats. at Large, 394,) confers upon the courts of the United States the power to make all necessary rules and regulations, for conforming the impanelling of juries to the laws and usages in force in the State.

This power includes that of regulating the challenges of jurors, whether peremptory or for cause, and in cases both civil and criminal, with the exception, in criminal cases, of treason and other crimes, of which the punishment is declared to be death.

The act of 1790 recognizes the right of peremptory challenge in these cases, and therefore it cannot be taken away.

But this recognition does not necessarily draw along with it the qualified right, existing at common law, of challenges by the government; and unless the laws and usages of the State, adopted by rule of court, allow it on behalf of the prosecution, it should be rejected, conforming, in this respect, the practice to the state law.

THIS case came up from the circuit court of the United States for the district of Kentucky, on a certificate of division in opinion between the judges thereof.

The point of difference was thus stated.

Statement of point of disagreement.

The statement of the point upon which the disagreement of the judges happened having been made, is in these words : —

Question of difference.

In the progress of the trial of this cause, and, after the jury had been in part selected, and other jurors were presented to the prisoner, he peremptorily challenged   one of them, when the question arose, whether the defendant was entitled to any peremptory challenges ; on which question the judges were divided in opinion. Whereupon, the point of division, and the grounds thereof, are ordered to be certified to the supreme court of the United States, for its opinion and direction to this court on the case certified.

And the cause was continued to await the instructions of the supreme court.   J. CATRON.

It was submitted upon printed arguments by *Mr. Cushing,* (attorney-general,) for the United States, and by *Mr. Underwood,* for the defendant.

Mr. Justice NELSON delivered the opinion of the court.

This case comes up on a certificate of a division of opinion between the judges of the circuit court of the United States for the district of Kentucky.

The prisoner was indicted for a misdemeanor in wrongfully deserting the mails of the United States, before delivering them to the proper officer or agent, he being a mail carrier at the time, and, as such, having the mails in charge. (§ 21 of act of cong., 3d March, 1825 ; 4 Stats. at Large, 107.)

A question arose, in impanelling the jury, whether the prisoner was entitled to a peremptory challenge of one or more jurors, upon which the judges were divided in opinion.

The act of congress passed 20th July, 1840, 5 Stats. at Large, 394, provides that jurors, to serve in the courts of the United States, in each State, shall have the like qualifications, and be entitled to the like exemptions, as jurors of the highest court of law of such State now have and are entitled to, and shall hereafter from time to time have and be entitled to ; and shall be designated by ballot, lot, or otherwise, according to the mode of forming such juries now practised, and hereafter to be practised therein, so far as such mode may be practicable by the courts of the United States, or the officers thereof. " And, for this purpose, the said courts shall have power to make all necessary rules and regulations for conforming the designation, and impanelling of juries, in substance, to the laws and usages now in force in such State; and, further, shall have power by rule or order, from time to time, to conform the same to any change in these respects, which may be hereafter adopted by the legislatures of the respective States for the state courts."

The court is of opinion that the power conferred upon the federal courts to adopt "rules and regulations for conforming the designation and impanelling of juries to the laws and usages in force at the time in the State," enables them to adopt the laws and usages of the State in respect to the challenges of jurors, whether peremptory or for cause, and in cases both civil and criminal, with the exception, in criminal cases, of treason and other crimes, of which the punishment is declared to be death.

The § 30 of the crimes act of 1790, 1 Stats. at Large, 119, provides, that if persons indicted for treason against the United States shall challenge peremptorily above the number of thirty-five of the jury, or if persons indicted for any other of the offences before set forth, for which the punishment is declared to be death, shall challenge peremptorily above the number of twenty persons of the jury, the court in any of these cases shall, notwithstanding, proceed to the trial of the persons so challenging, &c.

This act of congress having expressly recognized the right of peremptory challenge in the one case of the number of thirty-five jurors, and in the other of twenty, they should be regarded as excepted out of the power conferred upon the courts to regulate the subject by rule or order under the aforesaid act of 1840.

The right of challenge in the cases specified in the act of 1790, in respect to the number of jurors, is derived from the common law, which allowed thirty-five in cases of treason, and twenty in cases of felony.   4 Bl. Com. 354, 355; 12 Wheat. 483.

That law also gave to the king a qualified right of challenge in these cases, which had the effect to set aside the juror till the panel was gone through with, without assigning cause, and if there was not a full jury without the person so challenged, then the cause must be assigned or the juror would be sworn.

The court is of opinion that the right of challenge by the prisoner recognized by the act of 1790, does not necessarily draw along with it this qualified right, existing at common law, by the government; and that, unless the laws or usages of the State, adopted by rule under the act of 1840, allow it on behalf of the prosecution, it should be rejected, conforming in this respect the practice to the state law.

It does not appear in the case before us, whether or not the court below had adopted the state law under the act of 1840, as it existed at or previous to the proceedings certified, and hence we are not enabled to express any opinion upon the particular question certified. But the opinion expressed upon the general question will enable the court below to dispose of the case, without any amendment of the record, or further hearing of the case.

The cause is, therefore, remanded to the court below to proceed according to the foregoing opinion.

SUSAN E. CONNER, WIDOW OF HENRY L. CONNER, DECEASED, PLAINTIFF IN ERROR, v. WILLIAM ST. JOHN ELLIOTT, ADMINISTRATOR, AND DANIEL W. BRICKLE AND WIFE ET AL., HEIRS OF HENRY L. CONNER, DECEASED.

The first clause of the second section of the fourth article of the constitution provides that "the citizens of each State shall be entitled to all the privileges and immunities of citizens in the several States."

The court will not describe and define these privileges and immunities in a general classification, preferring to decide each case as it may come up.

The law of Louisiana gives a community of acquets or gains between married persons, where the marriage is contracted within the State, or where the marriage is contracted out of the State, and the parties afterwards go there to live.

The privilege thus conferred upon the wife, does not extend, by virtue of the clause in the constitution above quoted, to a native-born citizen of Louisiana, who was married while under age, in the State of Mississippi, in which State was her domicile together with her husband during the continuance of the marriage. Land in Louisiana, acquired by the husband during the marriage, was not subject to the Louisiana law, in respect to the community of acquets or gain.

This right was one which attached to the contract of marriage, which the State of Louisiana had a right to regulate; and was not one of the personal rights of a citizen, within the meaning of the constitution.

THIS case was brought up from the supreme court of Louisiana, by a writ of error issued under the 25th section of the judiciary act.

The case is stated in the opinion of the court.

It was argued by *Mr. Henderson*, for the plaintiff in error, and by *Mr. Benjamin*, for the defendants.

Mr. Justice CURTIS delivered the opinion of the court.

In the course of proceedings which were had in Louisiana, under the laws and in the courts of that State, to determine the rights of parties interested in the succession of Henry L. Conner, deceased, a citizen of the State of Mississippi, his widow, who is the plaintiff in error in this case, filed in the district court of the tenth judicial district of the State of Louisiana, a petition, claiming to be entitled to her rights of marital community, as they exist under the laws of that State. These rights having been denied by the district court, an appeal was prosecuted to the supreme court; and it was there held that inasmuch as the marriage through which the appellant claimed was not in fact contracted in Louisiana, nor in contemplation of a matrimonial domicile in that State, and the spouses had never resided therein; the wife was not a partner in community with the husband by force of the laws of Louisiana.

On this writ of error, it neither is nor can be denied that the supreme court of Louisiana has correctly declared and applied the law of that State to this case. But it is insisted that this law deprives the plaintiff in error, a citizen of the State of Mississippi, of one of the privileges of a citizen in the State of Louisiana, and therefore is in contravention of the first clause of the second section of the fourth article of the constitution, which provides that "the citizens of each State shall be entitled to all the privileges and immunities of citizens in the several States."

It appears upon the record that this question was raised by the pleadings, and presented to and decided by the highest court of the State; it is therefore open here, upon this writ of error, for final determination by this court, under the twenty-fifth section of the judiciary act of 1789, 1 Stats. at Large, 85.

It appears that the plaintiff in error, though a native-born citizen of Louisiana, was married in the State of Mississippi, while under age, with the consent of her guardian, to a citizen of the latter State, and that their domicile, during the duration of their marriage, was in Mississippi. But, while it continued, the husband acquired a plantation, and other real property, in Louisiana. If the marriage had been contracted in Louisiana, the code of that State, then in force, Code of 1808, art. 3, § 4, would have superinduced the rights of community. And at the time when the property in question was purchased by the husband, in 1841, the code of 1825, then in force, contained the following articles: —

"Art. 2369. Every marriage contracted in this State superinduces, of right, partnership or community of acquets or gains, if there be no stipulation to the contrary."

"Art. 2370. A marriage contracted out of this State, between persons who afterwards come here to live, is also subjected to the community of acquets with respect to such property as is acquired after their arrival."

And it is insisted that, as these articles gave to what is termed in the argument a Louisiana widow the right of marital community, the laws of the State could not constitutionally deny, as it is admitted they did in fact deny, the same rights to all widows, citizens of the United States, though not married in

Louisiana, or residing there during the marriage, and while the property in question was acquired.

In other words, that, as the laws of Louisiana provide that a contract of marriage made in that State, or the residence of persons there in the relation created by marriage, shall give rise to certain rights on the part of each in property acquired within that State, by force of the article of the constitution above recited, all citizens of the United States, wherever married and residing, obtain the same rights in property acquired in that State during the marriage. We do not deem it needful to attempt to define the meaning of the word *privileges* in this clause of the constitution. It is safer, and more in accordance with the duty of a judicial tribunal, to leave its meaning to be determined, in each case, upon a view of the particular rights asserted and denied therein. And especially is this true, when we are dealing with so broad a provision, involving matters not only of great delicacy and importance, but which are of such a character, that any merely abstract definition could scarcely be correct; and a failure to make it so would certainly produce mischief.

It is sufficient for this case to say that, according to the express words and clear meaning of this clause, no privileges are secured by it, except those which belong to citizenship. Rights, attached by the law to contracts, by reason of the place where such contracts are made or executed, wholly irrespective of the citizenship of the parties to those contracts, cannot be deemed " privileges of a citizen," within the meaning of the constitution.

Of that character are the rights now in question. They are incidents, ingrafted by the law of the State on the contract of marriage. And, in obedience to that principle of universal jurisprudence, which requires a contract to be governed by the law of the place where it is made and to be performed, the law of Louisiana undertakes to control these incidents of a contract of marriage made within the State by persons domiciled there; but leaves such contracts, made elsewhere, to be governed by the laws of the places where they may be entered into. In this, there is no departure from any sound principle, and there can be no just cause of complaint.

The law of the State further provides, that if married persons come to Louisiana to reside, and acquire property there during such residence, they shall be deemed nuptial partners in respect to such property; but if the domicile of the marriage continues out of Louisiana, the relative rights of the married persons may be regulated by the laws of the place of such domicile, even in respect to property acquired by one of them in Louisiana.

50 *

That the first of these rules, which extends the laws of the State to married persons coming to reside and acquiring property therein, is a proper exercise of legislative power, has not been questioned. But it is insisted that the last, which leaves the rights of non-resident married persons in respect to property in Louisiana to be governed by the laws of their domicile, deprives the wife of her rights as a citizen in property acquired by the husband during marriage in Louisiana. The answer to this has been already indicated. The laws of Louisiana affix certain incidents to a contract of marriage there made, or there partly or wholly executed, not because those who enter into such contracts are citizens of the State, but because they there make or perform the contract. And they refuse to affix these incidents to such contracts, made and executed elsewhere, not because the married persons are not citizens of Louisiana, but because their contract being made and performed under the laws of some other State or country, it is deemed proper not to interfere, by Louisiana laws, with the relations of married persons out of that State. Whether persons contracting marriage in Louisiana are citizens of that or some other State, or aliens, the law equally applies to their contract; and so, whether persons married and domiciled elsewhere, be or be not citizens or aliens, the law fails to regulate their rights. The law does not discriminate between citizens of the State and other persons; it discriminates between contracts only. Such discrimination has no connection with the clause in the constitution now in question. If a law of Louisiana were to give to the partners *inter sese* certain peculiar rights, provided they should reside within the State, and carry on the partnership-trade there, we think it could not be maintained that all copartners, citizens of the United States, residing and doing business elsewhere, must have those peculiar rights by force of the constitution of the United States, any more than it could be maintained that, because a law of Louisiana gives certain damages on protested bills of exchange, drawn or indorsed within that State, the same damages must be recoverable on bills drawn elsewhere in favor of citizens of the United States.

The rights asserted in this case, before the supreme court of Louisiana, are not privileges of citizenship; consequently, there is no error in the judgment of that court, which is hereby affirmed.

WILLIAM C. PEASE, PLAINTIFF IN ERROR, v. JOHN PECK, SURVIV-
ING PARTNER OF THE FIRM OF PECK AND WALTON.

Where a law, as published, has been acknowledged by the people and received a harmonious interpretation for a long series of years, the propriety may well be doubted
of referring to an ancient manuscript to show that the law as published was not an
exact copy of the original manuscript.

Moreover, in this case, a subsequent legislative authority sanctioned the law as previously published, and thereby adopted it as a future rule.

The original manuscript of the laws for the territory of Michigan left out the saving
of "beyond seas" in the statute of limitations, but the published law contained this
exception. It ought now to be considered as included.

As a general rule, this court adopts the construction which state courts put upon state
laws. But there are exceptions. Some of these exceptions stated.

THIS case was brought up by writ of error for the circuit court
of the United States for the district of Michigan.

The case is stated in the opinion of the court.

It was argued by *Mr. Lawrence*, for the plaintiff in error,
adopting also an argument filed by *Mr. Emmons* and *Mr. Grey*;
and for the defendant in error by *Mr. Badger*, upon a brief filed
by himself and *Mr. Carlisle.*

Mr. Justice GRIER delivered the opinion of the court.

Peck, the plaintiff below, declared against Pease in an action
of debt on a judgment obtained in the circuit court of the territory (now State) of Michigan, at the term of January, 1836.
The defendant pleaded the statute of limitations of eight years;
to which the plaintiff replied that he did not at any time reside
in the State of Michigan, but in parts "beyond seas," to wit,
in the state of New York.

The defendant demurred to the replication.

The objection to this replication is not to the construction of
the statute which is assumed by the plaintiff to govern the case,
or an allegation that, according to the settled construction of the
word "beyond seas," the replication is defective. But it is intended to deny that the statute of limitations pleaded has any
such provision in it. The question is, therefore, not what is the
construction of an admitted statute, but what is the statute.
For each party admits that if the statute be as claimed by his
opponent, his construction of it is correct.

By the ordinance of 1787, "for the government of the territory of the United States northwest of the River Ohio," it is
provided "that the governor and judges, or a majority of them,
shall adopt and publish in the district such laws of the original
States, criminal and civil, as may be necessary and best suited to
the circumstances of the district, and report them to congress
from time to time, which laws shall be in force in the district

until the organization of the general assembly therein, unless disapproved of by congress; but afterwards the legislature shall have authority to alter them, as they shall see fit."

By an act of congress of 24th April, 1820, 3 Stats. at Large, 565, the laws of Michigan territory in force, were ordered to be printed under the direction of the secretary of state, and a competent number distributed to the people of said territory.

In the volume of the laws so published by authority in that year, is a statute of limitations, which the governor and judges certify to have been "adopted from the laws of the State of Vermont, as far as necessary and suitable to the circumstances of the territory of Michigan."

The eighth section of this act provides that "actions of debt or *scire facias* on judgment must be brought within eight years after the rendition of the judgment," &c.

The 10th section enacts that "this act shall not extend to bar any infant, *feme covert*, person imprisoned, or beyond seas, or without the United States, or *non compos mentis*," &c.

On the 21st of April, 1825, the legislature of the territory, which had been now organized, appointed certain individuals to revise the laws of the territory. They were required "to examine all the laws then in force, to revise, consolidate, and digest them, making such alterations or additions as they may deem expedient."

On the 27th of December, 1826, the commissioners report to the legislature the statutes as revised by them, stating that considerable alterations and some additions had been made by them. These laws received the sanction of the legislature, and were published by authority, in 1827. By this it appears that they adopted the statute of limitations, and the 10th section thereof, from the published acts of 1820, and as stated above. Again, in 1833, "the laws of the territory of Michigan were condensed, arranged, and passed by the fifth legislative council," and were again published under authority of the legislature. The 10th section is again stated in the same words.

The law, as thus published, has been acknowledged by the people and the courts, and received a harmonious interpretation for thirty years. But it has lately been discovered that the text or original manuscript adopted by the governor and judges in 1820, differs from the printed statutes, as published by authority, as to the words of this 10th section. It reads as follows: "Persons imprisoned or without the United States," — having the words "beyond seas" erased; whereas the printed statutes retain the words "beyond seas," and add or interpolate the word "or."

It is no doubt true, as a general rule, that the mistake of a

transcriber or printer cannot change the law ; and that when the
statutes published by authority are found to differ from the
original on file among the public archives, that the courts will
receive the latter as containing the expressed will of the legislature in preference to the former.   Yet, as the people who are governed by the laws, and the courts who administer them, practically
know the law only from the authorized publication of them, the
propriety of recurring to ancient, altered, and erased manuscripts,
for the purpose of changing their construction after a lapse of
thirty years, and after their construction has been long settled by
the courts, and has entered as an element into the contracts and
business of the citizens, may well be doubted.   The reception
and long acquiescence in them, as printed and distributed by
authority, by those who had it always in their power to
alter or annul them, and did not, may justly be treated as a
ratification of them in that form by the sovereign people.   The
maxim *communis error facit jus*, though said to be dangerous in
its application, "because it sets up a misconception of the law,
for destruction of the law," might here find a safe and proper
application, and make it one of the "some cases" in which it is
said the law so favors the public good, that it will permit a common error to pass for right.   Noy's Maxims, 87, 4 Inst. 240.

But we need not have recourse to any doubtful speculations
in order to arrive at a satisfactory solution of this question.   The
laws reported by the governor and judges were intended to be
temporary, and to remain in force only till the territory should
be fully organized, as provided by the ordinance.   After such
organization, "the legislature is authorized to alter them as
they see fit."   Accordingly, when the territory of Michigan
was so organized, by the election of such council, legislature, or
"general assembly," they proceeded at once to have a code or
digest of the laws reported for the future government of the
territory, and they adopt, reject, alter, and add to the former laws
"as they saw fit."   After the promulgation of their code, that
of the governor and judges is entirely supplanted, and has no
longer any force or effect whatever.   Those who look for the
rule of action which is to govern them, seek it no longer in the
code which has been abrogated, and, having effected its temporary purpose, has become obsolete and null, but in that which
has the sanction of their own legislature.   The declaration of
the legislative will is to be sought from documents originating
with them, or published by their sanction.   The original documents reported by the judges may be the best evidence of what
statutes they intended temporarily to adopt, and what was their
will and intention, but cannot be received as any evidence of the
will and intention of a legislature ordaining a new and permanent

system of laws under powers delegated to them by congress and the people of the territory. It may well be presumed, that the legislature had no knowledge of this newly discovered erasure in the original, and supposed interpolation in the printed copy of the laws, reported by the judges in 1820; and that they adopted the law as they found it in the copy, — printed by authority, and "distributed to the people of the territory." They certainly had power to do so, and having done so, it would be folly to say that they intended to adopt some other words as the expression of their will, to be found only in a document reposing in the crypts of the secretary's office, and which they had probably never seen. But if we assume that they had seen this document, and were aware of its discrepancy from the published law, then their adoption of the latter would be conclusive. On either hypothesis this original document can furnish no evidence of the intention or will of the legislature. It must be remembered that there is no allegation or pretence, that the acts published by authority of the legislature differ from the original reported to them and adopted by them.

That is the only original, if there be any such in existence, by which the printed copy could be corrected or amended. But to correct or amend the declared will of the legislature, as published under their authority, by the words of a document which did not emanate from them, which it is most probable they never saw, or if seen, they did not see fit to adopt where it differed from the published statutes, would be, in our opinion, judicial legislation, and arbitrary assumption.

The only argument which has been urged, which could lead us to doubt the justness of this conclusion is, that the supreme court of Michigan have, it is said, come to a different decision on this question. We entertain the highest respect for that learned court, and in any question affecting the construction of their own laws, where we entertained any doubt, would be glad to be relieved from doubt and responsibility by reposing on their decision. There are, it is true, many *dicta* to be found in our decisions, averring that the courts of the United States are bound to follow the decisions of the state courts on the construction of their own laws. But although this may be a correct yet a rather strong expression of a general rule, it cannot be received as the enunciation of a maxim of universal application. Accordingly, our reports furnish many cases of exceptions to it. In all cases where there is a settled construction of the laws of a State, by its highest judicature, established by admitted precedent, it is the practice of the courts of the United States to receive and adopt it without criticism or further nquiry. But when this court have first decided a question arising under state laws, we do not feel bound to surrender our convictions on account of a contrary subsequent decision of a state court, as in the case of Rowan v. Runnels, 5 How. 139. When the decisions of the state court are not consistent, we do not feel bound to follow the last, if it is contrary to our own convictions, — and much more is this the case, where, after a long course of consistent decisions, some new light suddenly springs up, or an excited public opinion has elicited new doctrines, subversive of former safe precedent. Cases may exist also, when a cause is got up in a state court for the very purpose of anticipating our decision of a question known to be pending in this court. Nor do we feel bound in any case in which a point is first raised in the courts of the United States, and has been decided in a circuit court, to reverse that decision contrary to our own convictions, in order to conform to a state decision made in the mean time. Such decisions have not the character of established precedent declarative of the settled law of a State.

Parties who, by the constitution and laws of the United States, have a right to have their controversies decided in their tribunals, have a right to demand the unbiassed judgment of the court. The theory upon which jurisdiction is conferred on the courts of the United States, in controversies between citizens of different States, has its foundation in the supposition that, possibly the state tribunal might not be impartial between their own citizens and foreigners.

The question presented in the present case is one in which the interests of citizens of other States come directly in conflict with those of the citizens of Michigan. The territorial law in question had been received and acted upon for thirty years, in the words of the published statute. It had received a settled construction by the courts of the United States as well as those of the State. It had entered as an element into the contracts and business of men. On a sudden, a manuscript statute differing from the known public law, is disinterred from the lumber room of obsolete documents ; a new law is promulgated by judicial constrution, which, by retroaction, destroys vested rights of property of citizens of other States, while it protects the citizens of Michigan from the payment of admitted debts.

We think that such a case peculiarly calls upon us not to surrender our clear convictions and unbiassed judgment to the authority of the new state decision, and to render a judgment in favor of the plaintiff, which we do by affirming the judgment of the circuit court.

Mr. Justice DANIEL and Mr. Justice CAMPBELL dissented.

Mr. Justice CAMPBELL, dissenting.

The decision of this case depends upon the following facts. The territorial government of Michigan was organized under the ordinance of 1787, for the government of the Northwest Territory. The governor and judges of that territory "were authorized to adopt and publish such of the laws of the original States, criminal and civil, as may be necessary and best suited to the circumstances of the territory, and report them to congress from time to time; which laws shall remain in force until the organization of the general assembly therein, unless disapproved by congress. In 1820, the statute of limitations of Vermont was adopted by the council. That statute contains an exception which reads, " persons imprisoned, or beyond seas, without the United States."

The copy filed by the judges, and now found in the archives of Michigan, reads, " persons imprisoned or without the United States," the words " beyond seas " being erased in that copy. It is apparent that the two statutes are to the same effect.

The copy, as it is now found in the archives of Michigan, was reported to congress. The printed publication of the laws was as follows: " persons imprisoned or beyond seas, or without the United States." This error has been continued through the various publications of the laws of Michigan until the present time. But I have not been able to find that the statute, as published, has ever received the sanction of the legislative department of the government. The act, in the various reports and references of the legislature, has been described as an act of a particular title, or as included in the general term of " laws in force," without identifying it as the act published in any of the compilations which have been circulated through the State. I have no evidence of any series of decisions of the courts of Michigan on this subject; none was produced on the argument; and the public opinion that may exist in Michigan as to what makes its statute law, must be a most fallible rule of judgment. The statute laws of a State exist in a permanent form, and are unchangeable, except by public authority, and are not to be ascertained from any popular impression on the subject. If any mischief has arisen from the vicious publications, it belongs to the legislative authority of the State to afford the indemnity. It is admitted that the statute, as contained in the original roll, will bar the plaintiff's claim, and that he is within the exception contained in the printed laws. The question for the court is, what is the evidence on which it should depend to prove the existence of the statute of a State? The act of congress of the 26th of May, 1790, to prescribe the mode in which the public acts, records, and judicial proceedings, in each State shall be authenticated, so as to take effect in every other State, provides, "that the acts of the legislatures of the several States shall be authenticated by having the seal of their respective States affixed thereto," 1 Stats. at Large, 122.

This court, in the United States v. Amedy, 11 Wheat. 392, said, "no other or further formality is required; and the seal itself is supposed to import perfect verity. In Patterson v. Winn, 5 Pet. 233, the court said of the exemplification of a grant, that it is admissible in evidence, as being record proof of as high nature as the original. It is a recognition, in the most solemn form, by the government itself, of the validity of its own grant, under its own seal, and imports absolute verity as matter of record." We have before us an exemplified copy of the act of Michigan, and from that evidence we learn what is preserved in her archives as the act adopted by the governor and judges in 1820, and referred to in the subsequent reports and acts of her legislature as "An act for the limitation of suits on penal statutes, criminal prosecutions, and actions at law, adopted May 15, 1820.

The authorities are explicit to the effect that this evidence is the highest that can be offered of a statute. That the seal of the State, when properly affixed, is conclusive evidence of the existence of a statute, is the result of several State authorities. United States v. Johns, 4 Dall. 412; Henthorn v. Doe, 1 Blackf. 157; State v. Carr, 5 N. H. 367. The supreme court of Michigan have had this subject under consideration, and after repeated arguments and great deliberation, have decided that this printed statute does not form a part of the laws of that State, but that the original roll must be received as the exact record of the legislative will. The question is so entirely of a domestic character, and belongs so particularly to the constituted authorities of the State to determine, that I cannot bring myself to oppose their conclusion on the subject.

In my opinion the judgment of the circuit court is erroneous, and should be reversed.

This cause came on to be heard on the transcript of the record from the circuit court of the United States for the district of Michigan, and was argued by counsel; on consideration whereof, it is now here ordered and adjudged by this court that the judgment of the said circuit court in this cause be and the same is hereby affirmed, with costs and interests, until paid, at the same rate per annum that similar judgments bear in the courts of the State of Michigan.

Mr. Justice CAMPBELL and Mr. Justice DANIEL dissenting.

JACOB STRADER AND OTHERS, PLAINTIFFS IN ERROR, *v.* CHRISTO-
PHER GRAHAM.

Where a case is dismissed for want of jurisdiction this court cannot give a judgment
for costs.

74 THIS case was dismissed for want of jurisdiction, at December
term, 1850, 10 How. 82.

At the present term, *Mr. Crittenden,* of counsel for the defendant in error, moved the court to amend the judgment entered in
this cause at the December term, 1850, and to give a judgment
for the costs in this court in favor of his client.　Whereupon it is
now here considered by the court that this court cannot give a
judgment for costs in a case dismissed for want of jurisdiction,
and it appearing to this court that this cause has been dismissed
for want of jurisdiction, it is thereupon now here ordered by
the court that the said motion be and the same is hereby overruled.

INDEX

PRINCIPAL MATTERS.

BILLS OF EXCEPTIONS, (*Continued.*)

7. But to present a question to this court, the subordinate tribunal must ascertain the facts upon which the judgment or opinion excepted to is founded. *Ibid.*

8. Therefore, where there was a reference in the circuit court, and the bill of exceptions set out the objections to the award together with the testimony of the arbitrator who was examined in open court, and that testimony showed the facts upon which the objections were founded, it was a sufficient exception. *Ibid.*

9. If an arbitrator embraces in his award matter not submitted, and includes the result in a single conclusion, so as to render it impossible to separate the matters referred to from those which have not been, the award is bad. *Ibid.*

10. But in this case, the averments in the declaration and assignment of breaches in the covenant cover the ground upon which the arbitrator rested his award; and his conclusion is a final decision which this court cannot revise either upon the allegation of mistakes in law or mistakes in fact. *Ibid.*

BILLS OF LADING.

See COMMERCIAL LAW.

BOTTOMRY BOND.

See COMMERCIAL LAW.

CALIFORNIA.

1. Where there was a grant of land in California, subject to the condition that the grantee should build a house upon it, and have it inhabited within a year from the date of the grant, and also that he should obtain a judicial possession and measurement or survey of it, the evidence shows sufficient reasons for a non-compliance on the part of the grantee. *United States v. Reading*, 1.

2. This court again decides, as in Fremont v. United States, 17 How. 560, that a mere omission to comply with these conditions would not necessarily amount to a forfeiture, unless there were circumstances which showed an intention to abandon the property. *Ibid.*

3. Although the title did not become definitive until the grant was approved by the departmental assembly, yet an immediate interest passed by the grant from the governor, whose duty it was (and not that of the grantee) to submit the case to the departmental assembly, and, if they should reject it, then to lay the case before the supreme government of the Republic. *Ibid.*

4. If the governor failed to execute this duty, the title remained as it was after the grant was issued, and is sufficient for confirmation under the act of congress, passed on March 3, 1851, (9 Stats. at Large, 631.) *Ibid.*

5. The evidence in the present case shows that the grantee was a naturalized citizen of the Mexican Republic, and the fact that he joined the troops of the United States when war broke out with Mexico, furnishes no evidence of his intention to abandon the property, nor any reason why the grant should be forfeited. *Ibid.*

6. The title of the family of Arguello confirmed to the following described tract of land in California, namely, bounded on the south by the Arrogo, or Creek of San Francisquito, on the north by the Creek San Mateo, on the east by the Esteras, or waters of the bay of San Francisco, and on the west by the eastern borders of the valley known as the Cañada de Raimundo. *Arguello v. United States*, 539.

7. On the 26th of November, 1835, the governor of California gave an order that the petitioner should have a tract of land without specifying the boundaries, which was done by an order, having the formalities of a definitive title on the 27th. This latter document must govern the case. No good title is shown which can include the valley on the west.

8. The testimony upon this point examined. *Ibid.*

9. The decree of 1824 and regulations of 1828 forbid the colonization of territory comprehended within twenty leagues of the boundaries of any foreign state, and within ten leagues of the sea-coast, without the consent of the supreme executive power. *Ibid.*

10. But this restriction only included grants to empresarios, who intended to introduce large colonies of foreigners. It did not prohibit grants of land within those limits to natives of the country. *Ibid.*

11. The court again decides (as in United States v. Reading, page 1) that it was the duty of the governor of California, and not that of the grantee, to submit a grant of land to the departmental assembly. *United States v Cruz Cervantes*, 553.

12. And moreover, when the case was submitted, and a committee reported in favor of the grant, but no final action appeared to have been had upon the matter, the grantee should have the benefit of the presumption of the decision in his favor. *Ibid.*

CHANCERY, (*Continued.*)

21. The defendants were jointly interested with the complainants in one parcel embraced in the partition suit. The ancestor having conveyed away the property covered by the deed alleged to have been fraudulently obtained, the heirs had no interest in the partition of it. *Ibid.*

22. These proceedings being *in rem*, only operated in respect to the title as against them, upon that part of the property in which they had a joint interest. *Ibid.*

23. A stockholder in a corporation has a remedy in chancery against the directors, to prevent them from doing acts which would amount to a violation of the charter, or to prevent any misapplication of their capital or profits which might lessen the value of the shares, if the acts intended to be done amount to what is called in law a breach of trust or duty. *Dodge* v. *Woolsey*, 331.

24. So also a stockholder has a remedy against individuals, in whatever character they profess to act, if the subject of complaint is an imputed violation of a corporate franchise, or the denial of a right growing out of it, for which there is not an adequate remedy at law. *Ibid.*

25. Therefore, where the directors of a bank refused to take the proper measures to resist the collection of a tax, which they themselves believed to have been imposed upon them in violation of their charter, this refusal amounted to what is termed in law a breach of trust, a stockholder had a right to file a bill in chancery asking for such a remedy as the case might require. *Ibid.*

26. If the stockholder be a resident of another State than that in which the bank and persons attempting to violate its charter, or commit a breach of trust or duty have their domicile, he may file his bill in the courts of the United States. He has this right under the constitution and laws of the United States. *Ibid.*

27. The rights and duties of this court examined and explained, as an ultimate tribunal to determine whether laws enacted by congress, or by state legislatures or decisions of state courts are in conflict with the constitution of the United States. *Ibid.*

28. Where the State of Ohio chartered a bank in 1845, in which charter was stipulated the amount of tax which the bank should pay, in lieu of all taxes to which said company or the stockholders thereof, on account of stock owned therein, would otherwise be subject; and in 1852, the legislature passed an act levying taxes upon the bank to a greater amount and founded upon a different principle. This act is in conflict with the constitution of the United States, as impairing the obligation of a contract, and therefore void. *Ibid.*

29. The fact that the people of the State had, in 1851, adopted a new constitution, in which it was declared that taxes should be imposed upon banks in the mode which the act of 1852 purported to carry out, cannot release the State from the obligations and duties imposed upon it by the constitution of the United States. *Ibid.*

30. The case of the Piqua Branch of the State Bank of Ohio *v.* Knoop, 16 How. 369, again affirmed. *Ibid.*

31. In the State of Mississippi, a judgment of forfeiture was rendered against the Commercial Bank of Natchez, and a trustee was appointed to take charge of the books and assets of the bank. *Bacon* v. *Robertson*, 480.

32. Under the laws of Mississippi and the general principles of equity jurisprudence, the surplus of the assets which may remain after the payment of debts and expenses, belongs to the stockholders of the bank. *Ibid.*

33. The early and late English cases examined, as to what becomes of the property of a corporation whose charter has been forfeited by a judicial sentence. *Ibid.*

34. The modern rules of the English courts have been adopted in the United States, extending the protection of chancery over the civil rights of members of moneyed corporations, and recognizing the existence of distinct and individual rights in their capital and business. *Ibid.*

35. The trustee is estopped from denying the title of the stockholders to a distribution. *Ibid.*

36. The courts of the United States have jurisdiction over the case, and a bill can be maintained, filed by a number of stockholders owning one fifth part of the capital stock, suing for themselves and such of the stockholders as were not citizens of Mississippi, nor defendants in the bill. *Ibid.*

37. No objections to a master's report can be made which were not taken before the master; nor after a decree *pro confesso* can a defendant go before the master without a special order, but the accounts are to be taken *ex parte*. *McMicken* v *Perin*, 507.

CHANCERY, (*Continued.*)

88. An appeal will not lie from the refusal of a court to open a former decree; nor have the circuit courts power to set aside their decrees in equity, on motion, after the term at which they were rendered. *Ibid.*

CITIZENSHIP.

1. The change of citizenship from one State to another must be made with a *bond fide* intention of becoming a citizen of the State to which the party removes. *Jones* v. *League,* 76.

2. It was not such a *bond fide* change where the plaintiff only made a short absence, and it appeared from the deed under which he claimed that he was in fact prosecuting the suit for the benefit of his grantor, (who could not sue,) receiving a portion of the land recovered as an equivalent for paying one third of the costs and superintending the prosecution of the suit. *Ibid.*

3. In such a case, the federal court has no jurisdiction. *Ibid.*

4. The first clause of the second section of the fourth article of the constitution provides that "the citizens of each State shall be entitled to all the privileges and immunities of citizens in the several States." *Conner* v. *Elliott,* 591.

5. The court will not describe and define these privileges and immunities in a general classification, preferring to decide each case as it may come up. *Ibid.*

6. The law of Louisiana gives a community of acquets or gains between married persons, where the marriage is contracted within the State, or where the marriage is contracted out of the State, and the parties afterwards go there to live. *Ibid.*

7. The privilege thus conferred upon the wife does not extend, by virtue of the clause in the constitution above quoted, to a native-born citizen of Louisiana, who was married while under age, in the State of Mississippi, in which State was her domicile together with her husband during the continuance of the marriage. Land in Louisiana, acquired by the husband during the marriage, was not subject to the Louisiana law, in respect to the community of acquets or gain. *Ibid.*

8. This right was one which attached to the contract of marriage, which the State of Louisiana had a right to regulate; and was not one of the personal rights of a citizen, within the meaning of the constitution. *Ibid.*

COLLISION.

1. Where a large steamer was coming down Long Island Sound, on a foggy morning, with a speed of sixteen or seventeen miles per hour, in the direct track of the coasting trade, and run down a vessel which was lying at anchor, (the weather being perfectly calm,) the steamer was grossly in fault. *McCready* v. *Goldsmith,* 89.

2. The vessel at anchor cannot be considered in fault for omitting to have horns blown or empty barrels beaten. The usage that this is done in such a case is not established; and, moreover, it is doubtful whether such a precaution would have been of any service. *Ibid.*

3. Where a vessel was lying at anchor in the port of New York, and a steamboat came down the Hudson River with wind and tide in her favor, and also having several heavily loaded barges fastened on each side of her, and came into collision with the vessel which was lying at anchor, it was a gross fault in the steamboat to proceed, at night, on her way with a speed of from eight to ten miles per hour. *Steamboat New York* v. *Rea,* 223.

4. Moreover, the steamboat had not a sufficient look-out. *Ibid.*

5. The statutes of the State of New York, regulating the light which the vessel lying at anchor was to show, have no binding force in the present case. The rule for the decision of the federal courts is derived from the general admiralty law. *Ibid.*

6. Police regulations for the accommodation and safety of vessels in a harbor may be enacted by the local authorities. *Ibid.*

7. In a collision which occurred upon the Mississippi River between an ascending and descending steamboat, whereby the former was destroyed, the collision was chiefly owing to the neglect, by the ascending boat, of the rule which requires the ascending boat to keep near the right bank, and the descending one to keep near the middle of the river. *Goslee* v. *Shute's Executor,* 463.

8. Moreover, the ascending boat had not a sufficient watch, and in other respects its officers were to blame. *Ibid.*

9. Where a collision took place in the bay of Mobile between a schooner and a steamer, the latter was in fault. *Steamer Oregon* v. *Rocca.* 570

COLLISION, (*Continued.*)

10. The rule of this court, is, when a steamer approaches a sailing vessel, the steamer is required to exercise the necessary precaution to avoid a collision; and if this be not done, *primâ facie*, the steamer is chargeable with fault. *Ibid.*

11. Whether this rule be regarded or the weight of the testimony, the steamer must, in the present case, be considered in the wrong. *Ibid.*

12. The general rule is, for a sailing vessel meeting a steamer, to keep her course, while the steamer takes the necessary measures to avoid a collision. *Crockett v. Newton*, 581.

13. And though this rule should not be observed when the circumstances are such that it is apparent its observance must occasion a collision, while a departure from it will prevent one, yet it must be a strong case which puts the sailing vessel in the wrong for obeying the rule. *Ibid.*

14. The present is not such a strong case, and therefore the steamer must be condemned in the damages and costs resulting from a collision between herself and a sailing vessel. *Ibid.*

15. The general rule is, for a sailing vessel meeting a steamer, to keep her course, while the steamer takes the necessary measures to avoid a collision. *Ibid.*

16. And though this rule should not be observed when the circumstances are such that it is apparent its observance must occasion a collision, while a departure from it will prevent one, yet it must be a strong case which puts the sailing vessel in the wrong for obeying the rule. *Ibid.*

17. The present is not such a strong case, and therefore the steamer must be condemned in the damages and costs resulting from a collision between herself and a sailing vessel. *Ibid.*

18. Where a regulation was made in one of the harbors of the Mississippi River, assigning their positions to different species of boats, if the regulation was generally known, it was the duty of all persons to conform to it. *Culbertson v. Shaw*, 584.

19. Where a flat-boat was moored at the place designated for flat-boats, and a steamboat, in attempting to land, came into collision with and sunk the flat-boat, the steamboat must be liable for the damage done. *Ibid.*

20. When a steamer is about to enter a harbor, great caution is required. Ordinary care, under such circumstances, will not excuse a steamer for a wrong done. *Ibid.*

COLOR OF TITLE.

See LIMITATION, STATUTES OF.

COMMERCIAL LAW.

1. Where a bottomry bond was taken for a larger amount than was actually advanced, with a fraudulent purpose, to enable the owner of the vessel to recover the amount of the bond from the underwriters, the bond was void. *Currington v. Pratt*, 63.

2. Not only so, but the lender of the money loses his maritime lien upon the vessel for the sum actually advanced. *Ibid.*

3. Under the admiralty law of the United States, contracts of affreightment, entered into with the master in good faith, and within the scope of his apparent authority as master, bind the vessel to the merchandise for the performance of such contracts, wholly irrespective of the ownership of the vessel, and whether the master be the agent of the general or the special owner. *Schooner Freeman v Buckingham*, 182.

4. If the general owner has allowed a third person to have the entire control, management, and employment of the vessel, and thus become owner *pro hac vice*, the general owner must be deemed to consent that the special owner or his master may create liens binding on the interest of the general owner in the vessel, as security for the performance of such contracts of affreightment. *Ibid.*

5. But no such implication arises in reference to bills of lading for property not shipped, designed to be instruments of fraud; and they create no lien on the interest of the general owner, although the special owner was the perpetrator of the fraud. *Ibid.*

6. Though in such a case the special owner would be estopped, in favor of a *bonâ fide* holder of the bill of lading, from proving that no property was shipped, yet the general owner is not estopped. *Ibid.*

7. Where a cargo of potatoes was shipped at Hamburg to be delivered at New York, the evidence shows that they were in bad condition when shipped, and consequently the vessel is not responsible for their loss. *Ship Howard v. Wissman*, 231.

CONSTITUTIONAL LAW, (*Continued.*)

ney, took out letters of administration in the District of Columbia, and then signed a receipt as attorney for money paid by himself as administrator to himself as attorney for the Cherokee administrators, this receipt is good, and the surety upon his administration bond is not responsible to the Cherokee heirs. *Ibid.*

12. The Cherokee nation are so far under the protection of the laws of the United States, that they may be considered, for the purposes above named, as a State or territory of the United States. *Ibid.*

13. In a state of war, the nations who are engaged in it, and all their citizens or subjects, are enemies to each other. Hence, all intercourse or communication between them is unlawful. *Jecker* v. *Montgomery*, 110.

14. Cases mentioned, by way of illustration, in which property of a subject or citizen, found trading with an enemy, has been adjudged to be forfeited as prize. *Ibid.*

15. The interposition of a neutral port through which the property is to pass, does not prevent it from being confiscated. *Ibid.*

16. In the present case, the evidence shows that the owners of the ship and cargo knew that the destination of the voyage was to an enemy's port. Even if the owner of the vessel was ignorant of it, the fate of the vessel must be decided by the acts of those persons who had her in charge. *Ibid.*

17. It is generally the duty of the captor to send his prize home for adjudication; but circumstances may render such a step improper, and of these he must be the judge. In making up his decision, good faith and reasonable discretion are required. In the present case he was excusable for not sending home the vessel. *Ibid.*

18. Generally, the proceedings for the condemnation of property as prize, ought to be instituted in the name of the United States. The circumstances, which led to the use of the name of the captor, and the fact that no objection was made to it in the court below, prevent this court from pronouncing the objection to be fatal. *Ibid.*

19. The proceeds of sale were properly deposited in the treasury of the United States. *Ibid.*

20. A distress warrant, issued by the solicitor of the treasury under the act of congress passed on the 15th May, 1820, (3 Stats. at Large, 592,) is not inconsistent with the constitution of the United States. *Murray's Lessee* v. *Hoboken Land and Improvement Co.* 272.

21. It was an exercise of executive and not of judicial power, according to the meaning of those words in the constitution; and the privilege allowed to a collector to bring the question of his indebtedness before the courts of the United States, is merely the consent of congress to the suit, which is given in other classes of cases also. *Ibid.*

22. Neither is it inconsistent with that part of the constitution which prohibits a citizen from being deprived of his liberty or property without due process of law. The historical and critical meaning of these words examined. *Ibid.*

23. By the common law of England and the laws of many of the colonies before the Revolution, and of States before the formation of the federal constitution, a summary process existed for the recovery of debts due to the government. *Ibid.*

24. It does not necessarily follow that the adjustment of these balances is a controversy to which the United States is a party, within the meaning of the constitution. *Ibid.*

25. Under the power of congress to collect taxes and the exercise of that power by the act above mentioned, the warrant of distress is conclusive evidence of the facts recited in it and of the authority to make the levy, so far as to justify the marshal in making it; but the question of indebtedness may be the subject of a suit, congress having assented thereto, and the levy may provide security for the event of the suit. *Ibid.*

26. The article of the constitution, requiring an oath or affirmation for a warrant, has no application to proceedings for the recovery of debts, where no search warrant is used. *Ibid.*

27. The return of the marshal that he had levied on lands, by virtue of such a warrant, is, at least, *primâ facie* evidence that the levy was not irregular by reason of the existence of goods and chattels of the collector subject to his process. *Ibid.*

CONSTITUTIONAL LAW, (*Continued.*)

28. The second article of the constitution of the United States, section two, contains this provision, namely: "The President shall have power to grant reprieves and pardons for offences against the United States, except in cases of impeachment." *Ex parte Wells*, 307.

29. Under this power, the President can grant a conditional pardon to a person under sentence of death, offering to commute that punishment into an imprisonment for life. If this is accepted by the convict, he has no right to contend that the pardon is absolute and the condition of it void. And the court below was justifiable in refusing to discharge the prisoner, when the application was placed upon that ground. *Ibid.*

30. The language used in the constitution as to the power of pardoning must be construed by the exercise of that power in England prior to the Revolution, and in the States prior to the adoption of the constitution. *Ibid.*

31. The manner explained in which it was exercised in England and in many of the States. *Ibid.*

32. The language of the constitution is such that the power of the President to pardon conditionally is not one of inference, but is conferred in terms; that language being to "grant reprieves and pardons," which includes conditional as well as absolute pardons. *Ibid.*

33. The acceptance, by the convict, of the condition, was not given under duress in the legal acceptation of that term. *Ibid.*

34. A stockholder in a corporation has a remedy in chancery against the directors, to prevent them from doing acts which would amount to a violation of the charter, or to prevent any misapplication of their capital or profits which might lessen the value of the shares, if the acts intended to be done amount to what is called in law a breach of trust or duty. *Dodge* v. *Woolsey*, 331.

35. So also a stockholder has a remedy against individuals, in whatever character they profess to act, if the subject of complaint is an imputed violation of a corporate franchise, or the denial of a right growing out of it, for which there is not an adequate remedy at law. *Ibid.*

36. Therefore, where the directors of a bank refused to take the proper measures to resist the collection of a tax, which they themselves believed to have been imposed upon them in violation of their charter, this refusal amounted to what is termed in law a breach of trust, a stockholder had a right to file a bill in chancery asking for such a remedy as the case might require. *Ibid.*

37. If the stockholder be a resident of another State than that in which the bank and persons attempting to violate its charter, or commit a breach of trust or duty have their domicile, he may file his bill in the courts of the United States. He has this right under the constitution and laws of the United States. *Ibid.*

38. The rights and duties of this court examined and explained, as an ultimate tribunal to determine whether laws enacted by congress, or by state legislatures or decisions of state courts are in conflict with the constitution of the United States. *Ibid.*

39. Where the State of Ohio, chartered a bank in 1845, in which charter was stipulated the amount of tax which the bank should pay, in lieu of all taxes to which said company or the stockholders thereof, on account of stock owned therein, would otherwise be subject; and in 1852, the legislature passed an act levying taxes upon the bank to a greater amount and founded upon a different principle. This act is in conflict with the constitution of the United States, as impairing the obligation of a contract, and therefore void. *Ibid.*

40. The fact that the people of the state had, in 1851, adopted a new constitution, in which it was declared that taxes should be imposed upon banks in the mode which the act of 1852 purported to carry out, cannot release the State from the obligations and duties imposed upon it by the constitution of the United States. *Ibid.*

41. The case of the Piqua Branch of the State Bank of Ohio v. Knoop, 16 How. 369, again affirmed. *Ibid.*

42. The power of congress to regulate commerce, includes the regulation of intercourse and navigation, and consequently the power to determine what shall or shall not be deemed, in judgment of law, an obstruction of navigation. *Pennsylvania* v. *Wheeling Bridge*, 421.

43. The provisions of the act of congress passed August 31, 1852, (10 Stats. at Large, 112,) in its 6th and 7th sections declaring the bridges over the Ohio

CONSTITUTIONAL LAW, (*Continued.*)

    River at Wheeling and Bridgeport to be lawful structures at their then height and position, and requiring the officers and crews of vessels navigating the Ohio River to regulate their vessels so as not to interfere with the elevation and construction of said bridges, are within the legitimate exercise, by congress, of its constitutional power to regulate commerce. *Ibid.*

44. The said sections of the aforesaid act of congress are not invalid by reason of the compact, in respect to the free navigation of the Ohio River, made between the States of Virginia and Kentucky, with the sanction of congress at the time the latter State was admitted into the Union. *Ibid.*

45. Neither are they in conflict with the provision of the constitution of the United States, providing that "no preference shall be given by any regulation of commerce or revenue to the ports of one State over those of another." *Ibid.*

46. As a general proposition it is true, that an act of congress cannot annul a judgment of the supreme court of the United States, or impair the rights determined thereby, especially as respects adjudications upon the private rights of parties; and hence the decree of this court heretofore rendered in this case, so far as it respects the costs adjudged to the complainant, is unaffected by the act of congress referred to. *Ibid.*

47. But that portion of the decree of this court at the May term, 1852, in the case of the State of Pennsylvania *v.* The Wheeling and Belmont Bridge Company, which relates to the abatement of the bridge, proceeded upon the ground that the bridge was in conflict with the then existing regulations of commerce by congress, and was executory, depending upon the bridge continuing to be an unlawful obstruction to the public right of free navigation; and that right having since been modified by congress in the exercise of its constitutional power to regulate commerce so that the bridge is no longer an unlawful obstruction, the decree cannot now be enforced. *Ibid.*

48. After the passage of the act of congress referred to, the bridge no longer being an unlawful interference with a public right, the defendant's authority to maintain it, in its then position and height, existed from the moment of the enactment; for their authority then combined the concurrent powers of both governments, state and federal, and if these are not sufficient none can be found in our system. *Ibid.*

49. The complainant's motions for a writ of assistance to execute the decree of the 27th of May, 1852, by the abatement of the bridge and for a sequestration against the corporation and attachment against its officers for disobeying said decree are therefore refused; and the motions to punish the contempt of the corporation and its officers in disobeying the injunction granted by Mr. Justice Grier, on the 27th of June, 1854, are also overruled, and the injunction is dissolved. *Ibid.*

50. The decree for costs being unaffected by the act of congress, the motion for taxation and award of execution for their collection is granted. *Ibid.*

51. Where a suit was brought in the United States court by citizens of another State against a citizen of Mississippi, who appeared to the suit, pleaded and then died, after which the suit was revived against his administrators, and judgment obtained against them, the following proceedings of the probate court afford no bar to the recovery of the claim: 1. A declaration by the probate court that the estate was insolvent, and a reference of the matter to a commissioner in insolvency. 2. A publication notifying the creditors of the estate to appear and file their claims, or be forever barred of their demands. 3. A report by the commissioner, leaving out the claim in question, which report was confirmed by the court. *The Union Bank of Tennessee* v. *Jolly's Administrators,* 503.

52. Where the estate turned out not to be insolvent, but a fund remained in hand for distributees, the creditors can recover by a bill in chancery against the administrators, notwithstanding the proceedings in the probate court. *Ibid.*

53. The law of a State, limiting the remedies of its citizens in its own courts, cannot be applied to prevent the citizens of other States from suing in the courts of the United States in that State, for the recovery of any property or money there, to which they may be legally or equitably entitled. *Ibid.*

54. A statute of a State which forbids a suit from being brought upon a bill of exchange when protested for non-acceptance, can have no effect upon suits brought in the courts of the United States. So also if the statute seeks to make the right of recovery, in a suit brought in case of non-acceptance, dependent

52 *

CONSTITUTIONAL LAW, (*Continued.*)

upon proof of subsequent presentment, protest, and notice for non-payment. *Watson* v. *Tarpley*, 517.

55. The first clause of the second section of the fourth article of the constitution provides that "the citizens of each State shall be entitled to all the privileges and immunities of citizens in the several States." *Conner* v. *Elliott*, 591.

56. The court will not describe and define these privileges and immunities in a general classification, preferring to decide each case as it may come up. *Ibid.*

57. The law of Louisiana gives a community of acquets or gains between married persons, where the marriage is contracted within the State, or where the marriage is contracted out of the State, and the parties afterwards go there to live. *Ibid.*

58. The privilege thus conferred upon the wife does not extend, by virtue of the clause in the constitution above quoted, to a native-born citizen of Louisiana, who was married while under age, in the State of Mississippi, in which State was her domicile together with her husband during the continuance of the marriage. Land in Louisiana, acquired by the husband during the marriage, was not subject to the Louisiana law, in respect to the community of acquets or gain. *Ibid.*

59. This right was one which attached to the contract of marriage, which the State of Louisiana had a right to regulate; and was not one of the personal rights of a citizen, within the meaning of the constitution. *Ibid.*

60. Where a law, as published, has been acknowledged by the people and received a harmonious interpretation for a long series of years, the propriety may well be doubted of referring to an ancient manuscript to show that the law as published was not an exact copy of the original manuscript. *Pease* v. *Peck*, 595.

61. Moreover, in this case, a subsequent legislative authority sanctioned the law as previously published, and thereby adopted it as a future rule. *Ibid.*

62. The original manuscript of the laws for the territory of Michigan left out the saving of "beyond seas" in the statute of limitations, but the published law contained this exception. It ought now to be considered as included. *Ibid.*

63. As a general rule, this court adopts the construction which state courts put upon state laws. But there are exceptions. Some of these exceptions stated. *Ibid.*

COPYRIGHT.

1. On the 27th of December, 1847, George F. Comstock was appointed state reporter, under a statute of the State of New York, which office he held until the 27th of December, 1851. *Little* v. *Hall*, 165.

2. During his term of office, viz. in 1850, he, in conjunction with the comptroller and secretary of the State, acting under the authority of a statute, made an agreement with certain persons, that for five years to come they should have the publication of the decisions of the court of appeals and the exclusive benefit of the copyright. *Ibid.*

3. At the expiration of Mr. Comstock's term, viz. on the 27th of December, 1851, he had in his possession sundry manuscript notes, and the decisions made at the ensuing January term were also placed in his hands to be reported. Out of these materials he made a volume, and sold it upon his own private account. *Ibid.*

4. Whatever remedy the first assignees may have had against Mr. Comstock individually, they are not to be considered as the legal owners of the manuscript, under the copyright act of congress, and are not entitled to an injunction to prevent the publication and sale of the volume. *Ibid.*

CORPORATION.

1. For remedy of a stockholder in a corporation against the directors, see CHANCERY.

2. Where a corporation is sued, it is not enough, in order to give jurisdiction, to say that the corporation is a citizen of the State where the suit is brought. But an averment is sufficient, when admitted by a demurrer, that the corporation was created by the laws of the State, and had its principal place of business there. *Lafayette Ins. Co.* v. *French*, 404.

3. Where a corporation, chartered by the State of Indiana, was allowed by a law of Ohio, to transact business in the latter State upon the condition that service of process upon the agent of the corporation should be considered as service upon the corporation itself, a judgment against the corporation, obtained by means of such process, ought to have been received in Indiana with the same faith and credit that it was entitled to in Ohio. *Ibid.*

JURISDICTION, (*Continued.*)

over the succession of a debtor who was enjoying a respite from the claims of his creditors, for a certain time and died before the time expired; to the mode in which that jurisdiction should be exercised; to the propriety of collaterally attacking a sale made by its authority; to the point whether or not the death of the party transferred the proceedings to the court of probate, and to the mode in which the court of probate should exercise its jurisdiction; this court will adopt these decisions, and especially where many of them concur with the judgments of this court upon the same or similar points. *Ibid.*

33. The Louisiana cases and those of this court, examined. *Ibid.*

34. Where a suit was brought in the United States court by citizens of another State against a citizen of Mississippi, who appeared to the suit, pleaded and then died, after which the suit was revived against his administrators, and judgment obtained against them, the following proceedings of the probate court afford no bar to the recovery of the claim: 1. A declaration by the probate court that the estate was insolvent, and a reference of the matter to a commissioner in insolvency. 2. A publication notifying the creditors of the estate to appear and file their claims, or be forever barred of their demands. 3. A report by the commissioner, leaving out the claim in question, which report was confirmed by the court. *The Union Bank of Tennessee* v. *Jolly's Administrators*, 503.

35. Where the estate turned out not to be insolvent, but a fund remained in hand for distributees, the creditors can recover by a bill in chancery against the administrators, notwithstanding the proceedings in the probate court. *Ibid.*

36. The law of a State, limiting the remedies of its citizens in its own courts, cannot be applied to prevent the citizens of other States from suing in the courts of the United States in that State, for the recovery of any property or money there, to which they may be legally or equitably entitled. *Ibid.*

37. In order to give jurisdiction to this court, under the 25th section of the judiciary act of 1789, it must appear by the record that one of the questions stated in the section did arise, and was decided in the state court; and it is not sufficient that it might have arisen or been applicable; it must appear that it did arise, and was applied. *Maxwell* v. *Newbold*, 511.

38. This rule was established in the case of Crowell *v.* Randall, 10 Pet. 368, and has been since adhered to. *Ibid.*

39. Hence an allegation that "the charge of the court, the verdict of the jury, and the judgment below are each against, and in conflict with, the constitution and laws of the United States, and therefore erroneous," is too general and indefinite to come within the provisions of the act of congress or the decisions of this court. *Ibid.*

40. The clause in the constitution and the law of congress should have been specified by the plaintiffs in error in the state court, in order that this court might see what was the right claimed by them, and whether it was denied to them by the decision of the state court. *Ibid.*

41. By the general rules of commercial law, the payee or indorsee of a bill, upon its presentment and upon refusal by the drawee to accept, has the right to immediate recourse against the drawer. He is not bound to wait to see whether or not the bill will be paid at maturity. *Watson* v. *Tarpley*, 517.

42. A statute of a State, which forbids a suit from being brought in such a case until after the maturity of the bill, can have no effect upon suits brought in the courts of the United States. So, also, if the statute seeks to make the right of recovery, in a suit brought in case of non-acceptance, dependent upon proof of subsequent presentment, protest, and notice for non-payment. *Ibid.*

43. The decisions of this court upon these points examined. *Ibid.*

44. Where questions are certified up to this court, in consequence of a division in opinion between the judges of the circuit court, they must be questions of law and not questions of fact; not such as involve or imply conclusions or judgment by the judges, upon the weight or effect of testimony or facts, adduced in the cause. *Dennistoun* v. *Stewart*, 565.

45. The questions must also be distinctly and particularly stated with reference to that part of the case upon which such questions shall have arisen. *Ibid.*

46. The points stated must be single, and must not bring up the whole case for decision. *Ibid.*

47. Where a decree in admiralty was rendered in the circuit court upon an appeal from the district court, said decree being given *pro forma* because the presiding

LANDS, PUBLIC, (*Continued.*)

grantee should build a house upon it, and have it inhabited within a year from the date of the grant, and also that he should obtain a judicial possession and measurement or survey of it, the evidence shows sufficient reasons for a non-compliance on the part of the grantee   *United States* v. *Reading*, 1.

2. This court again decides, as in *Fremont v.* United States, 17 How. 560, that a mere omission to comply with these conditions would not necessarily amount to a forfeiture, unless there were circumstances which showed an intention to abandon the property. *Ibid.*

3. Although the title did not become definitive until the grant was approved by the departmental assembly, yet immediate interest passed by the grant from the governor, whose duty it was (and not that of the grantee) to submit the case to the departmental assembly, and, if they should reject it, then to lay the case before the supreme government of the Republic. *Ibid.*

4. If the governor failed to execute this duty, the title remained as it was after the grant was issued, and is sufficient for confirmation under the act of congress, passed on March 3, 1851, (9 Stats. at Large, 631.) *Ibid.*

5. The evidence in the present case shows that the grantee was a naturalized citizen of the Mexican Republic, and the fact that he joined the troops of the United States when war broke out with Mexico, furnishes no evidence of his intention to abandon the property, nor any reason why the grant should be forfeited. *Ibid.*

6. The act of congress passed on the 13th of June, 1812, (2 Stats. at Large, 748,) reserved for the support of schools in the respective towns or villages in Missouri "all town or village lots, out-lots or common-field lots, included in such surveys," (which the principal deputy-surveyor was directed in a preceding section to make,) "which are not rightfully owned or claimed by any private individuals, or held as commons belonging to such towns or villages, or that the President of the United States may not think proper to reserve for military purposes, provided that the whole quantity of land contained in the lots reserved shall not exceed one twentieth part of the whole lands included in the general survey of such town or village." *Kissell* v. *St. Louis Public Schools*, 19.

7. The act of 26th of May, 1824, (4 Stats. at Large, 65,) directed the individual claimants to present their claims within a specified time, after which the surveyor-general was to designate and set apart the lots for the support of schools. *Ibid.*

8. The act of 27th of January, 1831, (4 Stats. at Large, 435,) relinquished the title of the United States in the above lots to the inhabitants of the towns, and also in the lots reserved for the support of schools, to be disposed of or regulated as the legislature of the State might direct. *Ibid.*

9. In 1833, the legislature incorporated a board of commissioners of St. Louis public schools, and, in 1843, the surveyor returned a plat in conformity with the above laws. *Ibid.*

10. The title to the lots thus indicated by the surveyor as school lots enured to the benefit of the school commissioners. Until the survey, the title was like other imperfect titles in Louisiana, waiting for the public authority to designate the particular land to which the title should attach. *Ibid.*

11. The certificate of the surveyor is record evidence of title, and the question is not open whether or not these lots were out-lots or common-field lots, or other lots described in the statute. The title is good until some person can show a better. *Ibid.*

12. Such a better title was not found in an entry under the pre-emption laws of April 12, 1814, and 29th of April, 1816. The land in question was within the limits of the town of St. Louis, and was also reserved from sale. For both reasons it was not subject to pre-emption. *Ibid.*

13. The ignorance of the pre-emptioner that the land was reserved, does not prevent the entry from being void. *Ibid.*

14. The act of congress passed on the 4th of July, 1836, (5 Stats at Large, 107,) provided for a direct supervision by the commissioner of the general land-office over registers and receivers of the land-offices, and therefore their judgment is not conclusive in a case where additional proceedings were had before them in 1837. *Barnard's Heirs* v. *Ashley's Heirs*, 43.

15. The cases of Wilcox v. Jackson, 13 Pet. 511, and Lytle v. Arkansas, 9 How. 333, commented on and explained. *Ibid.*

16. Where a survey was approved on June 4, 1834, a selection made, under the au-

LANDS, PUBLIC, (*Continued.*)

52. It again decides, as in the preceding case of Arguello *v.* The United States, that the ten littoral leagues spoken of in the regulations of 1824 and 1828, do not mean prohibition of grants of land to native citizens for their own use. *Ibid.*

53. The title of lands held by the missions of California, was never vested in the church, which had only an usufruct in them; and in the present case, the mission assented to the grant in question. *Ibid.*

54. The 17th section of the regulations of 1828 has no application to the present case. *Ibid.*

55. Also, in 1833 and 1834, the government of Mexico passed laws to secularise the missions. *Ibid.*

56. Where there was a grant of land in California in 1843, with three boundaries and the quantity stated; and in 1845 a new grant was made which was approved by the departmental assembly, subject to the condition, that within four months a map of the land should be made; this was a condition subsequent, the non-compliance with which did not work a forfeiture of the grant, but only left the land liable to be denounced. *United States* v. *Vaca*, 556.

57. Moreover, the disturbed state of the country was a sufficient reason for not making the survey. *Ibid.*

58. Where there was a grant of land in California made by the governor to the secretary of the government, and neither the petition nor the patent stated the quantity, but the concession and direction by the governor to the proper officer to issue the patent, limited the quantity to eleven square leagues, this concession and direction constitute a part of the evidence of title, and are sufficient to make a good grant for that amount. *United States* v. *Larkin*, 557.

59. The petition to the governor was accompanied with a sketch or map giving the location and boundaries of the tract. The patent refers to this sketch, and by it the land can be located. *Ibid.*

60. The fraudulent nature of the grant was not made a question in the court below and therefore cannot be made here. Moreover, there is no evidence of fraud. *Ibid.*

61. The objections that the case was not submitted to the departmental assembly, and that judicial possession was not taken of the land, are overruled by the case of United States *v.* Fremont, 17 How. 542. *Ibid.*

62. Neither the act of the Mexican congress of 1824, nor the regulations of 1828, prescribe any particular form of grants or patents of the public lands. And there is no uniformity with respect to the conditions imposed upon the grantee, either in those which relate to the cultivation or taking possession of the land. The absence of the condition of settlement within a limited time will not avoid the grant in this case. *Ibid.*

LAWS OF NATIONS.

See CONSTITUTIONAL LAW.

LIMITATION, STATUTES OF.

1. A statute of the State of Illinois, passed in 1839, declared: "That hereafter every person in the actual possession of land or tenements under claim and color of title made in good faith, and who shall, for seven successive years after the passage of this act, continue in such possession, and shall, also, during said time, pay all taxes legally assessed on such land or tenements, shall be held and adjudged to be the legal owner of said land or tenements, to the extent and according to the purport of his or her paper title." *Wright* v. *Mattison*, 50.

2. What constitutes color of title, explained. *Ibid.*

3. What is color of title is matter of law, and when the facts exhibiting the title are shown, the court will determine whether they amount to color of title. *Ibid.*

4. But good faith in the party, in claiming under such color, is a question of fact for the jury. *Ibid.*

5. Hence, where the court decided that the color of title was not made in good faith, such decision was erroneous. It should have been left to the jury. *Ibid.*

6. An act of 1835, upon the same subject, passed by the State of Illinois, also examined and explained. *Ibid.*

7. The law of Missouri allows the lands of a deceased debtor to be sold under execution, but prohibits it from being done until after the expiration of eighteen months from the date of the letters of administration upon his estate. *Griffith* v. *Bogart*, 158.

53 *

MICHIGAN, (*Continued.*)

mineral lands, does not include section sixteen, which remains subject to the compact with Michigan. *Ibid.*

6. Under the operation of that act, and also the act of September, 1850, (9 Stats. at Large, 472,) a lease made in 1845, by the secretary of war, of some mineral lands, (including section sixteen,) did not confer a right upon the mining company, who were the assignees of the lease, to enter their lands and obtain a patent for section sixteen. *Ibid.*

7. It was not necessary for the State of Michigan to obtain the consent of congress before making a sale of the section. *Ibid.*

8. Whether or not the officers of the State of Michigan pursued the laws of the State in effecting the sale, is a question which the occupant of the land cannot raise in this suit. *Ibid.*

MISSOURI.

1. The act of congress passed on the 6th of March, 1820, (3 Stats. at Large, 547,) accepted by an ordinance declaring the assent of the people of Missouri thereto, adopted on the 19th of July, 1820, granted to the State for the use of schools the sixteenth section of every township in the State, which had not been sold or otherwise disposed of. *Ham v. Missouri*, 126.

2. This expression, "otherwise disposed of," does not include the case of an imperfect title, claimed to be derived from the Spanish governor, which had been rejected by the board of commissioners in 1811. *Ibid.*

3. The claim was confirmed in 1828 so far as to relinquish all the title which the United States then had; but at that time the United States had no title, having granted the land to Missouri in 1820, which they had a right to do. *Ibid.*

4. The proviso in the act of March 3, 1811, which forbade lands claimed before the board of commissioners from being offered for sale until after the decision of congress thereon, did not prevent a donation for schools, and, moreover, contemplated only a temporary suspension for the purposes of investigation. *Ibid.*

5. The act of congress passed on the 13th of June, 1812, confirmed the titles to out-lots in the town of St. Louis, in Missouri, upon certain conditions, and the act of 26th of May, 1824, required the performance of these conditions, and the boundaries of the lot to be proved before the recorder of land titles. *Savaignac v. Garrison*, 136.

6. Whether the lot and conditions came within the purview of the act of 1812, were questions of fact for the jury. The neglect to procure the survey and location under the act of 1824, did not forfeit the title acquired under the act of 1812. *Ibid.*

7. The case of Guitard et al. *v.* Stoddard, 16 How. 494, controls this case. *Ibid.*

NAVY, OFFICERS OF THE.

Where an officer of the navy was detached on special duty in France and a sum of money was transmitted to him by the secretary of the navy to be disbursed for medical attendance, the propriety of this act was peculiarly within the jurisdiction and discretion of the head of the department; and the officer cannot be charged with the amount so transmitted, by the accounting officers of the treasury department. *United States v. Jones*, 92.

PATENT RIGHTS.

1. Where there was an agreement between a patentee and an assignee that the latter should manufacture the machines for a certain time and upon certain terms, it is too late for him, when called upon in chancery for an account, to deny that the patentee was the original inventor of the thing patented. *Kinsman v. Parkhurst*, 289.

2. Even if the patent were invalid, yet that does not so taint with illegality the sale of the machines by the assignee, as to affect the claim of the assignor to an account of the sales. *Ibid.*

3. The agreement that one only of the parties should continue the manufacture was not void as being in restraint of trade. *Ibid.*

4. The assignee could not legally purchase the outstanding claim of a third person, and set it up against the patentee with whom he had an existing agreement, in the nature of a copartnership. *Ibid.*

5. If the assignee transfers his contract, the person to whom he transfers it is bound by the same equities which existed between the original parties to the contract, having purchased with a full knowledge of the state of things. *Ibid.*

6. If the report of the master was incorrect, exception should have been taken to it in the court below. It cannot be examined in this court · no exception having been taken. *Ibid.*

INDEX. 631

PENNSYLVANIA.
See CONSTITUTIONAL LAW.
PLEAS AND PLEADINGS.
1. Formerly, it was held, in some of the circuit courts, that the averment of citizenship in a different State from the one in which the suit was brought, and which it is necessary to make in order to give jurisdiction to the federal courts, must be proved on the general issue. But the rule now is, that if the defendant disputes the allegation of citizenship which is made in the declaration, he must so plead in abatement. *Jones* v. *League*, 76.
2. Where, in an action upon a sheriff's bond, the declaration did not charge the sheriff with a breach of his duty in the execution of any writ or process in which the real plaintiff was personally interested; but with a neglect or refusal to preserve the public peace, in consequence of which the plaintiff suffered great wrong and injury from the unlawful violence of a mob; the declaration did not set forth a sufficient cause of action against the sheriff and his sureties. *South* v. *State of Maryland*, 396.
3. The powers and duties of a sheriff explained, and the difference pointed out between his ministerial and judicial functions. *Ibid.*
4. It is only for a breach of his duty in the execution of the former, that the sheriff and his sureties are liable upon his bond, and the declaration in this case does not set out such a breach. *Ibid.*
5. Where a corporation is sued, it is not enough, in order to give jurisdiction, to say that the corporation is a citizen of the State where the suit is brought. But an averment is sufficient, when admitted by a demurrer, that the corporation was created by the laws of the State, and had its principal place of business there. *Lafayette Insurance Co.* v. *French*, 404.
6. If the judgment was recovered in Ohio against the company by an erroneous name, but the suit upon the judgment was brought in Indiana against the company using its chartered name correctly, accompanied with an averment that it was the same company, this mistake is no ground of error; it could only be taken advantage of by a plea in abatement, in the suit in which the first judgment was recovered. *Ibid.*

PRACTICE.
1. If the defendant in error files a copy of the record before the expiration of the time which is allowed to the plaintiff in error to file it, and afterwards the plaintiff in error files the record in proper time, the case made by the defendant in error will be dismissed. *Hartshorn* v. *Day*, 28.
2. Where the record is not filed by the appellant, within the time prescribed by the rules of this court, and the appellee files a copy of it, the appeal will be dismissed upon his motion. *The United States* v. *Fremont*, 30.
3. Also, where a mandate went down from this court to the district court of the United States for the northern district of California, and that court entered a decree according to the mandate, this furnishes no ground for an appeal, and the case will be dismissed upon that ground. *Ibid.*
4. A certificate from the clerk of the circuit court, that he cannot make out the record in time to comply with the 63d rule of this court, does not furnish a sufficient reason for an extension of the time prescribed by that rule. *Sturgess* v. *Harrold*, 40.
5. This court cannot grant a motion for the rehearing of a cause which has been transmitted to the court below. *Peck* v. *Sanderson*, 42.
6. A statute passed by the State of Illinois, on 3d March, 1845, permits matters both of fact and law to be tried by the court, if both parties agree. *Graham* v. *Bayne*, 60.
7. Where a case was tried in the circuit court of the United States, in which both parties agreed that matters of law and fact should be submitted to the court, and it was brought to this court upon a bill of exceptions which contained all the evidence, this court will remand the case to the circuit court with directions to award a *venire de novo*. *Ibid.*
8. A bill of exceptions must present questions of law. Where there is no dispute about the facts, counsel may agree on a case stated in the nature of a special verdict But to send the whole evidence up is not the same thing as agreeing upon the facts *Ibid*
9 Even if a special verdict be ambiguous or imperfect, if it find but the evidence of facts and not the facts themselves, or finds but parts of the facts in issue, and is silent as to others, it is a mistrial, and the court of error must order a

PRACTICE, (*Continued.*)

venire de novo. They can render no judgment on an imperfect verdict or case stated. *Ibid.*

10. This court again decides that a decree upon a motion to dissolve an injunction in the course of a chancery cause, and where the bill is not finally disposed of, is not such a final decree as can be re-examined in this court, under the 25th section of the judiciary act. *Verden* v. *Coleman*, 86.

11. Where the record contains only an agreed statement of facts, it is not in conformity with the eleventh and thirty-first rules of this court, and the case will be dismissed. *Curtis* v. *Petitpain*, 109.

12. Where different parties claimed a fund in the hands of the marshal, which had arisen from sales under an execution, a judgment of the circuit court on rules as to whom the money should be paid, is not such a judgment as can be re-examined in this court. *Ibid.*

13. Where a trial by jury is waived in the court below, and there is no special verdict or agreed statement of facts or bill of exception upon a point of law, this court cannot review the judgment of the court below. *Guild* v. *Frontin*, 135.

14. But having jurisdiction of the cause, and no error appearing upon the face of the record, the judgment will be affirmed. *Ibid.*

15. Where the United States brought a case up to this court as plaintiffs in error, and the attorney-general moved for a discontinuance upon the ground that he wished other questions to be presented upon the record, which he deemed necessary for a full elucidation of the case, the court, without expressing an opinion upon these other questions, will grant the motion made by the legal representative of the government. *The United States* v. *The Minnesota Railroad Co.* 241.

16. An original writ has fulfilled its functions when the defendant is brought into court. If lost, the court can provide, in its discretion, for the filing of a copy. *The York and Cumberland Railroad Co.* v. *Myers*, 246.

17. If several claimants of portions of an estate unite in filing a bill, this does not make it multifarious. The authorities upon this subject examined. *Shields* v. *Thomas*, 253.

18. The court in Kentucky having rendered a decree for the complainants, they had a right to file a bill in Iowa to enforce this decree. *Ibid.*

19. Where a petition is filed in a court of chancery by a creditor, praying to be admitted as a party complainant in a suit then existing, but the nature of the original suit is not made to appear, the proceeding is irregular, and cannot be sustained. *Ransom* v. *Davis*, 295.

20. Where a chancery suit involves matters of account, the action of a master should be had in the inferior court, and the items admitted or rejected should be stated, so that exception may be taken to the particular items or class of items, and such a case should be brought before this court on the rulings of the exceptions by the circuit court. *Ibid.*

21. Where a declaration in ejectment was served on the 15th of the month and the court met on the 27th, it was ten days before the commencement of the term. *Connor* v. *Peugh's Lessee*, 394.

22 Judgment being entered against the casual ejector, the tenant having neglected to make herself a party, cannot bring a writ of error to the judgment. *Ibid.*

23. A motion to set the judgment aside was an application to the sound discretion of the court below. No appeal lies from its decision, nor is it the subject of a bill of exceptions or writ of error. *Ibid.*

24. Where the clerk of the supreme court of a State neglects or refuses to make a return to a writ of error issued under the 25th section of the judiciary act, this court will lay a rule upon him to make return on or before the first day of the next term, or show cause why such return has not been made in conformity to law. *The United States* v. *Booth*, 476.

25. And where there is another case upon the docket involving the same questions the court will direct it to be continued, in order that both cases may be argued together. *Ibid.*

26. No objections to a master's report can be made which were not taken before the master; nor after a decree *pro confesso* can a defendant go before the master without a special order, but the accounts are to be taken *ex parte*. *McMicken* v. *Perin*, 507.

27. An appeal will not lie from the refusal of a court to open a former decree; nor have the circuit courts power to set aside their decrees in equity, on motion, after the term at which they were rendered. *Ibid.*

Cambridge : Stereotyped and Printed by Welch, Bigelow, & Co.

Lightning Source UK Ltd.
Milton Keynes UK
UKHW011310220119
335966UK00006B/162/P